AMBASSADOR OF AIR TRAVEL

THE UNTOLD STORY OF
LINDBERGH'S 1927-1928
GOOD WILL TOURS

Lindbergh standing by his NYP at the Seattle, Washington stop. Notice the Fairchild FC-2 escort plane in the background. PEMCO WEBSTER & STEVENS COLLECTION MUSEUM OF HISTORY & INDUSTRY

80 CITIES IN THE U.S., CANADA AND 15 COUNTRIES SOUTH OF THE BORDER

by EV CASSAGNERES

Library of Congress
Control Number 2006900321

ISBN 1-57510-125-4

First Printing: April 2006

This book is Part II in a series on the entire history of the NYP.
To obtain a copy of Part I, *The Untold Story of The SPIRIT OF ST. LOUIS,*
please contact the author through Pictorial Histories.

Cover photos: FRONT: CASSAGNERES COLLECTION. BACK: PHOTOGRAPHER EV CASSAGNERES

Cover Design and Graphics: Seiler Design & Advertising
Typesetting and Layout: Leslie Maricelli

PRINTED IN U.S.A.
BY UNITED GRAPHICS INC.
MATTOON, ILLINOIS

PICTORIAL HISTORIES PUBLISHING CO., INC.
713 South Third Street West, Missoula, Montana 59801
Phone (406) 549-8488 – Fax (406) 728-9280
Website – www.pictorialhistoriespublishing.com
E-mail – phpc@montana.com

Foreword

by Reeve Lindbergh Tripp

I have been told that the great difficulty about having "celebrity" parents is that any child of theirs must share a mother and father not only with siblings, but with the rest of the world, too. I suppose this may be true for some, but in my own experience one of the joys of my situation is that over and over, throughout life, the world gives my parents back to me in unexpected ways.

Everywhere I go, I have been fortunate enough to meet people who remember exactly where they were when they heard the news that my father had landed safely in Paris in May of 1927, at the end of his famous non-stop solo transatlantic flight in the "Spirit of St. Louis." Over and over, I have heard readers of all ages tell me how my mother's writings have changed their lives.

I meet my parents, both of them gone from the world now, in the minds and hearts of the people whose lives they have influenced, all over the earth. In this country, most recently, I have been touched and delighted to meet my father in the regional airports of my native New England, as well as in those in other regions of the country.

This happy circumstance is entirely due to my father's 1927-1928 "Guggenheim Tour." Thanks to the Daniel Guggenheim Fund, and to the Guggenheim family's generous philanthropic support of aviation in its earliest stages, my father and his airplane visited 48 states and 15 foreign countries during the months following his flight to Paris, with the purpose of promoting and publicizing aviation.

Thanks to Ev Cassagneres' new, thoroughly researched and documented account, I can trace that remarkable adventure in detail from city to city. I can hear the personal stories, appreciate the social and business climate of the day, and begin to understand as never before the extraordinary impact that this man and this airplane had upon the development of air travel in this country, and in the world.

Ev is an old friend, and one who has impressed me since our first meeting with his devotion to aviation history and his meticulous respect for every detail of historical truth. In one of his previous books, I learned a great deal about the little silver airplane my father flew and loved, the "Spirit of St. Louis"

itself, the Ryan NYP, the beautifully planned and constructed airplane that carried my father into history.

I learned, too, about the many people who financed, designed or built the aircraft, supporting the New York to Paris flight and therefore accompanying my father on his journey, even though they could not be in the cockpit with him.

In this new book, Ev brings the man and the airplane down from that long night over the Atlantic Ocean, and back from the glorious reception in Europe, and offers these two to the world in a different way, exactly as they offered themselves, during the carefully planned 22,000-mile Good Will tour of 1927 and 1928. The trip was designed to convince a skeptical population that air travel could be safe, reliable, and on time, and it succeeded beyond the wildest dreams of its planners.

I have learned things here that I did not know before, some of them touching on my own personal history. For instance, my father said he considered the flight he made to Mexico, where he met my mother, "the most interesting" flight he had ever experienced. including the flight to Paris. I think my mother would be gratified!

I learned that on the day my parents met, December 26, 1927, my father had also taken the comedian/philosopher Will Rogers up for a flight, in a Ford Tri-motor. I learned that during the time my father spent in Mexico on that visit, a Mexican aviator gave a toast at a dinner, extolling the fellowship of aviation. He said something that I know my parents and the other early aviators always believed, "We are all citizens of this immense country called sky."

It is such a pleasure to visit the places, meet the people, and hear the story of the further travels of this young man, my father, and his airplane. If you have said to yourself, as I did after reading my father's book, The Spirit of St. Louis, *"and then what happened?" nobody can give you the answer in more detail, or with more enthusiasm, than Ev Cassagneres. His book begins where my father's ended, and is a tribute to all those who witnessed and shared their next, world-changing adventure.*

Author's Note

Over the course of many years, I have often been asked what inspired my deep interest in Charles A. Lindbergh and the *Spirit of St. Louis.*

During the 1930s, I was one of that great throng of air-minded young Americans who would run outdoors at every opportunity to gaze upward at any airplane that might be passing overhead. I found I could not take my eyes off the airplane until it passed over the horizon and disappeared completely from sight. The shape, the sound, the direction and altitude of every airplane would be deeply recorded in my memory. I kept scrapbooks, built stick and tissue and solid models, rode my trusty bicycle many miles to local airports to watch the aviators fly their beautiful machines, dreaming about the day I might join their ranks.

I spent long hours reading model airplane magazines and books on flying. I had a particular fascination with Lindbergh and his flight from New York to Paris in 1927. In the course of my reading, I began to notice discrepancies and inconsistencies in writings about the famous flight, the design and building of the *Spirit of St. Louis* and Lindbergh's goodwill tours.

After I became a pilot in 1945, I continued to read about Lindbergh and the *Spirit of St. Louis* and noticed the errors continued to proliferate. In 1956 I had the opportunity to "check out" in a classic 1936 Ryan ST. From that moment, I was compelled–I had to learn all I could about the history of the *Spirit*, its manufacturer and its development.

I had always been inspired by Lindbergh and wondered how this little-known air mail pilot managed to become involved in the seminal 1927 trans-Atlantic flight. In light of the conflicting information I had already encountered, I developed an irresistible urge to dig deeper and find out the true story. I felt driven to fit the pieces together: not just to learn more, but also to better understand this key chapter of aviation and the crucial role that a small airplane and its pilot played in the future of commercial air travel and aviation in general.

In the thirty-eight years I have been involved in this project, it has continued to be both fascinating and satisfying–intellectually as well as emotionally. Perhaps it is just a basic human need to learn about the past in order to more fully appreciate the present and anticipate the future.

Researching the history of the *Spirit* was not without its challenges. I had to spend much time tracking down official documentation. When I did find original material (much of it dated 1927 and 1928), I often had to spend additional time scrutinizing this information to ascertain its accuracy and authenticity.

Data transcription often leads to typographical errors, misunderstandings and flat-out guesses. I attempted to distinguish fact from error throughout this research. Fortunately I have had access to a vast amount of historical, technical and photographic material which helped greatly in this effort.

Most important as accurate and trustworthy sources of information have, of course, been any writings by Charles A. Lindbergh, his wife Anne Morrow Lindbergh, and their daughter, Reeve Lindbergh Tripp. In addition, I have had the invaluable experience of spending time with the Lindbergh family, all of whom have generously shared from their hearts and personal archives.

I have also interviewed many people "who were there," via letter, telephone, in person and on tape, and listened to their stories and observations of how the experience affected their lives. I have collected photographs of the *Spirit* taken every place it ever landed, as well as the newspaper stories of Lindbergh's visits to every town, city or country stopped in or overflown on these tours. I was especially watchful for errors in newspaper stories. Unfortunately, in many cases, those are the only sources I was able to find on the events. I have attempted to qualify any information in this text that I feel questionable.

The original intent of this work was to convey a detailed documentation, as complete and accurate as possible, of the two goodwill tours in the *Spirit of St. Louis.* Lindbergh was the man responsible for the management, and determined every aspect of those flights.

This book is full of anecdotes, legend, and cold facts. I have attempted to weave all three elements into a useful story.

In 1968, upon learning of my project,

Lindbergh invited me to his home where he provided much valuable first-hand information. Since his death in 1974, his family has continued their interest in the progress of the project. Thus, my perception of Lindbergh is derived from knowing him personally, and I have tried to convey that image in this book.

In his own book, *The Spirit of St. Louis*, Lindbergh wrote, "No work is infallible; desire, records and memory combined cannot produce exactness in every instance; but sufficient effort has been expended on the pages of this book to warrant that in the majority of cases where there is conflict, accuracy will rest with the account carried herein" (pg 348). I would like to feel that way about my book as well.

Meeting Lindbergh

Early in this project I needed to address several questions to which I felt only Lindbergh would have the answers. But, aware of his great desire for privacy, I couldn't imagine how I would ever meet him.

Carl Schory, formerly of the National Aeronautic Association, suggested that I contact one of Lindbergh's close friends, Loren "Deak" Lyman, who lived near Lindbergh in Connecticut. I did, and three years later (February 1968) Mr. Lyman felt the time was right for me to write to Lindbergh to request a meeting, using Lyman as a reference.

To my great surprise and pleasure, I soon received a telephone call from Lindbergh himself, inviting my wife and me to join him and his wife, Anne, at their home for supper and a discussion of my project. During that meeting, on the eve of February 28, 1968, Lindbergh and I began a friendship that continued until his death. I found him to be a true gentleman–pleasant, gracious and quite accessible, with an incredible memory for detail and a quick and restless intellect. He did not waste words, always getting right down to the point in his answers and observations.

Since his death in 1974, many other questions have surfaced as I continued to collect information. I truly wish he were here to provide the answers. I will always be grateful for his friendship and generosity in sharing his thoughts so freely whenever we met.

Ev Cassagneres

Preface

Everyone knows the basic story of Charles A. Lindbergh and his *Spirit of St. Louis* making the first solo trans-Atlantic flight from New York to Paris, France, in 1927. But how many stop to think of the crucial role that the pilot and his airplane played in the future of commercial air travel and aviation technology today. What was learned as a result of that 1927-1928 effort laid the groundwork for modern aviation technology as we know it today.

In a converted San Diego, California, fish cannery, there existed a small airplane manufacturing company, founded in 1922 by T. Claude Ryan and known as the Ryan Flying Company and Los Angeles-San Diego Airline, which later became Ryan Airlines, Inc. In late 1926, the company had a high-wing monoplane, the Ryan M-1, in production. Several M-1s were flying air mail service on a regular basis between Los Angeles and Seattle for Pacific Air Transport (P.A.T.), an air mail carrier.

On February 3, 1927, the Robertson Aircraft Corporation of Anglum, Missouri, sent Ryan Airlines a telegram inquiring whether the small West Coast firm could build a Wright engine-powered airplane capable of flying from New York to Paris nonstop. The wire was signed by Charles A. Lindbergh, chief pilot. Lindbergh would be competing for a cash prize offered by entrepreneur Raymond Orteig for the first pilot to make the solo nonstop crossing.

It was clear that Ryan would have to re-engineer their existing M-1, incorporating aspects of a newly designed larger Ryan B-1 "Brougham," then under construction, for such a feat. They not only accomplished the engineering but did it in record time under the watchful eye of the daring pilot. The airplane proved to be up to the task, and the flight was so earth-shaking that the whole world was taken up by the marvel of the flight. The public demanded that Lindbergh follow up his feat by flying the *Spirit* around the country and into Canada, South America, and the Caribbean after his return.

Much has been written over the years about Lindbergh, but little attention has been paid to the airplane itself and the role it played in aviation's development.

This book on the 1927-1928 Lindbergh-flown goodwill tours in the *Spirit of St. Louis* has been written to fill that need.

Acknowledgments

This book about Lindbergh's post record-flight tours has not been written by myself only. The various abilities of many people and organizations have contributed and become part of whatever success this work may represent. Their cooperation and interest is without parallel. They have all been true collaborators. Their generous gifts of time, talent, experience, resources, and encouragement in varying degrees, have been a source of immense help and inspiration. I owe these special individuals and groups my deepest gratitude and appreciation, for without them I could not possibly have put this story of the goodwill tours together.

Having spent over thirty-five years doing extensive and exhaustive research, worldwide travel, telephone calls and letters by the thousands. I have found that a project of this complexity requires almost as many people and skills as was required to keep the *Spirit of St. Louis* in the air during its flying life as well as preserved in Washington, D.C.

Countless people went out of their way to have me as a guest in their home, feed me, and transport me from place to place. Often they would provided further leads or contacts, make suggestions, and offer access to their own personal archives or photographic collections.

Literally thousands of people played crucial roles in this work. Hundreds more took time to write, either longhand or by typewriter or computer, letters with detailed help and answers to my many questions. Many of these people would either donate or loan long-cherished photographs from their family photo albums, scrapbooks, or shoeboxes.

Encouragement from family, friends, business associates, pilots, authors, researchers and historians, writers (professional and nonprofessional), librarians, and even strangers, has been enormous. This alone has kept me going even at times when I was ready to give up in moments of discouragement. Space does not permit me to give credit to each and every individual.

Members of my immediate family deserve special mention for the hours, days and weeks away from them. Often while in such deep thought while in their company, I hardly knew they were even in the same room. However, their quiet support gave me the strength and determination to keep going to complete the work.

Over the years I have tracked down and made contact with scores of people "who were there," many of whom worked on the NYP in one capacity or another, or knew Lindbergh personally.

Countless hours have been spent scrutinizing photographs and their captions, checking and double-checking stories, anecdotes, and printed material for accuracy, details, and thoroughness to pinpoint dates and other data.

I have gathered primary data on the effect of the Lindbergh/*Spirit of St. Louis* flights on the development of air travel and aviation in general.

I would like to give special mention to Charles A. and Anne Morrow Lindbergh, Reeve Lindbergh Tripp, Wendy Lindbergh and Lars Lindbergh for their personal interest and help. The Lindbergh family was always available whenever the need for help arose.

A special thanks to Ruth Bauer, Ph.D., and her husband, Hans, son Paul, and daughter Betsy, for their friendship and encouragement. A special thanks to Ruth for her devotion, patience, and expertise, putting all of the manuscript on computer disc, while working from my rough typewritten drafts with all of their chicken scratches, and most of all for her untiring encouragement over so many years.

A special thanks to my good friend Candace Mcm. Routh, a business communications consultant, for her many hours of editing, constructive criticism and suggestions.

I would like to express my appreciation to local travel agent Bonnie Czuchra for her help in arranging my travel schedule to places far and wide to do research on this book. Most of the time she was able to get me a window seat so that I could see and appreciate some of the countryside, before or aft of the wing, of course. I would never pull the shade down while flying over this beautiful land.

Partial Listing of People
Charles A. Lindbergh, Anne Morrow Lindbergh, Reeve Lindbergh, Wendy Lindbergh,

Lars Lindbergh, John Underwood, William T. Larkins, Peter M. Bowers, Richard Sanders Allen, Dr. Paul E. Garber, Claude Ryan, Dan Hagedorn, Bob Bailey, William Wagner, Kirsten J. Cassagneres Salvador, Bryan Ev Cassagneres, Eline O. Cassagneres, Elizabeth Ferguson, Ed Morrow, Judith Schiff of Yale University, David Bilodeau of Yale University, Oce and Lorna Dotson, John Barker, George Gentsch, Nel MacCraken, Donald Keyhoe, Roger Thiel, Carol Keyhoe, Richard Hall, Robert Arehart, Mrs. Clyde Wann, Warren Shipp, Rogers Studio, Clarence Chamberlin, Mrs. Allen W. McCann Jr., Bob Cornwell, Stanley Jones, William F. Chana, Fred L. Barber, Binka Bone, Charles Hansen, Ed Eilertsen, Dennis Parks, Tom Poberezny, Susan A. Lurvey, Robin Williams, Ray Howland, Donna Recko, Eusabio Zambrano, M.D., Harvey Lippincott, William H. Gates, Jansz V. (Jack) Vander Veer, Francis J. Menez, Richard A. Washburn, Roy Meyers, Carlos Rosa Mejia, Dan Wykoff, Paul W. Looney, Carl J. Brobrow, Smithsonian Aeronautics Division, John E. Anstensen, Tom Heitzman, Maryann Bury, Charles F. Schultz, James B. Horne, Arvela Horne, Barbara Horne, William H. Shay Jr., Paul Shay, Steve Moisen, John Reznikoff, Stanley King, Dewey France, Joshua Stoff, Steve Mulligan, Benjamin R. Schlapak, Eleo and David Ammen, Ginny Hoffman, Bob Jones and Stan Cohen and Leslie Maricelli of Pictorial Histories Publishing Co. I would also like to express my gratitude to two good friends, Virginia "Ginger" Mountjoy and Lucie Douglass, for their individual expertise as we went into the final production and publication of this book, and David A. Douglass, posthumously.

Associations–Administrations-Institutions Armed Forces–Corporations

Ryan Aeronautical Company, Ryan Aeronautical Library; San Diego Aero Space Museum; National Air and Space Museum; American Aviation Historical Society; Federal Aviation Administration; National Archives; Library of Congress; Daniel Guggenheim Foundation; National Geographic Society; Experimental Aircraft Association; Aircraft Owners & Pilots Association; National Aeronautic Association; Airguide Publications, Inc.; Jeppesen Sanderson, Inc.; National Oceanic and Atmospheric Administration; Aviation Publication Service; United States Air Force Museum, Wright-Patterson Air Force Base; Pratt & Whitney Aircraft Company; Yale University, Sterling Memorial Library–Manuscripts and Archives; U.S. Air Force Association–Charles A. Lindbergh Chapter; Missouri Historical Society; Minnesota Historical Society; Charles A. Lindbergh Museum and Interpretation Center, Little Falls, Minnesota; The Charles A. and Anne Morrow Lindbergh Foundation; CAL/NX211 Collectors Society; Martin Luther King Library of Washington, D.C.; Anacostia Naval Air Station; Delta Airlines; Canadian Aviation Historical Association; Henry Ford Museum; Cradle of Aviation Museum; Museum of Flight, Seattle, WA; National Aviation Museum–Ottawa, Ontario, Canada; National Library of Canada–Ottawa, Ontario, Canada; National Archives of Canada–Ottawa, Ontario, Canada; American embassies of the countries of Mexico, Belize, Guatemala, Honduras, Salvador, Costa Rica, Panama, Colombia, Venezuela, Dominican Republic, Haiti and Cuba. Further listings and credits may be found in the contents of footnotes and endnotes.

Photographic Sources and Credits

Every effort has been made to credit the original photographer or any other appropriate person. However, photographs are frequently traded or sold, and the individual who snapped the camera shutter is often lost to history. For that reason the person who supplied the photo to this author is named in many cases where the original photographer is not known or doubt exists as to who the original photographer was.

Some photographs can be credited to the original photographer, such as Major Erickson of San Diego. Others were supplied by Ryan Company employees, pilots, Ryan or other aircraft owners, aviation enthusiasts/historians, collectors, people from the general public, libraries, historical archives, museums, educational institutions, commercial photographers or commercial photo archives.

I wish to credit Ryan Aeronautical Library, Ryan Aeronautical Corporation, San Diego Aero Space Museum, National Air and Space Museum, National Archives, Library of Congress, Leo B. Kimball Collection, Pratt & Whitney Aircraft Company, Charles A. and Anne Morrow Lindbergh Foundation, Missouri Historical Society, Minnesota Historical Society, Charles A. Lindbergh Museum at Little Falls, Minnesota, Cradle of Aviation Museum, Yale University Manuscripts and Archives; Experimental Aircraft Association, Donald E. Keyhoe Collection, National Geographic Society, Bettmann/Corbis Archives, Underwood and Underwood and miscellaneous libraries, universities, schools, institutions, individuals, and private collections.

In my teens while living across the street from a pioneer aircraft engine designer, who became my mentor, I was thrilled beyond all imagination when he offered his sizable collection of original glossy, often professionally taken, old aircraft photos and negatives, which included scores of NYP pictures. His name was Leo B. Kimball, designer of the Kimball "Beetle" radial engine. Many of these NYP photos I had never seen before or since. He gave them to me with the understanding that I would preserve them as best I could, and I have respected that wish.

Often a photo was found at a flea market or some other obscure location, with no information on the back. At a later date the same photo was found in a commercial photographic archive, for which there was a very high price for a copy, plus a high fee for publishing rights. Due to the lack of sufficient funds for this project, I often chose to use the same photo that was found at sources named above, as this photo quality was as good as the commercially supplied one. In some cases there are many duplicate photos of Lindbergh and the NYP, which were printed by the hundred in 1927 or later. This author has found that many of them ended up in private collections, but others found their way into commercial photographic archives, for which a large fee was charged for a print and publishing rights on top of that.

So it has been most difficult to make decisions regarding which photos to use for this book to more completely tell the story.

After this book is published I am certain that someone will appear who might know the answer to some questions I have been unable to answer before going to press. In addition, there is likely someone out there who will challenge some point I have made. Such people will say, "Why didn't you contact me?," I would have, had I known of their existence.

If I have made life a bit easier for the next generation of aviation historians, who may show an interest in continuing the research on these tours, then this work has not been in vain.

The tours came to represent a historical turning point. The world was at peace, and man had seemingly triumphed over nature, and especially the vast Atlantic Ocean. The tours were physical justification for man's and the aviation community's optimism, and the perfect backdrop for the advancement of air travel to what we have today.

Additional acknowledgments may be found at the end of each individual tour stop. They will include individuals as well as organizations, museums, libraries, archives, embassies and other government agencies.

The "brand new" Spirit of St. Louis shortly after rollout at San Diego in May 1927. RYAN AERONAUTICAL COMPANY

Table of Contents

Another look at the "brand new" Spirit of St. Louis shortly after
rollout at San Diego in May 1927. RYAN AERONAUTICAL COMPANY

ALBUQUERQUE BUSINESS COLLEGE

ALBUERQUE, NEW MEXICO

June 12, 1927.

Honorable Frank B. Kellogg,
Secretary of State,
Washington, D. C.

Sir:

The great achievement of Colonel Charles A.
Lindbergh in making the first non-stop aerial
flight across the Atlantic Ocean, has placed his
name on the Honor Roll of the Great Men of History.
And we rejoice that he is an American.

What more fitting tribute could be paid to
him than for the Government of the United States
to purchase his monoplane, "The Spirit of St. Louis,"
and place it, assembled ready for flight, in the
Smithsonian Institute as a permanent Memorial to
the noble flier and his great achievement, and there
to remain as "The Spirit of America," the harbinger
of peace, progress, and good will to the nation of
the earth?

Respectfully,

B. L. McDaniel

Principal Shorthand Department.

Copy

Introduction

After leaving the NYP at the Wright Aeronautical Corporation hangar at Teterboro, New Jersey, on July 4, Lindbergh was invited to the Guggenheim estate (Falaise) at Port Washington on Long Island, New York. It was during his stay there that Lindbergh worked on his first and most notable book, *We*. He completed the work in the incredible time of only two weeks, just before he was to leave on the goodwill tour.

Extensive work was accomplished at Teterboro (see Chapter 3) to prepare the NYP for the upcoming tour of the United States. The engine was removed for a top overhaul. A Splitdorf booster magneto was installed for easier engine starting. Several louvers were noticeably cut into the engine cowling, in order to give better cooling during hot weather in the desert areas of the West and Southwest. The oil tank was removed for repairs. A general overhaul of the airframe was done, similar to the present day "annual" license, and the liquid magnetic compass was swung at this time.

The Daniel Guggenheim Fund never did a finer thing for civil aviation and air travel than when it arranged and financed Lindbergh's "evangelical" U.S. tour. It was a remarkable demonstration of efficiency, dependability and safety of the airplane that was to break through the longtime public apathy and open the mind of the average citizen and politician to the possibilities of traveling by airplane.

This incredible tour would win more converts to the gospel of commercial aviation than any other single event in its history. Lindbergh and the tour personnel would be given such a welcome by the people of this country as had seldom been showered upon a private citizen at that time. Lindbergh's tactics followed those of the old barnstormers, but none of those gypsy aviators ever dreamed of the vast crowds that they would draw wherever they would land.

Through the press and motion pictures, Lindbergh's name and face were known to every man, woman, and child in the country. He became a household word. A hero of all heroes. Everyone knew who he was and what he did. And by this time the 120 million people in the United States, if not the entire world, knew all about his earlier accomplishments, family background, education, etc., but little knowledge about the famous airplane. This three-month tour would provide the opportunity to see, and inspect and photograph this wonderful airplane and watch and listen to it fly.

Hundreds of towns and cities across the nation requested a visit from Lindbergh. Scores of schoolchildren signed petitions for him to visit their school. State governors, powerful politicians, and other government officials and businessmen requested his presence.

Lindbergh insisted on breathtaking precision and regularity and strict adherence to the schedule in order to prove the dependability and reliability of air travel. They had scheduled to arrive at each stop at precisely two o'clock. As it turned out they did make that schedule, with some exceptions. Due to a thick fog at Portland, Maine, early in the trip, they were delayed, the only such weather-related circumstance on the whole trip. Other delays were due to either misunderstanding or misinformation with regard to the time zones, as you will see in the text.

The flight, *as planned*, would cover about 22,000 miles and would be completed with clockwork precision in three months. A carefully worked out itinerary was to involve all forty-eight continental states. It would include twenty-three state capitals, with a total of eighty "official" stops, of which eleven would be brief "touch" stops. Twenty-one were of longer duration, with ceremonies and speeches. They spent ninety-two overnights. Lindbergh would take up eight passengers in the NYP during the tour.

This grueling schedule placed tremendous physical strain on Lindbergh and his crew, not only from the flying itself, but from the demands of the programs at each stop. A physical examination was given to Lindbergh on two occasions, once at Chicago and another at Little Rock, Arkansas. He passed each perfectly with an A-1 rating.

The tour proved the strength of his determination and the accuracy of his careful, scientific planning and calculations. He was able to handle the constantly changing circumstances and un-

foreseen situations with ease, diplomacy and dignity.

Lindbergh attended sixty-five official dinners and banquets, participated in countless miles of parades, and was seen and heard by roughly 30 million people.

The flyer would make 144 speeches selling the virtues of the future of aviation and the need to develop airports, and safety and reliability in air travel for the general public. He attended receptions, meetings, and dinners, where more honors were showered upon him. At the end of the tour, the NYP had accumulated a total of 260:30 hours of flight time.

Looking at Lindbergh's running log, one will notice excessive flight time between some cities. This was due in part to the many requests from other cities whose inhabitants wished to see the NYP as it circled overhead, and in part to unforeseen weather conditions and head winds. The crew also at times spontaneously made extra detour flights for the purpose of exploration.

During the tour there were no forced landings, no overhauls, and no delays of any kind from mechanical difficulties. Both the NYP and its companion plane spent at least one night in each of the lower 48 states and flew in various kinds of weather conditions, including one night flight. Twenty-five percent of the terrain covered was mountainous. They did not follow any regular airways.

Thursdays and Saturdays were originally set up as rest days, although there were times when they did fly on those days to make up time, adhere to the schedule, or do local pleasure/passenger flights, or for some other reason.

Several days of vacation at Butte, Montana, were taken in early September at the camp of J. Carlos Ryan, a trustee of the Guggenheim Fund.

Each of the cities visited responded to the promotion of air travel. Other opportunities came as they flew over other cities and towns en route. At each of these places a specially printed address of greeting was dropped overboard by Lindbergh as he passed overhead. The text of these messages was:

Aboard *Spirit of St. Louis* on tour
Greetings:
Because of the limited time and the extensive itinerary of the Tour of the United States now in progress to encourage popular interest in aeronautics, it is impossible for the *Spirit of St. Louis* to land in your city.

This message from the air, however, is sent you to express our sincere appreciation of your interest in the Tour and in the promotion and extension of commercial aeronautics in the United States.

We feel that we will be amply repaid for all our efforts if each and every citizen in the United States cherishes an interest in flying and gives his earnest support to the Air Mail Service and the establishment of airports and similar facilities. The concerted efforts of the citizens of the United States in this direction will result in America's taking its rightful place, within a very short time, as the world leader in commercial flying.

(signed) Charles A. Lindbergh
(signed) Harry F. Guggenheim,
President
Daniel Guggenheim Fund for
the Promotion of Aeronautics
(signed) William P. MacCracken Jr.
Assistant Secretary of Aeronautics
Department of Commerce

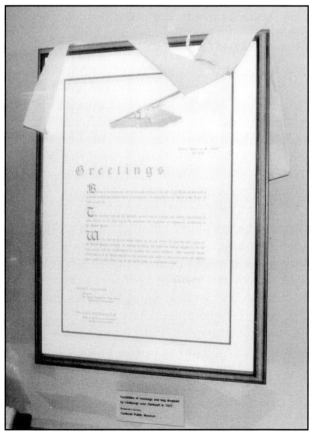

The message and bag dropped by Lindbergh over Oshkosh in 1927 is on display at the EAA Museum in Oshkosh, Wisconsin.

Rare photo of a man holding a special message of greeting that was enclosed in a canvas bag and dropped from the NYP with an orange streamer attached. Location of this particular one could be somewhere in Minnesota. THE CHARLES A. AND ANNE MORROW LINDBERGH FOUNDATION

Each of these messages was enclosed in a canvas bag, with an orange streamer attached to attract attention. One of these original messages exists and is on display at the Experimental Aircraft Association Air Museum in Oshkosh, Wisconsin.

Lindbergh's intimate knowledge of the air mail service, from his personal experiences, credited him with speaking with confidence and authority on the achievements and prospects for the future development of air mail. He had worked hard as an air mail aviator in those pioneering and difficult days in the previous years. He pointed out that in 1926 on six of the air mail routes in the country 34 million letters had been carried and four million miles flown.

His presentations were sufficient to convince the most hardened skeptic of the immense possibilities of commercial aviation. Not only did he direct his prophesies and appeals to the general public and ask for their support, but he was incredibly convincing in offering valuable advice to municipal authorities and politicians to establish new airports and to improve existing flying fields and their facilities.

Lindbergh stated in one of his speeches, "I believe that the best way to promote aeronautics in a given locality is to establish a well-equipped airport. The city will then be visited frequently by aircraft, thus allowing its citizens to become accustomed to the sight and performance of these modern means of transport. I believe that any city can work wonders with respect to its transportation problem by merely establishing an airport and using the airplane services wherever possible."

Lindbergh spoke with authority regarding the air transport industry and the problems it had been facing. After all, did he not prove the possibilities of long-distance flight over an unforgiving ocean, alone with a single-engine airplane and predicting the possibilities beyond anyone's wildest dreams?

As convincing as he was in his delivery during these many speeches, and his background experience in the industry, one could not help but be impressed with the man, his lifestyle, personality and dedication. Everyone just loved him, and all he stood for and believed in.

The Tour's Detailed and Careful Planning

Special goodwill tour regulations were implemented to insure the safety of Lindbergh and his crew.

Security regulations and standards were of top priority. They included a ban on flying escorts, whether military or civilian, although that was waived more than once.

Harry Guggenheim was in favor of a rule that any other aircraft were not to be in the air but should stay on the ground before the NYP arrived at each stop. Guggenheim was quite insistent, even though Lindbergh felt they should not order other pilots around and suggested he could keep clear of any other aircraft in the air. But Guggenheim was of the opinion that less experienced aviators might just collide with another machine. Lindbergh, after some thought, conceded, "All right, I'd rather not do it, but we can't have any accidents."

Additionally, there were to be no other aircraft on the landing field. That rule was broken a number of times as the tour progressed. Where one existed, a guarded hangar was to be provided for the NYP and the *Fairchild*, to protect the aircraft and offer inside space for mechanics to service, refuel, and do oil changes out of the weather.

As it turned out the rule was obeyed by both commercial and military pilots (with some exceptions), although the *Fairchild* had to police the area ahead of or before the NYP came into the area.

As for crowd control, in most cases the local and state National Guard were the main force, working with local police and in many cases the local Boy Scout troop or troops. They oversaw requirements for spectator viewing areas and adequate parking for automobiles. Many organizations wanted to be part of the parades in each city or town, but they were discouraged because it would take up too much of the precious time allotted for Lindbergh's parade.

Since any downtown areas would be too crowded and have inadequate parking areas, local parks or fairgrounds were selected for Lindbergh's daytime speeches, mostly to children and their parents.

Rules for the local celebrations were quite specific. Each city was allowed from 2:00 p.m. until 3:30 p.m. for welcoming ceremonies. From

3:30 p.m. until 4:30 p.m. was the time slot for Lindbergh to make an outdoor speech from a platform equipped with a sound amplification system.

Each evening there would be a banquet to start no later than 7:00 p.m. and at that time Lindbergh would speak for no more than fifteen minutes. The banquet guests were to be the local politicians, business people and other dignitaries from the area.

Finally, he would have to be in bed by 9:00 p.m. Rest was most important for Lindbergh and his crew, considering the hectic day-after-day schedule.

Advance man Milburn Kusterer would go to each one of the stops about two weeks in advance. He would work with the welcoming committee and other city officials, in order to fit in and coordinate Lindbergh's schedule with theirs. Kusterer traveled by train on the zig-zag route around the country.

During the planning stages of the tour, it was agreed they would make at least one overnight stop in each state. They discovered during the trip, however, that by error only a "touch stop" had been scheduled for two states, one of which was South Dakota. Lindbergh was not happy when he learned of this oversight.

He asked where they were planning to be on the next rest day, which was to be Denver. He said that they would have to do an overnight in South Dakota. He said, "We can make Pierre, South Dakota, that day and get back to Cheyenne on the next. That will give us a trip over the Bad Lands and the Black Hills, too. We can fly over the summer White House."

So, instead of flying from Denver directly to Cheyenne, they made the trip to Pierre, South Dakota.

"Two weeks till we get another rest," said Doc Maidment. Lindbergh answered unsympathetically, "We're getting to see more of the country, and we can rest at Butte. Remember, we get a week there." and that settled it.

On July 19 Lindbergh picked up the NYP at Teterboro, inspected the machine after its extensive overhaul, and made the thirty-minute flight from there to Mitchel Field, to be in position for the start of the goodwill tour, and that is where our story of the "Tour" begins.

Insurance

Lindbergh was apparently insured for life at $25,000; property damage, $10,000; fire, $15,000; public liability, $10,000 to $100,000.[1] It was considered today's "new business."

Further, regarding his insurace coverage while on the goodwill tour of the country, he was covered for fire, property damage and liability. It was underwritten by The Independence Companies, Philadelphia, Pa.[2]

Navigation Lights Situation

Throughout the flying life of the NYP, Lindbergh flew the airplane illegally with respect to night flights. In the original design, to save weight, there was no provision for navigation lights.

Lindbergh did, however, question such a requirement before leaving New York on the flight to Paris. He was granted verbal permission to fly without them by William P. MacCracken Jr.

In 1927 there were laws on the books, known than as Air Commerce Regulations, Department of Commerce, Aeronautics Branch, that became effective on December 31, 1926. The regulations read as follows:

Section 83, Lights

(A) Angular limits – The angular limits laid down in these rules will be determined as when the aircraft is in a normal flying position.

(B) Airplane lights – Between one-half hour after sunset and one-half hour before sunrise airplanes in flight must show the following lights:

1. On right side a green light and on left side a red light, showing unbroken light between two vertical planes whose dihedral angle is 100 degrees when measured to the right and left, respectively, from dead ahead and to be visible at least two miles.

2. At the rear and as far aft as possible a white light shining rearward, visible in a dihedral angle of 140 degrees bisected by a vertical plane through the line of flight and visible at least three miles.[3]

Now a goodwill tour of the United States was about to begin, and surely one would ex-

pect that Lindbergh might have to fly during some portion of night time. But no record of Lindbergh being approached or cited by someone from the Department of Commerce has ever been found. As you will see, he did encounter a night flight from Santa Fe, New Mexico, to Abilene, Texas.

Crew Luggage Carried on Fairchild

The Fairchild carried the following items on the U.S. tour:

4 special suit bags, which held 3 suits each

5 hand bags

2 briefcases

1 camera

Complete set of tools and spare parts for the J-5 engines in both airplanes and appropriate airframe parts for both aircraft.[4]

Course Plotted by the Author
(See also page 335)

When working out the plotting of Lindbergh's tour of the United States, the latest (1999-2000) Sectional Aeronautical Charts with a scale of 1:500,000 were used.

As a guide, Lindbergh's flight log, as printed in the book *Spirit of St. Louis* by Charles A. Lindbergh (pages 503-513), was used.

With a red pencil I drew a straight line from one point of reference (city, town, geographical location, etc.) to the next point of reference. A measurement in statute miles was recorded. If Lindbergh flew from one city/town in a straight line to the next city/town, I took the measurement, for instance, from the center of the city/town in each case.

All of the straight-line course distances added up to a total of 17,470 statute miles. To come up with a total actual distance, which would include his circling both cities/towns, airports or

other sites, I found it would be difficult if not impossible to measure on any kind of chart. Therefore, I averaged such circles as being at a minimum of five miles for one circle, to perhaps ten miles or more for two or more circles.

Lindbergh used only his watch plus the panel-mounted Waltham clock (model XA-15J) in the NYP to determine his flight time. But it is not known if he timed his actual flight time from engine start-up to engine shutdown, or from takeoff to landing touchdown time.

He did not have a Hobbs Meter or Recording Tachometer, such as is used in modern-day aircraft to record flight time.

Conclusion

As the years since have shown, the tour message came through. There was a major boom in American aviation development and rapid acceleration of aviation and aeronautical technology. Further advancement in research, engineering and freight, air mail and passenger volume and the number of new airports and air routes were documented in the years 1928 and 1929.

Yes, the tour WAS successful.*

Footnotes

1. *The Detroit News*, August 1, 1927, "The Insurance of WE."

2. Publication: *The Insurance Field*, #56, July-December 1927, 900 I17 full page advertisement, The Independence Companies, Philadelphia, Pa.

3. Taken from *Aircraft Year Book, 1927*, Aeronautical Chamber of Commerce of America, Inc., New York City, page 371.

4. *Flying With Lindbergh* by Donald E. Keyhoe, Grosset & Dunlap Publishers, New York, 1928. Published by arrangement with G.P. Putnam's Sons, page 141.

* The success of Lindbergh's tour can be shown by the response of various cities which he visited such as Jackson, Mississippi, where the citizens took a far-reaching step by approving a special bond issue, funds from which were to be used to acquire land and to build a municipal airport. This action marked the real beginning of the air age for Jackson (a common outcome in various cities across the U.S.)

CHAPTER ONE
THE GUGGENHEIM CONNECTION

A Swiss, who was born in 1827 and had lived in a ghetto, migrated to Philadelphia.[1] His name was Meyer Guggenheim, a physically small person with quick movements and sharp eyes, intuitive, farsighted, and full of vigor and stamina. He had many interests and was quick to understand the practical matters of life.

Meyer made his living by peddling pins, needles, lace, shoestrings, spices and other items carried in a backpack.[2] Some years later he became the owner of a small shop, an importer, a mine owner, a commission merchant, and eventually not only a millionaire but a multimillionaire.

Meyer married Barbara Meyer and had eight sons, one of whom was Daniel.[3] Like his father, he became a businessman and entrepreneur. Daniel was born in Philadelphia in 1856 and at the age of seventeen, when his formal education ended, was sent to take charge of the Swiss branch of a manufacturing and merchandising enterprise built up by his father.[4] Eleven years later he returned to the United States to participate in another family venture: mining and smelting.[5] Daniel subsequently became one of the world's most famous capitalists and philanthropists.[6]

Daniel's interest in aviation began almost by accident.[7] He had two sons, Robert and Harry Frank G. (born August 23, 1890), and when the United States entered into World War I both sons enlisted. Harry was a Navy lieutenant and served as a naval aviator in the United States Naval Aviation Forces in France, England and Italy. In 1918 he was commissioned a lieutenant commander and came home with a deep impression of the possibilities aviation might bring to his country. He was especially interested in peacetime aviation, which he felt might be one of the major forward surges in human development in his lifetime.

Unfortunately, in the years after the war, aviation experienced a time of troubles with little if any progress. Military pilots came out of the service expecting to find work in aviation but could only live a precarious life of performing aerial circus stunts at carnivals and country fairs, doing wing-walking, parachute-jumping, and taking passengers for rides. If they did not do any of that "barnstorming," they went into some other field of endeavor.

Some of these flyers were fortunate enough to find employment in flying the mail, following the inauguration of air mail lines by the United States Post Office in 1918. However, by the early 1920s it appeared that the development of aviation, once so hopeful, had become stalled for lack of public interest and government support.

In early 1925 Daniel had a very important conversation with his son Harry F. at their Hempstead House, a castle of gray stone near Falaise at Port Washington on the North Shore of Long Island. This talk related to the raising of $500,000 for the purpose of starting aeronautical education at New York University.[8]

That conversation opened a new chapter for the United States in the air. The father was planting a small seed from which has ripened the rich harvest of civil aviation in this country and would become the envy of the world. Daniel Guggenheim, who never in his life owned an airplane or an airline, or even a pilot's license, will never know how much he contributed to the aviation industry.

Daniel was known for his vision and broad philanthropic patriotism. He had a strong passion for providing opportunities for young men and enough insight to see that a new field lay ready for cultivation in aviation and air travel.

Thus was founded the Daniel Guggenheim School of Aeronautics at New York University. This was the root from which would spring the Daniel Guggenheim Fund for the Promotion of Aeronautics, a benefaction that resulted in the expenditure of more than $3 million allocated so that its influence may today be traced to every activity of aviation: to train men and women, for technical advancement, for safety, comfort and speed.

The fund was to have spectacular results in

helping for the first time to make Americans air-minded and to demonstrate that flight was a safe, practical method of transportation, that pilots could adhere to set schedules, and that long distances could be covered in a very short time.

The fund would sponsor "air tours" that would permit the public to see in person famous flyers and their airplanes, to listen to their predictions, and to witness demonstrations of their flying skill.[9]

The idea was sparked in Guggenheim's mind when, on May 9, 1926, Commander Richard E. Byrd in a tri-motor Fokker airplane named the *Josephine Ford* and piloted by Floyd Bennett, flew over the North Pole.[10] They had taken off from King's Bay, Spitzbergen, and returned sixteen hours later to world acclaim. It was after this flight that Guggenheim invited the pair to undertake an air tour of the principal cities of the United States.

That first "tour" began at Washington, D.C., on October 7, 1926, and made its first stop at Mitchel Field. After a circuitous route around the country, they returned and landed on Bolling Field, new Washington, D.C., on November 23, 1926.[11]

At the tour's completion, Harry Guggenheim had this to say:

"I think it a remarkable demonstration of the advances already made in aviation that the same plane which carried Commander Byrd and Pilot Bennett over the North Pole is able to complete a swing around the country with no more difficulty than would be found on a motor trip over present-day good roads."[12]

Lindbergh recalled years later,

"I first heard about it when I was a mail pilot on the St. Louis-Chicago route. I remember clearly being impressed by the fact that a great foundation had been established to encourage the development of aviation. I believe one of the more important results from the establishment of the Daniel Guggenheim Fund, certainly one of the most immediate results, lay in the confidence it implied in civil aviation in those early years, and in the respectability it gave the profession.

"The announcement of a multi-million dollar fund, created by a successful and respected businessman, had an extraordinary effect on morale and went far in supporting the claims of those of us who believed that the airplane had a brilliant future."[13]

By the time Lindbergh met Harry Guggenheim at Curtiss Field, Harry had become president and trustee of the fund. It was at that meeting that Guggenheim said, "When you get back from your flight, look me up."[14] Sometime later Mr. Guggenheim admitted to Lindbergh that he had not thought there was much chance that Lindbergh would make it back from such a flight. Lindbergh considered his invitation a gesture of politeness and promptly forgot about it.

But when Lindbergh returned to New York after the flight, many people advised him to contact Harry Guggenheim to express his desire to become involved in the development of aviation in this country.

When they did meet, on June 17, 1927, Lindbergh and Guggenheim together decided to do a three-month flying tour with the NYP, which the Daniel Guggenheim Fund would finance. As a result of this agreement, Lindbergh and Harry Guggenheim became good friends over the years. Guggenheim eventually appointed Lindbergh as an advisor to the fund.

At that first meeting on June 17, in the Operations Office at Mitchel Field on Long Island, New York, Donald E. Keyhoe, Lindbergh and Harry Guggenheim met to discuss a Lindbergh goodwill tour of the United States in the *Spirit of St. Louis.*

Donald Keyhoe was with the Department of Commerce, Aeronautics Branch, and was asked by that branch's Assistant Secretary William P. MacCracken to be Lindbergh's aide.

During the meeting Mr. Guggenheim said to Keyhoe, "The Colonel is leaving for St. Louis in a little while. I suggest that we go into the Operations Office and find a map. The colonel can indicate in general how he wants us to plan the tour, and we can work up the details later."[15]

Lindbergh suggested that it would be a straight business tour to promote interest in aviation.[16] In addition he said they would visit each of the states and as many representative cities as they could in the three months allotted for the trip. They would fly via the regular air routes, but would fly straight over the mountains in order to save time.[17]

- 8 -

From left to right, Lindbergh with President Calvin Coolidge and William P. MacCracken Jr., Assistant Secretary of Aeronautics, Department of Commerce.

Lindbergh said, "If the Department agrees to send a plane along, I'd like to have them pick Philip R. Love for the pilot. He's an inspector there, I think. I've known him in the Army and in the mail service. There isn't a better cross country pilot in the game. Besides, he's a good fellow and he'd be a help on this tour."[18]

Due to limited space inside the NYP, MacCracken suggested they have an escort airplane, which he would supply, that was owned and operated by the Department of Commerce. The airplane would carry a support group and equipment to accompany him on the flight.

Fairchild FC-2 Escort Airplane

The airplane was a recently built *Fairchild FC-2* (Fairchild Cabin No. 2) which was s/n 2, and carried registration number NS-7.[19] This airplane was powered by a Wright J-5 "Whirlwind" radial engine of 220 hp, the same type and model engine used in the NYP. It had a forty-four-foot wing span, an empty weight of 1,790 pounds, a gross weight of 3,225 pounds, could cruise at 103 mph and had a fuel capacity of seventy-five gallons. It could carry one pilot and four passengers. The fuselage was painted black, the wings and tail group international orange with markings on the wing, fin and rudder in black. The Department of Commerce Aeronautics Branch "winged" logo was painted on both sides of the fuselage.

The following was printed on the cockpit door:

United States Tour
Of
Charles A. Lindbergh
Under the auspices of
Daniel Guggenheim Fund
For The
Promotion of Aeronautics
Department of Commerce

And on the vertical fin:

Model FC-2
Fairchild Airplane Mfg. Corp.
Farmingdale, L. I., New York

MacCracken selected this airplane because of its high utility capabilities. It was often referred to as the one-ton truck of the air, a jack-of-all-trades aircraft. It was built in June 1927, just one month after the New York to Paris flight, by the Fairchild Airplane Manufacturing Corporation of Farmingdale, Long Island, New York, and was a high-wing monoplane. It was fully capable of carrying the necessary tools, spare parts and tour crew as well as other baggage and cameras.

Donald Keyhoe was one of the passengers. The other was Theodore "Ted" R. Sorenson, selected by the Wright Aeronautical Corporation as the engine and airframe mechanic for both airplanes. He was later replaced at Minneapolis by engineering mechanic C. C. "Doc" Maidment when Sorenson was recalled by the Wright Corporation.[20]

After the tour was over, the Fairchild was re-registered under the license C-9104, but further history and final disposition is not known.

On June 29, 1927, the Guggenheim Fund officially announced that Lindbergh would undertake a flight tour of the United States "for the primary purpose of stimulating popular interest in the use of air transport.[21]

"It will enable millions of people who have had an opportunity only to read and hear about the Colonel's remarkable achievement to see him and his plane in action. It is our belief that such an expedition…will strike the air-consciousness of the American people and give added impetus to commercial flying as a practical, safe, and useful means of transportation."[22]

This dream and foresight was shown in the nationwide tour of Colonel Charles A. Lindbergh in the NYP, thanks to the sponsorship and organization of the Guggenheim Fund.

The Fairchild FC-2, with registration N-57, was the U.S. Tour escort aircraft. FAIRCHILD REPUBLIC COMPANY VIA GEORGE CLAPP

A close-up view of the Fairchild FC-2 with Phil Love in the front (pilot's) seat, and Donald Keyhoe just stepping out of the cabin. LEO B. KIMBALL COLLECTION

Footnotes

1. *Seed Money - The Guggenheim Story,* by Milton Lomask, Farrar, Straus and Company, New York, 1964, first printing, pages 14, 15.

2. *Charles A. Lindbergh Autobiography of Values* Editor, William Jovanovich, Coeditor, Judith A. Schiff, Yale University, Harcourt, Brace Jovanovich, New York and London, 1977, pages 341,342.

3. *Ibid.*

4. *The Guggenheim Medalists,* G. Edward Pendray, Editor, The Guggenheim Medal Board of Award of the United Engineering Trustees, Inc. New York 1964, pages 11, 12, 31-38

5. *Ibid.* p 11.

6. *Ibid.* p. 11.

7. *Ibid.* p. 12.

8. *America Fledges Wings: The History of the Daniel Guggenheim Fund for the Promotion of Aeronautics,* by Reginald M. Cleveland, 1942, Pitman Publishing Corporation, New York and Chicago, page 1.

9. *Medalists Ibid.* page 31.

10. *Ibid.* page 31, 32

11. *Ibid.* page 33

12. *Ibid.* page 33

13. *Ibid.*

14. *The Spirit of St. Louis* by Charles A. Lindbergh, Charles Scribner's Sons, 1953, New York, page 168.

15. *Flying with Lindbergh* by Donald E. Keyhoe, Grossett & Dunlap, 1928, page 5.

16. *Ibid.* page 5.

17. *Ibid.* page 6.

18. *Ibid.* page 7.

19. *Journal of the American Aviation Historical Society* "Fairchild FC-2" by George H. Clapp, Winter 1982, Vol 27 no. 4, pages 280, 281.

20. *National Geographic Magazine,* January 1928, "Seeing America With Lindbergh" by Donald E. Keyhoe, page 17.

21. *Medalists Ibid.* page 34.

22. *Ibid.* page 34

October 4th, '27.

Mr. Perham C. Nahl,
6043 Harwood Avenue,
Oakland, Calif.

Dear Mr. Nahl:

In reply to your letter of September 23rd, I am pleased to grant your request and am sending you herewith Colonel Lindbergh's itinerary, which I think will answer your purpose.

Very truly yours,

Lewis Lee

START	ARRIVAL DATE
New York City	July 20
Hartford	" 20
Providence	" 21
Boston	" 22
Portland	" 23-24
Concord - N H	" 25
Springfield-Vermont	" 26
Albany	" 27
Schenectady	" 28 (touch Stop)
Syracuse	" 28
Buffalo	" 29 - 30 - 31
Erie	Aug 1 - (touch stop)
Cleveland	" 1 - 2
Pittsburgh	" 3
Wheeling	" 4
Dayton	" 5
Cincinnati	" 6 - 7
Louisville	" 8
Indianapolis	" 9
Detroit	" 10-11
Grand Rapids	" 12
Chicago	" 13-14
Springfield	" 15 (touch stop)
St Louis	" 15 - 16
Kansas City	" 17
Wichita	" 18
St Joseph	" 19 (touch stop)

TriCities	August 19th
Moline	
Davenport	
Rock Island	
Milwaukee	" 20 - 21
Madison	" 22
Twin Cities	" 23-24
St Paul	
Minneapolis	
Little Falls	" 25
Fargo	" 26
Sioux Falls	" 27 (touch stop)
Sioux City	" 27 - 28
Des Moines	" 29
Omaha	" 30
Denver	" 31 -Sept 1st.
Cheyenne	Sept. 2
Salt Lake City	" 3 - 4
Boise	" 5
Butte	" 6-7-8- -10-11
Spokane	" 12
Seattle	" 13
Portland	" 14 - 15
San Francisco - Oakland	" 16
Sacramento	" 17 - 18
Reno	" 19
Los Angeles	" 20
San Diego	" 21 - 22
Tuscon	" 23
Lordsburg	24 (touch stop)
El Paso	24

Santa Fe	Sept. 25th
Abilene (2 Hour stop)	" 25
Fort Worth	" 26
Dallas	" 27
Oklahoma City	" 28 - 29
Tulsa	" 30
Muskogee - Okla	Oct 1st (1 hour stop)
Little Rock	" 1 - 2
Memphis	" 3
Nashville	" 4
Chattanooga (1 hour stop)	" 5
Birmingham	" 5 - 6
Jackson	" 7
New Orleans	" 8 - 9
Jacksonville	" 10
Atlanta	" 11
Spartanburg	" 12 - 13
Winston Salem	" 14
Richmond	" 15-16
Washington	" 17
Baltimore	" 18
Atlantic City	" 19 - 20
Wilmington	" 21
Phila	" 22
New York City	" 23

-12-

CHAPTER TWO
ST. LOUIS - SELFRIDGE FIELD - CANADA - TETERBORO
June 17, 1927, to July 4, 1927

While the Guggenheim Fund was working out the details for the upcoming United States good will tour, and after Lindbergh attended numerous banquets and other honoring festivities, he prepared for another flight.

It would take him from New York to St. Louis to be honored by the city where his sponsorship was based, then on to Selfridge Field in Michigan, and Ottawa, Canada. From there he would fly down to Teterboro, New Jersey.

After the NYP's engine was given a careful inspection by Wright Aeronautical's R. Herald Kinkaid, Lindbergh took off from Mitchel Field at 8:18 a.m. on Friday, June 17, and headed west. His route took him over the Wright Aeronautical plant in Paterson, New Jersey, then over Columbus, Ohio, at 11:16 a.m. Shortly he was over Dayton, Ohio, where he was joined by an escort flight of thirty Army airplanes.[1] After Dayton he flew over Indianapolis, Terre Haute, Indiana, St. Elmo and Scott Field, Illinois, before landing at Lambert Field, near St. Louis. The flight took him 9:20.[2]

While he was on his way to St. Louis, a fog had formed over parts of the city, but by 5:00 P.M. as he approached the area, the fog apparently lifted enough for the people of that large Midwestern city to see the *Spirit of St. Louis* as it approached from the east. Many of them were on their rooftops to get a better view as he flew over.

He was met in the air, somewhere between Scott Field, Belleville, Illinois, and Lambert Field, by his old air mail and Army flying friend, Phillip R. Love. Love had taken off in another airplane with an Associated Press correspondent as his passenger to meet "Slim."[3]

When he landed at Lambert, Lindbergh was met by throngs of people, including troops from the 110th Observation Squadron of the 35th Division of the Missouri National Guard, and Mayor Victor J. Miller and Governor Sam A. Baker. The

NYP was rolled into one of the Guard's hangars for the night.

Lindbergh, together with his mother, who had arrived the night before from Detroit, spent that first night at the home of Harry French Knight, of the "We" group.[4] Knight's home was located in St. Louis County at Warson and Litzinger Roads. Accompanying Mrs. Lindbergh was Charles's uncle, acting Mayor Lodge of Detroit.

On Saturday morning he was mobbed again by people in the city, as a large parade made its way through the streets of St. Louis for seven miles. This was followed by a luncheon and banquet at the Hotel Coronado. In the afternoon there was a gathering on Art Hill in Forest Park, where Lindbergh gave a brief speech.

After the ceremonies in the park, he left for Lambert Field and shortly flew the NYP over St. Louis and the World's Fair grounds for thirty minutes for the benefit of the people unable to make it to the airport. Then he made another flight in a military TW.3 for forty-five minutes.

In the evening they held a banquet dinner given by thirteen hundred prominent citizens of St. Louis and the State of Missouri.

While in St. Louis Lindbergh was given a commission as colonel, Air Corps Reserve Corps of the U.S. Army by Secretary of War Dwight F. Davis. Governor Baker also presented the flyer with a commission as colonel in the air service of the Missouri National Guard.

During his stay in the Midwestern city, he got to fly other aircraft over the area. According to his log book they were a Curtiss P-1 "Hawk," an OX-5 powered Waco 10, and a Wright J-5 powered Curtiss A.T. 5.[5] Lindbergh also spent some time at the World War I Veterans Hospital at Jefferson Barracks.

On July 1 he left Lambert Field and made a flight of 5:10 to Selfridge Field at Mt. Clemens, Michigan. He flew via Ft. Wayne, Indiana, To-

1928 Date	Time Hr:Min	Flights		Total Flights	Total Passengers	Total Time Hrs:Min	Types						Chute Drops Total
							***** FLOWN BY MAJ. LANPHIER						
							****** FLOWN BY PHIL LOVE						
Jun 22	2:20	1	0	7209	5952	1855:00	P-1						177
"23	2:55	1	0	7210	5952	1857:55	P-1						
"24	1:55	1	0	7211	5952	1859:50	P-1						
"29	8:00	4	0	7215	5952	1867:50	P-1 ; A.T.5 (Whirlwind)						
"30	:15	2	0	7217	5952	1868:05	Waco 10 (OX5)						
July 1	5:30	3	0	7220	5952	1873:35	N.Y.P. — P1. ST. LOUIS TO SELFRIDGE *						
"2	4:10	1	0	7221	5952	1877:45	N.Y.P. SELFRIDGE TO OTTAWA, CAN.						
"3	1:10	1	0	7222	5952	1878:55	N.Y.P. LOCAL OVER FUNERAL						
"4	3:50	1	0	7223	5952	1882:45	N.Y.P. OTTAWA TO TETERBORO						
"19	1:40	5	8	7228	5960	1884:25	N.Y.P.; Fairchild K6 - Fokker Universal; Wright Sonia, Fokker J-5. TET. TO MITCHEL						
"20	1:35	1	0	7229	5960	1886:00	N.Y.P. MITCHEL TO HARTFORD						
"21	1:35	1	0	7230	5960	1887:35	N.Y.P.						
"22	1:35	1	0	7231	5960	1889:10	N.Y.P.						
"23	5:00	1	0	7232	5960	1894:10	N.Y.P.						
"24	2:45	1	0	7233	5960	1896:55	N.Y.P.						
"25	2:50	2	0	7235	5960	1899:45	N.Y.P.						
"26	2:10	1	0	7236	5960	1901:55	N.Y.P.						

Copy of Lindbergh's original pilot's log entries with notations on
right-hand side (upper case) by author for research clarification.

ledo, Ohio, and Detroit, Michigan.[6]

Selfridge Field History

A realtor by the name of Henry B. Joy in 1914 was enthused about the possible development of aviation and owned over six hundred acres of marshland just northeast of Mount Clemens, Michigan. Mr. Joy decided to develop the area as an airport, and it became known as "Joy Aviation Field."

For a time it was used by the Packard Motor Company, was later leased to the U.S. Government, and eventually (July 1, 1917) was activated as a military installation and renamed "Selfridge Field" to honor Lt. Thomas Etholen Selfridge.

Selfridge was the first military officer to design a powered airplane, the first to pilot such an aircraft and, ironically, the first to die in the crash of a powered airplane. He was the son of Rear Adm. Thomas Oliver Selfridge.[7]

Lieutenant Selfridge worked closely with Dr. Alexander Graham Bell at the latter's summer retreat known as Beinn Bhreagh (Scottish-Gaelic for "Beautiful Mountain"), which was located at Baddeck, Nova Scotia. Bell maintained a laboratory and carried on experiments of all kinds, including aeronautics, at this beautiful place.

The very first military personnel to occupy the field was Company G 33rd Michigan National Guard. Their duty was to prepare the airport for the soon to arrive 8th and 9th Aero Squadrons from Kelly Field, Texas.

In June 1919, just after the end of World War I, the famous 1st Pursuit Group returned from France and the military airfield became a pursuit (fighter) field. At this time the land was still owned by Mr. Joy, but in 1921 he sold the field to the government for $190,000.

Selfridge was designated as a permanent military installation for the 1st Pursuit Group, which included Capt. Eddie Rickenbacker, America's top World War I ace.

Up to this time Lindbergh had been the only pilot to fly the NYP since its inception. The commanding officer of Selfridge, who also commanded the 1st Pursuit Group, was Maj. Thomas G. Lanphier. Because Lanphier had let Lindbergh fly one of the country's latest Curtiss P-1 "Hawk" pursuit airplanes shortly after his arrival, Lindbergh allowed the major to fly the NYP, solo. Lanphier flew the airplane over

Lindbergh standing by the NYP at Mitchel Field on Long Island, June 16, 1927. From this photograph, which was reproduced hundreds of times over, this pose was duplicated often by sculptors and other artists. JOSHUA STOFF

Mitchel Field, June 17, just before Lindbergh took off for St. Louis. LEO B. KIMBALL COLLECTION

Lambert Field, St. Louis, Missouri, June 17. Lindbergh is shown with St. Louis Mayor Victor J. Miller. THE ST. LOUIS MERCANTILE LIBRARY

St. Louis, Missouri, possibly June 18. A Robertson Aircraft Corp. mechanic putting oil in the oil tank. Notice booster mag on top of right wheel chock and wire from it to the engine area, a temporary hook-up for starting.

Rare photo of the NYP at Selfridge
Field before his flight at Canada.
Notice hand pressure gun attached
and hanging from the cylinder of the
J-5 engine. Also notice where the
fabric has been repaired and painted
around left cockpit window. LEO B.
KIMBALL COLLECTION

Lindbergh is shown here
with Maj. Thomas Lanphier,
at Selfridge Field in Mt.
Clemens, Michigan, July 1.
AUTHOR'S COLLECTION

Selfridge for ten minutes on July 1, 1927. Lanphier was, incidentally, a close friend of Henry Ford.

Years later, when Thomas Lanphier and his wife were visiting with Mr. and Mrs. William Chana at their home in San Diego, he related the following story about that flight:

"I ran up to the door of the Spirit and shook hands with him through the open side window. After a few words of greeting, and with the engine still running, he said to me, 'Tom, I've never seen the *Spirit* in the air, would you mind taking it around the field?' Lindbergh stepped out and I swung myself up into the pilot's seat of the *Spirit*.

"You'd think I would have questions like, I understand that the airplane is a little unstable, will that be a problem for me? What's the best climb speed? There wasn't time to ask questions as Lindbergh patted me on the shoulder and closed the cabin door. You would think that for the ten minutes I was in the air I would have kept my eyes on the instruments and the limited vision out of the two side windows. But I can assure you, all that I could see in front of me were the big headlines on newspapers around the world that read, "LANPHIER CRASHES THE *SPIRIT*."[8]

To Ottawa, Canada

On July 2 Lindbergh took off from Selfridge and headed northeast for a flight of four hours and ten minutes, to land at the capital city of Ottawa, Ontario, Canada.

Lindbergh had earlier accepted an invitation from Canadian Prime Minister William Lyon Mackenzie King, not only to be honored by that country but to help celebrate their sixtieth anniversary of Confederation.

Lindbergh's plan was to fly into a makeshift airfield on Bowesville Road. Ottawa lacked a municipal airport to receive the NYP, so a private group known as the Uplands Syndicate made available a parcel of property on the Bowesville Road, adjacent to the Ottawa Hunt and Golf Club. The field was six and a half miles south of Parliament Hill in the city of Ottawa. It provided a firm and level surface with clear approaches from all directions. This included two grass runways, one 2,400 feet long and the other 1,800 feet, both 150 feet wide. A 100-foot-wide circle marked the intersection of each runway.

Refueling and servicing was arranged and handled by RCAF personnel. There were no hangars on the field. So a Royal Canadian Mounted Police Guard was provided to protect the NYP while there. A force of five hundred militiamen—representing the Princess Louise Dragoon Guards, the Third Field Company, the Third Signal Battalion, the Governor-General's Foot Guards and the Cameron Highlanders of Ottawa—provided security and crowd control.

The regular airport of those days at Rockclife was not considered (quite correctly, as things turned out) large enough or accessible enough at the time. As Lindbergh and his group of escort aircraft approached the field, horns of hundreds of motorcars blazed a welcome. The crowds flocking to the airfield created the worst

Line-up of Curtiss P-1 and P-1B airplanes that escorted Lindbergh into the Ottawa area on July 2. NATIONAL MUSEUM OF CANADA

The NYP has just landed at Uplands property at Ottawa, Ontario, Canada on July 2. NATIONAL ARCHIVES OF CANADA

Cowling removed for servicing the NYP at Ottawa. SAN DIEGO AEROSPACE MUSEUM

traffic jam Ottawa had ever encountered up to that time.

Lindbergh had taken off from Selfridge at 8:18 EST. He was accompanied by twelve Curtiss P-1B Hawk aircraft of the 1st Pursuit Group, U.S. Army Air Service, from Selfridge Field. The group was under the command of Maj. Thomas G. Lanphier. This armada of fast airplanes included Capt. Hugh M. Elmendorf, Lieutenants Victor H. Strahm, L.C. Mallory, J.J. Williams, K.J. Gregg, W.L. Cornelius, R. Keillor, E.H. Lawson, B.M. Hovey Jr., H.A. Wooding, J.G. Hopkins, and the commanding officer of the 27th Squadron, J. Thad Johnson.

The impressive formation reached Ottawa at 1:19 EDT, more than one hour after the expected time of arrival. The group did not know about Ottawa observing Daylight Saving Time.

Unfortunately this visit turned out to be more tragic than joyous. The Army airplanes formed a "Lufbery Circle" in preparation for landing. Five of the aircraft were in the circle when a collision occurred. Five others were already on the ground, including Lindbergh in the NYP.

Disaster struck when two of the Army aircraft collided, with one of them remaining in the air in fair shape. That one was piloted by Lt. H.A. Wooding. The other ship, flown by Lt. J. Thad Johnson, was in trouble. It went out of control, from the low altitude of the collision, and crashed. All of this was within sight of the welcoming crowd of thousands of people.

In a panic situation, Lieutenant Johnson jumped from the stricken airplane but was too low for the chute to open in time, and he was killed. Wooding landed safely.

It was another two hours before things quieted down enough for Lindbergh to give his brief speech, expressing his delight in helping the country celebrate its sixtieth birthday and bringing warm wishes and good will from the United States.

Prime Minister Mackenzie King, in welcoming Lindbergh to Canada, stated, "We feel more than highly honored that at this time of our national rejoicing you should come to us with a message of international good will. We believe you have to your credit the greatest individual achievement in the history of the world."[9]

Sometime later the Minister again expressed his admiration and impressions of Lindbergh when he said,[10] "A more beautiful character I have never seen. He was like a young god who had appeared from the skies in human form— all that could be desired in youthful appearance, in manner, in charm, in character, as noble a type of the highest manhood as I have ever seen."[11]

Because of the death of Lt. Johnson, most all celebrations were cancelled as the country went into a state of mourning.

Following lunch at Rideau Hall with the Governor-General and Viscountess Willington, Lindbergh visited sports activities at the Rideau Tennis Club, the Ottawa Rowing Club, and Landsdowne Park, accompanied by Mackenzie King and Hon. William Phillips, the newly appointed United States Minister to Canada. Lindbergh held a press conference at Laurier House (Sir Wilfrid Laurier) before attending a

Lindbergh with the NYP and Canadian military personnel. Notice the flyer has just his goggles on without his helmet, probably just too hot as the photograph was taken in July.
PUBLIC ARCHIVES OF CANADA VIA PETER ROBERTSON

state dinner in honor of Phillips at the Parliament Buildings during the evening.

After the evening dinner King presented Lindbergh with the Confederation medal, and then there was a reception at Laurier House. Lindbergh stayed there as the quest of the Minister. They did not retire until one a.m. as they spent some time discussing the possibility that they were somewhat distantly related.[12]

Prime Minister Mackenzie King arranged a state funeral to begin at 3:30 EDT on Sunday afternoon. The preparation of such a ceremony, combined with the necessity of holding an inquest, involved long hours of work for many people summoned at short notice on Saturday night. There was a brief service that took place on Parliament Hill. In the escort of the cortege to the train station there were cabinet ministers, government officials and diplomatic representatives and by the notes of Chopin's "Funeral March" played on the Peace Tower carillon.

According to local papers, approximately fifty thousand people lined the military cortege route from the East Block, where the service was held, out the Centre Gate to Wellington Street, then on to the train station where the casket was taken from the Royal Canadian Mounted Police drawn gun carriage and placed upon a train headed for Detroit. As the train headed west-

ward along the canal, Lindbergh, accompanied by several other squadron airplanes, flew low over it and scattered bunches of peony petals for remembrance and honor.

Sometime after the memorial the Prime Minister remarked, "I have seen nothing in my life so splendidly impressive, nothing comparable to it in an expression of national feeling expressed in international relations."[13]

The cost was also impressive: $10,271.60. This resulted in a certain amount of undignified behind-the-scenes haggling in order to pay all the bills.[14]

On Sunday night Lindbergh attended a private dinner at the County Club and stayed overnight at the Chateau Laurier.

For a while the field where Lindbergh and the Army squadron had landed was known as Lindbergh Field. But it was not to last. The name never really caught on and was dropped. It eventually became the present-day MacDonald-Cartier International Airport.

The Ottawa Hunt Club is still the local golf and country club located adjacent to the airport. Many people in the area still refer to the airport as Uplands, the name it acquired prior to World War II.

On Monday afternoon, July 4, at 1:30 EDT, Lindbergh took off from the Bowesville field and

Casket of Lt. J. Thad Johnson in the military cortege as it made its way to the railroad station to be sent back to Detroit. PUBLIC ARCHIVES OF CANADA VIA PETER ROBERTSON

headed directly south for Teterboro, New Jersey. The flight took three hours and fifty minutes.

Before leaving the Ottawa area, however, he circled in tribute over the city for thirty-five minutes.

A bit later, at 2:15 EDT, the 1st Pursuit Group of Curtiss Hawks and a Douglas transport airplane carrying spare parts for Lt. Woodring's damaged P-1 took off for Selfridge Field in Michigan.

Lindbergh was flying down to Teterboro to have some extensive work done on the NYP in preparation for the upcoming eighty-two city good will tour of the United States. (See chapter 3 for details of the work done at Teterboro.)

Prime Minister Mackenzie King was in the habit of recording personal and philosophical reflections in his daily diaries. With regard to Lindbergh's visit, it is interesting to read what he had to say.

"Indeed all thro' the last few days, with the carillon, the radio broadcasting, Lindbergh coming from the skies after his transatlantic flight, the sacrifice of this airman (Johnson) on the field of international goodwill, the (funeral) service and its associations–carillon, airmen, the US flag in our prlt [sic] (Parliament?) bldgs & on our streets, to see it was like Heaven itself coming near to earth, as if we were entering on a higher and loftier experience than ever before. Indeed, it seems to me as if Lindbergh was as a young god from the skies, bringing anew the message of Peace & Goodwill. ... It was the triumph of nationhood ... the beginning of a new epoch in our history. ... How strange all should centre about Laurier House and myself, even to Col. Lindbergh being my guest there! ... I feel I stumbled along the way, where I should have flown like a young god. ... Pray God there may arise a larger freedom and spiritual power to give to this nation the soul that God would have me give."[15]

Footnotes

1. Lindbergh Log (copy) of Spirit of St. Louis. Copy at the Missouri Historical Society, Jefferson Memorial, St. Louis, Missouri. Page 3.
2. *Ibid.*
3. *The Knickerbocker Press,* New York City, Thursday, June 18, 1927, "200,000 in 'Welcome Home' Roar To Lindbergh, Back With Stunts at St. Louis," Author unknown.
4. Letter to the author from Mrs. Martha Knight Clyde, March 31, 1999, grand-daughter of Harry French Knight.
5. Charles A. Lindbergh's personal pilot's Log. Copy at Yale University, Sterling Memorial Library, Manuscripts & Archives Dept., New Haven, CT. Log dated from November 11, 1926 to July 7, 1928.
6. Lindbergh Log, Spirit of St. Louis, *Ibid.*
7. Ref. Feeny, William D., *In Their Honor,* first edition, New York, Duell, Sloan and Pearce, 1963, p. 24
8. Personal interview by the author with William Chana, San Diego, CA, spring 1996.
9. Public Archives of Canada (PAC), W.L. Mackenzie King Papers, MG 26 J13, 2 July 1927
10. PAC, King Papers, MG 26 J13, 2 July 1927
11. *The Ottawa Evening Citizen,* July 4, 1927, Leslie T. Reissner, Ottawa, Ontario, Canada, Peter Robertson, Ottawa, Ontario, Canada, A.J. Short, curator, National Aviation Museum, Ottawa. Letter from him to author of 19 January, 1988.
12. *Ibid.* p. ?
13. PAC, Records of the Department of National Defense, RG 24 Vol. 4910, File 1008-9-4, 3 July 1927
14. PAC, King Papers, MG 26 J13 3 July 1927
15. *Ibid.*

December 6, 1927, showing the NYP having the compass aligned at Teterboro. Notice tri-pod on top. See also Frank Hawk's Ryan B-1, *Good to the Last Drop,* in the left background with registration #1105. BOB BORGHI

Another December 6 photograph of the NYP at Teterboro, during the compass alignment. Notice later wheels and Jorgenson clamps on fin and flair tubes installed on belly. Center wing tank has been removed. BOB BORGHI

CHAPTER THREE
TETERBORO STORY

The relationship of the NYP with Teterboro Airport in New Jersey is significant. The airplane spent more time there than on any other airport or flying field anywhere during its flying life. Numerous modifications, repairs, overhauls, and servicing were accomplished there. The NYP spent a total of sixty days (sixteen before the U.S. tour and forty-four after the tour) at Teterboro.[1] This pioneering airport, which has served the New York–New Jersey area, is still very much in operation today.

Built on land that was considered more than half salt marsh and cedar swamps, Dutch farmers found the area made for good pastureland, where they harvested coarse hay to provide bedding for their cattle.[2] As the Dutch are experts when it comes to dealing with water problems, they drained off portions of the land by digging ditches, thus transforming it into crop-producing soil.[3]

Teterboro is the smallest municipality (besides being an airport) in Bergen County, New Jersey. The airport is the largest tract of land in the borough.[4]

It had a rather short beginning.[5] It was known as Kuhnert's Aerodrome, was enclosed by a stadium-like nine-foot wooden fence and built in 1911.[6] Many early aviation pioneers flew out of there: Ruth Bancroft Law, Louis Bleriot, Frank Boland, and others.

The entire Aerodrome was destroyed by a freak tornado that passed through the area in 1912.[7] But in 1917, Charles, Paul and Walter Wittemann purchased the property from Walter Teter and in 1918 opened the Wittemann-Lewis Aircraft Company.[8]

As early as 1905 the Wittemanns, led by their imaginative and creative brother Charles, founded the first airplane manufacturing plant in the United States on their property on Staten Island.[9]

The Wittemanns deserve the recognition of being the people who put the grass strip on the map initially. They rebuilt World War I DeHavilland DH-4s to carry mail.[10] One of their planes flew coast to coast with the first bags of mail.[11] They built one Barling bomber, lost money, and went out of business.[12] Dutchman Anthony Fokker, at his general manager Bob Noorduyn's suggestion, moved into the large Wittemann hangar in 1924 and set up a manufacturing facility to produce the Fokker tri-motor monoplanes.[13] The large aircraft began to dominate the skies in the east, contributing to the new air travel industry. By the late 1920s nearly half of all passenger planes in the world were Fokkers. Teterboro was becoming well known all over the country.[14]

As the airport grew, prominent aviators became regulars at the field: Robert B. C. Noorduyn, Anthony Fokker, Bernt Balchen, Floyd Bennett, Roger Q. Williams, Clarence Chamberlin, Wiley Post, Juan Trippe, Richard E. Byrd, Bert Acosta, Amelia P. Earhart, Clyde E. Pangborn, Frank Hawks, Ivan Gates (Gates Flying Circus), Aaron "Duke" Krantz, and on and on.

Because the Wright company was located in nearby Paterson, New Jersey, they operated a hangar at Teterboro to install, test and maintain their engines. Company engineers and mechanics such as Thomas "Doc" Kincaid, Ken Boedecker, Ken Lane, Ben Zabora, Ted R. Sorensen and Charlie Kuss played an important role in tuning engines for many endurance flights, air racers, and long-distance record-breaking flights of that era.

Over many years this author has spent countless hours searching for documentation and photos to confirm the work done at Teterboro on the NYP, with little success. Work orders, bills and/or invoices have vanished over the years. The same is true for photographs, other than a few. The only accurate documentation to work from has been the NYP log, as found in Lindbergh's book, *The Spirit of St. Louis.* As to what work was done and when, only certain areas are accurate and others just speculation.

Lindbergh first landed the NYP at Teterboro on July 4, 1927, having flown in from Ottawa, Canada.[15] Sometime between the 4th and 19th of

Photographer B.P. Davidson shown with sons, Benjamin and Alexander. The Davidsons lived in Montclair, New Jersey at this time. STANLEY KING

Engine being removed from the airframe with mechanic Milton Wilson checking things out. Photographer B.P. Davidson. STANLEY KING

The Wright engine being either removed or re-installed at the Wright hangar at Teterboro, New Jersey airport. Photo taken either July 12th or 19th (notice original tires). Mechanic is Milton Wilson. Photographer was B.P. Davidson. STANLEY KING

Lindbergh shown in the cockpit of the Wright airplane, a Fokker S-3, June 16th at Teterboro. STAN JONES COLLECTION

Warming up for engine test at Teterboro Airport, July 18. STAN JONES COLLECTION

Engine test after overhaul at Teterboro Airport. STAN JONES COLLECTION

The Wright hangar after the successful engine test, July 18, Teterboro Airport. STAN JONES COLLECTION

July, the engine was removed for complete major or top overhaul. At this time, according to a letter dated August 15, 1978, to the author from Kenneth Lane, they installed a hand-cranked Splitdorf booster magneto to make it easier to start the engine. As can be seen in several photographs, the booster mag was mounted on the torque tube of the control stick, just forward of the stick itself, within easy reach of Lindbergh. The engine had about 93:40 hours total time at this point.

In Lane's letter he states, "I remember cleaning out the topsoil that had accumulated in the aft end of the fuselage. This was because all the men we had working in the hangar were too big to crawl through to the tail, and I had to strip down to my BVD's and do the job myself. It was a hot day, and I took out enough soil to start a small farm."

He went on, "I have been trying to recall the details of the work we did in preparing the Spirit for the tour but with little success. Alteration was a poor choice of term to describe the operation; most of the things we did were so minor in character that they made no lasting impression on my memory cells."

It was at this time that all of the louvers were cut into the engine cowling for cooling. That should take care of any engine overheating that might be experienced in the desert areas of the western and southwestern part of the country on the tour. Also the oil tank was removed for repairs. It is not known if this had anything to do with the crack that was found in Paris.

On July 19th Lindbergh flew the NYP from Teterboro over the greater New York metropolitan area to Mitchel Field on Long Island to be in position for the start of the US goodwill tour. It was a thirty minute flight.[16]

At the end of the tour on October 25th, he flew the NYP from Mitchel Field to Teterboro with a passenger, Milburn Kusterer, who was the advance man on the U.S. tour.[17] Again the engine was removed for a major overhaul. It had 355:25 hours at this time.[18]

Lindbergh recalled in 1958, "One day when I was taxiing the *Spirit of St. Louis* at Teterboro (New Jersey) airport in 1927, the earth over a small hole beneath the surface gave way, the right wheel dropped in, and the tail raised up just enough to bend the propeller before falling back into a three-point position. (This was the propeller that made the New York to Paris flight.) A new propeller was installed, and I do not know what happened to the old one—it was not badly damaged."[19]

After the engine was removed and disassembled in their experimental department,

Wright Whirlwind service plane in the hangar at Teterboro. It was a Fokker S-3 #1085. This is the same airplane used by Clarence Chamberlin to fly first "ship to shore" mail, from the ship, *Leviathan* to Teterboro. BOB BORGHI

Engine completely removed from the NYP in the Wright Aeronautical Corporation hangar, Teterboro Airport. MISSOURI HISTORICAL SOCIETY, ST. LOUIS

Raymond W. Young, the experimental test engineer at the time, wrote to Lindbergh with regard to their taking measurements of all the wearing parts which would be compared with those taken at a former disassembly. They found the engine in excellent condition and informed Lindbergh that it would be assembled with no major replacements. They had suggested that he come to the plant to inspect the various parts and that when he did arrive they would remove all the parts from safe storage and arrange them for his inspection.[20]

In a letter to Don Hall, Lindbergh said,

The "Spirit of St. Louis" has been in the Wright hangar at the Teterboro Airport since October 25th, but I expect to begin flying it again either this afternoon (December 5, 1927) or Thursday morning.

The motor was inspected and the plane completely checked over, both were found to be in excellent condition and practically no replacements made.

The valves were ground in the engine but even the rings were not replaced.

I have had two flares installed just back of the cockpit and will probably make a few flights at night.

As ever, Charles A. Lindbergh[21]

Sometime from November 25th to December 4th, the center 210-gallon wing tank was removed. A reason has not been determined. Allen William McCann Jr. was an office worker for Wright and had a small office in the hangar at Teterboro at that time. In an interview with his wife, Emma, in 1991, she related the story of the tank. After its removal it was placed in the corner of Mr. McCann's office. There was a fire that destroyed the office, causing the fuel tank to melt, except for the fuel tank filler neck and fuel cap and vent tube, which Mrs. McCann still has in her possession.

At the time of the tank removal, a large portion of fabric in that area had to be removed as well. That fabric still exists and is in the Lindbergh collection at Yale University, New Haven, Connecticut. There is a letter from Lindbergh to Mr. Lawrance dated January 23, 1929, that accompanies the fabric: "I am enclosing a piece of the fabric of the Spirit of St. Louis. This was cut away from the top surface of the wing when the center gasoline tank was removed during the preparation for the Mexico City trip. With best wishes, Charles A. Lindbergh." There is also a note that it is the property of Francis Lawrance, (son of Charles L. Lawrance).

Also, in a handwritten letter from Lindbergh to Knight, a copy of which is in the author's collection, is the following:

December 25, 1928
Dear Mr. Knight,
I am enclosing a small piece of fabric from *The Spirit of St. Louis.*
This was removed when the center wing gasoline tank was taken out in preparation for the Mexico City flight.
Sincerely,
Charles A. Lindbergh

It was at this time, December 5th perhaps (documented by photographic study), that the rudder was removed and the lower portion, from the bottom rib down, was removed of its fabric. The trailing edge tubing from aft of the lower rib down to the bottom of the tail post was also removed. No reports exist to explain why this was done, so it is assumed that due to all the landings on unimproved fields during the tour, the bottom of the rudder must have suffered some deterioration from mud, water and other miscellaneous debris.

A new trailing edge was made, clearly seen in many photographs, showing a much more gradual curve from the bottom of the tail post up to the aft of the bottom rib, eliminating that straight portion as made originally by Ryan.[22]

This is the same curve that can be seen on the airplane today at the National Air and Space Museum in Washington.

During my research I was contacted by Gordon Neddow of Manchester, Connecticut. He told me the story of his father, Lyle T. Neddow, who as a young man was working for a machine shop in Springfield, Vermont, as a machinist and tool and die maker in 1927 and 1928. He was sent by his company to the Wright plant in New Jersey to do the internal grinding for the cylinders for the NYP engine during one of its overhauls. He must have had quite a reputation to be asked to travel that far to do that kind of work.

On December 5th Lindbergh made one test flight of the NYP, and the airplane was put back into the hangar. The next day, the 6th, the compass was swung (see photo).[23]

According to an invoice dated December 7, 1927, from the Loening Aeronautical Engineering Corporation of New York City, they delivered on December 6th by truck to Teterboro two Standard Steel Propeller Blades, Drawing #1519 at cost f.o.b. Pittsburgh for a total cost of $223.59.[24] The question arises, were the old original blades discarded and replaced with these new blades, or are these the original blades which were overhauled in Pittsburgh and now ready for remounting on the airplane? He did test fly the NYP on the 5th. What set of blades was used for that flight? Also, was the original hub used? Are the blades now on the airplane in Washington the originals or the new/rebuilt ones?

On the 7th Lindbergh flew to Bolling Field, near Washington, D.C., to be in position for the Mexico City goodwill flight.

Teterboro Airport is still very much alive and well at this writing. Many New York and New Jersey Fortune 500 corporations hangar their aircraft there and Atlantic Aviation, the oldest FBO on the field, is still doing business there.

There is an official state museum dedicated to the history of the airport plus the New Jersey Aviation Hall of Fame and Museum and Lindbergh Aviation Center on the east side of the airport, all very much dedicated to preserving our aviation heritage.

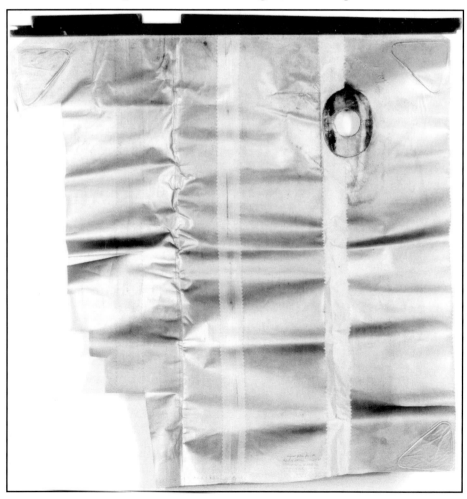

This is most of the fabric that was removed from the top center of the wing when the center fuel tank was removed on November 3, 1927, at Teterboro. It is in storage at Yale University.
CHARLES AUGUSTUS LINDBERGH PAPERS, MANUSCRIPTS AND ARCHIVES, YALE UNIVERSITY LIBRARY

Time Line for NYP at Teterboro 1927

July 4   Ottawa, Canada, to Teterboro
July 12   Engine removed, overhauled. Booster
          mag installed. All louvers cut into cowl
          for better cooling. Oil tank removed for
          repairs.[25]
July 19   Teterboro to Mitchel Field, Long Island

U.S. Goodwill Tour

October 25   Mitchel Field to Teterboro
             (Milburn Kusterer passenger)
             (prop incident?)
Nov. 3   Engine removed and inspected
             (@ 355 hours)[26]
             Center wing tank removed?[27]
             Replaced ignition wires with new
             Airtite cable
Nov. 4   Engine report. Two flares installed
             in fuselage, just back of cockpit.[28]
             Center wing tank removed?[29]
Dec. 5   Test flight. Rudder modified?
Dec. 6   New propeller blades delivered for
             NYP from Loening Corp. by truck
             (letter of Dec. 7, 1927)[30]
Dec. 7   Teterboro to Bolling Field,
             Washington, DC[31]
Dec. 13   Bolling Field to Mexico City

Breakdown of Dates

July 4 through 19   16 days
October 25 through December 7   44 days

Total time of 60 days at Teterboro

Footnotes

1. *The Spirit of St. Louis* by Charles A. Lindbergh, 1953, Charles Scribner's Sons, New York, NY, pages 505-06, 511.
2. *A Pictorial History, Teterboro Airport* by H.V. Pat Reilly, 1983. Published by Aviation Hall of Fame of New Jersey. pages 2-5, 8-9.
3. *Ibid.*
4. *Ibid.*
5. *Ibid.*
6. *Ibid.*
7. *Ibid.*
8. *Ibid.*
9. *Ibid.*
10. *Ibid.*
11. *Ibid.*
12. *Ibid.*
13. *Ibid.*
14. *Ibid.*
15. *The Spirit of St. Louis, Ibid.*
16. *Ibid.*
17. *Ibid.*
18. *Ibid.*
19. Letter from Charles A. Lindbergh to Mr. Chester C. Conner, Assistant Secretary, Aluminum Company of America, Pittsburgh, Pennsylvania, dated December 4, 1958, from Scotts Cove, Darien, Connecticut, Item I.
20. Letter to Col. Charles A. Lindbergh, Guggenheim Fund for the Promotion of Aviation, 598 Madison Avenue, New York, NY from Raymond W. Young, Experimental Test Engineer, Wright Aeronautical Corporation, Paterson, New Jersey, November 2, 1927.
21. Ref: Letter from Charles A. Lindbergh, dated December 5, 1927, (Racquet & Tennis Club, 370 Park Avenue on letterhead) to Donald Hall, c/o B.P. Mahoney Aircraft, San Diego, California. Original letter loaned to the author by owner Donald A. Hall, Jr. in 1989.
22. *Ibid.*
23. *The Spirit of St. Louis*
24. Invoice dated December 7, 1927 to Charles A. Lindbergh, c/o The Daniel Guggenheim Fund for the Promotion of Aeronautics, 598 Madison Avenue, New York, NY from Loening Aeronautical Engineering Corporation, New York, NY.
25. The Wright Engine Builder, March 1928: Issue 3, Vol. X, page 8, published by Wright Aeronautical Corp. for its employees, Paterson, NJ.
26. *Ibid.*
27. Letter from Charles A. Lindbergh to Charles L. Lawrance, dated January 23, 1929.
28. Letter from Charles A. Lindbergh, December 5, 1927, Racquet & Tennis Club, 370 Park Avenue, New York, NY, to Donald Hall, c/o B.F. Mahoney Aircraft, San Diego, California.
29. *Ibid.*
30. Conner letter, *Ibid.*
31. Careful study of original photographs in the author's collection revealed details and physical changes of the NYP structure, etc., from July 4, 1927, through December 7, 1927.

See and Welcome
COLONEL
LINDBERGH
To Los Angeles

AMERICA'S

L O N E

E A G L E

Tuesday, Sept. 20

Reduced Fares to Los Angeles

Going and Returning on September 20th only

From	Fare	From	Fare
Alta Loma	$1.40	Ontario	$1.35
Artesia	.65	Pomona	1.00
Azusa	.80	Redlands	2.25
Claremont	1.15	Rialto	1.85
Colton	2.15	Riverside	2.00
Covina	.75	San Bernardino	2.00
Etiwanda	1.55	San Dimas	.90
Fontana	1.75	Santa Ana	1.15
Garden Grove	1.00	Upland	1.25
Glendora	.90	Van Nuys	.65
LaVerne	.95	Whittier	.60
Monrovia	.65		

Purchase Tickets at Ticket Offices Before Boarding Train

PARADE - 2:30 P. M.
Starting at First and Broadway, south on Broadway to 12th Street; west on 12th to Figueroa, south on Figueroa to Coliseum.

Public Reception
At L. A. Coliseum - 3:30 p.m.

AVOID INTENSE TRAFFIC
TRAVEL VIA THE BIG RED CARS

PACIFIC ELECTRIC RAILWAY
PERMIT NO. 4504

Lindbergh was so popular that even some railroads reduced fares so the public would have the opportunity to see him. MUSEUM OF MOUNTAIN FLYING COLLECTION, MISSOULA, MONTANA

Chapter Four

The Tour Begins

Lindbergh in the NYP just before departure on the first leg
of the Goodwill Tour of the U.S., July 20, 1927. STANLEY KING

Goodwill Tour Personnel

Charles A. Lindbergh Pilot of NYP	Born: February 4, 1902 Died: August 26, 1974 Wife: Anne Spencer Morrow Children: Jonathan, Land, Anne, Scott, Reeve	Detroit, Michigan Maui, Hawaii
Philip Rockford Love Escort Pilot	Born: November 6, 1903 Died: June 1943 Wife: Eulalie F. Cook	Washington, D.C. Austin, NV air crash
Donald Edward Keyhoe Aide	Born: June 20, 1897 Died: November 29, 1988 Wife: Helen Wood Gardner Children: Kathleen, Caroline, Joseph	Ottumwa, Iowa
Cecil Charles Maidment "Doc" Engine Expert	Born: September 22, 1896 Died: December 27, 1970 Wife: Coral M.	London, England
Ted R. Sorenson Mechanic	Milburn Kusterer Advance Man (via train)	

Escort Airplane–Fairchild FC-2, Wright J-5 "Whirlwind," Registration No. N-S7, s/n 140

Passengers Carried in the NYP

Donald A. Hall	May 3, 1927	San Diego, Calif.
Major James Erickson (2)	May 3, 1927	San Diego, Calif.
A.J. Edwards (2)	May 8, 1927	San Diego, Calif.
O.R. McNeal (McNeel?)	May 10, 1927	North Island, Calif.
Brice Goldsborough (2)	May 13, 1927	Curtiss Field, Calif.
Kenneth Boedecker (2)	May 14, 1927	Curtiss Field, Calif.
Edward Mulligan	May 14, 1927	Curtiss Field, Calif.
U.S. Tour		
Henry Ford	Aug. 11, 1927	Detroit, Mich.
Edsel Ford	Aug. 11, 1927	Detroit, Mich.
Evangeline Lindbergh (mother)	Aug. 12, 1927	Grand Rapids, Mich.
B. Franklin Mahoney	Sept. 23, 1927	San Diego, Calif.
Donald E. Keyhoe	Sept. 30, 1927	Oklahoma City, Okla.
Earl C. Thompson	Oct. 4, 1927	Memphis, Tenn.
Gov. Harry F. Byrd	Oct. 16, 1927	Richmond, Virginia
Harry F. Guggenheim	Oct. 16, 1927	Richmond, Virginia
C.C. Maidment	Oct. 16, 1927	Richmond, Virginia
Milburn Kusterer	Oct. 25, 1927	Mitchel Field to Teterboro, NJ

Tour Crew Not Flown in NYP

Ted R. Sorenson

Two Additional Pilots Flew the NYP

Major Thomas Lanphier
July 1 & 19, 1927
Selfridge Field, Mich.

Philip Rockford Love
August 8, 1927
Louisville, Kentucky

(2) means two flights
No passengers were carried during the south of the border Tour.

1927 Date	Time Fits.	Flts.	Pass. carr'd	Total Flights	Total Pass- engers	Total Time Hrs. : Min.	NYP Types					Chute Drops	Total
Sept. 12	3:50	1	0	7300	5978	2038:00	N.Y.P.						17
" 13	5:15	1	0	7301	5978	2043:15	N.Y.P.						
" 14	4:45	1	0	7302	5978	2048:00	N.Y.P.						
" 16	7:10	2	0	7304	5978	2055:10	N.Y.P.	1 TEST FLIGHT @ MILLS FIELD					5 MIN.
" 17	3:00	2	0	7306	5978	2058:10	N.Y.P						
" 19	3:35	1	0	7307	5978	2061:45	N.Y.P.						
" 20	7:00	1	0	7308	5978	2068:45	NYP						
" 21	2:25	1	0	7309	5978	2071:10	NYP						
" 22	2:55	3	24	7312	6002	2074:05	Ford Tri-motor	SAN DIEGO					
" 23	5:10	2	1	7314	6003	2079:15	N.Y.P.						
" 24	5:35	2	0	7316	6003	2084:50	NYP						
" 25	4:05	1	0	7317	6003	2088:55	NYP						
" 26	8:35	2	0	7319	6003	2097:30	NYP						
" 27	2:00	1	0	7320	6003	2099:30	NYP						
" 28	3:00	1	0	7321	6003	2102:30	NYP						
" 30	2:40	2	1	7323	6004	2105:10	NYP	PASSENGER DONALD KEHOE					5 MIN.
Oct. 1	3:40	2	0	7325	6004	2108:50	NYP						

Copy of Lindbergh's original pilot's log entries with notations on
right-hand side (upper case) by author for research clarification.

Stop #1
Hartford, Connecticut

Often referred to as the "Insurance Capital of the World," Hartford, the capital of Connecticut, is located in the north-central part of the state. In 1633 the Netherlands established a trading post called the House of Hope on the future site of Hartford. It is located on the west bank of the Connecticut River, the longest river in New England.

The city was incorporated in 1784. Brainard Field, a small airport on the southeast side of the city, was built in 1920, and was the nation's first city-owned airport. It is protected from the Connecticut River by a dike along the western edge.

40 feet MSL. (Mean Sea Level)

JULY 20–21, 1927 (WEDNESDAY AND THURSDAY)

The NYP took off from Mitchel Field on Long Island at 12:30 in the afternoon, heading northeast and out over Long Island Sound toward the shores of Connecticut.

The Fairchild FC-2, carrying Love, Sorenson and Keyhoe, had taken off one-half hour earlier in order to prepare the welcoming committee at Hartford for Lindbergh's imminent arrival.

Just before the advance ship departed from Mitchel, however, Mr. Guggenheim gave them some last-minute instructions: "Colonel Lindbergh is the commanding officer. If anything very unusual comes up he will decide it. Goodbye and good luck."[1]

As the Fairchild headed out across the sound, they had to divert around a blinding rainstorm. After circumnavigating the storm and checking their course, they realized they had been following an incorrect map. This took up almost all of the half hour allowed for preparation at Hartford.

Phil Love, the FC-2 pilot, remarked, "This is the last time I'm going to sleep on this job, but for heaven's sake, don't tell Slim about it. He'll kill me for the next six months, getting lost on a simple little run like this."

The Fairchild finally landed at Hartford's Brainard Field at 1:45 P.M. As he looked out the window at the vast crowds at the airport, Keyhoe wondered what Lindbergh's thoughts would be on seeing this demonstration of the continued interest in him. This was their introduction to what would turn out to be a common sight at each stop for the rest of the trip. They figured they had better well get used to it.

In the meantime, Lindbergh had planned a slight detour, flying fairly close to his original New York to Paris route over Niantic, Connecticut. The annual Governor's Day ceremony was in progress at Camp Trumbull, home of the 169th Infantry of the Connecticut National Guard, taking place at Niantic. Governor Trumbull and the Mayor of Niantic were there. Lindbergh arrived overhead at about 1:50 and, in a low-level pass, attempted to drop a streamer with the standard message upon the Niantic camp, but it got caught on the tail skid, where it would stay until he landed at Hartford.

About the same time, the Governor, who wanted to be at Hartford for Lindbergh's arrival, climbed aboard a Guard airplane, piloted by Maj. William C. Ladd, and headed immediately for Brainard Field. He made it just in time.

Carol W. Kimball was a camper at the New London Girl Scout Camp at Gardner's Lake, about 13 miles north of Niantic, on the general route to Hartford, and she remembered that day in 1927. She and many other campers had assembled in a large open field to see Lindbergh fly over on his way to Hartford. Their counselors told them that Lindbergh would drop a message, but they waited in vain. In 1988 Ms. Kimball recalled the experience with tears in her eyes.

It was 2:00 P.M. and as Lindbergh lined up for the final approach, State Aviation Department inspector George Pranaitis and two members of the 188th Observation Squadron, Air National Guard, positioned themselves to direct Lindbergh to taxi to the protection of Hangar 1. At that moment there was a blast of automobile horns and factory whistles. Lindbergh acknowledged the greetings with a wave of his hand from the cockpit, as he could actually hear the noise over the drone of the Wright J-5 engine.

Brainard Field

In 1908 the Aero Club of Hartford was formed in Hartford, the insurance capital of the nation. The club president was Hiram Percy Maxim, who believed in the future of flying and wished for Hartford to share in this new industry.

Up to this time aircraft landed at Goodwin Park, the North Meadows, the South Meadows, open fields in West Hartford, the Hartford Golf Club, or any other suitable space.

It was about early 1921 that the South Meadows was selected as the site for the new airport. It was city-owned land and had to have 6,000 trees removed. On June 11, 1921, with an expenditure of almost $7,500, the airfield was dedicated and named Brainard Field in honor of former Mayor Newton C. Brainard. As a whole it was officially named the Hartford Municipal Airport. It was within one and one-quarter miles of the center of the city, although they had yet to build some roads so that it could be reached by automobile.

In the spring of 1923 a special hangar was built on the north end of the field for the 43rd Division Air Service, Connecticut National Guard, and the 118th Observation Squadron of that division.

The first CAM (Contract Air Mail) service route #1 flew from New Jersey to Hartford in July 1926.

The Hartford stop was rather timely, or propitious, coming just two years after engine maker Frederick Rentschler had joined forces with the Pratt & Whitney Tool Company to form Pratt & Whitney Aviation Company. The world-famous manufacturer did some of their first engine flight testing at Brainard.

Over 25,000 people were already on the field to greet Lindbergh. In the welcoming committee were Governor John H. Trumbull, acting Hartford Mayor Houghton Buckley and other city officials.

A speaker's stand was erected on the west side of the field. Sound and other equipment was supplied by the local Travelers Insurance radio station, WTIC, which broadcast the event over the radio waves.

Lindbergh gave the following speech:

"Hartford is the first stopping point on this tour of the United States in each state in the union. The purpose of this tour is to acquaint the people of the United States with aviation. This trans-Atlantic flight from

Lindbergh standing in front of the NYP at Brainard Field, outside of Hartford, Connecticut. RAYMOND B. HOWLAND

San Diego to Paris, including the trip from Washington to St. Louis by way of New York, or the test flight or exhibition flight, required less time than it takes for a train to go from New York to San Francisco. The next question that arises is "When is that service to be made available to anyone who wants to make a trip by air?" The answer to that depends almost entirely upon the air transportation facilities for the people who will be able to use them. We have some in the country which are struggling for existence. They are going to stay—they are going to make good. Some of them have already. But if we in the air mail could have fifty percent more postage than you people pay, the air mail would be a tremendous success today. And with that success would come the ability of the air mail contractors, engineers and followers to devote their time to improving that service.

"You have a wonderful air mail service throughout the states—better than anything in Europe. But that service will be improved as time goes on. Passenger service will follow the air mail. Plans along that line have been inaugurated on the continent—or will be within the near future. But not within a few weeks or a few months, and the number of lines that we have depends entirely upon the amount of use that you can give them. Transatlantic flying will not come in a short time, but it is still in the future. It will not come until the continent is crossed and re-crossed by passengers, mail, and express air lines. But inside of the next ten or fifteen years, possibly less, this country will have those lines, and we will also be developing every service not already developed by lines across the Atlantic."

John Hesselgrave wrote to the author: "At that time I was in the first year of Middletown High School. My friend Bob Provan and I had bummed a ride to Hartford in Bob's father's Fleishman Yeast truck. We left Middletown around 5 A.M. We were both Eagle Scouts and wore our uniforms. The news reel camera men tried to elbow us out of our spot near the speaker's stand at Brainard."

He did manage to take a picture of Lindbergh and others on the stand, selling enlargements of the picture and making enough money to purchase a used 4X5 Graflex. He later sold the camera when he learned how much it cost to maintain.

After the reception at the airport, the parade cars' entourage formed up outside Hangar 1. Lindbergh rode in a 1927 Packard touring car, supplied by Morton Treadway. It carried Con-

Shown during the parade into the city of Hartford. From left to right: Governor John H. Trumball, Lindbergh, and acting Mayor Houghton Bulkeley. LEO B. KIMBALL COLLECTION

necticut registration no. 493.

The entourage proceeded up Meadow Road to Wethersfield Avenue and on to the starting point of the parade opposite Colt Park. They proceeded up Main Street to Asylum Street, through the "tunnel" to the capitol grounds, where there was a private reception in the office of the Governor.

During the parade up Main Street some office girls in the Hartford-Connecticut Trust Building, lacking any type of official banner to hang out over Main Street, fashioned an ingenious though somewhat dubious honor to the hero, a collection of a half-dozen pastel smocks, sleeves tied together and dangled from an upper window.

Other office girls in an upper insurance office tore up everything but policies and bank notes in their frenzied excitement, while janitors emptied all the waste baskets out the window in jubilation.

Bushels of confetti created from all sorts of paper and cloth were showered down onto the parade route. They were every color of the rainbow.

A press conference was held in the Bond Hotel. It was at this meeting that Lindbergh would get a taste of what was to come at most of the upcoming stops around the country—the constant, endless questioning, cheering crowds, autograph hunters, reporters and photographers. Women reporters could be particularly aggravating, asking his opinions about love, marriage, or girls. "What has that to do with aviation?" became his stock reply.

While in Hartford that first evening, the State presented him with the Nathan Hale Medal at a banquet in the Hartford Club ballroom. Governor Trumbull explained that the Nathan Hale Sesquicentennial Medal was conferred upon Lindbergh because Connecticut found in the hero to whom it was host the same sterling attributes that had made the Coventry schoolteacher of a century and a half ago a national idol. Assistant Secretary of Commerce for Aeronautics, William P. MacCracken, also attended this banquet, as well as Benedict M. Holden, Toastmaster, and Houghton Bulkeley, acting Mayor of Hartford.

It was a gala evening, and one could hear a pin drop as Lindbergh was introduced and proceeded to give his talk on the future of aviation and air travel. This would be a talk he would have to give over and over, all over the country for the next three months.

Governor Trumbull had this to say about Lindbergh:

"Whatever we say here of the young man about whom this gathering centers, we are but echoing the thought and the word which have been universal since Le Bourget became an eastern terminus for most U. S. airlines.

"In the hearts of those of us to whom 'Aviation' has long been a vital word, there is a deeper sense of gratitude and wonderment than that aroused by the Trans-Atlantic feat itself. Our feeling has to do with the psychological rather than the physical; that Colonel Lindbergh should have accomplished *alone and in a few hours* what we others have together been striving for many years to bring about; the public attitude which is already tritely summed up in the phrase 'Air-Minded-ness.'

"It is here now, in Connecticut and in forty-seven other states. Considering the end in view, we are willing to incur the stigma of opportunism (if such there be) in accepting and making the most of this fact.

"But even though in Connecticut our own efforts had perhaps brought it nearer fulfillment than elsewhere, the Lindbergh impetus does not free us from the necessity to 'carry on.' And with the Connecticut public awake as now, with its lawmakers and executives alive to the responsibility, we shall not *lag* behind in the future exploitation of the air.

"Give us more good airports, and better roads connecting them with the commerce and industry to be served; give us more good men to operate, and more good planes to be operated; give us well-marked airways, with full facilities for fuel and service and safety to local or through air-traffic…. Granted these, the 'Air-Minded-ness' of Connecticut will never be questionable."[2]

LEAVING HARTFORD FOR PROVIDENCE, RHODE ISLAND

The next day, July 21, 1927, Lindbergh took off from Brainard Field at 12:20 P.M. to fly the second leg of the tour. After circling over Hartford, he headed north to fly over the city of Springfield, Massachusetts, and then headed

east toward Worcester.

Today Brainard Airport still exists in the same location it was in 1927. It is at an elevation of 19 feet MSL, and has two runways, one of which is 4,418 feet, paved, and a parallel 2,350-foot grass runway. It serves mainly general aviation.

A newer and larger airport, Bradley International Airport, 15 miles north of the city, serves both Hartford and Springfield, Massachusetts. It is at an elevation of 174 feet MSL, and has three runways. The main runway is 9,502 feet. The field serves major domestic airlines, some commuters, general aviation and the Air National Guard.

Footnotes

1. *Flying with Lindbergh*, Donald E. Keyhoe, Grosset & Dunlap, New York, NY, 1928.
2. Souvenir Program, June 15, 1977, Testimonial Dinner to Col. Charles A. Lindbergh given by the citizens of Hartford at the Hartford Club.

References

Newspapers
   The Hartford Courant (the oldest continuously published newspaper in the country)
   The Hartford Times
   New Haven Sunday Register
   The Waterbury Republican-American
   The Day Carol W. Kimball, New London, Conn., April 7, 1988.

Organizations
   Connecticut Aeronautical Historical Association
   The Connecticut Historical Society
   Connecticut Department of Aeronautics
   Connecticut Department of Transportation
   Brainard Airport (administration)
   United Technologies Corporation

People

Harvey H. Lippincott	William Foley
Vernon Muse	Harold Burritt
Raymond B. Howland	Mary Faircloth
Grace Martin	Leon Moquin
Frank Greene	John Wm. Ramsey
Donald V. Richardson	Bruce Hayden
Mel Rice	Peter Buckeley
Igor I. Sikorsky Jr.	Ruth Morrison
Sergei Sikorsky	Wilson H. Faude
Chuck Simmons	John Hellelgrave
Ronnie Officer	Suzanna M. Farina
Elizabeth & Richard Leonard	
Mrs. Elizabeth Leonardo	Milford F. Rhines
Phil Munson (England)	John Siska

STOP #2
PROVIDENCE, RHODE ISLAND

CAPSULE HISTORY OF CITY

Providence, Rhode Island, is the capital of the smallest state in the country and is the second largest city in New England. It was founded by Roger Williams, who called it Providence because he believed Divine Guidance had brought him there. The city is an important Atlantic Coast port.

The city lies about twenty-five miles from the Atlantic Ocean at the head of Narragansett Bay, and about forty-five miles southwest of Boston, Massachusetts.

Founded in 1636, it was the first settlement in Rhode Island. For many years both Newport and Providence were capitals of Rhode Island. In 1900 Providence became the only capital city.

80 feet MSL.

JULY 21-22, 1927 (THURSDAY AND FRIDAY)

The 119th Engineers had prepared an open field of the Quonset National Guard Campground site, which was normally used for military activities. The site was located 12 miles south of Providence, on the west shore of Narragansett Bay. The city did not have its own airport at the time. The Engineers laid out white sheets of canvas as a marker for Lindbergh to spot the open landing field.

Lindbergh came into view of Providence from the northwest and hovered over the city for fifteen minutes, and then headed over to the East Side and down the river over Sekonk and then over Providence Harbor and Narragansett Bay. He finally landed at Quonset Point at 2:00 P.M., after flying over East Greenwich, which he had flown over on his way to Paris.

- 39 -

According to the highly respected newspaper *The Providence Journal,* the smallest state in the union gave one of the largest and wildest receptions to Lindbergh accorded anywhere on the tour. People came from as far away as Vermont, New Hampshire, Connecticut, Massachusetts, and even Pennsylvania to get a glimpse of the flyer. Roads for many miles around were jammed with cars, horse-drawn vehicles, bicycles, and people on foot.

Within ten minutes of his landing, Lindbergh was whisked off in an eighteen-car motorcade going directly into the capital city of Providence, Rhode Island. He was received on the steps of City Hall by Mayor James E. Dunne, Councilman John W. Cunningham, Vice Admiral Guy Burrage of the cruiser *Memphis,* and Lt. Governor Norman S. Case.

After the reception at City Hall, the motorcade proceeded to Roger Williams Park where Lindbergh gave a brief talk on the development and future of air travel. During his talk he said,

"At Providence I find it takes an hour to come from the field where I landed to the city.... It took 45 minutes to come from Hartford to Providence. But here again I find that the condition is being remedied."

Over 700 city and state officials attended a banquet in the ballroom of the Biltmore Hotel in downtown Providence. The banquet was hosted by Henry D. Sharpe, a prominent Rhode Island citizen. Lindbergh and his crew spent the night in the State Suite of the hotel.

One reporter from *The Evening Bulletin* wrote: "Brightly dressed women of that huge crowd offered the age-old adulation of the female to the conquering male. From the careless flapper to the staid middle-aged matron, abandonment of reserve reigned."

His landing at Providence gave a boost to the people who were attempting to convince those in authority that a state airport was essential to the future of the state.

On June 2, 1927, it was announced that three

The NYP surrounded with people from the area shortly after Lindbergh landed at Quonset Point, south of the city. LEO B. KIMBALL COLLECTION

sites had been offered to Providence officials for a municipal airport. The first site was 100 acres at Buttonwoods, which was already being used as a landing place and would be available to the city for five years, free of charge. The other two sites were also in Warwick, several miles south of Providence. There was a 187-acre site near the Rumford rifle range, the Rumford range itself, and a site west of LaSalle Academy, south of the State House. The last site was the Gould farm near Georgiaville.

While all the discussion was going on, Lindbergh made his appearance. During that visit 300,000 people came to see him, 200,000 within the Providence city limits alone.

After spending the night in Providence, Lindbergh took off from Quonset Point at about 12:20 P.M. and headed for Boston. His log indicates he flew via Bristol, Connecticut (though author's research indicates it should be corrected to Bristol, R.I.), Pawtucket, Woonsocket, R.I., and then Worcester, Massachusetts, before landing at Boston.

Early in the January 1928 session of the General Assembly, a West Warwick senator presented a novel idea. Senator Alberic Archambault proposed that the Providence River from the New Haven railroad tracks to Crawford Street be bridged over, that the space made available to adjacent streets be used for the construction of an airplane landing field, and that Providence be authorized to issue one million dollars in bonds to carry out the work. No action was taken on this bill.

On April 16, 1929, a State Airport Commission was established, which was given the responsibility of selecting, obtaining and improving a site for a state airport. On July 2, 1929, the Commission, headed by State Senator Harry Bodwell, announced its decision to build an airport in the Hillsgrove section of Warwick, just south of the city. They made this decision based on the reasonable price of less than $100,000. The remainder of the available funds could be used for development.

On March 1, 1930, the first commercial airplane service to run on a regular schedule out of Providence was inaugurated, linking Providence by air with New York. The Eastern Air Express used tri-motored Fords for those first flights.

Lindbergh's efforts resulted in the voters of Rhode Island approving a state airport by a vote

A nice close-up of the NYP at Quonset Point during his visit to Providence. MS. MARJORIE ANGELL

of 76,281 to 9,369 in the general election of 1928. On September 27, 1931, the Rhode Island State Airport at Hillsgrove was formally dedicated. Over 150,000 people witnessed the accompanying aerial show. It was the first state-owned airport in the nation.

Today that airport is on the same site, and is known as the Green State Airport. Senator Theodore Francis Green's name was used to recognize him for his support of aviation at both the state and national levels. It is at an elevation of 55 feet MSL and has three runways, the longest of which is 7,166 feet. The field serves domestic airlines, some commuter aircraft, general aviation and military aircraft. It is located 6 miles south of the city near Interstate 95.

The old field at Quonset where Lindbergh landed is still there today. It became Quonset Point Naval Air Station and today is known as Quonset State Airport, open for civilian use. It is located in the town of North Kingstown, next to the West Passage of the Narragansett Bay. At an elevation of 19 feet MSL, it has two runways, the longer of which is 7,500 feet. Formerly a Navy base, it is now open to civilian aircraft and serves general aviation and the military. It is the home of the Quonset Air Museum.

Three miles north of Pawtucket, Rhode Island, and about 14 miles north of Providence is North Central State Airport, at an elevation of 441 feet MSL, with two runways, one of which is 5,000 feet. It serves mainly general aviation.

References

Newspapers
The Evening Bulletin
The Providence Journal
The Warwick Beacon

The Providence Journal-Bulletin
The Bristol Press, Bristol, Conn.

Organizations

State Airport System Inventory — Rhode Island
Statewide Comprehensive Transportation and
Land Use Planning Program, State House, R.I.

Bristol Historical & Preservation Society, Bristol,
R.I.

Roger Williams University Library, Bristol, R.I.

People

Mrs. Arthur K. Frazier	Elizabeth Jones
Barbara Einarsson	William Warburton
John Parker	Marjorie H. Angell
Walter Schiebe	Stephen A. Rongo
Deborah Barton	Ed Shea
Lawrance D. Webster	Barbara Shea
Norman Shorrock	Gregory J. Young
Wendel Pols	Ray Battcher
Howard Baker	Sean Paul Milligan
Donald A. D'Amato, City Historian,	
City of Warwick	Miss Pat Carbone

STOP #3

BOSTON

CAPSULE HISTORY OF CITY

Capital of Massachusetts, Boston is the largest city in New England. It lies on Boston Bay, which forms part of Massachusetts Bay, an arm of the Atlantic Ocean. The harbor is at the mouth of the Charles River, the innermost part of Boston Bay. Boston has been referred to as "Beantown," based on the ritual of eating baked beans and brown bread on Saturday nights. It earned the title "Cradle of Liberty" in the 1760s and 1770s when it led the American struggle for independence from Great Britain. It is also known for the Boston Massacre, the Boston Tea Party, and Paul Revere's Midnight Ride.

About 1620 William Blackstone, a British clergyman, was the first white man to settle on the site. The area was named for Boston, England, home of many of the original settlers. It became the capital of the Massachusetts Bay Colony in 1630 and was chartered as a city in 1822.

21 feet MSL.

JULY 22–23, 1927 (FRIDAY AND SATURDAY)

According to newspaper reports, there was some patchy fog coming off the Atlantic Ocean, but in between the patches Lindbergh was able to find East Boston Airport, as it was known then, located on the edge of Boston Harbor. The fog initially was apparently the worst on record for the area. Some ships ran aground or were anchored at sea awaiting clearance to enter the harbor of the big city. All sea traffic was at a standstill along the Massachusetts, New Hampshire, and Maine coasts. This would later present a problem to Lindbergh when he would fly, according to plan, from Boston to Portland, Maine.

He buzzed the field several times before turning on final approach, with a side slip to the left and the flair and landing. He taxied up to the hangar, where they put a dolly under the tail skid, turned him around, and rolled the NYP into the hangar. Lindbergh climbed out of the cockpit and was greeted by Mayor Malcolm E. Nichols and Governor Alvan T. Fuller, both of whom helped in getting the airplane pushed inside. After a brief ceremony at the airport, and instructions from Lindbergh about the care of the NYP now in one of the hangars, he climbed into the Mayor's limousine, sitting in back between the Mayor and Donald Keyhoe. They drove to the historic Boston Common where he gave his speech. He stressed the fact that airplanes can safely cross uncharted seas, that air travel is possible anywhere in the United States, and that it will become as commonplace as travel by train or automobile, and ever so much more satisfactory regarding time, comfort, and safety. He continued to show that the airplane could maintain its schedule almost to the minute, no matter how adverse the weather might be.

Also on hand to greet him were all of the New England governors: Ralph O. Brewster of Maine, Huntley N. Spaulding of New Hampshire, John H. Trumbull of Connecticut, John W. Weeks of Vermont, and Norman S. Case of Rhode Island. They were all in Boston preparing to leave by train for a governors conference on Mackinac Island, Michigan.

The only photo ever found showing Lindbergh taxiing in at East Boston Airport, near Boston Harbor. YALE UNIVERSITY, MANUSCRIPTS AND ARCHIVES

After a governor's reception at the State House, the entourage proceeded to the Ritz Carlton Hotel, where they dispersed for dinner. The Boston Council of Boy Scouts of America, including local Troops 15 and 9, were among the groups who honored Lindbergh at the State House.

While in Boston Lindbergh also visited the United States Naval Hospital at Chelsea. A total of 375 veterans were housed in the facility. Some were moved outside to the lawn. Others were moved to the nearest window. Three hundred other townspeople including the children of Chelsea had a chance to see Lindbergh from the front lawn of the hospital.

Lindbergh and his crew spent the night at the Ritz Carlton.

In a letter to the author dated July 20, 1991, Richard K. Morris of Deep River, Connecticut, remembered that day very well:

"Dad had packed our family into our car

early on Thursday, and they left their home at North Billerica and proceeded to Chelsea, where they had a good view of the parade route from a second floor room over a garage of a friend. We got there about 9 in the morning.

"Our hero was coming, and we forgot the long hours we had been waiting and the increasing discomfort from the sultry heat of that July day. First the motorcycle police, slowly pushing the straining masses of humanity back onto the sidewalk.

"Lindbergh sat bolt upright, lean and handsome, staring directly ahead. The entourage passed directly beneath us. The next moment was history. I shall always thank my late father for the arrangements he made that I might be a participant in this historical event. I could not have stood for hours in the broiling sun, as thousands of others did, for I wore braces on both legs. Yet the spot he had chosen made it all possible."

Other prominent oceanic flyers were in Boston as well, to be honored along with Lindbergh: Clarence D. Chamberlin, Bernt Balchen, Bert Acosta, Lt. George Noville, Boston native Lt. Albert F. Hagenberger, and Lester J. Maitland. The latter two were the first to fly nonstop from San Francisco across the Pacific Ocean to Hawaii.

The airport is still there today and is known as Logan International Airport. It is at an elevation of 20 feet MSL and has five runways, the longest of which is 10,081 feet. It serves most major domestic airlines, many commuter airlines, corporate and international airlines, helicopters, and some military aircraft.

Hanscom Field, near the town of Bedford, is about 12 miles east of the city, just off Route 128. The field is at an elevation of 133 feet MSL and has two runways, the longer of which is 7,001 feet. It serves mostly general aviation and some military aircraft.

References

Newspapers
The Boston Sunday Globe
Gloucester Daily Times
Portland (Maine) Press Herald
North Adams Transcript
Country Journal
The Bristol Press, Bristol, Conn.

Magazine
Air Travel Journal

Organizations
Massachusetts Aviation Historical Society
Winthrop (Mass.) Public Library

People

Tomas S. Cuddy II	J. L. Johnson Jr.
Richard K. Morris	George K. Sioras
Paul H. Comeau	Robert J. MacLeod
Waino T. Ray	Harry P. Mutter
Bob Whittier	Paul M. Bauer
Chester Lisak	Charles N. Cahoon
Peter G. C. Langmore	Mildred MacDonald
Mrs. Arletta W. Turini	Earl Harding Sr.
Thurman "Jack" Naylor	

STOP #4
PORTLAND, MAINE

CAPSULE HISTORY OF CITY

Portland, Maine, is located on the southwest coast of the state, about sixty miles southwest of Augusta, the capital of the state, on the Atlantic Ocean. The city is built on a narrow peninsula with a maximum height of 187 feet above sea level and overlooks island-studded Casco Bay to the east. Mount Washington and other mountains of the Presidential Range are to the northwest. To the south is Old Orchard Beach, a long stretch of smooth sand on the Atlantic Ocean.

The city was founded in 1632, first named Machigonne and later Falmouth. It has one of the finest harbors on the Atlantic Coast and is closer to Europe than any other trans-Atlantic port in the United States.

25 feet MSL.

JULY 23–24 (SATURDAY AND SUNDAY)

The flight from Boston to Portland, Maine, would be the only one in which Lindbergh was unable to be on time at the destination. His initial plan was to fly from the Hub City to Portland, then on to Concord, New Hampshire, and continue westward via Vermont. Here is what happened.

It was Saturday, July 23, and the fuel tanks of the NYP were filled. At 12:34 P.M. he took off from East Boston Airport and headed north. The same low, thick fog from Boston all the way up the coast to Portland, Maine, was still there.

In the meantime Love took the Fairchild up to check on weather conditions, and because the fog was getting worse, he could not get back down into Boston. He then decided to continue to Portland. He had left Sorenson and Keyhoe back at Boston, so they commandeered a state policeman, who drove them up the Boston Post

Lindbergh speaking with Capt. Robert S. Fogg on the Concord Airport as, possibly
Caleb Marston fuels the NYP on Saturday, July 23. DICK JACKSON

Road toward Portland. There they found Love
with the Fairchild. He had found a hole in the
fog and landed in a field at Dayton, Maine, near
the Biddeford line, owned by Harris Cole.

Lindbergh, in the meantime, had flown over
Lynn and Lowell, Massachusetts, and then
Nashua, New Hampshire, proceeding toward
Portland on top of the layer of fog. He somehow
found Portland, and circled over the city for two
and a half hours before deciding to head southwest and inland to Concord, New Hampshire.
He figured it would be far enough inland to be
free of fog, which it was.

Seven years before Lindbergh's flight to Paris,
prominent local pilot Robert S. Fogg and his
friend, Willis D. Thompson, cleared a patch of
land in Concord Heights, just east of the capital
city, for a landing field for airplanes. Lindbergh
and the NYP landed on this field at about 5:30

P.M. (4:35 P.M. local time) unannounced and
unexpected. He was not to be in Concord until
the 24th. He had been in the air for five hours on
a flight that should have taken no more than an
hour and a half or so.

The airplane was rolled into the hangar of
Robert Fogg, and Lindbergh was taken to the
home of host Col. Charles H. Mason, Director,
322nd Observation Squadron of the Organized
Reserves of New Hampshire. Colonel Mason and
his wife had a summer home at Farringtons
Corner, on the road from Concord to
Dunbarton. "Slim" (Lindbergh's nickname)
spent the night there, having a welcomed good
night's rest.

In 1927 Mrs. Edmond J. Belenger (nee
Yvonne Cartier) worked as a cook and maid for
Colonel Mason. She recalled that there were
eight or nine guests who sat down for dinner at

about 9:00 P.M. After dinner Lindbergh came into the kitchen to compliment her "Brown Betty." He gave her a $2.50 gold piece, which she has treasured all these years.

JULY 24 (SUNDAY)

Leaving Concord on the 24th (Sunday) at 10:05 A.M., Lindbergh headed northeast toward Portland. However, he did run into the same fog problem and had to circle over the city for

Lindbergh (near right wheel) and the NYP on Old Orchard Beach. Harry Jones in knickers. HARRY M. JONES ALBUM VIA LEO BOYLE

an hour and a half before deciding to head south along the beach areas where he found the fog lifting. Finally he landed on the beach at a point halfway between Grand Beach and Old Orchard (Old Orchard Beach area).

Again he surprised many people in the beach area, some out for their usual stroll. The beach was often used by flyers and there was a hangar there, owned and operated by another prominent local flyer, Harry M. Jones. The NYP

Old Orchard Beach, July 24, and the NYP safely in the Harry Jones hangar with a sand floor. Lindbergh by engine. CASSAGNERES COLLECTION

was immediately pushed into Jones's hangar for protection from the crowds of people who gathered there in short order. Many photographs were taken at that time. Many are in the author's

possession.

In a letter to the author from Domonique E. Bilodeau, dated December 14, 1993, she says, "I was twelve years old sitting with my father on the bulkhead in front of our cottage on Old Orchard Beach, next to the Harry Jones hangar, when Lindbergh circled twice over the area and my father remarked, 'that's Lindbergh.' The tide was high, and Lindbergh did what no other had done before or after, land his airplane at high tide."

In the meantime there were more than 5,000 people at the Portland Airport, which was a new field located in an area then called Scarboro, and presently known as Scarborough. The field was also known as Stroutwater Field.

Lindbergh was taken by automobile from Old Orchard to Scarboro to be officially welcomed by the people of Portland. There he was greeted by the reception committee, and shortly the motorcade headed for the city. All along the route the streets were lined with thousands of people.

He gave a speech at a grandstand at Deering's Oaks Park in Portland. In his talk he stressed the importance of people patronizing the United States Air Mail services.

He was impressed with the report of the city's plans for the new airport and updating its facilities for the future of air travel. He felt it was not necessary for him to elaborate on that fact, but to elaborate on air mail services instead. Lindbergh said that the air mail was barely keeping its existence and needed their support, so that when it reached a paying basis, improvements could be effected and efficiency reached. Then the air mail would give service equal to any other form of transportation. He believed their support would be repaid.

Slim and his crew attended a packed banquet at the Hotel Eastland that evening. In the absence of the Governor, who had left earlier that day for the conference in Michigan, he was welcomed by Councilor William S. Linnell for the State of Maine, and Chairman Philip J. Deering of the City Council.

While the NYP was at Old Orchard, Sorenson and a local mechanic assisted with the filling of the oil tank and doing other engine servicing.

Lindbergh left Old Orchard Beach on the morning of the 25th. He took off to the south and

Rare photo of the NYP at the
Scarborough Airport south of
Portland, Maine, July 25. IRA MILLIKEN

Another rare photo at Scarborough Airport as
Lindbergh is greeted by local Portland dignitaries,
July 25. OWLS HEAD TRANSPORTATION MUSEUM

immediately went into a left turn over the ocean. He circled about several times and then headed for Scarborough airport, five minutes away. He only stayed at Scarborough for a short time, where he expressed to the people his appreciation for the warm welcome of that Maine city.

The two airplanes took off and spent over a half hour circling the city, as promised, before heading out over South Poland, Maine, Mt. Hope, White Mountains, Lake Winnepesaukee, and Manchester, New Hampshire, landing at Concord, New Hampshire. He and the NYP and Fairchild were in the air for two hours and twenty minutes, taking in the sights of the White Mountains before proceeding to Concord.

Later the city of Portland built the present-day airport, known as Portland International Jetport, which is located just slightly west of the city and a bit north of the old Scarboro airport, no longer in existence. The field is at an elevation of 74 feet MSL and has two runways, the longer one being 6,800 feet. It serves many major domestic airlines, some commuters, general aviation aircraft and military aircraft.

References

Newspapers
Portland, (ME) Press Herald
Portland, (ME) Sunday Telegram

Organizations
Portland Public Library
Maine Aviation Historical Society

People
Mrs. Mary N. Sparrow	Judy and Ed Gardner
Lillian Weisz	Leo Boyle
Achilles Livada	Capt. Edward Nibur
Amy Calder	Heather Stafford
Arthur T. Forrestall	Ira Milliken
Harold Hutchinson	Gertrude Folz
Domonique E. Bilodeau	Dick Sherman
Mrs. Edmond J. Belenger (nee Yvonne Cartier)	

STOP #5
CONCORD, NEW HAMPSHIRE

Concord is New Hampshire's capital and the third-largest city in the state. It lies on the Merrimack River in south-central New Hampshire. The city was known as Penacook, named by the Penacook Indians, when it was founded in 1727, took the name Rumford in 1733, and assumed its present name in 1765. It became the state capital in 1808.

The last home of President Franklin Pierce still stands in the city.

290 feet MSL.

Hospital, miscellaneous State buildings and other significant sites to greet Army veterans, sick children, etc.

Lindbergh and his crew were taken to the Eagle Hotel in town, where they could relax before the evening festivities.

That night there was a banquet in the Bektash Temple, where Lindbergh gave a speech in which he touched on the subject of women flyers. A lady in the audience of 1,300 persons asked him what the possibilities were of women succeeding in the field of aviation. Lindbergh said, "I see no reason why women should not

The NYP in the hangar of the Concord Airport Corporation at Concord Airport.
ELINOR F. EVISON

JULY 25–26, 1927 (MONDAY AND TUESDAY)

After their scenic flight over the White Mountains, both airplanes came into Concord for the official visit about 1:22 P.M. (local time).

At Concord there was a parade from the airport across the Merrimack River into the capital city. A short press conference was held, then the parade continued throughout the city, with brief stops at the State Hospital, Centennial Home for the Aged, Memorial Hospital for Women and Children, the Margaret Pillsbury

succeed."

He continued, "I am sure that the next time I arrive in Concord you will have one of the best airports in New England. I do believe that when you have improved your facilities for air lines that you will support them to encourage the development of airports. You had already done this before we arrived. Therefore by request and for the first time on this tour I shall tell you something of my trip to Paris."

After a detailed account of his New York to Paris flight, he predicted that soon it would be possible to eliminate the danger to a flier encoun-

A nice close-up of Lindbergh in his pin-striped suit, by the nose of the NYP, and a clear view of the carburetor heat box. NEW HAMPSHIRE HISTORICAL SOCIETY #1755

tering sleet, such as he did over the Atlantic. He said, "This may be accomplished by running the exhaust through the wings and fuselage, thus preventing freezing to the wings which, when it occurs, may force a plane down by changing contours in as little as five minutes.

"I ask you to continue to support your airport and the eventual service which will come to it with the establishment of air lines."

JULY 26

Lindbergh and his crew arrived at the airport the next morning at 10:40 A.M. to find thousands of people already there and in the surrounding area to give him a send-off. He and the NYP took off to the south, circled over the airport and then the city and headed for Springfield, Vermont.

The airport at Concord is still on that original site and is known today as the Concord Municipal Airport. It is at an elevation of 346 feet MSL and has two runways, the longer of which is 6,005 feet. It serves some commuter aircraft, Air National Guard aircraft, and aircraft of the State Police and general aviation.

References

Newspapers
The Concord Daily Monitor

Magazines
Yankee

Organizations
Concord Public Library
New Hampshire Historical Society

People
Robert S. Fogg
Jack Ferns
Pat and Dick Jackson
Senator Warren B. Rudman
Warren M. Jenkins
Lee Ann Keniston
Yvonne Cartier
Herbert Hill *(Atlantic Flyer)*
Don Shea
Louis Hall
Mary L. Corrigan

Stop #6
Springfield, Vermont

The earliest known inhabitants of the area now known as Springfield, Vermont, were the Abenaki, an Algonquin tribe that maintained a hunting village in the area.

The first non-native settler in Springfield was John Nott, who paddled up the Connecticut River from Wethersfield, Connecticut, with two companions in 1751 and spent the spring and summer hunting and trapping in the area. Nott returned the following spring with his wife, Ruth, who was part Abenaki. They built a log cabin at the confluence of the Connecticut and Black Rivers. Other settlers arrived in the next few years from Fort #4 across the river in Charlestown, New Hampshire. The Crown Point Military Road was completed in 1760, linking Fort #4 with the fortress at Crown Point on Lake Champlain, making Springfield a point along this major commercial byway.

The town of Springfield was chartered in 1761 when New Hampshire Governor Benning Wentworth issued a land grant to Gideon Lyman and sixty-one other "proprietors," mostly from Northampton, Massachusetts. The town was named after Springfield, Massachusetts.

500 feet MSL.

July 26, 27, 1927 (Tuesday and Wednesday)

Lindbergh took off from the Concord Airport at about 11:45 A.M. and headed for Lebanon and Hanover, then Claremont, New Hampshire, and across the Connecticut River to Rutland, Vermont. The two tour airplanes spent time sightseeing the beautiful New England countryside. Lindbergh probably circled as the Fairchild landed ahead of him by thirty minutes at the Springfield, Vermont, field, then known as Hartness Field.

It was a hot summer day in Vermont, and the booths dispensing drinks in the vicinity of the field did a rushing business as the hour drew near and suspense became more pronounced.

A few minutes later the NYP was spotted by an alert Boy Scout, and after circling around the field several times, the airplane landed at exactly 1:55 P.M., five minutes ahead of schedule. But what about Hartness Field and aviation in Vermont in 1927?

All of the excitement of Lindbergh's flight to Paris was taken rather calmly until a telegram addressed to the "Mayor" was received on July

July 26 and the large welcome by the people of Springfield, Vermont. L.M. HOLLOWAY

On the roll-out just after landing at Springfield. MRS. LOIS M. PAQUIN

The NYP at Springfield with the Fairchild in the background just after they landed. MRS. LOIS M. PAQUIN

NYP and the Fairchild in front of the wooden hangar at Springfield. MRS. LOIS M. PAQUIN

12 from the Guggenheim Fund, stating that Springfield had been selected as the Vermont stop on the tour.

There was no mayor at the time, so the Western Union office turned the notice over to the County Sheriff, who in turn notified Municipal Manager Roy M. Wilcomb. A central committee was formed to make necessary arrangements.

The little town of Springfield was the only one in Vermont that had the foresight to establish a landing field for airplanes. Appreciation for such a place may be attributed to ex-Governor James Hartness, who grew up in this city. He was a veritable twentieth-century Renaissance Man. At age thirteen he left grammar school and went to work in a machine shop. Hartness became a successful inventor, manufacturer, astronomer and aviation enthusiast. By the age of forty he became president of the Jones and Lamson Machine Shop in Springfield and obtained the patent to the Hartness Flat Turret Lathe. He completed work on a "Newport Cottage" style mansion (now the Hartness House) and began work on his Turret Equatorial Telescope, one of the first tracking telescopes in the country.

Ten years previous to Lindbergh's visit, Hartness had the vision to establish the first airplane landing area in Vermont, at Springfield. He had the strong conviction and faith that the day would come when an airport would be an asset to Springfield. Hartness purchased 100 acres of land on which the field was established.

Mr. Hartness had obtained the first pilot's license in Vermont, one of only one hundred in the nation at that time.

Hartness was present at the committee meetings, and with his insight into the needs of the Lindbergh party and his ability for organization, made suggestions that eased the way of the committee to a great degree. Since that first announcement of the upcoming visit, the committee, as one reporter wrote, "had been right out straight"[3] working on the myriad details. The whole town, and even surrounding towns and villages, all volunteered their help, and in good old-time New England fashion. This was Vermont's party.

Hartness's pleas that other Vermont towns should also build landing fields may have been somewhat ahead of the times, but since that plea went unheeded many of the larger Vermont cities and towns have already had reason to regret that they, as well as Springfield, were not ready to welcome a Lindbergh landing.

It was a tremendous job for a small town, without facilities for the proper handling of such a crowd as came to Springfield, and for caring for the comfort and convenience of the crew. It would have been equally as tremendous a job in any city in the state. Vermont just wasn't equipped for such a rush. But the fact remains that Vermont took care of it, and that right well. Large cities where the flyer visited expressed wonder that Lindbergh should have included Springfield in his tour. The manner in which Vermont, and particularly Springfield, handled the difficult situation was their best answer. It was done and done well, with less confusion than had occurred in any place he had visited up to that time. About half the state was there to welcome Lindbergh.

Hartness, in the absence of Gov. John W. Weeks, who was at Mackinac Island in Michigan, was there that summer day to greet

Former Governor James Hartness meeting Lindbergh on July 26 at Springfield. MRS. LOIS M. PAQUIN

Lindbergh. Also in the reception committee was Lt. Gov. S. Hollister Jackson.

There was a huge crowd on hand to greet the tour flyers, estimated as 30,000, the largest assembly by far in the history of the town. The American Legion directed traffic, and the 1st Battalion, 172 Infantry, Vermont National Guard, policed the field. They were successful in providing proper clear space for the NYP to land, but less so in handling pickpockets. More than $1,000 was reported to police as having been stolen by the light-fingered gentry.

After Lindbergh was assured of the protection of the NYP, he was escorted to a small grandstand on the field to be officially welcomed. Mingled with the chorus of cheers and wild waving of hands, handkerchiefs, and hats as he mounted the stand, was the click of cameras. It was apparent that a likeness of the flyer would grace the photo albums of a great many citizens of the state within the next few days.

Lindbergh's speech at the flying field was a remarkably good estimate of the direction aviation would take. He felt there would be two lines of development, civil and military. He thought that transoceanic commercial flight would not come soon and that further research and development would be necessary.

After the thunderous cheering from the well-behaved crowd, Lindbergh was given the opportunity to speak.

"You in Vermont are particularly well suited to use aviation. Your country is rugged. You can't drive over the top of the hills, and you must detour around them. Or at least I think you must. You can take off here from Springfield and go in any direction regardless of the contour of the land. The time element is important. Fliers average a rate of about 100 mph, while on the ground 40 to 45 is about the best you can average.

"The development of aviation up to the present time has been largely along military lines. From now on there will be two lines, military and commercial. Commercial aeronautics possess possibilities of more economical transportation of freight and passengers."

Lindbergh gave one of his rare smiles during this time, and was clearly moved almost to tears from the reaction of the sincere Vermont people. He must have felt right at home. Most of them were farmers and country folk. Little was he or anyone else to know that many years later his daughter, Reeve, would be living permanently in Vermont, and that he would make his last flight as PIC (Pilot in Command) in that beautiful state.

He continued,

"Springfield is to be congratulated on this field. Probably it will be but a short time before you enlarge and improve it. It will not be a great while longer before you will be able to come out here, take a plane, go to Boston and from there to almost any part of the United States. Trans-oceanic planes will not soon come. Much research and development will be necessary before commercial flying to Europe will be practical. Thank you for your interest."

Time has proven the wisdom of Lindbergh's predictions at Springfield, and the foresight of the citizens of that small community, for their contributions to the continuing improvement of the airport, now known as the Hartness State Airport.

In addition to the citizens with their Brownie cameras, there were scores of newspaper photographers doing what they do best. This author wonders where all the pictures are today, as not many have turned up after exhaustive searching.

Five hundred representative Vermonters from around the state attended a banquet honoring Lindbergh, held that evening at the Community House. It was an invitational affair. Invitations were sent to heads of local government and civil and business leaders statewide. Lindbergh was given a gold commemorative medal at this affair.

Due to the small size of the town, the people had to look carefully for enough tables and chairs to accommodate the guests. Such places as the local churches, fraternal organizations, and private homes contributed. There were only 7,000 people living in Springfield at the time.

All the men who helped out with traffic direction and other sundry duties and responsibilities of crowd control were treated to a supper in the Methodist Church given by the ladies of that parish.

After the banquet Lindbergh and his crew

were given rooms (Lindbergh in #6) at the Hartness mansion, home of James Hartness. Today it is known as the Hartness House, one of Vermont's most famous mansions, where one can stay with real New England hospitality.

The final loose financial ends of the event were picked up at the 1928 annual town meeting, which voted to compensate the Springfield Manufacturers' Association for expenses it had incurred amounting to $1,302.81.

About two hundred people were at the airport the next morning (Wednesday, July 27) when the party prepared to leave for Albany, New York.

Before they left Springfield, Ted Sorenson gave both airplanes a thorough inspection, even before the pilots arrived. In spite of the careful security by personnel of the Vermont National Guard, souvenir hunters would not be denied, for a cotter pin, holding one portion of the engine cowling on the NYP was found to be missing and had to be replaced. After Lindbergh gave the NYP a complete pre-flight, the airplane was rolled out of the hangar, and shortly Sorenson hand-propped the airplane for startup.

At 10:20 A.M. Lindbergh and the NYP took off from Hartness and headed northwest a few miles to circle over Plymouth, the boyhood home of President Coolidge. The Fairchild left at 10:40 A.M. and headed directly to Albany. In the meantime Lindbergh changed his course to fly over Keene, New Hampshire, south to Brattleboro, Vermont, then directly west to Bennington, Vermont, and from there over to the scenic Catskill Mountains.

As a result of Lindbergh's visit to the Green Mountain State, a proposition was put forth in Burlington, then the capital, to establish an airport there and to name it in honor and dedica-

tion to U.S. President and Mrs. Coolidge, and should be known as Grace Coolidge Aviation Field in honor of the first daughter of this city and of Vermont ever to occupy the White House. Burlington did get an airport, but today it is known only as Burlington International Airport.

Hartness State Airport is still there on the same site as it was in 1927. It is at an elevation of 577 feet MSL, and has two runways. The longer is 5,498 feet. It mainly serves general aviation.

Footnotes

3. *Springfield Reporter*, Thurs., July 28, 1927, Springfield, VT

References

Newspapers
The Springfield Reporter, Thursday, July 28, 1927

Magazines
Northeast Weekend Flyers

Organizations
Town of Springfield, Vermont Annual report 1982
Vermont-Peoples National Bank of Brattleboro
Hartness Municipal Airport
Springfield Town Library

People

Richard Sanders Allen	Mary C. Barter
Mrs. Milton C. Baker	Roger Davis
Mrs. Anita Hudson	W. R. Batesole
Mrs. Lois M. Paquin	Russell Moore
Mrs. Oliver L. Lilley	L.M. Holloway
Simeon Donahue	Edward Eilertsen
Mr. Ludlow Richardson	
Preston A. Wheeler	
David M. Amidon	

Stop #7

Albany, New York

Capsule History of City

Albany, the capital of New York, lies on the Hudson River and is a busy shipping port, even though it is 150 miles from the Atlantic Ocean.

It is one of the oldest cities in the nation. It was named Albany by the British in 1664 in honor of the Duke of York and Albany. Its nickname is Cradle of the Union because Benjamin Franklin presented his Plan of Union there at the Albany Congress in 1754. It was the first formal proposal to unite the American colonies.

Albany lies on the west bank of the Hudson River in eastern New York State, near the meet-

ing of the Hudson and Mohawk Rivers. Albany, Schenectady and Troy form a combined metropolitan area.

Iroquois Indians lived in what is now the Albany area before white settlers arrived. In 1609 the English explorer Henry Hudson became the first white man to reach the site. Dutch settlers established a permanent community there in 1624, and by 1700 Albany had become the chief fur trading center of the American colonies and a busy port for river commerce. In 1797 Albany was chosen as the state capital.

200 feet MSL.

July 27–28, 1927 (Wednesday and Thursday)

After some low flying in the valleys of the Catskill Mountains, both airplanes headed to the Hudson River to avoid heavy rainstorms. In the wake of severe thunderstorms they went directly to the Albany Airport, just south of the city next to the river. This was the end of the first week of the goodwill tour.

The only airport for Albany at that time was on Van Rennselaer, or Westerlo Island, a low-lying tract at the city's south end, situated in the Hudson River at the mouth of the Norman's Kill. Known at the time as Quentin Roosevelt Field (in honor of the son of Theodore Roosevelt who was killed flying in World War I), the narrow,

former truck garden already had been found to be an inadequate landing site.

The NYP came in from the west, down the ravine of the Normanskill (the high bridges of the Thruway and Southern Boulevard were not there in 1927), and then side slipped to land on the field.

The *Spirit of St. Louis* touched down on the wet ground at 2:06 P.M., where Lindbergh was greeted by approximately 10,000 people. Initially he was met by Albany Mayor John Boyd Thacher, and the newly established "Albany Air Board," headed by Chauncey D. Hakes.

Under a heavy downpour Lindbergh was

Lindbergh with Albany Mayor John Boyd Thacher on July 27 under the wing of the NYP. COURTESY *THE TIMES UNION*, ALBANY, NY

This rare photo shows the NYP tied down on Westerlo Island, otherwise known as Quentin Roosevelt Field. Notice the tarp over the engine and "misty" look in the background. ELEANOR KIRCHNER

carried away quickly in the official car up South Pearl Street, "at a fast clip." An estimated 2,500 cars were parked on the island, but only a few were able to join the motorcade. Exits were jammed hours later as people and cars were still trying to leave the field.

The city celebrated a "half holiday," as another 30,000 people gathered in Lincoln Park. There Lindbergh gave his usual speech. However, he did foretell that letters would soon be sent from New York to San Francisco in less than twenty-four hours.

He had barely finished his talk when dark clouds and heavy rain again overcame the area, and everyone had to take cover. The entourage headed right away to Albany's downtown Ten Eyck Hotel on State Street.

While in the capital city, Lindbergh learned that the city was in the process of purchasing land just a few miles north of the city from the Niskayuna Shakers for a new airport. The Albany Air Board, of which Chauncey D. Hakes was chairman, drove him out to the Shaker farms to look over the proposed site, and Lindbergh gave it his enthusiastic approval.

The flyer recommended that the proposed airport have at least a 2,500-foot runway, perhaps two. A year later 225 acres were purchased from the Shaker community in Colonie for what is now the Albany County International Airport. Mayor Thacher proposed to name the new airport Lindbergh Field, but the idea was quietly dropped. Some of the first airlines to operate out of Albany were Eastern Airlines, Colonial Airlines, and later TWA, American, and Canadian Colonial Airways.

Today Albany International Airport, six miles northwest of the city, is at an elevation of 285 feet MSL, and has two runways, the longer one being 7,200 feet. It serves some major domestic airlines, commuter airlines, as well as general aviation and Air National Guard aircraft.

In a 1978 study it was found that about three to four thousand people use the airport every day, with some 575,000 passengers arriving annually and approximately the same number departing. The airport benefits the community with some $818 million in wages each year, a figure that is multiplied several times over as the wages are spent in the community.

In the evening the Albany Chamber of Commerce hosted a formal banquet at the hotel in Lindbergh's honor. Two dining rooms were used to accommodate 1,200 people. Lindbergh had part of his meal in one room and finished it in the other one, following which he was again called upon to speak.

On a hot and muggy Thursday morning, the 28th, the delivery of his laundry was delayed. It was 9:30 A.M. before he received the parcel. He was again driven in the official car to Westerlo Island where the NYP had been fueled and prepared for the next leg of the tour, to nearby Schenectady.

Normally a flight from Albany to Schenectady would only take about five or ten minutes, but Lindbergh elected to fly over Troy, across the river from Albany, and then up the Hudson Valley to Glens Falls, and a surprise fly-over of Lake George. From there he flew south to pass above Saratoga Springs and Ballston Spa. He would fly one hour and forty-five minutes before finally landing at Schenectady.

References

Newspapers
 The Times Union
 Troy Times
 The Knickerbocker Press

Organizations
 New York State Empire State Aero Sciences Museum
 Lockheed Air Terminal, Inc.
 Albany County Hall of Records
 Albany Public Library

People
Richard Sanders Allen
William Selfert Jr.
Howard Goldstock
Sara "Kim" Andrews
Mrs. Stacy Melvin
Mrs. Eleanor Kirchner
Ray Welt
Jackson Davis
Susan M. Gould
Jansz V. "Jack" Vander Veer

STOP #8
SCHENECTADY, NEW YORK
"TOUCH STOP"

CAPSULE HISTORY OF CITY

Schenectady is located fifteen miles northwest of Albany on the Mohawk River. Arendt van Curler and fourteen other Dutch pioneers purchased the site of the city in 1661. The English took possession of the city in 1664. It received its borough charter in 1765 and became a city in 1798.

It has been the home of the General Electric Company since the 1880s.

245 feet MSL.

July 28, 1927 (Thursday)

In the meantime, it seemed as though all of Schenectady County was flooding to the fields east of Thomas Corners in the East Glenville farmland, which would become the municipally owned Schenectady Airport. Inspired promoters had begun calling the stubby grass field "Port Schenectady."

Just about all of the businesses and city offices in town closed for the day to honor Lindbergh's visit. In charge of all arrangements was thirty-nine-year-old Henry C. Ritchie, General Electric's specialist in airport lighting and head of the local chapter of the National Aeronautic Association.

Schenectady was the home of the world-famous General Electric Company (GE), which in 1927 had pioneered some firsts in the electrical industry. The first home television reception took place at the Schenectady residence of Ernest F. W. Alexanderson. The Electric Refrigeration Department established the production of the "Monitor Top" hermetically sealed refrigerator, together with the all-steel cabinet refrigerator. GE played an important part in the launching of the S.S. *California*, the first large passenger ship with turbo-electric drive. With a cruising radius of 15,400 miles and speed of 18 knots, she was the largest electrically driven ship of her class in the world.

Mayor Alexander T. Blessing was there to officiate, with the head of the Chamber of Commerce, John F. Horman. Included was Martin P. Rice, head of GE publicity and broadcasting station WGY.

A well-behaved crowd on the field watched when at 11 A.M. Phil Love, piloting the Department of Commerce Fairchild FC-2, came into view and landed shortly thereafter.

Soon Lindbergh came into view and after circling came down and dragged the field to familiarize himself with the field surface to find the most suitable area to touch down. He did this at exactly 11:19 A.M. Lindbergh was the very first celebrated aviator to land there.

After introductions, the Mayor escorted the flyer over to a flag-draped reception stand on a flat-bed truck. During Lindbergh's talk he gave tribute to the progress of aviation and made a plea for airplane landing facilities at every major city. "I am glad," he said, "to find that Schenectady needs little prompting in this respect ... plans for the development of your port are magnificent."

The bunting-bedecked truck was driven all around the perimeter of the field, nearly pitching the guest over the tailgate. But he hung on, as cheers and concentrated tooting and cheering drowned out all other sounds.

Lindbergh on the left with his tour aide, Donald E. Keyhoe, and Henry C. Ritchie of the lighting department of the local General Electric Company. LARRY HART

The NYP under close guard by local police on what was once referred to as "Port Schenectady." LARRY HART

Lindbergh was on the ground for only an hour and a half before departing at 12:51 P.M. for Syracuse to the west. In the annals of the city, no public figure, before or since, has ever received such a tremendous reception.

In June of 1927, just after the NYP flight to Paris, the people of the area erected a sign on the field: "Lindbergh made his goal ... so can Schenectady!" At the end of that week exuberant Chamber officials announced that an excess of $121,000 had been pledged to the campaign, the start of building the Schenectady Airport.

Today the Schenectady County Airport is still there, at an elevation of 378 feet MSL and has two runways. The longer one is 7,000 feet. The field serves mainly general aviation and Air National Guard aircraft. On the airport grounds, housed in two buildings, one of which is the former hangar of the General Electric Company, is the Empire State Aero Sciences Museum.

References

Newspapers
The Schenectady Union-Star
The Post Dispatch
Schenectady Gazette
The Post Standard

Book
The General Electric Story 1976–1986: A Photo History. Schenectady, N.Y.: Hall of History Foundation, 1989.

Organization
New York State Empire State Aero Sciences Museum

People
Richard Sanders Allen   G. Asherwood
Marion J. Kimbrell   Roger Story
Ronald Arsenault
Jansz V. "Jack" Vander Veer
Larry Hart (City of Schenectady historian)

STOP #9
SYRACUSE, NEW YORK

CAPSULE HISTORY OF CITY

Syracuse is located close to Onondaga Lake, about 150 miles west of Albany, not far from the famous "Finger Lakes" region.

In 1570 the Onondagas' Indian chief, Hiawatha, chose the site as the location of the capital of the Iroquois Confederacy. The first Anglo-American settlers came to the area in 1788, and the city was founded in 1805. It is the home of Syracuse University, founded there in 1870.

Ephraim Webster became the first settler when he opened a trading post in 1786. The village was incorporated in 1825. It was once known as the Salt City because its major product was salt.

400 feet MSL.

JULY 28–29, 1927 (THURSDAY AND FRIDAY)

After leaving Schenectady Lindbergh flew over Little Falls, Utica, and Rome, New York. It was a beautiful day for this leg of the tour as he neared Syracuse.

Five local aviators greeted and escorted the famous flyer. Three of them were Dr. H. E. Luther, Ernie B. Hannam, and George Freeman.

Milburn Kusterer, the tour's advance man, had already met with Mayor Hanna to map out a reception plan.

Lindbergh was headed for what was then known as the Syracuse Airport Field (Amboy Field) at Belle Isle, out beyond the present state fairgrounds. He landed at 2:00 P.M., right on schedule.

The Fairchild had already landed a half hour before the NYP, and Donald Keyhoe expressed his pleasure at how well organized the reception committee was and how well behaved the crowd of citizenry was. Many businesses closed for the afternoon, and it became "Lindbergh Day" in Syracuse.

Lindbergh was greeted by the welcoming committee, including Mayor Charles G. Hanna and Florence E. S. Knapp, the New York Secretary of State as well as Dean of the College of Home Economics at Syracuse University. She would soon be running for reelection and according to newspaper reports took advantage of the situation to put herself in "front" of Lindbergh, as she and Mayor Hanna flanked the flyer in the back seat of the official Franklin open touring car (Syracuse was the home of the Franklin Automobile Company). The news photographers went crazy as a result, trying to get good shots of Lindbergh. She continued to wave her bouquet of pink roses as they drove into the city.

National Guardsmen, under the command of Maj. Harry E. Farmer, formed a solid line of soldiers around the perimeter of the field.

The official reception was at Syracuse

Lindbergh by the NYP at Syracuse Airport Field (Amboy Field) on July 28. CLEOTA REED GABRIEL

University's Archbold Stadium, where 25,000 people awaited his arrival and speech. Harry H. Guggenheim was expected to be in the reception group for Lindbergh's arrival.

By the time they reached the stadium, Mrs. Knapp had managed at least one or two more waves out of her roses. Lindbergh had little to say when he was given the chance on the platform, and shortly thereafter was escorted back into the car to be driven down off the hill to Hotel Syracuse, where a formal reception awaited him.

Four great flood lights were placed on poles surrounding the NYP so the people would be able to view the airplane during the day and into the evening as well.

The room Lindbergh occupied at the Hotel Syracuse was the same one used by former aviatrix Mrs. Aimee Semple McPherson.

While in Syracuse he met his first American Indian, Chief Harry Isaacs of the Onondaga tribe, who gave the flyer a bow and arrow. Chief Isaacs had carved it out himself especially for the occasion.

Syracuse resident Holland Redfield recalled the arrival of Lindbergh thus: "In July 1927, when only eleven years old, I trundled my battered Columbia bicycle to the top of a hill in Syracuse's east side Lincoln Park, arriving there early and then waiting for long hours searching the eastern skies for the *Spirit of St. Louis.* After flying over the city he touched down on the other side of town, at that time just an emerald green beautifully sodded field."

Sometime after, the Fairchild FC-2 with Phil Love at the controls took off for Rochester. Lindbergh lifted into the air with the NYP on Friday the 29th. He flew straight west toward Rochester with no detours.

Today Syracuse has the Hancock International Airport, which serves some domestic airlines and commuters, in addition to general aviation, Air National Guard and air cargo operations on the field. The field is at an elevation of 421 feet MSL, and has two main runways, the longer being 9,003 feet.

References

Newspapers
Syracuse Herald
Syracuse Herald-American
The Post Standard

Organization
Aviation Historical Society of Central New York

People
Peter Doyle Jr.
Holland Redfield
Cleota Reed Gabriel, Project Director, Light Work, documenting the history of photography in Syracuse
Lindsley A. Dunn, Curtiss Museum, Hammondsport, New York

Lindbergh is shown on the grandstand of Syracuse University's Archbold Stadium before giving his presentation over radio station WFBL and via loudspeakers in the stadium. CLEOTA REED GABRIEL

Stop #10
Rochester, New York
"Touch Stop"

Capsule History of City

The third largest city in New York State, Rochester is located along the Genesee River near its outlet into Lake Ontario. It is 70 miles northeast of Buffalo, New York.

The French established a post near the present site in 1710. However, the settlement was really established by New England people under the leadership of Nathaniel Rochester of Rochesterville in 1812. It was incorporated as a village in 1817 and chartered as a city in 1834.

It was originally called the "Flour City" because of its milling industries and also because of its nurseries, parks, and fruit and garden areas. The city leads in the manufacture of optical, surgical, dental, check-protecting and gear-cutting goods. It is also home of the world-famous Kodak Photographic Company. The George Eastman House is in Rochester, a museum of photography once the home of the founder of the Eastman Kodak Company.

515 feet MSL.

July 28–29, 1927 (Thursday and Friday)

Lindbergh flew west-northwest, and just north of the popular and beautiful "Finger Lakes" toward his next and brief stop in Rochester. The flight would take him over some pretty country and take one hour and fifteen minutes.

The old Britton farm, along Scottsville Road just south of the city, recently renamed the Municipal Aviation Field, on this day was already packed with 50,000 people anxiously awaiting the flying hero. The drizzle during the night had ended about 8:00 A.M. and the sky began to clear up, as automobiles began building up along the Scottsville Road. Local police, deputy sheriffs and the National Guardsmen were already in the area to help control the throngs of people that were expected for this special holiday.

Free parking space was provided to the crowds by Willis N. Britton, former owner of the flying field, on the 390-acre tract that he controlled on the Scottsville Road between the entrance to the field and the Flower City Gun Club, just beyond the Barge canal.

News of Lindbergh's imminent arrival reached many tourists in the area. They decided to divert their plans to include a stop at the airfield and asked if they could camp out during the night before his arrival. When re-

Just after landing Lindbergh is greated by Mayor Martin O'Neil and an officer of the local National Guard in addition to other dignitaries.

fused by the authorities, they drove south to find vacant fields in which they could pitch their tents in anticipation of his coming the next morning.

At precisely 11:00 A.M. and shortly after Lindbergh had circled over the downtown area of Rochester, he touched the wheels down onto the unimproved roped-off landing space.

Lindbergh was wearing his three-quarter leather jacket, covering his rumpled double-breasted blue suit. As he climbed out of the cockpit, the first person to greet him was Mayor Martin B. O'Neil, along with other dignitaries.

According to newspaper reports of the time, there were scores of photographers at the scene as Lindbergh climbed out of the NYP. They spent no less than ten minutes photographing him by the airplane, in every conceivable pose. This author wonders today whatever happened to those photographs taken by the many professional Eastman Kodak photographers. Only a handful of pictures have surfaced in later years.

Soon he was escorted to a nearby platform, where he gave his short, to-the-point speech, stressing the importance of the development of commercial aviation and predicting a glowing future for this local airfield, with regular mail and passenger service just around the corner.

As a result of his visit, he aroused tremendous enthusiasm, so that airport officials began to give serious thought to the establishment of a permanent air service for mail, merchandise and passenger services. In 1928 a hangar was erected on the new and dignified "Rochester Municipal Airport." Shortly runways were constructed and signal apparatus for navigation installed. It was known as the CAM 20 (contract air mail) on the air mail route between Cleveland, Ohio, and Albany, New York. The route was also known as "the lake level" because it generally followed a comparatively level region along the line of the south shores of Lakes Erie and Ontario and crossed near the region of the New York Finger Lakes.

The following day after Lindbergh's visit, the Army's latest blimp, the RS-1, visited the city. These two visits brought the city officials into a sudden conference and a definite announcement was made that the city airport would be equipped with hangar, runways, gasoline and oil station, etc., within the next sixty days.

The new airport was formally dedicated on August 16 and 17, 1930, and is still in operation as the Greater Rochester International Airport. It is at an elevation of 560 feet MSL and has three runways. The longest one is 8,001 feet. The field serves some major domestic airlines, commuter airlines, international operations, general aviation aircraft and Air National Guard operations.

When it came time to leave, George A. West asked Lindbergh if he could spin the propeller. Lindbergh did not want to take a chance so asked if West would sit in the cockpit while he (Lindbergh) spun the prop. Years later West said that he will never forget that day.

At noon Lindbergh took off, made one more circle over the city before heading west, then flew over Chili, Bergen, Batavia, and on to Buffalo.

While in Rochester he was presented with a pair of flying goggles by William Bausch, of the Bausch and Lomb Company, and a box lunch from Sibley's restaurant.

A nice close-up of Lindbergh in front of the NYP at Rochester, New York. CHARLES AUGUSTUS LINDBERGH PAPERS, MANUSCRIPTS AND ARCHIVES, YALE UNIVERSITY LIBRARY

The NYP being moved to a more secure location on the old Britton farm field. EXPERIMENTAL AIRCRAFT ASSOCIATION

PEOPLE WHO WERE THERE

David "Scotty" Caplan of Brighton, New York, remembers the excitement of that visit:

"I asked my parents if I could go and see him, and also take my younger brother with me. I was fifteen and Isadore was seven. As I held my brother's hand, we boarded a streetcar at Joseph Avenue, then transferred to another streetcar at Main Street, and again at Genesee Street. The line ended at Scottsville Road, and from there we walked to the Britton Road airport.

"Everybody scanned the sky to see who would see him first. It seemed we waited for at least two hours before he finally showed up."

In the ensuing years both boys became licensed pilots.

Also making his way to the field that day was Gus Konz, a musician who played and taught oboe with the Eastman Theatre Orchestra. He was so moved by it all he decided to become a professional pilot in 1929, eventually retiring as a captain from American Airlines at age sixty. Among Konz's oboe students was a precocious young man by the name of Mitch Miller.

Vic Evans, a seventeen-year-old boy and youngest Rochester pilot at the time, became, like Lindbergh, an air mail pilot. He also went with American Airlines, eventually flying DC-3 airliners. During one flight the stewardess came up to the cockpit to inform Evans that they had a celebrity on board, none other than Charles Lindbergh. Lindbergh was invited into the cockpit and they talked together for some time. Later Evans would brag to his grandchildren that he had taken Lindbergh for an airplane ride.

References

Newspapers
    Rochester Times Union
    Rochester Democrat & Chronicle

Organization
    The Rochester Historical Society

People
    Michael Zeigler of the
        Democrat & Chronicle
    Irving Wischmeyer
    James C. Reddig   Robert Bailey
    George A. West   Mrs. Edna B. Bell

Stop #11
Buffalo, New York

Capsule History of City

In the northwestern part of New York is the city of Buffalo, the second largest city in the state, located where the Niagara River empties into Lake Erie.

The Canadian city of Fort Erie, Ontario, lies across the Niagara River from the city of Buffalo. The world-famous Niagara Falls is located only about 16 miles north of the city.

In 1803 the Dutch-owned Holland Land Company established a settlement at the site, mainly because it was at the western end of an important Indian trail. The trail ran from western New York to the upper Great Lakes and Canada. This community was first named New Amsterdam and later changed to Buffalo, the name of a nearby creek, which became the official name in 1816.

Iroquois Indians lived near the site before white men arrived. The first white settler in the area was the French trader Daniel de Joncaire, Sieur de Chabert et Clausonne, who came in the 1750s.

599 feet MSL.

July 29–August 1, 1927
(Friday through Monday)

On his flight from Rochester, Lindbergh flew over Lockport, New York, and Niagara Falls, New York, as well as Niagara Falls, Ontario, Canada. As the two airplanes flew low over these spectacular waterfalls, the day was a bit misty with a low ceiling. Apparently the Fairchild FC-2 flown by Love was in the lead and suddenly had to climb sharply in order to avoid obscured high-tension lines. Love was concerned that Lindbergh, due to his limited visibility in the NYP, might not see the wires. But he decided to get out of the area, feeling they might not see each other and have a mid-air collision. When they finally neared the Buffalo airport, just east of the city, the NYP came out of the clouds in all its glory.

At that time Buffalo was a cradle of military aviation development. Such names as Curtiss, Fleet, Bell, Hall Aluminum Aircraft Company, Irving Air Chute Company, and Elias had put Buffalo on the aviation map.

The local airport was located in the town of Forks, New York, now Cheektowaga, and was dedicated in September 1926 and named the Buffalo Municipal Airport.

Lindbergh landed the NYP at 2:07 P.M. and shut down. He was greeted by Mayor Frank X. Schwab, Commissioner John J. Love, and Timothy J. Burns, the chairman of the reception committee.

Mechanics pushed both airplanes into Hangar No. 1, for protection from the throngs who swarmed all over the airport upon his arrival.

The NYP on the ramp at Buffalo Airport with some of the bystanders behind the fence. GEORGE BAILEY, ENGLAND

After the flyer was certain that the NYP was secure, he climbed into the Mayor's limousine for the parade into the city to participate in ceremonies at Delaware Park. The parade route was lined with thousands of people, all hoping to get a glimpse of the pilot. Two thousand Boy Scouts patrolled the line of march of the Lindbergh parade and aided the police in restraining the crowds.

Sirens were blasting during the parade, scaring some of the horses pulling horse-drawn vehicles, causing them to rear. Drivers pulled and yanked the reins to keep them from bolting.

At one point an eighty-nine-year-old lady, Mrs. Margaret Locke, visiting from Pasadena, California, and carrying a small American flag, slowly walked to the side of the car in which Lindbergh was riding. She took his hand and said, "Thank you for the great job you are doing for your country." Lindbergh squeezed her hand and smiled humbly, as she returned to her place on the curb.

He was escorted by the Mayor to the speaker's stand, where he gave his usual aviation promotional presentation. Lindbergh highly praised the airport and the people who were responsible for its creation, feeling it was one of the best he had seen. By stating this he had awakened an awareness in the local population to its potential and gave a boost to further develop-

ment. The people of Buffalo were quite proud of this asset, which today is known as the Greater Buffalo International Airport.

That evening he was guest of honor at a dinner at the Hotel Statler, attended by over one thousand people. The banquet was held on the 15th floor, in the suite of hotel manager Elmore C. Green. When Lindbergh was introduced during the affair, he had this to say in part: "You have an excellent airport here. It is one of the best upon which I have landed. I do not like to make comparisons between it and those at other cities. I will say, however, that you have a landing field here of which you may justly feel proud. There is little that could be done to make it better."

Saturday and Sunday Lindbergh and his crew spent at a friend's hunting lodge at Turkey Point, on the north shore (Canadian side) of Lake Erie, about eighty miles west of Buffalo. They were guests of Ward A. Wickwire of Buffalo and Timothy Burns, general manager of the Lackawanna plant of the Bethlehem Steel Corporation. They were all tired and needed a change of scene and some relaxation. This included swimming, fishing, picnicking, and boating on the lake.

In the meantime the NYP was put on exhibit at the Buffalo Airport, and people by the hundred passed by, while it was heavily

Another view of the NYP on the Buffalo ramp. Notice the hangar bunting. RICHARD STEPHENSON

One of the local mechanics servicing the engine of Lindbergh's plane. EILEEN M. VOGT

References

Newspapers
    Buffalo Evening News

Organizations
    Greater Buffalo International Airport
    Niagara Frontier Transportation Authority
    Buffalo and Erie County Historical Society
    Glenn H. Curtiss Museum, Hammondsport, New York

Book
    Buffalo Airport 1926–1976. Buffalo, N.Y.: NFTA, 1976.

People
    Alan Ward   Ken Taylor
    Mrs. Eileen M. Vogt   Russ Plehinger
    Paul E. Foersch   Charles F. Light
    George Bailey (England)

guarded by local police.

It was during this rest period that Donald Keyhoe had a discussion concerning taking photographs of Lindbergh with Keyhoe's own camera during the tour. Lindbergh gave his approval, but not many of the pictures have ever shown up.

According to newspaper reports of the time, Lindbergh had broken all of Buffalo's records for attracting crowds.

In 1929, as a result of his 1927 visit, a school was named after him—Charles Lindbergh Elementary School—which included kindergarten through sixth grade.

On the morning that Lindbergh planned to depart for Cleveland, he was delayed for two hours due to a lack of proper oil pressure. Because he always insisted on being at the airport each day more than a half hour before departure, time would be allowed for just such a problem. Mechanics had to remove the cowling and the oil pressure pump, inspect, prime and reinstall the pump, and replace the cowling.

One photograph shows the cowling removed and a mechanic adjusting the engine valves, as the valve cover plates are removed. No other documentation to confirm this service has been found.

After the problem was solved, he took off at 1 P.M. EDT and headed for Cleveland.

Today, the Buffalo-Niagara International Airport is on the same site as it was in 1926, five miles east of the city, along Interstate 90 (the New York Thruway). It is at an elevation of 724 feet MSL and has two runways, the longer of which is 8,102 feet. It serves many of the nation's major airlines, as well as international, commuter, general aviation and military operations.

A group of local citizens with the NYP for some reason. Wonder who they are and what the occasion was? GLENN H. CURTISS MUSEUM, HAMMONDSPORT, NY

STOP #12
CLEVELAND, OHIO

CAPSULE HISTORY OF CITY

The largest city in Ohio is located in the northeast part of the state, on the south shore of Lake Erie at the mouth of the Cuyahoga River. Due to the proximity of such waterways, and the convenience of shipping in huge supplies of iron ore and coal, it is a large steel producer.

Moses Cleaveland, a surveyor for the Connecticut Land Company, founded Cleveland in 1796. The site was purchased by the company from the State of Connecticut. Because of a newspaper misspelling in 1831, the city has been known as Cleveland. (The editor of the Cleveland Gazette and Commercial Register had dropped a letter from his masthead for it to fit across the page. He chose the first "a" in Cleaveland to be expendable.)

By 1832, the Ohio and Erie Canal was complete, and Cleveland, the northern terminus, had already doubled its population.

660 feet MSL.

AUGUST 1–3, 1927 (SUNDAY THROUGH TUESDAY)

After leaving Buffalo, they flew by Jamestown and Chautauqua, New York, then Erie, Pennsylvania, and along the south shore of Lake Erie. Lindbergh did circle Erie several times at about 2:15 EDT and continued on to Cleveland, landing there on Brook Park Airport at 2:22 P.M.

Soon after he landed, airport personnel pushed the NYP and the Fairchild FC-2 into the Ford Motor Company hangar, which was already decorated with flags and bunting for the occasion. It was planned to have both airplanes on display so people would be able to view them under the glare of floodlights through the night.

He was greeted officially by Mayor John D. Marshall, City Manager William R. Hopkins, Col. Carmi A. Thompson, Mr. and Mrs. Parmely Herrick and Parmely Jr.

An auto entourage made its way from the airport, past thousands of people, to Wade Park, near University Circle and north of the Art Museum. It was here that Lindbergh gave his first

talk, to a reserved audience of some 12,000 people, in addition to thousands of others who were unable to find room in the park.

Lindbergh went to the Cleveland Clinic hospital to pay a visit to Ambassador Myron F. Herrick of Cleveland, who had greeted him in Paris after his record-breaking flight from New York. Herrick was recovering from surgery and greeted the flyer in private, except for immediate members of the Herrick family.

Later in the afternoon Lindbergh gave the talk again at Wade Park and then was motored into downtown Cleveland, where they drove by a reviewing stand in front of City Hall.

That evening there was an official dinner at the Hotel Cleveland, broadcast by radio station WTAM, where he again spoke on the future of aviation, air travel and the air mail services. In his talk he said, "The United States is a peace-loving country, but we must have peace together with our self-respect. Cleveland already has shown that she will be a leader in aeronautics." He spoke about the NYP and stressed that

"... it will be possible to build airplanes that are much more efficient—and Trans-Atlantic service some day will be operated regularly.

Your city has done much toward establishing flying fields. They are the first need in making this country better equipped for air purposes. It is of little use for me to talk to you about airports and the possibilities of air transportation. You have foreseen that and built here one of the greatest airports in America and have patronized air transportation.

You have seen the development of air transportation as few cities have. I commend Cleveland for its air-mindedness."

After the banquet he was taken to the estate of Ambassador Herrick at Gates Hills, near Chagrin Falls suburb, where he was a guest until his departure for Pittsburgh on Wednesday morning.

In 1926 the former Steel Products Company

Three photos of the NYP at Brook Park Airport in Cleveland. ABOVE: CHUCK SIMMONS, BELOW: JIM KENNEDY

of Cleveland became Thompson Products, Inc., as a tribute to the founder and president. There were eighteen Thompson valves in the NYP Wright "Whirlwind" engine. The company also developed the experimental sodium-cooled cylinders for the Wright. They are still in business.

The Thompson Trophy became a symbol of speed records. It was one of the high stakes to go after at the famous "Cleveland Air Races" of the 1930s. Any picture map of the United States in the 1930–1940 period would show a horse in Kentucky, a car at Indianapolis, and the air races in Cleveland. The Thompson races were broadcast on radio all over the country.

Top pilots of the country were always there: such names as colorful Roscoe Turner, Amelia Earhart, Jimmy Doolittle, Howard Hughes, General Hap Arnold, Frank Hawks, Rudy Kling, Earl Ortman, Jack Story, Navy Lt. Al Williams, Charles "Speed" Holman, Doug Davis, and Benny Howard. The races were run by Cliff Henderson and his brother, Phillip, who were from Los Angeles and often brought along some famous movie star to be the queen of the show.

Wilbur Carpenter was thirteen years old when Lindbergh flew in to Cleveland on August 1, 1927. He was staying with his older

brother, Elwin, and his family on a farm about eight miles from the airport. At breakfast that morning Elwin said that they were going to see Lindbergh that day. Elwin's wife said, "No, we are not. There is too much work to do." But they all went anyway. Many years later Wilbur said that his appreciation and esteem for Elwin has never diminished from that day. They drove to the airport in Elwin's Model T Ford and joined an estimated 20,000 people. They did get to see the *Spirit of St. Louis,* but not Lindbergh himself. They were too far away to determine which of the men was Lindbergh.

On Sunday morning, August 3, while 25,000 people cheered a farewell, Lindbergh climbed into the cockpit and called out for "contact." A mechanic spun the propeller, but a fire burst out near the bottom of the engine. Dripping fuel had caught fire from the carburetor. A fire extinguisher promptly extinguished the flames, and Lindbergh climbed out, examined the area and found no damage. This information was from a news report. No further details have ever been found to confirm this incident.

At 10:31 A.M. Lindbergh finally took off from the airport, known today as the Cleveland Hopkins International Airport, and headed

southeast to Pittsburgh.

Today Cleveland Hopkins International Airport is still on the same site, at an elevation of 792 feet MSL. It has two parallel runways and one single, the longest of all three being 8,999 feet. It serves most domestic and international airlines, some commuter aircraft, as well as general aviation and military aircraft. The field is located none miles southwest of the city.

One mile north of the city, on the lakefront, is Burke Lakefront Airport, at an elevation of 583 feet MSL, and with two parallel runways, the longer of which is 6,198 feet. It serves mainly general aviation.

Ten miles east of the city is Cuyahoga County Airport, at an elevation of 879 feet MSL, with a single runway of 5,101 feet. The field serves mainly general aviation aircraft.

References

Newspapers
 The Kansas City Star
 Cleveland Plain Dealer

Organizations
 Cleveland Public Library
 The Western Reserve Historical Society
 Ohio History of Flight
 Museum—Columbus

People
 Fred C. Crawford   James J. Kennedy
 Beverly M. Calkins of Case Western
    Reserve University
 Wilbur A. Carpenter   Chuck Simmons

STOP #13
PITTSBURGH, PENNSYLVANIA

CAPSULE HISTORY OF CITY

As the country's largest inland seaport, Pittsburgh has been one of the great steel-making centers of the world. It is located in southwestern Pennsylvania, at the intersection of the Allegheny and Monongahela Rivers where they join to form the Ohio River. The city has had such nicknames as "Hearth of the Nation," "Iron City," "Steel City," and "Arsenal of the World."

Now known as the "Golden Triangle," Pittsborough was named in 1758 in honor of the British statesman William Pitt. At this time British troops built Fort Pitt near the fork of the Allegheny and Monongahela Rivers. It was under the direction of General John Forbes, who named it Pittsburgh.

745 feet MSL.

AUGUST 3–4, 1927 (WEDNESDAY AND THURSDAY)

On his way from Cleveland to Pittsburgh, Lindbergh flew the NYP over Gates Mills, Akron, Massillon, Canton, Alliance, Youngstown, Ohio, and Newcastle, Pennsylvania, just behind the Fairchild FC-2. He followed the Ohio River most of the way.

At 1:55 P.M. he circled over Pittsburgh and the University of Pennsylvania's Pitt Stadium and landed at 2:03 on Bettis Field (now Allegheny County Airport, AGC). Bettis was located about seven and a half miles SSE of the center of Pittsburgh, just west of Dravosburg, across the Monongahela River from McKeesport, and was under McKeesport jurisdiction.

Bettis Field was named after a Lt. Cyrus Bettis, who was a hero of Lindbergh's friend Maj. Thomas G. Lanphier.

Because the city knew of Lindbergh's impending visit, the mayor, Charles H. Kline, announced that there would be a half holiday during the afternoon, so many city offices and local businesses closed for the rest of the day.

A common problem during the tour was when the Fairchild first appeared near the airport, and due to its similar configuration to the NYP, the public was sure that it was Lindbergh. This happened at Pittsburgh, and the waiting throngs sent up an ear-deafening cheer. They were quieted, however, when from a loudspeaker a voice proclaimed that it was only the advance airplane.

Lindbergh just after he arrived at Bettis Field on August 3. HISTORICAL SOCIETY OF WESTERN PENNSYLVANIA

On this day as the hour drew near for his arrival, there were people everywhere. Over a knoll to the east of Bettis there was a 40-acre field. It was reported that not another person could have fit into that field without the aid of a shoehorn.

South of Bettis, behind another knoll, there was a camp meeting ground that held thousands of automobiles and more thousands of people.

Several local flyers felt it would be fun to be in the air when Lindbergh arrived, but they caused quite a stir from officials and possibly even Lindbergh. It was feared they might get in the way of the flyer as he attempted to line up for a landing.

After landing Lindbergh taxied the NYP up to the hangar and shut the engine down. He was met by David Bar Peat, airport manager, and introduced to Mayor Kline and Mayor George H. Lysle of McKeesport. He was also introduced as the youngest Colonel to the oldest Colonel in aviation, Col. Harry Fry, Commander of Rogers Field.

The single hangar housed three Wacos and nine mail planes, all owned and operated by Ball Air Lines (Clifford Ball and David Peat), under CAM 11. The three Wacos were NC 2574: "Miss Pittsburgh," "Miss McKeesport," and "Miss Youngstown." All three airplanes still exist to-

day.

The hangar at Bettis was rather narrow and would not be able to accommodate the NYP with its forty-six-foot wingspan. Ken Scholter, a local mechanic, came up with the idea to go into McKeesport, a steel town, and find some very large steel plates. He did this and put them into a strip, running from outside the hangar to the inside. They placed the wheels of the NYP on the already greased plates and slid the airplane sideways into the hangar for the night. This operation can be seen in some photographs. The Waco mail planes were left outside during Lindbergh's visit, and the public could then walk past the hangar to view the airplane.

The local Boy Scout troop was assigned to guard the NYP at Bettis. One of these Scouts was thirteen-year-old Charles A. Lindberg (without the "h"). On his own he had gone out and purchased a special cake to present to his hero. However, the Scout was not permitted to reach the flyer, which must have been quite disappointing to the young lad. The next day the Scout still had the cake, but little appetite for it.

Another Scout had better luck. Walter Hood won a contest for the best birdhouse built. The contest was sponsored by the Sun-Tele Bird House Club. When the gift was presented to Lindbergh the Scout got to shake his hand and

The NYP in front of the old air mail hangar at Bettis Field near Pittsburgh. HISTORICAL SOCIETY OF WESTERN PENNSYLVANIA

considered himself to be the luckiest boy in the world.

At 2:25 P.M. a parade of many automobiles, with Lindbergh riding with the Mayor and Donald Keyhoe in the lead car, left Bettis for Pitt Stadium, arriving there about 3:30 P.M. There the flyer gave his usual short speech, stressing the importance of further development of airports and aviation.

Soon the entourage left for the still existing William Penn Hotel, where Lindbergh and his

crew would stay for the night. He immediately ordered a sandwich and a glass of milk, as he had not eaten since that morning. Once this was accomplished, he met in his room with the local press until 6:45 P.M. when he had to get ready for the 7 o'clock banquet.

Lindbergh sat at the speaker's table with Mayor Kline, Don Keyhoe, Phil Love and tour mechanic, Ted Sorenson.

In his speech Lindbergh paid tribute to Samuel Pierpont Langley, who had conducted

A good portrait of Lindbergh with his escort pilot, Phil Love at Pittsburgh. Both seem to be in a happy mood. TRINITY COURT STUDIO, PITTSBURGH, PENNSYLVANIA

many experiments in aeronautics and aerodynamics in the Pittsburgh area. He also complimented the city for maintaining the lead in the development of the Pittsburgh-Cleveland air mail route success.

The Langley Beacon, commemorating the valor of the pioneers of aviation in the form of a powerful beacon to be erected at Pittsburgh's historic Point, was warmly endorsed by Lindbergh.

As he left the hotel the next morning Lindbergh was heard to say, "My stay here has been wonderfully pleasing, and I am delighted with the hospitality of your people."

It is interesting to note that the NYP propeller was manufactured by the Standard Steel Propeller Company of nearby West Homestead, a short distance south of the city. It is not known if Lindbergh was given a tour of the plant or met any of the firm's officers.

At precisely 1:15 P.M. on August 4, Lindbergh took off in the NYP and headed for Wheeling, West Virginia.

Bettis is no longer there. On the site in about 1949 the Westinghouse Company purchased the property to build a research and development laboratory, pioneering the development of an atomic reactor, and named the Bettis Laboratory.

Today in the Pittsburgh area, the main airport, which is located 12 miles northwest of the city, is known as the Pittsburgh International Airport. It is at an elevation of 1,204 feet MSL and has four runways, the longest one being 11,500 feet. It serves most major domestic airlines, some commuters, Air National Guard, and general aviation aircraft.

Four miles to the southeast is the Allegheny County Airport, at an elevation of 1,252 feet MSL with three runways. The longest one is 6,501 feet. It serves mostly general aviation, and some military.

There are many private and general aviation airstrips in and around the surrounding areas of Pittsburgh.

References

Newspapers
Pittsburgh Post-Gazette
The Pittsburgh Sun-Telegraph
The Pittsburgh Sun and the Pittsburgh Chronicle Telegraph
The Pittsburgh Press
Pittsburgh Gazette Times

Organizations
Historical Society of Western Pennsylvania
The Carnegie Library of Pittsburgh
Aluminum Company of America
Bettis Atomic Power Laboratory

People
Clifford Ball   Archie Defante
David Barr Peat   Jack Dernorsek
Robert Bailey
Kenneth W. Scholter

STOP #14
WHEELING, WEST VIRGINIA

CAPSULE HISTORY OF CITY

This industrial city is located on the east bank of the Ohio River about sixty miles southwest of Pittsburgh, Pennsylvania. Included in the city proper is mile-long Wheeling Island in the Ohio River. It lies on a level plain, which rises to steep hills along the Ohio River. Why this area was named Wheeling is not known.

Colonel Ebenezer Zane and his brothers founded Wheeling in the winter of 1769–1770. The state was formally admitted to the Union in 1863. Wheeling was the capital until 1870 and again from 1875 to 1885.

The 900-foot-long Wheeling Suspension Bridge, built in 1849, is one of the world's longest. The bridge is known as "Rainbow to Behold." 650 feet MSL.

Phil Love leaning out of the cockpit of the Fairchild FC-2 just after landing at Langin Field. TOM TOMINACK

The NYP landing at Langin Field, Moundsville, West Virginia, on August 4. TOM TOMINACK

The NYP just after landing at Langin Field in Moundsville. TOM TOMINACK

August 4-5 1927 (Thursday and Friday)

On his way to Wheeling, Lindbergh flew over East Liverpool and Steubenville, Ohio, and then down the Ohio River. He was headed for the Wheeling stop, a city without an airport.

South of Wheeling, and on the east side of a hook in the Ohio River, is the town of Moundsville. About three-quarters of a mile north of this town was a former Army airfield known as Langin Field. It was a north-south grass strip, about 3,000 feet long and 800 feet wide. It was located between the O.R.R.R. and B.&O. railroad tracks and the Ohio River on level ground in the rear of what is now Elby's Restaurant and Mini Mall.

In Marshall County, Langin Field was the halfway point between Washington, D.C., and Dayton, Ohio, for the U.S. Army. The Army operated the airport from about 1918 until Anthony Fokker of the Fokker Aircraft Company began to operate a test airport for his factory at Glen Dale, right next to Langin.

So in 1927 Langin Field, then owned by Dr. M. F. Compton, was the nearest flying field to

Wheeling, about thirteen miles to the south. This would be the field where Lindbergh would land.

Through the efforts of Moundsville Mayor Jesse D. H. Sullivan, the airfield grass was cut, weeds pulled, and bunting fastened to the existing airplane hangar. With the help of Dr. Compton and the local Chamber of Commerce, the field was spruced up and made ready for this biggest event ever for that small town. Even the local private homes were decorated for the occasion.

Thursday, August 4, was declared an official holiday, and a "Proclamation" was drawn up and signed by Wheeling Mayor William J. Steen. All manufacturers and businesses ceased their labors at noon, and flags were displayed all over the city.

Lindbergh made the trip from Pittsburgh in about forty minutes. He landed at 2:00 P.M. on Langin Field. Keyhoe, Love, and Sorenson and possibly Doc Kinkaid in the Fairchild had landed fifteen minutes earlier and were there to greet him as he climbed out of the cockpit.

He was immediately greeted officially by Mayor Steen, Mayor Sullivan, Harry P. Corcoran

Lindbergh standing with reception officials: Wheeling Mayor William J. Steen (holding straw hat); Harry P. Corcoran, Wheeling Chamber of Commerce; Mayor Jesse D. Sullivan of Moundsville; Lindbergh; Donald Keyhoe of U.S. Commerce Department; Peter Boyd, president of West Virginia chapter of the National Aeronautical Association; Charles O. Ephlin, Wheeling City Manager and "Miss Wheeling" Margaret Bright of Weirton. TOM TOMINACK

Lindbergh parade in Wheeling. WEST VIRGINIA STATE ARCHIVES, SCHLOSSER COLLECTION

of the Wheeling Chamber of Commerce, Wheeling City Manager Charles O. Ephlin, Peter Boyd of the National Aeronautics Association, and "Miss Wheeling," Mildred Bright of Weirton.

The NYP was rolled into the hangar and set up under guard by local police and Boy Scouts. Lights were provided so that people could view the airplane for the remainder of the day and into the evening.

Lindbergh and his crew were motored up State Route 2 to the fairgrounds in Wheeling, where he would be greeted by Governor Howard Mason Gore. The flyer gave his usual talk on the importance of the development of air travel and the building of airports. Adequate airport facilities for the city of Wheeling as a direct result of Lindbergh's visit were predicted by Mayor Steen.

The flyers were taken to the grounds of the Linsey Institute, and Lindbergh laid a wreath at the Louis Bennett Memorial Statue, "The Aviator." From there they all went to the Fort Henry Club, where they were given sleeping quarters and time to freshen up for the dinner that evening.

The evening banquet was held at the Scottish Rite cathedral, where the program was broadcast over radio station WWVA, one of the strongest radio stations in the country at the time.

After the evening festivities, they were taken again to the Fort Henry Club for a good night's sleep.

In the morning a local airplane manufacturing firm had the newly designed airplane on Langin airport to show to Lindbergh. It was named "The Lone Eagle" in his honor and was built by the Moundsville Airplane Corporation. It was a two-place bi-plane powered by the Kinner K-5 radial engine. Lindbergh did not have time to fly the airplane but did praise its designers for its potential and pleasing looks. It never did get into production.

Although Lindbergh was not scheduled to depart until noon, the surrounding roads and field were already crowded with people. He took off at 10:30 A.M. and circled over Langin Field several times, then headed north to again fly over Wheeling before heading west to Dayton, Ohio. The Fairchild FC-2 left just after the NYP and headed directly to Dayton to be in position and oversee the arrival plans for Lindbergh.

As a result of Lindbergh's visit, Wheeling had surveys made for an appropriate site. In 1939 a ground-breaking ceremony was held, and finally on November 1, 1946, the Wheeling-Ohio County Airport, located eight miles northeast of the city, was dedicated. The field is at an elevation of 1,195 feet MSL and has two runways, the longer of which is 5,000 feet. It serves some commuter airlines as well as general aviation and military.

Today Langin Field no longer exists, but just north about a mile or so on the old Fokker location, there was a small private grass strip, at one time shown on charts, listed under the name of Glendale.

References

Newspapers
  Moundsville Journal
  Moundsville Daily Echo
  The Wheeling Register

Organizations
  West Virginia Division of Culture and History
  Wheeling Area Historical Society

People
  Margaret Brennan, of the Wheeling Area Historical Society
  Richard Z. Richards   Ellen Dunable
  Evan M. Rogerson   George H. Evans
  Eleanor Harper Gay
  Thomas S. Tominack

STOP #15
DAYTON, OHIO

CAPSULE HISTORY OF CITY

Home of the Wright brothers, world-famous airplane designers and inventors, Dayton is located in the Miami River Valley in the southwestern part of Ohio. It is the sixth largest city in the state. The city is world famous as the "Home of Aviation," where the United States Air Force Logistics Command at the Wright-Patterson Air Force Base is located. The United States Air Force Museum is also located there.

Settlers from Cincinnati established the village of Dayton in 1796. The city was incorporated in 1805 and named for Jonathan Dayton, who owned land there. It received its charter in 1841. Jonathan Dayton, age twenty-six, was the youngest signer of the United States Constitution.

Orville Wright's home is located at Harmon and Park Avenues in Oakwood, a Dayton suburb.

745 feet MSL.

AUGUST 5–6, 1927 (FRIDAY AND SATURDAY)

In Dayton on May 20, 1927, Orville Wright spent the whole day at the home of his niece and nephew, Ivonette and Harold Miller. He did not own a radio at the time and wanted to keep abreast of Lindbergh's flight to Paris. He remained by that radio all day long, in a quiet and meditative mood.

Not long after the reports of the success of the flight, he had this to say in a letter to Maj. Albert B. Lambert of Dayton, dated June 9, 1927:

"The people of Dayton are most anxious to have Colonel Lindbergh come here as the quest of the city immediately after the celebration at St. Louis. I believe Dayton has had a longer and more intense interest in aviation than any other city of our country. For this reason it is able to appreciate to the full Colonel Lindbergh's wonderful flight. I am sure no city will give him a more cordial welcome.

"I am writing to you as an old friend in this art, hoping you will be glad to use your influence in giving Dayton her wish.

"Personally I have more than ordinary interest in Colonel Lindbergh; first, because he has so strikingly demonstrated the possibility of an art which I had a part in founding, and second, because his conduct in the midst of overwhelming popularity has been such as to command the admiration and respect of everyone.

"Please extend to Colonel Lindbergh my most cordial greetings with the hope that I may soon have the pleasure of his personal acquaintance." — *Orville Wright*

On his way from Wheeling, and after circling over Columbus, Ohio, Lindbergh was spotted at 12:46 P.M. over McCook Field at Dayton. He had arrived from the southeast. He did circle over the Gem City several times and touched down on McCook at 12:59. He taxied to the hangar on the east end of the field and was greeted by Al Johnson, president of the Johnson Airplane and Supply Company. It was then that Lindbergh realized he had made a mistake, landing one hour earlier than the usual planned arrival time of 2:00 P.M. Wheeling was still on Standard Time. Dayton was on Daylight Saving Time.

Lindbergh remained on McCook only a few minutes, taking off for Wilbur Wright Field, a few miles east, near the suburb of what is now Riverside.

He remained at Wilbur Wright until just a few minutes before 2:00 P.M. He then took off again and flew over to McCook for the official arrival.

Upon landing at McCook he was met by Mayor A. C. McDonald and Brig. Gen. William E. Gillmore, who gave a formal address welcoming Lindbergh to Dayton. Additionally, Perle Whitehead, executive officer of the Boy Scouts in Dayton, gave a presentation on behalf of the youth of the city.

One local remembered the event: "I was a

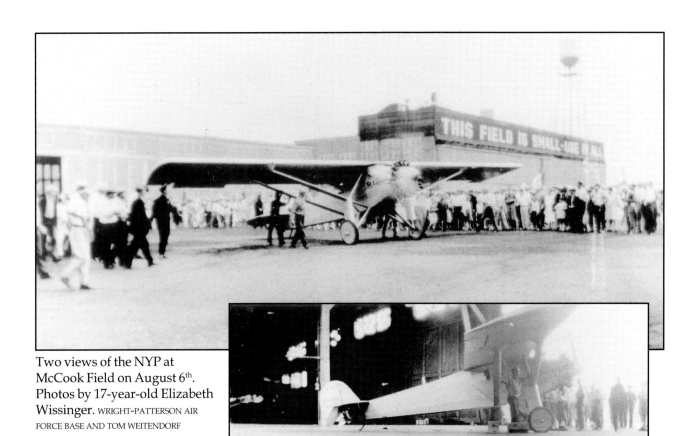

Two views of the NYP at McCook Field on August 6th. Photos by 17-year-old Elizabeth Wissinger. WRIGHT-PATTERSON AIR FORCE BASE AND TOM WEITENDORF

Orville Wright, Major J.F. Curry and Lindbergh at McCook Field. WRIGHT STATE UNIVERSITY

Boy Scout at the time Lindbergh visited Dayton, and was camping at the Scout camp known as Cricket Holler, which is still there. They all went at 'scout pace' or walked and trotted the seven miles to McCook Field. After Lindbergh landed, he taxied to about fifty feet of me, and I saw him get out of the cockpit. My dream of dreams. We scouts formed a cordon around the airplane, and I was about fifteen feet from the door. When we were relieved by the field officer, they walked back to the camp, and the best 'boy dreams' in the world. I earned the merit badge for a fourteen-mile hike." William E. Deis, eighty-two years old.

Joseph Moritz was nine years old at that time and remembered shaking hands with Lindbergh at the band stand at the old Veterans Home on West Shield Street in Dayton. "The parade of about five automobiles left McCook Field and started into town. Along the parade route there were little boys with faces newly scrubbed and shining, and small girls in crisp and beribboned organdies and parents distracted with the lures of street vendors offering their attractions to the young."

There were also interesting comments from the public. "Didn't that boy get thin," exclaimed one mother. Others would say, "He looks much better than when he was here before."

The next stop for the motorcade was the National Military Home, where Lindbergh was received by the residents, and then over to Woodland Cemetery, where he placed a wreath on the tomb of Wilbur Wright.

The ceremony at the Wright tomb ended the formalities for the afternoon. Lindbergh was then driven to the Miami Hotel in Dayton, where he and his crew could spend the rest of the time resting before the evening dinner program.

City and county offices were closed for the afternoon out of respect for Lindbergh's visit. A few stores and factories in the area did the same for their employees. Radio station WSMK gave periodic reports of the festivities of the day for its local citizens.

At 6:00 P.M. Lindbergh was driven to the National Cash Register (NCR) Cafeteria dining hall, where a dinner and banquet would take place. Lindbergh had requested that the affair be over by 9:00 P.M. He wished to retire early and plan with his crew for the next day's flight to Cincinnati.

In Lindbergh's talk he said,

"People throughout the country, both on the farms and in the cities, have now come to realize that aviation is a reliable means of transportation which has possibilities of furthering the development of our commercial life and social welfare. In almost every section the desire to do something to advance aviation locally has been expressed.

"In Dayton you people for two decades have been interested in aviation because it was in this city that the very first heavier-than-air–flight was contemplated, and it was here that the initial modest experiments with aircraft were made. The very name of Dayton is an inspiration in the world of aviation.

"You have one of the very best military airports in America, the Army's experimental division so the best that you can suggest is that the community live up to its reputation throughout the world and take all possible steps to encourage a larger and more worthwhile development of aircraft generally.

"It is rather significant that the plane which I brought to Dayton could take off tonight and land in most any distant spot in the United States in the morning and at a cost of only four cents per mile of travel."

Mr. Henry Rike of Rike's Department Store spoke about the city's intention to construct a municipal airport on an already owned tract some miles south and in use as a sewage leaching farm. Private interest eventually put money into an airport, known today as Moraine Airport.

Regretfully, Orville Wright, Governor Vic Donahey and Senator Simeon D. Fess were unable to attend the banquet.

After the banquet Lindbergh was invited to spend the night as the guest of Brig. Gen. William Gillmore and his wife at their home on Forrer Road in the Oakwood area of Dayton.

After a leisurely breakfast on Saturday morning, General Gillmore, Chief of the Material Division, Air Corps, gave Lindbergh a personal tour of the new Wright Field.

Also on Saturday morning the NYP was placed on display at McCook for public viewing

of the famous airplane.

Around noon the airplane was rolled out of the hangar, and after a preflight, Lindbergh took off at 12:45 P.M. and headed south for Cincinnati.

Today the modern Cox Dayton International Airport serves the area and is located about ten miles north of the city. The field is at an elevation of 1,009 feet MSL and has three runways. The longest is 10,901 feet. The airport serves major domestic airlines and commuter airlines as well as general aviation and military.

Within just a few miles is the Wright Patterson Air Force Base, with its world-renowned Air Force Museum and the Wright Brothers Cycle Company museum.

Additionally, there are many satellite general aviation airports and private airstrips, too numerous to mention.

References

Newspapers
Dayton Daily News

Organizations
United States Air Force historical archives, Wright Field
Dayton Public Library
Montgomery County Historical Society
United States Air Force Museum
Engineers Club
Wright State University Archives
Dayton and Montgomery County Library

People
Kate and Jack Tiffany   William E. Deis
Roger L. Miller   Albert J. Hobday
William Griesemer Jr.   Tom Weitendorf
Wilkinson Wright
  (grand nephew of the Wright brothers)

STOP #16
CINCINNATI, OHIO

CAPSULE HISTORY OF CITY

Cincinnati is located in the southwest corner of the state of Ohio, across the Ohio River from the northernmost point of Kentucky. A flat plain called the "Basin" is surrounded by hills on three sides. This is the Ohio River's mid-point and on the Mason-Dixon line. The city leads the world in the production of soap and playing cards and produces more machine tools than any other city in the country.

In 1788 settlers established a village called Losantiville on what is now the site of this city. The name was changed to Cincinnati in 1790 by Gen. Arthur St. Clair, the first governor of the Northwest Territory. This was to honor the Society of the Cincinnati, an organization that was formed by Army officers of the Revolutionary War in America.

550 feet MSL.

AUGUST 6–8, 1927 (SATURDAY THROUGH MONDAY)

After leaving Dayton and on his way to Cincinnati, Lindbergh flew over the Ohio towns of Franklin, Middletown, and Hamilton, eventually circling over the Kentucky hills and across the Ohio River before landing at Lunken Airport in the southeast corner of the city.

The history of this already established Cincinnati airport includes Edmund B. Lunken's father, who donated the land for Lunken Field in 1926. Edmund was known as "Ebby" to everyone. Originally the family name was "Lunkenheimer" but was changed to Lunken during World War I because of its German background. Ebby's father or grandfather founded the Lunkenheimer Valve Company, manufacturers of fuel and oil fittings.

Lunken Airport in 1927 was only a grass field with several hangars and that was all. Today it is a modern airport, thanks to Lindbergh's

1927 visit.

Shortly after Lindbergh landed at 2:00 P.M., the NYP and Fairchild FC-2 were rolled into a hangar and guarded by National Guard troops under the command of Major Hoffman. The public was allowed to view the airplane, at a safe distance but close enough to be photographed while it was there. Most existing photos only show it outside on the grassy field.

After preliminary introductions by the welcoming committee, a motorcade taking Lindbergh and his crew into the city was formed. They made their way to Redlegs Field, a baseball field where the Cincinnati Reds baseball team played. The field is no longer there. Lindbergh had made a special request to have many seats available free for the local schoolchildren at Redlegs Field.

Before Lindbergh gave his usual presentation, it was announced that Mayor Murray Seasongood was unable to attend the festivities due to the illness of his wife, who was at a hos-

Lindbergh just after landing at Lunken Airport, August 6th. STEPHEN B. SMALLEY

The NYP in full view of the public on the grass at Lunken Airport. BOB JACOBS VIA BOB BAILEY

Notice the bunting on the fence with American flags on posts surrounding the area. CASSAGNERES COLLECTION

pital in Rochester, Minnesota.

After Lindbergh spoke, Arthur E. Roberts, Scout Executive of the Cincinnati Council of Boy Scouts of America, made Lindbergh an honorary member of the Ku-Ni-Eh Society. It was an honorary society within the Cincinnati scouting area given to boys who attended the scout camp, Camp Edgar Friedlander. Lindbergh was then presented with an Indian headdress to commemorate his new membership.

Soon Lindbergh and his party were taken to Hotel Sinton, where they could relax in one of the most prestigious suites available at the hotel. This suite was once occupied by the late President Warren G. Harding, and later by Queen Marie of Romania.

Later that evening there was a banquet on the Roof Garden of the Gibson Hotel, where Lindbergh gave another speech. At this affair Judge Stanley Mathews, Vice Mayor, gave his official welcome to Lindbergh and stated that this visit was most timely because it had stirred up a much needed enthusiasm and inspiration for the development of the airport's facilities in the Queen City. Lindbergh's visit renewed a spirit to be manifested in the creation of a fund for this redevelopment. Mathews reviewed the local development of transportation with emphasis on air transportation and the need for improved airport expansion and the purchase of necessary equipment for the field.

Colonel C. Sherrill, City Manager, also declared that this event had emphasized the urgent need for an improved airport, for the rapidly increasing importance of commercial aviation regardless of cost. This airport could be compared favorably with other airports being developed around the country where they were spending millions of dollars to develop airports from scratch. Cincinnati already had an airport. It just needed to be improved upon, as the initial cost of land purchase had been paid. It would place Cincinnati on the main line of a number of important airways, and also improve the air mail service for the area.

On that same Saturday night, Phil Love gave a little romantic color to the tour when he disappeared for a while, returning to the hotel rather late. He knew a "nice young lady" in the area.

On Sunday, the 7th, the flyers' day off, the crew was loaned an automobile to tour both the countryside of Ohio and the nearby Kentucky hills. Lindbergh was driving when someone suggested they stop at a village drugstore for some refreshments. Keyhoe was elected to make the purchase. They had parked some distance from the store to have a bit of privacy.

While Keyhoe was waiting for the clerk to make up the order he spotted a small puzzle with the label "New York to Paris." It consisted of several wooden blocks that could be shifted in various directions. The purpose of the game was to move the "airplane block" from the New York corner to the Paris corner.

The clerk said that he thought it was quite easy and suggested that Keyhoe try it once. Keyhoe remarked, "We ought to have Colonel Lindbergh here to show us how to do it." The clerk remarked, "He could fly over there all right, but he'd fall down like anybody else on that puzzle." Keyhoe said, "How long would you give Lindbergh if he were here?" The clerk replied, "I would say he could not do it in four hours."

Keyhoe could hardly hold himself and keep a straight face, but he did purchase the puzzle and took it back to the car. When Keyhoe told Lindbergh about the conversation in the store, Lindbergh just grinned. Then his face grew serious. "Let's see it," he said. And all the way back to Cincinnati, Lindbergh was engrossed in the puzzle and just could not put it down. He could not wait to get to their rooms at the hotel to continue to try to solve the game. After about two hours or so he finally worked it out and announced, "There it is, now what do you say we order dinner. I am getting hungry."

When Monday morning came and it was time to prepare to leave, the crew could barely get Phil Love to wake up. Lindbergh remarked that in all the years he knew Love, he had never seen him like this and wondered if it would be a good idea to let him fly that day. Over the next two months he was apparently not the same man and had to be watched closely by his friends. The slightest mistake was instantly ascribed to "Cincinnati."

Today Lunken Airport no longer serves the general public for airline travel but is used for corporate and general aviation. As of 1984 it was the second busiest airport in Ohio. The airport is at an elevation of 483 feet MSL and has three runways. The longest is 6,101 feet.

A few miles southwest of the city, across the Ohio River and near the towns of Hebron and Limaburg, Kentucky, is the Cincinnati-Northern Kentucky International Airport, where many major airlines serve the area. It also serves general aviation and military operations. It is at an elevation of 897 feet MSL and has three runways, the longest of which is 11,000 feet. The other two are 10,000 feet long each.

References

Newspapers
   The Cincinnati Post
   The Cincinnati Inquirer

Organizations
   Missouri Historical Society
   Tribe of Ku Ni Eh of Camp Edgar Friedlander

People
   Richard V. Whitney   Hans Dam
   Howard M. Wilson   Lou Miller
   Jean D. Streeter
   Luke Feck, Editor of the *Cincinnati Inquirer*

STOP #17
LOUISVILLE, KENTUCKY

CAPSULE HISTORY OF CITY

The largest city in the state of Kentucky, Louisville lies on the Ohio River in north-central Kentucky, just across the river from Cincinnati, Ohio. Because of the twenty-six-foot-high falls of the Ohio River, it is sometimes called the Falls City.

One of the world's most famous horse races, the Kentucky Derby, is held at Churchill Downs in the city every year.

In 1778 a group of pioneers led by the explorer George Rogers Clark established a settlement on the site of what is now this large city. The next year Clark named the town for King Louis XVI of France to acknowledge France's help to the American colonies during the Revolutionary War (1775–1783).

450 feet MSL.

AUGUST 8–9, 1927 (MONDAY AND TUESDAY)

After leaving Cincinnati for the short flight to Louisville, Lindbergh flew over the towns of Lawrenceburg, Aurora, Rising Sun, and Vevay, Indiana, following the Ohio River. He circled the city and flew over Churchill Downs, home of the famous Kentucky Derby.

The only landing field at that time was Bowman Field, located about five miles ESE of the center of the city. It was the oldest, continuously operating airport in Kentucky at the time.

Sometime in 1919 Abram H. Bowman, a local man interested in flying, subleased the first fifty acres of land on the present site of the airport. In May 1920 he purchased a surplus Canadian Curtiss Jenny JN-4C "Canuck" and formed a partnership with Robert H. Gast to set up operations at the site on Taylorsville Road. Eventually Bowman became known as the "Father of Louisville Aviation." Bowman realized the importance of the airport becoming a site on the trackless air map, while many of Louisville's citizens still regarded air travel as a whim of the experimenters.

Because of the difficulties of convincing local leaders to develop the field for the city, a group known as the Aero Club of Kentucky was formed in 1922 to push for just such development.

In October of that year, terms of agreement were drawn up between the city of Louisville and the U.S. War Department, guaranteeing the use of Bowman Field, at a rental of one dollar annually. The city paid all expenses to have some hangars from Camp Henry Knox (now Fort Knox) moved to the Bowman site. The federal government designated the site officially as a landing field and established an Army Reserve Unit there. On Saturday, August 25, 1923, the field was officially dedicated by the Aero Club.

In 1928 the State Legislature passed a mea-

The NYP parked just in front of the Fairchild before going into the hangar at Bowman Field in Louisville. EDWARD PECK

sure authorizing the creation of the Louisville and Jefferson County Air Board to operate the field as a publicly owned facility. Later that year at their first air board meeting, directors were appointed by the mayor, William B. Harrison, and county judge, Henry I. Fox. The list read like a "who's who" of the Aero Club.

In 1927 Mr. Bowman, joined by the Louisville Board of Trade and other community-minded citizens, conducted a successful campaign to get voter approval of a $750,000 bond issue to finance the purchase of Bowman Field. The portion of the land not needed for an airport became Seneca Park. The campaign was inspired by Lindbergh's visit. (See letter.)

After flying over Louisville, Lindbergh landed the NYP soon after the Fairchild, touching down on Bowman at 2:02 P.M., taxiing to one of the hangars. There were 10,000 people already on the field, and 100,000 more lined the streets from the airport into the city to see him in the parade.

When Lindbergh climbed out of the cockpit, he was met by Mayor Joseph R. O'Neal and hundreds of Boy Scouts, the latter lining the way from the airplane to a previously erected speaker's platform.

At the stand Mr. Bowman said, "Louisville honors an ideal American. You came here to see the man who not only has done a big thing, but is continuing to do a big thing, meeting the men and women of this country. Louisville is honored in having him here."

In Lindbergh's presentation a few minutes later, he stressed the importance again of com-

mercial aviation development in the area.

The Lindbergh parade left the field and drove down Cannons Lane to Lexington Road, through Cherokee Park to Castleman Monument, and then down Broadway to Fourth Street to the Brown Hotel.

One newspaper reporter stated, "Not since Armistice Day in 1918 were the city streets so filled with people."

Later that afternoon he and Phil Love spent time in his room with an old flying friend from Brooks Field days, local plumber (See letter.) Russell Beeler. They enjoyed themselves for several hours, renewing their friendship and doing the usual hangar flying.

It was at the Louisville stop on Monday, the 8th, that Lindbergh let his flying friend, Phil Love, pilot the NYP around the airport one time, the only time that Love had soloed the NYP.

That evening there was a banquet at the Crystal Ballroom of the Brown Hotel, where more than seven hundred people gathered and where he was officially welcomed by Governor William J. Fields and Mayor Joseph R. O'Neal. Later in his speech Lindbergh stated, "Just as it was necessary for good roads to bring the age of the automobile, so it is now necessary for good airports to hasten the age of aviation."

The menu for that evening consisted of such delicacies as aspic Nova Scotia, hearts of celery, assorted olives, broiled breast of chicken on toast with bacon premier, new peas a la etuve, potatoes fondante Ireland, pear and cheese salad le Bourget, coupe Newfoundland, petit fours and coffee.

The Fairchild FC-2 escort airplane in front of the hangar at Louisville's Bowman field. EDWARD PECK

Escort pilot Phil Love standing with Lindbergh at Bowman Field. EDWARD PECK

While in Louisville, the NYP was hangared and serviced by the local Air Service Reserve Squadron, the 465th Pursuit. One of the squadron's members, Chester Lamppin, had an interesting experience while the NYP was outside the hangar for display and cordoned off with a rope and surrounded by a circle of viewers.

One of the viewers was an attractive young woman. She had motioned Chester to her and, while batting her eyes and flashing a big smile, asked quite sweetly if he would get her a souvenir off the NYP. Chester sensed an opportunity to score points with her but said, "Oh, no, I couldn't do that." But she continued to suggest that he find something small. Chester began searching for some way to meet the lovely girl's request to improve his chances of gaining her favor. Suddenly his eyes landed on the wheels. The canvas covers were laced on over the wire spokes, and he noted that one of these had a bit of unused lacing dangling loose. Carefully slipping a small knife from his pocket, Chester cut a bit of the spare lacing off and expectantly presented it to the foxy young thing. He was now all primed to engage her in "meaningful" conversation, perhaps even arrange an assignation in return for his favor. Instead, the pretty young lady flashed a smile, thanked him, and promptly disappeared into the crowd. The young woman's name is unknown, and that piece of lacing has disappeared.

Mary Roush, now of Brooksville, Florida, remembered going with her grandmother to see Lindbergh riding by in the parade. She also remembered the song "Lucky Lindy" and the picture of his plane that hung in her eighth grade classroom.

On Tuesday, the 9th, Lindbergh took off at 11:32 A.M. and headed for his next stop at Indianapolis, Indiana.

In 1938 paved runways were first put in at Bowman, and during World War II the nearby farm fields became a USAAF base, mainly for training combat glider pilots and air evacuation flight nurses.

The present-day large airport is Louisville International Airport, Standiford Field, located about four miles south of the city. This large, modern airport was built during World War II. It is at an elevation of 500 feet MSL and has three main runways, two of which are parallel. The longest runway is 10,000 feet. The field serves most major domestic airlines, some commuters, general aviation aircraft and the Air National Guard.

In and around the Louisville area are many private landing fields, and a couple of commercial general aviation airports.

References

Newspapers
Louisville Courier-Journal
The Louisville Times
The Tampa Tribune "Mailbag"
New Albany (Indiana) Tribune

Publication
Bowman Field, 60th Anniversary, 1918–1978, printed Sunday, September 17, 1978, by the Louisville and Jefferson County Air Board

People
Leland Hawes   Edward Peck
Robert Spiller   Douglas E. Studer
Charles W. Arrington

STOP #18
INDIANAPOLIS, INDIANA

CAPSULE HISTORY OF CITY

The capital and largest city in Indiana, Indianapolis is located in the center of the state. It is one of the largest cities in the country not on navigable water. It is sometimes known as the Crossroads of America because many highways and rail traffic meet there.

In February 1820 George Pogue and John McCormick and their families became the first white settlers in this area. A small group of Delaware Indians were living there as well. The ten-man State Commission felt that its central location and nearby navigable White River made it an appropriate location for the state capital. It was incorporated as a town in 1836 and as a city in 1847. The city was mapped out by Alexander Ralson, assistant to Pierre L'Enfant, who designed the city of Washington, D.C.

The city is known for the world-famous Indianapolis Speedway, built in 1909, home of the "Indy 500," an annual five-hundred-mile automobile race.

710 feet MSL.

AUGUST 9–10, 1927
(TUESDAY AND WEDNESDAY)

After leaving Louisville, Lindbergh flew over Camp Knox, Kentucky, then headed directly to Indianapolis in the "Hoosier" state.

At this time Indianapolis had an airport field known then as either Mars Hill or Stout Field, near Mars Hill and Maywood, suburbs southwest of the city. It was bounded on the east by Holt Avenue, on the north by Minnesota Street, the south by a line about one hundred yards south of Raymond Street (presently Airport Expressway) and on the west by Lyons Avenue or Taft Avenue south of Interstate 70. Stout Field was named after Lt. Richard Harding Stout, a National Guard officer who died on takeoff during a training flight. The place was also known as Mars Hill Municipal Airport and Stout-Cox airport for a time.

This field became the home base of the 113th Observation Squadron of the Indiana National Guard and its Armory, which are still on that site today.

The idea to have an airport at this city had been in the minds of a few air-minded people, and in late 1926 a corporation was formed to acquire and build an airport on the fifty-acre site. The first contract air mail flight into the field, as scheduled from Chicago, was on April 23, 1927. It was three months later that Lindbergh came to town to boost their enthusiasm and continue to stress the importance of a city airport.

The airport site was acquired from the state's holdings of prairie and from the Armory Board of the State of Indiana. Paul H. Moore, its first manager, was appointed by Mayor L. Ert Slack. Two large hangars were physically moved from Kokomo, Indiana, and erected on the new site.

Lindbergh landed at 2:00 P.M. He taxied to the two hangars, spoke briefly with Donald Keyhoe, and inserted the Pyralin windows into the NYP.

He was then greeted by Governor Ed Jackson, Mayor Duvall, William Fortune, and Wallace O. Lee, vice chairman of the welcoming committee.

Meanwhile the NYP was wheeled into one of the hangars, where it could be protected but viewed by a long line of spectators during the rest of the day. The hangar in which the NYP was housed was gaily decorated with blue, red and white bunting. The airplane was well guarded.

Soon Lindbergh was perched on the tonneau of a shining automobile and became the lead car in a thirteen-and-a-half-mile parade to the Coliseum of the State Fairgrounds in the north-northeast part of the city.

The motor car parade moved north on Holt Road to Washington Street to Illinois Street, around the Circle, then along Meridian Street to 38th Street to the Fairgrounds.

A group of boys that lived near the airport decided to build a model airplane to honor their hero. They found pieces of scrap tin to fashion into the model. In their enthusiasm they built a biplane rather than a monoplane, as is the NYP.

The only photo found showing the NYP just after it had landed at the only available grass field in the Indianapolis area on August 8. *INDIANAPOLIS STAR-NEWS*

At the Coliseum Lindbergh was presented with a bouquet of flowers by Miss Lucy Lindley of the Teachers College of Indianapolis.

There were about six thousand people at the Coliseum to greet the flyer. In Lindbergh's presentation he said,

"The purpose of this tour of the United States is primarily to encourage the building and equipping of municipal airports. Commercial aviation developed more rapidly in the last decade than the people have any knowledge of. The government has had to experiment with commercial aviation because it has been too expensive for private companies to consider.

"We now have planes that can fly one thousand miles without stopping and a cruising speed of 100 mph. We have now reached the place where it is necessary to have good airports. The airports soon will bring commercial activities, such as the air mail, express and passenger service, in addition to various other activities. I want to impress upon you that citizens of Indianapolis should get behind a program so that the city will be on the air map of the United States."

The program only lasted about ten minutes. Then the auto parade made a quick trip to the Columbia Club by way of Fall Creek Boulevard, then down Delaware to the club.

Lindbergh and his crew were escorted to the sixth floor to receive a few newspaper men at 4:30 P.M. and relax before the evening banquet at 6:00 P.M.

The next day while Lindbergh was preflighting the NYP, he noticed the left tire was quite low. The valve was leaking. After the valve was repaired a mechanic put more air in the tire. Soon Lindbergh climbed into the airplane, checked the instruments, and called out to the mechanic at the nose of the plane. The mechanic spun the propeller, but the engine failed to fire. He said, "Switch off," and the mechanic pulled the prop through again. With the switch on and with a final swing of the blade the J-5 finally caught.

Upon his departure to the northwest he turned right and made a point of flying directly to the James Whitcomb Riley Hospital for children. The hospital is located on the grounds of the present Indiana University/Purdue University. Many crippled children on white cots were outside in the yard and thrilled as he circled more than one time, much to their delight. One child said, "like a silver angel." Just before leaving he came quite low over the facility. He also circled the downtown business district of Indianapolis before heading north to Detroit.

Today one can fly in and out of the large, well-equipped Indianapolis International Airport, only two and a half miles from the original site where Lindbergh landed in 1927.

This new field is located 7 miles southwest of the city center. It is at an elevation of 797 feet MSL and has three main runways. The longest

of the two parallel ones is 11,200 feet. The field serves most major domestic airlines and some commuter airlines, as well as general aviation and military operations. The well-known Indianapolis Motor Speedway is nearby.

References

Newspapers
Indianapolis Star
Indianapolis News

Organization
Indianapolis-Marion County Public Library

People
Kenneth D. Wilson   Drina Abel
Barbara J. Gilles   Dale Glossenger

STOP #19
DETROIT, MICHIGAN

CAPSULE HISTORY OF CITY

A Midwest city famous for its American automobile production, Detroit lies on Lake St. Clair and the Detroit River on the southeastern border of the state of Michigan. It is often referred to as the Automobile Capital of the World, or Motor City. It is the largest city in the state.

The Wyandot Indians lived in the area before white men arrived. A group of French settlers, led by Antoine de la Mothe Cadillac, established the city in 1701 and called it d'etroit, or "City of Straits," which referred to the twenty-seven-mile Detroit River that connects Lakes Erie and St. Clair. The Detroit River, a segment of the international border between the United States and Canada, marks the only point where Canada lies directly south of the United States.

581 feet MSL.

AUGUST 10–12, 1927
(WEDNESDAY THROUGH FRIDAY)

On his way to Ford Airport at Detroit, Lindbergh passed over Kokomo and Fort Wayne, Indiana, and Toledo, Ohio. As he flew low over Fort Wayne, he dropped a signed message to the city.

On their way into Detroit the two tour airplanes flew along the Canadian border and over Windsor, Ontario, giving a morning view of the Auto City.

Appearing over the city about 1:30 P.M. through bright sun and blue sky, the NYP landed at Ford Airport. This landing field, established by Henry Ford, was located several miles to the west-southwest of the city in the Dearborn area. No longer in existence as an airport, Ford Airport today is located on the Ford Proving Grounds, part of Greenfield Village in the Detroit suburb of Dearborn.

One of the three NYP replicas used in the Warner Brothers movie *Spirit of St. Louis—1957* is located in the Henry Ford Museum, a few hundred feet from the site. The old airport site borders Oakwood Boulevard and Rotunda Drive.

In a holiday spirit, Detroit citizens felt a special kinship to the young flyer. City buildings as well as private homes were decorated with the Stars and Stripes and patriotic bunting.

After a perfect three-point landing at 2:00 P.M., Lindbergh taxied the NYP up to a Ford hangar, where the airplane and the Fairchild would be housed for two nights.

He was immediately greeted by Henry Ford, Edsel Ford, Mayor John W. Smith, and John C. Lodge, grand-uncle of Lindbergh.

At one of the parade cars nearby he was met by several members of his family: C. H. Land, brother of Mrs. Lindbergh, and Mrs. Edwin Lodge, widow of the great uncle of Lindbergh who had officiated at the birth of the flyer as the attending physician. Mrs. Lodge's children, Adelaide and Joseph, and Dr. Albert Lodge, another great uncle, were greeted. His mother,

Evangeline, was waiting for him in another car. Mrs. Lindbergh had on the same outfit that she wore when she attended the reception in Washington, D.C., held on his return from England aboard the Memphis. It was a blue and red polka dot chiffon gown and large black straw hat trimmed with white flowers. She carried a bouquet of yellow roses. Her son joined her in the car, with Mayor Smith and Mrs. Lodge on the folding seats.

The parade left Ford Airport and wound its way into the city by way of Oakwood Boulevard, Fort Street, and West Grand Boulevard, to the Northwestern Field, where he gave a heartwarming speech.

During the parade boys were seen pumping their bicycles excitedly in a vain effort to keep abreast of the parade and get a view of their hero. With wrinkled hands, older women shielded their eyes from the sun. A large, middle-aged man in shirt sleeves gazed hopelessly after the car passed by, when he realized it was too late to toss the humble bouquet he held in his hand.

On West Grand Boulevard a group of boys held two homemade banners. One said "Lindbergh, Our Hero" and the other "The Lindbergh Club."

The crowds lining the parade route were well disciplined, content with whistles, hand waving and pleasant remarks. However, as Lindbergh made his way up to the platform the crowds went berserk and had to be quieted by Clarence E. Brewer, Commissioner of Recreation, speaking into the microphone. Lindbergh was officially welcomed by Mayor Smith.

During Lindbergh's address he briefly interrupted the talk to explain that a Ford tri-motor was flying overhead.

After Lindbergh's presentation Mayor Smith stepped forward and said, "I want to introduce to you the proudest mother in the world." With that Mrs. Lindbergh rose, took a bow, and smiled.

En route from Northwestern Field to the hotel, the parade passed by his birthplace and former home at 1120 Forest Avenue. Here he and his mother spent some time sitting on the porch. Prominent World War I flying ace, Capt. Edward V. Rickenbacker, was part of the official welcome. On behalf of the J. L. Hudson Company, Rickenbacker presented a bronze memorial tablet that had been affixed to the front of the house. Mayor Smith gave a brief address of acceptance, and Miss Adelaide Lodge drew away the banner which had covered the tablet. The tablet was inscribed,

"This tablet marks the birthplace of
CAPT. CHARLES A. LINDBERGH.

The first aviator to fly from New York to Paris was born here February 4, 1902, the son of Charles A. and Evangeline Lodge Lindbergh.

After flying alone 3640 miles in 33-½ hours, May 20–21, 1927, Capt. Lindbergh was decorated by France, England, Belgium and Spain, and awarded the Distinguished Flying Cross by Calvin Coolidge, President of the United States."

From there the parade continued downtown to Michigan Avenue and the Book-Cadillac Hotel. Lindbergh and his crew were given a suite on the sixteenth floor, the same suite set aside for Queen Marie of Rumania when she planned to visit the city. It was a welcome rest period during which they could plan the continuation of the tour. Mrs. Lindbergh also had some private time with her son.

There were seven hundred prominent men and women of Detroit at the banquet that evening. The guests included Mr. and Mrs. Henry Ford, toastmaster Capt. Edward V. Rickenbacker, Fielding Harris Yost of the University of Michigan, Major and Mrs. Lanphier, and Henry Ford's son, Edsel.

In Lindbergh's talk that evening he stressed the importance of the development of aviation and air travel. After the banquet Lindbergh slipped away to spend the night at the home of Mr. and Mrs. Ford at Fair Lane, the family estate in Dearborn. Mrs. Lindbergh and the Lanphiers were also guests.

At the time of Lindbergh's arrival in Detroit, the Ford Company was heavily involved in aviation, and at the time getting into the production of the Ford tri-motor airliner.

Ford was also developing another airplane as well as the tri-motor. It was Henry Ford's dream of a "Model T" plane in everyone's garage, much as he had done with the Model T automobile. He wanted to produce airplanes that the average citizen could own and produce them on a production line basis.

It was in 1926 that twenty-seven year old Otto Koppen, an engineer from M.I.T., was hired to work in the Aviation Division of the Ford Company. Mr. Ford asked Koppen to design an airplane that anyone could fly—a Model T of the air, so to speak.

The airplane they came up with was called the Ford "Flivver." It was a single-place open-cockpit, low-wing monoplane powered with a

Supposedly Henry Ford is in the cockpit ready to take his first airplane ride with Lindbergh. Notice the bunting on the hangar which is part of the Stout Metalplane factory. STEPHEN J. HUDEK

The NYP in the hangar with the Ford Flivver #1 and the Fairchild escort airpane. TIM O'CALLAGHAN, PHOTO BY ED HEBB

35-hp Anzani engine. This prototype was registered experimental and carried no. 268 on the rudder. It was blue and yellow. Up to this time it had only been flown by Ford test pilot Harry J. Brooks.

On Lindbergh's "day off," the 11th, it was suggested that Lindbergh fly the Flivver. After discussing with Brooks the little airplane's flight characteristics and other details, Lindbergh climbed in, took off, and flew over the airport checking it out. He did several standard maneuvers, possibly steep turns, stalls, slips, climbs and glides, and came in for a smooth landing.

As Donald Keyhoe once remarked, during the tour there was a constant stream of requests to fly with Lindbergh, in *any* kind of airplane. Often these people indicated they would not fly with anyone else but would agree to go with him. As a result, many important converts were made. One of these was Henry Ford, who at the age of sixty-three had never been up in any kind of airplane. Many leaders in the aviation industry had urged him to fly, but he never did.

When Mr. Ford observed Lindbergh flying the Flivver that day, in addition to an Army Curtiss P-1 "Hawk," he was obviously impressed. When Lindbergh approached Ford and

suggested that he would like to take him up, Ford accepted without hesitation, most likely because it was a rare and special privilege to fly in the NYP and considering who the pilot was.

Ford mechanics had to work up a special rig on the right arm of Lindbergh's seat, including some sort of soft padding for Mr. Ford to sit on.

Lindbergh and Ford flew over the area for about ten minutes, so Ford could see the city of Detroit, Dearborn and Fair Lane, and his auto manufacturing facilities. Ford was sitting stoop shouldered with his legs drawn up close under him so Charles could reach the right rudder pedal with his right foot.

After the flight Ford remarked, "I never dreamed that I would look down on my enterprise from away up here." He was quite impressed.

Photo taken just after Henry Ford had his first airplane ride. He was apparently thanking Lindbergh for the generous opportunity. FROM THE COLLECTIONS OF HENRY FORD MUSEUM & GREENFIELD VILLAGE

Lindbergh also took Edsel Ford for his first airplane ride, which lasted about ten minutes, also in the NYP.

Soon Ford invited Lindbergh to fly the tri-motor. The airplane available was a model 4-AT-5, carrying temporary registration no. 3022. It was the fifth one built and known as the "tri-Ford." Harry J. Brooks was the pilot with Lindbergh flying in the co-pilot seat.

On board were Henry Ford (for his second flight but in his own airplane), Edsel Ford, Major Thomas G. Lanphier, William B. Mayo, Charles E. Sorenson, W. B. Stout (the designer), P. E. Martin, Mrs. Ray Dahlinger, and James Piersol. There are unconfirmed reports that one or two newspaper men were aboard as well.

During the flight Lindbergh offered his seat to Henry Ford, who accepted. He handled the yoke for a brief period. Again the Fords got to see their city and manufacturing plants from the air. They flew over the Belle Isle, Highland Park

and Lincoln plants as well as the plant at Fordson and the Dearborn Laboratories. That particular tri-motor was later lost in an accident on May 12, 1947, in Mexico.

On Friday, the 12th, Lindbergh was invited to Selfridge Field to fly another airplane, a flying boat.

At 11:16 A.M. that morning Lindbergh lifted the NYP off the Ford airport to head for Grand Rapids, Michigan, the next stop on the tour.

A few minutes later the same Ford tri-motor 3022 took off for Grand Rapids also. It was flown by Brooks, with Mrs. Lindbergh, Glenn Hopping, Andrew Nassam, Caspar D. Swenson, William B. Stout (president of Stout Air Services), Mrs. Stout, and Harold E. Cummings, a nephew of Stout, as passengers.

The Fairchild piloted by Phil Love took off shortly before the NYP and headed for Grand Rapids to prepare for Lindbergh's arrival.

Today one can find three major airports in

Aug. 19, 1927

Mr. Henry Ford,
Dearborn, Michigan.

Dear Mr. Ford:

Just a line to let you know that I certainly appreciate the honor of carrying you on your first flight and to thank you for your hospitality.

I expect to see Major Tompkins in a few days and hope to visit Detroit again soon after this tour ends.

Sincerely,
Charles A. Lindbergh

Letter from Charles Lindbergh to Henry Ford regarding Ford's first airplane ride. The letter, dated August 18, 1927, reads,

Mr. Henry Ford
Dearborn, Michigan

Dear Mr. Ford,
    Just a line to let you know that I certainly appreciate the honor of carrying you on your first flight and to thank you for your hospitality.
    I expect to see Major Tompkins in a few days and hope to visit Detriot again soon after this tour ends.
        Sincerely,
            Charles A. Lindbergh

FROM THE COLLECTIONS OF HENRY FORD MUSEUM & GREENFIELD VILLAGE

the Detroit area. One is the Detroit Metro–Wayne County Airport, located 15 miles south of the city. It is at an elevation of 640 feet MSL, has five runways, two parallel, and three parallel, the longest of which is 12,001 feet. The field serves all major domestic airlines and some commuter airlines, as well as general aviation and military.

Three miles to the east is a well-known airport from World War II, known as Willow Run Airport. It has five runways, the longest of which is 7,294 feet. It is at an elevation of 716 feet MSL and serves mainly general aviation. On the field is the Yankee Air Museum.

Two miles south of the city is Grosse Ile Municipal Airport, at an elevation of 591 feet MSL, with two V-shaped runways, the longest one being 4,978 feet. It serves mainly general aviation.

Three to four miles to the northeast is the Detroit City Airport, which serves mainly general aviation. It is at an elevation of 625 feet MSL and has three runways, the longest of which is 5,100 feet.

There are several smaller general aviation airports around the outskirts of the city, including one seaplane facility near Grosse Point.

References
Newspapers
   The Detroit News

Organizations
   Henry Ford Museum and Greenfield Village Research Center
   Detroit Public Library (Burton Historical Library)
   Selfridge Military Air Museum
   Florida Aviation Historical Society

Books
   The Ford Tri-motor 1926 - 1992-Larkins pages 160-162
   Flying with Lindbergh by Don Keyhoe
   The *National Geographic* Magazine, January 1928
   Lindbergh - His Story in Pictures-1929
   Ford News – Dearborn
   author needs to supply complete references

People
Janet Whitson	Robert Haley
Tim O'Callagan	Jeanette Bartz
Robert A. Stone	George Shaffer
Patricia Zacharias	

Stop #20
Grand Rapids, Michigan

Capsule History of City

The second largest city in the state of Michigan, Grand Rapids got its name from the rapids that are part of the Grand River, thirty miles east of Lake Michigan and sixty miles northwest of Lansing. Because of its extensive furniture-manufacturing industry, it is often called the Furniture Capital of America.

Louis Campau founded a fur trading post on this site in 1826. Earlier an Ottawa Indian village was there. Because of its close proximity to southern Michigan's great pine forest, it became the center of supply, distribution, and transportation for the lumber industry. In 1945 the city became the first in the country to add fluorides to its water to help combat tooth decay.

610 feet MSL.

August 12–13, 1927
(Friday and Saturday)

The flight from Detroit to Grand Rapids took two hours and five minutes, flying over Saginaw, the State Capitol at Lansing, and Iona, Michigan.

Riding in the Ford Tri-motor, Lindbergh's mother landed at 1:00 P.M., just after the Fairchild touched down on the old Kent County Airport, which was bordered by 32nd to 44th Streets between Division and Eastern. Lindbergh landed the NYP last.

The number of people on hand to greet the Lindberghs exceeded all records ever accorded anyone in western Michigan. It was reported that 100,000 people were already assembled at a local park where he was scheduled to give a speech and be welcomed to the city.

On Friday morning people by the thousands from outlying towns and villages were on their way, and thousands of automobiles lined the highways entering the city.

Colonel Lindbergh was greeted by Mayor Elvin Swarthout and other members of the reception committee. Lindbergh and the others were driven north in a parade that took them over the Grand River to the John Ball Park in the western area of the city.

Along the parade route the mayor pointed out a local streetcar, operated by the Grand Rapids Railroad Company, which was parked on the end of the Madison Line. It had been named for the flyer.

At the park Lindbergh shared the platform with his mother, Evangeline, and the Mayor. After the ceremonies at the park Lindbergh was driven to the Pantlind Hotel, and shortly thereafter slipped quietly away to meet with his mother back at the airport. It was to keep a promise that he would take her for a ride in the NYP. Mrs. Lindbergh sat on the right-hand arm rest, right next to her son, and they took off and flew for twenty minutes over the area. Her flight in the *Spirit of St. Louis* was not a novelty. She had flown with her son before he became famous.

Here is Lindbergh in the cockpit of the NYP with his mother, Evangeline Lindbergh. Photo taken at the time of his taking her for a ride in the famous airplane. LEO B. KIMBALL COLLECTION

At John Ball Park, and later at the banquet that evening in the Pantlind Hotel, Lindbergh advocated the construction of more airports, the teaching of aeronautics in schools, and the creation of more scheduled airline routes.

He went on to say that during World War I many technical developments and improvements in airplanes were made, but that this was military. "Now we are entering a new era, that of commercial aviation. These airplanes are much safer than military ones. I ask that you devote thought to aeronautics in relation to your city."

Ironically airline service between Grand Rapids and Detroit had been dropped two weeks before Lindbergh's visit. On the day he arrived, the Grand Rapids Flying Club and the Flying Service announced plans to reestablish commercial air service. About two years later Grand Rapids became a stop on a Detroit-to-Milwaukee route. James Van Vulpen, a local author, feels it was important that Lindbergh came here when he did and kept the dream alive because it came when they had taken a bit of a knock locally.

Former Kent County Director of Aeronautics Robert M. Ross said that Lindbergh's New York-to-Paris flight and subsequent tour were the most important development for commercial aviation. "There is no question about it," he said. "He established the silver bridge across the Atlantic. He proved it could be done. It was a real pioneering attempt. He opened up aviation, and he really fired the imagination of the whole population."

Eleven-year-old Stan Bosowski remembers standing at the entrance to John Ball Park, while someone was passing out a grape-flavored gum called Blatz gum. He has not seen any of it since.

Lewis Dereimer remembered that he was five years old and lived near Ball Park. His mother said that Lindbergh would be there soon, so he got on his tricycle and rode over to the park. When he got there the parade with all the motorcycle policemen and cars was just arriving, and he got scared. He put his tricycle in the bushes and ran home to hide in his room. Later he went back with his mother and retrieved the bike.

As a result of Lindbergh's visit, Albert H. Crane's father became interested in learning to fly. The family purchased a Piper J-3 "Cub" some years later, and most of the family learned to fly in that airplane. Several members of the family are still flying.

Mrs. Lindbergh was introduced to the audience by Congressman Carl E. Mapes. He commented that she was a typical American mother

of a typical American son.

James R. Fitzpatrick, vice president of the Haskelite Manufacturing Company of Chicago, presented an enlarged souvenir picture of the NYP, mounted, to Carl T. Batts, president of the Grand Rapids Flying Club.

Here the NYP is being wheeled either in or out of the hangar on Kent County Airport. GRAND RAPIDS PUBLIC LIBRARY

On Saturday, the 13th, Lindbergh and his crew arrived at the airport at 11:10 A.M. They immediately went into the hangar to preflight the NYP and the Fairchild and to fuel up, and at 11:35 he climbed into the NYP to prepare for departure.

Soon the Fairchild was in the air and at 11:45 Lindbergh took off for the next stop, Chicago. Once he was in the air he circled the airport several times, then headed over the city once again, and the Sunshine Hospital on Fuller Avenue as a special favor to the patients. It was a beautiful sunny, warm day for the flight.

Soon after Lindbergh was in the air, his friend Major Tom Lanphier took off in an Army pursuit airplane, circled the airport, and headed north to rendezvous with the NYP. They flew together for a while, then went south of the city, where Lanphier headed east to return to Selfridge Field, and Lindbergh flew to the west.

In the meantime Mrs. Lindbergh departed in the Ford for the flight back to her home in Detroit.

On his way to Chicago, Lindbergh flew first over Kalamazoo, then Benton Harbor, and St. Joseph, Michigan. Eventually he crossed the southern tip of Lake Michigan.

The old Kent County Airport is no longer on the same site as it was in 1927. The new Kent County International, also known as Gerald R. Ford International, is located six miles southeast of the city, close to Interstate 96. The field is at an elevation of 794 feet MSL and has three runways. The longest one is 10,000 feet. The airport serves most major domestic airlines as well as international flights, some commuter airlines, and general aviation aircraft.

References

Newspapers
   The Grand Rapids Press

Organizations
   Grand Rapids Public Library
   Grand Rapids City Museum

Publications
   James Van Vulpen, *On Wings of Progress: The Story of Kent County International Airport*, published by the Grand Rapids Historical Commission

People

Bob J. Tuinstra	Earl E. Spielmacher
Ms. Vera Klimer	Bob Hillebrand
Mrs. Arnold J. Osgood	Florence L. Mulick
Lewis Dereimer	Albert H. Crane

STOP #21
CHICAGO, ILLINOIS

CAPSULE HISTORY OF CITY

The "Windy City," as Chicago is sometimes referred to, is located on the southwestern shore of Lake Michigan, and covers an area that forms a semicircle curving from the Wisconsin border on the north into Indiana on the south, in the northeast portion of the state of Illinois. It lies on a flat plain and is split by the Chicago River that flows westward from Lake Michigan. Until 1900 the river flowed eastward into Lake Michigan, but it now flows westward. En-

gineers reversed the flow in order to prevent sewage in the river from polluting the lake, which supplies the city's drinking water.

The city is also known as "Chicagoland." Chicago comes from the Indian word Checagou. According to some historians the word means "skunk" or "wild onion," both of which were once abundant in the area.

Before any white people arrived, the local Indians used the area as a portage to carry their canoes from the Des Plaines River to the Chicago River, paddling on to Lake Michigan. The first white men to arrive in the area appear to have been two French explorers, Louis Joliet and Father Jacques Marquette, in about 1673. The first permanent settler was Jean Baptiste Point du Sable, a Negro, who established a trading post on the north bank of the river in 1779. Chicago became a city in March of 1837.

595 feet MSL

AUGUST 13–15, 1927
(SATURDAY THROUGH MONDAY)

One of the best known airports in the Chicago area has been Midway. Formerly the Chicago Municipal Airport, it was renamed Midway for the United States victory during World War II in the Midway Islands in the South Pacific. The field was officially opened on May 8, 1926, on three hundred acres of land. It is located about nine miles southwest of downtown Chicago, at Cicero Avenue and 63rd Street.

One of the first flying fields in the Chicago area was at Maywood, Illinois, known as Checkerboard Field. It was used by the U.S. Postal Service "air mail" services. The field was located at First Avenue and Roosevelt Road in Maywood. Lindbergh flew into and out of this field when he was an early air mail pilot.

As Lindbergh approached Chicago on August 13, 1927, he circled over the Straus Building, then over Grant Park and Soldiers Field and "The Loop," before heading for the Chicago Municipal Airport. Thousands of people, as well as foot police and motorcycle policemen, were already on the field. Just after he touched down, the motorcycle policemen escorted the NYP toward a large hangar operated by the Illinois National Guard. There was much confusion, and the mob of people was almost uncontrollable. It appeared they would get their hands on the air-

This is the NYP just after landing at Chicago with a large group of Chicago motorcycle policemen to escort him to the reviewing area. PHIL FELPER

plane and tear it apart. Mayor William Hale Thompson attempted to clear a path with his open car, which helped. He told Lindbergh that the airplane would be in good hands and taken care of and that they needed to be on their way in the parade. Lindbergh stated, "Go if you like, but I stay here to see that my plane is properly locked up and guarded." In the meantime the crowd of people threatened to break into the hangar, but the doors were closed and locked and guards stationed all around the building and adjoining areas.

Another view of Lindbergh in the NYP just after landing at Chicago. IMAGE COURTESY CORBIS

After the plane was secured, Lindbergh was escorted into a waiting automobile to be seated with William P. MacCracken, Assistant Secretary of Commerce; William R. Dawes, President of the Chicago Association of Commerce; and Mayor William Hale Thompson.

The parade pulled out of the airport grounds

and headed straight for the White Sox baseball park. At the park Lindbergh attended the Police Games, where he was asked to decorate a number of policemen and firemen, who had been winners of the Lambert Tree medals for heroism.

From here the parade proceeded to Soldier Field on the shore of Lake Michigan. After a few short introductory talks by officials, Lindbergh was introduced to the crowd assembled in the park. He said,

"Citizens of Chicago, Chicago has been in a position to observe the development of aviation as probably no other city in the world. About eight years ago the air mail was started. Since then the mail planes have operated more or less regularly. The operation was first in the daylight, and the mail was carried in connection with railroads. A few years later the night mail was inaugurated and the service was developed to such an extent as to send mail to New York overnight. You could send mail without losing any time between Chicago and New York. Pilots were flying in and out of Chicago in every direction, operating in almost every kind of weather. They were flying when most people would not care to be out of doors.

"We have had our troubles in aviation, just as other infant industry has. Planes were first used in Army and Navy maneuvers and needed greater strength than did commercial ships. This greater strength was needed for carrying bombs, torpedoes, and other paraphernalia of war. Weather conditions caused a great deal of trouble and still causes more or less trouble.

"Now we are entering the era of commercial aviation. It is necessary to have the cooperation of you and other citizens in aviation to accomplish what must be done. You have a good airport in Chicago. I understand that you intend to construct a land-

The NYP shown in the hangar at Chicago Municipal Airport (now Midway) on August 13th or 14th.
J & L COLLECTIBLES VIA BOB BAILEY

ing field on the lake front. If so, it will probably be one of the best, if not the best, in the country. By constructing this airfield on the lake front you will do more to put your city out in front of other large cities. New York has no airport, but is planning one. I hope Chicago will build one first. In closing, I want to thank you for the interest you have shown in my coming here."

From Soldier Field the entourage made its way to the Stevens Hotel in downtown Chicago, where Lindbergh and his crew held a brief press conference before retiring to their rooms for a rest before the evening program.

The evening banquet was held in the Grand Ballroom of the Stevens Hotel, under the direction of both the Mayor's Committee of Chicago and the Chicago Association of Commerce. William R. Dawes, President of the Chicago Association of Commerce, opened the program with a brief talk.

The banquet was further officiated by Chicago Mayor Thompson, Reverend Joshua Oden of the Irving Park Lutheran Church, Honorable William P. MacCracken, and Alderman Albert J. Horan, who presented a gift to the guest of honor.

Also attending were Maj. Gen. Roy D. Keehn of the Illinois National Guard, Postmaster Arthur Lueder, Chief of Police Michael Hughes and many others.

Many organizations had requested a chance to present a gift to Lindbergh, but there were so many that it was decided to limit the gifts to

three: a key to Lindbergh Field at Maywood, a statuette of him presented by the local Boy Scouts, and a book presenting the plans for a huge Lindbergh beacon light in Chicago (exact location unknown) given by Alderman Albert J. Horan.

On Sunday, the 14th, the Lindbergh crew spent the day in private to rest and have some recreation. They were invited to spend some time at the estate of Frederick Scott in Winnetka. They played baseball, went swimming and relaxed. Lindbergh slept late that morning and then attended a luncheon at the Belmont Hotel given by Mr. and Mrs. William P. MacCracken. Included at the luncheon were Philip R. Love, Theodore Sorenson, Donald Keyhoe, Milburne Kusterer, W. E. Herron, Robert Gast, Mrs. Simeon Lewis, mother of Mrs. MacCracken, and Clarence Young.

Lindbergh and his crew were dinner guests of Edwin P. Price at his home in Winnetka that evening.

During the day Secretary MacCracken informed the flyer that people were clamoring for the tour to be ended because they believed it was undermining his health. MacCracken suggested he undergo a physical examination to show that "you are in good condition." Lindbergh replied, "I am perfectly all right. I get enough sleep and have plenty to eat, and I can finish this tour. I don't say I'd want to do this all my life, but I'm going through with it."

After further persuasion Lindbergh did give in and was examined by MacCracken's father, Dr. William P. MacCracken Sr., who lived in the Chicago area.

That evening Lindbergh and Love spent an hour in his room with some old air mail flying friends, enthusiastically discussing those exciting days.

On Monday, the 15th, the flyers were up early to preflight the two airplanes. They took off at 9:25 A.M. and headed for Springfield, Illinois. After departure Lindbergh flew over the city, circling a few times, then headed west, circling over Aurora, then southeast to Joliet, and southwest to Peoria. From Peoria he flew south to Springfield.

Today the Loyola Emergency Services Building of the Loyola University Chicago Medical Center resides on the property of the old Maywood air mail flying field.

Chicago Municipal Airport, today known as Chicago Midway, is still in operation, with two sets of parallel runways and is mainly used by both private and corporate aircraft.

The main Chicago airport now is Chicago O'Hare International Airport, a hub for United Airlines, located about ten miles west of Chicago, just off Interstate 90. The field is at an elevation of 668 feet MSL and has multiple runways, the longest of the seven being 13,000 feet. O'Hare services all major domestic and international airlines, as well as many commuter airlines, some corporate, helicopters, and Air National Guard aircraft.

Another flight facility was Meigs Field, located on the shoreline of Lake Michigan, a short walk to the downtown loop. This field was used for private and corporate aircraft. Meigs was at an elevation of 593 feet MSL and had a single runway of 3,899 feet.

Located in the greater Chicago area are Romeoville, Lewis University–Joliet airport; Du Page airport in West Chicago, Schaumburg Reg airport, and Aurora Municipal Airport.

References

Newspapers
  Chicago Daily Tribune
  Chicago Herald Examiner
  Chicago Sunday Tribune
  Daily Journal
  Chicago Daily Journal
  Chicago Daily News
  The Sioux City Sunday Journal

Organization
  Chicago Historical Society

People
  Dale Caldwell   Abigail Smith, Ph.D.
  Miss Nel MacCraken   Ted Koston
  Bill Rose   John Wells
  Joanne Fitzgerald

STOP #22
SPRINGFIELD, ILLINOIS
"TOUCH STOP"

CAPSULE HISTORY OF CITY

The state capital and center of a rich farming area, Springfield lies near a central Illinois coal field, 200 miles southwest of Chicago and 100 miles northeast of St. Louis, Missouri.

The city was founded in 1818 and designated as the state capital in 1837. It was also the home of Abraham Lincoln from 1837 to 1861. He was born there in a log cabin, which still stands. Springfield was also the birthplace of poet Vachel Lindsay.

610 feet MSL.

AUGUST 15, 1927 (MONDAY)

They say history repeats itself, and in the case of Lindbergh he was again flying from Chicago to Springfield, Illinois. Only this was 1927, and he was not flying the night mail. He was in the *Spirit of St. Louis* and flying into this city to spread the gospel of air travel and the further advancement of aviation.

The site where he would land was the same thirty-five acre property that he had recommended for the first airport at the capital city. Developed by the Chamber of Commerce, it was located west of the city near the Beardstown

Road. Lindbergh at that time was chief pilot for Robertson Aircraft of St. Louis, Missouri. One can go there today and find a plaque which was erected by the Springfield Airport Authority and the Illinois State Historical Society in 1968.

On his way from Chicago to Springfield, Lindbergh flew west over Moosehart, south and over the Central State Fair at Aurora, then southeast to Joliet. From there he went a roundabout way to Peoria where he circled several times to drop the canvas bag message, then directly south to Springfield. This certainly was not the same direct-line route he used to fly the air mail between the two cities. He had been asked to overfly certain cities on the tour, and that is the reason for the zigzag route on this particular leg.

He landed on the Springfield airport, just west of the city at 12:04 P.M. and was met by a small reception committee: Will E. McConnell, George Bengel, L. L. Emerson, B. F. Meyers of Chicago, Postmaster William H. Conkling, John W. Sheehan Jr., V. Y. Dallman, Raymond Bahr, and Henry Mester.

At that time the field was known as the Old Southwest Airport and was operated by Frank Fleck Jr.

Springfield poured out a heartland of genuine warmth to "their Slim" as he had been known during his air mail days.

The NYP, with the engine still running and Lindbergh in the cockpit, is being moved by hand, just after landing on the Springfield Airport, also known as Southwest Airport.
SANGAMON VALLEY COLLECTION VIA
BERT THOMPSON

Lindbergh with, from left to right: Will H. McConnell; George Bengel; Donald Keyhoe; B.F. Meyers; William H. Conkling; John W. Sheehan Jr.; V.Y. Dallman; Raymond Bahr and Henry Mester, August 15th.

SANGAMON VALLEY COLLECTION & SISTER MAUREEN MAHAFFEY VIA BERT THOMPSON

After he was sure that the NYP was to be well taken care of during his short stay, he climbed into an open auto to ride in a parade through the city streets and out to the prominent Lincoln Tomb in the Oak Ridge Cemetery. There he was taken into the main office where he wrote his name on a page of the tomb register. At the bottom of the page his photograph had been pasted. He inscribed simply "C. A. Lindbergh, St. Louis." He autographed several photographs for Custodian H. W. Fay and wrote his name in autograph books for children, which Mr. Fay handed to him, and on a card which was to be given to former Lt. Gov. John G. Oglesby. Phil Love, Donald Keyhoe, and other committee members wrote their names under Lindbergh's. The ceremony ended with Lindbergh placing a large, beautiful wreath on the sarcophagus of Lincoln.

From there the party drove to the state arsenal where he was given the welcome of the State of Illinois at this capital city by Col. A. E. Inglesh, acting for Governor Len Small, who was unable to attend. He was introduced by Postmaster Conkling and shortly began his speech.

"A few years ago there were only two or three rebuilt war planes in your city. Just a little over a year ago the first airmail from St. Louis to Chicago was carried over the route through Springfield, and this city had an important part in the inauguration of that service.

"Springfield has already made a mark in airmail among cities many times its size, and you may well be proud of it. There is not another city in the United States of its size which has made a better record in airmail than Springfield, Illinois. You are to be congratulated. And in a large measure you have your postmaster Mr. Conkling to thank for this."

He continued his talk, and again referred to the city for their insight into the development of aviation.

"The city is to be congratulated for sup-

plying a landing field and in the cooperation which has been given the committee. But this field was selected only for temporary use. It is not a question of how small a field can be used but how large a field you must have in order to bring air service to your city and the big commercial airplanes which are marking the development of aeronautics.

"From what I have seen at Springfield and its airmail progress, I know that the citizens see the advantage of finding a better field for the future, and I look forward to the day when large planes from every part of the United States will come to this city's airport."

Secretary of State Louis L. Emerson was then introduced and presented the resolution adopted by the Illinois House and Senate in appreciation of Lindbergh's accomplishment at the time he made his world-famous flight.

"Colonel Lindbergh, the fifty-fifth general assembly of Illinois, before it adjourned, expressed its appreciation of your great and important service by resolutions unanimously inviting you to come to Springfield and Illinois over the route you previously flew in the airmail service. These resolutions accord you the admiration, the love and best wishes of the people of the State of Illinois." Two scrolls were tied with red, white, and blue ribbons and given to Lindbergh.

Then Mayor J. Emil Smith was introduced and voiced the official Springfield greeting to the young flyer.

In a few minutes the parade made its way out of the city and back to the airfield, where a ceremony for the renaming of the airport took place.

Because Lindbergh had helped to select the field and was the first to fly the mail to and from this city, he had endeared himself to Springfield, long before he won international fame and honor. So it was, therefore, only logical and fitting that when christening time came, the city should give their field the name of one upon whom not only the crowned heads of Europe but our own revered President bestowed the highest honor in his realm. Springfield was the first city in the United States acknowledged by Washington as having named their field "Lindbergh Field."

In a speech delivered by the President of the Springfield Chamber of Commerce, S. A. Barker, he went on to honor the hero and officially dedicated the field as Lindbergh Field.

Because Capt. Phil Love also flew the mail in and out of Springfield, the city honored him as well. He also congratulated the city for their forthcoming plans to build a new and larger flying field to handle faster and larger airplanes.

At 1:45 P.M. sharp Lindbergh departed for St. Louis, following behind the Fairchild, which was already underway.

Today Springfield has a large airport facility three miles northwest of the city known as Capitol Airport. The field is at an elevation of 597 feet MSL, and has three runways. The longest one is 7,999 feet. It serves many of the major domestic airlines, some commuter airlines, general aviation, and Air National Guard aircraft.

There are a number of privately owned satellite airstrips, mainly in the east, south, and west quadrants of the city.

The NYP on the field at Springfield showing some of the mounted National Guardsmen in the background. EULA MANLEY

References

Newspaper
Illinois State Journal

People
Job Conger   Mrs. Eula R. Manley
Bert Thompson

STOP #23
ST. LOUIS, MISSOURI

CAPSULE HISTORY OF CITY

St. Louis is the largest city in the state of Missouri, on the east-central border of the state on the west bank of the Mississippi River. It is about ten miles south of where the Mississippi meets the Missouri River.

The Missouri and Osage Indians lived on the site before French explorers arrived in the mid-1600s.

But let us digress to the origin of the naming of this large midwestern city, whose name was applied to the nose of the world's most famous airplane in aviation history.

Pierre LaClede, born in 1724 in the village of Bedous, in the lower Pyrenees, France, migrated to New Orleans in 1755 and became a trader by profession. In 1757 he formed a union with one Marie Therese Chouteau, separated from her husband with an infant son, (Rene') Auguste Chouteau. Together they moved north in 1763 to the east side of the Missouri River, where he established a trading post.

In 1764 he and his step-son established a village on the west side of the Missouri River, and named it St. Louis, in honor of Louis IX, one of the great kings of France.

King Louis, born in 1214, was a hero in every way. He came to the throne at age 12, and with his mother's tutoring became a pious, unselfish ruler. His reputation was that of a respectful, fair and just king.

Like Lindbergh, he traveled. He led a crusade to the Holy Land in 1248, and in 1270 another trip to Africa, where he died. He united the qualities of a "just and upright sovereign, a fearless warrier, and saint," according to biographical material. Louis was strong, idealistic, austere. His character and foundations were many. In 1297, twenty-seven years after his death, Louis was canonized; the man who was "every inch a king," thus became a saint in the Roman Catholic Church. The year of his canonization, 1297, carries the same digits as 1927, the year of Lindbergh's flight. (Excerpted from the book, The Untold Story of The Spirit of St. Louis, *by Ev Cassagneres.)*

455 feet MSL.

AUGUST 15–17, 1927
(MONDAY THROUGH WEDNESDAY)

Coming in from the north-northeast, Lindbergh circled over the business district of the city before heading toward Lambert–St. Louis Airport. He arrived over the field, circled and made a low pass, before touching down at 3:05 P.M. His usual ETA of 2:00 P.M. was missed due to the apparent extra time spent at Springfield.

There were 1,500 people on the field including many women and children, in addition to many of Lindbergh's old army friends from the 110th Observation Squadron of the 35th Division of the Missouri National Guard.

After landing he taxied right into the National Guard hangar and let the engine idle for a few minutes, finally cutting the mag switch.

The crowd attempted to break through the guard line, but the military men were able to hold them back in spite of the pressure.

There to greet him were Maj. Charles Ray Wassall, the commanding officer of the Missouri National Guard; Capt. William M. Robertson; Lt. George J. Stumpf; Capt. Russell Young, Lt. J. Johanpeter, all members of the Guard.

Earlier Lindbergh had requested that his visit to St. Louis be a relaxing and restful one and basically informal. Probably because he had been there before with the NYP, and would most likely spend some time there in the near future,

ORIGIN OF THE TERM "SPIRIT OF" ST. LOUIS

EXCERPTED FROM THE BOOK, *THE UNTOLD STORY OF THE SPIRIT OF ST. LOUIS*, BY EV CASSAGNERES

The name coined by Harold Bixby was not the very first time *"Spirit of St. Louis"* was created, however. It actually appeared for the first time in 1913. And in 1922, a movie was produced having as its title *"The Spirit of St. Louis."* Here is the story.

First conceived by the Chamber of Commerce of St. Louis in 1913 and revived by its successors in 1922-23 as a crusade for the good, the true, the beautiful and the proud, the city was to become a "New St. Louis." As stated by the Reverend Doctor W. C. Bitting, the city had emphasized virtues that could not be measured. Thus, he says, "A city is more than an assemblage of buildings with streets between them. It has a soul and an atmosphere and a social significance to which all material things should be made to minister."

A motion picture depicting the years from the city's beginning to the present was produced as a public spirited movement to acquaint the public with the city's heritage.

"The Spirit of St. Louis" was the first historical film of its kind ever produced by an American city. It was made by the Rothacker Film Manufacturing Company of Chicago and featured many highlights of the city's history and reflected the "Spirit of Achievement."

In the first scenes the movie showed King Louis IX as a crusader, leading his army against the Saracens in France, five centuries ago, in which he had a "big purpose," in comparison with the new St. Louis' big purpose in the founding of a great city.

---

the city respected his wish.

Officially Lindbergh and his crew had been offered a suite of rooms at the Hotel Statler, but he chose to spend the time with his friends of the 35th. Phil Love joined him.

At this time the 35th was having their annual two-week encampment on the field, which made the situation very attractive for Lindbergh. He wanted very much to spend some time with these men, as an old friend rather than a hero, and wished to be treated like any other human being.

A roadster was waiting to drive him to the Guard camp, driven by O. E. Scott, field manager at Lambert.

The squadron's canvas tents had been pitched on a grassy plot on the north side of the air mail hangars. Soon after Lindbergh arrived at the camp, he and Love were taken to be outfitted with a fresh set of uniforms for the occasion. Now he really began to feel at home. Having been a captain there previously, now he could wear the insignia of a colonel.

The Guard men all knew of Lindbergh's penchant for humor and practical jokes, and were dedicated to having some fun with him when he came into town this time. There was frank admiration and enthusiasm in the men's eyes but none of the ecstatic adulation that was showered upon him by the general public at every place he set foot during the tour. It was, "Hello Slim. How're you feeling?" or "Say, Slim, why

don't you get into uniform?"

He went into a tent to change into his colonel's uniform. It would be the first time he wore the eagles on his shoulder straps, but it failed to awe his friends.

After some photographs were taken of him and Love and the others, one of them said, "Slim, we're going to give you a ducking. You can come along peacefully or you can put up an argument and we'll carry you," which was a language he certainly understood. "I'll come along, but will not be responsible for what happens," he said.

His friends led him toward the hangar, and after arriving proceeded to perform the rite of getting his head wet. Master Sgt. Joe Wecker shoved the flyer's head under the water of a brimming rain barrel. The others held his hands and feet. The flyer came up sputtering, darted over to a bucket that was nearby, dipped up some water from the barrel and single-handedly routed the squadron. The fun had started. It became an old-fashioned rough-house. All this ended with Lindbergh seriously drenched which forced him to change back into civilian clothes. Many of his friends had to make their own clothes changes as well.

When asked what he wished to have for the evening meal, he said, "Anything but chicken; that's all I have had for the past two months." The cooks at the encampment worked up an elaborate menu for that first evening mess to show their respect for what the flyer had accomplished. The main meal was based around roast beef. The meal was held outside, around a U-shaped outdoor table. Lindbergh and his buddies were served roast beef, corn on the cob, potatoes, tomatoes and other foods of his choice.

There was no formal ceremony except for a small presentation of a silver and gold trophy to him by Master Sgt. Joseph Wecker, President of the 35th Division Air Corps Flying Club. This was to commemorate his trans-Atlantic flight. At this time he was requested to give a short speech.

"I haven't had time to think about a speech; I always talk about commercial aviation, but that won't work here. All I can say is that it's good to be back. I'd like to be back here for a couple of weeks. There are a couple of reasons why." He grinned at the ring leaders in the ducking episode earlier that afternoon.

Soon Lindbergh and Love got into some storytelling, with threats to pour more water on the other one if a certain story was told. Love had filled up three or four glasses of water in preparation for the duel.

Eventually Major Wassell "officially" signified that the supper was over. Two of the officers and Lindbergh took off for a short drive around the area and came back to spend what was left of the evening "hangar flying" with his flying friends.

Lindbergh spent that first night in one of these tents, and was perfectly content to do so, which is not surprising considering his background and interest in the outdoors.

The next day Lindbergh spent most of the time relaxing with his flying crew and squadron friends. He did attend a luncheon at the Hotel Statler. The luncheon was sponsored by

Lindbergh is shown standing next to Maj. C. Ray Wassell in the National Guard hangar at Lambert Field. PIERCE W. HANGE COLLECTION VIA MISSOURI HISTORICAL SOCIETY

the St. Louis Chamber of Commerce. In the audience were one hundred executives of St. Louis civic organizations and people from the Chambers of Commerce of many neighboring communities. They included Mayor Neun; Harold M. Bixby, President of the Chamber; and Carl F. G. Meyer, former Chamber President.

Lindbergh was requested to give a talk. He urged St. Louis to act soon to become a center of air travel and development. He said that here was an ideal stop on the proposed airway between New York and Los Angeles.

He continued,

"In the tour that I am making, under the auspices of the Guggenheim Fund for

The NYP at Lambert Field. Notice Louie's lunch shack and air mail planes in background, August 15th. PIERCE W. HANGE COLLECTION VIA MISSOURI HISTORICAL SOCIETY

Lindbergh with Maj. Phil Love, Capt. Russell Young, Brig Fen. Wm. A Raupp, Lt. Johanpeter, Lt. George Stumpf, Capt. Wm. Robertson and Maj. Ray Wassell, all members of the Missouri National Guard's 110th Observation Squadron, 35th Division. JIM D. LAURO VIA BOB BAILEY

the Promotion of Aeronautics, I have observed that every city is interested in making itself a flying center. None seems to realize, however, that it must get to work at once. Many cities once had the chance to be what Detroit now is in the automotive industry.

"Now, however, when they see the opportunity that Detroit seized, they realize that its position as an automobile center is impregnable. So it will be with aviation. Once the city will become the great center of aviation activity and that it will remain.

"Just what that will mean I don't know. I do not think aviation will ever equal the volume of the automobile business. But I do know that it will be one of the great industries and that the city where it centers will benefit vastly.

"You can do a lot in flying with a little money. My flight to Paris only cost about $13,500 and yet when I was preparing for it, many business men believed $15,000 was

too small an amount. Similarly they fail to realize the great opportunity that is offered. It seems too good to be true.

"Everyone asks me what can we do to be a flying center? The answer to that is, first of all, get a good airport. Here in St. Louis you have a good field, but it should be enlarged to get the AA rating from the National Aeronautic Association.

"Most important of all now you should have a good field within twenty minutes of the downtown district."

He urged that the authorities should "enlarge Lambert and equip it until it is the equal of the finest in the country."

He was given a rousing applause and spent the rest of the day in seclusion.

Years later John W. Rawlings wrote to this author saying, "I saw Lindbergh at Lambert Field, when I was seven years old. From then on I referred to an airplane as a 'Birdcar.' In a couple of years I was building model airplanes, and

Lindbergh sitting on one of the 50-gallon drums of aviation fuel given to him by the Missouri National Guard. MISSOURI HISTORICAL SOCIETY

eventually became a pilot in the military, all because of seeing Lindbergh at a young age."

Because one of the crew had slept late on Wednesday morning, there was a rush to get cleaned up, shave, pack and get from the hotel to the airport on time for a quick departure. They were due in Kansas City by 2:00 P.M., the pre-planned ETA, across the state of Missouri.

They climbed into the assigned car and took off at a very fast pace to the airport. Along the way they were pulled over by policemen who refused to believe Phil Love's story as to who they were and why they were speeding. When the flyers displayed their baggage, some of which clearly indicated it was Lindbergh, the officers were convinced and allowed them to get going. They reached their destination on time. Lindbergh was already there at the airport waiting for them.

Soon the two airplanes took off, and Lindbergh took up a westerly heading directly to the town of Chamois, then a west-southwest heading to Jefferson City, Missouri, and from there a long leg west-northwest to Kansas City.

Lambert–St. Louis International Airport is a modern, up-to-date airport serving this Midwestern city. At an elevation of 605 feet MSL, its longest runway is 11,019 feet. The field serves most major domestic and international airlines, as well as general and corporate aviation, the National Guard and other military aircraft. It is convenient to the city as it is only ten miles northwest of the business district.

In addition there are many satellite airports around the city, some of which are Creve Coeur Airport, just west of the city on the east side of the Missouri River, catering to general aviation (antique airplanes). St. Charles Airport is northwest of the city, and north-northwest is St. Charles County Smartt Airport.

Spirit of St. Louis Airport at 463 feet MSL is located just seventeen miles west of the city, with a 7,004-foot runway. This field caters mainly to general and corporate aircraft.

Across the Mississippi River in Cahokia, Illinois, is the St. Louis Downtown–Parks Airport (home of Parks Air College) at 413 feet MSL, and a main runway of 7,000 feet.

Northeast, about four miles east of the town of Alton, Illinois, is the St. Louis Regional Airport at 544 feet MSL, its longest runway being 8,101 feet.

References

Newspapers
   The St. Louis Times
   St. Louis Globe-Democrat
   St. Louis Post-Dispatch
   The Knickerbocker Press

Organizations
   St. Louis Public Library
   Mercantile Library
   St. Louis Historical Documents Foundation, 1952
   Missouri Historical Society

People

James L. Delaney	Maria Messina
Gerald A. Geiger	Jim Buckeridge
Ann Maupin	J.W. Franke
Bob Laudeman	Walter Goyda
Mrs. James M. Edwards	
Bob Broeg	(Edna M. Polson)
Ray Turnere	Gene Prucello
L.L. "Larry" Gray	Carl Masthay
Ralph Hermon	William D. Hobbs
Sue Ann Wood	Donald Ritchie
Helen M. Volpo	
Ms. Lori Calcaterra (Parks Coll.)	

STOP #24
KANSAS CITY, MISSOURI

CAPSULE HISTORY OF CITY

This unusual city lies in two states, Missouri and Kansas, but is considered to be one city separated by a street named "State Line Road." The larger part of the Midwest city lies in Missouri. It is not confined by state boundaries. However, the two politically separate cities form the Greater Kansas City area and meld into one economic complex. It is located on the western border of Missouri at the meeting point of the Kansas (or Kaw) and Missouri rivers.

The Kansas Indians lived at this site before the arrival of white settlers. In 1821 Francois Chouteau established a trading post on the bluffs of the Missouri River. In 1838 a group of investors purchased Chouteau's Landing and named it the Town of Kansas. Later it was called Westport and Westport Landing. In 1889 the official name of the city became Kansas City.

741 feet MSL.

AUGUST 17–18, 1927
(WEDNESDAY AND THURSDAY)

In 1927 there were two airports in the Kansas City area. One was known as the old Richards Field and the other the New Richards Field.

Due to heavy rains the day before Lindbergh's expected arrival, the people in charge of the reception plans were not certain at which airport they would have him land. But as it turned out they decided on the New Richards Field. Richards Field is named after Lt. John F. Richards. It is located on a sharp curve of the Missouri River, just east of the beginning of the Kansas River. The field is known today as the Downtown Airport, located in the southwest portion of North Kansas City, Missouri.

At the time of the event, and due to the heavy rains, plans called for Lindbergh, who was notified by telegram at St. Louis, to land in the south portion of the airport, which had been physically worked over and graded with drainage ditches to run off the rain water. On the arrival day it was in that area that most of the crowds,

including the officials, were congregated, including the Fairchild and its crew. They had already landed at 1:45 P.M. Because it was early, the Fairchild was mistaken for the NYP, which was common at many stops.

Flying in from Hampton Roads, Virginia Naval Air Base, that morning to greet Lindbergh were Lt. George Cuddihy and Lt. W. C. Tomlinson. Several Army pilots came in from Fort Riley and Fort Leavenworth, Kansas. There were approximately twenty-five airplanes on the field.

Soon Lindbergh appeared coming in from the east, and as usual he descended to a low altitude to circle around the business district and other parts of the city, then over the airport.

He came down to just a few feet above the ground and did a low pass to inspect the landing surface that had been prepared for him in the south portion of the field. He did not like the looks of things, especially the soft muddy ground, and felt that if he had a flat tire or went out of control he might ground loop into the waiting crowd.

So his plan was to circle the north end of the airport and see if that looked any better. The plowed surface there was also soft, but there were fewer people in that area, so that if he went out of control there would be less chance of running into anyone.

After circling the area and making a low pass there, he came in to land at 2:15 P.M. on a section 300 feet wide and 1,500 feet long. The landing was short, but successful.

However, after he shut down the engine, he had an additional problem. There were no restraining ropes or fences, police, or other guards at this end of the field, as they were all down in the south area. He had to get out of the NYP immediately and fend off the people who rushed over to touch the airplane, possibly doing damage.

He fought off the mob with angry determination. Finally they respected his concern and did back off. He held them off until the regular security people arrived to take over and move

the airplane to the fenced-off area in the south end.

Lindbergh kept the crowd at bay by picking up from the ground a piece of lath and swinging it with a vigorousness that meant business. He did all this singlehandedly. And there the crowd stayed, in a magic circle. As one reporter put it, "It took courage to cross the Atlantic, but it took spunk of a much more warlike nature to keep that crowd at bay."

Lindbergh refused to leave the spot where he landed until arrangements were made to get the airplane to a safe location. Guards from the 110th Engineers arrived to take over the duty.

Finally Lindbergh was officially greeted by George L. Goldman, acting mayor; Judge H.F. McElroy, city manager; William E. Mortin, chairman of the dinner committee; William P. MacCracken, assistant secretary of commerce in charge of aviation; and Donald Keyhoe.

In the meantime the NYP was given a close inspection by Harold Sorenson, other mechanics, and members from the Air Corps Reserve Officers Association. The moving of the airplane to a safe place was under the direction of Sorenson. The NYP was undamaged.

It was reported that as Lindbergh was preparing to enter the official car for the parade, a mob of people had broken through the guard lines and were again headed for the airplane. In fact, several small boys made it through, grasped the struts, and swung like apes hanging by their arms as they peered into the cockpit. Soon the guards regained control and everyone was held back until the NYP was secured in the wire enclosure.

During Lindbergh's arrival at the airport there were many photographers, both press professionals as well as people with Brownie cameras. They were all clicking away one shot after another.

Lindbergh climbed into the waiting car and sat with MacCracken, Keyhoe, Goldman, McElroy, and Poindexter.

Before the parade started Lindbergh was asked to take part in the official dedication ceremony for the new Richards Field. He was introduced by George L. Goldman. The flyer then said, "I take great pleasure in dedicating this field, and I thank you." And that was that.

The parade flowed through the streets of Kansas City to Muehlebach Field, at the corner of 22nd Street and The Paseo, where the 18th Vine Historic District and the Lincoln School are. There were 10,000 people gathered, mostly children and their parents, to listen to the flyer give his talk. After he was introduced by Mr. Goldman, Lindbergh said:

"You already have air mail here. But you probably will have air mail lines running in more directions in a short time. There is a very good opportunity here also for passenger lines. Eventually there will be a line from Los Angeles to New York and that route probably will be through Kansas City and St. Louis.

"In closing I want to thank you for your attention. I hope that you, as citizens of Kansas City, will see to it in the future that you patronize air activities, such as the air mail, and passenger service when it comes, as you have done in the past—with the greatest interest."

After that ceremony, the parade proceeded into town to the Hotel Muehlebach, where Lindbergh met briefly with the local press.

Just before he met with the press Lindbergh felt that he and Love needed a haircut. The barber was E. H. Smitherman who had his shop at the Hotel Muehlebach. He was asked to come up to the suite to cut their hair. Lindbergh said to the barber that he would like a trim and for him to use clippers at the edges. The barber asked him if he liked Paris, and Lindbergh said, "Lovely city." "Like it there?" asked the barber. "No, sure glad to get home," said the flyer.

Following the press interview he and his crew adjourned to the Hotel's presidential suite on the third floor. When the flyers were shown to their suite, they were too hungry to wait for the banquet dinner, so a light meal was served to them. They had not eaten since early that morning.

That evening the banquet was held on the roof garden of the Hotel President. Only men were allowed to attend. There were about 530 men present. The weather was favorable for the outdoor event.

At the head table Lindbergh sat with Governor Paulen, William MacCracken, Keyhoe, and H. F. McElroy. Rev. Roy Rutherford returned thanks for the food.

William MacCracken was the first speaker.

"The aeronautical fraternity, the people of America, the world, in fact, appreciate mightily the achievements of this young man. They honor him for his flight from New York to Paris, but they honor him even more for his conduct since that flight.

"If Kansas City wishes to express its admiration for our hero it can do it best by acquiring in fee simple the new Richards Airport and making it the best in the country. Then patronize the air mail and develop all the phases of commercial aeronautics. If Kansas City wishes to further express its admiration it behooves every person to make this airport a reality that never can be taken away. Colonel Lindbergh's dedication is a

prepared for him, if the wind was all right.)

"Less than six months ago I was working on a survey of the possibility of an air passenger route from St. Louis to Kansas City. I found it would take about two and one half hours to make the flight, but that it would require two hours more for passengers to go to and from the airports of those cities.

"Kansas City has done away with half of that problem by establishing a new airport five minutes from the heart of the city. That begins to make the route probable, whereas six months ago it was doubtful. You may find parallel cases in other cities contemplating air routes."

Rare photo of the NYP at Kansas City. It is sitting in some soft ground on New Richards Field.
R.G.MOULTON OF ENGLAND

wonderful start toward this end."

Lindbergh was finally introduced.

"Let me make myself clear why I did not land on the runway at the field. Due to the newness of the field causing the soft runway, I could not take a chance of landing there. Had my landing gear plowed into the soft ground, or a tire blown out, the ship might have swerved into the crowd. After looking over the airport, I felt it was safer to land on the north part of the field. (He planned to take off on the runway that was

He continued to explain the future plans and possibilities of commercial aviation and passenger services that would be possible for Kansas City and the surrounding area.

At the end of his talk he said,

"In closing, I want to thank you, as citizens of Kansas City, for the interest you have tonight. In the future I wish you would devote that interest to the development of commercial aviation."

Lindbergh's speech was recorded by radio station WOQ. A year later Lou Holland learned of the recording, and Lindbergh was now head of a technical committee to select a headquarters for Transcontinental and Air Transport. Holland played the recording to Lindbergh. After listening to his own speech, he persuaded the committee to agree on Kansas City as the headquarters for the airline, later to be known as TWA, Trans World Airlines.

Sometime during his stay in Kansas City, Lindbergh had an opportunity to visit with some of his flying friends and do some "hangar flying" or shop talk. Thomas P. Nelson, a National Air Transport pilot who formerly flew the air mail with Lindbergh, was there, as well as the well-known John T. "Tex" LaGrone, another flyer known to the aviation fraternity. They talked about flying people and different types of airplanes. Lindbergh discussed taking Henry Ford in the NYP for his first plane ride. They apparently had "a grand old time."

The next morning, the 18th, Lindbergh took off from Richards Field at 10:46 A.M. Then the Fairchild, with Governor Paulen as its passenger on his first airplane ride, and Keyhoe and Sorenson took off and headed for Wichita. Lindbergh headed south-southwest to Osawatomie, then south-southeast to Fort Scott, and from there south-southwest to Girard.

While flying over Girard, the Crawford County Fair was in progress. He came in from the east, circling the town square and coming over the county courthouse. At this point he dropped the canvas bag message. After Girard Lindbergh flew west-northwest to Chanute, and from there directly west to Wichita.

On this same day (the 18th), Jack Dempsey had lost his heavyweight boxing title to Gene Tunney at Philadelphia a year before and had gone into training for a September 22 rematch.

Babe Ruth and his New York Yankee teammate, Lou Gehrig, had each hit 38 home runs for the season, and it appeared unlikely that the Sultan of Swat would equal his record of 59 home runs in the 1921 season.

The airport that Lindbergh landed on at Kansas City is still there, and is known today as the Kansas City Downtown Airport. It is at an elevation of 759 feet MSL. Its longest runway is 7,001 feet. It caters mainly to general aviation.

Today the main airport for the city is the Kansas City International Airport. It is located 15 miles northwest of the business district, at an elevation of 1,026 feet MSL and has parallel runways, the longer being 10,801 feet. It services all of the major domestic and international airlines, and some commuter, military, and general aviation aircraft.

References

Newspapers
Kansas City Journal
Kansas City Star
Kansas City Times

Organizations
Kansas City Public Library
Frontiers of Flight Museum, Dallas, Texas

People
Lynn Wendl   John D. Milbourn
Perry McCormick   D. Carpenter
R.G. Moulton (England)

Stop #25

Wichita, Kansas

Capsule History of City

Wichita, Kansas, can be found in the south-central area of the state, where the Little Arkansas and Arkansas Rivers meet.

The first people known to live in the area were the Wichita Indians. In 1864 James Mead and Jesse Chisholm established a trading post on the site. In the early years Wichita was known *as a real cowboy town. Legendary American pioneers drove Texas Longhorn cattle along the Chisholm Trail, fattened them on Kansas grass, and then shipped the animals from Wichita to distant markets.*

White men settled about 1870 when they incorporated the place as a town. The city received its charter in 1886.

1,300 feet MSL.

AUGUST 18-19, 1927
(THURSDAY AND FRIDAY)

Wichita is sometimes referred to as the air capital of the world. In fact it is only one of many other air capitals of the world. Pioneers in the aviation manufacturing industry in Wichita were Clyde V. Cessna, Walter H. Beech, and Lloyd C. Stearman. Today Cessna and Beechcraft are two of the largest American producers of light aircraft, besides Piper in Florida, formerly of Pennsylvania.

In 1927 the city had its own airport, which was located east of the downtown area, on the south side of Central Avenue. It was owned and operated by the Swallow Airplane Mfg. Co. Both the Swallow Airplane factory and the Travel Air Mfg. Company were right on the field. The airport consisted of a large open rectangular field. Aircraft could land in any direction, depending on the wind.

With thousands of people all around the landing field, the very first airplane to appear as the hour neared for Lindbergh's arrival was the Fairchild. The big airplane landed at 1:30 P.M. to prepare the welcoming committee and others involved with the event.

The five-passenger Fairchild had on board the Governor, Ben S. Paulsen, on his first airplane ride, along with pilot Love, Donald Keyhoe, and Ted Sorenson. Due to the extra person on board and to save weight, Lindbergh's "complimentary baggage" was shipped from Kansas City via a National Air Transport mail plane, flown by George Grogran. It was the wardrobe of the tour party, consisting of long leather covered bags, from the top of which peeked the hooks of coat hangars, plus other suitcases and portfolios. The air mail was extremely light on this flight.

The Wichita committee was instructed to keep the field clear. There should not be any other aircraft in the air over the field during the arrival of Lindbergh in the NYP.

Mrs. Paulsen, the Governor's wife, who had arrived the night before, was on the field and, looking up, said, "There he comes. There's Lindbergh," as he was sighted coming in from the east.

Shortly the NYP circled over the business district a few times, then flew over the airport, did a low pass, and came around for a three-point landing.

As he climbed out of the cockpit, Lindbergh's first words were, "Keep that crowd back," to George Comstock, airport manager of National Air Transport, who was the first to greet him. He had taxied up close to the TAT hangar, where the NYP would be put in overnight. He followed closely as the mechanics put the plane in the hangar.

In a few minutes J. H. Turner and Governor and Mrs. Paulen welcomed the flyer to Wichita. Then they climbed into a waiting car for the parade. Lindbergh sat in the rear with Mayor A. J. Coombs, the Governor, Mrs. Paulen behind her husband, and Lindbergh.

The parade made its way along Central Avenue to Riverside Park, where about 20,000 people were already jammed into every available space to greet the NYP pilot and to hear his speech.

The first to address the crowd was Col. H. G. O'Dell, who then introduced Mayor Coombs. The mayor gave a short address and then turned the microphone over to Harrison Albright, who spoke about his experience of being in Europe at the time of Lindbergh's arrival in Paris.

Then Mayor Coombs introduced the Governor, who expressed his appreciation for Lindbergh's kindness in seeing that he had a ride in the Fairchild from Kansas City to Wichita. The governor also said that he was proud of Kansas on this occasion and proud of Wichita because this city had contributed so much to aviation. Then he introduced Lindbergh.

The flyer said that he knew Wichita, as every aviator of the time did. He wasted no time on nonessentials. He knew he was in an aviation town and there was no need to plead for support of the cause. "The people of this city have shown, as have very few cities, that they are extremely interested in aviation. They always have followed its history. Therefore I am not going to talk to you about its development or much about its possibilities."

He did go into other details of the development of commercial aviation and its needs, and in closing said, "You are fortunately situated here in the center of the country. Air lines must come to you. From the Atlantic to the Pacific coast. From the Gulf to Canada they will pass through here.

"It is not necessary for me to talk to you about

patronizing aviation. Wichita has shown it is alive to its opportunities in this respect. I can only thank you and hope that in the future you will show even more interest."

Because there were so many children in the park, it was the appropriate time to honor the winner of a model airplane contest sponsored by the *Wichita Eagle* newspaper. The winner was Paul Eugene Zeigler. Lindbergh himself made the presentation and autographed the model of that famous Travel Air monoplane, the "Woolaroc," which was flown by Arthur Goebel to Hawaii.

After the ceremonies at the park, Lindbergh was driven to the Hotel Lassen, where he was given a suite of rooms for himself and his crew. He met briefly with the local press.

In the evening he attended the banquet on the mezzanine floor, which was sponsored by the Wichita chapter of the National Aeronautic Association and the Wichita Flying Club. There were 600 guests at the banquet. Lindbergh was introduced by J. H. Turner, who was also chairman of the Aviation Committee of the Chamber of Commerce. Lindbergh gave his usual commercial aviation development proposal and the importance of Wichita being a very strong part of the commercial aviation system in the country.

The next morning an escort of motorcycle police accompanied the cars, driven by J. H. Turner and L. S. Seymour, taking the tour party to the airport.

After taking off, Lindbergh circled the airport and the city, headed north-northeast to Junction City, and then to the Fort Riley military reservation in Kansas. After circling both of those places, he headed east-northeast to Fort Leavenworth military reservation, Kansas, which is just north of the town of Leavenworth, on the west side of the Missouri River. From there he flew north-northeast directly to St. Joseph.

While Lindbergh was in Wichita he was asked if he would like to fly several locally built airplanes, which he accepted. One was an American Eagle and the other appears to have been a Travel Air 6000 monoplane, with a Wright J-5 engine. Both flights were solo. According to his pilot log book, they were flown on August 18th for a total time of twenty minutes.

Today Wichita is still very much involved with aviation. The old Municipal Airport is in the same location, and now is occupied by Raytheon-Beech Aircraft Company. It is at an elevation of 1,273 feet MSL, with a more or less north-south runway of 8,000 feet, and caters mostly to general aviation aircraft.

Just north of Beech is the Rawdon airport. Several miles southwest of Rawdon Field is the Cessna Manufacturing Company airport at an elevation of 1,378 ft MSL and a single north-south runway of 3,873 feet.

Just south of Cessna is McConnell Air Force Base, which has the Air National Guard on the field as well as the Kansas Aviation History Museum.

Northeast of the city is Jabara Airport, and to the southwest is the new Wichita Mid-Continent Airport, at an elevation of 1,332 feet MSL, with the longer of two parallel runways being 10,200 feet. The airport serves most of the major domestic airlines, as well as commuter and general aviation.

References

Newspaper
  The Wichita Eagle

Organizations
  Wichita Public Library
  Kansas Aviation Museum
  Cessna Aircraft Company
  Beech Aircraft Corporation
  Aviation Data Service, Inc.
  Boeing Wichita

People
  Olive Ann Beech   Brett E. Lovett

Lindbergh has just arrived at the Wichita Airport on August 18. HERB HOLLINGER

Ole C. Griffith   Clarence W. Stach   Dick Wilson   Herbert Hollinger
Charles H. Crane   R. O. Wilson   Harry Adams   Dave Franson
Dorothy Dickerhoof   Robert J. Pickett   Mary Jane Townsend, M.L.S.

STOP #26
ST. JOSEPH, MISSOURI
"TOUCH STOP"

CAPSULE HISTORY OF CITY

On the east bank of the Missouri, in the northwest part of the state of Missouri is St. Joseph, fifty-five miles northwest of Kansas City. It was the home of the famous outlaw, Jesse James, and the Pony Express launched its famous mail service from this city.

In 1826 St. Joseph was founded by Joseph Robidoux, a French fur trader, and received its city charter in 1851.

800 feet MSL.

AUGUST 19, 1927 (FRIDAY)

On their way from Wichita to St. Joseph, it was noted by Donald Keyhoe in the January 1928 issue of *National Geographic* that St. Joseph was always a town that was enthusiastic in supporting aviation. He felt sorry that they could not spend more than an hour at the city.

The two airplanes had flown over the vast expanse of prairie, with its grid system, and felt quite secure that there were so many open flat fields in case of an emergency landing.

In Wichita they had been awakened at 3:30 A.M., which the crew was not happy about, in order to make the one-hour stop and then continue on to Moline, Illinois.

In 1927 St. Joseph had a landing field just west of town on the Missouri River bluffs at the foot of Chestnut Street near Wyeth Hill. Interstate 229 runs through the property today, where the field is bordered by County Road 00. The airport was named Rosencrans Field, after Guy Rosencrans, killed in France in World War I.

Lindbergh was expected to land at St. Joseph at 10 A.M., but actually set the NYP down at 9:30. He was welcomed to the city by Mayor Louis V. Stigall, National Guard officers, including Cols. William E. Stringfellow, Joseph A. Corby, John D. McNeely and Capt. Max Habeker. Also in the welcoming party were L. B. Clough, manager of the local Chamber of Commerce, and Mr. and Mrs. W. H. Rosencrans and their granddaughter Helen Dittemore of Kansas City.

Five-year-old Walter Drannan remembered years later that the weather was quite hot that morning. The main hangar was located at the north end of the field just across the road from Texter's General Store. "Most of the folks in our neighborhood walked down Chestnut Street and around the bend to Texter's store and indulged in a bottle of soda, an extravagance in those days. Then they followed the gravel road east across the railroad tracks and up the hill to where it petered out as a cow path trailing along the crest."

It was a dramatic moment as Lindbergh came into view. Children shrieked, women suppressed sobs, and men felt a surge of pride in their breasts as the NYP landed.

Lindbergh was ushered into a Lincoln car and was driven all around the airport so the 20,000 people could see him, then was escorted up to a quickly made stand to speak very briefly over radio station KFEQ over remote radio equipment made possible by the Gazette newspaper.

He explained the purpose of the tour which was to promote aviation throughout the country and went on to say, "It makes very little sense to fly for two hours from one city to another and then fly for another two hours to find a place to land." He congratulated the city for the airfield he had just landed on. Mr. Clough presented Lindbergh with a wooden model of the NYP that had been hand-carved from wood taken from the Pony Express Stables, located at

10th and Penn.

Joseph Gibson, then six and a half years old and very small, remembered, "We lived on the north side of the 'old car barns,' and my mother and I walked all the way to the airport from there."

Local airplane designer George A. McClennan had built a new airplane at Rosecrans Field and asked Lindbergh if he would like to fly her. It was a biplane named the "Bird Wing" and was powered by a Curtiss OX-5 90-hp water-cooled engine. Lindbergh took it up for a few minutes and after landing complimented McClennan on the airplane's easy handling characteristics. Shortly he took McClennan and flying enthusiast Carl Wolfley up for a local ride.

Promptly at 10:30 A.M. he and the Fairchild took off for Moline, Illinois.

Today St. Joseph is served by a large, modern airport, Rosecrans Memorial, located across the Missouri River about three miles northwest of the city in Buchanan County, Kansas. The airport is at an elevation of 826 feet MSL and has two runways, one of which is 8,059 feet in length. The airport serves mainly general aviation and aircraft of the Air National Guard.

References

Newspapers
   St., Joseph, Missouri Gazette
   St. Joseph News Press

Organizations
   St. Joseph Area Chamber of Commerce
   Patee House Museum
People

Gary Chilcote	Mrs. Ellen Jones
Shirley S. Hatfield	Walter Drannan
Joseph M. Gibson	Fred Canfield
Jack D. Magee	Bob Laudeman

The NYP shown on Rosencrans Field at St. Joseph, Missouri, August 19th. PATEE HOUSE MUSEUM

From left to right: J.D. McNeely, W.E. Stringfellow, Lindbergh and J.A. Corby, the committee that received the flyer for the short visit. SHIRLEY S. HATFIELD

Lindbergh and Stearman company officers, left to right: Deed Levy, Lindbergh, Walter Innes and Earl Schaefer. All of the men were National Guard colonels. Could that be the "Bird Wing" Lindbergh test flew? HERB HOLLINGER

STOP #27
MOLINE, ILLINOIS

CAPSULE HISTORY OF CITY

Often referred to as the "Plow City," Moline is located on the Mississippi River, adjacent to Rock Island and East Moline, Illinois, opposite Davenport, Iowa. These unique communities are known collectively as the Quad Cities, which united the states of Iowa and Illinois along the great river. All are linked by several bridges. Moline is 150 miles from Chicago.

The name Moline is from the French word moulin (or the Spanish word molino), meaning mill, probably suggested by the water power of the Mississippi River. The city is of Belgian ancestry. It was laid out in 1843, and four years later John Deere located his plow factory there. 585 feet MSL.

AUGUST 19–20, 1927
(FRIDAY AND SATURDAY)

On their way to Moline, the tour party flew over Ottumwa and Muscatine, Iowa. Early that morning hundreds of people streamed on to the airport to have a good viewing spot for Lindbergh's arrival. In addition, many airplanes flew in from miles around. There were already locally based airplanes of the Campbell-DeSchepper Company parked on the grass. Scores of people arrived on the roads in automobiles, bicycles, and walking. Soldiers from the Rock Island arsenal were stationed early on the field to be ready to guard the two airplanes during the visit.

Lindbergh came into view and landed at 2:03 P.M. on part of the present-day site of the Quad City International Airport. It is just south of the Rock River, south of Moline. The Fairchild had arrived at 1:30 P.M.

The original thirty acres of land was known as far back as 1919 as Franing Field. Later it had one hangar owned and operated by N.A.T. (National Air Transport, Inc.). That original site is located on the northeast corner of the present airport, close to the curve of 27th and 1st Avenue. It is off the end of Runway 23, between the runway and the curve of the road.

Lindbergh immediately taxied the NYP into the N.A.T. hangar, where it was roped off to protect it from the crowds. It was put on display there all Friday afternoon so streams of people could pass by, take pictures, and view the airplane.

Kenneth Lee, a retired instrument maker at AMETEK in East Moline, then a pilot, recalled the mechanics had removed the cowling of the NYP for some reason, possibly to check the oil and other mechanical details.

After securing the airplanes, Lindbergh was ushered into a waiting Packard Phaeton automobile to begin the parade into town. He was first welcomed by U.S. Army Col. D. M. King, Commanding Officer of the Rock Island Arsenal, whom he sat next to in the car. The Fairchild had arrived at 1:30 P.M.

The parade proceeded through East Moline, Moline, Rock Island and Davenport, Iowa, across the Mississippi River. A newspaper article stated, "Never since the signing of the Armistice had such a crowd turned out and shown more signs of irrepressibility. As Lindbergh proceeded slowly through the streets the welcome accorded him in each of the cities grew in intensity."

The parade proceeded to the Rock Island Arsenal where Lindbergh expected to meet with the press and then relax before the evening banquet. The six P.M. banquet took place at the Rock Island Arsenal Mess Hall and was attended by over 1,400 people. He was welcomed by Mayor John H. Siefken of East Moline, Moline Mayor

The NYP in the hangar at what was known then as Franing Field. DR. WARREN STREED

Claude W. Sandstrom, Rock Island Mayor Chester C. Thompson, and Mayor Louis E. Roddewig of Davenport, Iowa. Senator M. R. Carlson was also at the banquet as well as Augustana College of Rock Island President D. Gustav Andreen.

With great enthusiasm over the upcoming visit of Lindbergh, one East Moline resident, Leonard Saunders, decided to "re-body" his 1922 Ford Model T to look like the NYP. He was a carpenter so he took off the roadster tub, turtle deck and fenders, and replaced these components with a wood-framed airplane body. The rear of the car was covered with aluminum painted canvas. That section had a working tail assembly, which in turn was connected to the Model T's steering gear. The rudder turned as the car changed direction.

The front of the car was hand-formed of sheet steel and then painted to resemble the engine-turn Damascene that duplicated the NYP cowling. The propeller was carved from a 2-x-6-foot plank of wood. The spinner was made of an automobile headlight bucket mounted opposite its normal direction.

He built a replica Wright Whirlwind engine using parts of a Chevrolet four-cylinder, overhead valve engine, such as rocker arms and spring assemblies.

A six-foot-wide top wing was attached to the body with struts constructed of scrapped Model T Ford steering columns.

This "Spirit of Youth" aero-car had been constructed in less than two months. The NYP Model T was used in the parade, and he met

Here the NYP is shown on Franing Field. Also seen is the right wing tip of the Fairchild FC-2. DR. WARREN STREED

Lindbergh as well. The machine was driven around town for a few years until he sold it in 1929.

Lindbergh and his crew were the overnight guests of Col. And Mrs. King at their home on the arsenal island. Lindbergh occupied the bedroom in Quarters One, which today is known as the Lindbergh Room in honor of his visit.

The flyers were at the airport early on Saturday morning to preflight both airplanes. Soon they rolled out of the hangar, and preparations were made for departure.

The NYP engine was started with Lindbergh inside. Then he stepped outside for a brief conversation with Donald Keyhoe. Mr. Keyhoe relayed to *The Daily Dispatch* representative that Lindbergh would pose for one picture by the airplane, which he did. He then climbed back into the cockpit and took off at 11:30 A.M.

The Moline Quad City International Airport is still there on the same site. It is at an elevation

Lindbergh with from left to right: Col. D.M. King, Mayor John H. Siefken, Mayor Claude W. Sandstrom, Lindbergh, Mayor Louis E. Roddewig and Mayor Chester C. Thompson.
METROPOLITAN AIRPORT AUTHORITY VIA MICHAEL J. HANEY A.A.E.

of 590 feet MSL and has three runways, the longest of which is 10,002 feet. The field serves some of the domestic airlines and commuter airlines, as well as general aviation.

To the northwest, just 5 miles north of Davenport, Iowa, is the Davenport Municipal Airport, at 733 feet MSL, with two runways, the longer of which is 5,501 feet. It serves mainly general aviation in addition to military aircraft of the Air National Guard.

References

Newspaper
The Daily Dispatch, Moline

Organizations
Metropolitan Airport Authority
Moline Public Library
Moline Historical Society
Rock Island County Historical Society

People
Dr. Warren R. Streed   James Irish
Irene Christofferson   Sue Ribro
Michael J. Haney, A.A.E.

Stop #28
Milwaukee, Wisconsin

Capsule History of City

This coastal city is located in the southeast part of Wisconsin, on Lake Michigan, and is the largest city in the state. It has been known as the beer capital of the country, and lies on a bluff overlooking a crescent-shaped bay. The Kinnickinnie, Menomonee, and Milwaukee Rivers flow through the city to the bay. Milwaukee's name comes from the Milwaukee River.

The Rox, Mascouten, and Potawatomi Indians hunted in the area before the first white settlers came. The first white was Father Jacques Marquette, a French missionary, who just stopped by the site for a brief visit in 1674. A later fur trader by the name of Jacques Vieau opened a trading post there in 1795. In 1833 the town of Juneau was founded on the east side of the Milwaukee River. Milwaukee received its city charter in 1846.

635 feet MSL.

August 20–22, 1927
(Saturday through Monday)

On the way from Moline to Milwaukee, Lindbergh and the NYP flew over Dixon and Rockford, Illinois, and then Beloit, Wisconsin, before heading northeast to Milwaukee.

Shortly before Lindbergh was to arrive, the reception committee was in a quandary as to which of the two existing airports they should have him land at—Maitland Field on the lakefront (Lake Michigan) or General Mitchell Field, near the town of Cudahy. Many people, including local experienced flyers, suggested the latter because it was the local base for the air mail service and the recently inaugurated passenger air service. Some of them felt that Maitland Field was unsafe. Mitchell was about five miles south of the center of the city.

On the morning of his arrival, the weather was clear and a bit cool. At 2:00 P.M. the NYP was seen overhead and shortly Lindbergh landed at Mitchell Field and immediately taxied to the hangar where the airplane was put inside.

He was met by Mayor Daniel W. Hoan of Milwaukee, and Charles C. Younggreen, president of a Milwaukee advertising agency and a World War I aviator.

After arrangements were made for the care of the NYP and the Fairchild, Lindbergh and his party were driven in a parade into the city. They motored out of Mitchell east to Cudahy, then north via Kinnickinnic Avenue to Broadway and Clybourn Street, west on Clybourn to 26th Street and north to Wisconsin Avenue, then

east to Juneau Park on the shore of Lake Michigan, where Lindbergh was scheduled to give his usual presentation to the public.

A stand had already been erected on the Lincoln Memorial Bridge, where the official welcome was presented. Lindbergh was then introduced by Chauncey W. Yockey, a local attorney.

He said in his talk that the airplane had a definite place in the commercial life of the country and that it was possible to build commercial planes for purely commercial purposes. One of the most urgent needs was to have fields close to centers of towns similar to the one that was here under construction.

From Juneau Park the entourage made its way to the Hotel Astor, where Lindbergh remarked, "This is the most orderly reception of any I've received so far." When asked by a reporter what the average man could do to help promote aviation, Lindbergh said, "The average man can promote aviation by backing the development of air fields and by patronizing air facilities."

That evening they held a banquet attended by over 800 people. Mayor Hoan in his speech said, "Lindbergh did more for us in Europe than all of our diplomats in the last one hundred years. Personally, I'd rather have Lindbergh in the capitals of Europe tonight than all the ambassadors, all the consuls—and all the whole shootin' match."

Lindbergh in his speech said, "It has been with great satisfaction that I witnessed today how Milwaukee has connected the theme of aviation with this visit. The purpose of this tour is to promote aviation in the United States, and I feel that here it has been accomplished."

In his closing remarks he said, "In conclusion I want to thank the people of Milwaukee for the interest they have shown and sincerely hope you will continue to show this interest in aviation."

Because Sunday the 21st was the crew's day of rest at this stop, they were invited to spend some time at industrialist Clarence Falk's country estate on Green Bay Road. Others who attended were Charles Younggreen, Alderman Cornelius Corcoran, John Anderson, vice president of The Milwaukee Electric Railway and Light Company, and Stuart Auer, local realtor and World War I aviator, Lt. Albert E. Hegenberger and Lt. Lester Maitland. They did some swimming, played ball, walked on the property, and generally relaxed.

Sometime during the visit to Milwaukee, the NYP had developed a puncture in the right wheel, as shown in a photo in the author's collection. It was jacked up in front of the hangar, the wheel removed, repaired, and remounted. Richard W. Carter, now of Prescott, Arizona, recalled, "I can't tell or remember if the two fellows working (in the photo) on the wheel are taking the cover off, prior to its repair, or checking things over after I laced it back on. I have a strong hunch that I am sitting in the shade while the mechanic in coveralls is making sure I did the job right. His name, if the person shown in the coveralls was the head mechanic there, was Lester Ball. I remember him well. The one in the knickers could have been Stan LaParle, pilot."

On Monday morning, the 22nd, Lindbergh took off at 11:10 A.M. to fly to Madison, Wisconsin.

Today General Mitchell International Air-

In front of the Milwaukee County Airport hangar, three men are fixing a puncture on the NYP. LEO B. KIMBALL COLLECTION

A clear view of Lindbergh and details of the engine and cowling, etc. PHOTO BY A.F. TOEPFER VIA GEORGE HARDIE JR.

port still exists at the same location, only considerably expanded over the years. The airport is 723 feet MSL and has five runways. The longest is 9,690 feet. The field serves most all domestic airlines, some commuter airlines, general aviation, and Air National Guard aircraft.

Only 5 miles northwest is Timmerman Field, at an elevation of 745 feet MSL, with two paved runways, the longest of which is 4,107 feet. In addition there are two parallel grass runways, one for each paved one. The longer grass runway is 3,251 feet. The field is used mainly for general aviation.

References

Newspaper
The Milwaukee Journal

Organizations
Experimental Aircraft Association
Milwaukee County Historical Society
Sioux City Sunday Journal

People
George A. Hardie Jr.   Norm Petersen
William Feeny   Tom Poberezny
Don Swanson

As usual, hundreds of people gathered at the airport to welcome Lindbergh and see the NYP in the flesh. EXPERIMENTAL AIRCRAFT ASSOCIATION

STOP #29
MADISON, WISCONSIN

CAPSULE HISTORY OF CITY

Madison, Wisconsin, is the capital of the state and the second largest city in Wisconsin. It is the home of the largest campus of the University of Wisconsin and is on an isthmus between Lakes Mendota, Monona, and Wingra in the western part of the state. It is one of the country's most beautiful state capitals because of its proximity to these lakes.

Winnebago Indians lived in this area before whites. The first white was James D. Doty, a former federal judge, and Stevens T. Mason, governor of the Michigan Territory, who purchased the site in the 1830s. In 1836 the first legislature of the Wisconsin Territory made Madison the capital. The first white settlers were Eben and Rosaline Peck, who arrived from nearby Blue Mounds in 1837. They erected a

hotel for the workers who built the capitol building. The community did not exist at this time. The place functioned as a capital in 1838, was incorporated as a village in 1846, and was incorporated as a city in 1856.

The University of Wisconsin was established in 1848.

860 feet MSL.

AUGUST 22–23, 1927
(MONDAY AND TUESDAY)

On his way to Madison, Lindbergh flew over Waukesha, Fon du Lac and Oshkosh, Wisconsin, before heading southwest to the capital city. He dropped his autographed and ribboned documentary message on the town of Fon du Lac.

As he flew over Madison he circled the capi-

-119-

tol dome several times before heading south to the local airport, then known as Pennco Field— later Royal Airport—to land at 2:00 P.M. The Fairchild had already arrived at the airport at 1:36 P.M.

Lindbergh taxied the NYP up to the hangar and did not leave until it was placed inside. Because of the forty-six-foot wingspan, the airplane could not be pushed or wheeled straight into the hangar and had to be rolled several times, back and forth, in order to fit. Local Alderman Bernard Mixtacki said that the metal hangar that housed the NYP was condemned by the city of Monona years later, and it was purchased and reassembled at Truax Field by an aircraft flying school and is in use today.

Pennco Field was developed by Howard A. Morey, then chief pilot for the Madison Airways Corp. The name Pennco came from the Pennsylvania Oil Company, a Madison company that provided fuel for airplanes. The name was changed to Royal Airport when the Royal Rapid Transit Company, a bus service, decided to initiate commercial air service and advanced Howard Morey money to purchase a Travel-Aire cabin plane.

The land where Royal Airport was located is now the site of South Towne Mall parking lot and the south Beltline, routes twelve and eighteen, in the suburb of Monona. The only thing marking the location of Royal Airport now is a street in the area named Royal Avenue.

At the time of Lindbergh's visit, there was only one other airport near Madison. It was located at 2520 Coolidge Avenue, at the north end of North Street, just south of the site of the present Madison airport, near the Oscar Mayer plant. It was a separate operation and did not last very long. A housing project incorporating Myrtle Drive and Aberg Avenue (Route 30) and Shopko occupies the site today.

The city went all out to welcome the aviator and closed local businesses and city, county, and state offices to pay tribute to him.

After the airplane was secure, Lindbergh was then welcomed by the committee—Governor Fred R. Zimmerman; Glenn Frank, President of the University of Wisconsin; Mrs. Marvin B. Rosenberry, former Dean of Women at the University; and Mayor A. G. Schmedeman, chairman of the reception committee.

A motorcade, with Lindbergh in the lead open car, made its way around Lake Monona to Atwood Avenue, up East Washington Avenue to Capital Square, and then out to Camp Randall Stadium of the University of Wisconsin.

Upon reaching the stadium Lindbergh was escorted to the speaker's stand by Burr W. Jones, former Chief Justice of the State Supreme Court.

In his presentation Lindbergh stressed the importance of establishing a new airport for the

An excellent and rare photo of the NYP in the hangar at the old Royal Airport, known then as Pennco Field, August 22nd. PHOTO BY HOWARD MOREY COURTESY FIELD MOREY

capital city. He continued with the state of air travel and aviation in general around the country, noting, for example, business advantages in having an up-to-date and modern airport there in Madison.

From the stadium the parade made its way to the Memorial Union Building, where Lindbergh placed a wreath. He and his crew were taken to the Hotel Loraine, where he was interviewed by the press and given a chance to rest before the evening festivities.

Over one thousand businessmen attended the six o'clock banquet, held at the local Masonic Temple. Col. J. W. "Bud" Jackson presided. Speakers were the Honorable Robert M. LaFollette Jr., United States Senator; Major Alvin C. Reis, Assemblyman, Madison District; Carl A. Johnson, President of the Gisholt Machine Company, and Lindbergh.

In his address Lindbergh again stressed the importance of more airports in the state and went on to say that America has lagged behind Europe in the development of aviation and commercial air travel. He said, "Following the war the balance in American aviation was still largely military and it was necessary for the government to subsidize the construction of planes for commercial use, but today the institution is soundly established on its own feet."

"Madison must not be lax," said Col. Jackson, "We ought to take some positive step right here and now to start our commercial aviation program."

Lindbergh had said, "I hope you will devote part of your time in the future to what will be and what is rapidly becoming one of the world's greatest industries. The development of commercial aeronautics will be very rapid from now on."

About 1928 the committee arranged for the city to purchase a large marsh off Packers Avenue to build a newer airport to serve the city. The development of the site did not take place for some time, partly due to financial difficulties due to the Depression. It was owned by the Raemisch family, who rented it to local farmers.

However in 1933 as part of the federal gov-ernment subsidies in the early days of the Roosevelt administration, money for the development of the airport became available. Howard Morey was hired by the city to organize the project and become its first manager. In the 1930s Northwest Airlines operated in and out of the field, and in 1942, with the country at war, the airport was taken over by the military and named Truax Field.

It is presently known as Dane County Regional Airport. It is at an elevation of 887 ft MSL and has three runways, the longest one being 9,005 feet. Most major domestic airlines and some commuter airlines operate in and out of the field as well as general aviation and the Air National Guard.

Sometime after World War II, Howard Morey opened his own airport, Morey Field, in the town of Middleton, and it is still there on Airport Road. It is at an elevation of 926 ft MSL, and has a single paved runway of 2,971 feet and two grass cross runways. It is a general aviation airport, and is 5 miles northwest of the city. It was recently purchased by the city of Middleton which was planning to do some improvements.

Ten miles east of the city along Interstate 94 is the Blackhawk Airport, which serves general aviation. At 920 feet MSL, it has two runways, the longer of which is 2,953 feet.

About twelve miles northwest of the city is Waunakee Airport, at an elevation of 950 feet MSL, with a single runway of 2,230 feet. It is a residential general aviation community.

According to the St. Louis Chamber of Commerce, sometime during Lindbergh's Madison stay it was reported in the local paper that 34,000 people throughout the United States had already received an autographed photo of Lindbergh and the NYP. These photographs, produced in quantity through the courtesy of the Daniel Guggenheim Fund for the Promotion of Aeronautics, were sent by air mail to these people. They were persons who wrote their request and sent it by air mail to Col. Lindbergh, care of the St. Louis Chamber of Commerce with a ten-cent stamp for return air mail.

Lindbergh When A Student at University of Wisconsin

Charles Lindbergh and his mother, Evangeline, rented an apartment on the top floor of a three-story house at 33-35 North Mills Street. Since then the interior has been extensively re-modeled, but the exterior of the house still appears much like it did in 1921. He also lived for a short time in a basement apartment of a house at 1803 Vilas Avenue belonging to E.C. Smith at that time.

While at the university he studied chemistry, engineering, drawing, English, mathematics and shop. He was also enrolled in physical education and ROTC military drill. He became the best shot on the ROTC rifle team. His grades were below average, and he was "encouraged" to withdraw.

Personal Recollections

B. Arden Taylor:

"I was fourteen years old when Lindbergh flew into Madison. My father had a Model T Ford sedan that I borrowed to drive out to the airport. I drove on a one-lane cement road around Lake Monona. The NYP was immediately wheeled into a metal hangar at the west end of the field. I was able to position myself in front of a small window on the north side of the hangar. From there I got an excellent view of the airplane.

"The traffic jam on the way home was so great that the old Model T boiled over, but we finally made it anyway."

Joseph Masino:

"I was one of five Boy Scouts who were assigned to guard the airplane and work at the airport during the visit. I was thirteen years old. We stood at attention and saluted as he came by and shook each of our hands. It was a big thrill for us." He said the NYP came in from the northeast.

Vincent L. Esser:

"The citizens really got excited that Lindbergh was coming to Madison. My father worked at a large company here and the plant closed down so people could go to the Royal Airport to see him.

"When the day came my father drove Mother, brother Ken, and myself out to the airport in our 1925 four door Chevrolet to watch.

"There was a huge crowd standing all around the field's edge and waiting. Finally someone with good eyes shouted, 'There it is!' and soon that little plane came into view for all to see. It landed and taxied up to the hangar area. Everyone watched as he got out and strolled up to the welcoming committee to shake hands. I wasn't more than fifteen feet away from him as he passed by in the car later. Wow, was I impressed that I had gotten so close. It truly made my day."

After spending the night at the Hotel Loraine, the tour crew was out at the field early, preflighting both airplanes. (Today the Lorraine Hotel is a state office building.)

Before Lindbergh left he mentioned, "Madison certainly was 100 per cent. I appreciated very greatly what the people here have done for me."

There were about 2,000 people at the airport to witness his 10:10 Tuesday morning departure for Minneapolis.

On his way he flew over Portage and La Crosse, Wisconsin, and Winona and Red Wing, Minnesota. He was to drop his messages on these towns.

When Lindbergh flew over LaCrosse, Wisconsin, his route called for circling the town. Robert J. Swennes recalled, "My friend Norm and I posted ourselves where we had a clear, unobstructed view, listening intently, scanning the horizon with concentration we waited for what seemed hours, hoping to get a glimpse of the airplane. Then suddenly there it was, low and near enough for us to see Lindbergh at the controls. We jumped up and down waving as hard as we could, filled with excitement. "Does he see us?" one of us asked, and then we saw him wave back. We were sure it was for us alone, maybe it was, and nothing our parents said could discourage that interpretation. There were many influences in my life in the years that followed, but it was at that moment I promised myself that someday I would be a pilot."

References

Newspapers

Wisconsin State Journal
The Capital Times
The Community Herald, Monona, Wisconsin

Organizations

State Historical Society of Wisconsin
University of Wisconsin, Madison Archives
Madison Area Technical College
Minnesota Historical Society
Rock County Historical Society
Trachte Building Systems, Inc.
Historic Madison, Inc. – Thomas D. Brock,
Editor

People

William D. Feeny	Thomas D. Brock
Field Morey	Martin Robbins
Joy Bartol-Snyder	B. Arden Taylor
Orton E. Martinson	Mayor Paul R. Soglin
Sandy L. Kampen	Gregory Lehman
Maurice J. Montgomery	Dr. Glenn Frank
Barnard Schermetzler	Steve Stucynski
J. Frank Cook	C. P. Montgomery
Lois Wuilleumier	David Benjamin
Joseph Masino	Bernice Woll
Barnard Mixtacki	Dr. T. W. Tormey Jr.
Dale Thompson	Mrs. Jean A. Dollard
William F. Steuber	Dorothy Swennes
S. R. Stroud, Atty.	Vincent L. Esser
Halsie J. Taylor	Walter A. Ftautschi
Dorothy S. Lamm	Abigail Curkeet
Bruce Baldwin Mohs	Lisa Spencer
Sequel C. "Duke" Johnson	

STOP #30
MINNEAPOLIS AND ST. PAUL, MINNESOTA

CAPSULE HISTORY OF CITY

The largest city in Minnesota is Minneapolis, located on the west side of the Mississippi River and across from the city of St. Paul, the state capital, on the east side of the long river. It is also the home of the University of Minnesota, one of the largest in the country. The two cities are often referred to as the "Twin Cities."

The name Minneapolis comes from the Indian word minne, which means water, and the Greek word polis, which means city. This name was derived because of the twenty-two natural lakes that lie within the city limits. It has the nickname "City of Lakes."

Apparently, the first people on the site were the Sioux Indians who farmed and hunted there. A Belgian explorer and missionary named Louis Hennepin was the first white man to visit in 1680. This great city changed its name from All Saints to Minneapolis in 1852 and received its city charter in 1866.

St. Paul, the capital, was first known as a settlement with the name "Pig's Eye." Led by a wild French-Canadian whiskey trader, Pierre

"Pig's Eye" Parrent and a motley group of undaunted squatters moved to a river landing near Fort Snelling, giving the new settlement its unusual name. The name lasted until Father Lucien Galtier erected a log chapel to his patron saint, St. Paul, and persuaded the local people to rename the town for this more subdued personage. Sioux Indians were the first people there, also, and the city was incorporated in 1849 and received its charter in 1854.

Minneapolis 840 feet MSL; St. Paul 780 feet MSL.

AUGUST 23–25, 1927
(TUESDAY THROUGH THURSDAY)

Winona was the first town in Minnesota to receive the message dropped from the NYP, and it was during the last of several passes over the city, on his way to Minneapolis, when Lindbergh released a canvas bag with a bright orange streamer. There was a scramble to be the first to pick up the item and read the message. It was known that each greeting was autographed by the flyer.

At 12:50 P.M., only a little over an hour away from the Twin Cities, the people of Red Wing gave Lindbergh a hearty welcome by ringing the fire bell and shrieking the industrial whistles. People were on top of many buildings in the town and on the roof of the local newspaper. On the *Republican* building a white "R" had been painted for identification in keeping with pre-arrangements by the Guggenheim Fund. It advocated that communities mark their names or initials on roofs to assist aviators who might otherwise be forced to fly low enough to read railroad station signboards. After circling the town for ten minutes or so, Lindbergh continued on the old air mail route toward the Twin Cities.

At 1:34 P.M. he was sighted over the St. Paul Municipal Airport (Holman Field, presently St. Paul Downtown Airport). He circled and then passed over the area and proceeded to Wold-Chamberlain Field at Minneapolis, where he landed at 2:03 P.M.

Lindbergh was supposed to land and taxi to the 109th Aero Squadron Air Guard hangars. In spite of police patrol in the airport area, the crowd of over 20,000 people broke the lines to rush out onto the field after he landed. Because of this mass of people, he made a right turn and taxied over to the air mail hangar in the middle of the field, where the NYP was immediately pushed in and the doors closed.

The confusion that all of these people created delayed the planned schedule for the parade, which did not get underway until sometime later.

Earlier that morning, at 7:15 A.M., Evangeline, Lindbergh's mother, had arrived at the Great Northern station aboard a train from Chicago.

Back at the airport, Lindbergh boarded a car, sharing a space with Minneapolis Mayor George E. Leach and St. Paul Mayor Lawrence C. Hodgson. In the next car were Mrs. Leach, Mrs. Hodgson, and Evangeline Lindbergh.

From the airport the parade went on 34th Avenue South to Minnehaha Parkway and then westward on the parkway to Park Avenue, Tenth Street to Nicollet Avenue, Nicollet to Second Street, to Third Avenue, and over the Third Avenue Bridge to University Avenue. In St. Paul the parade went on University Avenue to Robert Street, to Fillmore Avenue, to State Street to St. Lawrence Street and the Holman Airport. It

was 3:30 P.M. when they reached the field. There Lindbergh gave his usual presentation, stressing again the general needs and future of commercial aviation in the United States.

The flyer's official appearance in the Twin Cities ended that evening with a banquet at the Saint Paul Hotel. At that event Lindbergh was presented a commemorative medal from the state by Governor Christianson. Also that evening, in honor of Mrs. Lindbergh, a dinner was given in the Italian Room of the Hotel Radisson, at the same time as the banquet for her son in St. Paul.

Because Lindbergh was returning to his home state of Minnesota, he received "a glad and unprecedented ovation from his home community and took deep pride in what he had done," according to state historian Theodore C. Blegen.

A statement was made in the *Minnesota Journal* that "the homecoming of Colonel Lindbergh to the soil of Minnesota is an affair of the heart." He was even referred to as the "blond Viking of the air." Someone suggested that the state be renamed Lindberghia and that Lindbergh be made head of a "Boy's Aviator" movement. To the Minnesota press Lindbergh was a "world air hero," an "intrepid flier," and "a gallant and sensible young man."

The *St. Cloud Daily Times* stated that Lindbergh received a greater reception than any plaudit accorded a victorious Roman general. And a *St. Paul Pioneer Press* editorial writer concluded that "for once the world stopped its quarrelling and united for a moment to applaud a young man who had accomplished a feat of outstanding and extraordinary heroism."

Because of the constant demands on his time at each of the stops, Lindbergh found that time in the air between stops was the most restful. He often flew long detours in order to add to that time alone.

As was customary during the tour, the group would set aside two days out of each seven for rest and recuperation. So the 24th was a rest day. Lindbergh was hoping to spend considerable time with his mother and half-sister, Mrs. Eva Lindbergh Christie, or other relatives who had come there especially for that purpose.

Charles and Evangeline were able to spend a few hours at the Lowry Hotel in St. Paul, where he was staying. She drove over from her own

A good aerial view of Wold-Chamberlain, as the crowd waited for Lindbergh's arrival. Notice the Fairchild FC-2 is already there, in front of the open hangar door. MINNEAPOLIS PUBLIC LIBRARY

hotel, the Radisson in Minneapolis.

WHEELS STORY

Also on the 24th a major change took place on the NYP. Lindbergh had decided to have the original 32" x 4" wheels and tires changed to 30" x 5" ones. This was to give good handling and support on muddy and soft sod-type landing fields during the tour, as he was flying into many unimproved airports or cow pastures.

The work was accomplished at one of the Air Guard hangars at Wold-Chamberlain by a mechanic from the 109th Observation Squadron of the 34th Division of the Minnesota National Guard named Harry A. Hansen. He was a mechanic with the Base Detachment of the 109th. In a letter to the author dated January 15, 1976, he stated that the wheels were replaced as a safety precaution.

Hansen took possession of the original

wheels "until such time as the Colonel requested their disposition." In a letter dated March 28, 1928, to Lindbergh from Hansen, he stated that inasmuch as it seemed to lay claim on them, he took possession the day after Lindbergh left for Little Falls. Hansen apparently kept the wheels in the supply room of the 109th. He claimed he crated the wheels and sent them to the Smithsonian in Washington, D.C. They have been in cold storage there ever since.

It also appears that Arthur G. Hallaway shipped the wheels to the Smithsonian about July 1935. In a letter written in longhand by Lindbergh to Hallaway he stated: "Dear Mr. Hallaway. I have just received your letter forwarded from the Smithsonian Institute. I want to thank you very much for shipping the wheels from the *Spirit of St. Louis* to the Smithsonian. I deeply appreciate your taking care of them for so long a time. Sincerely, Charles A. Lindbergh."

Hansen claimed that the replacement wheels

The NYP is shown in one of the hangars at Wold-Chamberlain Field, a rare photo. DONOR UNKNOWN

might have come from a Hisso powered PT-3 trainer.

While they were at Minneapolis, the Wright Corporation recalled Theodore (Ted) R. Sorenson, the engine and airframe mechanic for both airplanes. He was replaced by C. C. "Doc" Maidment, who was to take up Sorenson's responsibilities.

On Thursday morning the Fairchild with Phil Love flying was the first to take off for Little Falls. He had as his passengers Evangeline, Kehoe and Maidment. Evangeline wanted to be at the next stop for the festivities.

In the meantime Lindbergh flew in a detour that took him over Savage, Shakopee, St. Cloud, Melrose, and Sauk Centre, Minnesota, all quite familiar places to him as he was growing up and during his barnstorming days.

MINNEAPOLIS–ST. PAUL AIRPORTS

In 1915 the Twin Cities Motor Club built a two-and-a-quarter-mile auto speedway in the area of what is now Minneapolis St. Paul International Airport. The concrete racetrack was not very successful and soon closed. In 1920 the Aero Club of Minneapolis leased the land, and the dirt area in the center of the track became the local airport. The first hangar was built to accommodate the U.S. Air Mail service.

The field was eventually named Twin Cities Airport and then Wold-Chamberlain, to honor two men who were killed in action in France in World War I. For a time it was also known as the Minneapolis Municipal Airport.

In 1926 Northwest Airways (now Northwest Airlines) won the government contract and acquired the only hangar on the field other than the 109th Air Guard hangars. It was then known as the air mail hangar.

With a growing cargo market, the field became a major distribution center for many corporate headquarters companies with major branches here and several foreign firms.

Many airports from coast to coast rely on "MSP" as their "North Coast Gateway" to Asia and Northern Europe. There is direct service now to London, Amsterdam, Frankfurt and Tokyo, connecting to many additional destinations in Europe and Asia. According to a recent study, each new international route established means from $100 million to $300 million annually injected into the local economy.

The field is at an elevation of 841 feet MSL and has three runways, two of them parallel. The longest runway is 11,006 feet. A fourth runway is under construction. This airport is also used for general aviation and military aircraft of the Air National Guard and Air Force Reserve.

There are many satellite airports around the Minneapolis/St. Paul cities, most of which are for general aviation. Holman Field, now known as St. Paul Downtown Airport, is still there at an elevation of 705 feet MSL with three runways. The longest one is 6,711 feet. The field caters mainly to general aviation. The airport is located along the Mississippi River, just one mile south of the city.

Ten miles north of the Twin Cities, in the town of Anoka, is the Anoka County–Blaine Airport, at an elevation of 912 feet MSL, with two runways, the longer of which is 4,855 feet. It is a general aviation field, and well known for the many antique/classic airplanes based in its several museums.

References

Newspapers
    Minneapolis *Star Tribune*
    St. Paul *Pioneer Press*

Organizations
    Minneapolis Public Library
    St. Paul Public Library
    Lindbergh Foundation
    Minnesota Historical Society
    North St. Paul Museum & Historical Society
    Hennepin Historical Museum
    The Minneapolis/St. Paul International
Airport
    Minnesota Aviation Hall of Fame

Minnesota Air Guard Museum

People

Jim B. Horne	Bruce Larson
Noel Allard	Robert J. Swennes
William Halverson	Loren C. Hansen
Harry H. Hansen	Baldwin Hallaway

Bob Franklin	G. W. Christie
Liz Murphy	Charles Kapsner
Douglas H. Fredlund	Tony Bour
Wallace R. Forman	Luther Noss
Mayor Donald M. Fraser (Minn.)	
Earl J. Levens	

STOP #31
LITTLE FALLS, MINNESOTA

CAPSULE HISTORY OF CITY

The town of Little Falls is located on both shores of the Mississippi River in north-central Minnesota. It is named for the rapids that supplied power to the town's lumber, paper and flour mills.

In June of 1853 during an abnormally high flood stage the steamboat "North Star" passed over the falls on the only recorded northward journey to Itasca, Minnesota.

The town was home to Charles A. Lindbergh during most of his youth.

1,100 feet MSL.

AUGUST 25–26, 1927
(THURSDAY AND FRIDAY)

At 12:15 P.M. on his way to Little Falls, Lindbergh flew low over the town of Savage. Mayor Charles F. McCarthy said he circled the village three or four times, coming down to scarcely more than one hundred feet. He apparently dropped a message. This was the same town where he had a forced landing in 1923.

Shortly after 1:00 P.M. he circled St. Cloud, and the local paper reported that he was so low they could see the "Lone Eagle" leaning far out of his cabin waving to those in sight.

He dropped the printed promotion for commercial aviation on St. Cloud, where it landed on St. Germain Street. Then he flew west to Melrose where his grandfather, August Lindbergh, had settled in the summer of 1859, after arriving from Sweden. It was about 1:20

P.M. when he circled for a brief time over the old homestead at the western limits of the city.

Lindbergh attempted to drop the canvas bag with his message on Melrose, but the bag had snagged on the tail and never made it to the ground. Lindbergh did get the message to them when he mailed it by registered mail from his stop at Fargo, North Dakota, a few days later.

At 1:30 P.M. he appeared over Sauk Centre and dropped greetings there. Loren C. Hansen remembered her father saying that Lindbergh flew over Sauk Centre during the tour and dropped a message to the town. She has no idea where that message would be today. Then he headed for Little Falls.

Because he had grown up there, Little Falls would be a special stop for the flyer. It would be very special for the town as well. In fact, it would be the most memorable day in Little Falls history.

For weeks their "Homecoming Committee" and the whole town prepared for his visit. One of their newspapers had printed that the visit "was more important than one from the President of the United States."

The old family car, a 1916 Saxon, which had been driven by Lindbergh often, was found rusting away. It was fixed up and displayed as one of their prized possessions. The media went all

The NYP is shown parked on the Jacob Brutcher farm on the north side of town. CHARLES A. LINDBERGH HOUSE

out in their coverage of this event.

Well-known flyer Charles "Speed" Holman was instrumental in selecting the landing site, a sixty-acre field on the Jacob Brutcher farm north of town.

It was announced in the papers that on "Lindy Day" businesses would be closed for the day, and there would be limited postal service.

On the arrival day the sun was out bright and hot. Lindbergh landed precisely at 2:00 P.M. in a three-point landing on the grass. After taxiing to a stop, he climbed out of the airplane and all of Little Falls went wild.

The reception at Little Falls was restrained and orderly, a remarkable display of plain, old-fashioned appreciation for the feat of a native son.

However, it was unfortunate that even in 1927 the overenthusiasm of some of his admirers caused them to get carried away. The Lindbergh home was vandalized for souvenirs. They kicked in some windows, picked up any loose items and generally defaced the home. Some items, including a number of books from the library of Charles A. Lindbergh Sr., were taken.

The ensuing parade included many bands and drum corps from several Minnesota communities, floats (including the Saxon car on a flatbed truck), an old tractor that was used on the Lindbergh farm, replicas of the NYP, the Eiffel Tower in Paris, and the Statue of Liberty in New York. The parade included a marching delegation of five hundred children.

He was more familiar with people in that parade than in any of the others he had witnessed so far on the tour. It was estimated that 50,000 people were along the parade route, re-

Notice a coil of rope is ready for tying down the NYP. In the background is the Fairchild escort airplane.

CHARLES A. LINDBERGH HOUSE

gardless of the August heat.

The colorful parade ended at the Morrison County Fairgrounds south of the city where several speakers paid tribute to Lindbergh. Among them were Mayor Austin L. Grimes, Congressman Harold Knutson, Senator Chris Rosenmeier, Governor Theodore Christianson, Swedish Consul Nils Leon Jaenson of Minneapolis, and Dr. C. H. Longley of Little Falls.

In his talk Lindbergh said, "I have looked forward for a long time to coming back to Little Falls and I regret that I can stay but one day now that I am here." He went on to say that "the tour was to hasten the time … (in which) this country will fly" and said that twenty-five years of development in aeronautics had been more rapid than advances in any other form of transportation and cited construction materials, design, and weight as problem areas that had been successfully overcome.

He urged that people "differentiate between commercial, experimental, and military aviation" and pointed out that the safety record of regularly operated airlines equaled that of other types of transportation.

Lindbergh reminded the Little Falls residents that they could fly to Minneapolis in one hour. Land travel took three hours. He admitted there were still problems such as landing planes in fog and financing the high cost of flying, but he was optimistic about solutions. He noted that the fuel cost of the NYP was less than four cents per mile.

Then he went on to predict that "the day is coming when airlines will be more extensive than our present day railroad lines," and that "we may expect to see regular passenger service to Europe—when flying boats will render a regular service." Lindbergh concluded his presentation by calling for construction of more airports near the centers of cities and for standardization of air laws.

In the evening hours he attended events at the Elks Hotel where he gave another speech. A number of musical presentations were rendered.

The next morning (the 26th), he viewed the family home and the pleasantly wooded areas along the Mississippi River where he had spent many happy hours as a boy.

After Lindbergh's visit to his home state, residents there reaffirmed their own loyalty and virtue to their beloved state and country. Lindbergh firmly maintained during the tour that its pur-

Another view of the Fairchild FC-2 escort airplane. CHARLES A. LINDBERGH HOUSE

pose was only to promote commercial aviation. This was not a personal journey. He continued to push for more airports, uniform air laws, perfection of aeronautical equipment, and expansion of commercial airlines.

Lindbergh wrote a letter that was printed in the *New York Times* back in 1927 that stated, "I remember nothing about the stops in Minnesota that would justify the term 'hysterical.' I recall the days in Minnesota as having been surrounded by above-average dignity and interest in the future of aircraft. I remember clearly the lack-of-pressure feeling I had at Little Falls, the feeling of getting back to some degree of normalcy and the kind of human relationships I had known before my Paris flight. It was a great relief."

He took off from Little Falls at 11:30 A.M. and headed over the west-central portion of the state to Fargo, North Dakota. It was reported that on the way he had to deal with gusty winds.

Today there is one airport in Little Falls, Morrison County Airport. It is at an elevation of 1,122 feet MSL and has one paved runway of 4,500 feet, and one grass runway of 3,010 feet. It is a general aviation field located 2 miles south of the town, along state route 10.

The Lindbergh Interpretation Center is located on the west side of Little Falls, and includes the Lindbergh Park and the old homestead where the flyer grew up.

References

Newspapers
Star Tribune
Pioneer Press

Organizations
Minneapolis Public Library
Lindbergh Foundation
Minnesota Historical Society
North St. Paul Museum & Historical Society
St. Paul Public Library
Hennepin Historical Museum
Charles A. Lindbergh House and Interpretation Center

People

Noel Allard	James B. Horne
Bruce Larson	Liz Murphy
G. W. Christie	Charles Kapsner

STOP #32
FARGO, NORTH DAKOTA

CAPSULE HISTORY OF CITY

Fargo, North Dakota, founded in 1872, was named after George Fargo of Wells Fargo Express Company. It was located on the eastern border of North Dakota, in the fertile Red River Valley, the bed of prehistoric glacial Lake Agassiz. The city shares economic and cultural ties with its sister city, Moorhead, Minnesota, across the Red River.
900 feet MSL.

AUGUST 26–27, 1927
(FRIDAY AND SATURDAY)

After leaving Little Falls, Lindbergh flew over the town of Lake Itasca, where the Mississippi River flows out. It starts at the town of Bimiji and then on to the south-southwest toward Fargo.

The only landing field available at that time was located on the south side of 19th Avenue at the corner of 13th Street, now University Drive, and running west to Dakota Drive North. It was

just south of the present-day Hector International Airport. The site was on what is today the northern border of the North Dakota State University campus.

Lindbergh was first spotted over Moorhead. From there he headed west to downtown Fargo. He circled a few times, then made a right turn toward the field and landed on the grass at the prearranged time of 2:00 P.M.

Among the guests of honor who met him there was his sister, Mrs. George W. Christie of Red Lake Falls, Minnesota. The party included her husband and Dr. Robert L. Christie. Also there to greet the flyer were Fargo Mayor J. H. Dahl; Moorhead Mayor B. T. Bottolfson; Congressman O. B. Burtness of Grand Forks; Congressman J. H. Sinclair; Congressman Thomas Hall of Bismarck; E. J. Schenberg, President of the Fargo Commercial Club; Hon. Albert Prefontaine, Minister of Agriculture and Immigration, Province of Manitoba, Canada; Murray A. Baldwin, president of the Fargo Aeronautic Club; and F. E. Ferguson, Secretary to Mayor Ralph Webb of Winnipeg, Canada.

Sometime after the NYP landed, a high wire fence was constructed around it and the Fairchild for protection. National Guardsmen were assigned to patrol the area. This compound was located in the southeast corner of the field.

Later that day a reception was held for Mrs. Christie at the home of Dr. Elizabeth Rindlaub

from 4:30 to 5:00 P.M., according to Miss Clara Richards, president of the Quota Club.

The parade wound through the local streets and then east to El Zagel Park, where the El Zagel Golf Course is located today. Lindbergh was officially welcomed to the city by the chairman of the Welcoming Committee, Murray A. Baldwin. Lindbergh gave his usual speech at the park, emphasizing his belief in the future of aviation and air travel and the need for more airports.

At 6:30 P.M. a banquet was held at the Masonic Temple in Fargo, where Lindbergh gave a fifteen minute speech. Following the banquet an official Lindbergh Day dance, sponsored by the American Legion, was staged at the Winter Garden.

One of Lindbergh's old flying friends, H. J. Lynch, sometimes known as "Shorty" or "Cupid" Lynch, was there to greet the flyer. At this time Lynch was president of the Chicago Northwest Air Transport Company. The two spent some time together reminiscing over the times they had while barnstorming through the West with "Banty" Rogers, in the summer and fall of 1922. At that time Lindbergh worked as a mechanic, parachute jumper and wing-walker.

Lindbergh stayed in the Gardner Hotel. While looking out the window, he noticed a sign across the street that said, "Mortuary, Welcome Lindbergh 100 years from now, Undertaker." He thought for a moment and then said, "Well,

Clearly the NYP appears to be in soft ground, unless it was dug in to keep the wind from blowing it around.

Appears the Fairchild FC-2 is having its oil changed or some other maintenance performed. CHARLES A. LINDBERGH HOUSE

I'm a son of a gun," and that was all he said.

Col. Lindbergh and his crew arrived at the flying field at 7:00 A.M. on Saturday morning the 27th to begin preflighting the two airplanes. Before climbing into the cockpit he spent some time with his friend "Shorty" Lynch, explaining the workings of the NYP. He gave Lynch a chance to sit in the cockpit for a short time. Soon the engine was started, and he taxied to the north end of the field. The ground was a bit muddy from rains during the night, so he moved rather slowly. He then turned into the wind and took off at 7:40 A.M. The Fairchild took off next and headed southeast toward Sioux Falls, South Dakota. After lift-off Lindbergh circled the field several times as a final salute to Fargo before heading in a southwest direction.

In less than two hours he was over Aberdeen. Whistles blared in that small town as he came lower above the Crown County Courthouse, where he dropped the canvas bag message. The little daughter of Sheriff Geisler was the first to reach the spot and so became the proudest youngster in the city.

Lindbergh headed straight south, flying over the city of Redfield just before 10:00 A.M. Again he dropped the canvas message which was picked up by Tony Olding, Chief of the Redfield Fire Department, where it remains today as a reminder of the brief flyover of the hero.

From Redfield he flew south-southeast toward the town of Huron. He arrived over the area at 10:28 A.M., circled over the town three times, and then continued toward Mitchell and Sioux Falls. It is not known if he dropped the usual message on Huron.

At 11:05 A.M. he flew over Mitchell, dropping the message there. It missed the top of the Mitchell Republican Building and the Western National Bank Building by scant feet and fell to the ground at the corner of Third Avenue and Main Street. The parcel was picked up by Leo McIntyre, a thirteen-year-old boy, and was soon posted on display in the window of the Nicolls-Kress Pharmacy at that very corner.

He continued on eastward to Sioux Falls, where he was expected at noon for a quick stop before continuing on later that day to Sioux City, Iowa.

Today the Hector International Airport, named for Martin Hector, president of the Fargo National Bank, as mentioned earlier, is located three miles northwest of the city, and is at an elevation of 900 feet MSL. It has three runways, the longest of which is 9,546 feet. The field serves most major domestic airlines, commuter airlines, some international flights, general aviation, crop dusters, and Air National Guard aircraft.

Also in the surrounding area is West Fargo Utility Airport, 6 miles northwest of the city. It is at an elevation of 896 feet MSL, and has a single 2,400-foot runway. It is a general aviation field, with crop dusting aircraft, ultralights and some parachute operations.

References

Newspapers
    The Fargo Forum
    The Jamestown Sun

Organizations
    Fargo Public Library
    North Dakota State University

People
    John McElroy
    J. D. Lamb
    Richard J. "Dick" Pratt

Stop #33

Sioux Falls, South Dakota

"Touch Stop"

Capsule History of City

The city of Sioux Falls, South Dakota, was settled in the 1850s, mostly by Norwegian, English and Scottish immigrants. This area was noted for its proximity to stone quarries and the possibility of harnessing the Big Sioux River for water power. These immigrants were quite skilled in stonecutting. The city was first settled in 1856. High-altitude balloons are developed and manufactured there and are world famous.

August 27, 1927 (Saturday)

Sioux Falls in 1927 did not have its own airport. But about eight miles north, in the town of Renner, with a population at that time of less than one hundred, there was a flying field established in 1925 apparently by Harold Tennant. It consisted of 118 acres of meadowland, which was leased from George Renner.

The field was named or known as Renner Field, a smooth, flat hay meadow, a half-mile long north and south and 2,000 feet wide east and west.

When plans were being formulated for the tour, Ben B. Lawshi, secretary of the Sioux Falls Chamber of Commerce, was told that Sioux Falls was one of the planned stops. Shortly an airport committee was formed, headed by R. G. Coon, president of Coon Auto Company. They were to put together a plan to welcome the flyer.

On August 17th Milburn Kusterer, the advance agent, arrived in Sioux Falls from Fargo to meet with the committee to help make the final arrangements for the event. Kusterer was shown the Renner airfield site, where he approved it for landing.

Kusterer emphatically suggested that no airplanes would be sent to serve as escort to Lindbergh on his way into Renner. All aircraft must be down by 11:00 A.M.

Clyde W. Ice was a prominent old-time pioneer aviator in North Dakota, a legend in his own right. At this time he was chief pilot of Rapid

Air Lines of Rapid City. He recalled years later the story of Lindbergh coming to Sioux Falls.

He had heard by the grapevine that an air show was being planned for a new air strip there (Renner). They wanted Charles Lindbergh to be the first to land there, unbeknownst to Ice. He went on to say, "Here I came in, and landed—didn't even know he [Lindbergh] was coming!" So Ice was really the first to land on this "new" flying field.

People began arriving at Renner from many miles around by horseback, wagons, carriages, bicycles and autos. They said that never before had there been such an evacuation of its citizens from Sioux Falls.

At 11:30 A.M. the Fairchild arrived to assist in the preparation of Lindbergh's arrival. It was reported that by that time 30,000 people had already arrived at the field.

About eight minutes before noon the NYP flew in from the west and circled over the Sioux Falls business district, then over the various residential areas before heading north to Renner.

As soon as he climbed out of the airplane, he was greeted by the reception committee and led to the already constructed speaker's stand on the field. After a few remarks from Robert R. Montgomery, president of the Chamber of Commerce, Lindbergh was officially welcomed to the city by Col. Boyd Wales, commanding officer of

The NYP taxiing in with the Fairchild in the foreground. DR. CLAYTON F. SMITH

The NYP on Renner Field with Lindbergh between the two men behind the wing strut. LEO B. KIMBALL COLLECTION

The Fairchild escort airplane being looked over by the military and local officials. JOHN MCKILLOP

the 147th Field Artillery, who was appointed by Governor W. J. Bulow, who was unable to attend. Sioux Falls Mayor Thomas McKennon was also present.

Lindbergh gave his usual speech, stressing the need for an updated and modern airport for Sioux Falls, closer to the city rather than at the present location. "I want to thank you for the interest you have shown in coming here today in the hope that this field or one that may be better situated will be developed into a first-class airport for your city. I thank you."

The Chamber of Commerce secretary Ben B. Lawshi in his brief talk said,

"We have learned that air transportation has passed from the uncertain, experimental stage to that of practical reality. It is our job to give further impetus to this new means of transportation by providing municipal landing fields. South Dakota cannot afford to be backward in providing this kind of encouragement. It is up to us to put ourselves on the air map of the United States with sufficient numbers of good airports to attract to us our full share of the business of the air. The hope is that today we shall all leave this field with our job clearly in mind and determined to do all we can in our own communities to foster air transportation."

The entire program lasted only about thirty minutes. The NYP was moved back from the viewing point out to the field to be ready for departure. After Lindbergh climbed into the cockpit, Phil Love pulled the prop through and got the J-5 started. Lindbergh took off at 12:40 P.M. After circling over the field and waiting for the Fairchild to get airborne, he headed south directly toward Sioux City, Iowa.

Lindbergh's challenge provided a new dimension of urgency and promise for air-minded Sioux Falls citizens and civic leaders. A few weeks after Lindbergh's visit, City Commissioner Ellis O. Smith secured an eighty-acre parcel of land for a municipal airport. It was located southwest of the city, south of West 41st Street, on the east side of the Sioux River in the area of the Western Mall.

Renner Field continued to operate, closing in January 1935. On September 15, 1939, the Sioux Falls Municipal Airport was founded and located at a new site three miles northwest of the city beyond Elmwood Park and Golf Course. It included 478 acres of prime land for future expansion.

On March 7, 1955, it was renamed Joe Foss Field in honor of Joseph J. Foss, a South Dakota World War II ace and former governor of the state, at an elevation of 1,429 feet MSL. It has three runways, the longest of which is 8,999 feet. It serves some domestic airlines, commuter airlines, general aviation aircraft and Air National Guard aircraft.

Joe Foss knew Lindbergh briefly when the two met in the South Pacific during World War II, when Lindbergh was there as a consultant to the Air Corps. In later years Foss always referred to his "friend," "Charlie" Lindbergh. Lindbergh made it very clear in his own writing that he never liked being called Charlie or Lindy, Lone Eagle, or Lucky Lindy.

References

Newspapers
  Sioux Falls Press
  Argus Leader

Rapid City Journal

Organizations/Publications
    Minnehaha County Historical Society
    Sedgwick, Rhonda Coy, *Sky Trails, the Life of Clyde W. Ice*

People
C. John McKillop   J. G. Nikkels
Mr. Miller   Rev. Dr. Clayton F. Smith
Richard J. (Dick) Pratt, CLU (Fargo, N.D.)
Robert Kolbe

Stop #34
Sioux City, Iowa

Capsule History of City

Sioux City, Iowa, is geographically located at the juncture of the Big Sioux and Missouri Rivers and is one of the country's leading livestock and grain centers.

It was named for the Sioux Indians and was laid out in 1854 by John K. Cook.

1,110 feet MSL.

August 27–29, 1927
(Saturday through Monday)

The only landing field existing at that time near Sioux City was a municipal airport known as Rickenbacker Airport. By 1:00 P.M. it was reported that 20,000 people were already gathered at the field to witness his arrival. The Fairchild had already landed, and the crew assisted in getting the NYP into a specially built enclosure.

Lindbergh was greeted by the reception committee consisting of Mayor Stewart Gilman, B. H. Kingsbury, Audley Johnson, Ralph J. Haley, Sheriff John Dahlin, Councilman T. L. Taggart, Harry Burdick, and U.S. Army Maj. J. H. Jones.

The parade made its way to the Interstate Fairgrounds, where Lindbergh was introduced to the audience and then gave a brief speech.

After this gathering the parade proceeded into the city area and to the Martin Hotel. After spending some time with newspaper reporters, he adjourned to his room to rest for the evening's program.

The welcoming committee had done such a superb job of organizing the arrival plans and parade for 2:00 P.M. that many people missed it. So it was suggested they do another parade, to which Lindbergh agreed. Many who had expected to view the parade at the appointed time later realized that it had already occurred. Not wanting to disappoint the people, another parade was scheduled, which drew many more people than the first one.

In the evening at the banquet at the Hotel, Lindbergh gave his usual address with regard to commercial aviation and the need for modern airports.

Later in the evening a former flying student of Lindbergh's came to the hotel and the two spent a half-hour discussing their former flying days. Churchill (first name unknown) asked if Lindbergh would land the NYP at his airstrip near Battle Creek, but with such a tight schedule, Lindbergh said he could not but that he would at least fly over the site.

Four local boys had won first prize for their model airplanes. They were seated at an honor table. The committee thoughtfully hung these models from the ceiling at the banquet.

On Sunday, August 28, the airport at Mason City, east of Sioux City, was to be dedicated. An air show was part of the program, and three flyers from Selfridge Field in Michigan, flying Curtiss P-1 Hawk fighters, were to take part in

This one photo exists showing the NYP with the cowling removed, a bench below the engine area and other equipment. Apparently an oil change was done while at this stop. BOB BAILEY

The NYP being moved to a better location on the field at Rickenbacker Airport. SMITHSONIAN INSTITUTION

the show. Knowing that Lindbergh was in Sioux City, Col. Hanford MacNider, acting Secretary of War, made arrangements to have the three P-1s flown to that city. Lindbergh was given the use of one of them. Upon arrival they did a three-ship inside loop before landing. Then Lindbergh in one of the P-1s and two other pilots went up for a demonstration flight. He flew the right wing position when they did the first of four V-shaped elements. They demonstrated military formations and closed their presentation with a Lufbery Circle. Then the three airplanes flew back to Mason City.

On Monday morning, the 29th, Lindbergh took off and flew over Battle Creek, just a short flight southeast from Sioux City, to swoop low over Churchill's flying field, as promised. Then he and the Fairchild continued southeast to Des Moines.

Today one can fly into and out of the modern Sioux Gateway Airport, located about six miles south of the city near Sergeant Bluff, Iowa. It is at an elevation of 1,098 feet MSL and has two main runways. The longer one is 9,002 feet. The field serves most major domestic airlines, commuter airlines, general aviation and Air National Guard.

Three miles southwest of the city in South Sioux City, Iowa, is Martin Airport, at an elevation of 1,100 feet MSL, with a single runway of 3,281 feet. It is mainly a general aviation field, with some glider, crop duster operations, and ultralight aircraft as well.

About one mile north of North Sioux City, Nebraska, is the Graham Airport. It is at an elevation of 1,106 feet MSL and has a single 2,237-foot runway. It is a general aviation airport.

References

Newspaper
Sioux City Journal

Organization
Herbert Hoover Library

People
Ann H. Pellegreno

Stop #35
Des Moines, Iowa

Capsule History of City

Des Moines is located at the fork of the Raccoon and Des Moines Rivers and was established in 1843 as the military garrison Fort Raccoon. It was changed by the War Department to Fort Des Moines. The name was drawn from the vocabulary of the French voyageurs who had christened this river "La Riviere des Moinesk," River of the Monks. The state capital was moved to Des Moines from Iowa City in 1857. It is the largest city in Iowa. At this time the city had one landing field site near the *present town of Altoona (exact location unknown).*
805 feet MSL

August 29–30, 1927 (Monday and Tuesday)

Ninety minutes out of Sioux City, Lindbergh arrived over the city of Des Moines at 1:50 P.M. He had promised to do a flyover of the Iowa State Fairgrounds, just east of the city. He did, as 63,000 people watched in awe. This was a promise to pay his respects to the Iowa institution, the Fair. Instead of the usual outburst of

cheers, a hush fell over the crowd.

Soon he headed northeast toward Altoona, where 3,500 autos and 20,000 people awaited his arrival. After landing he taxied into the white-fence-post-and-chicken-wire corral which was prepared for the occasion, as they did not have a hangar.

He was welcomed at the airport speaker's platform by Governor John Hammill and Mayor Fred Hunter of Des Moines and George Yates, president of the Des Moines branch of the NAA (National Aeronautical Association) in addition to being the chief photographer of the *Register* and the *Tribune* newspapers.

In his talk Lindbergh said, "Two years ago it was my privilege to land on the Des Moines airport, or rather the Airport of Des Moines with an Army plane from Richards Field. Today I find upon landing that the city has provided a suitable airport for practically any type of airplane. Des Moines has been farsighted enough to provide that airport, and the only remaining thing for your city is to patronize the activities in the air."

After the parade Lindbergh was driven to Hotel Fort Des Moines, where he rested until time for his appearance at 6:45 P.M. at a banquet attended by 500 people at the hotel.

After taking off at 12:03 on the 30th, Lindbergh headed southwest to fly over historic Fort Des Moines. From there he flew directly west to the next stop at Omaha.

A few airports had been built and dedicated in Iowa before his 1927 visit. There were scores of flying fields built and improved soon after his first visit to the state. The citizens began to support airports, and thousands turned out to enjoy air shows and ceremonies dedicating an airport.

Today Des Moines International Airport is a

The NYP is shown in the corral of the Des Moines stop. NOEL ALLARD

modern facility located three miles southwest of the capital city. It is at an elevation of 957 feet MSL and has three runways, the longest being 9,001 feet. It serves most major domestic airlines, some commuters, general aviation, some military, cargo aircraft, and Air National Guard aircraft.

Three miles north of the city is the Des Moines Morningstar Airport, at an elevation of 805 feet MSL. It has a single grass runway of 2,065 feet and is a general aviation airport, with some helicopter operations.

One mile southeast of the town of Ankeny, and five miles north of Des Moines, is the Ankeny Regional Airport, at an elevation of 903 feet MSL. It has two main runways, the longer one being 5,500 feet. It is a general aviation field.

References

Newspapers
 Des Moines Register
 Sioux City Daily Tribune

Publications
 Flying with Lindbergh by Donald E. Keyhoe

People
 Noel Allard   Ann Holtgren Pellegreno

STOP #36
OMAHA, NEBRASKA

CAPSULE HISTORY OF CITY

The largest city in Nebraska, Omaha (from the Omaha Indians), a word meaning "above all others on a stream," is located on the eastern border of the state. The tribe gave most of its hunting grounds to the United States in 1854. That year the Council Bluffs and Nebraska Ferry Company, a land development firm, founded the town of Omaha. The city is located on the west bank of the Missouri River and was once called "the crossroads of the na-

tion." It is one of the world's largest cattle market and meat-packing centers.
1040 feet MSL.

AUGUST 30–31 1927
(TUESDAY AND WEDNESDAY)

At the time the landing site was known as Carter Lake Field. The site is located between the lake and the Missouri River northeast of downtown Omaha. The surface of the field at that time was a large, poorly drained pasture. There was no hangar on the field. The American Legion had been trying to raise money to build a $30,000 building and to encourage the city to construct dikes and a drainage system.

Prior to Lindbergh's arrival the Airfield Committee erected a fenced area for the NYP and the Fairchild. In case of rain they were prepared to flag the dangerous, soft areas of the field.

There was an airfield known as Ak-Sar-Ben Field (Nebraska spelled backward), which was on what today is the Ak-Sar-Ben Field and Coliseum at Center Street and 63rd Avenue. It had an air mail hangar up until 1924 when it was destroyed by high winds. Air mail activities were then moved south of the city to Fort Crook.

Ak-Sar-Ben had been a Lincoln-Standard and Curtiss Jenny rebuilding facility for barnstormers after World War I through the 1920s. Banty Rogers and Lindbergh often landed there for OX-5 parts and for airplane repairs.

Sometime before Lindbergh's arrival, M. V. Robins, the official meteorologist, gave an optimistic twist to the formal forecast of "partly cloudy tonight and Thursday, not much change in temperature." He said, "From present indications I would say Lindy should have good flying weather on his flight here from Des Moines."

To protect both airplanes a corral of strong wire fence was built on Monday. The enclosure would be patrolled by companies of the 134th Infantry, Nebraska National Guard and members of the Naval Reserve. All of these men were under the command of Col. Amos Thomas.

At about 1:27 P.M. the Fairchild appeared at the field and landed. Soon Lindbergh flew over the city and then circled the airport several times to check out the landing surface before he lined up for a landing into the wind. He made the approach from northeast to southwest, making a perfect three-point landing on the turf of Carter Lake Airport.

After climbing out of the cockpit and having a discussion with Keyhoe and Maidment, he was greeted and welcomed by Governor McMullen; Mayor Dahlman (on crutches); John Hopkins, acting Mayor and chairman of the welcoming committee; Senator Howell; Maj. Gen. H. A. Smith, commanding the 7th Corps area; Congressman Ashton C. Shallenberger of Alma, Nebraska; and Gould Dietz.

Soon he was escorted into an open car for the parade, which then proceeded through the city streets to southwest of the center of the city, to stop at Ak-Sar-Ben Field, where a speaker's stand had been erected for the occasion. Lindbergh was then introduced by the Governor.

Lindbergh gave his usual presentation, again stressing the importance of more airports, commercial aviation and the future of the industry, strongly suggesting the public's interest in traveling by airplane.

After a rousing cheer from the people in the park, estimated to be seven to eight thousand, Lindbergh and the entourage paraded downtown to the Hotel Fontenelle. At the hotel he and his crew were given a suite of rooms on the fourth floor. He held a press conference for a while, then adjourned to his room for a rest and shower before the upcoming banquet at the same hotel.

Boys in one of the neighborhoods had "chipped in" and erected a small sign to greet Lindbergh which read, "The Gang Welcomes Lindy," which drew a smile from the flyer as he passed by. At 22nd and Cass Streets a small boy had climbed up into a tree, using a pillow to make his long stay comfortable. He had made sure that he would be able to see the flyer over the heads of the crowd.

A Ford roadster with three youthful occupants bearing a sign "Lindbergh Special" preceded the parade by five minutes. They waved gracefully, acknowledging the crowds on either side of the parade route.

At the press conference Lindbergh mentioned that the last time he was in Omaha was in 1923 and said that he did not get the reception he had received then. He believed his first flight to this city was in a Nebraska aircraft plane, possibly a Lincoln-Standard Tourabout.

He went on to comment, "It is hard to give

On Carter Lake Field, C.C. Maidment, the Wright service man, can be seen below the nose possibly doing an oil change. LEO B. KIMBALL COLLECTION

The NYP tied down for the night at Carter Lake Field with a tarp over the engine. MARK C. WALKER JR.

Lindbergh is in the third auto, with motorcycle police escort during the Omaha parade, on 17th Douglas Street on August 30th. Note the photographer on the corner of the building on the left. MARK C. WALKER JR.

specific suggestions on your air field after only one landing, but the airport is in a good location, and we had no trouble. Development of an airport and promotion by the public of its use is the important step for any city to take."

Local resident John L. Kennedy compared Lindbergh with the pioneers of covered wagon days. "This has been a marvelous day for Omaha. I have lived here for forty-five years and never have I seen such an outpouring of humanity, such joy and admiration. But the people of Omaha are not awake or they would not have failed to respond to the airport fund."

"Colonel Lindbergh, when you go to the Great Beyond, no matter where you are, there will be no little monument or large mausoleum to mark your final resting place. People will not look for it on earth, in any country. But in the air—ah, they will see it there: 'Spirit of St. Louis' in the air as a living monument to the man who dared and to his great achievement."

Commissioner John Hopkins said, "All the glory of Lindbergh's triumph shall be for the furtherance of aviation, and we love him. He has come to help us with our problem. The Lord knows we need this inspiration. Worthy young men of Omaha have tried to raise a few paltry thousands to equip our airfield. I have faith in Omaha and her people. I believe we can put it over. The next time Col. Lindbergh honors us with a visit, we want something better than a barbed wire fence to wrap around his priceless plane, and I ask now that everyone here who will pledge their support will not be disappointed."

The next morning, Lindbergh was in the air by 7:45 A.M. on his way to the next stop, Denver. Lindbergh took a rather zig-zag route over Columbus, Lincoln, Hastings, Kearney, Lexington, and McCook, Nebraska, then Bird City, Kansas. He flew over Bird City, where he went with his exhibition parachute in 1922 to join "Shorty" Lynch and Holmes A. "Banty" Rogers while barnstorming and doing exhibition flights. It was at Bird City that he said he started his "professional" career in aviation and left his status as a flying student at Lincoln.[8]

They were flying a Lincoln-Standard Tourabout. He said that flying was more of an art and less a science in those days. More depended on the man and less on the machine.

You had more the sense of flying when you went up; it was less mechanical. Instruments were only referred to for checking your own feelings and estimates. One flew on fabric and wood and wire through sheer skill and daring.

From Bird City the group flew to Imperial, Nebraska, then directly to Denver. It is not known if Lindbergh dropped the canvas bag message on any or all of those towns and cities.

Before the party departed from Omaha, Phil Love remarked to someone there that the Omaha Airport had "room for improvement" and that the field is a little soft, but that arrangements for the program were good.

So what does Omaha have for an airport now? On the very same piece of property there is a modern airport, Eppley Airfield, with long runways and a modern airline terminal. It is at an elevation of 984 feet MSL. The longest of three runways is 9,500 feet. It serves most domestic airlines, some commuter airlines, general aviation, and some military. In fact, there is a perimeter roadway on the west side of the Missouri River that is named Lindbergh Plaza.

There are about five satellite airports around Omaha, one of which is Offutt Air Force Base, located south of the town of Bellevue, Nebraska. It is at an elevation of 1,048 feet MSL and has a single 11,700-foot runway. It is strictly a military airport.

Footnotes

1. *The Wartime Journals of Charles A. Lindbergh,* pg. 221, Harcourt Brace, New York

References

Newspapers
  Scottsbluff Star-Herald
  World-Herald (Omaha) or *Omaha World-Herald*
  Evening World-Herald
  Morning World-Herald

Organization
  Mobile Oil Corporation (Mary C. Keane)

People
  Harold W. Dubach   Archie Block
  Mark C. Walker Jr.

STOP #37
DENVER, COLORADO

CAPSULE HISTORY OF CITY

Denver, the capital of Colorado, lies on the South Platte River, ten miles east of the Rocky Mountains. It is known as the "Mile High City." Gold prospectors founded the city in 1858 as part of the Kansas Territory, and it was named after James W. Denver, the governor of the territory. The city today covers 95 square miles.

5,595 feet MSL.

AUGUST 31–SEPTEMBER 1, 1927
(WEDNESDAY AND THURSDAY)

Lowry Field was located just a short distance northeast of the center of the city at the time of the Lindbergh visit. The site today is occupied by the Park Hill Golf Course, which is bordered by E 35th Street, Dahlia Street, Colorado Boulevard and Smith Road. There was one hangar on the field at the time, Hangar No. 1 of the National Guard.

Fifty thousand people assembled on the field that bright, sunny day. There were people and cars as far as one could see. Streets and private homes were decorated with bunting, flags, and other decorations hours and days before his arrival. Homeowners on the route found their yards and front porches crowded with friends and strangers. It was estimated that three hundred thousand people lined the parade route.

Early that morning at the Children's Hospital, nurses had moved bedridden patients to the windows of their rooms. Wheelchair patients were moved to balconies and children who could walk were guided to other viewing locations. Sick and maimed patients were also moved to windows and balconies.

The evening before, the *Denver Post* said that all Denver was "on tip-toe of eagerness." It was the greatest welcoming effort for any one individual in the history of the city. One old-timer said it was even greater than when President Theodore Roosevelt was welcomed at the capital decades before.

Appearing out of the east, the NYP came into view about 1:40 P.M., somewhat ahead of schedule, and made a low pass across Lowry Field. After weeks and weeks of planning, this was designated as "Lindbergh Day" for Denver.

After the engine was shut down and the NYP placed in the hangar along with the Fairchild, Lindbergh was greeted by C. A. Johnson, a member of the welcoming committee, along with Colorado Governor Bill Adams of Alamosa, dressed in high-heeled cowboy boots and sombrero. Included were Denver Mayor Ben Stapleton (Stapleton Airport); Claude K. Boettcher, parade chairman; band coordinator Henry Sachs; as well as Police Chief R. F. Reed and Manager of Safety Reuben W. Hershey.

A fourteen-year-old Boy Scout, Bill Madsen, one of four hundred volunteers, was there that day. His job was to hold the end of a rope which stretched around the hangar parking area. Folks would rush up against the rope and stop and smile. His station was at the gate that opened onto Dahlia Street. With his idol, Lindbergh, he was at the starting point of the parade. Lindbergh's vehicle stopped not six feet from him, and looking down from his perch, Lindbergh said, "Hello, young man! How are you today?" In later years Madsen said he was petrified that the hero had spoken to him, and he was speechless. Then Lindbergh said, "It's great to be a Boy Scout, son. Keep up the good work!" Madsen snapped to attention with the typical Boy Scout three-finger salute. The incident lived in Madsen's mind throughout his life.

The parade proceeded by way of local streets to City Park, Cheesman and Washington Parks, then through the downtown area of Denver, back over the 20th Street Viaduct, out to the Children's Hospital and to the Brown Palace Hotel. He and his crew were given a presidential suite there.

That night Lindbergh gave his speech to a standing-room-only audience in the Colorado Room of the Cosmopolitan Hotel. The banquet hall could accommodate only one thousand persons, so the *Post* rented the City Auditorium to handle the overflow. Arrangements were made to transmit Lindbergh's speech to the auditorium

by wire through "the most powerful electrical amplifiers in the West." There was no charge for people attending.

The *Post* also arranged with a local music company for an extra fillip (echoic extension). The firm brought to the auditorium its latest model of the Automatic Orthophonic Electrola made by the Victor Talking Machine Company, and would play a record of Lindbergh's speech in Washington, D.C., and a welcome by President Calvin Coolidge. The American Legion planned a dance at the auditorium following the evening program. (in Denver?)

Before and during Lindbergh's visit, plans were made to memorialize him in Colorado. It was suggested that a highway, lake or river be named after the flyer. Finally they named a local well-known mountain after him. It was a mountain in the Hell Hole Gorge, rising to an elevation of 11,920 feet between two living glaciers. On February 9, 1961, Lone Eagle Peak was "so named to commemorate the first solo airplane flight across the Atlantic Ocean in 1927." Supposedly the peak is located in the Indian Peaks area of Colorado's Front Range along the Continental Divide, northwest of Denver. Crater Lake is at the foot of Lone Eagle Peak.

The *Post* sponsored a model airplane contest for young people, offering top prizes of $50, $30, and $20 in gold. Ten other winners would get an airplane ride in a Colorado Airways, Inc., Ryan M-1 airplane (registration no. 3122).

By visiting a Piggly Wiggly grocery store before "Lindbergh Day," every boy and girl who was accompanied by an adult would receive a free Piggly Wiggly Lindy Lid, a cap they could wear at the parade.

At the Brown Palace Hotel Lindbergh granted a ten-minute press conference, where he kept trying to convey to the impatient reporters that "I don't want to talk about myself. I'm making this flight in the interests of commercial aviation."

The menu at the banquet that night included fruit surprise, consommé aviation, pascal celery, pecans, mixed olives, broiled spring chicken, au gratin potatoes, mountain peas in butter, hearts of lettuce with thousand island dressing, mousse Lindbergh, petite fours, rolls, and demitasse. They were simple dishes, according to the hotel's chefs, as a concession to Lindbergh's preference for plain food.

Completely forgetting to acknowledge the presence of the distinguished guests, Lindbergh began his talk.

"Denver could be a natural center for the nation's commercial aviation. Its high altitude would offer no handicaps to the new, supercharged aviation engines that were being built. The unusually clear atmosphere, with only rare clouds and fog, would be ideal for aircraft movements.

"Here in Denver today it is possible to fly across the mountains in any direction or across the plains to the Atlantic coast, Mexico, Canada, or any other place to which it is desired to go. There is another advantage to air transportation here in the West. That is the fact that an airplane can follow a straight course over the mountains. It is not necessary to wind about over passes or to tunnel through, but it is entirely practicable to fly directly over the top.

"Denver is so situated that almost any part of the United States is overnight from this city. We could take off here tonight and land in New York or San Francisco early tomorrow."

He closed by predicting that "given a good airport Denver would be the greatest air center in the West. I hope you will devote part of your attention in the future to the establishment of an adequate airport here."

The NYP on Lowry Field at Denver, Colorado on August 31st before leaving for Pierre, SD. DENVER PUBLIC LIBRARY: WESTERN HISTORY COLLECTION, HARRY RHOADS RH 894

The next morning there were an estimated 5,000 people on Lowry Field, waiting to see Lindbergh depart. He arrived there just after 8:00 A.M., spent some time preflighting the NYP, as did Phil Love, pilot of the Fairchild. Both airplanes had been guarded all night by men from the 120th Observation Squadron of the Colorado National Guard from Fort Logan.

After an easy start he took off at 8:23 A.M., heading directly toward the Fitzsimons Veterans Hospital where he made several low passes around the facility. A young veteran with tears in his eyes stood in a doorway of Ward E-2. He waved wildly at the NYP and recalled the days he shared flight training with Lindbergh as a fellow cadet at Kelly Field in Texas.

Lindbergh did another low pass over Lowry and then headed northwest. On his way to Pierre, he first flew over Rocky Mountain National Park, 14,255-foot-high Long's Peak, northwest of Denver, Greeley, Colorado, then on to Scotts Bluff in Nebraska.

Lindbergh first appeared over historic Scotts Bluff National Monument, and then circled the city several times. He dropped his message of greetings at the south door of the Methodist Hospital and dipped his wings to honor Lt. J. L. Daniels and Robert Barlow, injured aviators who were convalescing there. Soon he headed northeast toward Pierre, South Dakota.

It was estimated that seven to eight thousand people had gathered on the streets of Scotts Bluff to see the hero. The message he dropped was lithographed on a 22 X 29 inch sheet with CAL's signature in ink. Written in pencil was, "To the City of Scottsbluff." The canvas bag container was sixteen inches long and was weighted down by size 16 shot. Attached was the usual five-foot-long orange colored streamer. The message was picked up by Chief of Police Guy Carlson and was taken to the sickroom for the two injured men to see and then turned over to the mayor.

Mayor Ben Stapleton exhorted Denver business leaders to get behind a move to build an airport. On the afternoon of October 18, 1929, Governor Billy Adams was the main speaker as a gravel runway and a few scattered buildings were dedicated as the new Denver Municipal Airport, which was named Stapleton Airport to honor the Mayor. Stapleton Airport today is closed to aircraft movements, as is Lowry Air

August 31st with Lindbergh by the cockpit of the NYP and Donald Keyhoe on the right. Other man unknown. DENVER PUBLIC LIBRARY: WESTERN HISTORY COLLECTION, HARRY RHOADS RH 188

Force Base just south of Stapleton. To the east of Lowry is Buckley Air National Guard Airport, a single strip of 11,000 feet.

Today one can fly into the immense new Denver International Airport, one of the largest in the country. It is located about twenty miles northeast of the capital city. The airport is at an elevation of 5,431 feet MSL and has five runways oriented north-south and east-west. All of the runways are 12,000 feet in length. The field serves all major domestic, international, and commuter airlines. There are also cargo aircraft operations at the airport, as well as a small amount of general aviation aircraft.

Other airports in the Denver area include Front Range, Centennial, Aurora, Jeffco, Tri-County, Brighton Van-Aire, and numerous private turf strips all around the satellite area of the big city.

References

Newspapers
Denver Post
Rocky Mountain News

Organizations
Denver Public Library
United States Air Force Academy – Library and Archives
Colorado Aviation Historical Society
New World Airport Commission
Civil Air Patrol – National Historical Committee

Publications
Empire Magazine
Talon, cadet magazine of the USAF Academy

People
Neil King   Miss Barcley Howarth
Louis Henke Jr.   Eleanor M. Gehres
Doris J. Shaw   Andrew T. Kennedy Jr.
William D. Madsen, Lt. Col. CAP
George M. Fuller

STOP #38
PIERRE, SOUTH DAKOTA

CAPSULE HISTORY OF CITY

Located in approximately the center of the state, on the east bank of the Missouri River, Pierre, the state capital, was named for Pierre Chouteau, an early fur trader. The first settlers arrived in 1878. It became the state capital in 1889, soon after South Dakota was made a state.

1,484 feet MSL.

SEPTEMBER 1–2, 1927 (THURSDAY AND FRIDAY)

The only flying field available at the time was located three miles north of the city, in the shadow of historic Snake Buttes. It was once the place of worship of local Indians.

This airport was Class A rated and on virgin prairie soil. It was known variously as Pierre Port or Planes Field. When Lindbergh was expected to visit the capital city, a group of American Legionnaires volunteered their time to mark out the field according to Department of Commerce regulations. They used whitewash to mark a 200-foot-diameter circle in the middle of the almost perfect square of land, just on the south side of Snake Butte, east of Highway 14. The markings were readily visible from a considerable distance in the air. They also outlined the word "PIERRE" in large white letters on the slope of the Butte, a short distance from the field.

Flying conditions that day were perfect, with a bright sun, a mild breeze from the south and unlimited visibility. Lindbergh's ETA was set at 4 P.M. that day. He actually arrived at 3:59 P.M. after a 6:35-minute flight from Denver.

September 1 was originally designated as the next rest day, which was to be at Denver. Lindbergh's crew, sometime before the Denver stop, had realized that by error only a touch stop had been planned for two states, and one of them

was South Dakota. When this was brought to Lindbergh's attention, he clearly was not pleased. He reminded them that one of the main ideas of the tour was to spend at least one night in each state. So they had to work out a plan to make Pierre an overnight stop. Lindbergh suggested that on the normal rest day at Denver, they would fly to Pierre, stay overnight, and the next day fly on to Cheyenne. He realized also, after suggesting this change of plan, that it would give them a chance to fly over the Bad Lands, the Black Hills, and the Summer White House at Hermosa. When some of the crew complained about the loss of a rest day, Lindbergh reminded them that they were getting to see a lot of the country, and that a whole week's vacation was awaiting them at Butte, Montana. The matter was settled.

After landing at Pierre, he was officially welcomed by Governor W. J. Bulow, Mayor John E. Hipple, and other members of the reception committee. There were approximately 3,500 people on the field at his arrival.

It appears that the NYP was refueled sometime after he landed and began the festivities. In one photo, Clyde Ice can be seen assisting with the refueling.

Shortly he was again put in an open car,

Lindbergh just after arrival at Pierre being greeted by the reception committee. MILLER PHOTO VIA J.G. NIKKELS

The NYP and Fairchild tied down for the night at Pierre Port, September 1st. MILLER PHOTO VIA J.G. NIKKELS

driven by Dan Lawrence, for the parade into the city and to the capitol steps, where it was reported that thousands of people were assembled to hear what Lindbergh would have to say. In his presentation he stated that he "wished the people in the sparsely settled Midwest to have an opportunity to see the trans-Atlantic plane, as they could not have otherwise. Pierre is located near the center of a territory in which the airplane has many uses which it would not have elsewhere" (this was the apparent reason for electing to pay a special visit to this city). He continued, "This territory is just as good for aviation purposes as any other, and the airplane has an advantage here over other modes of travel." He went on to mention the advantages of developing the air mail system, air-express, and passenger service for the area.

At 7:00 P.M. he was a guest at the home of the Mayor on Highland Avenue. At 8:00 P.M. he was escorted to the Capitol, State House Grounds, by the American Legion Scots Band, where there was a short talk by the flyer. In his introduction, Governor Bulow said, "Lindbergh crossed the ocean and came back to tell about it. Someday some man is going to leave the earth, perhaps on a trip to the moon, and come back to tell about it."

That evening Lindbergh stayed in the St. Charles Hotel in Pierre. The local paper said that he did not retire early which was his custom, but spent some time at the American Legion bowery dance, appearing on the platform but not speaking.

The next morning, after first starting the engine on the NYP, there appeared to be a problem with one of the oil lines, and the engine was shut down. The problem was checked and repaired, with the loss of a half hour. He finally took off at 9:30 A.M. sharp and headed for Chey-

enne, Wyoming.

On the way he flew over Philip, then Hermosa, the summer home of President Coolidge. Here he dropped a message to the President, as the latter stood in front of the executive offices of the game lodge and enthusiastically waved at the flyer. Then he flew north to Rapid City, where he dropped the usual message, where the populace turned out in full force to get a glimpse of the NYP. The message was picked up by Eugene Berry and was last reported being on display in the window of the *Rapid City Journal* business office.

He circled the city twice and then headed northwest and out over Cowboy Hill, straight for Spearfish and Deadwood, South Dakota, before crossing the border into Wyoming. The people at Spearfish had not been alerted that the flyer would pass over their area, therefore not many of them were there for the occasion, according to the Spearfish *Queen City Mail.* In fact, not many people who *did* see the airplane go over realized what they were looking at. Then Lindbergh headed straight for Cheyenne, Wyoming, over beautiful, desolate countryside.

Pierre Regional Airport is the present-day field for the city, located northeast of the city, east of State Route 14 and just off Airport Road. It has two runways, the longer of which is 6,891 feet. The airport is at an elevation of 1,742 feet MSL. It caters to most domestic airlines and some commuter lines as well as general aviation. There are no other airports in the Pierre area.

References

Newspapers
Rapid City Journal
Pierre Daily Capitol Journal
Spearfish Queen City Mail

Organizations
None

People
J. G. Nikkels   C. John McKillop
Margaret Fossum Forgette (Lindbergh Foundation)

CHEYENNE, WYOMING

CAPSULE HISTORY OF CITY

Cheyenne is one of the most historic towns of the Old West and is the capital and largest city in Wyoming. It is located in the southeastern corner of the state. Maj. Gen. Grenville M. Dodge, chief engineer for the Union Pacific Railroad, selected the site of Cheyenne in 1867. It is named after the Cheyenne Indians, a warlike tribe of the plains.

SEPTEMBER 2–3, 1927 (FRIDAY AND SATURDAY)

The Cheyenne air mail field was the only facility available at that time, and it was located north of the city, on the site of the present airport. It is at the north end of Central Avenue, which runs into U.S. Route 85-87. There was one hangar located on the field at that time.

One-half hour after the Fairchild landed, Lindbergh was spotted over the city where he circled several times before touching down at 1:58 P.M. He had arrived over the area from the north. After landing he taxied directly to the hangar where the NYP and the Fairchild would be housed behind locked doors for the night.

Shortly after Lindbergh and his crew landed, they were assured that the aircraft were secure. They were officially met by Governor Frank C. Emerson, Mayor C. W. Riner, Gen. Dwight F. Aultman, and chairman of the local committee, Wilfred O'Leary. In a few minutes the parade left the field and headed down Central Avenue to 16th Street, then west to Carey Avenue and north to Frontier Park, located northwest of the city, near Sloahs Lake and Lake Absarra.

At the park the 1st Infantry from Fort Russell "Parade of the Troops" entertained the crowd until the parade arrived and the dignitaries had mounted the grandstand. Children of Cheyenne and the rest of the state filled the lower deck of the grandstand and were given front seats. Lindbergh spoke for about ten or fifteen minutes. Then the party paraded downtown to the Plains Hotel, where he and his crew held a press conference.

After a rest period at the hotel, the crew, committee, and other VIPs made their way to the local Masonic Temple, where the evening banquet began at 7:00 P.M. There were six hundred people attending the sold-out banquet that evening. The dinner was provided by the ladies of the Presbyterian Church. They were swamped with requests to volunteer as servers. This was a switch, as in the past they had difficulty finding people interested in helping out with *any* church activities.

In Lindbergh's two presentations he stressed the importance of commercial air travel with improvement of the local flying field.

It was noted during his visit that at this time widespread airlines in Germany were doing a thriving business, with a total of 56,268 passengers having been carried for a total of four million miles and the loss of only four people in mishaps.

In the year 1926 there was only one air fatality for every million miles flown in the United States. Lindbergh pointed out that aircraft engines are much more reliable these days, and that aviation and all its branches have been reduced to such a science that one can hardly continue to classify flying as a more hazardous occupation, pastime, or mode of transportation

After Lindbergh's arrival, a Ms. Bonnie Gray appears to be "worshipping" the NYP for some reason. Quite dramatic. WYOMING STATE MUSEUM VIA LEIGH A. MEYERS

Appear to be some local aviators having their picture taken standing near the NYP. PAT HALL

Wonder who the little boy is and where he might be today? PAT HALL

than automobiling. He brought forth an honest and justifiable change in the people's mental attitude that was to bring to aviation the great progress that it deserved. He also pointed out the fallacy that air travel belonged to the ultra-hazardous class, for authentic figures reveal a degree of safety for airplanes that automobiles would have difficulty reaching.

Lindbergh and his crew were at the field bright and early the next morning to prepare for the next leg of their tour—Cheyenne to Salt Lake City, Utah, where they would fly over some of the most desolate and beautiful Western terrain yet encountered. The seven hour and thirty-five minute flight took him over Laramie, Parch, and Rawlins, Wyoming, Craig, Colorado, and on to Mt. Pleasant, Utah, before continuing on to Salt Lake City.

Lloyd J. Jensen remembered Lindbergh flying over the town of Mt. Pleasant, Utah. The town mayor waved a flag at the flyer, and Lindbergh dropped his message bag. Jensen said that there was a family by the name of Lindbergh in town. It has never been confirmed that this was the reason for flying over this little town in the middle of the state.

It was during this flight that Lindbergh climbed the NYP up to 19,800 ft altitude, possibly to get over the Rocky Mountains as well as the High Uintas Mountains in Utah.

Today one can fly in and out of the city by way of Cheyenne Airport, a very modern facility north of the city. It has a 9,175-foot runway at 6,156 feet MSL. The field serves some domestic airlines, commuter airlines, Air National Guard, and general aviation.

Only a couple of private airstrips exist in the area of Cheyenne now.

References

Newspapers
  Wyoming Eagle
  Wyoming Tribune-Eagle

Organizations
  State Historical Museum
  Cheyenne Airport
  University of Wyoming – American Heritage Center

People
  Leigh A. Meyers   Walter M. Jeffries Jr.
  Pat Hall   John E. Hanks
  Rhonda Sedgwick Stearns

Stop #40
Salt Lake City, Utah

Capsule History of City

Salt Lake City is the capital of Utah and the largest city in the state. It is located in a spectacular setting in the north central part of the state near the southeast corner of the Great Salt Lake, in the Salt Lake Valley at the foot of the Wasatch Range of the Rocky Mountains. Before white men found the area it was inhabited by the Paiute, Shoshoni and Ute Indian tribes. James Bridger and other American trappers visited the area in 1824, but in 1847 a group of Mormons led by Brigham Young established the site and named the city after the Great Salt Lake. Young proclaimed to his followers, "This Is The Place," for which the city is famous. The Mormons had traveled across the country to escape persecution and to be able to worship in their own way. The city was incorporated in 1851 and became the territorial capital in 1856.

4,330 feet MSL

September 3–4, 1927
(Saturday and Sunday)

Salt Lake City had an airport at the time Lindbergh came to town, known then as Woodward Field. It was named in honor of a local pilot, John P. Woodward, who was killed when his airplane crashed into a ledge of rock near Tie Siding, Wyoming, during a snowstorm. Woodward Field was at an elevation of 4,301 ft MSL and covered 105 acres of flat, open plain four miles west of the city. It was an ideal location close to the city, and there was unlimited room for expansion.

Woodward Field was on the north side of North Temple Street, west of the city near Sperry Way, which today would be the southeast corner of the present Salt Lake City International Airport. Later hangars were built for Western Air Express, Inc., the Boeing-Hubbard Line, and the Varney Line. All contract air mail routes were privately owned and operated. It was also known as Salt Lake City Airport. Also on the

field then was the 10th Army Air Reserve Corps under the command of Lt. Russell L. Maughan, the Utah flier who became famous for his dawn-to-dusk flight across the continent in a Curtiss Pursuit PW-8 on June 23, 1924.

Lindbergh was usually quite punctual but arrived over Salt Lake almost an hour early. He spent time circling over Bingham copper mine, Utah Lake, and the Great Salt Lake before setting down on the airport.

The Fairchild came into view before the NYP and soon landed to supervise the upcoming celebration. At precisely 2:00 P.M. Lindbergh touched down on the field, and taxied up to one of the hangars, most likely the Western Air Express hangar. He was officially greeted by Mayor C. Clarence Meslen, Governor and Mrs. George H. Dern, Congressman W. H. King, E. O. Leatherwood, Congressman Donald B. Colton, Col. Walter B. McCaskey, Senator Reed Smoot, and Chairman Ben F. Redman.

Soldiers from Fort Douglas were already assigned to control the many thousands of people at the airport and along the parade route into Salt Lake City. Lindbergh was escorted to the waiting car, where he climbed aboard and sat up on the top of the back seat along with Mayor Meslen and Governor Dern. The car was driven by Thomas F. Kearns, president of the Salt Lake Tribune Publishing Company. The parade started from the field and headed east on North Temple Street and into the city.

Some of the local citizens viewing the NYP on Woodward Field at Salt Lake City. LEO B. KIMBALL COLLECTION

Streets along the parade route were decorated with bunting and flags. Young patients at the L.D.S. Primary Children's Hospital located on North Temple Street were taken outside to watch the parade and wave to their hero. On the north side of the Brigham Young Monument, the flyer saw a twelve-by-twelve-foot portrait of himself.

All state and city offices closed that day at noon, including the stores in the city so that customers as well as workers could view the parade. Closing time was signaled by blowing the steam whistle at the Denver and Rio Grande Railroad shops.

The parade headed for Liberty Park on 9th South and 6th East where an archway formed by two immense paper sego lilies designed by Jack Sears was mounted. Sears was one of Utah's best known artists. On top of the archway was a replica of the NYP, covered with blue flowers, and a portrait of Lindbergh painted by Mrs. Sears. The parade went all around the outside drive of the park. Each of Salt Lake's schools had an assigned spot around the route for the students to stand. Boy Scouts in uniform policed that portion of the parade. Then the parade headed down the center drive where a crowd of 10,000 people jammed around the bandstand. From the car to the stand Lindbergh walked through a double line of two hundred beautiful girls from every part of the state. They were dressed in their finest summer dresses and each held a bouquet of flowers. During this procession the band played "Ain't She Sweet."

The NYP being guarded by National Guard troops on Woodward Field. The nose of a Douglas M-2 can be seen in the background. LOUISE B. APOSHIAN

Harry L. Finch, the City Commissioner of Parks, was master of ceremonies. Senator William H. King and Congressman E. O. Leatherwood said a few words before Lindbergh was given the stand. He began with, "What the next ten or fifteen years will bring can only be judged in the light of developments of the last decade. From a converted Army crate and a little stunt flying we have progressed to especially designed passenger planes having enclosed cabins, upholstered seats, heating equipment, ventilation systems, lights and other improvements."

Lindbergh urged cities, commercial companies and states to improve immediately and prepare for the swiftly developing new conquerors of the air. "Those who have the facilities and the proper regulations in the beginning will be forever the air centers," he said. "Four foundations for proper air commerce are: airworthy craft, competent pilots, suitably equipped airways and airports, and standard air traffic rules.

"If Salt Lake wishes to be a center of aviation and air travel, they had better improve the local airport and its facilities. This would include the removal of high tension wires near the field at that time." He said that local pilots would be the best people to offer their suggestions related to how to improve the flying field.

Following the address Lindbergh handed medals to the four winners of the model airplane contest conducted by the City Recreation Department. The winners were L. Clark Jacobsen, Joseph Wade, Merlin Behunin, and Theodore Marx.

Donald Keyhoe also had some words to say.

The entrance to Liberty Park was appropriately decorated. Notice the car on the left and the driver hand-cranking the engine that must have stalled. KLAMATH COUNTY MUSEUM

"Cities without airports are finding themselves in the same class as coastal cities without harbors. Naturally, those cities which possess good airports will attract present and future air commerce."

After the ceremonies the parade proceeded to the Hotel Utah, arriving at 4:00 P.M. After a brief meeting with the press, the crew spent time resting in the Presidential suite before the evening banquet, which was held at the Tabernacle.

That evening the world-famous Tabernacle was filled to capacity as music was played by the 38th Infantry band from Fort Douglas. Additional music included selections by the Mormon Tabernacle Choir and an original organ fantasy, "The Winged Ambassador," composed by Professor Edward P. Kimball. Senator Reed Smoot gave an address of welcome. Governor Dern mentioned that Lindbergh was "the most popular hero America has ever had."

During Lindbergh's presentation that evening, he predicted that the time would come when a person could fly from Salt Lake City to New York in twenty-four hours and be in Europe within three days.

Viola A. Stout wrote, "I was in bed with a newborn baby when Lindbergh came to Salt Lake City. I would have liked to have been at the airport to greet him and also to have been at the meeting in Liberty Park and the Tabernacle on Temple Square to hear his speeches. Not able to be present I nevertheless shed tears of joy and waved a flag for him from my bed of confinement, such was my admiration and feelings for Lindbergh and what he accomplished."

At the Children's Hospital Lindbergh presented the patients with a box of candy that had originally been placed in his care. He said that he seldom ate candy and felt it would be more appreciated by the children. Along the shining top of the box Lindbergh wrote, "To The Kids From Lindy."

"Good Bye," "Good Luck," and "God Speed" were heard all over the airport as Lindbergh came out the next morning to preflight the NYP. People had arrived before dawn so they would not miss his departure. There were approximately 20,000 people on the field that morning to say "Good Morning" and "Good Bye."

Shortly after he took off he headed out to Saltair, then made a 180-degree turn and headed back, very low, over Woodward Field, waving out of the cockpit to say goodbye. Then he headed north toward Ogden.

PERSONAL MEMORIES AT SALT LAKE CITY

George D. Evans remembered that a local candy company sold "Lindy" candy bars at the Salt Lake City occasion.

Helen McKean was thirteen years old and incapacitated by an accident to her foot the day before. She was determined to walk on her crutches the five blocks to see Lindbergh at Liberty Park.

Nine-year-old F. Richard Pugmire said he was there and that Lindbergh landed from north to south. Pugmire rode his bicycle seven miles from his home to the field.

Amelia Bennion remembers her mother giving permission for "Sunday Best" for an important day in her early life when she was eight years old. She wore a new voile dress as the family traveled downtown to help welcome the aviator. They arrived at Liberty Park and maneuvered to the curb for a child's space. "All at once everyone was looking, not up the street, but directly at me." Someone exclaimed, "Oh look!" A huge butterfly hovered over Amelia's head and landed right on her shoulder, nestling into the soft folds of her lovely yellow dress. They said, "The butterfly thinks she is a flower."

"I dared not move," Amelia remembered, "nor could I let go of this incomparable feeling of happiness at being me. Yes, I was as beautiful as my favorite doll."

OGDEN, UTAH

It was Sunday morning when household chores and preparations for the meetings of the Sabbath Day in Ogden were filled with excited talk of what was soon to be. Those people at church had a difficult time paying attention to anything but the imminent happening then only moments away.

Soon he came into view. The work chores and meetings in churches came to an end with everyone running out into the streets. Lindbergh dropped his canvas bag message, "To the city of Ogden, Utah." Luke Wheelwright retrieved the

message on the ground near the Orpheum Theater and then turned it over to Jesse S. Richards of the Ogden Chamber of Commerce. Lindbergh circled three times over the city and then disappeared to the northwest heading for Boise, Idaho. In admiration and awe the people of Ogden waved and tipped their hats to say goodbye. They returned to their homes and previous tasks. Those who returned to the church houses didn't return to their lessons, however. The remainder of the meeting time was spent in very animated talk as people excitedly recounted what happened. They were seeing something new and so different everyone was out gawking. Most had seen an airplane before, but what they had seen was very small and seemed like a toy in comparison. Often what they saw had an open framework—no sides, no door, just wings and a motor. Lindbergh's plane was so big that they were amazed at the size and that an object so big could be flying. They were afraid that it might just fall down. They were all keyed up beyond comprehension. They were yelling, waving flags, hats and handkerchiefs, banging cans, pounding drums, shooting off guns, making all kinds of noises, anything that would add to the celebration. The noise was deafening, the mood almost hysterical.

Because it was Sunday they were all thinking in very religious terms, "What has God wrought?" from Numbers 23:23, and this bore more powerfully into their minds than ever before. "Make a joyful noise unto God," the Scripture told them. Outside their meeting places they had done just that. What a great development they had seen that day which they considered to be part of the handiwork of God for the benefit and blessing of His children. Lindbergh's accomplishment filled the people with pride and patriotism for their country and was further evidence to them that they lived in a land chosen above all other lands, for which they would always be grateful.

Mrs. Peter T. Takler (Mary Ethel Jones) remembered being in grade school in Ogden when the principal decided the flight was a historic event. "He dismissed us long enough to go out on the playground and watch the flight go over us. The sun shone brightly."

He flew over the town of Oakley, Idaho, on his way to Boise. Dorothy Smith Whitely remem-

bered while living there that Lindbergh flew over the town in tribute to Mrs. Lena B. Price, mother of Noel Davis, whose flight preceded Lindbergh's but was not successful. The people of the town met on Tabernacle Hill and surrounded Mrs. Price. He dropped a message to her.

Because Salt Lake City had been so ideally located, both geographically and topographically, the local airport was at the heart of a vast stretch of level plain, isolated from all obstructions to landing and taking off.

Today the Salt Lake City International Airport occupies the same basic property where Woodward Field was located, north-northwest of the city, four miles west of the business district, just off Interstate 80. It is at an elevation of 4,227 feet MSL, with 12,000-foot runways and a modern airline terminal. The field serves most domestic and international airlines, some commuter airlines, general aviation, and Air National Guard operations.

Seven miles southwest of the city is Salt Lake City Municipal Airport No. 2 with a single runway of 5,860 feet, at an elevation of 4,603 feet MSL. The field is mainly used for general aviation and Air National Guard operations.

Three miles southwest of the town of Bountiful, and about 3 miles northeast of Salt Lake International, is Skypark Airport. It is at an elevation of 4,234 feet MSL, with a single north-south runway of 5,250 feet. It is a general aviation field.

References

Newspapers
Salt Lake Tribune
Deseret News
Daily Spectrum, St. George, Utah
Salt Lake Telegram
Daily Herald, Provo, Utah

Organizations
Utah State Historical Society
Salt Lake City Public Library
Air National Guard
Charles Redd Center for Western Studies, Brigham Young University
Heritage Associates

People
Donald R. Hall, retired teacher
Richard Berghout   Justin C. White
Debbie Hellberg   Mrs. Peter Takler
Dr. Steve Lacy, of Footprints from the Past Museum
David C. Montgomery, Ph.D., Brigham Young University
Delores Hansen Auger
Sgt. Gilles Gohier   Dorothy B. Wetzel
James Allen Smyth   Dale J. Bain
Joseph D. Staker   George Evans
Pat L. Farr   Mrs. Alice H. Stokes
Grace D. Day   Ida M. Nelson
Vera Paget   Ruth O. Thompson

Parry D. Sorenson   Jessie L. Embry
Whitney D. Hale   W. Glenn Swaner
Willis G. Nelson   Mrs. Merlin Behunin
W. Dee Halverson   Amelia A. Bennion
Florence E. Holsinger   Ethel R. Johnson
Everet D. Wood   Clyde O. Porter
Louise B. Aposhian (Louise B. Boehme)
Mrs. Arthur B. Williams
Lillian S. Huish   John Quincy Adams
Letha L. Wilcox   Lloyd J. Jensen
Dorothy Smith Whitely   Luacine P. Bunnell
Charles E. Jeffery   James H. Budd
F. Richard Pugmire   Thomas J. Parmley
Helen McNair (nee McKean)
Dorothy E. Jacob   Marjorie A. Jones

Stop #41
Boise, Idaho

Capsule History of City

The largest city and capital of Idaho, Boise is located beside the Boise River in the west-central portion of the state.

Sometimes called "The City of Trees," stately old trees still line the streets of Boise. It got its name from French-Canadian trappers—les bois in French meaning "the woods," or boise meaning "wooded."

The city was founded in 1863 as Fort Boise, a military post. It received its charter in 1864. The city is also home to the Boise State University and regional medical centers.

2,704 feet MSL.

September 4–5, 1927 (Sunday and Monday)

Boise had a municipal airport at the time. It was a wild forty acres a half-mile south of town and was known as "College Field," but sometimes called Ridenbaugh's Island, since a south branch of the Boise River encircled it at the base of the bench. The field was located where the present-day Boise State University campus is now located, along the south side of the Boise River and on the north side of University Drive. It was somewhere between Capitol Boulevard and Broadway on the east side.

After leaving the Salt Lake City area, Lindbergh and his crew flew over Bingham and Ogden, Utah, then Oakley and Twin Falls, Idaho. The flight took them four hours and thirty minutes. Lindbergh was nearly an hour overdue, so it was almost 3:00 P.M. by the time he was spotted in Boise coming in from the southeast. Soon he came in low over the "barracks field" and then turned toward the main thoroughfare of the city. It was standard procedure for Lindbergh to fly over the barracks so that the former servicemen in the hospital could see the NYP.

On the day before Lindbergh's scheduled arrival, people came to Boise by the hundreds from eastern Oregon as well as southern Idaho. They came by train, bus, auto, and interurban streetcar. The local hotels were crowded with most of these people. The downtown buildings were decorated with flags and buntings. Store

Here the NYP taxies in for Lindbergh's visit on the College Field at Boise, Idaho. IDAHO STATE HISTORICAL SOCIETY

windows were also decorated, and newspaper ads ran welcoming messages and pictures of the flyer. On the day of his arrival, autos lined the Mountain Home Highway for miles and nearly every vantage point along the bench overlooking the airport. Thousands of people lined the parade route between the airport and the fairgrounds, where he would give his outdoor speech.

One person who remembered being there when Lindbergh landed is Arline Martindale Scott Brinton, now living in Salt Lake City. She was eight years old at the time and traveled with her three aunts from Pocatello to Boise on the train. Their fathers worked for the Union Pacific Railroad, so they had passes. They also had relatives to stay with in Boise. They arrived early on the morning of the flyer's arrival and were able to find seats on the lower bleachers. They waited for several hours. When Lindbergh landed everyone stood, waved their arms, stamped their feet, and screamed in excitement. She had hoped to meet Lindbergh and marry him.

A special reception committee consisting of Leo J. Falk, Governor H. C. Baldridge, Mayor Walter F. Hensen, Boise architect Col. Frederick C. Hummel, and Col. M. G. McConnell of the Idaho National Guard received Lindbergh shortly after he landed.

Phil Love was invited out to the fairgrounds to hear his flying friend give the regular talk to the assembled throngs. He refused, saying, "No thanks, I don't believe I will. I haven't been in very many auto accidents." He then turned to give instructions about putting the Fairchild into the hangar. He planned to go straight to the hotel where he could wash up. "I generally hear Lindbergh whenever he speaks, but sometimes I miss."

When asked about why they were an hour late arriving at Boise, Lindbergh said, "Say, by the way, we were mightily distressed that we should get in here an hour after you people were expecting us. But we were informed in Salt Lake that there is a difference of an hour in time between here and Salt Lake and that Lindbergh was expected here at 2 o'clock, Boise time. That, we thought, gave us another hour. Instead, we learn we have been holding up the proceedings."

From the airport the parade of cars went directly to the ADA county fairgrounds, where Lindbergh gave his speech.

In his talk he said, "People throughout the country both on the farms and in the cities have now come to realize that aviation is a reliable means of transportation which has possibilities of furthering the development of our commercial life and social welfare. ... In almost every section the desire to do something to advance aviation locally has been expressed. This trip is made solely to interest people in the possibilities of commercial aviation.

"This trip is being undertaken in no sense as a personal journey. It is an opportunity for me, as one interested in forwarding aviation, to join with local civilian gatherings all over the country to promote the cause. I hope such a purpose will be accomplished, but it cannot be accomplished by a limited number of people. The great development which will make the United States take its rightful place in leadership can only be accomplished by the united efforts of people all over the country."

He declared that regular trans-Atlantic travel is bound to come, but before this the United States will be criss-crossed with a vast network of commercial airways over which aircraft will fly on regular schedules, carrying passengers, freight, and express. Next year will see fifteen-passenger planes

In the hangar at Boise is Col. Frederick C. Hummel and his son, Charles F., in front of the NYP. ARTHUR A. HART

Seen with Lindbergh shortly after his arrival, from left to right: Leo J. Falk; Gov. H.C. Baldridge and Mayor Walter F. Hansen. IDAHO STATE HISTORICAL SOCIETY

on most of the regular routes now established for mails.

"Just what the next ten or fifteen years will bring in aviation is hinted at in the developments of the last ten years," Lindbergh said.

After his presentation at the fairgrounds he was taken to the Veterans' Hospital where he spent some time with many of the disabled war veterans. From there he went to the Owyhee Hotel in downtown Boise. Here he met with the press and had something to eat. Then he and the crew took their usual rest and spent time discussing the next day's flight to Butte, Montana.

At the banquet that evening there were five hundred guests who gave a rousing cheer as Lindbergh entered the room and took his place among the other dignitaries. At the appointed time of seven o'clock, Boy Scout buglers sounded "assembly" for the hero. Lindbergh congratulated the committee for how well everything went at the airport, crowd control, the caring of the NYP and the Fairchild, all of which he deeply appreciated.

After some vocal songs by Mrs. Alice May Carley Lamb, a Boise singer, she was followed by Governor H. C. Baldridge, who spoke briefly about the development of transportation and particularly in relation to world peace. Lindbergh was then introduced. He spent some time telling of his New York to Paris flight and then got into the importance of air transportation development and the need for better air-

ports and navigation systems. At 9:00 P.M. the banquet was over, and the flyers retired to their suite of rooms in the hotel.

The plan was to depart from Boise at 10:15 A.M. and head northeast toward Butte, Montana. On this leg they would fly over the rough and jagged Sawtooth Mountain Range, one of the most isolated areas of the country they would encounter during the tour.

The crew was warned by the locals that the land between Boise and Butte was so precipitous that no one could sleep safely in a camp without tying himself to a tree to keep from rolling down hill. (Folklore?) It was further suggested that they deviate around the worst stretches. Lindbergh replied, "That's where the airplane beats other forms of transportation. How long does it take to go to Butte by railroad?" He was told about nineteen hours. "We'll make it in a little over three hours," he said. "That's two-thirds of a day saved."

Lindbergh noted that there were some power lines they would have to clear during their take-off. He cleared the wires by a safe margin, but the Fairchild with its load of three men and equipment cleared it by scant inches, uncomfortably close.

During the flight over these rugged mountains, Lindbergh had fun going over ridges and down into canyons, completely in his element, according to his aid, Donald Keyhoe.

Today the city of Boise has a very modern airport with two long parallel runways, one 10,000 feet long. It's known today as Boise Gowen Air Terminal. The airport is located about four miles south-southwest of the city on the south side of Interstate 84, bordered on the south side by Gowen Road. It is also known as Boise Municipal Airport on local road maps. The field is at an elevation of 2,868 feet MSL and serves most domestic airlines, some commuter airlines, general aviation and fire-fighting aircraft (hot air balloons at the fairgrounds nearby).

References
Newspapers
  Idaho Daily Statesman
  Idaho Statesman

Organizations
  Idaho State Historical Society
  Boise Cascade Corporation

People
Edward L. Scott
Arthur A. Hart
Carlos Schwantes

Connie Abel
Dick King
Arline Martindale

Scott Brinton
Mrs. William Demond

Robert R. Auth

Stop #42
Butte, Montana

Capsule History of City

Butte, Montana, is called "the city that is a mile high and a mile deep." It lies on a plateau (butte) in a rich mining district near the southwestern part of the state. It is the fourth largest city in Montana and often referred to as the "richest hill on earth" because of its high production of copper and other minerals. It is the home of the Montana College of Mineral Science and Technology.

Placer mining for gold first attracted settlers in 1864. The town was laid out in 1867 just west of the Continental Divide.

5,765 feet MSL.

September 5–6, 1927 (Monday and Tuesday)

In this city where wealth and fame had been won hundreds of feet underground even though the city itself is more than a mile above sea level, preparations to welcome the world's most famous flyer were underway.

They were well prepared with fifty special policemen and 64 special deputies on duty, plus 66 enlisted men and four officers from Fort Missoula to control the crowd and keep things safe for the two airplanes expected shortly.

At this time Butte had an airport that was located just south of Elizabeth Warren Avenue and north of Four Mile Road, just east of the present Route 393 (Harrison Avenue) on the west, near the present Mountain View Cemetery. Mount Highland Drive runs south off Elizabeth Warren to the middle of the old field, which is now part of the existing airport.

The Fairchild arrived about one-half hour before the NYP, coming in from the southwest. When Lindbergh came into view people stam-

peded into a "wild western" welcome like no other in the history of the city. Before landing Lindbergh circled over the city, including Anaconda Hill, with a low pass over the airport. Coming in at 1:50 P.M. for a perfect three-point landing, he taxied up to the hangar. He was met by Phil Love and Donald Keyhoe.

In spite of the carefully made plans for security, the mob of people broke through the police lines and headed toward the NYP. But a line of automobiles, with the mayor and the reception committee in them, made a line between the crowd and the airplane, giving time for the security people to hurriedly erect a fence to protect the two airplanes and get them into the hangar.

Lindbergh had flown the 245-mile leg from Boise to Butte in just three hours and thirty-five minutes, including his circle over the city. He averaged 75 mph. They had flown over some of the most rugged mountain ranges in the country.

Shortly after landing, Lindbergh inserted the windows on each side of the cockpit before stepping out. He was met by Love and Keyhoe and then officially by Mayor M. Kerr Beadle and Chauncy L. Berrien, chairman of the Chamber of Commerce.

One of the first persons to warmly greet him and shake his hand was an old-time flying friend, Harold "Shorty" J. Lynch. They had flown in an air circus together in 1922. Also there to shake his hand was Mrs. Ralph McLeod of Philipsburg. Both had graduated from the Little Falls, Minnesota, High School in the class of 1918.

A group photograph was made of Lindbergh standing with Mayor Beadle, Mrs. Beadle, Mrs. McLeod, Harold Lynch and Chauncey Berrien.

Shortly he boarded the Mayor's car, sitting with Donald Keyhoe, the Mayor, and William Downing. They drove out of the airport property, then north on Harrison Avenue to Clark Park, a ball park where Lindbergh would give his usual address.

The grandstand at Clark Park in Butte was filled for Lindbergh's speech. WORLD MUSEUM OF MINING

After Lindbergh's speech the entourage motored into town by way of Harrison Avenue, Front Street, Montana Street, Park Street, Excelsior Avenue, and then east on Broadway to the Hotel Finlen. After a short meeting with the local press, the flying crew rested for the evening banquet.

The banquet was held at the Temple Ballroom. His friend "Shorty" Lynch was seated with Lindbergh, the Governor, the Mayor and other officials. In the Governor's introductory speech he said that he understood that the flyer and his crew were tired at this point in the tour, and the speakers would make their presentations short. With that he wished for Lindbergh's eternal welfare to be long and lasting. On behalf of the city of Butte, Mayor Beadle mentioned that one of the reasons the city loved Lindbergh was that the flyer had written to the Mayor requesting that the grandstand at Clark Park be reserved for the children.

Introduced by Harry Gallway, toastmaster, Lindbergh urged the development of aviation and airports and generous patronage of the air mail, air express and the passenger lines to come as the surest way of making aviation supreme in a democratic country.

"I am not going to be able to talk to you this evening on anything but aviation and subjects bearing upon it. What I say I will try to tell you conservatively, and as far as I know it will be the truth and the entire truth. In considering the advancement of aviation it will be necessary to take into consideration the past. None of us knows exactly what the future of the airplane will be. But we do know that within our lifetime the airplane will become one of the greatest means of transportation because of its speed, because of its independence from obstacles that hamper land and water transportation, and because of its economy of operation.

"Aviation, as you already know, has been in existence less than twenty-five years. Less than a century ago steam transportation was first brought into existence. For the first years of steam transport, trains stopped running at night, the danger being considered too great in the darkness. Today we're flying not only night and day, but in good weather and bad.

"What holds aviation back today is that it is not yet practical for planes to land in a dense fog or to fly in stormy weather when sleet forms an ice-coating on the wings of the plane."

The *Spirit of St. Louis* on the ground in Butte. WORLD MUSEUM OF MINING

He continued to trace the development of aviation from the Wright brothers to the present (1927). He said that forced landings were more or less a thing of the past.

"The most important thing at present is the development of airports. I understand that the Butte airport has been enlarged and improved in the last few weeks. Yours is the spirit that will help to take this nation to the forefront in aviation. We need the same cooperation from every city in the country. Build airports. Develop them. Equip them well. Then patronize aviation activities. Keep Butte in the foreground in western aviation."

During the dinner the Butte Mines Band, under Sam Treloar's baton, played popular and patriotic numbers. At the speakers' table, in addition to Lindbergh, were Mrs. Harold Lynch, Mr. and Mrs. McLeod of Philipsburg, John S. Mooney, Chauncey L. Berrien, Philip Love, and E. E. Maidment of the Wright Aeronautical Company.

A contest, sponsored by the *Butte Miner*, was held to name the airport. The prize was thirty-five dollars. Each contestant would have to write about one hundred words stating the reason for the name selection.

The next morning (Tuesday, September 6), Lindbergh and his crew were up early, had breakfast, and headed out to the airport. They were accompanied by Mayor Beadle, C. L. Berrien, Al Wilkinson, and "Shorty" Lynch. After saying that this would be "just a jaunt to take a few photographs" before arriving at 2:00 P.M. at Helena, their next stop, Lindbergh took off at 7:45 A.M. This was to be a secret trip, so no one was informed why they left so early when it was only fifty statute miles from Butte to Helena.

After the Fairchild rose up to join the NYP, both flew off to the north. On this trip Keyhoe had made sure his two cameras were ready, and he had enough rolls of film on hand.

The NYP framed between the struts of the Fairchild, taken by Donald Kehoe. WALTER M. JEFFRIES JR.

Another photo taken from the Fairchild by Donald Kehoe of Lindbergh looking out of the cockpit window of the NYP.
WALTER M. JEFFRIES JR.

BUTTE TO HELENA
BY WAY OF GLACIER NATIONAL PARK

This was the first time on the tour that Lindbergh and his friends deviated from a more reasonable route between cities in order to see some spectacular scenery. Lindbergh had always wanted to see Glacier National Park, and now was his chance. He was sure they could still make their usual 2:00 P.M. ETA at Helena. After leaving Butte, the two airplanes flew out of their way to the next stop. Initially heading north, they first flew over Swan Lake Camp, Highgate, and on up north to be over the Continental Divide where it crosses into Canada. From there they headed eastward and over Cleveland Mountain, then northwest around Glacier National Park, and southeast to Blackfoot, near Browning. Then they went northeast to Sweetgrass, Montana, and north to Milk River in Alberta, Canada. Finally they headed south to Great Falls, and then on to Helena.

GREAT FALLS "FLY OVER"

Arriving over Great Falls, the two airplanes came swooping down low at exactly 1:15 P.M. Sirens from the Central Fire Station, the Great Northern Railway shops, and a local smelter announced their arrival before they had crossed the Missouri River.

Lindbergh dropped his canvas bag with the usual message, and it landed at Central Avenue and Third Street, in the middle of town. According to one newspaper, it struck the shoulder of Miss Mingeberg Myhr, proprietress of Peacock Shop in the Liberty Theater Building. She then fell to the sidewalk. (The story has not been confirmed, however.) The bag was opened by Mayor Harry Mitchell.

From there they proceeded to Helena.

References
(see second Butte stop)

STOP #43
HELENA, MONTANA

CAPSULE HISTORY OF CITY

Helena is located just north of Butte on the Continental Divide, in west-central Montana. It was never a regular residence for any Indian tribes, but was visited often by Blackfeet and Salish hunting parties. Members of the Lewis and Clark Expedition were the first white men to visit the area.

Owing its existence to a few prospectors, who named it the "Last Chance Gulch," they had found gold where the city's Main Street now runs. In October 1864 a group of settlers had a "town" meeting and decided to name the place Helena, because John Somerville, one of the settlers, and his wife were from Helena, Minnesota. Others at the meeting did not like the way he pronounced the name — HEL-ena — so they suggested it be "Hel-NA." The city became the territorial capital of Montana in 1875 and the state capital in 1889.

4,155 feet MSL.

SEPTEMBER 6–7, 1927
(TUESDAY AND WEDNESDAY)

The only airport at the time was called the "Municipal Airport," but in reality it was the Municipal Golf Course. The local police department, in addition to the Regimental Headquarters Company of the Montana National Guard, was assigned to patrol the field to keep law and order upon Lindbergh's arrival. A special en-

Both the NYP and the Fairchild tied down at the Municipal Golf Course at Helena. MONTANA HISTORICAL SOCIETY

A good side view of the NYP showing it tied down at the Municipal Golf Course at Helena. L.H. JORUD PHOTO VIA MONTANA HISTORICAL SOCIETY

closure was built to house the two airplanes since a hangar did not exist at that time.

The Fairchild came into sight and landed at 1:43 P.M., and Lindbergh landed a few minutes before 2:00 P.M. He was greeted by Governor John E. Erickson, Mayor Percy Witmer, Scott Leavitt, Thomas A. Marlow, former Governor Sam V. Stewart, A. M. Holter, W. A. Campbell, E. J. Murphy, Brent N. Rickard, Fred Kessler, and E. W. Brown.

He was escorted to the waiting car of C. B. Power and sat in the rear of the open car between the governor and the mayor. From the airport the motor parade made its way to the State Fairgrounds, where more than 25,000 admirers were waiting to see Lindbergh and hear what he had to say. The *Helena Independent*

The NYP over the Rockies during the western part of the tour. KEYHOE PHOTO VIA WALTER M. JEFFRIES JR.

newspaper printed that "women fainted and children screamed" as the throng pushed forward to get a better view of Lindbergh. Governor Erickson introduced the flyer. Lindbergh said, "Commercial aviation is safe. Mail and express services are the forerunners of a network of passenger lines. We need the cooperation of the American people in making possible this great advancement in transportation."

He was then escorted to the Placer Hotel, where he was given a suite of rooms on the fourth floor. One thousand fifty people attended the banquet held that evening at Helena's Algeria Shrine Temple. One writer years later said that Lindbergh was seated at the head table, with two young princesses from the state fair seated on either side of him. He gave another talk on the future of air transportation and the need for airports and further development of the industry, promoting the use of the air mail system and standardizing the country's airports.

HELENA TO BUTTE
VIA YELLOWSTONE NATIONAL PARK

After breakfast the next morning, the flyers were at the airport early to do a preflight of both airplanes. They were leaving early because they wanted to visit Yellowstone National Park in Wyoming. The airplanes were refueled, the oil checked, and the rocker arms greased as necessary. They took off at 10:05 A.M. and then circled the city several times before heading eastward toward Billings, east of the mountain ranges, out in the plains area.

There was a new airstrip at Billings on the

Another Keyhoe photo of the NYP over the Rocky Mountains. WALTER M. JEFFRIES JR.

rim rocks above the city. It was hoped he might land on it to check it over. However, he ignored this new strip and flew west of the city to circle over his old airstrip in the cow pasture, where he had operated from during his barnstorming days.

While over Billings he dropped the canvas bag with the message and then turned southwest, flying over Cody, Wyoming, toward Yellowstone National Park.

Lindbergh enjoyed this flight, flying low into the beautiful valleys and canyons, close to the many rock walls, over isolated lakes, low over a beautiful flowered valley, over some evergreen forest and more mountain peaks. In the Fairchild Love was not able to play-fly. He was carrying a load of three people, baggage, equipment and much fuel. They had to stay rather high to clear the mountains and to get through many passes, holding a straight line course to the next checkpoint or scenic view.

They flew over Yellowstone Lake and from there directly west to go over "Old Faithful," the famous geyser. Then they proceeded over Mammoth Hot Springs and the Grand Canyon of Yellowstone before heading for Butte.

On their way back to Butte, the Fairchild was running low on fuel. Communicating by sign language they headed straight rather than make any more detours.

It was on this leg that the clouds forced them down into the valleys between the mountains, causing them to scud run at less than 100 feet above the ground, landing at Butte at 4:11 P.M. after a flight of six hours and five minutes.

HELENA IN THE FUTURE

Possibly as a result of Lindbergh's 1927 visit to Helena, there exists today a modern airport. It is Helena Regional Airport with its longest runway at 9,000 feet. It is located on the eastern edge of the city near Interstate-15 and Highway 287. The field is at an elevation of 3,874 feet MSL and serves some of the major domestic airlines, as well as commuter lines and general aviation.

To the northwest is Fort Harrison AAF airport, a dirt strip of 2,800 feet at an elevation of 4,050 feet MSL. A short distance east of the main airport is a private strip named Woods, a dirt field 2,500 feet long, at an elevation of 3,850 feet MSL.

The golf course where Lindbergh landed is still there on the north side of the city and is now called the Bill Roberts Golf Course.

References

Newspapers
  Helena Daily Herald
  Montana Record-Herald
  Great Falls Tribune
  Helena Independent

Organizations
  Montana Historical Society Library
  Cascade County Historical Society

Publications
  Montana — A State Guide Book
  Montana and the Sky, by Frank W. Wiley
  "Oh, How We Loved Lindy," by Jeff Birkby, published in *Montana Magazine* by American Geographic Publishing, Helena

People
  Skeeter Carlson

The Spirit of St. Louis over Yellowstone Lake in Wyoming, taken by Donald Keyhoe from the Fairchild. WALTER M. JEFFRIES JR.

BUTTE, MONTANA

SECOND VISIT AND VACATION

SEPTEMBER 7–12, 1927
(WEDNESDAY THROUGH MONDAY)

After landing for the second time at Butte, one of the first persons to greet them was advance man Milburn Kusterer, who had ridden the train from Helena to Butte earlier that day. Kusterer was concerned that it had taken so long to fly the fifty miles from Helena to Butte. Lindbergh explained to him that as they flew over the Old Faithful geyser, they spent a long time waiting for it to spout, which it did not do. Kusterer was still puzzled even when Lindbergh said they only flew a short way off the course to Butte. Lindbergh always had a straight-faced, clever sense of humor.

VACATION

That evening the NYP was placed in a hangar for the night, while the Fairchild, with its folding wings, was housed in a newly built adjoining hangar. They all had supper with "Shorty" Lynch at the New Finlen Hotel and then were escorted by J. Carlos Ryan to his home up in the mountains for a four-day vacation. Lynch was included. It was on Elbow Lake in the Swan Valley area. Elbow Lake is 43 miles south of Swan Lake and forms the headwaters of the Swan River.

This vacation trip was arranged by John D. Ryan, chairman of the board of the Anaconda Copper Mining Company and also a director of the Guggenheim Fund.

On Thursday the group left by auto and went by way of Anaconda, Philipsburg, and Drummond. The first stop was made at noon at the summer home of Walter McLeod, president of the Missoula Mercantile Company at Seeley Lake. They had lunch there and then continued on to the camp.

Also joining Lindbergh at the camp was J. R. Hobbins, vice president of the Anaconda Copper Mining Company; Cornelius F. Kelley, president of Anaconda; L. O. Evans, an Anaconda attorney; Col. D. G. Stivers of Anaconda's legal department; J. E. Woodard, president of Metals Bank and Trust Company in Butte; Nills Florman of New York City; Louis Evans; Dr. R. C. Monahan of Butte; Frank Kerr, general manager of the Montana Power Company; and J. Carlos Ryan, the host.

While Lindbergh and Keyhoe were at the camp, Maidment and Love were engaged in servicing work on both the Fairchild and the NYP in their respective hangars. They did an oil change and general lubrication in addition to checking over the air frames for any necessary repairs.

On Sunday night Kusterer left Butte by train and headed for Spokane, Washington, to make arrangements at the next stop for Lindbergh's visit on Monday the 12th.

Lindbergh took off at 11:10 A.M. and took a basic northwest heading toward Spokane, flying directly over the town of Anaconda, then Bonner and Missoula in Montana, then over Wallace, Idaho, and over Lake Coeur d'Alene and the city of Coeur d'Alene in Idaho, and on to Spokane. He was in the air three hours and fifty minutes.

Today Butte has Bert Mooney Airport with a 9,000-foot main runway at an elevation of 5,545 feet MSL. The field is located on the edge of the south side of the city. The main runway (No. 15) at the north end of the airport is on the property where Lindbergh landed in 1927, just east of Mountain View Cemetery. This airport serves some domestic and commuter airlines, as well as general aviation.

References

Newspapers
  Butte Miner
  Butte Daily Post
  Montana Record-Herald
  Anaconda Standard
  Great Falls Tribune
  Idaho Daily Statesman

Books
  Montana and the Sky, by Frank W. Wiley
  Montana — A State Guide Book

Organizations
  Montana Historical Society Library
  Cascade County Historical Society

People
  Debbie Hellberg P. T. McDermott Jr.
  Skeeter Carlson
  C. Owen Smithers, photographer, Butte, 1927

Lindbergh and friends enjoy a break between stops. A short vacation was taken about halfway through the U.S. tour at Elbow (now Lindbergh) and Seeley lakes.
PICTORIAL HISTORIES PUBLISHING COMPANY

STOP #44
SPOKANE, WASHINGTON

CAPSULE HISTORY OF CITY

Spokane is located on both banks of the Spokane River near the eastern border of Washington and about fifteen miles west of Idaho. Two waterfalls in the middle of the city furnish hydroelectric power and add to the scenic beauty of the city.

Fur traders entered the area in the early 1880s. The town of Spokane Falls was officially laid out in 1878. The Northern Pacific Railroad first reached the site in 1881, and in 1889 a fire destroyed the business section of the city. Residents rebuilt the city and renamed it Spokane in 1890.

1,900 feet MSL.

SEPTEMBER 12-13, 1927
(MONDAY AND TUESDAY)

In 1927 the only airport was Buell Felts Field at Parkwater. The field is still in operation at the same location. It is located about five miles east of the center of the city, along the south bank of the Spokane River and across the river from the Sekani Boy Scout Camp. It is a mile or two west of Millwood. At the time of Lindbergh's visit it was a grass field, with several National Guard hangars.

On this day there was still unsettled weather

in the area with occasional light rain, rather cool, and with temperatures below normal.

At 1:55 P.M. Lindbergh was spotted over the city as he made his usual low pass above the business district. The Fairchild had already arrived at 1:15 P.M.

As Lindbergh came into the area a bald eagle was seen circling the infield of the Interstate Fairgrounds at about 1:45 P.M. The eagle then flew off to the east after circling the airport several times.

Lindbergh landed at 2:04 P.M., and as he taxied toward the hangars a small dog came out of nowhere and chased the airplane across the field until the NYP came to a stop. At this point the dog sat on its haunches and barked a welcome, then trotted off the field.

After the flyer climbed out of the cockpit, he gave instructions for servicing the airplane with fuel and oil. He was first met by Keyhoe and then Mayor Charles Fleming; Governor Roland H. Hartley; Harlan I. Peyton; Maj. John R. Fancher, Commanding Officer of the National Guard Flying Squadron on the field; C. V. Haynes; Frank Davies; Mayor Thomas G. Aston, and Walter Evans. Soon he was escorted to an open Lincoln car and sat between Mayor Fleming and Major Fancher. This car was the fifth in a caravan of twenty-one.

The parade of cars made its way to the Interstate Fairgrounds, located just south of the airport on the south side of Broadway. The motorcade came into the east gate of the park, and 15,000 people cheered. The area was cleared and guarded by police, Army troops, Boy Scouts and National Guardsmen. Troops from the 4th U.S.

Lindbergh has the honor of fueling up the NYP at Spokane with Red Crown gasoline, the choice of the times. EXXON MOBIL CORPORATION

A good overall view of the refueling by Lindbergh at Felts Field in Spokane. SAN DIEGO AEROSPACE MUSEUM

Infantry at Fort George Wright guarded Lindbergh throughout the day.

Beside the racetrack, seated on park benches just below the grandstand, the combined bands of North Central and Lewis and Clark High Schools waited for the arrival of the flyer. Lindbergh had requested that many children be present. Nearly every child carried some souvenir or flag to wave.

After a short talk Lindbergh and the entourage proceeded into the city directly to the Davenport Hotel. The flyers were given a suite on the mezzanine floor. At this time he held a brief press conference.

The evening banquet was held in the Marie Antoinette Ballroom of the hotel. Ticket prices were four dollars per plate. Lindbergh stated,

"We have today advanced to a stage where the airplane is entirely practical. Commercial aviation compares in safety

Lindbergh shaking hands with a Spokane official after landing. Donald Keyhoe in the raincoat. EASTERN WASHINGTON STATE HISTORICAL SOCIETY

with all other means of transportation. The development of the past has been during the brief period of a quarter of a century. Less than twenty-five years ago the first flight was made. Today we have advanced. That is an example of the engineering accomplishment of the past few years. The airplane is changed from that of 1903, one which could not take off from the ground, that could remain in the air only a few seconds, to the modern machine with the modern equipment that can fly over 100 miles an hour, carrying a load equivalent to its own weight, with motors up to 1,000 hp which could almost be placed under the hood of an auto.

"The average man and woman knows nothing about airplanes but must begin a study of aviation, the same as my parents did when the automobile first came into general use. We must be air minded. Everyone will find flying necessary in time to come."

Interviewed by an Associated Press reporter who asked for a statement on recent developments in trans-oceanic flying, he replied,

"Transoceanic flights which have been accomplished demonstrate the feasibility of air transportation between continents. The trend of future development should be toward making air transportation practical under all conditions. Years of development and scientific research will be required before such regular inter-continental service can be successfully inaugurated. During this experimental period we may expect casualties, yet to totally restrict hazardous flight would have the same effect on the future of trans-oceanic flying as the air mail would have experienced had it been abandoned by the government during the heavy casualty period of its pioneering days.

"The result of total restriction might be compared to the effect on aviation in general had legislation been enacted against all flying during the first few years following the flight of the Wright brothers, when, hour for hour, any flight was more dangerous than trans-oceanic flying is at present.

"The pioneering and development of al-

most every advance in the air is marked by the loss of its explorers or its scientists. Yet they would be the last to request that the advancement of the cause for which they gave their lives be retarded.

"Hazardous flights should not be prohibited, but they should be attempted only after careful study by experienced personnel with the best of modern equipment and for a definite purpose. In the future expeditions should be organized and prizes offered under conditions which promote the development of safer travel.

"Safety of travel does not rest alone in the perfection of plane and engine, but equally important is highly trained personnel, accurate weather information and other navigation aids, including a means of radio communication for use in case of a forced landing."

The next morning after preflighting both airplanes, Lindbergh took off from Felts Field at 8:44 A.M. and headed south-southwest toward Walla Walla, Washington, 125 miles away. It was rainy and overcast, not very good flying weather.

The first part of the trip was over two- and three-thousand-foot elevations of the mountain range. They had difficulty staying away from the highest elevations because of low ceilings and reduced visibility. Many of the passes were filled with clouds. However Lindbergh was able to climb up on top and hold a compass heading until he found a hole on the other side of the high elevations. He could then drop down to follow the ground and continue on in fair VFR (Visual Flight Rules).

The Fairchild had to detour far to the south. They found Cispus Pass, which they were able to fly through, close to Mount Adams. Almost within sight of Portland, Oregon, they followed the Columbia River, flying north to Seattle.

The Veterans Hospital at Walla Walla had sent a request asking Lindbergh to fly over the facility and the town. He responded favorably, arriving over the area about 10:30 A.M. He dropped the canvas bag with the message, which landed on the hospital grounds. Several flocks of ducks flew over the city at the same time, heading south to warmer weather. Just before the NYP came into view in the rainy con-

ditions, some startled pigeons were seen flying in a dozen directions at once.

Mr. Kern, Walla Walla superintendent of schools, asked the principals of the schools to call a fire drill just as the flyer came into view. The children piled out of classrooms to get a glimpse of the NYP. A reporter claimed that Lindbergh flew low over each school and waved to the children.

From there Lindbergh flew on to Pasco, dropped a message bag, and went on to the Yakima Fairgrounds. He headed northwest via Naches Pass on the north side of Mount Rainier, over Enumclaw and Auburn, on to Renton, and then into the Seattle area. On the way he circled over the Children's Orthopedic Hospital on Queen Anne Hill.

Today Spokane has several good airports, but Spokane International Airport is the main airport. Located a few miles west of the city at 2,372 feet MSL, it has a 9,000-foot main runway. It serves all major airlines and some commuter lines, as well as general aviation, cargo aircraft, and some military.

In addition, Fairchild Air Force Base is located about four miles west of the International Airport. The field has a 13,900-foot runway at an elevation of 2,462 feet MSL, and handles all military operations. Felts Field is at an elevation of 1,953 feet MSL and has two runways, the longer of which is 4,500 feet. It serves general aviation. A few miles south of the city are five private grass airstrips.

References

Newspapers
Spokane Press
Spokane Daily Chronicle
Spokesman–Review
Walla Walla Union-Bulletin

Organizations
Mobil Oil Corporation
San Diego Aerospace Museum
Eastern Washington State Historical Society
Cheney Cowles Museum

People

Ralph Nortell	Vance Orchard
Jerry L. Cundiff	Catherine Graves
Dr. Robert Henderson	Mrs. Lawrence Bernard
Doris and Ed "Skeeter" Carlson	
Larry B. Allen	Ernie Bursey, Ph. D.

Stop #45
Seattle, Washington

Capsule History of City

The largest city in the state of Washington, Seattle is located on the east shore of Puget Sound, about 125 miles from the Pacific Ocean, via the Strait of Juan de Fuca. It is a major shipping point of the Pacific Northwest and a gateway to the Orient as well as to Alaska. It is often called the Emerald City, situated between the rugged Olympic Mountains to the west and the volcanic peaks of the Cascade Range to the east. Famous Mount Rainier lies southeast of the city. The city lies on a narrow strip of land between Puget Sound and 18-mile-long Lake Washington. There is a series of locks and a ship canal feeding into Lake Union.

Before white men came to the area it was inhabited by the Duwamish, Snohomish, and the Squamish Indian tribes, where they fished and hunted. In 1851 a group of Illinois pioneers led by Arthur A. Denny settled at Alki Point on the Puget Sound. The town of Seattle was established on the shores of Elliott Bay in 1852. Seattle received its city charter in 1869.

This city is the home of the well-known Space Needle (607 feet high), constructed for the 1962 World's Fair, and has a city monorail system. It is also home of one of the world's largest airplane manufacturers, the Boeing Commercial Airplanes.

510 feet MSL.

September 13–14, 1927
(Tuesday and Wednesday)

The Naval Air Station was the only airport for Seattle at that time. It was also used by the Army at Sand Point, which is located northeast of the downtown part of the city on the shore of Lake Washington. Located between Pontiac Bay and Wolf Bay, that property today is shared by the Warren G. Magnuson Park, National Oceanic and Atmospheric Administration, and the U.S. Naval Support Activity, Seattle.

It was raining at Sand Point, and it was planned to put the NYP in the back National Guard or Army hangar on the field.

The NYP landed at precisely 2:00 P.M. and taxied directly inside the Army hangar, where Lindbergh shut down the engine. He was met by Mayor Bertha K. Landes; James W. Spangler, president of the Chamber of Commerce; Rear Adm. S. S. Robison; Brig. Gen. Richmond P. Davis; Lt. Cmdr. John H. Campman, in charge of the flying field for the Navy; and Maj. H. C.

The NYP is seen here in a slip as he made his approach for a landing at Sand Point. Notice the many boats in a choice location for this exciting event. PEMCO WEBSTER & STEVENS COLLECTION MUSEUM OF HISTORY AND INDUSTRY

K. Muhlenberg, who was in charge of Army flying activities in the area.

Lindbergh was whisked over to the yacht *Alarwee*, owned by A. S. Eldridge, where he had time to change clothes and have lunch. The yacht then conveyed Lindbergh around Lauralhurst Point (now Webster Point) to the University of Washington Stadium escorted by harbor patrol and police boats. At University Stadium Mayor Landes was the first to officially welcome the flyer. She mentioned that one of her interests was the future plans of the city for a new airport so that Seattle "will take its place in the front ranks and become the aviation center it is destined to be."

Then Brig. Gen. Richmond P. Davis, Commanding General of Fort Lewis, commented, "Your ideals are our ideals and to a man we are

A wonderfully clear view of Lindbergh by the NYP at the Naval Air Station at Sand Point, Seattle. PEMCO WEBSTER & STEVENS COLLECTION MUSEUM OF HISTORY AND INDUSTRY

behind you in our endeavor to awaken the air consciousness of our country. We take pride in what will be accomplished in the future, and we feel you are a messenger to the whole world in aviation, which is destined to play an important part in the future relations of all nations. We are with you and we pledge to you and your coworkers our undying support."

Lindbergh then came to the microphone to give his talk. "Seattle and other cities need the immediate construction of airports. Automobiles were hindered in advancement until the development of hard roads. Aviation will be similarly hampered until there are more airports, and planes will only reach a state of perfection when there are airports to encourage their use."

Then a motorcade proceeded from the stadium to Volunteer Park, driving all around the park roads so that the crowds of schoolchildren assembled there would have a chance to see their hero.

His enthusiastic reception at the park was not confined to men, women, and children, according to one newspaper reporter. Many dogs barked their approval and welcome. A howling chorus covered the entire scale. Great Airedales growled a bass as the beloved flyer approached. Collies, tugging and struggling, sang baritone. Fox terriers, white, black, and spotted, yapped their admiration in tenor. Freckled hands throughout the line were seen to lift Fido above little shoulders for a glimpse of the hero. And there was not a cat in sight.

After a short address at the park he continued in the parade to downtown Seattle to the Olympic Hotel to rest up with his crew, plan for

the next leg, meet with the press, and get ready for the evening program.

To attract attention to the Seattle visit, a movie theater exhibited an aircraft air-cooled radial engine. A local businessman was overheard saying that he thought they had the wrong propeller on that engine.

While in Seattle Lindbergh met with a grand-uncle, Francis C. Land, then eighty-one years old, who lived in poverty in downtown Seattle after a lifetime of wandering. He was feeble but able to attend all of the festivities. He had been given a new suit and a clean shave, and felt proud of who he was. His eyes brightened and there was a spring to his step as he got ready to meet with his grand-nephew.

Five-year-old Billy Boeing, son of a world-famous airplane builder and designer, had a chance to meet Lindbergh. The boy said, "I like him. I was wishin' he'd take me up. Dad and those mail men have taken me up in their big flies, and Lindbergh's looks as pretty to me as any of them. Can't he, Daddy?" The boy did get a hug from Lindbergh, however.

A well-known Ryan B-1 Brougham, (s/n 33) christened the "Queen of the Yukon," was in the area at that time. Clyde G. Wann, Andy D. Cruickshank, and mechanic Ed Smith were leaving Seattle to attempt a nonstop flight from there to White River. Wann was one of the officers of the Yukon Aircraft Company.

At the banquet that night in the Spanish Ballroom the first speaker was the Mayor. Additional speakers were Senator Jones; Lt. Governor Lon Johnson; Robert S. Boyne, Chairman of the Chamber Airport Committee, and President Spangler, who introduced Lindbergh. Lindbergh

gave his usual talk and retired to the hotel.

Lindbergh left the following morning, and after flying over the city, he headed south to Portland, Oregon.

Three major airports serve the Seattle area today, including Boeing-King County International, where one can find the famous Boeing airplane manufacturing facilities. The Boeing-King County International Airport is at an elevation of 18 feet MSL, and has two runways, the longer of which is 10,000 feet. Many test flights of Boeing-produced airplanes are made from this field. There is also much military and general aviation aircraft operating from this airport. The famous Museum of Flight is on the field, with an excellent history display of the early days of Boeing.

South of Boeing-King County, in Tacoma, is the Seattle-Tacoma (Sea-Tac) International Airport with its 11,900-foot main runway, at only 429 feet MSL. It serves most major domestic and commuter lines, as well as some military and general aviation aircraft.

East of the city of Seattle, about a mile west of the city of Renton and just northeast of Sea-Tac, is the Renton Municipal Airport. It is at an elevation of 29 feet MSL, and has a single runway of 5,379 feet. There are several fixed base operations on the field, besides numerous seaplane aircraft operations, banner towing, and other general aviation aircraft.

There are many satellite airports of all sizes and shapes around this northwest metropolitan city, including many seaplane operations. Flying in and out of Seattle can be one of the most spectacular experiences due to the beautiful scenery of the Cascade Mountains, the Olympic Peninsula, and the snow-capped peaks of Mount Olympus and Mount Rainier.

References

Newspapers
Seattle Daily Times
Seattle Star

Organizations
Museum of Flight
Seattle Public Library
University of Washington Library
Seattle Historical Society
Museum of History and Industry

The NYP in take off position on a rainy morning headed for Portland, Oregon. PEMCO WEBSTER & STEVENS COLLECTION MUSEUM OF HISTORY AND INDUSTRY

People
Denis Parks   Fred H. March Jr.   Howard Fox   Ginny Lyford
Peter M. Bowers   Tracy & Scott Cutler   James Campbell Sr.
Larry B. Allen   Merle Olmsted   Fedora & Rod MacKenzie
                                                        Mr. and Mrs. Guenther Schmidt

STOP #46
PORTLAND, OREGON

CAPSULE HISTORY OF CITY

Portland, Oregon, is the state's largest city, a major center of industry and trade, and Oregon's principal commercial center. It is an important West Coast port and lies on the northern boundary of Oregon, near the meeting place of the Columbia and Willamette Rivers. The city lies on the west bank of the Willamette River. Two land developers, Asa L. Lovejoy of Boston and Francis W. Pettygrove of Portland, Maine, founded the city in 1845. Ocean-going ships reach the city by way of the Columbia and the Willamette. Each of the two men wanted to name the city after their home city, so they flipped a coin, and Pettygrove won.

Portland is often called the "City of Roses" due to its many private and public rose gardens. The flower thrives in Portland's mild and moist climate.

The city also lies at the northern end of the fertile Willamette Valley. Mountains of the Coast Range rise twenty miles west of the city, and the view eastward is spectacular when one sees snow-capped Mount Hood.

Chinook Indians lived in what is now the Portland area before white people first arrived there. The city was incorporated in 1851. 25 feet MSL.

SEPTEMBER 14–16, 1927
(WEDNESDAY THROUGH FRIDAY)

The only airport serving the Portland area was sometimes referred to as Harris-Rankin Airport, a grass strip 800 feet wide and 1,500 feet long. It was run by famous aviator Tex Rankin and C. B. Harris. The field was located on Swan Island, north of the city, along the north side of the Willamette River and the south side of Willamette Boulevard, below the existing cliffs. The airport was established in the mid-1920s at the behest of the city council, which had decided the city needed an airstrip to accommodate the latest in transportation. It was constructed by the Port district and dedicated on September 14, 1927, at the time of Lindbergh's arrival. Airline service began in 1931 with Pacific Air Transport (PAT), run by Vernon C. Gorst of North Bend, Oregon, with Ryan M-l airplanes. They flew air mail on Contract Airmail Route 8 (CAM #8). Today the site is known as Swan Island Industrial Park, and includes the Port of Portland and the University of Portland.

The field did not have a hangar in 1927 so a pole structure with a tarp cover was erected to house the NYP and the Fairchild before Lindbergh's arrival.

After leaving Seattle, Lindbergh flew over the city of Tacoma, then directly to Fort Lewis. He then headed southwest to Olympia and west to Aberdeen on the Chehalis River near Grays Harbor.

From Aberdeen he took an east-southeast heading to fly over the towns of Centralia and Chehalis, where he dropped a canvas bag. His next fly-over was at Home Valley, Washington, east of Portland and from there directly to Portland. It was a warm, clear day for flying.

As he approached the city, he first circled over the business district and then the Veteran's Hospital. In the meantime the Fairchild had circled over Pearson Field in the small town of Vancouver, Washington, at about 1 P.M. before landing a few minutes later at Swan Island. As Lindbergh came over the field and made his landing at 1:59 P.M., twelve cannons of the battery of the Oregon National Guard were fired for a roaring salute to the flyer.

Most business establishments in Portland and the surrounding area closed for the afternoon to honor the visitor and give people a chance to see and hear Lindbergh while there. At noon that day the steamer Portland slid away from

Terminal No. 1 and headed for Swan Island with 400 people who were part of the reception committee. They were the only ones allowed on the island upon the flyer's arrival. The public was not permitted to come over to the field from the mainland.

After both airplanes were placed safely into the makeshift hangar under the protection of the National Guard, Lindbergh was met by Mayor George L. Baker, Governor L. L. Patterson, and Edgar R. Piper, managing editor of the *Oregonian*. Shortly Lindbergh was given a bouquet of roses by Dorothy Mielke, the present rose queen.

Soon Lindbergh and his crew were taken aboard Julius Meier's nearby yacht, *Grace*, where they motored over to the battleship *Oregon*, tied up by the north end of the Broadway Bridge. The party was whisked through the battleship and up to the street level, where the automobile parade was forming up.

Lindbergh was escorted to a waiting car driven by the Mayor's chauffeur, Orville Larson, where the flyer rode with Mayor Baker and Governor Patterson. The entourage proceeded to the United States Veteran's Hospital, then to Holladay Park and from there to the Benson Polytechnic School playing field. The parade drove around the infield of Benson Field and out again, continuing across the Burnside Bridge to the west side and on to the Multnomah Stadium.

Up on 12th Street a small orchestra of children beat the tops of pans together as cymbals when he passed them.

The Stadium was filled to capacity with schoolchildren and their parents or escorts. The Oregon National Guard band entertained the people, in addition to an eighty-piece harmonica orchestra, including soloists.

Lindbergh gave a ten-minute talk, again stressing the importance of commercial aviation, the need for modern airports, and people to develop an interest in air travel.

The next stop was the Multnomah Hotel, where they were given a suite of rooms on the fifth floor. The waiting press asked Lindbergh what he thought of Swan Island Airport. He responded, "Well, it's narrow; the length is fine, but it isn't large enough for a Class A rating. It should be 2,500 feet in every direction to get that."

A reporter then asked if that was why he

The NYP is shown in the open air makeshift hangar at Swan Island. Notice the hand-cranked oil pump on top of the barrel, with hose. ALLEN BENTZ

circled around before landing. Lindbergh said, "I always do that to see if there are any holes or obstructions. The visibility from my plane is fair. No, I'm not using a periscope."

"Why did you fly up the Columbia River?" asked another newspaper person. "Well, I had a tail wind on the way down, and I was a little ahead of time, so I went up the river. On the way down here I flew over Tacoma, Fort Lewis, Olympia, Aberdeen, Centralia, Chehalis and some Columbia River towns."

After the press conference Lindbergh retired to their suite of rooms. A former teacher of chemistry and physics at Little Falls High School came to the hotel to visit. She was Justine Dahm, now Mrs. Guy A. Jollvette, living in Portland. Lindbergh immediately recognized her, much to her surprise and delight.

An eight-year-old boy by the name of Donald Tucker had written to the mayor requesting an introduction to Lindbergh, so that he could ask for an airplane ride with the famous flyer. The mayor wrote back to the boy that it would be impossible, but that he would see that the boy was introduced to Lindbergh at some point in the visit. The introduction took place in the hotel sometime after the press conference. The boy was thrilled. His parents had made sure that he was all dressed up, wearing highly polished tan shoes, a brilliant sweater and knickerbockers, face shining from a recent scrubbing and eyes large with excitement through horn-rimmed glasses. He had shaken the hand of his hero. Lindbergh said that he regretted he could not take Donald for an airplane ride.

After this the crew of flyers spent time preparing for the evening banquet, which was held in the Arcadians Gardens at the hotel.

On Thursday the 15th, Lindbergh and his party spent most of the day in their suite—relaxing, sleeping, and planning for the next flight on the tour. Lindbergh slept for thirteen hours straight, getting up at noon.

A number of people remembered that exciting time in the City of Roses, all of them expressing to this writer that they never forgot it.

Paul Fischer was at Swan Island and had his picture taken with Lindbergh. He was sixteen years old and one of the winners of a model airplane contest.

Judges and winners of a model airplane contest at the time of Lindbergh's visit, left to right, rear: Lt. Okley G. Kelly; Art Mckenzie and Howard French. Front row: George Farrah Jr.; Louis Procter; Paul Bauer and Paul Fischer. PAUL FISCHER

Danny Grecco, prominent local aviator, known as the dean of Oregon aviation, claimed to have worked on the NYP at Swan Island, doing some fabric repair work to the left elevator.

Edith M. Bunch was seven years old then, and her father kept her out of school so that she could attend the festivities at the stadium. At the time she did not realize the importance of the event and what a memorable day it would be.

Cecile M. Morris was a senior at Jefferson High School, within walking distance of Swan Island. The principal let school out that afternoon so that they could see Lindbergh land. Her husband, whom she was dating at the time, installed the loudspeaker equipment at Multnomah Stadium.

Sylvia G. Gettig was a student at the old High School of Commerce in Portland (now Cleveland High School). The students were taken to Multnomah Stadium to see Lindbergh. It was a big thrill, and she remembered it the rest of her life.

James W. Daniels was an eight-year-old boy living in the University Park area of Portland at that time. He said that Swan Island airport was just being developed as a flying field then. They lived not far from a bluff that overlooked the island. He has remembered the sound of the NYP engine all these years.

Marion M. Sharp was ten years old. She lived about twelve blocks from Swan Island and was one of six children. Their mother walked them to the airport to see Lindbergh. It was an exciting event for them and they often remembered the privilege. Her husband remembered riding his bicycle to the site at the time. They did not know each other then.

Jay Ellis Ransom was thirteen years old and rode his trusty old bicycle, aptly named "Heap," and said the NYP flew along the east side of the river, from south to north along the bluff and then tilted the airplane's right wing sharply downward and waved to all of those eagerly watching him.

Rodney W. Samson was with the 116th Engineers, Oregon National Guard. He was asked to report to the Armory with seven others, dressed in their best uniforms, complete with Springfield rifles and side arms, and to stand by. They were taken to the Multnomah Stadium to be the Honor Guard to Lindbergh. Everything was calm and the crowd hung on Lindbergh's every word until the end of the speech. Then thousands of people wanted to shake the flyer's hand, and in the panicking mob, Rodney and his fellow Guardsmen were trampled on, thrown down, walked on, and had their uniforms ripped. But they did manage to get Lindbergh into the limousine that sped out of the stadium. He was proud to have been there.

After spending two nights at the Multnomah Hotel, the crew left at dawn on Friday by way of the Stark Street boat landing and were taken via a police patrol boat, *F. W. Mulkey*, to Swan Island. Once there Lindbergh made a quick pre-flight, climbed into the cockpit, and started the engine.

The NYP took off at 6:55 A.M. after a 35-second roll down the runway. Two minutes later the Fairchild took off and headed directly south. Lindbergh headed north to fly over Vancouver,

Washington, and back south over Portland for one last time.

From there he flew to Silverton, Chemawa (former Indian reservation but no longer there), Salem, south-southwest to Corvallis, south through the Willamette Valley to Eugene, and then over some beautiful country on a southeast course to Crater Lake at Crater Lake National Park. After the lake he headed southwest to Medford, Oregon, and then south-southeast to Mount Shasta, California, then Anderson (south of Redding), Red Bluff, and directly south-southwest to San Francisco. He dropped the canvas bags on Corvallis, Salem, and Eugene, Oregon. He circled Silverton, Chemawa, and Medford. The day was bright sunlight and clear for the entire flight south to San Francisco.

Today the Portland International Airport serves the city, and it is located on the south side of the Columbia River, about five miles north of the city's business district. This modern field is at an elevation of 27 feet MSL and has a main runway of 11,000 feet. It is served by many of the major airlines. The Air National Guard is on the field, and there are some general aviation aircraft operations as well.

There are a number of satellite general aviation airports around Portland that serve the area. These include the Portland Troutdale Airport, located 10 miles to the east of the city along the Columbia River. It is at an elevation of 39 feet MSL and has a single 5,400-foot runway. The field is mainly a general aviation facility. It is close to the well-known Columbia River Gorge.

In Vancouver, Washington, Pearson Airport still exists at the same location, just across the Columbia River, a bit northwest of the new Portland International Airport. It now has a paved east-west runway of 3,275 feet at an elevation of 25 feet MSL. It is a general aviation airport.

References

Newspapers
Sunday Oregonian
Oregonian
Oregon Daily Journal
Oregon Sunday Journal
Northwest Magazine

Organizations
Portland Public Library
Oregon Historical Society

People

Bryan Ev Cassagneres	Mrs. Sylvia Gettig
Alvin L. Andrews	Margarit Batty
Paul Fischer	Doyle Sells
Mrs. Jessie Parmer	James Daniels
Edith M. Bunch	Mary Banton Larsen
Marion M. Sharp	Jay Ellis Ransom
Frederick Kildow	Eugene A. Cabler
T. V. Ridgway	John Elott
Mary M. Worthylake	Rodney W. Samson
Max Schulze	Allen Bentz
Herb Hill	Cecile M. Morris

Stop #47
San Francisco, California

Capsule History of City

It was in 1595 that the Spanish explorer *Sebastian Rodriguez Cermeno* found what was then known as Drake's Bay. He renamed it *"Puerto de San Frencisco"* (Port of St. Francis), which established the name San Francisco for the area.

The first white men to view the site in 1797 were scouts of a Spanish expedition under *Gaspar de Portola.* On September 17, 1776, the Spaniards dedicated the Presidio (military post) of San Francisco. California became part of Mexico in 1820. In the interim the place became known as Yerba Buena, but was officially named San Francisco in 1847. The city was incorporated on April 15, 1850.
65 feet MSL.

September 16–17, 1927 (Friday and Saturday)

The first airport was planned by San Francisco's city engineer, and the Board of Supervisors accepted his plan. Mills Estate was the

best location from which to do further studies into the building of a municipal airport for the city. The property was located on the eastern edge of the city limits of San Bruno, on the San Francisco Bay about thirteen miles south of San Francisco.

The committee approached Ogden Mills, executor of his father's estate, suggesting the city lease a part of the family holdings in San Bruno for use as a temporary airport site. It was not near any high-tension power transmission lines. It was the most northern site on the Bay's shore free of climatic drawbacks. The former pasture land was dedicated on May 7, 1927, by Mayor James Rolph Jr. as a municipal airport.

Soon one steel hangar was erected and others were being constructed when Lindbergh arrived. The field had been equipped for night operations and had an administration building, in addition to a meteorological office, hospital and restaurant. It was considered one of the finest airports in the country. Timing was just right. Two weeks after the airport dedication, Lindbergh flew to Paris, proving again that aviation was the upcoming latest in transportation. The Mills Field site is still there, and today is known as the San Francisco International Airport.

There was a faint haze as Lindbergh arrived over the Golden Gate and circled the city several times while the Fairchild went ahead and landed at Mills Field to prepare for the flyer's imminent arrival. Despite the planning and the police and R.O.T.C. officers on duty at the airport for crowd control, thousands of schoolchil-

dren ran out onto the landing area. Lindbergh had to make several low passes before the area was cleared for a safe landing and he was sure he would not hurt anyone.

The Fairchild landed at 1:41 P.M., and Lindbergh touched down a few minutes after 2:00 P.M. He landed on what is today the north end of the San Francisco International Airport.

After landing and taxiing into a specially erected fence near the one hangar on the field, he had a few words with his aid, Donald Keyhoe. He was officially met by Mayor James Rolph Jr., who was dressed in an immaculate Palm Beach suit with matching hat, and City

Lindbergh with the San Francisco Mayor, James Rolph Jr., sometimes called Sunny Jim.
SAN FRANCISCO PUBLIC LIBRARY

Well-protected by a chain link fence, the NYP is seen on the old Mills Field, south of San Francisco. PETER M. BOWERS COLLECTION

Another view of the NYP at Mills Field with the tail skid on a bicycle wheel type dolly and within the fence enclosure. MRS. MARGARET NAYE

Supervisor Jesse Colman. It was reported in one newspaper that Lindbergh ordered one hundred gallons of fuel to be put in the NYP at this time.

Officials had planned to have Lindbergh sign in the new log book for the airport and also to preside over the turning of the earth to break ground for a new hangar. However, this event had to be postponed until the next day when he was to leave for Oakland because of the large and unruly crowd on the field.

From the airport Lindbergh was taken in Mayor Rolph's automobile north to the Ferry Building at the northeastern end of Market Street. He rode in the rear of the car with the Mayor and Mr. Colman. The parade began at the Ferry Building and then headed down Market to the center of San Francisco known as the Civic Center. The City Hall and the Library are still there.

After formalities in the Mayor's office in City Hall, Lindbergh came out onto a balcony and was introduced by the Mayor. Before Lindbergh gave his talk there was a display of fireworks for the children assembled on the Civic Center grounds.

Earlier Milburn Kusterer had made his way to the Civic Center where schoolchildren and citizens were assembled, to work out plans for the event. He said, "This is the finest and most beautiful setting in America for a Lindbergh reception. You can accommodate one of the largest crowds, and I believe that your reception will be one of the most striking of any city this Colonel has visited."

In Lindbergh's talk he said,

"Citizens of San Francisco, I am making this tour of America to help promote the science of commercial aviation. This is in the interest of present day aviation, but looking toward the future of this science from its splendid development today.

"In organizing this tour, we decided that the most important step in the future of aviation was to assist in the establishment and equipping of adequate airports. Therefore I would like to impress upon you the necessity of a progressive air development program in your city and in your state to keep San Francisco and California in the foreground of American aeronautics. I want to thank you all for the welcome I have re-

ceived here today, and I hope that you will turn part of your energies toward the development of an air program for your city, and I thank you."

It was at this time that he was given a gold plaque by the Royal Aero Club of Sweden by the Swedish Council.

From the Civic Center he was driven to the Bellevue Hotel, where he met for half an hour with the press and then was shown to his room on the seventh floor to relax and clean up before the evening banquet. The hotel was Lindbergh's for the day. Guests had to depart and/or enter by way of a rear elevator as the lobby and front area were under guard by police Capt. Arthur Layne of the Central district and a detail of men from the 381st Air Service Squadron U.S.A.R. plus squads of plainclothesmen.

During the press interview there were many questions about his private life. However, he tactfully said, "I'm sorry, but I'll have to ask that our public and private life be distinctly differentiated."

The evening dinner banquet was held at the Palace Hotel in downtown San Francisco.

While Lindbergh was in this large metropolitan city, a Chinese couple living there named their first child after the flyer, "One Long Hop."

While Lindbergh was in the hotel room that evening he had an opportunity to meet briefly with Lt. George O. Noville, one of the aids in the Byrd transatlantic flight.

While in San Francisco Lindbergh made a short visit to the Guggenheim Aeronautics Laboratory at Stanford University in Palo Alto.

Early on the morning of the 17th, the crew had their breakfast in their room and soon the hotel manager, Tommy Hull, made arrangements to have the flyers leave by way of a rear exit to avoid the crowd already assembled in front of the hotel to wish him farewell.

They were out to the field earlier than expected and Lindbergh was then given the opportunity to "officially" sign in the log book, which he did by putting in the NYP license number NX-211 and his pilot's license number T (Transport) #69.

The party that escorted Lindbergh from the city out to Mills Field included William G. Herron, vice-president of the Boeing Air Transport Company, Vance Breese of the Breese Aircraft Corporation and his wife, and Walter T. Varney, air mail operator and his wife and daughter, Virginia, and Lt. Noville.

Before he left the Bellevue Hotel, Lindbergh was visited by Kenneth C. Boedecker, Wright Company representative, who he knew at Curtiss Field in New York before the flight to Paris.

After the preflight of both airplanes, the NYP took off at 10:04 A.M. (the Fairchild seven minutes later) to the south, and then west toward the Pacific Ocean to take a look at the Seal Rocks and the Cliff House, including a wrecked ship at the entrance to the harbor. Finally they headed toward the redwood forests and Mount Tamalpais, near Micasio Reservoir. Shortly they flew low over the University of California at Berkeley.

Today the main airport for this city is the San Francisco International Airport (formerly Mills Field) with four parallel runways, the longest of which is 11,870 feet. The field is at an elevation of only 11 feet MSL and is served by most of the country's major airlines in addition to many foreign airlines.

Also in the San Francisco area one can find across the San Francisco Bay the Metropolitan Oakland International Airport and the Hayward Airport south of Oakland. Further south, just south of the southern end of the Bay, is Moffett Federal Airport (Navy), Palo Alto Airport, and farther south, San Jose International Airport. Many outlying satellite airports serve general aviation, including San Carlos Airport, a small general aviation strip along Interstate 101, northeast of Palo Alto. San Carlos is at 5 feet MSL, with a single runway of 2,600 feet.

Going farther southeast, in chronological order, one will find first Moffett Federal Airport in the town of Mountain View. Next is San Jose International 2 miles northwest of that city, and then Reid-Hillview Airport east of San Jose.

References

Newspapers
San Francisco Chronicle
San Francisco Examiner
Oakland Tribune

Organizations
San Francisco Public Library
San Francisco Historical Association
Northern California Chapter, American Aviation Historical Society
St. Louis Mercantile Library Association

People

William T. Larkins	Peter M. Bowers
Art Schefler Orestes	Walter M. Jefferies Jr.
Guy Falbo	Eva Machado
Mrs. Margaret Naye	Mel Patterson
Peter M. Bowers	
Jim and Betty Rollison	
Mrs. Carol R. Hughes Floto	

STOP #48
OAKLAND, CALIFORNIA
"TOUCH STOP"

CAPSULE HISTORY OF CITY

Located in what is known today as the San Francisco–Oakland Metropolitan Area, this city is on the eastern shore of San Francisco Bay, about six miles east of San Francisco. The great San Francisco–Oakland Bay Bridge connects these two large northern California cities. It varies from sea level to 1,500 feet in elevation.

Its original inhabitants were the Ohlone Indians. Spanish explorers were the next people to come to the area in 1770. In 1820 the site of the city was included in a Spanish land grant given to Luis Maria Peralta, a Spanish soldier. Sometime later, lawyer Horace W. Carpentier, a settler, obtained a town charter for Oakland and became its first mayor in 1852. Two years later Oakland received a city charter. Its name comes from groves of oaks where the first homes were built.

25 feet MSL.

September 17, 1927 (Saturday)

The only possible land site for an airport became available many years later, when the Board of Port Commissioners of Oakland negotiated for the purchase of 600 acres of land, known then as Bay Farm Island. The site was located south of Alameda Island and about twelve miles south of the business district of Oakland.

The site was geographically advantageous with clear approaches. On June 3, 1927, Assistant U.S. Secretary of War (Army) F. Trubee Davison met with the Oakland Board of Port Commissioners, suggesting an interest by the Army to use this land for a take-off point. Work began almost immediately and proper grading was done for a 7,000-foot runway.

Because of the New York to Paris flight by Lindbergh, a spark was lit to fly the Pacific, with the possibility of a first attempt at a nonstop flight, 2,416 miles to Hawaii, which had not been attempted before. On June 28 Lt. Lester Maitland and Lt. Albert Hegenberger took off in a Fokker C-2 bomber. Exactly 25 hours and 49 minutes later, they set the *Bird of Paradise* down at Oahu's Wheeler Field. One writer said shortly after, "The Pacific has been Lindberghed!"

The first civilians to fly from Oakland to the islands were Ernie Smith and Emory Bronte in the *City of Oakland*, on July 15. Many flyers entered the Dole race, sponsored by pineapple magnate James Dole, to fly the same route, all departing from this new airport at Oakland. The prize was $25,000. On August 16, the day before Lindbergh's arrival, Art Goebel, a Hollywood stunt pilot, with Navy Lt. William V. Davis as navigator, flew the Travel Air *Wooleroc* (NX 869) from Oakland to Wheeler Field at Oahu, winning the prize. The flight took 26 hours, 17 minutes, and 33 seconds. The Dole Race was also known as the "Pineapple Derby." Oakland Airport became a well-known airfield, with much publicity, proudly announcing the names of many of the nation's famous flyers there.

By July 1927 the airport was in full swing, becoming one of the best in the area. It became the focus of world attention during an important time in the development of aviation and air travel.

After making a low pass to check out the

The only photo ever found of the NYP at the old Bay Farm Island airport site for Oakland. Notice how low the trailing edges of the elevators are, actually touching the rough ground. FROM THE COLLECTION OF "SANDY" SANDERS, A NOTED ALAMEDA, CALIFORNIA PILOT, VIA RONALD T. REUTHER

newly graded surface of the airport, Lindbergh landed at about 11:30 A.M. to a highly controlled and well-behaved crowd of thousands of people.

After landing and being directed to park the NYP and Fairchild in a wooden fenced enclosure, he was greeted by Fred Caldwell, chairman of the reception committee and acting mayor. Mayor William H. Parker was ill. Once Lindbergh was certain the NYP was in good hands, he climbed into a waiting automobile and was driven a short distance to a speaker's stand on the airport grounds. Here he took part in the official dedication of the new airport and spoke a few words. Accompanying Lindbergh on the stand was William H. Parr, a member of the Board of Port Commissioners.

It was at this time that Lindbergh unveiled a brand new plaque honoring the Maitland-Hegenberger flight to Hawaii. It was set in a base of concrete in the airport turf.

Lindbergh said, "It's fitting that an airport as excellent as Oakland's should have been dedicated by such a flight as Lieutenants Maitland and Hegenberger accomplished." He also complimented the city for their new airport and stressed the importance of more airports around the country. Then he was driven back to the NYP and prepared to leave for the next leg of the tour. He took off at 12:25 P.M.

He had been asked to circle the Veteran's Hospital at Livermore, so he flew fifteen miles out of the way to satisfy this request. From Livermore he continued east to Lathrop and then northeast to Stockton. From there he went directly north to Sacramento. This flight took one hour and thirty-five minutes.

Robert P. Keller, a lieutenant general in later years with the Marine Corps, remembered being on the field at Oakland when Lindbergh visited during the tour. "I was then seven years old when my two elder brothers and I were taken to the airport. Lindbergh arrived and was ushered to a platform from which he addressed the vast and idolizing multitude. I was far too short to see him. My nine-year-old brother Harry was strong and obliging enough to hoist me onto his shoulders. I was then able to behold this tall, slender, boyish-looking man. What he said, I do not recall. I do recall being struck by an extraordinary case of hero-worship, the effect of which lasted for years."

Keller met Lindbergh in person during World War II in the South Pacific on Green Island in June 1944, when Lindbergh came there as a military advisor.

In celebration of the opening of the Oakland Airport and Lindbergh's visit, festivities continued well into the night. At 7:30 P.M. Lindbergh turned on the new street lighting system (airport?). This was done long distance by pressing a button during the banquet at Sacramento.

There were fireworks, music and dancing at the Municipal Auditorium. It was a historic holiday. An Aviator's Ball, the peak of the day's celebrations, took place at the Oakland Municipal Auditorium. Music was provided by Lynn Pryor's augmented orchestra. Horace Heidt was the guest conductor. It was also the seventy-fifth birthday of the city of Oakland.

Today, on the same exact site, one can fly in and out of the Metropolitan Oakland (Metro Oakland) International Airport. The field has a northwest-southeast runway of 10,000 feet at an elevation of 6 feet MSL, with two modern airline terminals, and is served by most of the major airlines in the country.

References

Newspapers
  San Francisco Chronicle
  San Francisco Examiner
  Oakland Times
  Oakland Tribune

Organizations
  Western Aerospace Museum
  San Diego Aerospace Museum
  Tower Aviation Services

Publications
  A Chronology of World Aviation, by Lt. Col. Gene Gurney, USAF (New York: Franklin Watts, 1965)

People
  William T. Larkins   Clifford W. Archer
  Genny Carlson   Alice S. Perry
  Ronald T. Reuther   Lawrence C. Ames Jr.

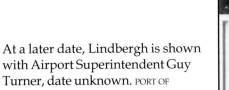

At a later date, Lindbergh is shown with Airport Superintendent Guy Turner, date unknown. PORT OF OAKLAND ARCHIVES

Stop #49
Sacramento, California

CAPSULE HISTORY OF CITY

The state capital, Sacramento, is located at the junction of the Sacramento and American rivers in the Sacramento Valley, about eighty-five miles northeast of San Francisco.

It is a historic city of the American West and was founded as a town in 1849 by John A. Sutter Jr., son of the Swiss pioneer who established the first white settlement in the area. The city was named for the river. In 1860 and 1861 daring riders of the Pony Express carried the U.S. Mail between the city and St. Joseph, Missouri.

Sacramento was incorporated as a city in 1850 and became the state capital in 1854.

30 feet MSL.

SEPTEMBER 17–19, 1927
(SATURDAY THROUGH MONDAY)

In 1927 there were two airports in the city. One was known as Irwin Airport, located four miles south of the business district. It was a municipal airport owned by J. F. Irwin. Today it is named Sacramento City Executive Airport or Sacramento Executive Airport.

The other field was Mather Field, which still exists on the original site and is about nine or ten miles east of the center of the city, just south of State Route 50.

It was a bright and sunny day as Lindbergh came into view from the south and circled the business district of the city several times. He landed ten minutes late, about 2:10 P.M., on Mather Field to a roaring crowd of 200,000 people. He was greeted and welcomed by Governor C. C. Young and Mayor A. E. Goddard.

Lindbergh taxied the NYP right up to the California National Guard hangar. The Fairchild had already arrived at 1:40 P.M. to be ready to give instructions to the ground personnel for the care of the NYP.

Also in the welcoming committee was pioneer railroad man John E. Lonergan, an engineer on the C. P. Huntington No. 1 steam engine. Lonergan drove the first locomotive over the Central Pacific line. Lonergan's eyes were wet with tears as he gripped Lindbergh's hand, as one pioneer to the other, and he whispered to the flyer, "God bless you, boy."

The large red automobile of Fire Chief M. J. Dunphy was provided to carry Lindbergh in the parade. Others in the car were the Governor, Keyhoe, the Mayor, and Darwin J. Smith, local aid to Lindbergh. Before Lindbergh arrived, the band of the 184th Infantry played for the crowd at the airport. The parade proceeded along Folsom Boulevard the full fourteen miles into the center of the city. They stopped at Moreing Field for a reception and went from there to the Hotel Senator.

That evening during the banquet Lindbergh pressed a button at 8:00 P.M. to turn on the new lights in the downtown area of Oakland.

The day of the 18th, Lindbergh and his crew rested in their hotel suite. It was reported that some friends did manage to pay a visit to him, but their names are not known at this writing.

On Monday the 19th they were up and out to the field early. Both airplanes were preflighted and fuel taken on. At about 10:24 A.M. they took off for Reno, Nevada. The Fairchild headed directly to Reno. Lindbergh flew west to Livermore flying low around the hospital several times. The veterans at Stockton had said that he did not fly over the hospital at Livermore but some other building when he was on his way from Oak-

The NYP in front of the hangar at Mather Field in Sacramento, California, with a curious crowd just behind the fence. WAYNE MOTE

Another view of the NYP at Mather Field. Notice the young lady checking the EIC drive cups on the top of the fuselage behind the cockpit. HAROLD W. TURNER, PHOTOGRAPHER

land to Sacramento. He then took a direct heading for Reno over the Sierra Nevada Mountains.

After Livermore he flew over Lake Tahoe, then north of Reno to Pyramid Lake and Smoke Creek Desert before making a 180 to fly south to Reno.

Today the capital city still has the use of Mather Field in its original location. Now it has a main runway of 11,301 feet at an elevation of 96 feet MSL. The airport handles mainly general aviation activities and corporate aircraft.

There is, however, a main airport for the city, which is Sacramento International Airport, located about twelve miles to the northwest off Interstate 5. It has two main runways of 8,600 feet each at an elevation of 28 feet MSL. There are two airline terminals which handle most of the major American and international airlines.

Northeast of the city is the former McClellan Air Force Base, and several miles south of the city is Sacramento Executive Airport, formerly Irwin Airport.

References

Newspapers
Sacramento Bee
San Francisco Chronicle
San Francisco Examiner

Organizations
California State Library

People

Alston W. Sutton	Harold W. Turner
Wayne Mote	Barry E. Wackford
Dick Hoerle	Mrs. Ann M. Bernard
Godfrey Amacher	J. J. Ralph
Merle Olmsted	Mrs. Doris Mehren
A. C. McJenkin	Robert Handsaker

A rare photo of the entrance to Mather Field at that time.
BARRY WACKFORD

STOP #50
RENO, NEVADA

CAPSULE HISTORY OF CITY

Known as the "Biggest Little City in the World," Reno, Nevada, is located along the Truckee River on the northwestern border with California, in a very sunny and dry climate. It is north-northeast of Lake Tahoe and within sight of the Pine Nut Mountains, the Virginia Mountains, and the Sierra Nevada Mountains in nearby California. The University of Nevada is located here as well as many gambling businesses.

Reno was founded in the spring of 1868, when surveyors for the Central Pacific Railroad laid out a right-of-way through the Truckee Meadows. Myron Lake, owner of much of the downtown area land, donated this area for a depot. Railroad officials named the fledgling community in honor of General Jesse Lee Reno, a Union officer who had been killed in battle in Maryland in 1863. The officials, Charles Crocker and Mr. Mills, who had known General Reno personally, wished to select short names easily spelled and remembered.

4,490 feet MSL.

SEPTEMBER 19–20, 1927
(MONDAY AND TUESDAY)

Reno did not have an official airport at the time, but an air mail field known then as Blanch Field. It was located on the west side of Plumas Street, south of Urban Road and Skyline Boulevard, north of West Moana Lane. Today the Washoe County Golf Course occupies the site at the fifth fairway.

During the afternoon of the 19th, Governor Fred B. Balzer issued a proclamation calling attention to the arrival of Lindbergh. State offices, schools, and businesses were closed for half a day from noon on. A special fare was offered on the trains of the Virginia & Truckee Railroad so no one would miss the event.

Various mothers clubs and other women's organizations of Reno contributed five dollars from each club to a fund for the purchase of an airplane pin to be given to Lindbergh's mother as a gift from the mothers of Reno.

The mountains in the area were white with fresh snow at the higher elevations in the district around Mount Rose and the mountains north and south of it.

Lindbergh was sighted over Reno at 1:40 P.M. After circling the field and doing a low pass, he landed in the southwest corner of Blanch Field at 1:55 P.M., about ten minutes after the Fairchild. He immediately taxied the NYP into the hangar before shutting down the engine. The hangar doors were closed. After he had removed his leather jacket and flying helmet, he was met by Keyhoe. He then shook hands with Mayor E. E. Roberts and Judge Frank H. Norcross, who represented the Governor.

The NYP in front of the hangar at Blanch Field in Reno. Names of the people in the photo are unknown. D. DONDERO COPYRIGHT

Under guard in the hangar at Blanch Field. Who is the little boy? D. DONDERO COPYRIGHT

A waving sea of humanity accompanied the parade with cheers, shouts, and flag waving. The parade went out of the airport grounds on to Plumas Street, heading north into the city.

The entourage passed near City Hall, then out onto 2nd Street and Riverside Drive to Idlewild Park, on the north side of the Truckee River, near McKinley Park Recreation Center.

Dr. Walter E. Clark, president of the University of Nevada, and Professor B. D. Billinghurst, Superintendent of Schools, were in charge of the celebration at Idlewild Park. Lindbergh made his way to the speaker's stand and was introduced by Mayor Roberts. The park was filled to capacity with children and their escorts.

Lindbergh stated that airplanes of today are reliable, fairly economical and high in performance. Public confidence can be created in the airplane by a combination of four things, in which the government is taking a vital part: airworthy and adequately maintained aircraft, competent pilots, suitably equipped airways and airports, and standard air traffic rules.

Students from the university had assisted in policing the grounds, and the crowd was orderly, giving vent to its enthusiasm with hand clapping and cheers.

The welcoming committee was approached by many people who wanted special attention and had requests. One woman wanted Lindbergh to cut a birthday cake at a party she was giving that night. Another wanted him to pose especially for her camera, and any number of other people believed he should have graced their dinner table the evening of his arrival. The committee's answer was, "We'll ask Colonel Lindbergh."

From the park he was driven, again through streets filled with men, women, and children, to the Riverside Hotel, where he held a press conference. He told them, "The Reno field is entirely too small for planes, the type of which will be seen in the near future. It must be enlarged to take care of the gigantic airlines which are bound to come."

In the evening he gave another presentation outside in Powning Park. Original plans called for the banquet to be held in the Granada Theater, but because the weather was favorable, the committee decided to hold the meetings outside.

Lindbergh on the speakers stand at Idlewild Park in Reno. NEVADA HISTORICAL SOCIETY VIA JOHN CURRAN

At Powning Park he spoke again about the future of air travel and the importance of building new and modern airports, with the suggestion that Reno do just that as soon as possible.

Before he appeared at Powning Park he was a dinner/banquet guest of Mayor E. E. Roberts that included city councilmen, the Governor's representative, county commissioners, and the official committee. They discussed the future of Reno in the national air transportation system.

After Powning Park he and his crew retired to the Riverside Hotel for rest and time to plan their long flight the next day to Los Angeles.

After an early breakfast on Tuesday morning, the flyers left Reno and took a south heading toward Carson City and then Yosemite National Park. They flew around the park enjoying the bird's eye view of some beautiful waterfalls and mountain peaks, and flew on down along the Sierra Nevada mountain range. They flew over Death Valley and from there over Borax Flat and on to Los Angeles.

People Who Were There

Mrs. Jane W. Inglehart. As a child she and her brother and their mother had just arrived in Reno in September 1927 for a stay of several weeks. They were housed in the Riverside Hotel by the Truckee River. Her father, back in Massachusetts, contacted Mr. Harold Bixby to request a meeting with Lindbergh for his children. They were in the crowd at the airport when Lindbergh flew in, and it was near-hysteria to hail the flyer. The next day it was arranged for them to meet the pilot. They waited with tremendous excitement in the corridor outside his room until Lindbergh's representative, Keyhoe, motioned for them to come into the room. They were told to sit on a sofa until the door to one of the rooms opened and Lindbergh came in. Her instant impression, "He was tall, handsome, and a perfectly immense hand grasping mine." She thinks they were both struck dumb simply being in the presence of the man. After she left she remembered announcing to her mother that her right hand was no longer going to be washed because it was now holy ground. (After about twenty-four hours she was persuaded to reverse this stand.)

Halcyon McEachern Pinney. Halcyon was seven years old at that time, and there was such a large crowd that she could not see Lindbergh and started to cry. A man in the crowd lifted her up and carried her on his shoulders so that she could see. She remembered most the kindness of someone to a little girl who so much wanted a glimpse of the famous man.

John Curran. John Curran was there with his school class from western Nevada. He remembered that the only hangar was a low, galvanized iron-covered frame building covered with a few signs, and a larger sign with black letters proclaiming the U.S. Mail Terminal. Three or four DeHavilland biplanes were tied down close to the hangar.

He said that when Lindbergh finally landed and stepped out of the cockpit, he was escorted over to the speaker's stand by Mayor Roberts. He appeared to be a very unassuming and unchanged person, even after what he had accomplished. The children were given a chance to see the NYP up close. Each of them brought back to Carson City a feeling of pride, along with the realization we had been close to a great moment in our history.

Lindbergh had impressed the city officials so much that they began a search for a new airport site, all within two months of his visit. One piece of land northwest of Reno was considered, and also Spanish Springs Valley, but they did not decide one way or another. In July 1928 Boeing purchased 120 acres of land southeast of town on the Walts and Kietzke ranches, east of State Route 395. Sometime later Washoe County officials put in a road, E. (East ?) Plumb Lane, from South Virginia Street to the site. Then runway grading began. The first landing on the airfield was on October 25. Three weeks later William H. Boeing flew in for the dedication of the facility, christening it Hubbard Field.

Today that field is known as Reno-Tahoe International Airport. At an elevation of 4,421 feet MSL, it has a main runway of 11,000 feet with a parallel one at 9,000 feet. It has service from many of the nation's major airlines.

About ten miles north-northwest of Reno is Reno-Stead Airport, where the well-known Reno Air Races are held each fall. That airport is at an elevation of 5,046 feet MSL and has a main runway of 8,080 feet.

References

Newspapers
Reno-Gazette Journal
Nevada State Journal
Reno Evening Gazette
Carson City Daily Appeal

Organizations
Sparks Heritage Foundation
Nevada Historical Society

People

Mrs. Jane W. Inglehart	Frances Gale Parker
John Curran	Phillip Earl
Margaret Flavel Cates	Helen Bledowski
Don Dondero	Margaret Bradshaw
Melva Anderson	Carol R. Floto
Ruth J. Williamson	Rollan Melton
Dorothy Goetz	Edward H. Knauf
E. Elaine Deller	Mrs. Roy Rohr
Anne Elliott	Harold Curran
Earl Surine	Col. Don Schwartz
Alan Stephen	
Mrs. Merlyn Pinney (Halcyon)	

STOP #51
LOS ANGELES, CALIFORNIA

CAPSULE HISTORY OF CITY

Los Angeles, California, the largest city in the state, is located on the Pacific Coast in southern California. The city is about 130 miles northwest of San Diego and 350 miles southeast of San Francisco. It is the third largest city in the country, after New York City and Chicago. It is most famous for the film industry in Hollywood.

During the 1500s a branch of the Shoshoni Indian tribe lived in a village called Yang-na, along the Los Angeles River near what is presently the downtown area.

In 1542 a Portuguese explorer working for Spain by the name of Juan Rodrigues Cabrillo discovered the Yang-na village. He marked the site on his map and continued to explore the California coast. But it was not until 1769 that a Spanish Army captain, Gaspar de Portola and Juan Crespi, a Franciscan priest, led an expedition north from San Diego to Monterey Bay. When they reached Yang-na, Crespi noted in his diary, "a delightful place," and suggested it had all the features necessary for a large settlement. They named the area "Nuestra Senora la Reina de Los Angeles de Porciuncula, meaning "Our Lady the Queen of the Angeles of Prociuncula."

Under Mexican rule years later, Los Angeles alternated with Monterey as the California capital. The first white man to reach L.A., as it is known today, was Jedediah Smith in 1826, an American fur trapper. On April 4, 1850, Los Angeles was incorporated as a city, and five months later California became a state of the United States.

275 feet MSL.

SEPTEMBER 20–21, 1927
(TUESDAY AND WEDNESDAY)

In 1926 the Los Angeles Chamber of Commerce published a survey with the suggestion that thirteen possible land sites be considered as good locations for a municipal airport. One of these sites was known as Vail Field (named for W. R. Vail, managing trustee of the Vail Company). Vail was located in the town of Montebello, east-southeast of Los Angeles, at the intersection of Telegraph Road, where Garfield and Yates Avenue converge, and between the Southern Pacific and Santa Fe railroad tracks. It was about 7.3 miles from the Arcade Station in Los Angeles, the passenger and mail center of the city.

The land consisted of roughly 400 acres, with all of it usable for a landing field. The surface soil was fertile clay loam suitable for sodding, packing, or any other necessary treatment. It was oriented for an east-west runway. The absence of surrounding hills made it attractive for flight operations.

For two years up to Lindbergh's arrival, Western Air Express had been operating out of the field quite successfully. Douglas M-2 airplanes were being used, and the operation gained a reputation for being profitable and well managed. Western Air Express later became known as the "Lindbergh Line." Western Air Express operated between Los Angeles and Salt Lake City, flying the mail (CAM #4) and later carrying passengers.

On the day of Lindbergh's expected arrival, the enthusiasm of the people of Los Angeles was beyond imagination. Many of them camped out at Vail Field as early as the previous day. Some folks prepared a reserve seat by parking their cars in the line and then returning to their homes in a friend's auto, to return the next day to the same spot.

At 11:00 A.M. on Tuesday, Wendell Graham, a youthful amateur aviator, wanted to get a good view of Lindbergh, so he decided to "fly in." It cost him a county traffic tag. The young pilot circled Vail field several times, and then landed his Jenny behind the line of parked automobiles and taxied up to the deadline established for cars, only to be greeted by County Motorcycle Officer Boycott, who issued the tag. The pilot said that

it was worth the tag to get a good view. His passenger was his father, P. C. Graham.

A wire fence, 13,000 feet in length, had been installed all the way around Vail Field. The 160th Infantry, local police, and reserves from the Navy and Marines were ready for the throngs of people. Even provisions for emergencies were set up at the local hospitals. The event had been well organized. The J. B. Ransom Corporation offered free parking space at their facility nearby.

Considered one of the greatest shows in southern California history, upon Lindbergh's arrival old men threw their hats into the air, women cried, and others shrieked, cheered, and roared until their voices were exhausted.

Lindbergh first appeared above the city at 1:40 P.M. and proceeded to circle over Hollywood, then over the business district of the city, and then headed east toward Vail Field.

After circling the airfield several times, he landed with a slight bounce at the southeast end of the airport. He was seen to side-slip before the flair for the landing. Soon he taxied toward the air mail hangar and then fifty feet to the left of the hangar into a wire enclosure that had been made especially for the NYP and Fairchild. He was guided in by Keyhoe and Love.

About 350 guardsmen, under the command of Col. Harcourt Hervey, formed a giant human "V" extending from the entrance to the enclosure out into the field. Lindbergh was officially welcomed by Mayor George M. Cryer and the welcoming committee, in addition to pilots of both Western Air Express and Pacific Air Transport, and other highly distinguished men and women of California.

Lindbergh is shown on top of the cowling checking the fuel at Vail Field. It appears that an oil change was done at this time. DUSTIN W. CARTER

After the official reception and securing both airplanes, Lindbergh was escorted into a car and the parade began to form. They went out of the field beginning at First and Broadway and continued through the thousands of people lining the parade route to the Exposition Park Coliseum. He rode with Mayor Cryer and President E. F. McGarry of the Chamber of Commerce. There were thirty cars in the entourage, which included many police motorcycles as escorts.

About 60,000 people, mostly children, crowded the Los Angeles Coliseum. It was the greatest welcome accorded anyone in the city's history up to that time.

In his short talk at the Coliseum Lindbergh said,

"This tour you have heard so much about was conceived and is being carried out for the one and only purpose of promoting commercial aviation in this country to a practical basis.

"Commercial aviation should be distinguished from pioneer aviation because there is a vast difference between them. Divided into their respective classifications, commercial aviation chiefly deals with passenger, express and mail carrying, the latter being the only well-developed division of commercial aviation today. While the pioneering division includes development of designs, testing and experimentation, the latter coming under the category of hazardous flights."

Later on in his talk, he complimented the California flyers who conquered the Pacific Ocean in the first nonstop flight in a commercial plane from California to Honolulu, won by Art Goebel, who was introduced to Lindbergh at the Coliseum. Lindbergh again stressed the importance of building more airports and improving air navigation and the development of airliners and airlines.

Lindbergh said, "I plead with you to voice your belief in the need of a municipal airport. Support the air mail, and if you haven't sent a letter today, go when you leave here to the nearest mail box and send one to Grandpa, Grandma, or anyone else you can think of."

People in the Coliseum were entertained by the 160th Infantry Band and the Roberts Golden

State Band. The children there were entertained with paper airplanes, and apple cores and spit balls filled the air before the flyer entered the west tunnel.

In the afternoon Lindbergh was the guest of honor at the Fiesta Ball Room of the Ambassador Hotel where members of the Hollywood crowd suspended their work and other operations for a short time to show honor to the outstanding star of the air. Hostesses were Mary Pickford and Marion Davies, famous actresses. It was a break in the usual routine for Lindbergh and his crew, and he enjoyed the festivities.

After the Hollywood party Lindbergh spent some time with the press before retiring to his suite in the Ambassador, before the evening festivities.

The official banquet was tendered by the Chamber of Commerce. Speeches were given by the Mayor and other dignitaries, before Lindbergh was introduced to give his usual aviation promotional talk. The flyers retired for the night at 9:00 P.M.

While Lindbergh visited Los Angeles it was announced that all air mail posted in southern California during his stay was or would be posted to delivery to anywhere except Arizona, New Mexico, and western Texas. It was sent as a tribute to the flyer according to formal requests made by the Chamber of Commerce and postmasters throughout the area. For the past fifteen months Vail Field was where every record air mail load had been flown out. Cost then was ten cents per half ounce to send a letter anywhere. Any postage stamps could be used, and air mail could be dropped into any mail box.

Early Wednesday morning Lindbergh was met at the hotel by Louis B. Mayer, who was waiting to take the flyer out to the Metro-Goldwyn-Mayer Studio in Culver City for a tour of the famous facility. He was the guest of actress Marion Davies in her studio bungalow. He enjoyed the break from the routine schedule of the tour and seeing how motion pictures were produced. At 10:15 A.M. they drove him back to Vail Field. He had been riding in a car with William Hearst.

On Wednesday morning there was no official ceremony for Lindbergh as he prepared to depart for San Diego. A special police detail was assigned to the field to control any crowd that might gather.

The NYP in front of the hangar at Vail Field, next to a Western Air Express Douglas M-2 mail biplane. RYAN AERONAUTICAL COMPANY

After preflighting both airplanes they took off from Vail at 11:30 A.M. and headed over Pomona, California, and then toward San Diego.

Earlier he had been requested to circle over the ranch of corn flake king, W. K. Kellogg, which was near Pomona. If Lindbergh would agree, Kellogg would establish an up-to-date airport for the community. It would be a first-class field with hangars and a repair shop or shops. At noon Lindbergh did fly over the ranch and also the Los Angeles County Fair at the same time. The fairgrounds were about two miles from the Kellogg ranch.

Kellogg kept his promise and built an airport on the ranch. It was named Rodgers Field, because Cal Rodgers landed there in 1911. It was rather modern for the time, with lights for night operations, etc. It was closed in 1932.

Today one can fly into or out of the Los Angeles International Airport, or "LAX," as it is known to most people who use the facility on a regular basis. The field is located at Century and Sepulveda Boulevards. It began in the late 1920s on a small patch of land. The airport still has parallel runways, the longest being 7 left and 25 right at 12,091 feet. The field is at an elevation of 126 feet MSL and handles most of the world's major airlines in addition to local commuter airlines and a large air freight terminal.

At one time there were 101 airports in the greater Los Angeles area, but only fifty-six in operation at any one time. Due to so much world-class airline traffic, military flights, and general aviation in and around the L.A. area, it is one of the most congested and complicated air traffic areas in the country.

In the early days up to World War II, LAX was known as Mines Field. (It was officially Los Angeles Municipal Airport, however.) The name Mines came from the name of the realtor who handled the purchase of the land by the City of Los Angeles. It officially became "LAX" in October 1949 when it was named the Los Angeles International Airport.

References

Newspapers
Los Angeles Times
Arizona Gazette

Organizations
Los Angeles Department of Airports
American Aviation Historical Society – Journal
University of California – Davis
San Diego Aerospace Museum
Ryan Aeronautical Corporation
Sterling Memorial Library – Yale University

People
Merle C. Olmstead
John Underwood
C. John McKillop
Arthur C. Barth
Chan Robinson
Douglas M. Bielanski
Charles W. Winburn
Dustin "Dusty" W. Carter
Ethel L. Pattison
Barney Gambrell
William Wagner

STOP #52
SAN DIEGO, CALIFORNIA

CAPSULE HISTORY OF CITY

The second largest city in California, San Diego lies in the southwestern corner of California as well as of the United States, just nineteen miles north of the Mexican border on the Pacific Ocean. The city has one of the finest deep water harbors in the country. Large aircraft manufacturers and a large U.S. Navy base have made the city a major industrial center, and tourism is heavy all year long due to the excellent climate.

This coastal city has been called the "Cradle of California Civilization." The first people living on the site were the Diegueno Indians. The first European to see the place was most likely Juan Rodriguez Cabrillo (see also Los Angeles, stop #51), a Portuguese explorer, in 1542.

However, no whites settled in the area until 1769, when Spanish soldiers built a presidio in what is now the Old Town area of the city. A Franciscan priest, Junipero Serra, established San Diego de Alcala, California's first mission, in the presidio in 1769. The city was organized as a town in 1834 and became a city in 1850. In 1867 Alonzo E. Horton, a businessman, bought land which is now in the downtown area of San Diego. He laid out an area and named it New Town, which is near the present city wharf.

In the 1900s large fish canneries were established along the waterfront, one of which pro-duced, besides fish products, one of the most famous airplanes in history.
20 feet MSL.

SEPTEMBER 21–23, 1927
(WEDNESDAY THROUGH FRIDAY)

At the time of Lindbergh's return to San Diego, the old Dutch Flats was still very much in business, but now referred to as "Mahoney Field" or "Mahoney Airport."

On the day of his arrival, the city declared the day a holiday, closing most businesses and schools. People by the thousands were lined up around Dutch Flats and along the parade route from the field to Balboa Park Stadium. The stadium itself was filled beyond capacity with bands, military people, thousands of schoolchildren, their parents and teachers, and other dignitaries.

Lindbergh and the NYP were returning home to where the "roots" of the NYP began in essence. After leaving Los Angeles and flying over Pomona, he took a direct route to San Diego for his "homecoming."

The Fairchild had flown into Dutch Flats Mahoney Field first to prepare the welcoming committee and other appropriate people for Lindbergh's arrival. A special wire enclosure had been erected just outside the old hangar to protect the NYP, and to be able to do some servic-

ing.

Soon the NYP was spotted over the city, where it circled the business area as well as Balboa Park Stadium, and slowly let down to fly a low pass over Dutch Flats. Lindbergh touched down at 1:58 P.M.

Just after Lindbergh landed at San Diego. On the far left is Will Rogers. Three men on far right, left to right: Donald Hall, B.F. Mahoney and Donald Keyhoe. BUNNEL PHOTO SHOP

He was met by B. Franklin Mahoney; Donald Hall; humorist Will Rogers, who was the former mayor of Beverly Hills near L.A.; Howard Wroth, president of the San Diego Chamber of Commerce; Mayor Harry C. Clark of San Diego; and others.

Once the two airplanes had been made secure, a parade formed. It began at B Street and Kettner Street. Donald Hall sat in the front seat with Lindbergh. A. J. Edwards and B. F. Mahoney sat in the back seat.

Also in the parade were a Marine detachment, men from the Naval Training Station and "fleet air," the USS *Omaha* and the USS *Holland*, the Naval Reserve, California National Guard, San Diego High School ROTC, the Grand Army of the Republic in automobiles, Sons of Civil War Veterans, United Spanish War Veterans, Veterans of Foreign Wars, American Legion and the Disabled Veterans of World War I, the Coast Artillery from Fort Rosencrans, and a personal escort by the Cavalry around Lindbergh's car, in the "royal" formation. Also the Ladies of the D.A.R. were marching in the parade, along with the Salvation Army, the Daughters of Veterans, and Women's Auxiliary, Bennington Camp. About ten motorcycle policemen covered the parade route to keep order.

The NYP being thoroughly checked over by the original builders of the airplane. This was done at the former Dutch Flats, later known as Mahoney Airport. SAN DIEGO AEROSPACE MUSEUM

After things quieted down at the Balboa Stadium, Howard Worth, presiding, introduced Dr. Roy Campbell, the toastmaster. He in turn introduced the Mayor, who extended a welcome to Lindbergh.

During the afternoon a "park" for lost children was established. It was a clearing house for parents to sort out their offspring and apply appropriate and necessary discipline.

At the stadium Lindbergh was presented with many gifts, one of which was a parachute. It drew a smile from just about everyone. Lindbergh was already a member of the famous Caterpillar Club.

Attending the ceremony was Georgia "Tiny" Broadwick, the first woman to parachute out of an airplane successfully (June 21, 1912). She had flown in from Portland, Oregon, just to see Lindbergh.

It finally came time for Lindbergh to give his talk, and because others had spoken on the technical side of commercial aviation, he decided to speak on the building of the NYP in San Diego.

"The ship was constructed and tested almost exactly sixty days after the order was placed. I do not know of any other place where such a feat would have been possible, and I am in a position to speak, for I looked around a lot before I placed the order.

"It was necessary to construct a ship that would prove to be practically perfect on its test flights. There was not the opportunity to make extensive and expensive tests and still be ready to make the flight at the time I considered to be most opportune. It was necessary to build a ship that would

make in safety a flight that was longer than any flight that had been made at that time.

"The engineering problems too were great. The previous distance record was about 3,300 miles, made with a motor of higher horsepower and a plane of more expensive construction and design. Yet in sixty days after the order was placed, the plane was taken to Camp Kearny and tested for load. It was one of the few times on record that the performance was up to the theoretical plans. I may say that the performance of the plane has surpassed the theoretical performance.

"After we left San Diego and St. Louis, the plane was inspected in New York, and it was not necessary to make any real changes. It was in almost exactly the same condition as when it left San Diego. It reached Paris the same way. It was necessary there to recover part of the rear of the fuselage, but that was not due to faulty construction. It seems that there were some souvenir hunters in Paris, and I do not think they were all Parisians, for I have seen since my return to this country, pieces of silver cloth marked 'Spirit of St. Louis.'

"The plane has now traveled nearly 25,000 miles, and is still practically in its original condition. It is in excellent shape. The motor, which was of course not built in San Diego, has not yet been overhauled, and it is still in its original condition after 270 and some odd hours in the air. The condition of this ship indicates the present state to which the building of aircraft for commercial aviation has reached.

"If the same plane were to be used for commercial purposes, it would carry four passengers beside the pilot, at an approximate cost of four cents per mile for fuel. The fuel on the trip from New York to Paris cost less than $4,000. On the matter of original expense the airplane cannot yet compete with the automobile, because there is no real quantity production of aircraft. But it has been proved that it is possible and practicable to operate air lines at a profit even with the present equipment. It will be more profitable in the future when manufacturing is on a quantity production basis and the original costs will not be so high."

Lindbergh went on to talk on commercial aviation development and the need for airports. He mentioned that the wonderful weather in the San Diego area is ideal for flying, and that it is almost impossible that San Diego should not back this air program.

"I appreciate your interest and the compliments you have paid me," he concluded. "You are to be congratulated on having the industry that constructed this plane. I hope to be able in the future to devote a part of my time to the development of aviation in this city and this state."

After the festivities at the Balboa Park Stadium, Lindbergh was driven to the home of Franklin Mahoney on Point Loma. Here he met for a time with the local press and spent some needed time resting. The banquet that evening, which began at 6:00 P.M., was at the Hotel de Coronado on Coronado, near North Island. Also on that evening of his first night at San Diego, a special dance was held at the Mission Beach Ballroom in honor of the flyer and was known as the "Lindbergh Souvenir Ball." Hundreds of Lindbergh souvenirs were given away at this event. Music was provided by the Carr Brothers Band, playing popular big band music of the time.

After remarks by several local dignitaries honoring Lindbergh at this banquet, American humorist Will Rogers, also a lover of aviation, was introduced to the audience and had, in his characteristic drawl, the following to say:

TRIALS OF A HERO

"That was pretty good applause you gave me. You know, I never done nothing more than make a non-stop jump from Hollywood to here. It's hard to say anything now that will be of interest when you come to see Lindbergh, so I'd like to say a few words for Tijuana. That town, you know, isn't very beautiful. It don't appeal to you much when you look at it. It don't hardly give you an eyeful, but it sure does give you a mouthful."

Up to this time the hero of the occasion had looked pretty tired, and was making every ef-

fort to seem appreciative of what his friends were doing for him. But at Rogers' remarks he began to forget his weariness, and his smile broadened and finally became just a boyish grin that eventually was nothing less than hearty, convulsing laughter.

"You know, this is pretty hard on this boy here, and ever since he made that flight a few months ago he has had to sit, night after night, and listen to all this applause. Every amateur orator in the world has tried out on him, so I'm not going to try to use any big words on him tonight.

"I would like to speak, though, about my operation. You know, Slim here, belongs to that aviator's club, the Caterpillar Club. Now I haven't got time to discuss it right now, but all you folks who belong to the other society just stay after dinner and we'll compare experiences.

"It's hard to tell what to do for this boy. Everybody has compared him with all the big men of history that ever went anywhere. They compared him with Napoleon. I suppose they meant well, but what did he do? He crossed the Alps. You know they say an army travels on its stomach, and we know darn well Lindbergh traveled a lot faster than that. And besides, Lindbergh came back, and what did Napoleon do? He went into a tailspin at Waterloo and was a complete washout at St. Helena.

"Up at Spokane the other night they compared him to Nero. And shucks, Nero was nothing but a fiddler, and he wasn't very good at that. And as far as I can find out he never went any place but to a fire.

"One of these orators called him Columbus, the modern Columbus of the air. Now you can't compare their feats. Columbus, he was lost when he found this country. He had all of North and South America for a landing field, and he'd have been a great bird if he couldn't of landed on one of them.

"And then they say this boy is an ambassador. That's not so. An ambassador is sent by one people to fool the people of the country he goes to about the people of the country he comes from. This boy is anything but that. An ambassador has to look you in the eye and lie to you.

"And he has been called an inspiration to our youth. I hope that's not so, because if they all try what he did there won't be anybody left. I know I don't want my two boys to try it.

"So they can't give him credit for being any of these great men, but there is one thing he really did do what is worth talking about. He is the first man who ever took a ham sandwich to Paris.

"You know his plane was made here in San Diego and all that. But Los Angeles is determined to get in on the credit, and you can't count them out of it. They claim that they raised the pigs that were cured into the ham that went into the sandwich. The pigs were raised on Hellman's ranch, and were cured by Joe Toplitsky.

FOOD FOR THOUGHT

"But the thing that I'm wondering about is what this boy really thinks of this talk that he has to sit and listen to every night. I don't know what he thinks, but if I had to listen to it, I'd get in that plane and start across the Pacific with only ten gallons of gas in the tank. And if I never get back I'd think the Lord had been good to me. He must be glad to fly alone, and to get up in the air where he can go so fast that nobody can catch him and say 'sign this.'

"I'm sorry that the Army had to get in on this tonight. Major Macaulay, you ought not to of brought Latin into your speech. There are a lot of Navy people here tonight that didn't understand it. All these admirals are up in the air about it.

"When we get to thinking and talking about being the leading nation in the air, we don't want to get all swelled up because three of our boys flew across the Atlantic. The important thing is what 110,000,000 people are going to ride in and where are they going to land? Look at that Italian that had his plane burn up out here at Roosevelt Dam. He had the backing of his government and all he did was to sit down and send a telegram to Mussolini—collect—and they sent him another plane that night.

WIRE TO COOLIDGE

"Now if Lindbergh had broken down near Paris, can you imagine what would have happened if he had wired Coolidge collect? If he had sent for another plane there wasn't another like it, and Congress would have had to be called to convene and filibuster for a few months before they would even appropriate enough for a ticket back home.

"The next war is going to be in the air. They won't shoot you in the next war. They'll just drop it on you. They won't give you a gun and a pair of puttees and tell you to fight. They'll put an airplane in your hand and tell you to go up and see if you can come down on purpose. And this is the only nation in the world that uses the air for speaking purposes exclusively.

"Don't get so excited about this air mail. You can get a letter there faster, but when you get it, it is only a real estate advertisement. And if you are in a real hurry you can telegraph and that's faster. It is more important to carry males than mail.

"Now I don't generally compliment people, but I've got to change my style tonight. I've been reading about this boy in the papers, mostly because what he did was the only clean thing in the papers in years. Mostly they are filled up with big headlines and stories about walking across the desert and leaving no tracks.

PRAYED FOR HIM

"But we have a real regard for this boy. He went across the ocean on the strength of more prayers from more people of more nations than ever before. In your lifetime and my lifetime we will never again know about another man alone out over the middle of the ocean. He is the first and only one to do that.

"If you live a hundred years from now you will never again see or hear of anything that will give you such a thrill as what this boy did. The armistice didn't give us a kick like this. We were expecting that, but this gave us the biggest kick that any of us will

ever know.

"It is pretty bad for a comedian to get serious, but when I have been talking about this thing I can't help it, and I always get a little serious. I'm a tough bird, but this feat got me. Every time I read about it, it gives me a kick all over again.

"This is the first time in history that I have been complimentary," and as he turned toward Lindbergh, he said, "I hate to do it, but I guess this time I'll have to compliment you."

The End

After the banquet Lindbergh and Rogers were invited to the Russ Auditorium at San Diego High School, where they were initiated into the Ancient Egyptian Order of Sciots. After that ceremony Lindbergh spent the night at the Mahoneys' home.

Thursday the 22nd was to be a day of rest for Lindbergh and his crew, but he ended up with a rather busy day. After all, it **was** San Diego, birthplace of the NYP.

Lindbergh flew as pilot in command (PIC) in Jack Maddux's first Ford 4-AT-7 tri-motor, s/n 7, C 1102 on a flight from San Diego to Los Angeles (Vail Field) and return. Rogers was in the right seat on the first leg, which departed Dutch Flats at 8:30 A.M. Their passengers were Jack Maddux; Mr. And Mrs. Will Rogers; Harry H. Culver, founder of Culver City; Mayor Harry Clark of San Diego; Howard Worth of the Chamber of Commerce; Judge Benjamin F. Bledsoe; C. C. Tanner, a Los Angeles business-

Lindbergh shown with some people next to what may be the Maddux Ford 4-AT-7 tri-motor that Lindbergh flew on September 22nd. WILLIAM T. LARKINS

man; and George L. Eastman, vice president of the Los Angeles Chamber of Commerce.

On the return flight they had as passengers Dr. Ford A. Carpenter in charge of the aeronautics department of the Los Angeles Chamber of Commerce; J. L. Van Norman; Charles E. Lindblade; Norman Chandler; Col. Perry Widener; Mayor Clark; Mr. Worth; and B. Franklin Mahoney as co-pilot.

This was an inaugural flight to set up regular, scheduled trips between the two cities. They would plan on carrying passengers as well as light freight and on occasion offer local sightseeing flights. The plan was to eventually extend trips to Arizona and Texas.

They returned to San Diego later in the morning, just in time to attend a luncheon/banquet, during the regular lunch break at the Ryan-Mahoney plant.

There were long tables set up in the shop where the NYP had been constructed. Lindbergh was the honored guest of the employees, which he enjoyed thoroughly.

He was asked to say a few words, and he

This is the banquet in the old fish cannery that was in celebration of Lindbergh's success. Most of the B.F. Mahoney (Ryan) employees are there, September 22nd.
PHOTO BY ERICKSON

briefly brought up the subject of the J-5 running a bit rough over the mountains on his flight from San Diego to St. Louis. He thought at first one of the fuel tanks was running dry. As it turned out it was carburetor ice, which was corrected with a carburetor heater at New York before the flight to Paris.

Lindbergh said, "I was rather surprised yesterday when very little mention was made of the qualities of the *Spirit of St. Louis*. In other cities the plane was mentioned prominently and its airworthy qualities lauded. Here in San Diego they present me with a parachute." Everyone laughed at Lindbergh's reference that his ship was regarded here as unsafe.

Toward the end of his talk he said, "At this time I want to thank you all, especially the older employees, for the work which you did in constructing the plane. It is this organization which can do much to keep San Diego and California in the forefront of aviation."

On that morning Lindbergh learned that three young Boy Scouts from Mexico had hiked all the way from Mexico City to San Diego to see, hear, and greet the flyer. The boys were P. Novello, A. Ondareo and E. Lopez.

Because the NYP was now back at its birthplace, it made sense to have these original mechanics, builders, and technicians go over the airplane with a fine tooth comb.

Through the good memories of Ed Morrow, Dan Burnett, and Jon Harm van der Linde and a close study of original photographs, this writer was able to determine the extent of mechanical work and servicing. No documents have been found to substantiate this work.

The full engine cowling was removed, which would indicate an oil change, and general inspection of that area of the air-frame and engine controls, etc.

Rocker box covers were also removed, indicating that they were checking the valve tappet clearances and adjustments, etc.

A proud Jon Harm van der Linde posing by the airplane he helped build and who oversaw much of the servicing at San Diego during the tour stop there.
RYAN AERONAUTICAL COMPANY

The Hamilton Standard propeller was removed, and possibly checked for balance, pitch, and general clean up. The edges of the blades were filed and dressed, considering the many undeveloped landing surfaces the airplane had operated off so far on the tour.

While the Hamilton Standard prop was off, they also checked the magnetos and forward part of the engine, including the prop spinner and shroud assembly.

A temporary wood Hamilton propeller was mounted on the crankshaft in the meantime, so that they could check compression and timing of the ignition system, and perhaps even run the engine. Note: The wood prop included a spinner shroud, which might indicate it was borrowed from one of the Ryan B-1 Broughams. The shroud showed the swirling (Damascene) as was on the original.

It appears that the left (and possibly the right) landing gear shock cord fairing was removed to check the shock cords, fittings, and structural integrity of that area.

The tail skid assembly was removed, possibly for the same reason—shock cords and structure.

The airplane was generally cleaned up, all of the fabric areas were checked for wear and tear, general condition, and repaired where necessary.

Tires were checked for general condition and proper air pressures.

C. C. "Doc" Maidment (Wright J-5 expert) did most of the engine servicing, as a photograph shows him wearing white coveralls, with "Wright" written or printed in an arc across the back.

A photograph exists in this author's collection showing an attractive young lady by the name of Mrs. Violet Khene sitting in the cockpit of the NYP at Dutch Flats. The photo, dated September 21, 1927, was taken directly into the cockpit from the right side of the airplane with the cockpit door in the fully open position. The picture clearly shows the instrument panel (side view only) and other controls and fuel valving, etc.

The picture is interesting in that it shows a rather large round or circular instrument mounted on the lower part of the panel, just below the Air Speed Indicator. The instrument has an adjusting knob on the bottom in the six

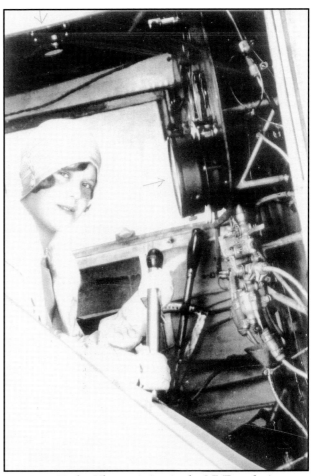

Mrs. Violet Khene sitting in the NYP cockpit, taken on September 21st. Notice the Kollsman "Super Sensitive Altimeter" (arrow) on the instrument panel. COURTESY STANLEY JONES

o'clock position. The full face cannot be seen, nor has a full face view photo been found, so there is a question of its identity.

There appears to be a large flange on the rear of the case touching the wood panel. When this writer physically checked the original NYP in Washington, one hole of about 3/8" diameter can be seen just below and to the left of the fuel primer. There is an additional 3/8" diameter hole just below and a little to the right of the Air Speed Indicator. It is assumed, therefore, that they are there for the mounting of the instrument.

So the question is, how long was the instrument mounted in the airplane, and why? Going back to the San Francisco stop, we find, according to Lindbergh's flight log, that he made a five-minute flight (test ?) while in that city on Friday, September 16. No reason for the flight is given. Moreover, he was invited to visit the Guggenheim Aeronautics Laboratory at

Jon Harm van der Linde working on the engine area. Notice the Hamilton wood propeller mounted temporarily. SAN DIEGO AEROSPACE MUSEUM

Stanford University in Palo Alto. Also during this time he had a brief visit with Kenneth C. Boedecker of the Wright Company, who was in the area for some reason. Was there some connection with all of this? Perhaps the instrument was installed there and test flown, to be used or tested during his flight to Reno and then south to L.A. and San Diego.

No documentation or other additional photographs on the subject have surfaced showing the instrument before San Francisco.

Two early aircraft instrument experts were consulted. Roy Meyers and Jack Sprinkle feel the instrument in question may have been some kind of test instrument, possibly an aneroid barometer. Most likely this would be to test the accuracy of the existing Neko standard altimeter which was permanently mounted on the panel. Both gentlemen estimate the size to be about 7.5 to 8.0 inches in diameter, a common size at the time. Apparently there was at that time an al-

Phil Love, the escort pilot, pulling the propeller through on the NYP. Notice Ryan M-1 in the background. DONALD KEYHOE COLLECTION

timeter of 7.5 inches diameter with an adjusting screw or knob at the bottom.

A test instrument of the aneroid type would have been much more sensitive than the standard altimeter. Such a barometer would have one rotation of the needle to equal 1,000', whereas a similar pressure change (1" HG) in a normal altimeter would only move the needle a few feet in altitude.

If this was in fact a test instrument to test the existing altimeter, would the purpose have been to check the latter while flying over the Rocky Mountains? Lindbergh might have been using it as a primary instrument when its accuracy was essential to his flight environment over the mountains or water at night or IFR.

The accuracy of the NYP's primary altimeter would be of concern to Lindbergh because it would have to be extremely accurate while flying over very high terrain in the western part of the country. But he had already been flying over high mountains before he reached San Francisco. One wonders therefore if the instrument was installed earlier, and the San Francisco test flight was for some other reason.

These conclusions are largely based on deduction rather than on concrete facts because a photo or other official documentation has not turned up showing its face for further positive identification.

Photographs of the instrument panel during the tour are scarce at best. However, there is one good photo of it, while Keyhoe leans into the cockpit for something, that was taken at Spokane, Washington. The instrument is not on the panel. So it must have been installed either at Seattle or later Portland, Reno, Sacramento, Oakland, San Francisco or Los Angeles. It does show up in one photo taken at Los Angeles.

In the May 1928 issue of *National Geographic* Lindbergh wrote: "Since the transatlantic flight I had added a Kollsman supersensitive altimeter to my instrument board. Without this addition, blind flying at 150 and 200 feet over the coast line would have been impossible."[4]

Early the next morning, the 23rd, Lindbergh took B. Franklin Mahoney up for a local five-minute ride over San Diego in the NYP. Mahoney was his thirteenth passenger.

Copy of an original Flight Certificate of B.F. Mahoney Aircraft Corp., that was issued to a Pearle M. Lock on August 15, 1927. Although the certificate reads Ryan Monoplane, the watermark is the "Spirit." CASSAGNERES COLLECTION

SAN DIEGO TO TUCSON

After taking off from Dutch Flats in the early morning, Lindbergh headed east toward the Rocky Mountains, a bit north of Barrett Lake and the Morena Reservoir and near Los Pinos Mountain. His basic course paralleled the southern border of the United States with Mexico. Soon he was over the little city of El Centro, California, and from there he flew south-southwest to Mexicali, just over the border into Mexico.

Again he took a direct easterly heading toward Yuma, Arizona, and eventually flew east-southeast to Tucson, flying over some fairly desolate country in the Mohawk Valley and Mohawk Mountains, near the Sand Tank Mountains and near the Aguirre Valley, and the Roskruge Mountains and on into the Tucson area.

SAN DIEGO AREA NOW:

The old Dutch Flats site was barren for many years until the United States Postal Service purchased the land and built a large post office and regional center on the site. There is nothing visible of the old flying field anymore.

However, along Harbor Drive you will find San Diego International Airport, Lindbergh Field. It is at an elevation of 14 feet MSL. Its main runway is 9,400 feet long. Most major airlines of the country fly in there, in addition to corporate and commuter airlines, foreign airlines, and some military. It has two modern terminals and all of the facilities of a modern airport.

Across the harbor North Island still has a

Naval Air Station, Halsey Field. On the outskirts of San Diego there are several general aviation airports: Brown Municipal Airport, Gillespie Field in El Cajon, Montgomery Field in San Diego, and Miramar Mitscher just north of Montgomery, which is north of the city. The famous glider center south of Del Mar, known as Torrey Pines, is still there. This is where Lindbergh, with the help of Hawley Bowlus, soloed a glider and taught his wife, Anne, in a Bowlus glider.

SAN DIEGO GREETING TO LINDBERGH
- AUTHOR UNKNOWN -

On greeting you today, San Diego can add no new extravagance to the acclaim that has been yours for five months past. Applause has perhaps become wearisome to you. But we ask you to remember that we have thought of you as "our" Lindbergh, that we have taken a pride more intimate than the national pride in you and your exploit, and that our greeting to you here is the release of genuine, spontaneous and somehow personal enthusiasm that we have felt here since you first calmly hopped to St. Louis on the first lap of your famous flight.

We cannot but give you something more than the crowd's admiration for a brave man and a gallant adventurer. In all the noisy jubilation of the day's program, we hope you will sense a gratitude more profound than words will describe.

Through the glorious thrill of your first exploit, you have somehow added things that are deeper and more enduring. With

skill and courage you have also other qualities that have shown themselves very clear and shining in every episode of this great adventure of yours. Those things, God-given, it is futile to praise. But gratitude makes a little tightening of the throat when we remember how gallantly you have kept them untarnished.

And, then, another gift to those you have already given. Let us continue to think of you as we have in the past—as a knight loyal to his knightliness, even while crowds and rulers shower their favors. And today let us feel that you are "ours"—and that you have come home.

Footnotes

4. *National Geographic* article, May 1928, *To Bogota and Back by Air*, pg. 530.

References

Newspapers
  San Diego Union-Tribune
  Los Angeles Times
  Western Flying

Organizations
  Ryan Aeronautical Corporation
  Ryan Aeronautical Library
  San Diego Aerospace Museum
  Solar Turbines Incorporated
  San Diego Public Library
  Bunnel Photo Shop
  American Aviation Historical Society
  National Aeronautic Association
  National Geographic Society

People
  Claude Ryan
  Jerry Ryan
  William Wagner
  Ed Morrow
  Jon Harm van der Linde
  Walter Locke
  Stan Jones
  George D. Hall
  Donald Hall Jr.
  Nova Hall
  Greg Williams
  T. Aubrey Smith

  William F. Chana
  William Immenschuh
  Raymond Wagner
  Elizabeth Ferguson
  "Dapper" Dan Burnett
  Lorna & Oce Dotson
  Mrs. Nancy Getz
  Mrs. Earl Prudden
  Donald Keyhoe
  Hawley Bowlus family
  John M. MacDonald, Jr.

STOP #53
TUCSON, ARIZONA

CAPSULE HISTORY OF CITY

Tucson, Arizona, is one of the sunniest and driest areas of the United States and is a favorite area for retired people. It features a beautiful desert and is surrounded by four mountain ranges: the Santa Catalinas to the north, the Rincons to the east, the Santa Ritas to the south, and the Tucsons to the west. It is located on the Santa Cruz River in the south-central part of the state, about sixty miles north of the Mexican border at Nogales. The University of Arizona is located here.

In 1700 a Spanish Jesuit, Eusebio Francisco Kino, established the San Xavier Mission at the nearby village of Bac. Nearby were the American Apache Indians. An old nickname was "The Old Pueblo," which referred to a previous walled presidio in the town.

The city officially became part of the United States with the Gadsden Purchase in 1854. It served as capital of the Arizona Territory from 1867 to 1877.
2,390 feet MSL.

SEPTEMBER 23–24, 1927
(FRIDAY AND SATURDAY)

Because of the town's strategic location, numerous traveling flyers, mainly military, would stop there for service or to be put up as guests of the Old Pueblo Club. The town did have an Aviation Committee under the Chamber of Commerce but no airport. The traveling aviators would land at the fairgrounds.

In order to accommodate a flying circus in 1919, a tract of land on Oracle Road, where the Amphitheater High School now stands, was cleared for the air show and named Sawtelle Field.

On May 9, 1919, Mayor O. C. Parker received a letter from the U.S. Air Service asking

the town to build an airport. The site selected was four miles south of town on the Nogales Highway. This new field was named McCauley Field, changed to Fishburn Field, and later to Tucson Municipal Flying Field in 1920. It was the first city in the country to use municipal funds to purchase land for an airfield.

In 1924 a well-known barnstormer and flight instructor by the name of Charlie Mayse came there and opened a flying school on the field as a fixed base operation.

After careful study they found that they needed a new site, a larger and flatter area, and in 1925 the land southeast of the city where the present Davis-Monthan Air Force Base is located was acquired for the new Municipal Airport (purchased with municipal funds). Now the city could lay claim to the largest municipal airport in the country, about 1,280 acres. Timing was right, so that when Lindbergh was scheduled to make an overnight stop in Tucson, this would be the ideal time for an official dedication of the new airfield.

Through the cooperation of the local utility companies, the Army, and the Chamber of Commerce, the water, lights, sewers, and other improvements were installed by the time Lindbergh was to arrive. Even a "Lindy Light" was installed, a large rotating beacon, funded by public subscription and in full operation at that time.

There were about 20,000 people already at the airport that day awaiting his arrival. Neal Pennington, a University of Arizona student at the time, remembered that the entire roadside from the airport into town was packed solid on both sides with automobiles, and that he had never seen anything like it before or since.

At this time Davis-Monthan was located at the intersection of Alvernon and Aviation. The field was named for 1st Lt. Samuel H. Davis and 2nd Lt. Oscar Monthan, two early Tucson military flyers.

Lt. Albert A. Horner was the leader of a detachment of troops sent from Nogales to protect the flyer and his airplane. "We roped off the airplane to protect it from the crowds, who wanted to touch it or take pictures," he said. So they handed their cameras to Horner and his men who took the pictures for the people. (This writer wonders where the pictures are today, as very few have surfaced over the years.)

Local florist Hal Burns had constructed es-

Shown is the well-known "Cactus" plane built by local florist, Hall Burns, just for the occasion of Lindberg's visit. It was meant to resemble the NYP. ARIZONA HISTORICAL SOCIETY

pecially for the celebration a "Cactus Plane," a quasi-replica of the NYP made entirely out of local cactus plants. It drew much interest and headlines in the local newspapers. It was referred to as the "Spirit of Tucson." The actual material was ocotillo spines and saguaro ribs, prickly pear tunas and a barrel cactus split in half for the nose section. Burns spent about a week putting it all together. At the request of the reception committee it did not carry any advertising, and was built right on the field. When it was shown to Lindbergh, he remarked, "You don't want me to get into that, do you?"

That day was "Lindbergh Day" in Tucson, so businesses, offices, and schools were closed, and Arizonans poured into the small city from all over the state. Even a special train was put together to carry the Governor and other dignitaries from Phoenix down to the city. Other dignitaries arrived from Mexico.

Lindbergh had already been spotted over Calexico at 10:35 A.M. and Yuma at 11:05 A.M. before coming over Tucson. He came in from the northwest and circled the center of the city before heading southeast to Davis-Monthan. At

Here is the NYP kicking up some sand/dust on the Tucson Municipal Airport. NATIONAL ARCHIVES

The NYP creating more dust as it and the Fairchild prepare to
shut down their engines just after arrival. ARIZONA HISTORICAL SOCIETY

precisely 2:00 P.M. the wheels of the NYP touched down on the turf field, and shortly taxied up to the large corrugated metal hangar. Written on the roof of the hangar was "Tucson El 2500."

The Department of Commerce Fairchild had already landed about thirty minutes earlier to prepare the crowd for the upcoming event.

Lindbergh was soon greeted by Barry Holbert, representative of Mayor John E. White, and Kirk T. Moore, head of the aviation committee. He was also welcomed by the Gold Star Mothers, whose own sons gave of their lives in the air service.

Soon Lindbergh and his crew were put into a Packard car and driven through the local streets to the United States Veterans Hospital at Pastime Park, where he would greet veterans of the war for a short period. From there the parade motored to the University of Arizona football field, directly to the center of the field where a speaker's stand had been erected. Lindbergh's car was driven by Herbert Chambers, a city councilman.

Harry Holbert, a spokesman for the city, introduced the flyer to the 5,000 people in attendance. Lindbergh spoke clearly and distinctly.

"Citizens of Arizona, we are just beginning the third lap of our tour which is taking us to all the important cities in the country. This tour was organized for the purpose of promoting aviation in the United States, and it is under the auspices of the Daniel Guggenheim Fund for the Promotion of Aeronautics.

"There is no other means of transportation by which a tour of this schedule could be made. Only once during this entire tour have we been delayed and that was not due to mechanical trouble, but due to weather conditions in the New England states. Airplanes of today are reliable, fairly economical, and high in performance. The engine in the *Spirit of St. Louis* is the same in which the trip across the Atlantic was made.

"Your interest in aviation is manifested by your attendance here today and by your splendid airport in Tucson. It should be the object of every city to maintain equally as good airports as here, and that is one of the purposes of this tour. I thank you."

Soon he was driven into town to the Santa Rita Hotel to rest with his crew before the evening banquet. Before retiring to his suite he met with the press for a short time.

The banquet that evening, announced as informal, was held at the University of Arizona commons. One of the events on the program was for Lindbergh to personally meet with four young boys, winners in the *Arizona Daily Star*'s model airplane contest. The boys were Bob Quesnal, Bill Quesnal, Lansing Bronson, and Joe Liera.

Attending the banquet were high-ranking military and civil Mexican people, along with officials of the State of Arizona, among whom was acting Governor James Kerby. A fellow flyer was also there, Martin Jensen, who had flown in the Dole race to Hawaii.

Three Mexican governors were in attendance including Mexican aviators, all guests of the city. Permission for two Mexican airplanes to enter the United States in order to participate in the celebration had been granted by the State De-

partment.

While in Tucson Lindbergh met with the Mexican officials at the Old Pueblo Club. Attending was Maj. Gustave G. Leon of the aviation forces at Ortiz, Sonora, who gave a brief talk. After meeting and shaking hands with Lindbergh he said, "I was so moved that I could hardly say what I wanted to." Lindbergh replied, "I particularly appreciate your tribute because it comes from a brother officer from a sister nation."

On the morning of the 24th, Lindbergh took off from Tucson at 7:45 A.M. and flew due east to Silver City and Ft. Bayard in New Mexico before heading southwest to Lordsburg, the next stop on the tour.

Today Davis-Monthan Air Force Base still exists, and is on the same site as it has always been, where Lindbergh landed in 1927. It is at an elevation of 2,704 feet MSL and has a 13,000-foot northwest-southeast runway. It has not been precisely determined where Lindbergh landed in 1927 on the site, but assumed in the more or less northwest area of the airfield, about 4.5 miles southeast of the center of Tucson. Today it is home to the 355th wing, HQ 12th Air Force.

In later years, about 1940, the city purchased roughly 4,000 acres of land about two miles directly south of the old Charlie Mayse Field, to build yet another major airport. It is known today as the Tucson International Airport. It is at an elevation of 2,641 feet MSL. Its longest runway is 10,996 feet. It is equipped with arresting gear on both the main runway and the secondary runway of 7,000 feet. The airport handles most major airlines, as well as corporate and some general aviation aircraft and military.

The famous Ryan Field, several miles west of the city, is still in existence, servicing mostly general aviation airplanes. The airport is well known for the thousands of pilots it trained in Ryan PT-22 airplanes during World War II.

References

Newspapers
Arizona Gazette
Arizona Republican
Arizona Daily Star

Organizations
Arizona Flyways
Arizona State University
The Arizona Historical Society
Department of Library, Archives and Public Records, State of Arizona

Publication
Sky Pioneering, by Ruth M. Reinhold

People
Senator Barry Goldwater
Richard Sanders Allen

Robert W. Ost	Arv Schultz
Ole C. Griffith	Robert Jackson
Ruth M Reinhold	Scott Gifford
Al Gonzales	Carl Bernhardt

STOP #54
LORDSBURG, NEW MEXICO
"TOUCH STOP"

CAPSULE HISTORY OF CITY

Lordsburg, Hidalgo County, is located in the southwest corner of the state of New Mexico, just a few miles west of the Continental Divide, about seventeen miles east of the border of Arizona. When the Southern Pacific Railroad came into the area, one of their engineers was Delbert Lord. He established a string of eating houses along the line from the west, in the area of the Lordsburg site. Thus the town was officially founded in 1860/1880, and named after Lord — Lordsburg.

The Lordsburg area is a great stock-raising region. In addition to high-class sheep, goats, and poultry, it has produced some of the finest herds of purebred Herefords to be found in this area of the country.

A former resident of Lordsburg was the notorious bandit, Billy the Kid. In the early years Geronimo and the Indians of the region were very hostile.

"Stagecoach," one of the greatest Hollywood movies ever made, was filmed at Lordsburg.

Within sight of Lordsburg, on an 8,000-foot peak, a Solar Radiation Observatory was established by the Smithsonian Institute Research Department of the Federal Government. Their mission has been to make round-the-world reports, showing the weather conditions two weeks in advance. The lab is located on the south peak of Big Burro Mountain.

The city is noted, as is New Mexico, for its continuous sunshine and generally pleasant climate. The average annual temperature at one time was 63.4 F and average summer temperature has been a comfortable 72.3 F. Average winter temperature is 45.2 F, which strengthens the tourist trade.

4,200 feet MSL.

SEPTEMBER 24, 1927 (SATURDAY)

As it turned out, Lordsburg would be the smallest town the crew would visit during this eighty-city goodwill tour. At this time there was an open flying field, just southeast of the little western desert town. It was just an open area without much in the way of service facilities. It had a corrugated-type hangar on the field.

As usual, the Fairchild landed first, at about 10:30 A.M. Keyhoe was quite concerned about the large crowd already on the field, including all of the children of the town. He did not see many policemen or other guards around. He was told "not to worry" and was assured that the people of Lordsburg would be well behaved and not get out of control.

Arrangements had been made with the Scott Auto Company to receive three cases of Mobil Oil B for the NYP and the Fairchild.

Soon the NYP was spotted over the town and landed a few minutes later to the excitement of everyone. As at other stops, all businesses and schools were closed for the day, and everyone was there on the airfield. Because of its western heritage, there were scores of mounted cowboys and cowgirls in colorful compact groups wearing their traditional chaps and spurs.

These western people were not mob hysteria prone and conducted themselves in a respectful manner. It is said that 10,000 people were there. Most of that number had come from far and wide, as the town had only 1,600 residents at that time.

Soon after Lindbergh landed and parked the airplane, he climbed out of the cockpit and immediately was welcomed by Lordsburg's ambassador at large, Willard Holt, editor of the local paper, the *Lordsburg Liberal*. Holt was also the personal representative of the New Mexico gov-

Taken just after Lindbergh arrived on the open field outside of Lordsburg. JOHN A. JOHNSON

ernor, and George W. Hanner, the Mayor of Lordsburg. He was also welcomed by G. P. Jeffus, President of the Chamber of Commerce; Charles Fuller, Chairman of the Board of County Commissioners; and B. H. Cross, Clerk of the District Court.

The costumed cowboys and cowgirls put on a horsemanship demonstration for the flyers. The little town could not put on an elaborate parade, but they could do this in appreciation for his visit and in honor of their hero.

Apparently there was a picture taken of these hard-working range folks, near the *Spirit of St. Louis*, but this writer has yet to find one. In

Lindbergh is seen on the speaker's stand that was set up on the field. JOHN A. JOHNSON

fact, not even one photo of the NYP at Lordsburg has shown up at this writing.

After being driven around the airport, Lindbergh said a few words to the assembled crowd: "Mr. Chairman, citizens of New Mexico, Lordsburg is one of the smallest cities included in this tour of the United States. We do not believe in measuring a city by its size as much as by what it does, and by your establishing this airport you have set an example for the cities of the United States."

Lindbergh spoke as usual on the development of commercial aviation and airports and the importance of air travel and the future of the industry.

In closing he said, "I want to compliment

The NYP on the open desert field outside of the little Western town. JOHN A. JOHNSON

A good view of the NYP with the mountains in the background and some of the local people and the Fairchild just to the right. JOHN A. JOHNSON

you as citizens of Lordsburg and your fair state in establishing this airport. I thank you very much for your interest, and I certainly appreciate the work you have done here, and what you have done in arranging for this visit. I thank you."

Shortly the Fairchild took off and headed for the next stop at El Paso, Texas. Lindbergh took off from Lordsburg at 11:25 A.M. Mountain Time. The two airplanes flew along the edge of the United States and Mexican border to get a view of Juarez and that part of the country that

C.C. Maidment on the left, Phil Love in the center and Donald Keyhoe, in hat, on Maidment's right. Other man in hat is unknown. WILLARD E. HOLT PHOTO

lies below the Rio Grande River at that point.

Lordsburg today still has an airport on the same site, on the southeast side of the city. It is known as Lordsburg Municipal Airport, at an elevation of 4,278 feet MSL, and with one 5,011-foot-long paved runway, in addition to a 2,655-foot dirt runway. The field has one fixed base operator.

References

Newspapers
Lordsburg Liberal

Organizations
Lordsburg Hidalgo Library

Publications
"In the Shadow of the Pyramids," bicentennial, 1776–1976
"The Story of Lordsburg," by Col. Willard F. Holt, manager of Lordsburg Chamber of Commerce
"Fourth Estate," by John Schimmel, from the *Lordsburg Liberal*

People
Marlene Siepel   Jeanne La Marca   Mrs. Brenda Collins   Gail Hall
                                          Donald R. Lavash, Ph.D.   John A. Johnson

STOP #55
EL PASO, TEXAS

CAPSULE HISTORY OF CITY

El Paso, Texas, is located at the extreme western end of the largest state in the country, on the border with Ciudad Juarez, Mexico, and Santa Teresa and La Union in the southeast corner of New Mexico. The city is on the north bank of the Rio Grande River.

Manso and Suma Indians were the first people to live in this area. About 1598 the Spanish explorer Juan de Onate arrived at this location. He named the site El Paso del Norte (The Pass of the North). Spanish priests established a mission there in 1659. In 1682 the mision (sic) Nuestra Senora del Carmne, the eastern suburb of Ysleta, was established and is the oldest settlement in Texas.

In 1848 the United States Army established an infantry post at El Paso, which today is known as Fort Bliss. El Paso was incorporated as a city in 1873. The famous Mexican bandit Chief Pancho Villa used El Paso as his headquarters during the early 1900s.

In 1848 the Treaty of Guadalupe Hidalgo established the Rio Grande as the boundary between Mexico and the United States. The river divided El Paso del Norte into two settlements, El Paso and what later became Juarez on the Mexico shore.

3,760 feet MSL.

SEPTEMBER 24–25 1927
(SATURDAY AND SUNDAY)

In 1927 the only flying field in the El Paso area was a strip lying between the municipal golf course and what was to become Biggs Air Force Base, then no more than a balloon hangar out in the open desert.

This site, acquired by the Army, was named after James B. Biggs, an El Pasoan who was killed in air combat in France in 1918. The field was operated by the government, and was at an al-

Here the NYP is being re-fueled and having the oil changed at Biggs Field. Notice older type of fire extinguishers on the ground near the right wheel.
EL PASO PUBLIC LIBRARY

titude of 3,900 feet MSL. At that time it was 2,000 feet square and was located just northeast of the city, a bit south of the military reservation. Biggs was officially named on January 5, 1925, and was also known as Fort Bliss.

Lindbergh day in El Paso was a holiday. Banks were open only until noon, and other businesses and schools closed for the day's festivities in honor of the flyer's upcoming visit.

It was about 1:53 P.M. when Lindbergh came into view and flew over the city before making a smooth landing at 2:00 P.M. on the Fort Bliss landing field. The Fairchild had already arrived there at 1:25 P.M. There were about 5,000 people on the field to see him come in.

The NYP in front of the balloon hangar on Biggs Field. Looking in the window of the NYP is Dick Laudeman. Leaning on the strut is Floyd Huff. BOB LAUDEMAN

After landing, both airplanes were placed in a wire enclosure so that people could view them and take pictures but not get their hands on the machines. At night they would be placed inside the balloon hangar and guarded all night by a squad of twenty-five men of the 141st Infantry of the National Guard.

Lindbergh was met by Mayor R. E. Thomason and Myrtil Coblentz, chairman of the welcoming committee.

Some of the people were so excited that some men forgot the ordinary way of clapping their hands together to make applause. They stood transfixed, pounding one fist after another into the palm of the other hand. There was no sound.

Lindbergh rode in a car with the Mayor and Mexican pilot Emilio Carranza, known in that country as the "Lindbergh of Mexico," who had flown in from Mexico City for the event.

One little girl on Montana Street wasn't going to be disappointed by not seeing the flyer. She came out on a pair of homemade high stilts. A little boy in a homemade airplane sat gazing adoringly at the greatest aviator of them all.

The parade entourage went directly to the El Paso High School stadium. There Lindbergh gave his speech saying, "We are entering a new era of commercial aviation. I would like to impress on you the necessity of beginning an airport program for your city. ... El Paso is very favorably suited for the development of aviation and should co-operate in the promotion of air industry. In 1928 or 1929 you will see regular air service passing through El Paso."

The El Paso people thought he was a prophet with honor, who could electrify any crowd he talked to, and things began to happen.

After the festivities at the high school stadium he was driven to the William Beaumont Military Hospital, where some of the war veterans were grouped on the front lawn, thrilled that Lindbergh stopped there and gave a brief address.

From there the parade went directly to the Hotel Paso del Norte, where Lindbergh would meet with the press at 4:30 P.M. Then he and his crew would retire to their rooms on the fourth floor of the southwest wing for a rest and time to plan for the next day's flight.

At about 7:00 P.M. Lindbergh was taken to the banquet in his honor at the Hotel Hussmann.

At the banquet Lindbergh broke one of his tour rules by autographing a sketch of himself by local artist Floyd Crews of the Art Guild. It was Lindbergh's gift to the new El Paso Art Guild.

That night the Hotel Hussmann was decorated with a Spanish theme, and there were many Mexican officials in attendance. These officials were from the Mexican government, and the town of Ciudad Juarez, in Mexico just across the Rio Grande River. Five hundred and thirty-eight guests were there. Lindbergh was presented with a large flaming red sombrero, a red and green serape, and a carved Mexican cane. The audience cried for him to put on the hat, which he did. It brought the house down.

Finally he was introduced by Mayor R. E. Thomason, and gave his usual talk, concentrating on the development of aviation, especially commercial flying, and the importance of developing more airports around the country.

"Within a short time this country will be transversed by three transcontinental trunk air routes; one from New York to San Francisco, the second from the state of Washington east, and the third in the south from Southern California."

At the banquet Lindbergh presented Carranza with a pair of silver-rimmed goggles, which had been autographed in pen on the strap and said, "To the Lindbergh of Mexico." Carranza was thrilled beyond words.

According to the hotel manager, Paul Harvey, the next morning Lindbergh ordered orange juice, cream of wheat, scrambled eggs, milk and toast. Then he and his crew were driven out to the airfield, and soon preflighted both airplanes. The Fairchild was in the air by 9:25 A.M. After shaking hands with the Mayor and some others, Lindbergh climbed into the NYP and took off at about 9:46 A.M. After circling over the city and the military area, he headed north-northwest over and along the Rio Grande River, over Las Cruces. From there they took a more northerly route, possibly (not confirmed) just to the east of Elephant Butte Reservoir near the present town of Truth or Consequences, known then as Hot Springs.

Continuing north along the river with the Los Pinos Mountains on their right, still following the river, they flew over Albuquerque. From there they took a northeast heading for just

north of the Sandia Mountain area directly to Santa Fe.

The first little airport was dedicated on September 8, 1928, two weeks less than a year since Lindbergh's visit. That was the year before C. R. Smith and Stillman Evans, a friend of then-Mayor Thomason, came to see the latter about landing airplanes they were using to promote an air service in the area. That service became one of the nation's largest, American Airlines, of which Smith became president.

Today on the site where Lindbergh landed, the Biggs AAF (Army Air Force) airport is still there. At an elevation of 3,946 feet MSL, it now has a paved northeast-southwest runway of 13,600 feet.

Just east of the city about four miles is the new El Paso International Airport. At an elevation of 3,956 feet MSL, it has two main runways, the longer being 11,009 feet, which runs northeast-southwest, and a second east-west runway of 9,015 feet in length. They have a modern terminal and handle most major domestic and international airlines, as well as commuter, corporate, cargo, and general aviation aircraft.

Southeast of the city there is a general aviation airport known as West Texas, at an elevation of 4,007 feet MSL with a 7,030-foot runway that runs east-west. The field is about eleven miles southeast from the city.

References

Newspapers
El Paso Times
El Paso Evening Post
El Paso Herald

Organization
El Paso Public Library

People
Wayne Daniel   Bob Laudeman
William J. Nelson

STOP #56
SANTA FE, NEW MEXICO

CAPSULE HISTORY OF CITY

Santa Fe, New Mexico, the capital of the state, is located near the Sangre de Cristo Mountains.

It was chosen as the provincial capital in 1609–10 by the newly appointed governor, Don Pedro de Paralta. He named the city La Villa Real de Santa Fe de San Francisco de Asis—the Royal City of the Holy Faith of St. Francis of Assisi. It would become the oldest continuous seat of government in the United States. In time the name was shortened to Santa Fe.

It is the home of Saint John's College and the College of Santa Fe. There is a Museum of International Folk Art, the Hall of the Modern Indian, the Laboratory of Anthropology, and the Museum of Navaho Ceremonial Art.

6,300 feet MSL.

SEPTEMBER 25, 1927, TO MIDNIGHT THE 26TH (SUNDAY P.M. TO MONDAY A.M.)

According to Donald Keyhoe, an "accidental arrangement" of a "touch stop" instead of an overnight stop in New Mexico caused their plans to change, so that a night flight would be necessary to keep things going and make their obligations on time. Therefore, Santa Fe would not be an overnight, but a touch stop.

At this time the only field ever used by passing aviators was located quite near the mountains. This field had been used only a few times since the first airplane landed there a decade earlier. This site would not be suitable for Lindbergh, so another place was found.

Because of the impending arrival of Lindbergh, Governor Dillon had transmitted a letter to the Santa Fe Chamber of Commerce asking that the name Santa Fe be placed in large white letters on a black background on a large roof with an arrow pointing toward a new land-

Someone is seen shoveling dirt or sand in front of the left wheel to make a pit to roll the wheels into to act as a chock. A National Guardsman watches. WAYNE MOTE

The Fairchild FC-2 escort airplane is seen taxiing in to be near the NYP at Santa Fe, New Mexico. PHOTO BY RAMONA B. LATIMER

ing field, which was now being prepared in a hurry. This new site was five miles southwest of the city. It straddled the Cerrillos Road just south of its junction with the Albuquerque Road. It was 500 feet wide and over 1,000 feet long, with the Cerrillos Road in the center of the field. So the landing area was oriented southwest-to-northeast. They ran two-strand barbed-wire fence along both sides of the "runway." The Cerrillos Road was then blocked at both ends of the parallelogram.

On the northwest corner of the field they erected a corral enclosure, 125 feet long by 80 feet wide, to house the two tour airplanes and to protect them from the public. One hundred National Guardsmen would act as sentries to patrol the area, with over sixty of them mounted on horseback.

After circling over the city, the Fairchild came into view and landed on the "new" airfield at 1:30 P.M. and immediately taxied into the wire enclosure.

When Lindbergh came into view and made a low pass over the field, he came around, and when turning to final approach there must have been a gust as he slipped to view the makeshift runway, because he landed not quite as smoothly as the FC-2, according to one reporter. The crowd was mesmerized and most likely did not notice the imperfect landing. They were now seeing this famous airplane and almost forgot to wave and shout their greeting.

Lindbergh climbed out of the cockpit and removed his flying helmet and goggles, revealing his ordinary gray business suit. He first shook hands with Mayor Ed L. Safford and Colonel King, then Governor R. C. Dillon, and many other officials. He boarded the Governor's car and headed out of the airfield's grounds toward the city.

On their way they passed children at the Santa Fe Indian School and New Mexico School of the Deaf, in addition to other parochial and public schoolchildren. They continued on to the La Fonda Hotel to rest and spend time planning for the upcoming night flight to Abilene. He also spent some time with the local press.

At 5:00 P.M. he was taken to the State House and the Governor's office, and escorted outside to a portable speaker's stand on the Statehouse steps. He was officially presented to the citizens, and then spoke about the future of commercial aviation.

He said, "While the city's high altitude formerly was a disadvantage to aviation, improvements being made to airplane engines mean Santa Fe has the same opportunities for air development as any other city."

He envisioned regular trans-Atlantic airplane travel in the not-too-distant future. Before

National Guardsmen are seen handling baggage for Lindbergh and his crew shortly after they landed at Santa Fe. PHOTO BY RAMONA B. LATIMER

Fueling the NYP for an upcoming night flight. Mr. V.G. East is seen holding the can at the rear of the truck. BERT DAVIS

that would be accomplished, however, Lindbergh predicted that the United States would be crisscrossed with a vast network of commercial airways, over which aircraft will fly on regular schedules carrying passengers, freight, express and mail.

He suggested good aircraft maintenance and inspections, pilot training, well-kept landing fields and airports, and the design of standard air traffic rules.

After the event on the capital steps, Lindbergh and his crew were escorted back to the hotel to sleep before their proposed night flight.

Shortly after midnight the flyers were awakened, given some food, and driven over to the flying field. While there and during the preflight, Katherine Stinson, sister of the famous aviator Eddie A. Stinson Jr., who lived in the area, paid a visit to Lindbergh and wished him well on this flight. She said she would like to have traveled with him.

Using automobile lights at either end of the field (road), they started their engines with the use of flashlights. Lindbergh took off first and headed into the night sky. The Fairchild fol-

lowed, and they took up a southeast heading just south of Thompson Peak, toward Santa Rose, continuing on to Gallaher and possibly north of Lubbock. From there for some reason they took a northeast heading to Roaring Springs, then changed heading again to go southeast to Stamford, Texas, and then directly south to Abilene.

While on this night flight Lindbergh, who had his flashlight on board, stayed to the left of the Fairchild, and blinked his light occasionally toward the FC-2 to let them know where he was and that he, in fact, *was* still out there.

Lindbergh could see the FC-2. They had red and green navigation lights on the wing tips and one white taillight on top of the rudder. Soon they ran into a deck of clouds, and both airplanes climbed up on top to avoid hitting any mountains that might be hidden in the clouds below. It was two hours or so before they could let down and take a look at the ground to locate their position. They were temporarily lost, as they had no way of knowing what their drift might have been. They looked for signs on buildings for a town name but found nothing, then came across a railroad line and began to follow it. It took them directly to Abilene. Lindbergh had already landed there.

Dear Don,

You suggested that Santa Fe would be a good altitude test for the plane.

I took off from the field there at 2:45 A.M. so do not know the exact length of run required but it was not long, and I was carrying about 175 gallons of gasoline in addition to my baggage. Soon after taking off we encountered fog and storms which required flying at about 12,000 ft in order to stay above.

I found a hole to get down through soon after daybreak but Love was over the clouds for about five hours before he could get down.

(The letter goes into other matters on a new design for Hall to work on.)

As Ever,

Charles A. Lindbergh[5]

Today Santa Fe has a municipal airport nine miles southwest of the city, but not in the same location as the one Lindbergh landed on. This airport is at an elevation of 6,348 feet MSL and has a modern terminal. There are two runways,

with the main one 8,342 feet long and the secondary one 6,307 feet long.

There are no other airports or even private strips in the Santa Fe area. The nearest are San Juan Pueblo North, just north of the town of Espanola off Interstate Route 285. The other one is just east of the town of Los Alamos and is named Los Alamos Airport.

Footnotes

5. Excerpt from a copy of letter from Lindbergh to Donald Hall, dated October 2, 1927, from the Hotel Marion, Little Rock, Arkansas. A copy of the letter is in the author's collection. Ref: Santa Fe night flight to Abilene, Texas.

References

Newspapers
Santa Fe New Mexican
Santa Fe Reporter

Organizations
State Records Center and Archives
Museum of New Mexico

People
Wayne Mote   William Sauter
Bert Davis   John K. Lucas
Paul Murphy   Ramona B. Latimer
Mrs. Winnabelle Beasley
Richard C. McCord   Donald Hall Jr.

STOP #57

ABILENE, TEXAS

"TOUCH STOP"

CAPSULE HISTORY OF CITY

The city of Abilene is located in the west-central part of the state of Texas, in Taylor County, and was named after the Kansas cattle town of Abilene. The site had been occupied on and off by various nomadic Indian tribes and United States military personnel in the early days, but eventually became a railroad town site. Here it was bisected by the Texas and Pacific tracks, which run east-west.

The town was started by a group of ranchers and land speculators. The Indians were driven out in the 1870s. The city was officially established about March 1881 and incorporated in January of 1883.

1,708 feet MSL.

SEPTEMBER 26, 1927
(NIGHT FLIGHT) (MONDAY)

About three miles east of town and one mile east of Lytle Lake, there existed a small airport in 1927. The original land there was purchased by Dr. Ramsey and J. McAlister Stevenson. It was named Kinsolving Field, after Maj. Grady Kinsolving. At this time it was just an open field of 2,640 by 1,320 feet, with one hangar.

Having separated from the Fairchild sometime during the early morning, Lindbergh had flown directly toward Abilene after he flew over Stamford.

A siren on top of the big hangar sounded as soon as he was spotted over town, which was about 9:25 A.M. Soon he flew over the field, made his usual low pass to check the surface, and touched down at the extreme northwest corner of the field. He taxied into a previously built wire fence enclosure in the southeast corner of the field, where National Guard troops were stationed to protect the area. At about 9:45 the Fairchild came into view and in several minutes landed and also came into the wire enclosure.

As soon as the airplane was secure, Lindbergh met Mrs. Dan Moody, wife of Texas Governor Dan Moody; Mildred Paxton; Abilene Mayor Thomas E. Hayden Jr.; and Charles William Bacon, president of the Abilene Chamber of Commerce. It was at this time that Lindbergh signed the airport guest book.

The NYP and Fairchild were put in the hands of L. E. Derryberry, chief pilot and manager of the West Texas Air Transport, Inc., which was based on the field. Boy Scouts from the Baptist and Methodist troops were assigned the task of

protecting the NYP as soon as it had arrived. They circled the airplane while holding hands to form a ring around it. One of the scouts, Paul A. Corley, remembered years later that when Lindbergh returned to the field to prepare for his departure, he patted Paul on the back and said, "Thank you, guys," and then left for the next stop.

In a few minutes Lindbergh was escorted to a waiting car, an old Nash, and seated in the back with Mrs. Moody and the Mayor.

Abilene had 30,000 residents and 2,000 college students at that time. These throngs were augmented by at least 40,000 other West Texans in the crowd that was there for the celebration.

Because this was a rather small west Texas town, they made it an all day celebration, even though the famous flyer would only be there for a couple of hours. Events started in the morning before he even arrived, and went into the night, and even into the early morning hours of the next day.

There was a football game in the afternoon between Anson and Abilene High Schools. In the evening there was a gala dance affair at the country club for "The Spirits," a group of young ladies. The dance began at 10 P.M. and went until two the next morning. Music was provided by the Mickey Rathbone orchestra.

One of the highlights was the assembling of about seventy of the most beautiful young ladies of west Texas. They were wined and dined and appropriately called "The West Texas Spirits." The local newspaper was full of stories on the attributes of each girl, and detailed descriptions of what each one was wearing. Lindbergh could have had a date with any one of them, but was obviously not interested.

After introductions at the airfield, the pa-

The only photo found of the NYP at Abilene. It shows L.W. (Bernie) Burnett Jr. standing on the wheel. BERNIE BURNETT

rade finally got underway and proceeded westerly into the city to Federal Lawn in downtown Abilene.

At first there was some commotion about a "throne" that had been prepared on the back seat of the Nash for Lindbergh to sit on so folks could see him better. He flatly refused to be part of such an arrangement and made it clear that he preferred to sit on the regular seat. He felt the public could still see him, or he might stand at times so he could be seen a bit easier.

At the speakers' platform Lindbergh was introduced by Mrs. Moody. In his address he had this to say: "Mrs. Moody and citizens of West Texas. Texas has always been one of the foremost of our states in the development of aviation, both civil and military. During the war, Texas was an example of the achievements in aviation for many of the states of the union. You have here ideal flying conditions. A southern route from the Pacific to the Atlantic will naturally pass through your state. Your flying conditions in relation to others are among the best. You have natural territory available for flying and training and, in short, the natural adaptation of the state of Texas is excellent for flying conditions."

His talk went on into the development of aviation and commercial air travel with the usual remarks as given at all the other stops. After the talk he was given some lunch and then driven back to the airport to prepare for his departure and that of the escort airplane.

A touching sidelight happened during the parade when Lindbergh spotted a lone figure at a railroad crossing. A lady was holding a four-year-old boy in her arms so that he could see the hero. A tattered old sweater sheltered her and the boy from the cool morning air. It was apparent that she had known what hard work was because she looked tired and worn. She was heard to whisper to the boy, "That's him! That's him!" The boy was showing signs of realizing that an unforgettable event in his life was about to happen. The woman had a look of bewilderment as Lindbergh noticed her and the boy and saluted.

During his visit in town he was apparently taken over to the *new* Hilton Hotel to sign the register so his name would appear at the very top—as their first guest.

L. W. "Bernie" Burnett Jr. was at the airport

for the arrival of Lindbergh with his grandfather, E. N. McCluskey. Young Bernie had his picture taken while standing on the right wheel of the NYP and never forgot the day. Because Bernie was primarily interested in the airplane, he passed up the chance to go into town for the Lindbergh speech. That one event inspired him to make a lifelong career as a pilot. He retired after more than fifty years in the cockpit of corporate airplanes, from Cubs to jets. He was in one of the first classes to graduate from Lear jet school.

At 11:08 A.M. Lindbergh took off for Fort Worth to the east after circling over the little city a few times. The two-hour-and-fifteen-minute flight to Fort Worth started out by flying northeast over Hubbard Creek Lake near Breckenridge, directly to Jacksboro, then east over Lake Bridgeport to the town of Bridgeport, Texas. The last leg took him from there southeast to Fort Worth and the Meacham Municipal Airport there. An apparent weather system along that route moved eastward bringing rain to the Fort Worth landing area.

Today there is an airport on the exact same site in Abilene called Abilene Regional Airport. It is at an elevation of 1,790 feet MSL and its longest runway is 7,202 feet. It serves mostly general aviation and some regional and national airlines.

Just north of Abilene Regional is Elmdale Airpark, a general aviation field. Several miles to the southwest is Dyess Air Force Base, which has been there for many years. Dyess has a 13,500-foot runway.

References

Newspapers
Abilene Morning News
Abilene Reporter News
Abilene Daily Reporter

Organizations
Abilene Public Library
Museums of Abilene, Inc.
Abilene Preservation League
Hardin-Simmons University
Burnett Farm and Ranch

People

Jack Holden	B. W. Ashton, Ph.D.
Janis C. Test	Jennifer Garner
Bernie Burnett	Ms. Ruby Perez
Jack W. Townsley	Richard T. Veigel
Jack North	A. B. Shelton
Rick W. Sisk	Jesse Chase
Nancy Robinson Masters	

STOP #58
FORT WORTH, TEXAS

CAPSULE HISTORY OF CITY

Fort Worth, Texas is located on the Clear Fork of the Trinity River in North Texas.

In June 1849 Army Major Ripley A. Arnold established a military post on this site to protect early settlers from Indian attacks. When the Army personnel left the post in 1853 the settlers used the Army buildings for storage. The post was eventually named for Maj. Gen. William J. Worth, a hero of the Mexican War, hence Fort Worth. It is still often referred to as "Cowtown" because of its history as a center for marketing and processing cattle. It was incorporated as a city in 1873.

670 feet MSL.

SEPTEMBER 26–27, 1927
(MONDAY AND TUESDAY)

In 1927 an airport known as the Municipal Airport, sometimes referred to as the Fort Worth Airport, existed in the northwest part of the city. It is five miles from the central business district on North Main Street. The field consisted of 745 acres of open land, so airplanes could land in any direction depending on the wind, typical of the day. Today the field is known as Fort Worth Meacham International Airport.

Because Fort Worth was one of the largest cities at the time in Texas, there were thousands of people waiting for Lindbergh's arrival—many at the Municipal Airport, others along the proposed parade route, and still more at Panther

The NYP in the hangar at Municipal Airport with the engine area being checked by the tour's mechanic as Lindbergh looks on. CHANDLER ROBINSON

Park near downtown. Twelve aviation cadets had flown in from Brooks Field earlier that morning to greet the flyer. He was scheduled to give his usual talk at the park to local schoolchildren and their parents.

Soon the NYP was spotted coming in from the north, after circling the business section of the city. He came over the field with a low pass and made his final approach from the north, landing to the south on the sod field in a cloud of dust.

He turned around and taxied up to the hangar area where the NYP was immediately put into a wire enclosure near the hangar to protect it and the Fairchild from the crowds and still be visible enough for them to take pictures and view the airplane. The area was surrounded by National Guard troops and local Boy Scouts for security. Lindbergh landed at 1:57 P.M. The Fairchild had already landed at 1:20 P.M. with Keyhoe, Love, and Maidment, to prepare for Lindbergh's arrival.

Several officials greeted him after he stepped out of the cockpit; one was Major Fitzgerald, who was in command of Brooks Field in San Antonio when Lindbergh was training there, another was Sgt. E. F. Nendell of Kelly Field, who trained with Lindbergh there. Also present were Gov. Dan Moody, Atty. Gen. Claude Pol-

lard, Lt. Gov. Barry Miller, speaker R. I. Bobbit and others.

Several bands, including the 144th Infantry Band of the Texas National Guard, the local high school bands, and others, were at the airport to entertain the crowds.

The parade moved down Old Decatur Road, then to North Main, working its way into the city proper and to Panther Park. At the park Zane Irwin, daughter of Mr. and Mrs. W. H. Irwin, presented a bouquet of flowers to Lindbergh on behalf of the public schoolchildren of Fort Worth.

Lindbergh was introduced to the audience by the Governor and gave his usual speech. After these festivities he was taken to the Texas Hotel, where he met with the press before retiring to the presidential suite until the evening activities.

That evening the banquet at the Texas Hotel's Crystal Ballroom was packed to capacity with 800 guests. Lindbergh again was introduced by the Governor, who called him "the most beloved peace-time hero in the world." He presented his talk on the future of commercial aviation and commended Fort Worth on their fine municipal airport. After the banquet there was an informal reception in the flyer's suite for some close friends and officials.

There was also a ball at Casino Park on Lake Worth, open to the public, which was followed by a "Lindbergh" fireworks display over the lake.

When the guests had departed, Lindbergh and his crew were discussing the rest of the tour. They considered it a milestone, figuring the remaining flights would be shorter. Soon they

Here the NYP can be seen in front of the hangar with a water tower and smoke in the background. JOHN KOTZ JR.

would head for the Atlantic side of the country and up the East Coast to the last city.

Maidment remarked that he was happy it would be only a half-hour flight to their next stop at Dallas. But Lindbergh countered with, "That's too short a flight. It isn't worth taking off for such a little hop. I've already told two mayors we'd fly over their cities before going to Dallas. But it'll be only about two hours." And that settled the matter.

The next morning was rainy and overcast so the flyers slept for most of the morning. Out at the field the two airplanes were kept in the hangar for most of that morning. Because they were so well sheltered, the preflight routine would be much more comfortable and thorough, even though Lindbergh usually spent considerable time with his preflight.

At noon the field was quite soggy and muddy. During the take-off he used about three-fourths of a mile before leaving the ground, then gradually held her down to build up flying speed. Eventually he flew back over the field as a final salute to the city, in appreciation for their hospitality. He circled the field three times before heading southeast.

When Lindbergh left the Fort Worth area, he headed southeast to the town of Alvarado, then south to Hillsboro, northeast to Waxahachie, where he circled several times, finally heading north to Love Field after a two-hour flight, just as he had planned.

The old Municipal Airport is still on the same site but today is known as Meacham Field, named after former Mayor H. C. Meacham. Its formal name is Fort Worth Meacham International Airport. It is at an elevation of 710 feet MSL, with the main and longest runway 7,501 feet. It services corporate and general aviation air traffic and some military.

Seven or eight miles southwest of Meacham is the Naval Air Service Fort Worth Joint Reserve Base, Carswell Field, on the south shore of Lake Worth. Elevation is 650 feet MSL, with a 13,500-foot runway.

References

Newspapers
  Fort Worth Star Telegram
  Fort Worth Press

Organizations
  Texas State Library (Austin)
  Dallas Public Library
  University of Texas (Dallas)
  William E. Jary Research Library

Publications
  Adolphus Hotel Banquet Program, Sept. 27, 1927

People
  Capt. Chandler A. Robinson   John Kotz Jr.
  Mrs. William Dods Hawkins
  Morgan W. Vaught   Mrs. Leslie Irvin
  Mrs. H. V. Frances Whitson
  Mr. Willian E. Jary Jr.   Mrs. Lindy Berry
  Mr. C. C. Risenhoover

Stop #59
Dallas, Texas

Capsule History of the City

Dallas is the second largest city in Texas, second to Houston. Located on the rolling prairies of north-central Texas, about thirty miles east of Fort Worth, it is sometimes called the "Big D."

Historians believe that the city was named for George Mifflin Dallas, former vice president of the United States from 1845 to 1849 under President James K. Polk. The actual site was founded by John Neely Bryan in 1841. It be- *came the county seat in 1846 when Dallas County was created. It was incorporated as a town in 1856 and as a city in 1871.*
512 feet MSL.

September 27–28, 1927
(Tuesday and Wednesday)

In 1927 the local airport for the city was, and still is, known as Love Field. At the time of Lindbergh's visit, the city was in the process of purchasing the airport, which would make it a

municipal field. At that time there were several fixed base operators (FBOs) on the field, including the large chain known as Curtiss Aeroplane & Motor Corp. There were several hangars on the field at the time, all numbered from one to at least six.

A cold and shivery rain started falling at daybreak that morning, which cut the crowds of people almost in half. Love Field became soggy and muddy. The rain continued intermittently during the morning of September 27, according to meteorologist Dr. Joseph L. Cline. He hoped that the skies would clear by nightfall, and that the next day (Wednesday) would clear with cool weather coming in from the northwest. The temperature had dropped from 85 to 55 degrees F in only a few hours on the afternoon of Lindbergh's arrival.

There was only about a thousand-foot ceiling by the time Lindbergh was due, with some light drizzle and rain. He was in and out of the clouds as he made his way north and came into view over the city, which he circled a number of times. He made his usual low pass to check on the surface, which was clearly very wet and soggy. The wind was blowing from the north, so he landed to the north. It was reported that he came to a stop near Hangar 5.

He taxied the NYP right into the hangar to get out of the rain and let the engine run several minutes before cutting the mixture control to kill the engine.

While sitting in the cockpit he took off his leather flying coat. Donald Keyhoe stepped up to the door and said something to Lindbergh, just before the flyer stepped out of the airplane to meet the welcoming committee. As Lindbergh stepped out, the local aviation cadets stood at attention, a bugle blew, and the crowd went wild with cheering.

The first to shake his hand was Mayor R. E. Burt, as the official welcome. He was then escorted to a speakers' stand or platform just outside the hangar. The stand was already hooked up with loudspeakers so the crowds around the field could hear him. This part of the program was the "dedication" of the airport, even though the sale of the field to the city had not been offi-

The NYP in what appears to be the Curtiss Company hangar at Love Field (could possibly be Kansas City.) Notice the Curtiss Jenny wings up in the storage racks above. The airplane was being fueled at the time of this picture. FROM THE COLLECTION OF THE TEXAS/DALLAS HISTORY AND ARCHIVE DIVISION, DALLAS PUBLIC LIBRARY

cially made as yet.

At this reception were Postmaster John W. Philip, Col. William E. Easterwood Jr., Mayor Burt, and President E. R. Brown of the Chamber of Commerce. Dr. Carl C. Gregory of the local First Methodist Church gave the invocation. In the invocation Dr. Gregory said, "Thank God for the advance made in this age, for the type of man who is this day a guest of Dallas asking for the continuance of the progress of aviation that would bring about universal peace."

Then the Mayor stated that they had talked and dreamed of aviation, but done nothing un-

This photo shows part of the parade and throngs of people along the parade route in downtown Dallas. FROM THE COLLECTION OF THE TEXAS/DALLAS HISTORY AND ARCHIVE DIVISION, DALLAS PUBLIC LIBRARY

til Lindbergh came. Now they were far more interested in the subject. From that day on the plan was to improve Love Field and commercial aviation in general in the area, indicating Lindbergh's usual influence on the industry throughout the whole nation.

The original plan called for the parade to proceed to the Fair Park stadium for a talk to the local schoolchildren, but because of the inclement weather the plan was scratched, and his talk at the airport was considered the main presentation.

Soon Lindbergh was whisked into a waiting car to begin the parade into the downtown area, between thousands of parked cars. Drivers and passengers and thousands more, in colorful raincoats and umbrellas, lined the sidewalks along the route.

They made their way to the Hotel Adolphus in the business district of the city. He and his crew were given a suite of rooms on the fifteenth floor to rest after he met with the press for a half hour.

The banquet that evening was in the junior ballroom of the hotel. Toastmaster for the event was E. R. Brown, Dallas Chamber of Commerce president. Others on the reception committee were Lloyd M. Long and P. D. Lampert, who were both in charge of the NYP and FC-2 out at the field, and Senor Cosme Hinojosa, Postmaster General of the Republic of Mexico. Gov. Dan Moody was also present.

Lindbergh said, "The best way any city can promote aviation is to see that a well equipped airport is provided. In that way the city can become and retain a place on air lines and attract other machines so that its citizens can see at first hand how these modern means of transportation perform with reliability and a high degree of efficiency.

"Through the use of the development already here at your airport, in the support of the agencies of air mail and its allied services, you will best insure further development. You must keep Dallas and Texas on the air map of the United States, and the best way is to get behind your air program wholeheartedly."

It also appears that at the time of Lindbergh's visit, the movie "The Lone Eagle" was playing at the Odeon Theater.

Because of his visit, and what he did for aviation, the city decided to name an extension of Skillman Avenue "Lindbergh Boulevard." However the name was removed about 1940. It was caused by an isolationist speech Lindbergh made as part of the America First Committee attempting to keep the country out of World War II. The name was never replaced. So the name Lindbergh in Dallas has never been popular with some of the people, the press, or the politicians. It has been the only city in the United States to take this stand, and it has made research there very difficult, if not impossible.

But in April 1975 the situation changed. A housing development was underway at the location of the old White Rock Airport, a few miles northeast of the city, just off John West Road. One street there is named Lindbergh Drive. According to the city's urban planner, Jo Anne Yadack, "It seemed appropriate, since it was an old airport, and they wanted to keep the aviation theme."

When Lindbergh took off from Love Field on the morning of the 28th, he circled over the airport as well as the city. He then took up a direct northerly heading, flew over Denton, and from there over Gainesville, passing on the west shore of Ray Roberts Lake. Continuing north he flew over Ardmore and then Sulfur and Paul's Valley in Oklahoma before arriving over Oklahoma City. The weather was still raining with low ceilings.

Love Field is still there on the same site as it was in 1927. It appears that Lindbergh landed somewhere in the northeast corner of the field. The field is at 487 feet MSL, and its longest runway is 8,800 feet. There are many fixed base operators on the field, in addition to a modern terminal that handles most of the country's major airlines, including commuter, corporate, general aviation aircraft and some international movements as well. Also right on the field is the Frontiers of Flight Museum.

There are just too many airports in and around the Dallas and Fort Worth areas to mention here. However, there is one extremely large airport that serves both cities. It is the DFW (Dallas-Fort Worth International) Airport. At an elevation of 603 feet MSL, its two longest runways are 13,400 feet each. The airport serves most of the major airlines of the world and also has facilities for general aviation aircraft, which in-

cludes corporate jets.

References

Newspapers
Dallas Morning News
Daily Times Herald

Organizations
University of Texas at Dallas

Frontiers of Flight Museum
City of Dallas
Dallas Public Library

People
Capt. Chandler A. Robinson
Phyllis R. Moses   C. V. Glines
Emilio Salazar   Eleanor Nelson
Bill Pritchett   D. F. Whitehurst

Stop #60
Oklahoma City, Oklahoma

CAPSULE HISTORY OF CITY

Capital and largest city in Oklahoma, Oklahoma City is located on the North Canadian River, close to the geographic center of the state. Five Indian tribes lived on what is presently this great city — Cherokee, Chickawaw, Choctaw, Creek, and Seminole. It was made into a reservation for those tribes in the early 1880s by the government of Oklahoma Territory.

On the afternoon of April 22, 1889, the government opened the area for white settlement, and by that evening, after a great land rush, about 10,000 settlers had arrived on the site. The land claims surrounded a Santa Fe Railroad station. The city literally blossomed overnight.

It was incorporated as a city in 1890, and in 1910 Oklahoma City replaced Guthrie as the state capital.

1,200 feet MSL.

SEPTEMBER 28–30, 1927
(WEDNESDAY THROUGH FRIDAY)

The city had a municipal airport in 1927 located at or on the west side of May Avenue, near the corner of 29th Street and extending as far south as 36th Street and west to about Independence. The 2,640-foot dirt field was at an elevation of 1,300 feet MSL. Woodson Park occupies that site today, and Route 44 runs through the park. Burrell Tibbs was the local fixed base operator and manager at the time. The field was four miles from the center of the city to the southwest. It was known as Munici-

pal Aviation Park at that time. The field was used by the U.S. Air Mail system also.

Nearly all of the 150,000 inhabitants of Oklahoma City, in addition to thousands of other people from around the state, were in the city to welcome the flyer on a rainy, overcast day.

The first airplane to arrive was the Fairchild, landing at 1:30 P.M. The State Fair was on at this time, and everyone there had expected that Lindbergh would fly over the event before landing. Everything came to a standstill as he was sighted over the city. He came over and circled, most likely coming in low as a salute. Thousands

The NYP in front of the NAT hangar where it is obvious that the 47-foot wing span of the NYP will not fit in the hangar. R. LEE FISH PHOTOGRAPHER VIA STEVE JOHNSON

of visitors, employees, performers, and hamburger and peanut venders gathered in open spaces to watch him fly. People yelled out, "There he is, there he is." "I saw him through the window," and the place went wild.

A wire enclosure had been built to protect

Tied down in the rain at Oklahoma City with a tarp over the engine. R. LEE FISH PHOTOGRAPHER VIA STEVE JOHNSON

the NYP and yet make it viewable for the public to take pictures. There was one hangar on the field that had NAT (National Air Transport) printed on a sign on the front of the building. A photo shows the NYP tied down, facing toward the hangar, making it obvious that its wing span is much too long to fit into the small hangar.

When Lindbergh first appeared over the city about 1:00 P.M., he circled over the business district and also circled several times over the tuberculosis hospital for the disabled veterans. The facility housed about 100 veterans. Then he headed southwest to the Municipal Airport. He circled the field, made a low pass, and came around for a smooth landing on the soft, wet surface at 2:00 P.M., his ETA.

After taxiing into the wire enclosure in front of the hangar, he stepped out of the cockpit and was greeted by Governor Johnston, Mayor Walter Dean, Ed Overhoiser, H. C. Martin, chairman of the Chamber of Commerce Aviation Committee, and Donald Keyhoe. Lindbergh had put in the windows of the cockpit before he stepped to the ground.

The newspapers said that many cameras clicked at the time of his arrival and while he was getting out of the airplane. (This writer wonders where all of those pictures could have gone as not much has shown up after exhaustive research.)

Soon he entered a car driven by Tom Reed and sat in the back with the governor and mayor, with Don Keyhoe riding up front. The parade route was lined on both sides with thousands of people, all the way to their first stop, the grandstand at the fairgrounds, where he gave his usual talk on commercial aviation.

Then they drove over to the University Hospital where crippled children were out at the

curb and in wheelchairs or on cots. Lindbergh's car slowed down so that he could wave and nod his head toward them. They were all quite thrilled.

From there they drove to the university, and as they rode along interesting remarks in the crowd could be heard: "Just think, he flew across the ocean—alone"; "He looks exactly like his picture"; "We've seen him, and that's enough. A fine boy, isn't he good looking?"; "Hey, Lindy, look this way."

Soon after arriving at the university campus he was asked to turn the first shovel of dirt to begin the construction of a new building. It would be the Lindbergh Hall of Fine Arts.

Later that afternoon he gave another talk to a crowd of about 4,000 people on the university campus:

"Citizens of Oklahoma City, I am here to talk about aeronautics and its future. It has reached a stage where it can't progress without the aid of the citizens.

"In the past it was mostly in the hands of the military authorities. It made little difference whether the citizens were interested in aviation. Now it is different. Today we must have good airports, properly situated. The construction of airports is the most important thing for aviation now. Practically every important city will have centrally located airfields.

"I would like to impress the citizens of Oklahoma City with the necessity of getting behind the needs of aviation."

Shortly the entourage made its way to the Huckins Hotel in town, where Lindbergh met with the press and then adjourned with his flying crew to their suite. One of the press reporters asked Lindbergh what he thought of the Oklahoma City airport.

Lindbergh said, "Well, it ought to be larger and it needs other improvements. The citizens here ought to co-operate in improving it. Now please understand I mean this only to be constructive criticism. The airport here is just as good as a great many others, but almost every airport in this country needs to be improved. Oklahoma City is not a bit backward in aviation. ... The location is good. And four miles from the center of the city was not too remote."

At the banquet that evening, held at the Shrine Temple, Masonic banquet hall, Lindbergh presented another serious talk on the development of aviation, airports and especially commercial air travel.

Thursday the 29th was the day of rest for the flyers. Not much information has been found to indicate just how they spent that time. Most likely they just relaxed in the hotel suite all day and spent time planning the navigation for the next leg of the trip. Early that evening Lindbergh and the others did manage to slip out of the hotel unnoticed to a waiting car driven again by Tom Reed to be shown around the city. It was reported that several people had visited the suite on Thursday evening, but no further information as to who or why is available.

The flyers slept a bit late on Friday morning before being driven out to the airport to prepare for their departure.

The weather improved enough for Lindbergh to take Donald Keyhoe up for a long-awaited five-minute ride in the NYP over the area. This experience is best understood in his words.

Keyhoe relates: "In spite of a keen satisfaction and a definite thrill at being privileged to fly in the transatlantic plane with the man who had piloted it across the sea, I did not neglect to watch his handling of his plane.

"I had had experience as a pilot and had covered many thousands of miles with capable flyers, but that flight with Lindbergh was a lesson in complete mastery and understanding of an airplane.

"From the second of taking off he was utterly at ease, although, to me, that blank wall of instrument board in front of us was at once disturbing. Yet it did not bother Lindbergh, in spite of the added handicap caused by my being seated on the right arm of his chair, so that one of his two small windows was half-way hidden.

"He climbed quickly up to an altitude of 2000 feet and then throttled the engine so that I could hear him speak.

"Watch the action on this stall," Lindbergh said, somewhat as an experienced automobile salesman might have called attention to a good point in his car.

"He pushed the throttle ahead once more and waited until the *Spirit of St. Louis* had picked up speed of about ninety miles per hour. Then he pulled back evenly and deliberately on the control stick, until the nose of the plane had risen at a steep angle, and I could see a wide margin of sky under the wing. The plane slowed to a stalling speed.

"Notice that it doesn't fall off on either side," commented the Colonel, nodding toward the wing tip, which hung parallel with the horizon even as the nose began to drop earthward.

"The *Spirit of St. Louis* pointed itself downward without jerking, picked up speed and went ahead into straight flight as he pushed the stick to its normal position. After a moment he throttled the engine again and pointed to the altimeter.

"We lost less than 200 feet on that stall," he observed. "That's why I'm safe in bringing the plane in so slowly in small fields. It won't fall off on one side unexpectedly.

"A second later he was banking into a vertical turn, with the wings pointing straight at the uninhabited stretch below. Smoothly, we pivoted for a complete turn, Lindbergh effortlessly keeping the tell-tale "bubble" in the position of a perfect bank, his eyes on the ground beneath.

"As he leveled off for a gentle landing a few minutes later, the hundreds of people along the side of the airport began to push forward. Then, for the first time during the flight, I saw a faint sign of uneasiness in Lindbergh's manner — a tension that had nothing to do with the actual flying. For in that brief trip he had shown that he is without nerves when in the air."[9]

Keyhoe went on to explain how good a flyer Lindbergh was, how well he knows his airplane, and how thorough he is when the opportunity would come to fly some new machine. "He tests each one thoroughly, scientifically."

Keyhoe said, "I happened to be in the advance plane when he first flew it (location and date unknown). Within five minutes I had seen a complete tryout of maximum climbs, steep turns, stalling point, perfor-

mance when stalled, handling with idling engine, gliding and finally flying with hands off the controls. As he ended this brief but complete test, he nodded to himself and turned around. "Handles all right, considering all that baggage in the rear," he commented. And with that he closed the throttle and went down for a landing as smooth as though he had flown this particular plane for years."[6]

Lindbergh took off and after circling over the city a few times headed to the northeast directly to Stillwater. Then he headed directly to the town of Pawhuska, circling there as well.

He took up a southeasterly heading, flying by the eastern edge of Skiorook Lake (there now but possibly did not exist in 1927) and then directly to Tulsa, arriving over the city at about 1:45 P.M.

Today the old Municipal Airport does not exist. It is the site of Woodson Park. However, about a mile or two to the southwest is the newer Will Rogers World Airport. It is at an elevation of 1,295 feet MSL with a 9,802-foot runway. A modern airport, it handles most all major airlines, both domestic as well as international, general aviation, and the Air National Guard.

Oklahoma City is blessed with several other airports in the area such as the Wiley Post Airport, seven miles northwest of the city, which is mainly general aviation and some military.

The closest airport to the city is the Downtown Airpark, located only two miles southwest of the business district. At 1,180 feet MSL, it has a 3,240-foot runway. The field caters mainly to general aviation but also the 45th Infantry Division Museum. In addition there is the National Cowboy Hall of Fame, and the Omniplex, a conservatory planetarium, science, and airspace museum.

Several miles to the southeast is Tinker Air Force Base, at an elevation of 1,291 feet MSL, with an 11,000-foot runway.

Oklahoma City is well known in the aviation industry because the Federal Aviation Administration's main headquarters is located there at the Will Rogers World Airport.

In 1929 the American Society of Mechanical Engineers decided to create an aeronautical medal as an award for meritorious service in the advancement of aeronautics. The medal therefore was named the *Spirit of St. Louis Aeronautical Medal,* a very prestigious award. The first recipient of this medal in 1929 was Daniel Guggenheim. Second was Paul Litchfield in 1932, who devoted much of his time to the development of lighter-than-air craft in America.

In 1935 Will Rogers, before his untimely death, also received the medal. His wife, Betty Rogers, received the medal at her home in Santa Monica, California, after the death of her husband. Rogers was a close friend to Lindbergh and had flown with him several times later on in years after Lindbergh was married.

Footnotes

6. *Flying with Lindbergh,* by Donald Keyhoe, Grosset & Dunlap Publishers, New York, published by arrangement with G.F. Putnam's Sons, 1928, pgs. 229-233.

References

Newspapers
Daily Oklahoman
Oklahoma City Times

Organizations
Metropolitan Library System
Oklahoma City University

Publications
Jennys to Jets: The Life of Clarence Page, by Odie B. Faulk (Oklahoma Heritage Association, Western Heritage Books, 1957).
The Life of Wiley Post, by Bob Burke (Oklahoma Heritage Association, 1998).

People

Betty Flinta	Tom Solinski
Philip Vickers	Kathy Triebel
Mary Lee O'Neil	Steve Johnson
Robert Reed	Sublett Scott
Cliff Lang	W. L. McManus
R. Lee Fish	Larry Johnson

STOP #61
TULSA, OKLAHOMA

CAPSULE HISTORY OF CITY

The second largest city in Oklahoma, Tulsa is located on the Arkansas River, about 105 miles northeast of Oklahoma City. The name is derived from the Creek Indian tribe word Tullahassee or Talahassee, meaning "old town." In the 1830s the Creeks, who were from Tallassee, Alabama, settled in this area. Archie Yahola, one of their members, presided over tribal council under a huge oak tree. The tree was called Council Oak in 1838, and it still stands today.

Another Creek, Lewis Perryman, opened a village trading post on the Arkansas River in 1848. A post office was established by Lewis Perryman's son, George, on his ranch in 1879. The city was sometimes called Tulsey Town. It was incorporated as a town in January of 1898 and received its city charter in 1908.

Because of the oil boom in those days, Tulsa became known as the "Oil Capital of the World."

677 feet MSL.

SEPTEMBER 30–OCTOBER 1, 1927
(FRIDAY AND SATURDAY)

Tulsa's local airport in 1927 was known as McIntyre Airport. The field was located on the southeast corner of Sheridan Road and Admiral Place, five miles east of the downtown area of the city. It is no longer in existence. It was at an elevation of 750 feet MSL and covered an area of 1,500 feet by 3,500 feet and had some hangars on the field.

The Fairchild was the first airplane spotted as it flew over Reservoir Hill airplane marker and then headed for the airport. It was about thirty minutes ahead of Lindbergh. Many people thought it was the NYP and sent up cheers and waved handkerchiefs.

As the time approached for the big event, America's Highway 66, known then as the Main Street of America, was packed almost solid with automobiles, and

it became impossible to move along the route near the airport.

Soon Lindbergh appeared over Tulsa, circled the business district, and then headed east for the airport. On his way he circled the fairgrounds several times.

After landing he taxied the NYP into the wire enclosure, where the Fairchild had already been placed. The crowds at the field went wild, but with the help of local police and National Guardsmen, they were kept back in line until the two airplanes had been secured in the enclosure.

Lindbergh was welcomed by J. Frank Natchett, chairman of the reception committee; Art Goebel, the Pacific flyer; Mayor Herman F. Newblock; and Donald Keyhoe. Goebel gave a cheerful "howdy" to Lindbergh when the latter stepped from the cockpit. After the flyer made sure all was satisfactory with the NYP, he climbed into a waiting automobile, sitting with Mayor Newblock, Art Goebel, Donald Keyhoe and a twelve-year-old boy named Paul Day, the winner of an essay contest for young people.

The parade of cars left the flying field and proceeded down Sheridan Road to 21st Street. It then headed west to the Fairgrounds for a reception.

In a big field just east of the Fine Arts building, adjoining the Tulsa State Fairgrounds, a stand was erected and Lindbergh was welcomed by the people, including hundreds of children. The International Petroleum Exposition was in progress at this time, so they were included in

The NYP taxiing in at McIntyre Airport at Tulsa on September 30th. CHESTER L. PEEK

From left to right: Lt. Strickland; Mayor Herman F. Newblock; and Art Goebel just after Lindbergh landed. CHESTER L. PEEK

the program. W. G. Skelly was president of the Exposition. Art Goebel was included in the program. Paul Day was also included.

On the speakers' stand the Mayor stepped up to the microphone and introduced Lindbergh to the waiting throng. One could hear a pin drop as the flyer stepped forward. He urged the people of Tulsa to adopt a progressive air development program and to carry it through. He said, "In a few years we can expect to operate planes under any conditions and to be able to land on fields that cannot be seen a few feet above the ground."

Then Mayor Newblock introduced Art Goebel, who did not speak but accepted and acknowledged the cheers and applause accorded him.

In a few minutes everyone climbed into the waiting cars. The parade through the Tulsa streets started by going west on 21st, proceeded into the city center, and to the Mayo Hotel. The procession slowed down as it passed St. John's Hospital to greet its white-robed patients.

At the hotel Lindbergh met briefly with the local press, answering many questions on aviation but not on anything personal. After the press conference Lindbergh and his crew retired to their suite for some rest and cleanup before the evening program.

Lindbergh's visit brought many other airplanes and some well-known pilots to be a part of this celebration. Art Goebel had flown the Travel-Air "Woolaroc" into McIntyre from Muskogee. He had Frank Phillips along as a passenger. Goebel had just won the Dole Race and the $25,000 prize (see Oakland, California, stop #48).

Frank Hawks flew a Ryan B-1 Brougham in from Spokane, Washington. Al Henley piloted a B-1 Brougham that belonged to Robert F. Garland, a Tulsa oil executive. Phil Ball, owner of the St. Louis Browns baseball team, flew in to Tulsa in his Ryan B-1 Brougham that was piloted by Frank Dunn. Walter Beech was there with one of his bi-planes, in addition to a Jenny, Canuck (Canadian) Jenny, Swallow, Waco, Eaglerock, and some other Travel Airs.

As the winner of the essay contest entitled, "What Lindbergh Means to Me," Day was rewarded with a ride in the car with Lindbergh in the parade and was allowed to sit near the flyer on the speakers' stand at the park.

In Day's writing he said, in part,

"Lindbergh means to me faith, determination, preparedness, and bravery. He had faith in his enterprise and hoped for a successful end. He did not depend altogether on himself, but put equal faith in his plane and himself.

"He had determination to make Paris and put his heart and soul in doing this, and prepared himself and plane to the best of his ability and did everything in his power to make it a success. He had bravery or he would not have ventured alone into the unknown regions of the air above the Atlantic, where already the fate of two men was unknown.

"Lindbergh because of his excellent qualities means to me faith, determination and preparedness and bravery, which can be combined in every boy along with the unconceited air of "Lindy," which gained him many friends and admirers such as myself."

Other winners were Ernest Clulow, Randall Simmermacher, Robert Gilmore, and Phil Claxton. They were also given the chance to ride in the parade, in a separate car.

Comments from local children were printed in the local paper. They are included as they wrote them.

"The reason I want to see Lindbergh is to no how brave he is & so I will to talk to him and would like to go up in a air plane some day too."
–Captola Garrison

"Lindbergh mean to me a grate man of are country and he is as clumbis to me. Clumbis was the firs man to go on boat across the atllenty and lendy was the firs sto go across in a aprine and he is one fasmo man." –*Royal Klinger*

"I think Lindbergh is a young boy who tried to set a record for boys who are growing up in America to be determined. Lindbergh is a very famous for his flight o'er the ocean. He was brave, bold and had courage or else he would never flew o'er the ocean." –*Author Unknown*

"Lindbergh is a type of boy who would never be a coward. He made America do it again. I believe Lindbergh is very glad to come to Tulsa and I hope he will have a very good reception Friday, September 30, 1927." –*Charlotte Chouteau*

"Is why I am interested in Charg Limdberg is because he flewed across the amtie ocean without falling. He is the onley wone that hasn't fell. He is known all over the world of being the greatest flier. We are glad to have him to come to Tulsa." –*Mary Elizabeth M'Furron*

The banquet that evening was held on the sixth floor of the Mayo Hotel in the Crystal Ballroom. The celebration was run by Harry Smith, secretary of the Mid-Continent Oil & Gas Association and chairman of the committee in charge. A charge of four dollars was made for each guest. Space was limited to 620 people so careful selection was made to insure that a representative group of the local businesses would be there.

The toastmaster was N. A. Gibson. Other speakers were James A. Veasey, general counsel of the Carter Oil Company, and Professor Josh Lee of the University of Oklahoma.

On Saturday morning Lindbergh expressed his appreciation to Mr. McIntyre, "We certainly appreciate the manner in which you handled the situation at the landing field. The entire affair in Tulsa went very smoothly and it was a pleasure to come here."

Lindbergh asked the airport manager to extend his personal thanks to the many people who were responsible for the care of the NYP and Fairchild, and in keeping the record crowds in order.

On this morning there were an estimated 1,000 people at the field to see Lindbergh again and to watch his every move before he left for the next stop. They were treated to Lindbergh's careful pre-flight before climbing in and getting ready to go.

The NYP and Fairchild engines were started, including Art Goebel's "Woolaroc." Lindbergh took off first at 9:30 A.M. followed by the Fairchild and then Goebel. The NYP began circling the airport. As Goebel climbed over the field and came in close beside the NYP, the two famous airplanes circled the field together. Once again Lindbergh headed for the downtown area of Tulsa to circle before taking up a southeast heading toward Muskogee. At this point Goebel flew on to Oklahoma City and then Ponca City. It was the first time both airplanes had ever been together at one place and flown together. This departure was one of the highlights of the Tulsa visit.

On the flight from Tulsa to Muskogee, Lindbergh and the Fairchild flew directly in about one hour to the next stop, passing close to the eastern edge of the Arkansas River.

Today there are multiple satellite airports around Tulsa to accommodate passenger travel as well as corporate, sport, and recreational flying.

Tulsa International Airport is at an elevation of 677 feet MSL and its longest runway is 10,000 feet. The field accommodates all major domestic and international airlines, as well as commuter, general aviation, corporate, military and helicopter travel. The airport is located five miles northeast of the downtown district. McIntyre Airport no longer exists.

Four miles to the northwest is the Tulsa Downtown Airpark, a general aviation field. It is at 725 feet MSL. Its only runway is 2,965 feet long.

About five miles to the south of the city at 638 feet MSL is the Richard Lloyd Jones Airport, which serves mainly general aviation, including corporate. It has two parallel runways, the longer of which is 5,107 feet.

Seven miles east of the downtown district is the Harvey Young Airport at 750 feet MSL. This field has a north-south runway of 2,580 feet. It serves mainly general aviation. A grass or turf runway is on the east side of the paved runway.

One of the local newspapers carried the following advertisement –

THE MAYO
TULSA

No. 39481
CASHIER –   Date – 9-30-1927

Please Pay HOTEL MAYO TOGGERY

Shirt	$5.00
Sox	$4.50
Underwear	$9.00
Ties	$9.00
Ties	$5.00
	$32.50

Suite 1016
Col. Lindbergh Party
By C. R. Love

THE COLONEL KNOWS
WHAT'S WHAT

We feel very much complimented that the above bill of goods was delivered for Colonel Lindbergh from our Hotel Mayo Toggery last Friday.

The Colonel is an exceptionally well-dressed man and with the stores of every big city in America to choose from we are indeed flattered that he should favor us with his patronage.
Renberg's
The Store of Quality

References

Newspapers
  Tulsa Tribune
  Tulsa Daily World

Organization
  Tulsa City-County Library System

Publications
  The Spartan Story, by Chet Peek, with George Goodhead

People

Dana Christian	Chester L. Peek
Charles W. Harris	Steve Johnson
Matthew E. Rodina Jr.	Bob Pickett
Fred Huston	Beryl Ford

Stop #62

Muskogee, Oklahoma
"Touch Stop"

Capsule History of City

The city of Muskogee lies in rich farming country in the east-central part of the state of Oklahoma.

In the 1870s the white settlers gave the city its name. The site had been occupied by the Creek Indians, whose language was known as "Muskogee." The city is located on the Arkansas River Navigation System and is the seat of Muskogee County.

602 feet MSL.

October 1, 1927 (Saturday)

At the time of Lindbergh's visit, the only airport there was (and still is) known as Hatbox Field and was located on the western edge of town.

At about 10:15 A.M. the NYP was spotted in the northwestern sky. Lindbergh came down low over the Veteran's Bureau Hospital at Honor Heights, circled several times, and then flew directly over the business area of the city. He circled several times before heading back over the airport.

Soon he came down for a low pass over the field, swooped up and around to the north, and turned to land at 10:20 A.M. There were 15,000 people already on the field awaiting his arrival. Before he landed large groups of schoolchildren had been especially assembled in a section of the field. Another area had a group of war veterans to see the hero. After Lindbergh turned the NYP around, he taxied slowly past the children before shutting down the engine and climbing out of the cockpit.

He was immediately met by Lt. Auby Casey Strickland, the commander of Hatbox Airport. Also greeting him were Mayor Paul C. Williams and Paul Hyde Davies, president of the Muskogee Aviation Club.

A pouring rain at the time of his arrival put a damper on the festivities.

Lindbergh rode in the back seat of an open touring car driven by Lt. Strickland. The mayor rode in front with Strickland. They drove out of the airfield onto 40th Street to Okmulgee Street, heading west into town. Along the route another 45,000 people were there to witness this historic event.

The entourage came back to Hatbox. On the north end of the field they halted momentarily in front of the assembled hospital veterans. Then they made their way to the children assembled near the NYP, where he gave a three-minute speech standing in the rear of the car.

"The main purpose of this tour is to increase interest in aeronautics." He said that Muskogee was known throughout the entire country for its splendid Hatbox Field and that he hoped that strides in commercial aviation and in military flying would continue as they have in the past. "We would like to spend more time in this city, and many other cities, but only three months have been allowed to make the tour. I want to thank you for the welcome which I have received here."

Right after this he was presented with a solid silver wings pin by Lieutenant Strickland's wife, Mary Adele, otherwise known as Maridel, originally from El Paso, Texas. Lieutenant Strickland had been one of the advanced instructors at Kelly Field when Lindbergh was a student pilot in training. The wings were given on behalf of Muskogeeans and their visitors. Lindbergh said, "That's nice. It's the first pair of wings I have ever been given."

After a few words with the Stricklands, he autographed three books for some friends. Then he climbed into the cockpit and started the "Whirlwind," taxied into position, and took off to the south. After climbing he circled the airport several times and headed east to fly again over the business district of the city. On the eastern boundary of the city he made a point of circling over the Oklahoma School for the Blind, so that students there who could not see him could at least hear the sound of his engine as he passed over.

After leaving Muskogee, Lindbergh took a southeast heading, flew over the southern tip of Tenkiller Ferry Reservoir, and flew directly to Fort Smith. He circled several times, then headed north-northeast to fly over Van Buren. From Van Buren he took a southeast direction to Boonville, and from there east-southeast directly to Little Rock. He was in the air for two hours and forty minutes.

Today Hatbox Airport still exists on the same site as it was in 1927. It has a 3,800-foot runway, and the field is at 627 feet MSL elevation.

About six miles south of the city is Davis Field, at an elevation of 610 feet MSL. The longest runway is 7,200 feet. The airport caters to general aviation.

References

Newspapers
Muskogee Daily Phoenix
Sacramento Union

Organizations
Eastern Oklahoma District Library System

People
Mary Lee Strickland O'Neal, author
Paula N. Stump   Malcolm Rosser
Cliff Lang

The only picture of the NYP at Muskegee ever found. Shows the airplane on Hatbox Field.
Lt. A.C. Strickland, commandant of the field, is standing next to Lindbergh. CLIFF LANG

Stop #63
Little Rock, Arkansas

Known as the "City of Roses," Little Rock is located on a rocky bluff overlooking the Arkansas River on the north side of the city. It got the nickname because of the profusion of roses in its residential areas. The site is in the geographical center of the state of Arkansas.

The first people living in this area were the Quapaw Indians. Since then it has become the largest city in the state. In 1820 the legislature of the Arkansas Territory chose the city to be the territorial capital, while only a handful of people lived there at the time. It has been the capital ever since.

William Russell, a land speculator, established Little Rock in 1820. The site lay on the smaller of two rock bluffs that flank the Arkansas River. The bluff had been known as Little Rock for many years.

300 feet MSL.

October 1– 3, 1927
(Saturday through Monday)

Little Rock Airport in 1927 was located one-and-one-half miles southeast of the city business district and is still on the same site. It sits at an elevation of approximately 287 feet. The National Guard had at least one hangar on the field at the time.

The first airplane to be seen over Little Rock was the Fairchild, which landed at about 1:30 p.m. on Little Rock Airport. At about 1:45 p.m.

the NYP circled over the business district of Little Rock, including North Little Rock, before heading southeast toward the field, where Lindbergh did a low pass before coming in for a landing at 2:00 p.m. He taxied up to the National Guard hangar immediately.

The airplane was placed inside a wire enclosure, near the Guard hangar in the southwest corner of the airport. Six units of the Arkansas National Guard were placed on duty at the airport to guard both of the tour airplanes during the time they would be there.

Lindbergh was greeted by the Little Rock acting Mayor Hon. Joe H. Bilheimer Jr., acting Governor Hon. Harvey Parnell, and J. Gilroy Cox, chairman of the welcoming committee. Mr. Cox would also be the driver of the car in which Lindbergh would ride into town. Mayor Moyer, J. Curan Conway, and Russ Lawhorn were also present.

Lindbergh was placed in Car No. 5, along with Donald Keyhoe, who was in the front seat. Lindbergh stood on the floor in the rear for most of the way along the route. There were approximately 75,000 people standing along the parade route.

The long entourage proceeded through Little Rock, across the Arkansas River to North Little Rock, and directly to the Fort Roots Veterans Hospital. From there they made their way back to the capitol in downtown Little Rock, where Lindbergh gave a brief speech.

Esma Smith Fitzgerald lived on a cotton farm. She remembered that she had picked three

These two views from over the railroad tracks show the NYP taxiing into the reception area at Little Rock. CHESTER R. GOODWIN

hundred pounds that day so they could go to see Lindbergh at Little Rock. They took a bus to the city and saw him at the capitol and heard his speech.

Mrs. Mary Crothers remembered being six years old when her grandmother, Molly Martin, took her to see the flyer at the capitol. She held her grandmother's hand tightly, pushing through the crowd on Fifth Avenue (now Capitol Avenue) to the foot of the capitol steps. "I looked up and saw the tall, handsome, young Charles Lindbergh standing near the top of the steps. His appearance made an impression on my mind that I'll never forget. He looked to me as if he were a Greek deity standing above the crowd."

Later in the afternoon or evening Lindbergh was driven to the Hotel Marion, where he met briefly with the press before he and his crew retired to their hotel suite. It was during October 2nd that he drafted a handwritten letter of three pages on hotel stationery to Donald Hall in San Diego. In the first part of the letter he gave the details of their night flight from Santa Fe to Abilene, Texas, a few days earlier in the week.

The banquet that evening was held at the Albert Pike Memorial Temple in Little Rock. Toastmaster for the evening was Alfred G. Hahn, president of the Little Rock Chamber of Commerce. The president of the local chapter of the National Aeronautics Association, Moorhead Wright, presided. Maj. J. Carroll Cone, governor at large of the NAA, also presided.

Sitting near Lindbergh at the banquet were four boys, guests of the Lindbergh reception committee, who had been winners in a model airplane contest. They boys were Albert Gebelin, Robert Coker, David Walt Clark and Paul Nash. They were thrilled to shake hands with the famous flyer. Lindbergh himself presented the awards to the boys.

Paul Nash eventually learned to fly and in 1935 had purchased an old World War I Jenny, recovered the plane, and flew it most of the summer. Later that year, in December, he lost his life in an auto accident in which he was the only passenger. He also was a parachute rigger and had made several freefall jumps successfully.

Lindbergh was due for a physical, which he had with Capt. Phillip E. Thomas Jr., a flight surgeon of the National Guard. Lindbergh passed in excellent physical condition. The sur-

Two men by the names of "Mac" and "Goodwin" standing by the NYP at Little Rock. ROBERT B. WHITE, MD

geon was from the 154th Observation Squadron of the Arkansas National Guard. The physical was done shortly before noon on the 2nd at the airport, under the regulation known in Army parlance as "609." At the time this was the regular six-month check, a requirement of his Air Transport Pilot rating. While he was at the airport and visiting with this unit he was given a new flying suit, which was contributed by a local manufacturing plant.

After an early breakfast on the morning of the 3rd, the flyers were driven out to the airport to prepare for their departure.

Lindbergh took off at 11:00 a.m. and circled briefly over this capital city as well as North Little Rock before heading for the next stop, Memphis.

When the tour was originally planned, the group had been requested to land at Nashville, the capital of Tennessee. However, while they were in Little Rock they received word late one night that the Governor of Tennessee had just passed away. They were to be at the capital on the second day following, which would be the 4th or the 5th. After some discussion with his crew

Lindbergh decided it was best not to go there under the circumstances. He and his crew would dominate the local scene, which would not be respectful to the governor, his family, and the city. However, they could visit Memphis, where a committee there had earlier asked for his presence.

Soon he took up a south-southeast heading following the Arkansas River, to Pine Bluff, and from there east-northeast to fly over the town of Helena, Arkansas, on the west side of the Mississippi River, and then northeast to Memphis. He was in the air for three hours.

He had arrived over Pine Bluff at 11:20 a.m., circled the business district and dropped the canvas bag message, which landed in the center of Main Street at about the intersection of Barraque Street. Before coming over the center of town he circled over the local airport, Toney Field.

Today there are three or four airports in the Little Rock area, and the old field where he landed is now known as Adams Field. It is at an elevation of 262 feet MSL. Its longest runway is 8,273 feet. It serves most all domestic airlines as well as commuter, general aviation, and military aircraft.

North Little Rock Municipal Airport, located six miles north of the city at an elevation of 545 feet MSL, caters mainly to general aviation aircraft. Its longest runway is 4,462 feet. Just southwest of the city center is another airport, privately owned and operated, known as Worth James Airport.

References

Newspapers
Arkansas Democrat Gazette

Organization
Historical Aviation of Arkansas, Inc.

Publication
Jefferson County Historical Quarterly, vol. 21, no. 1 (1993)

People

Chester R. Goodwin	Donald Hall, Jr.
Dave Wallis	Reba McClain
Elizabeth Godfrey Page	Max L. Calkin
Ruth Dearing*	J. M. Lemley
Esma Smith Fitzgerald	William L. Blair
Muriel C. Sinnott	Loretta James
May Hope Moose	Rev. David N. Noose
Mary Crothers	Edgar E. Ashcroft
Robert B. White, M.D.	

*Ruth Dearing is the daughter of Phillip E. Thomas Jr., the surgeon who gave Lindbergh his physical at Little Rock.

STOP #64
MEMPHIS, TENNESSEE

CAPSULE HISTORY OF CITY

The largest city in Tennessee, Memphis is located in the southwest corner of the state, on a bluff on the east bank of the Mississippi River. It was named for the ancient Egyptian capital of Memphis, which lay on the Nile River.

The first people in the area were the Chickasaw Indians. Then in 1541 Spanish explorer Hernando de Soto arrived on the site and became, it appears, the first white man to see the Mississippi River. In 1673 Louis Joliet, a French-Canadian explorer, and Father Jacques Marquette, a French missionary, visited the site to trade with the Indians.

In 1682 a French explorer, Robert Cavelier,

Sieur de la Salle, built Fort Prud'homme near what is now the city and claimed the area for France. By the 1700s Great Britain, Spain and France claimed the Tennessee region but in the late 1700s the United States government gained control of the area. In 1818 the U.S. government purchased much of western Tennessee from the Chickasaw Indians. It was finally organized as a settlement and named Memphis in 1819 and incorporated as a city in 1849.

331 feet MSL.

OCTOBER 3–5, 1927
(MONDAY THROUGH WEDNESDAY)

One of the earliest airports that existed in

the Memphis area was known as Armstrong Field. It was named after Lt. Gulon Armstrong, a Memphis pilot who was killed in World War I. The field was dedicated on Armistice Day, November 11, 1926. It was located on the south side of Willington Road, between Fite Road and Lucy Road, in Woodstock. The site is about eleven miles north of Memphis. Louis L. Carruthers and several other local flyers formed the Memphis Aero Club, which leased this field to get it started as a flying field. Today there is a marker erected by the Memphis-Shelby County Airport Authority and the Shelby County Historical Commission. The marker commemorates the fact that Lindbergh landed there during the 1927 tour.

It appears that Lindbergh's original plan was to fly to Nashville, the capital. However, shortly before the tour flyers were to come to Tennessee, Governor Austin Peay had died on Sunday night, October 2. So the route was changed to visit Memphis. It might have had something to do with the fact that the Navy ship (*USS Memphis*) that brought Lindbergh and the NYP back from England was named for the city.

The NYP was seen coming in from the southwest, over the city, which he circled a few times before heading north to Armstrong Field. Thousands of people were all around the field cheering and yelling as he came into sight. The Fairchild had already landed at 1:26 P.M. It was now just several minutes before 2:00 P.M., right on schedule.

A circle of Armstrong Airport, a low pass down the 3,000-foot turf runway, and coming around, he made a perfect three-point landing.

This is the historical plaque on the site where Lindbergh landed the NYP at Memphis, which is still an open field. EV CASSAGNERES

The crowd went wild.

As he taxied into a wire barricade on the south end of the field, where the Fairchild had already been placed, he shut down the engine. He climbed out to shake hands with Mayor J. Rowlett Paine and several other people on the welcoming committee.

A sixty-foot square tent was provided as a shelter for the NYP and Fairchild. National Guardsmen were assigned to stand guard around the area to protect both airplanes.

No time was wasted in getting Lindbergh into a waiting automobile, after he was asked to pose for dozens of photographers who wished to take his picture by the airplane. (This author wonders where all those pictures have gone, as none have been found in the city of Memphis.)

In the car Lindbergh rode with Mayor Paine, Donald Keyhoe, and C. Arthur Bruce. Close behind came a car bearing Capt. Henry E. Lackey, former commander of the *USS Memphis*.

The parade of cars soon made its way out of the field property for the long drive south into the city. Their first stop was Overton Park golf course, where they stopped just east of the Soldiers Memorial.

This visit was a bit timely because Capt. Lackey happened to be in town at this time. Lackey, when commanding the *USS Memphis*, brought Lindbergh and the NYP (in crates) back to the United States after the New York to Paris flight. When the *Memphis* docked at the Washington Navy Yard and Mayor Paine came aboard, Capt. Lackey apologized for the way the dining table looked. He told the mayor he was a bit embarrassed by the fact that a ship like the *Memphis*, which entertained royalty in the foreign ports, had no decent silverware service.

That was all Mayor Paine had to hear. When he returned to his home he began a drive to raise $6,000 to purchase a silver service for the famous ship. Boxes for contributions were set up all over Memphis and word got around to local businesses and schools. Soon the funds rolled in. It took less than three months to raise the money. Fifty-seven pieces of sterling silver were

purchased. This was sufficient to serve the complement of the formal dining salon of twenty-two persons on the ship.

Therefore, when Lindbergh came to town, what better time would there be to make this presentation. At Overton Park, Lindbergh was asked to do the honors in handing over this wonderful gift.

The mayor was behind all of this and ordered all businesses and schools and other offices in the city to be closed for the afternoon. He had fifty-seven Eagle Scouts on the platform at Overton to hold up the fifty-seven pieces of silver during the official presentation.

Before getting into the ceremonies, Mayor Paine stepped to the front of the platform, raised his hands, requested silence, and expressed his sorrow for the death of their governor. As thousands stood with bowed heads, a bugler sounded taps.

After Lindbergh presented the gift, Capt. Lackey spoke: "I accept this service on behalf of the Navy and am but sorry that a majority of its officers are not present to see the fine spirit of the people of this city, which presents it to us." When referring to the service which the ship had so proudly performed for Lindbergh, he said, "And I have an abiding opinion that she will always happen to be present when needed." He then complimented the city as being fully worthy of its honor, and humorously added that it was perhaps best that he had been assigned other duties in the Navy rather than as commander of the ship, for he felt that he would be tempted to give too many parties with this beautiful silver service to adorn his table.

That same silver served on the ship until the ship was decommissioned in 1946. The Navy returned it to the city as a historical memento. For many years it was on display in the "Silver Room" of the old Memphis Pink Palace Museum. Sometime later it was boxed up and stored in the attic of the museum.

In Lindbergh's address at the park, he said,

"We have reached a stage in aviation where it is extremely necessary to have the cooperation of the people of the United States before we can turn the airplane into its fullest commercial use. In the past twenty-five years development in the aeronautical industry has been towards the time when the airplane would reach that stage of perfection that it could be a benefit to commerce. We have now reached that period. Without further development the airplane has already proved itself to be a great development over other means of transportation in relation to speed. We cannot, however, place this new means of transportation before you for use in daily life without your cooperation; first, in the development of municipal airports, and second, in the patronage of the air lines which these airports bring."

He continued with the same insight into the development of the industry that he had at all the other tour stops, but in closing he said,

"Before closing I want to bring before you again the necessity of conducting a progressive air program for your city in order to keep your city in the foreground of American aeronautics. I want to thank you for the interest shown here and for the welcome I have received. I hope that you will devote a portion of your interest in the future of aviation in relation to your community. I thank you."

From the park Lindbergh was driven to the Hotel Peabody, where he met briefly with the press, and then retired to his suite of rooms. While meeting with the press he said, "Mud Island would make an excellent flying field—a fine field, if it was built properly." He said he had observed the island as he circled over the area and saw that the island, just behind the Federal Building, would make an ideal site. Floyd Bennett, who had piloted Cmdr. Richard E. Byrd's airplane over the North Pole, had made a similar statement in the fall of 1926.

In a question posed by one of the members of the press, with regard to his pay, he said, "I receive no pay for this tour. This is in the interest of aviation." He explained how the Guggenheim Foundation was the full sponsor of the trip. Lindbergh took this one opportunity (as he most likely did at some of the other stops) to explain to the press the term "We."

"'We' doesn't mean what it sounds like. What I really meant by 'We' is not myself

and ship, but my organization. The men who backed me and who made the flight possible. I am really sorry that such an idea has been obtained by the American public and am glad to correct it at this time."

In the beautifully decorated banquet hall at the Hotel Peabody that evening there were five hundred people in attendance. Dean I. H. Noe delivered the invocation, and while everyone was having the meal the hotel orchestra entertained with appropriate music. When it came time for the program, Earl Thompson, one of Lindbergh's backers, gave a brief presentation, as did Federal Judge Harry B. Anderson. Some of the distinguished guests—Lt. Phil Love, Capt. Lackey, Maj. N. Crawford, Capt. Donald Keyhoe, C. Arthur Bruce, who was president of the Memphis Chamber of Commerce, and Louis Carruthers—were introduced.

Before introducing Lindbergh, Louis Carruthers, president of the Aero Club, said, "There is a great need of Memphis for an adequate airport." He hoped that Lindbergh's visit would implant the thought of this necessity in the mind of the public.

Finally Lindbergh was introduced and said,

"Cities which expect to profit from this new, but now thoroughly tried, medium of commerce and travel must have adequate airports. These airports must be more than large and well equipped. They must be as near as possible to the business district of the city. If it takes an hour to get by automobile from the business section to the airport, there is a great loss in valuable time."

He continued into his usual speech from there.

The next day, the 4th, was to be Lindbergh's and his crew's rest day, but it turned out to be a "busman's holiday." They took advantage of the day off to have Maidment, with the help of the local mechanics, check both airplanes over thoroughly. They were both in excellent shape, considering the wear and tear of the trip. Even though the servicing gave both aviators an extra sense of security, it nevertheless did not cause them to be any less thorough with their preflight procedures.

Sometime in the morning a Buick sport model was loaned to the flyer so that he could drive around the Memphis area and see the sights without being disturbed by the public or the press. Lindbergh disguised himself, which he became expert at in later years. He had as his passengers Earl Thompson and Lake Hayes, a Memphis attorney.

The party passed through Overton Park and by the Soldiers Monument. Lindbergh found the wilderness portions of the park of special interest, and he admired the city for its work.

They drove out to Armstrong Field, where the two tour airplanes were being worked on. Sometime during the afternoon the NYP was ready, and arrangements were made to take it for a local flight with Earl Thompson as a passenger. They were in the air for twenty-five minutes, and Thompson became the only member of the original "WE" group to ride in the famous airplane.

After the NYP flight another airplane was offered to Lindbergh, a rather new early version of the Ryan B-1 "Brougham" with a Wright J-5C engine. Most likely it was serial number 35 and carried registration number C-866. The airplane belonged to the Von Hoffman Aircraft Company, a Ryan dealer based at St. Louis, Missouri.

This is probably the Ryan B-1 "Brougham," s/n 35, that was flown to Memphis and the airplane Lindbergh flew as mentioned in the text. This photo was taken at San Diego when the aircraft was new.
UNDERWOOD, COLLINGE & ASSOCIATES

Lindbergh spent considerable time with his inspection and preflight. Then he and his passengers were ready. They were Earl Thompson, Capt. Vernon Omlie of the Mid-South Airways, Inc., and Milton D. Girton, who was the general manager of the Von Hoffman Company. They flew straight and level over the local area, so Lindbergh could feel out the new ship. They were in the air for ten minutes. In Lindbergh's pilot log he entered the flight and referred to the

airplane as a B-2.

On Wednesday morning, the 5th, Lindbergh and his crew were up early, had their breakfast and left the hotel at 4:40 a.m. The Fairchild took off at a few minutes after 5:30 a.m. and headed for Chattanooga.

After saying good-bye to everyone, Lindbergh took off soon after 5:35 a.m. He circled over several areas around Memphis, then took up a heading for Chattanooga, which was planned to be a "touch stop." Lindbergh flew east-southeast, crossing the Tennessee-Mississippi border, then continuing on directly to Florence, Alabama. He circled over Florence, then headed a bit south, over Wilson Lake, to circle over Muscle Shoals, Sheffield and Tuscumbia, Alabama, all grouped together within a few miles of each other. From there he took a direct east northeast heading to Chattanooga, having flown for four hours and forty minutes.

Today Armstrong Field no longer exists, other than an open field. However, just east about a mile is the Charles W. Baker Airport. It is at an elevation of 247 feet MSL and has a 3,499-foot runway. The field caters mainly to general aviation.

Memphis now has a main airport, known as the Memphis International Airport, located three miles south of the center of the city. It is at an elevation of 335 feet MSL. Its longest runway is 9,319 feet. The airport services all major and some international airlines and some general aviation aircraft. Additionally, the renowned national air freight company Federal Express, better known as Fed-Ex, is based on this airport, delivering freight all over the world.

References

Newspapers
  Commercial Appeal
  Memphis Press-Scimitar

Organizations
  Memphis Shelby County Public Library and Information Center
  Memphis Shelby County Airport Authority
  Memphis Public Library
  University of Memphis Library

People
  Stephen K. Freeman   Michael Waldbillig
  Robert C. Hill   Cathy Evans
  Judy Brown   Edwin G. Frank
  Janice Young   James L. Delaney
  Patricia M. LaPointe

STOP #65
CHATTANOOGA, TENNESSEE
"TOUCH STOP"

CAPSULE HISTORY OF CITY

The city of Chattanooga, Tennessee, lies on both banks of the sharp Moccasin Bend of the Tennessee River, just north of the Georgia boundary in the southeast corner of the state.

The first inhabitants of the area were the Chickamauga, a branch of the Cherokee Indians. These Indians were conquered in 1794, and then moved west in 1838. Around this time John Ross, a chief, operated a trading post on the site, called Ross's Landing.

The city is located in a beautiful mountain area, ranges of the Appalachian Plateau, the Appalachian Ridge and Valley Region, which surround the city. Lookout Mountain stands to

the south. The Creek Indians called this mountain Chat-to-to-noog-gee, meaning "mountain rising to a point." So the city received this present name when it was incorporated as a town in 1839. It received its charter as a city in 1851.

675 feet MSL.

OCTOBER 5, 1927 (WEDNESDAY)

One airport existed at Chattanooga in 1927, known as Marr Field, controlled by the Chamber of Commerce. The field was located one and one-half miles northeast of the city. It was southeast of the railroad tracks, and south of the Chickamauga Creek in East Chattanooga. As

near as can be determined, it was near the intersection of Dodson Avenue and Glass Street. The property consisted of an area 3,300 feet by 1,050 feet at an elevation of 900 feet MSL. It had some hangars and was near the present site of the Holsum Bread Company.

At the crack of dawn many carpenters and some small boys arrived at Marr Field to be ready for the Lindbergh arrival. Refreshment stands were quickly erected, and by 8:00 a.m. throngs of people had arrived to get a good spot for the event. The 6th Cavalry Band from Fort Oglethorpe played martial airs, marching through East Chattanooga on their way to the airfield. They gave some entertainment in addition to being on guard with over four hundred soldiers from their post.

While searching the sky for the arrival of the NYP, the people were thrilled when they were sure they had spotted the airplane. It turned out to be a chicken hawk, circling high overhead. The bird was first sighted by a youngster, who shrilled out, "There he is, there's Lindy." But other sharper eyes revealed and destroyed the illusion.

There were hundreds of little boys who were running about in the dust and yelling out, "Kin ye see 'im? Say, has he flew over yet?"

One newspaper reporter noticed one lean, lanky lad who was riding a bicycle in a most capable fashion. He was making good speed, and that it would be a patent that among the confreres for sometime hereafter he will be a "man who."

At about 10:10 a.m. the Fairchild was spotted over the city, and shouts went up that it was Lindbergh. Soon the airplane landed, and most people then realized that this was the escort ship. As soon as the Fairchild had landed and taxied in, it was surrounded by a cordon of eighteen Eagle Scouts, and when the NYP came in they

extended the circle to include it as well, to guard both airplanes from the crowds.

These Eagle Scouts remained at their guarding posts all during the time of the Lindbergh visit, right up to the time both airplanes started their engines to depart. These scouts were from Troop 20 at the local Methodist church. Some of the scouts were Arthur J. Hitchcock, John Vass, Elmer Farmer, Stanley Farmer, Burch Cooke, Warren Smith, Roy Smith, Fritz Englehardt, and Wallace Page.

Coming in from Muscle Shoals, and along the Tennessee River, the NYP soon came into view at about 10:17 a.m. Lindbergh first flew over North Chattanooga and then the business district of the city, before circling and heading for the airport out east-northeast of the city. Factory whistles blew, as mounted soldiers began to patrol the streets from the airport all the way into town.

Soon Lindbergh came over the field, circled and came down for a pass across the open area, climbed up and around and came in for a perfect three-point landing on the turf. It was 10:30 a.m.

He taxied up to one of the hangars, shut down the engine, and climbed out of the cockpit. He was first met by Mayor Ed Bass; then Col. Walter Marr (for whom the field was named); J. T. Lupton, the Coca-Cola tycoon; committee chairman John Lovell; and Col. T. A. Roberts, Commander of the Fort Oglethorpe garrison.

Lindbergh was escorted to a waiting automobile. He was seated with the mayor, Lupton, and Col. Roberts for the parade into town. As the parade passed the Chattanooga High School the cadets in battalion formation presented arms in salute to the flyer as he passed by. The school band played a martial air.

The parade proceeded to the downtown area and stopped at a speaker's stand, on an old truck on the corner of Broad Street between Ninth and Eleventh Streets.

Here Lindbergh gave a brief talk, "I regret very much that it is impossible to spend as much time here in Chattanooga as I would like." He explained that they only had three months to

The NYP on Marr Field being guarded by local Eagle Scouts, all of whom must have been thrilled. GEORGE S. CAMPBELL

cover eighty stops, so the schedule had to be trimmed here and there. He spoke in his usual way on the development of commercial aviation and building more airports. He said, "I want to thank you for coming here and listening to what I have told you, for the welcome Chattanooga has given me. I hope in the future you will devote a part of your interest to aeronautics in this city and put on a program of activity which will result in the establishment of an adequate airport in Chattanooga."

After other remarks from the Mayor and the presentation of a scroll from the city, Lindbergh was driven back to Marr Field to prepare to leave for the next stop. He had been in town for only an hour.

His speech to the people and politicians of Chattanooga made an impression. The chairman of this event was John Lovell, and the new airport in another location, which is still in existence, is named after him.

In the assembled crowd in town, an older woman was overheard telling her granddaughter, "Now you can tell your great-grandchildren that you saw Lindbergh."

The crowd that had assembled at Marr Field to see his arrival did not disperse, but were still there upon his return so they would not miss his take-off.

He climbed into the NYP cockpit, put on his helmet and goggles, got the engine started, and took off down the field at precisely 11:30 a.m. He circled the airport several times and then flew over the downtown district again, before heading southwest to Birmingham, Alabama. After leaving the area, Lindbergh flew more or less a straight line course southwest to Birmingham. The flight took two hours and thirty minutes, passing just east of Guntersville Lake.

Marr Field is no longer there, but the city does have a modern airport at Lovell Field. It is located about five miles east of the city, on the east side of the South Chickamauga Creek. It is at an elevation of 682 feet MSL and has a main runway of 7,401 feet. It services most domestic airlines as well as commuter, general aviation, and military aircraft.

References

Newspapers
  Chattanooga Times
  Chattanooga News-Free Press
  Chattanooga Daily Times

Organizations
  National Caves Association
  Chattanooga-Hamilton County Bicentennial Library
  Leo B. Kimball Collection
  The Bettmann Archive

People
  George S. Campbell   Mrs. Tarbell Patten
  Barbara Munson   Mrs. D. F. Black
  Mrs. Blondie H. Smith   Arthur J. Hitchcock
  Ned Irwin   Wiley O. Woods Jr.
  Mrs. Jewell Cartwright Giuliano

The NYP taking off from Marr Field on October 5th after the "Touch Stop" heading for Birmingham, Alabama. LEO B. KIMBALL COLLECTION

STOP #66

BIRMINGHAM, ALABAMA

CAPSULE HISTORY OF CITY

Birmingham is the largest city in Alabama. It is located in the north-central part of the state in the Jones Valley, at the foot of Red Mountain in the foothills of the Appalachian Mountains.

The first Indian tribes in the area were the Choctaw, Creek and Cherokee Indians, when they hunted in the valley. The first white settlement was in 1813.

This large southern city was founded in 1871 and incorporated as a city later that same year. Its nickname is Magic City because the population grew so rapidly between 1880 and 1910.

The city was named for the large, English steel-producing city of Birmingham. There was an abundance of iron ore, coal and limestone, essential ingredients for steel production, which contributed to the early growth of the city.

583 feet MSL.

OCTOBER 5–7, 1927
(WEDNESDAY THROUGH FRIDAY)

In 1927 Birmingham had an airport named Roberts Field, which had been built in 1922. Its primary use was as a base for the Alabama National Guard's 106th Observation Squadron, under the command of Maj. Sumpter Smith. At that time they had several hangars.

The field did not have runways or lighting for night operations. For a while Glenn E. Messer operated an aerial charter service. The people of the city and their leaders realized the airport needed a modernization program, and the coming of Lindbergh would encourage an update of the airport.

Roberts Field is no longer there. At the time it was located in what is now the suburb of Thomas, on the north side of Route 20/50 and south of Village Creek, west of the reservoir, and east of Brock Industrial Drive at the end of Roberts Industrial Drive.

Historian Blaine A. Brownell once said, "The business of Birmingham in the 1920s was busi-

ness." Thus it was not surprising that airline service was one of the city's objectives in 1927. There were about a half-million people living there at the time, a city with some of the most impressive downtown office buildings in the South.

On the day before Lindbergh's arrival all kinds of activities were going on to welcome the flyer. Decorations for the event sprang up overnight—banners were unfurled, flags hung everywhere, and pictures of Lindbergh were seen in every section of the city. Toy airplanes were visible in children's hands. Local jewelry stores almost ran out of field glasses. Two bands, the Birmingham Police Band and the Avondale Mills Band, welcomed the aviator.

The reception committee, including S. F. Marn, C.A.W. Berney Perry, Thad Holt and Frank Savage from the Junior Chamber of Commerce, was headed by Major Smith of the 106th Squadron. The local government declared it officially as "Lindbergh Day." Schools and businesses were closed early so that students and workers could see Lindbergh.

As preplanned, this would be heralded as Air Carnival Week at Roberts Field. The event was under the direction of the 106th Squadron, based on the field. Wednesday would be solely devoted to Lindbergh's arrival and visit to the city. However, during the other days of the carnival there would be passenger rides, parachute jumps, night flying exhibitions, and stunt fly-

An aerial view of a portion of Roberts Field as it looked in 1926 showing the Air National Guard buildings. ALABAMA AIR NATIONAL GUARD AND SOUTHERN MUSEUM OF FLIGHT

ing. All money received by the squadron during this week would be directed toward the further development of a municipal airport. In the past Roberts Field had been supported by money donated personally by members of the squadron.

After circling the city twice, Lindbergh headed west to Roberts Field, did a low pass, and landed at precisely 2:00 p.m. The Fairchild with Love, Keyhoe, and Maidment had already landed at 1:20 p.m.

The NYP on Roberts Field on October 5th shortly after Lindbergh landed. ALABAMA AIR NATIONAL GUARD AND SOUTHERN MUSEUM OF FLIGHT

Lindbergh taxied up to one of the National Guard hangars, and after conferring with Don Keyhoe, the NYP was rolled in. Also in the hangar was the Fairchild, with the wings folded to conserve space. A section of the hangar had been wired off, forming a passageway down which spectators could pass and inspect the NYP under the glare of floodlights.

Local people strain to get a glimpse of the NYP as it was being rolled into the Air Guard hangar at Roberts Field. ALABAMA AIR NATIONAL GUARD AND SOUTHERN MUSEUM OF FLIGHT

A liberal portion of the field had been set apart with a barbed wire fence, behind which automobiles of spectators could be parked.

Soon Lindbergh was escorted into a waiting automobile, seated between Lt. Governor Davis and Major Smith. The entourage sped off and headed, via a short cut, directly to Fair Park. It was about 2:18 p.m. when his car entered the gates to the park, where thousands of schoolchildren were waiting to hear what he had to say. Lindbergh gave a short speech stressing the importance of the advancement of air travel and the building of airports.

After the events at the park the parade proceeded into the city proper and to the Tutwiler Hotel. The parade route was crowded with spectators: farm girls in gingham dresses, debutantes in chiffon and satin, crying babies. Limousines, bicycles, and wagons followed the parade route. Overheard remarks included, "Lindy needs a hair cut"; "Ain't he cute, ain't he precious"; "Why, he didn't even speak to me"; "Oh, ain't he darling"; "They say them French girls kissed him something awful."

He held a press conference at the hotel shortly after his arrival. Then he and his crew made their way to the Louis XIV Suite assigned to the party.

It appeared that Lindbergh would often do the unexpected. For instance, when reporters of the *Birmingham Press* were escorted to the parlor of his private suite, they had decided that Lindbergh should occupy a very comfortable chair with soft cushions and luxurious dimensions. When he came into the room he surprised everyone there by pushing a bowl of pink roses aside to sit on the table.

The banquet that evening was held at the Municipal Auditorium and was attended by 1,500 people at $3.50 a plate. Toastmaster Hugh Morrow introduced Governor Bibb Graves. Governor Graves said that next in importance to air mail and landing fields, the greatest need of the hour is oratorical terminal facilities. "I need not remind you that we are honored by the presence of many notable personages, distinguished speakers, consisting of several ex-governors, a United States Senator, and numerous Congressmen, but it has fallen to my lot to introduce the man who will present your distinguished guest, Col. Charles A. Lindbergh, in whose honor this hour's blaze of eulogy is kindled."

One speaker remarked, "His coming to our midst has quickened the pulse and reanimated the heart of this entire commonwealth. It has

done more than anything else to encourage the hope that Birmingham has long indulged for a transcontinental air mail and commercial route that will permit her people and her industries to share in breaking down the barriers of time and space and bring them in closer communion with the rest of the country."

Lindbergh said, "Starting in 1928 we will probably see the greatest progress commercial aviation has ever known." He went on to say that he considered two classes of aviation, pioneer and commercial, the latter of which the public should take an invigorated interest in.

He stressed the need for Birmingham to build a municipal airport in 1928. It was rather timely due to the indecision over whether to continue to use Roberts Field for the air mail service, which had delayed any progress, or to find another site.

He said, "We are asking you to build not only for the present but for the future. Your city and state need the cooperation of every citizen to bring about better air facilities. It is obvious that the more people see airplanes the more confidence they will have in their performance. To this end it is most important that well-equipped airports be established. I believe that any city can work wonders with its air transportation probably by merely establishing an airport and using the airplane service where possible. An airport should of course be large enough for safety of operation and should be easy to access. Eventually centrally located municipal fields will assume the status of our present railroad terminals which are merely points for boarding and leaving trains."

After his nine-minute talk, the audience applauded for a long time. The opinion heard was that the people had caught his spirit and were determined that a new era of aviation throughout Alabama should come.

It had been decided that Birmingham would be one of the rest stops on the tour. So all day Thursday they did what they wanted to do. Most of the morning was spent recuperating from the elaborate welcome Lindbergh had received the day before. However, in the afternoon he and Love obtained a car and drove all over the city, returning to the hotel at about 6:00 p.m. They were never recognized during the trip. Their time was also spent relaxing, hangar flying, and planning for the next leg to Jackson,

Mississippi.

Early Friday morning the tour flyers went out to Roberts Field. The guards helped get the two airplanes out of the hangar, and after a thorough preflight by both pilots, they climbed in to get their engines started. All of this happened while a crowd of 25,000 people gathered all around the airport to witness his departure.

Lindbergh took off at 1:30 p.m. and flew around the field several times, then over the city, before taking a heading west. While he circled the field, the shrieking of automobile horns could be heard over the shouts of the people.

As planned, the Fairchild took off just after the NYP and circled the field too, before heading for Jackson, to be there before Lindbergh.

Lindbergh flew almost directly west to Columbus, west again to Starkville, then west-northwest to Maben and Mathiston, all in Mississippi. From Mathiston he flew southwest, passing on the west side of the Ross Bernett Reservoir which is just before Jackson. On this last leg he followed right along what would become the Natchez Trace Parkway.

Seeing Lindbergh in Birmingham as an eight-year-old had a strong effect on Joe Turner. At a more mature age, when Pearl Harbor was the topic of discussion, he quit the University of Alabama to become a cadet at Maxwell Field Army Air Base in Montgomery, just a few days before Christmas. He hoped to become a pilot. The powers-that-be decided he would make a better navigator due to his test scores, not to mention that his legs were too short to reach the rudder pedals. So, he was off to Mather Field in Sacramento, California, to navigation school

Regular airline service was inaugurated on May 1, 1928, connecting Birmingham with New York in only one day, via the air mail service. It was not long before people were making the flight to the Big City to visit relatives or do business. This small beginning was a significant one considering Lindbergh's visit and its later contribution to air travel in the United States. Lindbergh's 1927 visit was unique in itself, as the story appeared as a special feature in the special Centennial issue of the *Birmingham News* in April 1973.

Although Roberts Field no longer exists, Birmingham does have, most likely as a result of Lindbergh's 1927 visit, a modern airport, the Birmingham International Airport. It is located four

miles northeast of the city. Its main runway of 10,000 feet is at an elevation of 644 feet MSL. The field serves most major airlines of this country as well as other parts of the world, in addition to military, commuter, corporate, and general aviation.

References

Newspapers
   Birmingham News
   Post Herald
   Birmingham Age-Herald

Organizations
   Birmingham Public Library
   Montgomery Airport Authority
   Southern Museum of Flight
   Alabama Air National Guard, HQ 117th
Air Refueling Wing

People

Frank Nash	E. W. Stevenson, M.D.
Deborah Stone	Dr. Wesley Newton
Alton G. Hudson	Col. Stan Pruet
Joe Turner	Bob Blackwell
M. Sgt. Warren Hood	Martin J. Derity
Lawrence Pearson	
Col. William J. Copeland	

STOP #67
JACKSON, MISSISSIPPI

CAPSULE HISTORY OF CITY

As state capital of Mississippi, Jackson is the largest city in the state. Often called the "crossroads" of the South, it is located on the west bank of the Pearl River in central Mississippi.

A trading post called LeFleur's Bluff was established by Louis LeFleur about 1780. The state legislature in 1822 appointed a commission to locate a state capital nearer to the center of the state, moving it from the temporary capital at Columbia. In 1821 LeFleur's Bluff was chosen and named in honor of the seventh president of the United States, Andrew Jackson.

940 feet MSL.

OCTOBER 7–8, 1927 (FRIDAY AND SATURDAY)

In 1927 Davis Field was Jackson's local airport, sometimes referred to as the Davis Stock Farm. It is the present-day Hawkins Field. That site is located three miles northwest of the business district of the city. At the time of Lindbergh's visit, it was just an open grass field.

Lindbergh first appeared over the city about 1:30 p.m. and soon flew away to the northwest for ten or twelve miles, caused by some misdirection that he must have received. Love, with Keyhoe and Maidment, climbed into the Fairchild, which had already arrived at Davis Field, when they realized their friend might be lost. They took off, found the NYP, and directed the famous flyer to follow them to Davis Field. So Lindbergh then landed at 2:07 p.m., missing his usual ETA by only seven minutes.

William Ewing, a reporter with the *Clarion-Ledger*, remembered that the NYP came in from the west, landing in front of a reviewing stand on the field. Lindbergh made a perfect three-point landing from the south, turned around, and taxied into a temporary wire hangar already prepared for him. Lindbergh was dressed in a brown business suit, white shirt, and tie. He was greeted by Mayor Walter A. Scott, Commissioners Hawkins and Taylor, American Legionaries, National Guard and Reserve officers, in addition to some 3,000 others on the field. Gen. Curtis T. Green and Keyhoe were also present.

The NYP is shown shortly after landing on Davis Field. WILLIAM H. EWING VIA MRS. BETTYE ANN EWING

Lindbergh being greeted by Jackson Mayor Walter A. Scott on Davis Field. WILLIAM H. EWING VIA MRS. BETTYE ANN EWING

Shortly the NYP was prepared to be refueled by the Standard Oil Company truck.

After instructions from Lindbergh on the care of the NYP, he and the Mayor were escorted to a waiting car to be taken out of the field and line up for the parade into town. The autos sped away, going through Livingston Park to Capitol Street, and proceeding east on Capitol to the Capitol Building, arriving at 3:00 p.m.

After some formalities, Lindbergh was introduced to the assembled crowd of children and their parents. He said, "We have reached a stage in aviation where it is extremely necessary to have the cooperation of the people of the United States before we can turn the airplane into its fullest commercial use." He continued to expound on the development of air travel and the need for modernizing airports. He elaborated on the air mail system, where it stood, and where it would be going in the future.

After his talk at the Capitol, he was whisked off to the Edwards Hotel, where he had a brief press conference before he and his crew retired for some rest in the guest suite.

While in his room that evening, Lindbergh had agreed to visit briefly with seven-year-old Walter G. Johnson Jr., who had missed seeing the flyer earlier that season in St. Louis. This meeting was by special arrangement. "Lindy," the boy said, "I'll bet I'm the only boy seven years old that's had an interview with you." And Lindbergh replied, "And if you were a little bit older I'd bet from that grip you gave me that you were a politician." The colonel remarked later that the boy was "an unusually bright chap."

In the evening the banquet was held in the New Masonic Temple. It was the only place in town that could accommodate such a large gathering.

As guests were arriving and being seated at the banquet, a concert was given by the Wahabi Temple Band. Guests were directed to their seats by the Dan Beard troop of Eagle Scouts. Dinner was served by about sixty school and college girls, while the orchestra from the Institute for the Blind played numerous selections throughout the evening. Five hundred people attended the affair, each paying $5.00 for the privilege.

Several speakers were introduced before Lindbergh spoke. Among them was Gov. Dennis Murphree, who had the following to say in his welcome to the flyer: "You came not for self-glorification, not for self-advertisement, but with the distinct purpose of fanning the birds of interest in the new business of aviation. It is a message of a new industry, an industry which in all probability, in the future will to a large extent, revolutionize transportation." He went on to say, "It is with pleasure that I tell you that our state has caught the spirit of progress, that in many towns and cities in Mississippi in the very near future, regular landing fields will be completed, and that in this line as well as in others the future lies bright before us. I welcome you to the Magnolia State."

Mayor Scott pointedly stated, "We know that you are here today for the sole purpose of promoting aviation. Therefore, I am sure the most pleasing statement I could make to you is that the Jackson Chamber of Commerce, all of the civic clubs and the city officials are of the unanimous opinion that to do our part in developing commercial aviation, the city of Jackson must at once provide a first-class fully equipped airport. I am glad to announce to you that on tomorrow the voters of Jackson will go to the polls and vote on a bond issue to provide the necessary funds to purchase and equip a Triple A municipally owned and operated airport."

He urged every man, woman, and child to remind the people to go to the polls to vote. He said that the city that fails to go on air routes might just as well be off the main line of the railroads. Keep Jackson abreast of the times, he urged. "Let us tomorrow prove to Colonel Lindbergh that we mean what we have said to him today."

Finally Senator Harrison said that he would do everything in his power for the promotion of the air services of the United States.

When Lindbergh was finally introduced he spoke in a clear, audible tone, and showed unusual poise in delivering the eight-minute talk. He did give evidence of boyish shyness, but launched into his argument directly and spoke with great earnestness.

He briefly reviewed the development of aviation from the Wright brothers to the present. He believed that up to the time of the Great War (World War I) aviation was considered an amusement for thrill-seekers, but finally received its first great impetus with the creation of Army and Navy air forces between 1914 and 1918. He said the major step in the United States came with the creation of the air mail service in 1919, and with altitude records, distance and endurance records. But now with the wholesale establishment of airports in this country, it showed signs of catching up with developments made in Europe since the war.

Jeff Meaders remembered being in Jackson when Lindbergh landed at Davis Stock Farm. Along with several other chaps, Meaders rode his bicycle from his house to the Capitol Square. Several of these boys ended up in the aviation business as a result of seeing Lindbergh at that time. Meaders helped fuel the NYP. In later years he became a flight instructor and flew into his eighties.

The next morning the flyers left the hotel after a hearty breakfast and were driven to the field, where they went through a thorough pre-flight exercise. An estimated 1,500 people who wanted to witness the departure of the two airplanes had already gathered on the field, despite the drizzling rain and overcast. After taking off at 10:41 a.m., Lindbergh came back around to make a low pass twice for the benefit of the crowd and took up a heading to the south-southeast. Five minutes later the Fairchild took off and headed in the same direction. The escort plane would take a direct heading toward New Orleans, the next stop on the tour.

Shortly Lindbergh came over the town of Columbia, circled several times, and headed southwest to Franklinton. From there he took up a direct southerly heading, flying across Lake Pontchartrain toward New Orleans.

Today Jackson's Hawkins Field, at an elevation of 342 feet MSL, is still there, with the longest runway being 5,387 feet. The field services mainly general aviation, including corporate aircraft.

Five miles east of the city is Jackson International Airport. This major airport is at 346 feet MSL and has parallel runways, the longest of which is 8,501 feet. The airport serves most major foreign and United States airlines, in addition to general aviation.

The Williams Airport is three miles northeast of Raymond, Mississippi, and about fifteen miles west of Jackson. It has a single runway of 3,992 feet at an elevation of 246 feet MSL.

The Mississippi Agriculture and Forestry/ National Agricultural Aviation Museum is located in the Jackson area.

References

Newspapers
Jackson Daily News
Clarion-Ledger

Organizations
City of Jackson, Department of Administration, Records Division
Jim Hankins Air Service, Inc.
Mississippi Department of Archives and History

People

Cyrilla J. Duprel	Jim Hankins
Gary Pettus	Mrs. Curtis L. Johnson
Jeff Meaders	John Hey, M.D.
Tom Littlejohn	Mrs. Jana John
Steve Owen	James H. Lacey Jr.
Gilbert J. Jally	Bettye Ann Ewing
Kenneth H. Kraft Jr.	Mayor Frank E. Melton

Pat Fordice, former first lady of Mississippi
Robert M. Walker, Chief Administrative Officer

STOP #68
NEW ORLEANS, LOUISIANA

CAPSULE HISTORY OF CITY

One of the great cities of the United States, New Orleans, Louisiana, is the largest city in the state. Located on the Mississippi River on the Gulf of Mexico in the southeastern portion of the state, it is an important link between the Mississippi River and the Atlantic Ocean to the east.

It is often called America's most interesting city. It has many reminders of Old Europe and the Old South, with both the historic French Quarter as well as the exciting Mardi Gras festival, important links to the past.

The city was founded in 1718 by Jean Baptiste le Moyne, Sieur de Beinville, the governor of the French colony of Louisiana. The site was chosen on a curve of the great river because it was protected from hurricanes and tidal waves. In 1722 Beinville established the town as the capital of the colony and named it La Nouville Orleans (New Orleans) after the regent of France, Philippe, Duc d'Orleans.

Over the early years the city was under three flags: France in 1800, then the United States, and Spain, all in less than a month. It was incorporated in February 1805, and when Louisiana joined the Union in 1812, the city became the first capital of the state.

5 feet MSL.

OCTOBER 8–10, 1927
(SATURDAY THROUGH MONDAY)

In about 1925 George A. Hero donated one hundred acres of land located south of New Orleans in the little town of Belle Chasse for an airport. It was between the low waters' edge of the Mississippi River and the easterly right-of-way of what is now Louisiana State Highway 23. The site work was completed in 1926 and the airport was named Callendar Field.

Rain fell throughout the area as Lindbergh and the Fairchild came across the lake and over the city of New Orleans. Lindbergh circled over the high buildings of the business district and soon headed for the airport to the south-south-east. It was about 1:30 p.m., a bit early for his usual ETA of 2:00 p.m. He circled the airport several times and made a low pass to check the landing surface, which was wet and soggy. The landing went fine, and he taxied up to and into the hangar, with the help of many people pushing on the struts.

He was met by Mayor Arthur J. O'Keefe and other officials of the welcoming committee.

Sometime after he arrived the NYP was serviced with fuel by five-gallon cans from a "Standard Motor Oil" truck of the Standard Oil Company of Louisiana.

Hundreds of cars were lined up on the roads leading to the field, but no one was allowed on the airport property at that time, except official greeters and others associated with the airport operations.

Because it was the only stop in Louisiana, there were many special excursion trains that came from all over the state bringing thousands of people.

At the field one lad had been waiting since early morning. He could not restrain himself when the NYP came into sight, and ran all over the area shouting, "There's Lindbergh! There's Lindbergh!"

Another youngster said, "I touched the car he was riding in." A young lady mourned that her make-up had been ruined by the rain and that she would not be able to put up her best appearance for the Slim Eagle.

Here the NYP is being put into the hangar on Callendar Field outside of New Orleans. Lindbergh had just arrived and taxied the NYP into the hangar.
RON ARSENAULT

A boy of ten or eleven fell headlong into a puddle, gave a few feeble kicks like a fish, and hauled his soaked body erect, saying, "I should've brought my water wings."

The NYP was put on display on Sunday from 9:00 a.m. to 5:30 p.m.

Miles and miles of ticker tape and hundreds of pounds of waste paper were thrown out of windows along the parade route. It resembled a snowstorm, something that would be unheard of in the South. The flags and banners on the street were wet and drooping.

An old, blind newsman, standing at University Place and Canal Street, exhibited much enthusiasm when he heard the police motorcycles approach. He made his way to the curb and stood there, cheering and waving his hat. The crowd pushed him away from his perch, but as he attempted to get back there, he was seen smiling as if he had actually seen Lindbergh.

The entourage made its way slowly along the parade route to the Tulane Stadium. There was so much rain that the Lindbergh car's ignition system got soaked and the engine quit. They switched cars somewhere along the route, then made it safely to the stadium. Lindbergh sat atop the open car during the driving rain. He said that if people had to stand out there in this rain, he could sit there for several hours.

The local newspaper reported that there were thousands of schoolchildren at the stadium to greet and to hear their hero. (However this writer received an anonymous letter from a New Orleans lady who claimed this was not true, the reason being that it was just too rainy and cold, and that part of his visit was called off for fear that all the children would catch cold and get sick.)

From the Tulane Stadium he was taken to the Roosevelt Hotel for the usual press conference and some rest from all the activities.

During the parade they passed bedraggled bits of bunting and homes with children's faces peering through window panes. They continued through Gretna and into the center of the city.

The evening banquet was held in the Roosevelt Hotel with many local business people, political personalities, and others of note in the city.

The next day, Sunday, was to be a rest day for the tour flyers. For the crew, most of that day was spent servicing the two airplanes and attending to any necessary repairs.

However, for Lindbergh, it became another flying day, but not in the NYP. By some previous arrangement, he was invited to visit the Pensacola Naval Air Training Base in Pensacola, Florida. The Navy sent a P&W Wasp-powered Curtiss Hawk to New Orleans for Lindbergh to use to fly over to Pensacola. The Hawk's pilot was a friend of Lindbergh, 1st Class Seaman E. E. Laudenbache.

After the airplane had landed, Lindbergh suggested to Don Keyhoe that he spend some time with the aviator during the day. Lindbergh was sure it had spoiled the pilot's Sunday, so he asked Keyhoe to "make him feel at home as much as you can."

Lindbergh flew the high-powered little biplane fighter to Pensacola, where he was the guest of Adm. Frank H. Upham, Commandant of the Pensacola Naval Air Station. Lindbergh was treated royally and given a complete tour of the famous base.

He spent the night at the base, and at 5:13 a.m. on Monday he and two other Hawks took off for New Orleans. Lindbergh needed to be back in time to pick up the NYP for their next leg to Jacksonville. One of his escort planes was piloted by Cmdr. Ralph A. Davison, Chief Flight Instructor of Pensacola. The identity of the other escort aviator was not known. Lindbergh and the one escort landed at Callendar at 6:30 a.m. The second escort did not show up as expected. Someone suggested that the Navy plane had fallen into a thick growth of trees near the airport. Lindbergh remarked to Love that they had better find the ship and inform the airport people of its exact location so they could reach the pilot. With Lindbergh in the NYP and Love in the Fairchild, they took off. Lindbergh covered the southern half while Love covered the northern half.

Neither pilot could find the Hawk, so they landed and discussed the situation with the man who had reported it in the first place. The man gave a vague reply when asked more details. The two airplanes went up again, and upon landing, this time were informed that the Navy pilot had managed to glide across the Mississippi.

Apparently the Hawk flown by Davison had engine trouble just as he was nearing Callendar

Field. The aviator nursed the airplane into the water of the Mississippi, near Scarsdale, and close to the west bank. Later he said that he was banking to line up for a landing when the engine quit, possibly due to a broken fuel line. The airplane turned over and sank, but the flyer was able to swim clear and make it to shore.

Lindbergh passed a message on to Davison saying, "I'm sorry you had any trouble," and then remarked that they had better get going for the leg to Jacksonville. Lindbergh had put forty minutes on the NYP during the search.

Soon Lindbergh and the Fairchild were in the air again, departing from Callendar Field. It was still an overcast day with rain. He circled over the field several times and then over the city. He took up a heading of east-northeast, along the coast toward Biloxi, Mississippi. He flew east along the Gulf of Mexico coastline to Pensacola, circling the Navy base a few times. Then they headed east again, directly to Tallahassee, the capital of Florida. It was 12:15 p.m. when he circled over the city and dropped the canvas bag message. The bag fell in the capitol yard and was picked up by a group of young women, who were state employees.

The flight then headed east again directly to Jacksonville, where they landed after a five-hour-and-thirty-minute trip.

Raoul Jordan, a retired New Orleans Steamship Company executive whose office was in the business district at that time, remembered, "Lindbergh flew extremely low over the city before landing, probably due to the storm and low ceilings."

Mrs. A. Thompson Mayfield was a starry-eyed college student at that time, and as an aviation enthusiast, she was up in the middle of the night to be sure she did not miss Lindbergh when he was scheduled to depart the next morning. She helped push the NYP out of the hangar, but could not get any closer to him than that. She went home and cried for two days, she was so consumed with adoration for the man.

Today Callendar Field still exists on the same site and is known as NAS New Orleans, JRB. The place where Lindbergh landed is now a wooded corner of NAS NOLA. The longest runway is 8,000 feet, at an elevation of 3 feet MSL.

The New Orleans International–Moisant Field is located on the western edge of the city. It is at an elevation of 6 feet MSL. Its longest runway is 10,080 feet. The airport serves most domestic airlines, European and other international airlines, commuter, and general aviation aircraft.

Along the shore of Lake Pontchartrain to the east of the city is Lakefront Airport at an elevation of 9 feet MSL. Its longest runway is 6,879 feet. It serves mainly general aviation including corporate operations.

References

Newspapers
  New Orleans Times-Picayune Item-Tribune
  Kansas City Journal Post Magazine

Organizations
  New Orleans Public Library, Louisiana Division
  The Historic New Orleans Collection, Kemper and Leila Williams Foundation
  Twenty-first Judicial District Court, State of Louisiana

People
Kathleen Gess	Pete Lucas
Charles Hoerske	Mary Ann Aucoin
Thelma J. Rainey	Marie I. Messina
Bertha B. Murrhee	Edwin James Blair
Mrs. A. Thompson Mayfield	
Diane Robbins	George A. Hero III
John Burke	Sue Hibben
Nancy Burris	Ronald Arsenault
Pamela D. Arceneaux	Waldemar S. Nelson

The NYP is fueled up. Notice C.C. Maidment, in white coveralls, just under the prop spinner. RON ARSENAULT

STOP #69
JACKSONVILLE, FLORIDA

The largest city in the state of Florida, Jacksonville is located in northeastern Florida, midway between Atlanta, Georgia, and Miami, Florida.

The first people in the area were the Timucua Indians, many years before the first white man. In 1564 a group of Huguenots under the leadership of Rene de Laudonniere built Fort Caroline in this area. The city stretches along both banks of the St. Johns River and is bordered on the east by the Atlantic Ocean.

It was developed around a "ford" (shallow place) in the St. Johns River. Isaiah D. Hart, a Georgia plantation owner, moved to the area in 1821 and founded the city. He mapped out the town and named it Jacksonville after Andrew Jackson, seventh president of the United States, who at the time was provisional governor of the Territory of Florida. It was chartered as a town in 1832, and as a city in 1859.

20 feet MSL.

OCTOBER 10–11, 1927
(MONDAY AND TUESDAY)

The city did not have any regular airline or air mail service in 1927. Florida Airways had begun air mail and passenger service on April 1, 1926, but despite this effort, they went out of business later that same year. The public lacked any confidence in air travel in Jacksonville, as in the rest of the country. As John P. Ingle Jr. put it many years later, "The air age was knocking at America's door and no one was listening."

However, by 1927, a municipal airport was under construction and would be named Imeson Airport. In order to be ready for Lindbergh's visit, a special effort was made to whip it into some kind of shape. Imeson was located about six miles north of the business district. It was bordered on the west by Main Street (Route 17/5), on the north by just below Cedar Bay Road, on the south by Gun Club, and on the east by just east of the present Canada Drive. The property today is bisected by Route 163. The Sears Catalog and Distribution Center is almost in the center of the old airport.

Jacksonville hotel owner Robert Kloeppel offered a $1,000 prize to supplement Raymond Orteig's original $25,000 prize to be given to the aviator who first flew to Paris from New York. Kloeppel sent a telegram to Lindbergh in Paris saying that the money had already been deposited and would be delivered to the flyer as soon as he could come to Jacksonville to claim it. Lindbergh did agree to come to the city.

Low overcast skies and very poor visibility hung over the city of Jacksonville all morning and into the early afternoon as thousands of people awaited Lindbergh's arrival. Due to the heavy rains over the city area, Lindbergh had to delay his flight over the stadium, as previously planned, and go directly over to the airport. He landed in a downpour. He came into sight and circled over the downtown area several times and then flew north to the airport. He came down rather low after circling the field, made a low pass, and came around and landed on the wet field.

There were one hundred National Guardsmen stationed on the field for security, to protect not only the landing runway area but the NYP and Fairchild when they got there. This was in addition to a contingent of Boy Scouts, local police, and traffic coordinators. A specially prepared wire enclosure was placed around the two airplanes for their protection in a way that the planes could be visible to the crowds of

The NYP at Imeson Airport. Man in dark suit is Thomas C. Imeson, city commissioner of highways, airports and the local radio station. Other man is unknown. JOHN P. INGLE JR.

Lindbergh with (on left) Hotelman Robert Kloeppel and Capt. Raymond W. Cushman, chair of the Aviation Committee. CASSAGNERES COLLECTION

people. (Because of the rain it is apparent that not many pictures were taken of the NYP, as only a couple have shown up over the years.)

Lindbergh was welcomed by a special committee consisting of Mayor John T. Alsop Jr., George B. Hills, president of the Chamber of Commerce, Thomas N. Imeson, Dr. Ralph N. Greene, and Capt. Raymond W. Cushman, chairman of the Aviation Committee.

The city's children were let out of school at noon, and local businesses excused employees to watch the parade, but remained open to serve the numerous visitors in town.

After both airplanes were secured and attended to by Love, Keyhoe, and Maidment, the parade was organized and cars lined up outside the airport grounds. Lindbergh rode in an open touring car, with the top down at his request, so the people could see him during the parade, in spite of the rain.

There were local bands and floats (no pun intended) in the entourage, which eventually made its way to the stadium, the present-day Gator Bowl. There were 10,000 seats at the stadium, all of which were filled. Many more people stood outside the fence in order to see the famous flyer as the parade entered the gate.

In Lindbergh's talk he predicted that airplanes would soon be built that would be faster, bigger, and more dependable. He said that scheduled airlines would soon span the entire country. He strongly urged Jacksonville to plan ahead for needed facilities to promote and encourage aviation and air travel.

After his appearance at the stadium, he was driven with his crew to the Hotel George Washington. He was met there by Robert Kloeppel, who gave him the $1,000 check. After spending some time with the press, the flyers were shown to their suite for clean up and rest.

In the evening Lindbergh was the honored guest at a lavish banquet at the hotel. Included in the guest list were the elite of Jacksonville: business people, politicians, and other influential people. During the banquet there was a presentation of the Hotel George Washington Transatlantic Flight Fund. The benediction was given by the Reverend Sam I. Smith, president of the Jacksonville Ministerial Alliance.

After these formalities Lindbergh was introduced by Mayor Alsop.

Lindbergh said: "Jacksonville is the turning point of this tour which has been underway for three months and covered more than 20,000 miles. We passed over the wildest and most mountainous portions of the United States. This is a striking example of the efficiency of modern equipment used by planes and motors as shown by the flight here today. We have used two ships in the flight and have not been delayed by mechanical trouble as shown by our schedule. The total life of the airplane now exceeds that of the automobile."

He went on to tell about the air mail records and miles covered by that service.

He continued, "The development of aviation and the accomplishments of the aeronautical engineers have convinced the world of the practicality of airplanes."

The rest of his talk covered the usual promotion of the future of air travel, building more airports, and developing the industry. He stressed the urgent need for the people to use the air mail and passenger services in the near future. He also expressed his appreciation to the city for its hospitality and kindness.

October 11th as Lindbergh was preparing for the take off for Atlanta, Georgia. G.P. HARRY

The next morning Mr. Kloeppel drove Lindbergh and his crew to the airport for their departure to the next city. Although there were some breaks in the clouds allowing the sun to show through here and there, some low clouds and drizzle stayed in the area.

After a thorough preflight of both airplanes, the NYP took off, followed by the Fairchild with Love, Keyhoe, and Maidment. Lindbergh came back across the field several times before taking up a heading for the city, where he circled a number of times as a farewell gesture.

Once again the airport was closed officially to continue the work necessary to render it fully completed. The building of Jacksonville's first municipal airport had been slowed by financing difficulties and the lack of regular airline service since the demise of Florida Airways in 1926. However, since Lindbergh's visit, the local industry saw a marked shift in sentiment. Construction of their field quickened. It finally opened in 1928 with a large steel hangar and other necessary buildings.

Pitcairn Aviation began their air mail service to the city on the same day the airport opened. Pitcairn operated between Miami, Atlanta, and New York, with connections to other airlines along the way, providing access to the entire air mail system of the country.

Jacksonville became the Florida headquarters for Eastern Air Transport, later to become Eastern Airlines.

An interesting note is that 150,000 people greeted the flyer. When the census was taken a year later for the city, it was found that the population was 129,549. This gives an idea of the number of visitors, mostly from other parts of Florida.

After circling the city, Lindbergh took up a south-southwest course heading down to the little town of McRae, Florida, which he circled several times. He then headed north directly to Vidalia, Georgia, and from there northeast to Millen, Georgia. Both airplanes dropped low over the area. This was a personal greeting to Miss Alma Galbreath, a nurse who had tended to Phil Love, when he was in the hospital as a patient there. In 1925 Love had been working as a duster pilot in southern Georgia. He had been flying over cotton fields with a chemical load to kill the boll weevil. He had contracted a case of slow arsenic poisoning, and while flying at a low altitude became unconscious and crashed. So Love insisted that on this leg they fly over the spot where he crashed. Love's second rendezvous was with the nurse, by pre-arrangement. They found her waving. The two had developed a correspondence and the plan was for her to wear a red dress and be outside the hospital, perhaps on the roof. Love dropped a note, but it is not known what it said. Local people were sure it was a girlfriend of Lindbergh.

After circling that small town Lindbergh headed roughly northwest to Atlanta.

Jacksonville Municipal Airport no longer exists, and has been replaced with Jacksonville International Airport, which is located nine miles north of the city, several miles from the original airport. It has a 10,000-foot runway, and is at an elevation of 30 feet MSL. The airport serves all major airlines, both U.S. and foreign. Additionally, the field services corporate and other general aviation aircraft, as well as some military.

On the St. Johns River, south of the city, is NAS Jacksonville Towers. Two airports southwest of the city are Herlong, at an elevation of 87 feet MSL, catering to general aviation with the longest runway of 4,000 feet, and NAX Cecil Airport, used by the Navy.

Directly west at 99 feet MSL is NOLF Whitehouse Airport, and to the east, just on the east side of Duval, is Craig Municipal Airport, at an elevation of 42 feet MSL, with the longest runway of 4,007 feet. It serves mainly general aviation and the National Guard.

References

Newspapers
Florida Times-Union
Jacksonville Journal

Organizations
Jacksonville Public Library
Jaxport, Jacksonville Port Authority
Jaxport Magazine
Florida Aviation Historical Society

People
Victor W. Tatelman
John E. Anstensen
Roland F. Spicer
John P. Ingle Jr.
Mrs. Sara R. Jochnowitz
Jack V. Casamassa

Bob Evaul
Mark Miller
Oran Barber
G. P. Harry
George R. Hindall

STOP #70
ATLANTA, GEORGIA

CAPSULE HISTORY OF CITY

Capital and largest city in Georgia, Atlanta is located on the Piedmont Plateau in northwestern Georgia. Because of its abundance of dogwood trees, it is often called "Dogwood City." The beautiful Blue Ridge Mountains lie just northeast of the city.

The Creek Indians were the first people on the site in about 1821. In 1836 the state began building the Western and Atlantic Railroad in this area, near a town called Terminus, which was the end of the line. This town was renamed Marthasville in 1843. In 1845 J. Edgar Thompson, a railroad engineer, renamed the town Atlanta, after the Western and Atlantic Railroad. It was incorporated as a city in 1847. But it was not until 1868 that this large city became the capital of the state.

1,050 feet MSL

OCTOBER 11–12, 1927
(TUESDAY AND WEDNESDAY)

In 1909 there was a famous old speedway on the site where in 1927 the city acquired 300 acres from a private estate by means of a five-year lease with option to purchase. This was to build an airport. While a race track, it was used by such notable auto racers as Barney Oldfield, Louis Strong, and George Robertson, who sped around the two-mile oval. It was known as Hapeville Speedway. In 1927 when Lindbergh landed, the old track was clearly visible. This site, Candler Field, was located eight miles south of the city. It was in the process of being improved under the direction of Alderman W. B. Hartsfield. It had recently been graded and seeded. A 60-foot-by-120-foot large white hangar with "Pitcairn Aviation" painted over the door was completed.

Tuesday, October 11, was declared as "Lindbergh Day" in Atlanta. Unfortunately, the rainstorm that had been in the South for several

days was still lingering around the Atlanta area before heading east out to sea. By the time Lindbergh arrived, there were only lingering rain showers over the city.

Lindbergh came over Atlanta, circled the business district a few times, then headed south to Candler Field. He circled the field several times, did a low pass, and came in for a perfect three-point landing at 2:00 p.m. CST. There were a reported 50,000 people already gathered on the airport before he got there. The Fairchild had already landed about thirty minutes earlier.

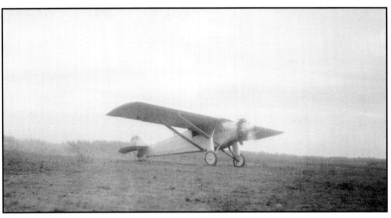

Lindbergh was directed into air race pilot Doug Davis's hangar, which had been built on the airport a short time before. The reception committee met him there. He inserted the windows, checked other details, and climbed out to be met by Gov. I. G. Hardman, Mayor I. N. Ragsdale of Atlanta, Henderson Hallman, president of the Atlanta Aero Club, William H. Hartsfield of the aviation committee of the City Council, and Col. Charles H. Cox, Commander of the 122nd Infantry National Guard. Mayors from surrounding towns were also present.

The Fairchild was rolled into the hangar, where its wings were folded to be kept safe from the throngs of people.

Cars from all parts of the state were showing up in the city early that morning. Local pilots were doing a thriving business taking people up for scenic rides. It seemed as though everyone wanted to fly. Vendors of soft drinks and hot dogs also did a record business. Even the peanut venders did better than if it had been a circus day.

Many Georgia military schools—Georgia Military College of Milledgeville, Riverside Military Academy of Gainsville, and Georgia Tech—

were on the field to welcome the hero.

Soon the parade of cars was formed up, with Lindbergh in the fourth car with Keyhoe, Henderson Hallman, and Colonel Cox. The third car carried Phil Love, Capt. O. L. McLain, a representative of the Department of Commerce in Atlanta, and a Pathe Newsreel representative.

As soon as the parade got underway, C. C. Maidment, the mechanic, gave the NYP a bath, changed the oil, tested the fuel, and supposedly patched a number of tears in the wings. Wherever gasoline did not clean the fabric areas, he painted the silver with new silver dope. He was

The NYP has just landed on Candler Field and Lindbergh is taxiing toward the Davis hangar. COURTESY OF THE ATLANTA HISTORY CENTER

assisted by some Candler Field mechanics.

The parade went from the airport through College Park, then Hapeville and East Point, where schoolchildren and others were gathered to say hello. From there they went to Pershing Point, where Lindbergh placed a wreath upon the World War I memorial, and then to Base Hospital #48 of the Disabled Veterans of World War I. From there they went to Grant Field to greet 20,000 people.

In his talk at the park he said, "Regular passenger service in airplanes between populous centers will be established on a permanent basis in a few years and in some parts of the country in a few months. Establishment of airports with adequate facilities for planes, with proper equipment for repairs, and with conditions as near perfect as possible to assure safe landings is the first essential that will aid development of air navigation. Those cities which provided such facilities and those sections of the country which have them in the larger number will be the first to reap the benefits of air traffic. ... I expect to arrive in New York October 23rd and shall then discuss for the first time my permanent plans for the future. Of course I feel now that what-

The NYP and Lindbergh are shown in Doug Davis' hangar shortly after he arrived at Atlanta being met by some of the reception people. COURTESY OF THE ATLANTA HISTORY CENTER

ever these plans are they will be connected with aviation."

The parade made its way into the city to the Biltmore Hotel. A short press conference was held, after which the flyers were escorted to their suite for some rest.

At the banquet that evening at the Ansley Hotel, only a few people spoke before Lindbergh, so that he could retire early. The speakers were Governor Hardman, Mayor Ragsdale, and Mr. Hallman. Lindbergh gave his usual pep talk about air travel.

PERSONAL RECOLLECTIONS

Richard L. Nagle (from Norcross, Georgia): "My brother John and I were taken by our father to Candler Field to see Lindbergh. The anticipation and excitement was very high. Suddenly we spotted the plane as a small speck in the southeastern sky. When the plane landed a cheer went up from the crowd. Brother John grabbed my hand and we ducked under the rope, running towards the runway in the distance. The police yelled and tried to stop us but to no avail. We got to the plane just as the prop took its last turn. Lindbergh opened the door and stepped out. He looked a bit surprised. He said something like, 'Well, well, are you boys the welcoming committee?' Soon he was taken to the speaker's stand. Our moment of glory was over. We were both severely reprimanded, but we got a good bit of mileage out of that experience."

Gloria Cassity Stargel: She remembered her parents relating the following story of that day: Her dad, Woodie Cassity, was a tall, ruggedly handsome Irishman. He and his wife were invited to the evening banquet, and when Mr. Cassity walked in the guests mistook him for Lindbergh and they all stood up with a thunderous applause. Daughter Gloria did not know how her father got out of that one, but suspected that his fair Irish complexion must have turned crimson.

Gloria also remembered that her brother, at the age of three in 1927, was with his father at the field when Lindbergh landed and that the airplane's prop-wash turned up so much dust, hitting him in the face, that he tried to hide from it all by getting between his father's legs seeking shelter.

It was about 9:15 A.M. the next morning when Lindbergh and the crew left the Biltmore Hotel suite. He was driven to Candler Field by Henderson Hallman, general reception committee chairman, and Colonel Cox.

The airport was intermittently bathed in sunlight as holes in the clouds allowed the early morning sun's rays to shine on the field. After a thorough preflight Lindbergh took off at 10:00 A.M. He made several farewell passes over the airport, to the delight of the 2,500 early risers. Then he headed for the business district, where he circled several times to say good-bye.

Shortly after Lindbergh departed, the

Fairchild took off, accompanied by two Pitcairn Mailwing bi-plane mail planes. The two pilots were Jim Ray and L. H. Elliott. They were to escort Lindbergh to Philadelphia, home of Pitcairn Aircraft Corporation, including the stops in between.

Lindbergh headed in an east-northeast direction, directly to Athens, Georgia. On their way they passed over Stone Mountain. Deciding to go lower for a closer look at the monument, they ran into some severe turbulence, and Lindbergh nearly ran into some high tension lines.[10]

He came over Athens, Georgia, at 12:10 p.m., circled twice, dropped the canvas bag message, and continued in the basic same direction to Greenwood, South Carolina, while crossing the Savannah River at about Calhoun Falls at Richard B. Russell Lake. He was over Greenwood at 1:05 p.m. and dropped a bag.

After flying around Greenwood he took up a north-northeast heading to fly direct to Spartanburg, South Carolina.

Only a few days after Lindbergh's visit, work was started on a two-million-candle-power revolving beacon and extensive other lighting equipment for Candler Field in Atlanta. All of this included boundary lights and hangar flood lights. It was the latest manufactured by General Electric. A local flyer, Beeler Blevins of Atlanta, purchased a Ryan B-1 Brougham, s/n 44, #1962, and went into the flying business there.

Not too long after that a gesture of honor was given to the hero flyer. The city decided to rename Mayson Avenue Lindbergh Drive. The street runs east from Peachtree Road to Piedmont Road, at the old Mayson homeplace.

Today the main commercial airport for Atlanta exists on the very same site as Candler Field, but is now known as Hartsfield-Atlanta International Airport. It is at an elevation of 1,026 feet MSL with four parallel runways, the longest of which is 11,889 feet. The airport services all major U.S. and European airlines, as well as commuter, corporate, and some general aviation and military.

Eight miles northeast of downtown is Dekalb-Peachtree Airport. It is at an elevation of 1,002 feet MSL. Its longest runway is 6,001 feet. The field serves mostly general aviation, including corporate operations and some military. To the northwest is Dobbins ARB, and farther to the northwest is Cobb County-McCollum, both of which are in the city of Marietta.

Surrounding the city of Atlanta, in the Class B airspace, are many private and general aviation airports, one of the highest concentrations of airports around a major city that one can find anywhere in the country.

Footnotes

10. The full story can be read on pages 267-268 in Donald Keyhoe's book, *Flying with Lindbergh*.

References

Newspapers
Atlanta Constitution
Atlanta Journal

Organizations
Atlanta Fulton Library
Atlanta Historical Society, Inc.
Atlanta History Center
Pullen Library, Georgia State University

Another view of the NYP in Doug Davis' hangar at Candler Field. COURTESY OF THE ATLANTA HISTORY CENTER

Publications

Legacy of Wings: the Harold F. Pitcairn Story, by Frank Kingston Smith (New York: Jason Aeronson, Inc., 1981).

Atlanta and Environs: A Chronicle of Its People and Events, by Franklin M. Garrett, vol. 2 (New York: Lewis Historical Publishing Company, Inc., 1954).

People

Kathy and Larry Lee	Neil L. Fraser
Horace Steele	Binca Bone
Martin L. Zellman, Ph.D.	Steve Pitcairn
William R. Davis Jr.	Fred L. Barber
Clyatt W. James Jr., M.D.	

STOP #71
SPARTANSBURG, SOUTH CAROLINA

CAPSULE HISTORY OF CITY

Located in the northwestern part of the state of South Carolina, Spartanburg is fifteen miles from the North Carolina border. It is sometimes called the Hub City of the Southeast.

This city was chosen as the seat of Spartanburg County in 1785. Both the town and the county are named for the Spartan Regiment, a South Carolina militia group that fought in the Revolutionary War. Spartanburg is a leading textile manufacturing city and also a trading center of a peach-growing region.

875 feet MSL.

OCTOBER 12–14, 1927
(WEDNESDAY THROUGH FRIDAY)

On September 10, 1927, just one month before Lindbergh's visit, the Spartanburg Municipal Airport was officially opened. However, it was in early June 1926 when an aviation committee composed of three men—J. C. Grier, Maj. B. Manning, and R. Z. Cates—began accumulating information on the "Piedmont Route," one of three southern routes being considered by the U.S. Post Office Department for the establishment of an aerial mail route. It was part of the route between New York and Atlanta. A contract to carry the mail was let to Pitcairn Aviation, Inc., of Philadelphia on February 23, 1927. Spartanburg would become an official stop on this air mail route.

At the dedication, officials of the Department of Commerce, the Pitcairn Company, and the U.S. Post Office and Chambers of Commerce were in attendance. Cost for the 105 acres was $20,000. After grading, building a hangar and other physical necessities, the total cost came to $46,000.

The first airplane to land on the site, some months before the official dedication, was a Navy airplane, piloted by A. W. Smith of the Department of Commerce, and Charles I. Stanton. This site was, and still is, located just three miles southwest of the center of the city.

The first airplane sighted by the throngs of Spartans, as they refer to themselves, was the Fairchild. It came over the city, arriving from the southern horizon, then circled the new airport and landed. It was immediately placed in the hangar, as Keyhoe met the reception committee with instructions for the care of the NYP, which would arrive in about thirty minutes.

Lindbergh was spotted over the city, after circling over Duncan Park Stadium, at about 1:45 p.m., before he headed south to the airport. He circled, made a low pass, and came around for a three-point landing at exactly 2:00 p.m.

The NYP was then rolled into the Pitcairn hangar, but could still be seen by the public. Lindbergh was met by Gov. John G. Richards, Mayor Ben Hill Brown, and President H. A. Ligon of the Chamber of Commerce. After some formalities and careful instructions from the flyer, he was whisked out of a side hangar door to a waiting car.

The parade of cars moved briskly along Otis Boulevard in Converse Heights and on to Duncan Park Stadium. He was greeted there by parents and children singing "America."

Mayor Brown was the Master of Ceremonies, and Dr. Henry Nelson Snyder, President

of Wofford College, introduced the famous flyer. His talk was the usual, stressing the need for airports, airport improvement, releasing the necessary funds for the development of air travel and the air mail system, the design and building of safer and larger aircraft, and development of navigation aids. He received rousing applause.

After the festivities at Duncan Park, the entourage made its way into the city business district and the Cleveland Hotel, where he held a short press conference with the local media.

Eleanor Louise Smith, a student at Converse College, remembers the event:

"I was torn between my determination to ask a question and my fear of blurting out an ungrammatical sentence—college girls do get into the habit, it seems.

"Time slipped by, and at last the thought that the interview would soon be over without my having said a word unless I spoke up at once, spurred me to the point of utterance. I could not let it be said that I had interviewed Lindbergh without opening my mouth. Surprisingly enough, my voice sounded very calm and even intelligent, and I made no grammatical errors in putting a question about future transatlantic flights.

"Colonel Lindbergh said that further attempts were, in his opinion, unnecessary and impractical for the present. A successful flight had been made and energies should be devoted toward perfecting safety equipment.

"The Colonel was not at all the aloof man of the parade. He smiled often, the famous "Lindy" smile, and even laughed a bit. There was a warmth in his manner which was charming. He was perfect master of himself and of the situation and was at all times very impersonal. Through his poise and self-possession came a strain of the boyish modesty which has endeared him to millions."

After about fifteen minutes the interview was over. Colonel Lindbergh shook hands with everyone again. When he reached Eleanor he said, "I'm glad to have met you." "Probably he said the same thing to everyone," Eleanor said, "but I like to think that we were the only ones favored thus."

After the press meeting he and his crew retired to their suite for some rest and cleaning up.

Because there was not a suitable room in Spartanburg for a banquet/dinner, the Chamber of Commerce requested the dining hall of Converse College. It was a girls' college, only a few blocks from the downtown area of the city. Permission was granted for the affair that would draw several hundred quests.

The female student body went wild with enthusiasm. The girls had to have their evening meal elsewhere, but still could linger on the porches and in some of the halls until the flyer arrived. They were given strict instructions regarding stealing his buttons or some other memorabilia, and they complied.

Donald Keyhoe approached the woman in

The NYP parked near a water tower on the Spartanburg Airport. CASSAGNERES COLLECTION

charge, Mary Wilson Gee, and said that Lindbergh was quite shy and had a horror of going through a line of girls. She assured him that her girls would not harm him in any way.

At the appointed time he was driven to the college and came up the front steps, where a group of students sang a special song of greeting, in addition to the college song.

Finally he went inside and along the hall, through a veritable lane of girls, and into the dining room. It was one of the few places on the tour, according to him, that someone did not try to snatch something off his clothes.

The dining hall was filled with leaders from Spartanburg and the state. Behind the chair at which Lindbergh would be seated, the girls had arranged a great display of gold and purple chrysanthemums, the college colors, so that he seemed about to be taking his place on a throne. He did not care for this kind of thing and asked that they be removed.

Senator E. D. "Cotton Ed" Smith and Mayor Brown sat on one side of Lindbergh. Mr. Ligon, Governor Richards, Mrs. Richards, and Dr. Pell sat on the other side.

Lindbergh was introduced, and there came a hush over the hall as he began to talk. He made his usual presentation for the advancement of aviation and air travel. The place went wild with cheers and clapping. He left the hall and was driven back to the hotel for a good night's rest.

Never before had a guest of Converse been so well received or idolized by the student body than when Lindbergh came there. It was a notable occasion for the school. They had often had statesmen, famous lecturers, poets and novelists and famous preachers, including Carl Sandburg, the biographer. But nothing so impressed the people at Converse.

A letter from a Converse student that was written to a friend follows.

"How can I ever tell you the wonderful news? Colonel Lindbergh is coming to Spartanburg. He will be in Converse tonight – Lindy himself, real true, true and no foolin'. We can hardly breathe, we're so excited.

"A little Freshman wants to know how she may get a peep at Lindy while he's at Converse. A very ingenious person would have to devise a way to do that successfully. It has been suggested that one become a maid for the evening and by chance serve his table. One never knows. Many casualties are expected in the rush, such as broken necks from falling over Main banisters. But what is that when Lindbergh is to be seen?

"Did you know that aeroplane riding is quite the fad here? It is certainly the thing to do, for it has been authorized by our dean. Many are planning trips, and one of our Seniors seriously considers going home to Texas by plane. Are we progressing?

"Wish you were here to cheer with us. Let's give fifteen now for Lindbergh."

Signed – Polly Parrott (?)

Sometime while Lindbergh was in Spartanburg, he had noticed a Pitcairn biplane parked at the back of the hangar. He was immediately impressed with its good looks, and asked if he could fly it. Permission was granted, and he put on an exhibition of aerobatics, and was the first person to fly the airplane outside of Pitcairn pilots. It was probably a PA-5 model.

The people of Spartanburg devoted tremendous time to the success of Lindbergh's visit. The whole affair came off without a hitch. The city deserved the highest praise for the manner in which it represented South Carolina. It was the welcome of a city on a scope that would have done credit to a municipality with double the population. The "City of Success" got the swing of metropolitan ways and knew much about pep, community enterprise, and loyalty. The city made a marked success of its "Lindbergh Day." It was the largest crowd ever assembled in the state to greet one man, the young, blue-eyed blond boy from the West. As a host the city was thoughtful and thorough, and it showed the state how it could be done.

Today, on the same site, the Spartanburg Downtown Memorial Airport, at an elevation of 801 feet MSL, is very active. It has a 5,202-foot runway and services most major domestic airlines, as well as general aviation, commuter airlines, corporate and some military aircraft.

There are no small airports in the surrounding area of the city with the exception of Greenville-Spartanburg International Airport, located about fifteen miles west-southwest of the center of the city. The field is at an elevation of 964 feet MSL and has one runway 11,000 feet

long. It serves most major domestic airlines, commuter lines, and general aviation and corporate aircraft operations and some military.

References

Newspapers
Parley Voo (Converse College)
Spartanburg Journal
Spartanburg Herald
Herald-Journal
Anderson Independent

Organizations
Spartanburg County Library
Converse College Library and Mickel Library – Wade M. Woodward
B & B Studio (photography), Tommy White
Spartanburg County Historical Association
South Carolina State Archives
South Carolina Library
Regional Museum of Spartanburg
City of Spartanburg–Frank G. Anderson

People
Dr. Alan Stokes   Beth Bilderback
Carolyn Creal   Charlotte Huskey
Gary Henderson   Steve Pitcairn

STOP #72
GREENSBORO, NORTH CAROLINA
"TOUCH STOP"

CAPSULE HISTORY OF CITY

This North Carolina city is located about 85 miles northwest of Raleigh, the state capital, in the north-central part of the state.

The city was named for Maj. Gen. Nathanael Greene, commander of the Continental Army at the Battle of Guilford Courthouse in March of 1781. It was chartered in 1808.

840 feet MSL.

OCTOBER 14, 1927 (FRIDAY)

Greensboro had an airport in 1927 which was located seven miles west of the city, and is still there. It was known then as either Guilford Airport, after Guilford County, or Lindley Field. Pitcairn Aviation operated one hangar at the time of Lindbergh's visit. They were part of the CAM 19 air mail route.

On the day of the expected arrival of the flyer, the field and parade route into the city were jammed with thousands of people. Shouts and screams went up from the throngs when he was first spotted over the area at a little after 11 a.m.

The Fairchild had already arrived a few minutes earlier, and Keyhoe was giving instructions to the reception committee. The NYP landed

about 11:30 a.m.

Lindbergh was met by Gov. Angus W. McLean, Mayor E. B. Jeffress, and Guilford County Commission Chairman J. A. Rankin.

After further introductions and assurance to Lindbergh that the NYP was in good hands, he boarded an open car, sitting in the rear between Governor McLean and Mayor Jeffress. The touring car was a 1927 Cadillac. They proceeded out of the airport grounds to Friendly Avenue and into the business district of the city. On their way into town they passed by the North Carolina campus and Greensboro College.

William S. Russell Sr. was a cadet at Oak Ridge Military Institute, about ten miles from the airport. They were invited to witness the landing and to salute Lindbergh when he stepped out of the cockpit. Lindbergh saluted back. Russell remembered the thrill of being allowed to look inside the cockpit. It was the first weekend that the cadets were allowed to have a pass to go home. Russell planned to hitchhike home to Sanford, North Carolina, with his friend, Gaither Scott. They were surprised when the very same Cadillac that Lindbergh had ridden in came along. The driver picked them up, and they just HAD to ride on the top of the rear deck, as Lindbergh did, where they could wave to everyone as they left the airport.

October 14th, "Touch Stop" at Greensboro's Guilford Airport, the NYP is shown in front of another Pitcairn hangar. ARCHIVES DIVISION, GREENSBORO HISTORICAL MUSEUM, GREENSBORO, NC

Lindbergh and the entourage arrived at Greensboro's War Memorial Stadium, where he gave his usual speech. In his talk he complimented the city on establishing Lindley Field and said, "We should turn our eye to the future and we are here to ask the cities and counties to construct and maintain airports. ... We are inaugurating the air routes of the future."

After his presentation Lindbergh and the other officials were driven back to the airfield, where he said good-bye to everyone, checked over the NYP, and took off for Winston-Salem at 1:30 p.m.

After taking off, Lindbergh circled the airport and the city several times, then took up a westerly heading. However, it is not known what his exact route was (it is not in his log book), so why it took forty-five minutes to make a direct fifteen-statute-mile flight is not known. Most probably he circled over several little towns on the way, plus his time over both Greensboro and later Winston-Salem.

As a result of his visit, that old airport in Greensboro has stayed in business all these years, and today is a modern airport. The present name is Piedmont Triad International Airport. It is at an elevation of 926 feet MSL, with a main runway of 10,000 feet. It handles any domestic and foreign airlines, many commuter airlines, plus some military and general aviation.

References

Newspapers
Greensboro Daily News
Greensboro Daily Record

Organizations
Greensboro Public Library
Greensboro Historical Museum

People
Mike Edwards   Page Parker
R. L. Beall   Kenneth V. Brugh Jr.
Bob Benbow   W. D. Wilkinson
J. Stephen Catlett   William S. Russel Sr.
George J. Pollock Jr.

Lindbergh can be seen in this photo standing with his head near the number 2 on the wing, apparently speaking with some of the local officials on October 14th. ARCHIVES DIVISION, GREENSBORO HISTORICAL MUSEUM, GREENSBORO, NC

STOP #73
WINSTON-SALEM, NORTH CAROLINA

CAPSULE HISTORY OF CITY

Winston-Salem, home of the tobacco industry, lies in the central-northwestern part of the state of North Carolina, about thirty miles from the Blue Ridge Mountains.

This area dates from 1753, when a group of Pennsylvania Moravians purchased a large tract of land in the North Carolina Piedmont. The settlement was called Bethabara, which meant "House of Passage" or "Temporary Home." They prospered, and it became a trading and crafts center. In 1766 Salem (from Shalom, Hebrew for "Peace") was built nearby as the Moravians' permanent settlement.

The city of Winston, founded in 1849 because of its extensive tobacco industry, surpassed Salem. The two towns, known as the Twin Cities, consolidated in 1913.

860 feet MSL.

OCTOBER 14–15, 1927
(FRIDAY AND SATURDAY)

One of the earlier airfields in the area was known as Maynard Field, on the east side of Winston-Salem. It became outmoded, so the citizens made plans for a new airport. In the summer of 1927 Miller Municipal Airport was built on the old county farmlands just outside the city, beyond the Fairgrounds on the Walkertown Road to the north- northeast.

On August 5, 1927, Reynolds Airways, Inc., established a fixed base operation on Miller Field. It was owned by Dick Reynolds (from the R. J. Reynolds Tobacco Company family). The airport was named after Clint Miller, who contributed the money to build the first hangar.

From the end of August to the time Lindbergh was expected, construction on the airport was in high gear. Four-way runways were expanded to 1,600 feet long and approximately 450 feet wide. Lighting for night landings was installed, and an all-steel hangar was completed with electricity installed on October 12. Cinders and gravel were spread on the ground in front of the new hangar.

On the day of Lindbergh's arrival, the dedication and official opening of Miller Municipal Airport would take place. In the afternoon there was only a small crowd of people, including state and city officials, on the field. A much larger crowd had been expected. Because of this, one of the city officials made several telephone calls

Some time after Lindbergh's arrival at Miller Field at Winston-Salem, NC. THOMAS H. DAVIS

to such places as Owens Drug Store, O'Hanlons, and other popular local establishments to urge more people to come for the celebration. By the time Lindbergh was sighted over the city, several thousand people appeared in the area. It was a momentous occasion.

The sky was clear, and since the storm had passed through, the ground had a chance to drain off and become firm again. It was just about 1:45 p.m. when Lindbergh first appeared over the city, coming in from the east. He flew over the City Memorial Hospital, circling around the building and dipping his wings, before heading for the business district. After that he flew north-northeast to the field, made a low pass, and came in for a smooth landing at exactly 2:00 p.m.

The Fairchild, with passengers Phil Love, Donald Keyhoe, and C. C. Maidment, had landed a half hour earlier to prepare the welcoming committee for Lindbergh's arrival.

Wearing a dark blue pinstripe suit, white shirt, and blue tie, Lindbergh was met by Gov. Angus W. McLean and Mayor Thomas Barber. After the flyer was assured of the security of the NYP, he was asked to say a few words at the official dedication and opening of the new airport in a christening ceremony.

Major Thomas Barber standing with Lindbergh next to the NYP, October 14th. PHOTOGRAPH COLLECTION, FORSYTH COUNTY PUBLIC LIBRARY

Then he was whisked off in a private car to begin the parade into town. They first went into the heart of the city and out to Hanes Park, where there were already 25,000 people, mostly schoolchildren and their parents, waiting for him. The car stopped beside Wiley School (now Wiley Middle School) and he walked to the speakers' stand in the park. Both Mayor Barber

and William M. Hendren, a local attorney, gave brief talks before the flyer was introduced.

It was a five-minute talk, centering on the advancement of aviation and air travel. In closing Lindbergh said, "I want to bring before you again the necessity of conducting a progressive air program for your city in order to keep your city in the foreground of American aeronautics. I want to thank you for the interest here and for the welcome I have received. I hope that you will devote a part of your interest in the future to aviation in relation to your community. I thank you."

It was sheer pandemonium as Lindbergh left the park. Females large and small, old and young, moved fast toward the chair he had sat in on the platform. They crushed it and broke it into small fragments for souvenirs. One girl, with an axe, proceeded to chop up the planks upon which the aviator had stood, and the pieces were passed around the crowd.

The entourage then drove into town again to the Robert E. Lee Hotel. Here he and his crew were given a special suite where they held a press conference, and then spent some time relaxing before the evening banquet.

During the parade and the melee at the park, perfect order (other than the chair and plank incident) was maintained by the local police, scores of American Legion members, and Company G of the North Carolina National Guard.

In the hotel that evening the banquet hall was lavishly decorated. A facsimile of the NYP, in many colored roses, hung over the head table. Wreaths, flowers, and trailing vines were everywhere, including a large "L" with tremendous chrysanthemums and roses. Mayor Barber was the toastmaster.

Only a select few of the state and city dignitaries and leading citizens of Greensboro, High Point, and Winston-Salem were invited to this special event. They included Mayor Barber of Winston-Salem, Mayor E. B. Jeffress of Greensboro, Fred N. Tate, Chairman Publicity Bureau of High Point Chamber of Commerce, and North Carolina Governor A. W. McLean. Background music was provided by the Buccaneers Orchestra from the University of North Carolina at Chapel Hill.

During the evening a surprise announcement was made. Mr. Robert E. Lasater, a public-spirited citizen and general manufacturing manager

of the R. J. Reynolds Company, had purchased the airport property for $100,000 from Forsyth County and transferred it over to the Winston-Salem Foundation for the city. This donation guaranteed the permanence of the airport for the future. The Miller Municipal Airport Commission would continue to be in charge of the actual operations for ten years.

William Ritter commented many years later, "When the announcement was made, their faces showed an expression like what would appear on the face of a Democrat on learning that a Republican had been elected to the Presidency."

On the morning of the 15th, Lindbergh and the Fairchild took off from Miller Airport, circling over the field and then the downtown area. They then took up a heading to the northeast directly to Danville, Virginia. He circled there several times and headed east-northeast to South Boston, Virginia. Circling there, he headed northeast directly to Richmond, Virginia, the next stop.

Miller Field still exists on the same site, but is known today as Smith Reynolds International Airport. It is at 970 feet MSL, and its longest runway is 6,655 feet. It serves some domestic and commuter airlines, corporate and general aviation.

Some private airstrips are located around the Winston-Salem area, mostly in the southwest.

References

Newspapers
Winston-Salem Journal

Organizations
Forsyth County Public Library (Jones Collection)
Wachovia Historical Society
Vineyard Plaza Shoe Shop (Kay Conrad, D.S.S.)
Old Greensboro Preservation Society

Publication
Aviation Magazine (August 15, 1927), p. 384

People
Thomas H. Davis, Piedmont Airlines
Molly G. Rawls   Gary S. Sigvaldsen
Robert F. Highsmith   Cassaundra Sledge
Frances B. Heath   Bob Beall

Stop #74
Richmond, Virginia

CAPSULE HISTORY OF CITY

Richmond, state capital of Virginia, is located on the James River about 125 miles west of the Atlantic Ocean and 100 miles south of Washington, D.C. It served as a capital of the Confederate States of America during the Civil War. It possibly has more monuments and museums than any other city in the South.

In about 1609 Capt. John Smith purchased some land near the Richmond site from an Indian chief named Powhatan. Thus was founded a settlement that he called "None Such." In 1737 the land was officially surveyed by Col. William Byrd and named Richmond, for Richmond, England. The community was incorporated in 1742 and designated as the state capital in 1779.

160 feet MSL.

OCTOBER 15–17, 1927
(SATURDAY THROUGH MONDAY)

Some of the earliest beginnings of the development of the art of flight happened in Richmond. The area possessed a heritage of flight that predated any other airport. It began in the Civil War era on the very site where Lindbergh landed during his goodwill tour, Byrd Airport. Within ten or twelve miles both Union and Confederate Aeronauts rose above the trenches in balloons to observe the enemy during battles fought there in the 1860s.

In the 1800s some Richmond citizens conducted experiments with gliders and more balloons. One of the latter claimed to have reached an altitude of 5,000 feet. In September 1909 the first heavier-than-air flight was made at the state fairgrounds by Charles Willard, who worked for Glenn Curtiss.

This shows the tremendous crowd and public interest in his visit to Richmond with the NYP outside the Pitcairn hangar.
WALTER M. JEFFERIES JR.

In the town of Sandston, the Curtiss Company established a large airplane assembly plant within a half-mile of where Byrd Airport is presently located.

The first stable aviation activity for the city was established as an airport known then in the mid-20s as Eagle Rock Airport. It opened about 1925 and was later known as Hermitage Field.

But in January 1927 two significant aviation events happened in Richmond. Lt. Comdr. Richard E. Byrd had just returned from his first Arctic explorations, and the city was quite eager to honor him for this accomplishment. The city council had been considering the creation of a municipal airport, and decided to name it after this famous Navy officer. So the Byrd Airport was named before it was constructed. The council had been looking for a site, and it happened that famous pilot and speed king Roscoe Turner found it, quite by accident, when he had been circling over the area of Sandston looking for a place to land his Standard biplane. It was January 20. He landed on a dirt road in what is now the northwest portion of Byrd Airport.

Turner had been invited to Richmond to establish an aviation business and flying field. He had landed near a pasture located about five miles east of the city. It became his base of operations known as Roscoe Turner Flying Service. He registered the field under the name of Richmond Air Junction.

Extensive construction was completed on this airport and it would now be designated as one of the air mail stops between New York and Atlanta. Eventually Pitcairn Aviation took over the operation of the field and completed the building of a new hangar on October 12, just in time for Lindbergh's arrival.

There were 10,000 people on Byrd Field on the day that Lindbergh was expected. The weather was clear with a 2,000-foot ceiling of broken clouds, and the field was in very good condition for "Lindbergh Day."

At 1:30 p.m. the Fairchild FC-2, with Phil Love piloting, and passengers Keyhoe, Maidment and Kusterer, landed at Byrd Field. Keyhoe met briefly with the welcoming committee and the Pitcairn staff, under the direction of Harold F. Pitcairn, to prepare for Lindbergh's expected arrival and the care of the NYP.

Virginia National Guard troops, under the direction of Maj. W. W. Poindexter, were already in place on the field to keep law and order and control the crowd. They were reinforced by local police and Boy Scouts.

Many aircraft flew in for the celebration, including two Ford tri-motors, a deHaviland from Langley Field, flown by Edward A. Hillery with Lt. R. R. Gillespie, and another deHaviland of the 58th Squadron. A second group of airplanes included three Martin bombers of the 2nd Bombardment Group, and an Army Air Corps Fokker. These airplanes had arrived from Langley, Bolling Field, Quantico, the Hampton

Roads Naval Base, Detroit and other points. Several air service technical school Curtiss Hawk pursuit planes and several Pitcairn airplanes were also there.

Lindbergh came over Richmond's business district about 1:45 p.m., then over the fairgrounds, before heading east toward Byrd Field. He came in low across the field, much to the delight of the masses of people, and came around for a smooth landing on the turf. It was exactly two o'clock.

He taxied the airplane into the Pitcairn hangar, and detailed arrangements were made for its care. The Fairchild was already inside. He was met by several people from the welcoming committee, including Mayor J. Fulmer Bright.

After a short talk by the flyer, he formally dedicated the airport in honor of Richard Evelyn Byrd. Then he and other dignitaries were escorted into waiting automobiles for the parade into town. The parade went through city streets to the Virginia State Fairgrounds, where there was already a gathering of thousands of schoolchildren and their parents. This was the official public reception for the flyer. Lindbergh gave his usual speech on the development of commercial aviation, and the present safety record of air travel and aviation.

John Stewart Bryan presided at the ceremonies at the fairgrounds. Rev. J. J. Scherer, D.D., pastor of the First English Lutheran Church, pronounced the invocation. Mayor Bright presented the Richmond medal of distinguished service to Lindbergh. Then the party went to the Governor's mansion in the city for a luncheon for Lindbergh and his crew. He was greeted by Commander Byrd, Harry F. Guggenheim and Gov. Harry Flood Byrd.

Lindbergh was given a room in the mansion, where he could meet with the press and then relax with his crew before the evening banquet. As Lindbergh arrived at the mansion, members of the reception committee and their wives, Army, Navy, and Marine officers went down the receiving line in the lovely right-hand room of the mansion—the old Blue Room—to shake hands with Lindbergh.

In his presentation to a captive audience at the mansion, he said, "I would like to ask that all you people help the field of aviation to become greatest in America, and to aid in establishing methods of safety and reliance which will

work toward this end." His talk was brief; his topic, aviation and its future.

In the meantime the NYP was put on display in the Pitcairn hangar, where lights were provided in the hangar as well as all over the airport so the public could come and view the famous airplane well into the evening of Saturday night.

After leaving the mansion at three o'clock, they toured Fort Gregg, Fort Harrison, and other landmarks of Richmond.

The five-course banquet that night was held at the auditorium of the Jefferson Hotel. There were five hundred prominent city and state officials and businessmen there to honor Lindbergh. As he made his way to the celebration, the National Anthem was played on the chimes of the St. James Church in his honor. People were even crowded into the balcony at this lavish banquet.

Toastmaster was Eppa Hunton Jr., who, in his introduction to the audience said that Comdr. Richard E. Byrd was unable to attend the banquet. No reason was given. Harry Guggenheim was there and in his address he said, "As long as there are Lindberghs and Byrds, we of the nation need never worry that we will sink into the mire of materialism. Some have said the age of supreme courage and chivalry died in the Middle Ages. But, with the advent of Lindbergh and Byrd, that age has been reawakened."

In one of his presentations in Richmond, Lindbergh reminded Virginians of the early explorers—of the members of his own Nordic race who were the first Europeans to reach America; of Christopher Columbus, who opened the New World; of the Cabot brothers, Henrick Hudson and John Smith, of Boone, Lewis and Clark, and young Washington. He said that Virginia contributed to the development of America hundreds of such explorers, and Virginia is able to appreciate pioneers of the air as well as the pioneers of ancient trails over water and forest.

The Richmond stop included one rest day, the 16th. There were to be no public functions or celebrations of any kind on this day. Most of the day was to be spent at the Governor's mansion.

However, in the morning Lindbergh made four flights over the local area; three in the NYP and one in a Pitcairn. The three flights in the NYP were to take up passengers. His first pas-

Close-up view of Lindbergh in his blue suit standing by the Fairchild FC-2 escort airplane at Byrd Airport, October 16TH. LINDBERGH PICTURE COLLECTION, MANUSCRIPTS & ARCHIVES, YALE UNIVERSITY LIBRARY

senger was Harry Flood Byrd for ten minutes. His next passenger was Harry Guggenheim for ten minutes, and finally a five-minute flight with mechanic C. C. Maidment.

On his fourth flight he flew a Pitcairn PA-3 Orowing, an open cockpit bi-plane, similar in appearance to the Curtiss Jenny. He was up for ten minutes flying over the Virginia countryside

A mechanic (Maidment?) working on the Wright J-5 engine, possibly the left magneto. GEORGE R. NELSON

to enjoy himself, flying over the beautiful country at slow speed.

Also on that same morning the Fairchild was flown to Washington, D.C.'s Bolling Field to make preparations for the arrival of Lindbergh the next day. For him this would be strictly a business visit.

In the afternoon, at the Governor's invitation, Lindbergh was driven after supper in the Governor's limousine around the Richmond historic area, including such places as Fort Gregg, Fort Harrison, and other landmarks in the city. They also went to "Westover," the ancestral home of the Byrd family. They were received at Westover by Mr. And Mrs. Richard Crane and their guests, and returned to the mansion at 5:55 p.m.

During that day 15,000 automobiles were involved in traffic tie-ups, as people made their way out to Byrd Field to catch a glimpse of the famous NYP and take pictures. It was one of the worst traffic tie-ups ever seen in the city. Some fender benders happened, and tempers flared.

After a good night's rest, the flyers were up early in the morning of the third day, the 17th. They consumed a substantial breakfast before they were taken out to the airport.

A thorough preflight was given by both pilots to both airplanes. Lindbergh lifted off the field at 10:30 a.m. The weather was clear except for some scattered clouds at 2,000 feet. Lindbergh bade a cordial farewell to Col. John W. Williams of the Governor's staff and other officials who had accompanied him to the airport.

He circled the field once and then came down low over the length of the field as a final farewell, much to the delight of everyone there that morning. Soon he headed northward toward Washington, D.C., his next stop.

Today Byrd Field is still on the very same site. It is now known as Richmond International (Byrd Field). It is at an elevation of 168 feet MSL and its longest runway is 9,003 feet. It serves all of the major domestic and commuter airlines, corporate and general aviation and military.

Also around the Richmond area are three other airports, mostly served by general aviation aircraft. Eight miles north is Hanover County Municipal in Ashland. New Kent County Airport is located three miles southeast in the town of Quinton. It is at an elevation of 123 feet MSL, with a single 3,600-foot runway. Several airports can be found on the outskirts of Richmond, many in the northeast quadrant. Most of them are grass strips.

References

Newspapers
Richmond Times-Dispatch
Richmond News Leader

Organization
Richmond Public Library

Publication
The Capital Region Airport Commission Presents: "Golden Wings" over Richmond 1927-1977, by John Tegler (Arnold, Md.: Wings Publishing Co., 1977).

People
Donald Foster	John T. Molumphy III
Shannon Humphries	Dan Hagedorn
Arthur Pullin	Joan Lowden
Ray Fredette	Ruth Reel or Reed
George R. Nelson	Walter N. Jefferies Jr.

Stop #75
Washington, District of Columbia

CAPSULE HISTORY OF CITY

Known as the heart of the nation, Washington, D.C., is the capital of the United States. It is located on the Potomac River between Maryland and Virginia, about 38 miles southwest of Baltimore, Maryland. It is one of the most beautiful centers of a national government in the world.

George Washington, the nation's first president, chose this site for the city in 1791. He hired the famous French engineer Maj. Pierre Charles L'Enfant to lay out the city. This location was once a swamp, with some scattered villages of Powhatan Indians living there.

It was in 1783 that the Continental Congress decided to set up a federal city as a permanent site for its meetings. The city was named in honor of George Washington.

It is here, at the National Air & Space Museum, on the south side of the Mall, that Lindbergh's Spirit of St. Louis is preserved and on display.

25 feet MSL.

OCTOBER 17–18, 1927
(MONDAY AND TUESDAY)

This flight from Richmond into Bolling Field was not publicized and was reported as a "business trip." It is not known what time he reached the field, but it is assumed, because of the time en route of one hour and fifteen minutes, to have been approximately 11:45 a.m.

Just after landing, Lindbergh was met by William P. MacCracken Jr., Maj. H. S. Burwell, Commanding Officer of Bolling Field, and several other people. With MacCracken they motored to the White House for a luncheon with President Coolidge.

In his meeting with the President, he said, "The best way to cut down the tragedies is to have the flights properly organized. The majority of the transoceanic flights start out without proper organization, experience, and equipment. I think it would be foolish for the Federal Government to enact legislation in an attempt to curb interoceanic flying. ... The immediate future of aviation is in the development of our transcontinental lines instead of transoceanic lines. ...We need considerably more transcontinental air development. I see no reason why we should not have service stations en route in transcontinental flying, but that is a matter for engineers to determine."

He stayed overnight (location unknown) and was to leave the next morning for Baltimore, the next official stop.

His business in the city also had to do with the last-minute details of completing the tour, meeting with the Department of Commerce Aeronautics Division, and making arrangements for his upcoming South-of-the-Border goodwill flight.

Lindbergh left Bolling Field and flew directly to Logan Field at Baltimore, with no stops or circling of towns during the fifty-five-minute flight.

Bolling Field is no longer an operating military airport, but some of the large hangars remain and are used for various government offices.

On the Anacostia side, next to the Anacostia River, one can find some of the hangars still there, although it is not an operating airport, either.

Washington National Airport, named Ronald Reagan Airport, serves the nation's capital. Located just minutes away from the capital, along the west side of the Potomac River, it is at 16 feet MSL and its longest runway is 6,869 feet. The field serves all of the major airlines as well as some international airlines, some commuters, corporate, a small assortment of general aviation aircraft, and military.

There is also the Washington Dulles International Airport, twenty miles west of the capital. It is at an elevation of 313 feet MSL, and its longest runways are parallel at 11, 501 feet. The airport serves all of the major airlines of the country as well as international with some commuter, corporate and general aviation movements. The National Air & Space Museum has an annex facility there for their larger historical aircraft collection, most of which is on display and open to the public.

Just a few miles northeast of the city is the oldest registered airport in the nation—College Park, a single runway of 2,600 feet, at an elevation of 50 feet MSL. It is used mainly by general aviation aircraft. An aviation museum is located there.

(No photos have ever been found for this stop.)

References

Organizations
National Air and Space Museum (Smithsonian)
Library of Congress
National Archives
National Geographic
Martin Luther King Jr. Memorial Library
Washington Navy Yard, Archives
United States Navy
United States Air Force
Pentagon

People

Roger Thiel	Paul E. Garber
Donald Engen	Nel MacCracken
Richard Hall	Russell Quackenbush
Harold & Leona Nielsen	
Frances & Leonard Wood	
Eline Nikkels Cassagneres	
Johns Hopkins University	

Stop #76
Baltimore, Maryland

Capsule History of City

Baltimore, a large port city, is located on the Patapsco River, about two-thirds of the way up the Chesapeake Bay, in the north-central part of the state of Maryland. It is the only American port with two links to the Atlantic Ocean, the Chesapeake-Delaware Canal to the north and the Chesapeake Capes to the south.

The Susquehanna Indians were the first people living in the area. The first white settlers came in 1661. The city of Baltimore was founded in 1729 by an act of the Provincial Assembly and incorporated in 1797. This new place was named in honor of the Lords Baltimore, the family that controlled the colony of Maryland.

101 feet MSL.

October 18–19, 1927
(Tuesday and Wednesday)

Baltimore's airport in 1927 was known as Logan Field, located in the town of Dundalk, southeast of the center of the city. It was operated by Third Corps Air Office and the Maryland National Guard, leased from the Flying Club of Baltimore. There was a low overcast and heavy rain all day long on the day Lindbergh flew into Baltimore. It was two days after the closing of the Baltimore & Ohio Railroad's successful Fair of the Iron Horse at Halethorpe. The event drew people from all over the world. It was a celebration of the birth of the B. & O. but also the railroad industry.

Lindbergh standing with local officials in front of the NYP on Logan Field. UNIVERSITY OF MARYLAND

There were one thousand brave souls already on the field awaiting Lindbergh's arrival, and five hundred National Guardsmen were on hand to guard both airplanes in a special fenced enclosure near Hangar 1 in the south end of the field.

Lindbergh flew over the financial district downtown, and then over some of the outlying neighborhoods, turning east toward Logan Field in Dundalk. He landed at precisely 2:00 p.m.

After shutting down he was greeted by Mayor William F. Broening, who gave the flyer a yellow slicker as they made ready to climb into an open touring car to head to the Baltimore Stadium. Also there to greet him were W. Frank Roberts, general manager of Bethlehem Steel and chairman of the reception committee, Roland Marchan, and Frederick W. Huber. The commander of the 3rd Corps Army Area, Maj. Gen. Douglas MacArthur, was also present.

There were some 25,000 people along the auto route to the stadium. The entourage en-

circled the War Memorial and the City Hall, and then made its way to the stadium.

At the stadium he was officially welcomed by Gov. Albert C. Ritchie and other officials of the city and state. There was no "formal" street parade, but word traveled through the crowd with information regarding the route he would most likely take. There were many people standing with umbrellas to see their hero.

Many schoolchildren were already in the stadium with their parents. Crouched by the speakers' stand were twenty Blackfoot Indians, led by Chief Two Guns White Calf. It was estimated that a total of 30,000 people were there as he arrived and was serenaded by the Municipal Band playing "Hands across the Sea."

Lindbergh sat on the speakers' stand to the left of Mayor Broening, along with Police Commissioner Gaither, Chief Inspector Henry, and John Philip Hill, the former representative in Congress.

The flyer gave a short talk expounding on the future of air travel and the development of commercial aviation. He was hailed as the "New Columbus" by Mayor Broening, and soon he and the entourage made their way into town to the Emerson Hotel, which had been provided by

This is the Fairchild FC-2 escort airplane on Logan Field at Baltimore. UNIVERSITY OF MARYLAND

Bromo-Seltzer founder Capt. Isaac E. Emerson.

Lindbergh had a lunch of oyster stew, crackers, and coffee, and at the same time addressed questions from the press. He and his crew then retired to the twelfth-floor suite at the Emerson.

That evening the banquet was held at the Lyric Theatre, attended by 1,200 prominent citizens, the Governor, the Mayor, and some federal officials. In a brief speech Lindbergh said, "Someday soon, thanks to radio beacons and other devices, passenger planes will be winging through the skies by the hundreds." He elaborated further on some of the developments presently underway and planned for the future, and then suggested, "If you citizens of Baltimore expect to keep in the forefront of the coming great air program, you must get behind your state and municipal aviation program."

The next morning the crew slept in and then was driven out to the airport to prepare to leave for the next stop.

Lindbergh took off from Logan Field at 12:05 p.m. and took up a direct heading for Atlantic City. Right after lift-off he flew over the field, then made several circuits around the city, taking a direct easterly heading for Atlantic City. It is not known if he circled any other towns on the way or dropped the canvas bag anywhere during the two-hour flight to the coastal city.

The Fairchild took off shortly after Lindbergh. They had a passenger on board for this short flight, Maj. Clarence M. Young, Chief of the Air Regulations Division of the government's Aeronautics Branch of the Department of Commerce.

Logan Field was closed many years ago. However, there are several airports around the city of Baltimore. The main airport that serves both Baltimore and Washington, D.C., is Baltimore–Washington International, at an elevation of 146 feet MSL. The field has a main runway of 10,502 feet in addition to other runways. It is served by most major domestic airlines as well as international and commuter airlines, some corporate and general aviation and military aircraft. It is located nine miles south of the city.

Martin State Airport, nine miles east, was established originally for the Glenn L. Martin Aircraft Company. It is at an elevation of 22 feet MSL and has a single runway of 6,996 feet. The field serves mainly general aviation aircraft including corporate and National Guard operations.

There are a number of satellite general aviation and private airports around the Baltimore area.

References

Newspapers
  Baltimore Sunday Sun
  Baltimore American
  Sun. Baltimore

Organizations
  University of Maryland College Park
  Museum and Library of Maryland History
  Maryland Historical Society
  Enoch Pratt Free Library
  University of Maryland Baltimore County – Albin O. Kuhn Library and Gallery

People
  Karen Fishman   Les W. Hendrickson
  Morton Kuff   Robert B. Meyer Jr.
  Jacques Kelly   Claire Pula
  George W. Heston

STOP #77
ATLANTIC CITY, NEW JERSEY

CAPSULE HISTORY OF CITY

Atlantic City, New Jersey, a large seaside resort, is located on the Atlantic Ocean on the southeastern coast of the state, about 140 miles south of New York City. The city is built on Absecon Beach, an island about ten miles long and three-quarters of a mile wide. This island is separated from the mainland by a narrow strait and by meadows that lie partly under water during high tide. Atlantic City has a boardwalk along the beach that is seven miles long by sixty feet wide.

The city began as a fishing village in the late 1800s at the north end of Absecon Island and was incorporated in 1854.

10 feet MSL.

OCTOBER 19–21, 1927
(WEDNESDAY THROUGH FRIDAY)

Atlantic City got an early start in aviation because its wide, smooth beach between low and high tide marks made a natural runway for airplanes to take off and land. Such an advantage was not enjoyed by other metropolitan cities.

The term "airport" was coined in Atlantic City to designate its first flying field. Prior to this they were known as aerodromes or landing fields. It was not, however, the first municipally owned flying field. Henry Woodhouse, one of the owners of the field when it was opened on Saturday, May 10, 1919, is claimed by aeronautical men to have coined the word "airport." Newspapermen, however, claim the honor for William B. Dill, then editor of the *Atlantic City Press*. No actual record exists to prove either claim.

The first idea of bombing from the air was supposedly born there when Glenn H. Curtiss, a pilot, during a 1919 air carnival dropped oranges to prove that accurate hits could be made. He dropped the oranges close to the yacht *John E. Mehrer II*, splashing water on the passengers. Later he dropped more fruit within a small circle on the beach. An Army officer said that it showed the day of battleship bombardment of enemy cities was coming to a close.

The first attempt to cross the ocean was made from Atlantic City when polar explorer Walter Wellman launched in the dirigible *America*, but a storm forced him down and the idea was abandoned.

The first use of a rocket plane was demonstrated there when William G. Swann, a local stunt flyer, flew the first rocket-powered glider in history from Steel Pier. A single rocket was used, and he made a perfect landing on the beach. It became a Pier attraction.

On Saturday, July 8, 1922, the city purchased the airport from private owners, and the athletic field created there was named for Edward L. Bader, then mayor of the resort. It has been impractical to enlarge this airport because it is surrounded by the inland waterway and a state highway.

So it was in 1927 that Bader Field was the only airport available for Lindbergh to land on in this latter part of his goodwill tour. The field still exists on the same site. It was listed at that time in the American Aircraft Directory as being only 900 feet square.

Because Bader Field was on the short side for an airport, both airplanes had to be careful when approaching and setting up for their landing, especially the Fairchild with its heavy load. Also the recent rain had left the ground soft and muddy.

At about 1:30 p.m. the Fairchild arrived, and with Phil Love piloting, made a short approach and full stall landing without nosing over, much to the delight of his passengers, Keyhoe, Maidment and Clarence N. Young.

Men from the Atlantic City Police Department guard the NYP on Bader Field, where it was tied down. ATLANTIC CITY FREE PUBLIC LIBRARY

Flying under a gray overcast with some rain, Lindbergh circled over the city and along the beach area, then over the airport to survey the situation.

Guards were stationed at the end of the runway. In case he ran long they could grab the wing tips and struts to keep it from rolling into muddy ground at the end. He made a very low pass to check the surface, and at that time signaled the guards to step back away from the runway in case he ground-looped so he would not hit any of them. He made several false attempts to land, each time a bit slower than the last. Then he climbed up to 500 feet, circled the field again, and came in on a long, flat glide. One could hear a pin drop as it appeared that "this was it!" He had the NYP quite slowed up, with the engine barely turning over, as he passed over a bordering fence and settled down smoothly, with 100 feet to spare. A ten-year flying veteran remarked, "I never saw anything like that before. That, gentlemen, was a landing!"

After landing and taxiing to a stop, Lindbergh climbed out of the cockpit and was greeted by Mayor Anthony M. Ruffu and other reception officials. He was then escorted over to the balcony of a flying club house, where he gave a short speech, and then climbed into the Mayor's car to ride into town.

The NYP and Fairchild were placed immediately in a hangar to be put on display until their departure on Friday. Heavily patrolled by local police, firemen, National Guard and Morris Guards, space at the airport was roped off so that thousands of the local people could view the planes.

In his brief talk at the field, Lindbergh said, "Of course no one can accurately forecast the final effects of aviation upon the world. We can go ahead a few years and show the general trend beyond that, but no one can tell just how far flying will take us.

"It will have a great effect just as have steamships, railroads and automobiles. But I believe the change will come more quickly because the airplane has developed more rapidly. In less than twenty-five years it has grown from the crudest experimental stage to a safe, reliable carrier with many conveniences and comforts.

"The best basis for estimating the future is to look at the present. You can see that Europe seems to have everything its own way in regard to commercial lines. On many of these lines they are using large multi-engine cabin ships, equipped as comfortably as Pullman cars. They run on regular schedules and are used by travelers just as we use our own trains in the United States."

The group left the airport in several cars and drove over a pontoon bridge over the Inside Thorofare (inland waterway) to the Ritz-Carlton Hotel. During the drive into town, they did a tour of the city and the famous Boardwalk, and then went to City Hall to have a conference with the Mayor and the reception committee. From there they went to the hotel where Lindbergh held a short press conference. Then he and his crew retired to their hotel suite for some rest.

In the evening the banquet was held at the Hotel Chelsea. There were nine hundred of the city's important business officials and their wives present. The banquet was toasted by Congressman Bacharach. The only other address on aeronautics was by Clarence M. Young, until Lindbergh was introduced. Lindbergh gave his usual talk, first touching on the reason for the goodwill tour and the development of commercial aviation.

Then he said, "We do not know the exact future of aviation, all we know is that it is in a rapidly developing stage, and it is on the way to become one of the chief industries. The air mail lines have already been in existence some years, and it is possible now to transport mail from New York to San Francisco in a day and a half.

"It will not be long when regular passenger lines will be operating over the air mail routes. In order to make them safe, adequate airports must be established in the most important cities.

"Atlantic City should have a commodious and well-equipped airport. It would be a valuable asset to your city, which entertains millions of visitors, to have a passenger air line carrying visitors from the large centers of population to the seashore.

"At the present time an aviator has great difficulty in making successful landings at the field. The runways should be at least

2500 feet long, but are only about 1000 feet. This alone is a great handicap, but can no doubt be remedied to some extent by enlarging the present site of the field. We must build primarily for safety. The possibility of anyone but a skilled pilot operating a plane does not seem practicable, at least during the present time. Before such changes can be made aviation must be put on a sound foundation, with the public wholly back of it."

Thursday was set aside as a rest day for the flyers. They relaxed and spent time working out the navigation for the remainder of the trip. They did, however, manage to use a car provided by the mayor to tour around the famous resort city.

Lindbergh left Atlantic City on Friday, taking off at 12:10 p.m., and flew first over Mays Landing, a few miles northwest of the city, and from there again northwest to Salem, New Jersey. He dropped the canvas bag message on both of those towns. Fighting a strong west headwind, he flew from Salem northwest to Wilmington, Delaware, his next stop.

Today Bader Field is still on the same location at an elevation of 9 feet MSL. It has two runways, one of which is 2,830 feet long. It serves mainly general aviation and some corporate aircraft. This historically significant airport, unfortunately, has had some serious difficulties over the years and has been fighting for survival.

Nine miles northwest of the city, in the town of Pomona, is the main airport, Atlantic City International, at an elevation of 76 feet MSL. It has two runways, the longer of which is 10,000 feet.

The Federal Aviation Administration Technical Center is located on Atlantic City International Airport. It is a center of engineering, evaluation and research and development services for the industry.

References

Newspapers
  Atlantic City Daily Evening Union
  Pleasantville Press
  Daily Record – Morristown, New Jersey
  The Press – Atlantic City
  Atlantic City Daily Press
  The Sunday Gazette – Atlantic City

Organizations
  Newark Public Library
  New Jersey Historical Society
  Atlantic County Historical Society
  Atlantic City Free Public Library
  Aviation Hall of Fame of New Jersey

Publications
  The Book of the Boardwalk and *The Atlantic City Story*, by Frank M. Butler, 1952, The 1954 Association, Inc.

People
  Irene Brostow   H. V. Pat Reilly
  Cheryl Turkington   Terry Auchard
  Robert Blackwell   Alice Critchley
  Elizabeth Ehrhardt   Elsa Meyers
  Bill B. Nash   Marie E. Boyd

Stop #78

WILMINGTON, DELAWARE

Capsule History of City

Wilmington, Delaware, the largest city in this small state, is located on high ground next to the Delaware River in the northern section of the state. At this point the Delaware River receives the waters of Brandywine Creek and the Christina River. The city is 27 miles southwest of Philadelphia, Pennsylvania.

The first settlement on the site was known as Fort Christina. The city was founded in 1638 under the direction of Peter Minuit and his people from Swedish Colonists. In 1655 the Dutch, under Peter Styvesant, took possession of the land there and renamed it Altena. In 1664 the site was taken over by the British and the name was changed to Willington in 1731, in honor of Thomas Willing, the man who laid out the town. The name became Wilmington in 1739 when it incorporated as a borough.

It is the home of world famous E. I. Du Pont de Nemours and Company, started in 1802 by Eleuthere Irenee du Pont de Nemours as a powder mill.

135 feet MSL.

October 21–22, 1927
(Friday and Saturday)

As near as can be determined, about 1924, a private airstrip was established by Henry Berlin du Pont. It consisted of about forty-five acres and had one hangar. In April 1926 the property was transferred by William and Anne du Pont to the Delaware Land Development Company (a holding company) established by the du Pont family. This change was made to eliminate legal repercussions, since Henry's flying friends would often fly in to visit.

That original hangar was painted and the rest of the field was spruced up for the arrival of Lindbergh.

To control the thousands of people awaiting his arrival, the Delaware National Guard, the State Police, and the local police were called in. Soldiers from Fort du Pont had established their camp in the rear of the hangar and were preparing their midday lunch. The wind sock on top of a pole on the ridge of the hangar indicated a strong west wind, which would help Lindbergh and the Fairchild to land on this short runway.

Soon the NYP appeared over the city, circling several times before heading northwest to fly over du Pont Field. Lindbergh arrived over the field at 1:55 p.m., circled several times, making a low pass to check the short runway. The NYP came in for a landing into a northwest

wind at 2:00 p.m. It was a cool and pleasant day with a 25 or 30 mph wind, which helped him slow down for the soft and wet runway.

He was met by Milburn Kusterer, Frank V. du Pont, the chairman of the reception committee, Governor Robert P. Robinson, Mayor George W. K. Forrest, Henry Berlin du Pont, Gerrish Gassaway and others.

The Fairchild, its wings folded, had been placed in the hangar. The NYP was in a fenced area in front of the hangar, visible to the public and available for photos.

On this same day the annual session of the forty-six Kiwanis Clubs of the Capital District was opened in the Barry Room of the Hotel du Pont Biltmore. Wilmington was overflowing with humanity on this day, and some people more than likely had a difficult decision to make as to which event they wished to attend. Per-

Above: Henry B. du Pont with Lindbergh in front of the NYP at Dupont Field near Wilmington, Delaware, October 21st. COURTESY HAGLEY MUSEUM AND LIBRARY

At left: In the parade Lindbergh is in the back seat next to Governor Robinson. Seated in front were Mayor Forrest and Frank du Pont. Next to the driver is Mr. Kusterer, advance man for the tour.
LEO B. KIMBALL COLLECTION

haps many of them split up their time between Kiwanis and Lindbergh.

An attractive sport model touring car of dull gray was provided for Lindbergh, who rode in the back seat with the Governor. Also in the car, seated in front of Lindbergh, were Mayor Forrest and Frank V. du Pont, while Mr. Kusterer rode next to the driver. There were six cars in the motorcade, which made its way out of the airport and headed toward town and the Baynard Stadium, still in existence. There were fifteen to twenty thousand people on the field to greet the flyer.

Accompanied by motorcycle police, the cavalcade traveled at eight miles per hour, out on Center Road to Kennett Pike and into town.

Before Lindbergh's arrival the stadium was filled to capacity with children and their parents. One child in the bleachers spied an approaching auto and cried, "Here's Lindy." Immediately, one whole section of the bleachers was emptied and a swarm of children ran to meet the approaching car. They found out their mistake, however, and surged back into their seats. It was not Lindbergh yet.

At the stadium Lindbergh was presented and gave his usual promotional aviation speech and was given rousing applause. Then he and the Mayor and the Governor left the area, and the parade made its way into the city to the du Pont Biltmore Hotel, where he held a press conference and was escorted to their suite of rooms for some rest.

In the evening the banquet was held at the same hotel, where seven hundred people had assembled, including many of the local and prominent business people and city and state officials.

In Lindbergh's presentation he said that the du Pont field was not long enough for commercial aircraft to make landings and take-offs. It should have at least 2,500-foot runways, he said. Then he continued to elaborate on the future of aviation: the need for safety improvements for navigation, the building of larger airports, and the establishing of airways around the country.

After the banquet Lindbergh was presented to the Kiwanis Capital District dinner-dance in the ballroom of the hotel, before retiring to his room. He was not asked to give a talk.

Also after the banquet six Boy Scouts were escorted up to Lindbergh's room. They were there to present him with a model they had made of the NYP. The boys were Richard Breneman, Harry Essig, William Schreckengust, Charles MacLay, Robert Hammaker, and Stanley Caplan. They were accompanied by Winfield H. Lobam, a member of the faculty of Camp Cartin

Lindbergh with Miss Emily Bissell as she presented him with the special packet of Christmas Seals to be delivered to Philadelphia, October 22nd. GEORGE FREBERT

The NYP in front of the newly painted du Pont hangar, where it was refueled by what was to become the well-known Atlantic Aviation of today.
CHRISTOPHER J. PRATT, V.P.
ATLANTIC AVIATION

Junior High School in Harrisburg, where the model was made.

While in Wilmington Lindbergh was signed up for membership in the local chapter of the Red Cross. Miss Lillian Chrichton, a popular member of the younger set in the city, got his signature. This took place in the hotel where the unit had a booth, conducting their annual roll call campaign. It was by special arrangement through the Guggenheim Corporation that the flyer was given this membership.

The next day he was asked to carry on the NYP a special packet of Christmas Seal stickers to Philadelphia. Prominent Delaware resident Emily Perkins Bissell of Wilmington had introduced the original Christmas Seal in the United States in 1907 to raise money for a tuberculosis clinic. Miss Bissell handed the packet to Lindbergh and asked if he would present them to Mrs. George Horace Lorimer, a member of Philadelphia Mayor Kendrick's reception committee, to which he agreed.

Lindbergh took off at 12:55 p.m., circled the field several times, then flew over the city again as a farewell to everyone. He then headed north toward Philadelphia. On his way he flew over Chester, Pennsylvania, northwest to Media, circling the great city before heading southeast toward the Philadelphia Airport.

Today the du Pont Field is no longer there. In its place one can find Barley Mill Plaza, a group of professional buildings, just west of Mount Olive Cemetery and south of the railroad tracks, near the intersection of Lancaster Pike (Route 48) and Center Road (Route 141).

Today Wilmington's main airport is the New Castle County Airport. It is at an elevation of 79 feet MSL and has three runways, the longest of which is 7,181 feet. It is located four miles south of the city along Interstate 95. It serves some major airlines, commuters, corporate and general aviation, and National Guard aircraft.

References

Newspapers
Wilmington Morning News
Evening Journal
Sunday Morning Star
Every Evening

Organizations
Wilmington Library
Hagley Museum and Library – Manuscripts & Archives Department
Dover Litho Printing Company
Atlantic Aviation Corporation
Eleutherian Mills Historical Library

Publications
Delaware Aviation History, by George J. Frebert and Debbie Haskell (Dover, Dela.: Dover Litho Printing Company).
Professional Pilot Magazine – Washington, D.C.

People

Renee Gimski	Marge McNinch
George Frebert	Christopher J. Pratt
Betty-Bright P. Low	Philip Rice
Jon M. Williams	

STOP #79
PHILADELPHIA, PENNSYLVANIA

CAPSULE HISTORY OF CITY

Known as the "birthplace of the United States," Philadelphia, Pennsylvania, is located at the southeastern tip of the state. It is on the western and northern side of the Delaware River, linking it with the Atlantic Ocean. The smaller Schuykill River winds through the central portion of the city into the Delaware River.

This city is also known as the "City of Brotherly Love." The name Philadelphia means "brotherly love" in Greek.

William Penn, an English Quaker, founded this city, also known as Quaker City, in 1682. The city is the home of the original Declaration of Independence and the United States Constitution. Thomas Holme, a surveyor, laid out the site and called it "greene countrie towns". Therefore it became one of the first cities in the country that was built according to plan. It was the

nation's capital during most of the Revolutionary War. Then the capital was moved from this great city to Washington, D.C. in 1800.
100 feet MSL.

OCTOBER 22–23, 1927
(SATURDAY AND SUNDAY)

The site in South Philadelphia of the Philadelphia Municipal Airport, as it was then known, was deeded or obtained by conversion of city property and condemnation of additional ground. It was managed by a Board of Control, representing the city, State of Pennsylvania National Guard, and the concessionaire.

The airport at that time was reachable by Island Avenue and Tinicum Avenue, near 83rd Street, which is the northeastern area of the present Philadelphia International Airport.

There were five hundred policemen under the command of William Connelly, and hundreds more National Guard troops of the 103rd Aerial Squadron on the day of Lindbergh's arrival. A barbed-wire enclosure had been erected outside one of the Guard hangars, where the NYP could be parked so the public could see it and take pictures. In the evening, the NYP, along with the Fairchild, was rolled into the hangar.

At about 1:45 p.m. Lindbergh appeared over the business district of this large city, circling over the buildings at a very low altitude, probably less than five hundred feet, according to reports. The weather at this time was somewhat cloudy but dry. Soon he came over the airport and circled several times, made a low pass, and came around for a smooth landing at precisely 2:00.

He taxied into the wire enclosure, where the Fairchild had already been placed, having landed thirty minutes earlier. After shutting down and climbing out of the NYP, Lindbergh was met by Director of Public Safety George Elliott, who was acting as mayor for Mayor W. Freeland Kendrick, who was under orders by his doctor to be confined to his home to nurse a bronchial cold.

The first order of business was for Lindbergh to pass along the box of Christmas Seals that he had carried from Wilmington for Emily Bissell to Mrs. George Horace Lorimer and her committee in charge of the sale of the seals.

A few minutes later he was asked to raise a new flag over the airport, officially dedicating the new and still uncompleted field.

Lindbergh was then escorted into a waiting car to be driven along a parade route through thousands of people, to the Municipal Stadium for the official welcoming ceremony. This was on the site where the present-day Veterans Stadium is located at the south end of Broad Street.

He was welcomed by thousands of people,

The *Spirit of St. Louis* in front of the National Guard Hangar at the Philadelphia Municipal Airport in South Philadelphia. Lindbergh had just landed and can be seen as he left the airplane to be welcomed. CASSAGNERES COLLECTION

many of whom were children and their parents. The entourage drove into the stadium, and there was a parade around the track, led by many Boy Scouts with American flags. By this time the sun was shining brightly.

He was introduced to the audience and started his usual presentation on aviation development.

Toward the end of his speech he said, "We need your cooperation and backing for the program you have inaugurated, if you want to keep Philadelphia in the foreground of aviation. Your interest in the airport of Philadelphia is everything that makes for the support of aeronautics and generally must be continued and intensified.

"I thank you sincerely for the reception that has come to me in Philadelphia and I ask that you shall keep alive your interest in aviation for Philadelphia's sake as well as for the development of this new factor in civilization."

From the stadium he was driven to Independence Hall in Independence Square. Here he reverently laid flowers at the base of the Liberty Bell, symbol of the Spirit of America.

From there he was again driven through the streets of the city, up Broad Street to the Academy of Music, where he greeted two thousand Boy Scouts who filled the auditorium. Because he was running behind schedule he was unable to give a speech there, although he was introduced by director Elliott.

At the request of the Mayor, Lindbergh made a last-minute stop to visit with children at the Philadelphia Home for Incurables. Then the entourage went to visit with the war veterans at the Naval Hospital, and from there to his ninth-floor suite at the Bellevue-Stratford Hotel for a brief meeting with the press and some rest.

At the banquet that evening, held in the Bellevue-Stratford auditorium, he was introduced and immediately started into his regular speech.

The address was somewhat brief and to the point. "During the last few years aviation has progressed so rapidly that it is difficult to keep up with it. The first flight was made two decades ago, and it attracted more skepticism than it did admiration.

"It was beyond the conception of the average man or woman at that time that someone had actually taken off and had remained aloft in a heavier-than-air machine for a matter of a few minutes. It seemed inconceivable to the average mind that such a thing could be possible.

"Wilbur and Orville Wright, America's pioneers in the original development of aviation, soon convinced a doubting world that the seemingly impossible had been accomplished. However, exhibition flights of from five to ten minutes, principally at county fairs, were the order of the day in that early phase of aviation. Some flights often ended in disaster."

Then he went into the development of aircraft for both the war effort as well as the later air mail service and other advancements in the industry.

He again urged the city of Philadelphia, as other American cities, to further develop and improve the present airport and to enlarge the runways. However, he felt that the airport was a bit far from the business district of the city, and that it should be moved to a closer location.

His closing statements centered on other future developments in aviation, air travel, the building of airports, and engineering and safety.

After the banquet he did not get directly to bed, as his schedule had called for at all of the previous stops. He was asked to attend another function. This time he went to the Penn Athletic Club, where they held a "smoker." Here he was presented with a solid gold plaque, emblematic of the life membership in the club. Attending this gathering was another trans-Atlantic flyer, Clarence Chamberlin, who came there from New York for this special occasion. After the presentation there was vaudeville and musical entertainment.

This was the last official city on the United States goodwill tour that Lindbergh would visit. He would not have to give any more speeches until the next goodwill flight, "Below the Border," beginning in December.

The next morning Lindbergh in the NYP and his crew in the Fairchild took off from Philadelphia. Lindbergh circled the field several times with a low pass, then headed over the city, circling the downtown area a few times before heading on a north-northwest direction to fly

over Trenton, New Jersey. He dropped the canvas bag message while circling the capital city. From there he took a direct heading northeast to New York City, heading east to Mitchel Field on Long Island.

Today the Philadelphia Municipal Airport, now known as the Philadelphia International Airport, is still located on the same site as it was in 1927. It is at an elevation of 22 feet MSL and has three runways, the longest of which is 10,499 feet. Five miles southwest of the city business district, it serves all major domestic as well as international airlines including corporate and general aviation aircraft.

Ten miles northeast of the city is the Northeast Philadelphia Airport at an elevation of 121 feet MSL with two runways, the longer being 7,000 feet. It caters mainly to general and corporate aviation.

Three miles north-northwest of the city is Wings Field at an elevation of 301 feet MSL with a single runway of 2,625 feet. One of the oldest in the area, it is strictly a general aviation airport.

Just on the edge of the Class B airspace is the well-known old Willow Grove NAS JRB Airport with its single 8,002-foot-long runway.

References

Newspapers
Philadelphia Inquirer
Evening Journal – Wilmington, Delaware

Publication
Aircraft Year Book, 1927 (New York: Aeronautical Chamber of Commerce of America), p. 107.

People
Stephan Pitcairn	Charles Henry
Leonard W. Ziemek	Harry P. Mutter
Joseph N. Lunardi – St. Joseph University	
Milton Sheppard	

Stop #80
Long Island, New York
"Mitchel Field"

Capsule History of City

Mitchel Field was located in Mineola, on Long Island in New York State, and was operated by the U.S. Army in 1927. It was located two miles northeast of the Hempstead Reservoir and about fifteen miles east of New York City.

October 23–25, 1927
(Sunday through Tuesday)

The Fairchild had already arrived on the field thirty minutes earlier, when Lindbergh was seen approaching. He circled several times and came in for a landing at precisely 2:00 p.m.

There were an estimated two thousand people on the field to greet the flyer and to see him make the last landing of his tour of the United States. Harry F. Guggenheim, President of the Guggenheim Fund for the Promotion of Aeronautics, sponsor of the flight, was one of those people.

Lindbergh taxied up to one of the hangars which was used for visiting airplanes, shut her down, and stepped out of the cockpit to a group of press people. When asked what his future plans were now he replied, "To drop out of the public view for a while." Then he was asked if he would enter into politics or join the Department of Commerce, to which he replied, "Absolutely not. You can make that as definite as you like. I have no intentions of doing that. When I know myself what I'm going to do, I'll announce it."

He continued when asked about how he felt, "I never felt better in my life. No, banquet food didn't seem to do me any harm."

When asked about the airplane, Lindbergh said, "The *Spirit of St. Louis* is in fine shape. It gives more revolutions per minute now than when it was new. But this looks like a good time to do it so I'm going to have it completely overhauled. That's never been done since it was built, you know. No, it isn't destined for a museum yet. Eventually, but not now."

He did not comment on the success of the tour, but suggested that other people would have to. In a statement by Guggenheim, William P. MacCracken and Harry S. New, postmaster-general, they said how the tour had stimulated interest in flying, in the air mail, and in construction of airports. That was the end of the interview with the press.

From here Lindbergh was driven to the home of Harry Guggenheim out at Falaise, at Sands Point on Long Island, where he spent time vacationing and writing his book, *WE*.

On October 25th, Tuesday, he flew the NYP from Mitchel Field over the city of New York directly to Teterboro Airport, to leave it with the Wright Aeronautical Company for servicing. He had as his passenger for the forty-minute flight Milburn Kusterer, the advance man, whose job had just ended. It was Kusterer's first ride in the famous airplane.

Mitchel Field is still partly there, but not as an airport. Only some of the hangars are there, and they make up the Cradle of Aviation Museum, which has a fine collection of historic aircraft and other related memorabilia and a library.

For continuation of the NYP's life at Teterboro, see chapter 3, "The Teterboro Story."

Some time after the tour ended, Donald Keyhoe asked Lindbergh when he planned to bring the NYP to the Smithsonian. Lindbergh replied, "I'm not going to let anyone know when I bring it. In fact, I don't know myself. But I think I'll come in when they aren't expecting me."

When suggested by Keyhoe that it might be a bit hard to give up the old ship, Lindbergh said, "It's just as good as ever. I could take it out and make a lot more jumps with it—but I guess it belongs to the country."

An aerial view of Mitchel Field (in foreground) with Curtiss and Roosevelt Fields in the background, August 3, 1927. MRS. ELLEN W. DIOGUARDI

The final stop, and Lindbergh shown taxiing the NYP just after landing at Mitchel Field on October 25th. This appears to be the last photo taken of the NYP on the U.S. Tour. LEO B. KIMBALL COLLECTION

Lindbergh is shown here at Mitchel Field with Commanding Officer, Brigadier General Benjamin D. Foulois, soon after Lindbergh had landed. MRS. ELLEN W. DIOGUARDI

𝔗𝔥𝔢 𝔑𝔞𝔱𝔦𝔬𝔫𝔞𝔩 𝔊𝔢𝔬𝔤𝔯𝔞𝔭𝔥𝔦𝔠 𝔖𝔬𝔠𝔦𝔢𝔱𝔶

PROGRAM

8:00 P. M. MUSIC BY THE UNITED STATES ARMY BAND

  March—"Heroes of the Air"........*Clark*
  Selection from "Blossom Time"....*Romberg*
  "Brazilian Caprice" ....*Burks*
  March—"Young Veterans".........*Frazee*

8:35 COLONEL CHARLES A. LINDBERGH, MRS. EVANGELINE LINDBERGH AND OFFICIAL PARTY enter

8:45 THE PRESIDENT OF THE UNITED STATES AND MRS. COOLIDGE ARRIVE

DR. GILBERT GROSVENOR, President of The National Geographic Society, presiding

Presentation of the Hubbard Medal of The National Geographic Society to Colonel Lindbergh by
  THE PRESIDENT OF THE UNITED STATES

COLONEL CHARLES A. LINDBERGH responds

The Assistant Secretary of Commerce for Aëronautics, HON. WILLIAM P. MACCRACKEN

Motion pictures epitomizing the epochal achievements of Aviation from the first flights of Orville and Wilbur Wright to the present, collected and presented through the courtesy of Paramount-Famous-Lasky Corporation.

On the platform are:
THE PRESIDENT OF THE UNITED STATES AND MRS. COOLIDGE
COLONEL CHARLES A. LINDBERGH
MRS. EVANGELINE LINDBERGH
HON. WILLIAM P. MACCRACKEN
Assistant Secretary of Commerce for Aëronautics
HON. EVERETT SANDERS
Secretary to the President of the United States
DR. GILBERT GROSVENOR
President of The National Geographic Society
DR. JOHN OLIVER LA GORCE
Vice-President of The National Geographic Society

MR. BERT ACOSTA	LIEUT. ALBERT HEGENBERGER
MR. BERNDT BALCHEN	MR. MARTIN JENSEN
MR. WILLIAM S. BROCK	MR. CHARLES LEVINE
MR. EMORY BRONTE	LIEUT. LESTER MAITLAND
MR. CLARENCE CHAMBERLIN	LIEUT. GEORGE NOVILLE
MISS RUTH ELDER	MR. EDWARD P. SCHLEE
MR. ARTHUR GOEBEL	MR. PAUL SCHLUTER
MR. HARRY F. GUGGENHEIM	LIEUT. ERNEST L. SMITH
MR. GEORGE HALDEMAN	DR. ORVILLE WRIGHT

November 14, 1927

Although there was room for only 6,000 National Geographic Society members at the ceremonies, over 30,000 requested tickets. Here they are gathered before the doors of the headquarters on Sixteenth Street long before the actual distribution of tickets began.

President Coolidge addresses the National Geographic Society on Colonel Lindbergh's achievements.

President Coolidge presented the National Geographic Society's highest award, the Hubbard Medal, to Colonel Lindbergh before 6,000 members in the Washington Auditorium. The medal bears the following inscription: "Awarded by the National Geographic Society to Charles A. Lindbergh for his heroic service to the science of aviation by his solitary flight from New York to Paris, May 20-21, 1927."

Chapter Five
South of the Border
Introduction

Charles Lindbergh had flown across the Atlantic Ocean in the NYP, connecting two continents. He had flown an impressive "goodwill tour" of the United States in the NYP, again putting air travel and aviation in general on the map. This combination of man and machine had boosted air travel beyond all expectations, worldwide, and was now going to embark on yet another "goodwill" flight.

Young Lindbergh, so mature for his age, had carefully thought out his plan for promoting aviation and working it into modern transportation, to be accepted by the general public. He felt that this development would or could be made in three stages. The first stage would be to fly within the continents. The second stage would be to fly between continents, and the third stage to cross oceans from hemisphere to hemisphere. He also felt that aviation would bring the remotest corner of the known world within a few hours of a metropolis, making any geographical location on earth accessible to mankind.

Lindbergh predicted that one could fly comfortably over tropical equatorial jungles as well as the cold and inhospitable Arctic. Additionally, he predicted that airplanes would fly for thousands of miles and carry many passengers for a cost of only a bit more than rail travel.

At the end of the goodwill tour of the United States in the fall of 1927, Lindbergh was introduced to the new U.S. Ambassador to Mexico, Dwight W. Morrow, a New York financier and philanthropist. Morrow had been appointed by United States President Calvin Coolidge to head a board to investigate the conditions of American aviation.

Morrow had developed a high respect for this young flyer, and valued the latter's opinion and suggestions. Lindbergh was invited to the Ambassador's apartment at 4 East 66th Street in New York City for a conference. It was at this meeting that Morrow invited him to fly the NYP to Mexico City. In a country where few railroads existed, the airplane could easily be the only feasible means of transportation over rough terrain and for long distances.

Morrow's suggestion was made in response to an invitation by Mexican President Plutarco Elias Calles. The rest of the south of the border flights and visits were made in response to invitations by the governments of the countries Lindbergh visited.

Lindbergh obviously was impressed with Morrow's insight. This could be a world advertisement of the possibilities of commercial air travel. This would give him the opportunity to accomplish several objectives on a single flight. This could develop good political friendship toward the country of Mexico, but more importantly the flyer could demonstrate even more clearly the capabilities of the then "modern" aircraft and air travel. This would not be a flight that would be considered a "stunt."

His navigation and routing between cities and countries was planned just as a commercial flight might have been planned. The routes could be practically identical to the routes that would have been flown for commercial purposes. Aviation would receive publicity that it did not have to pay for, and for which it would never be able to pay.

After his visit to Mexico City he could continue south to Central and South America to help link together the continents of the Western Hemisphere. This would give aviation and air travel greater political significance.

He strongly felt that he could fly from Washington, D.C., nonstop to Mexico City, thus linking the two nations' capitals for further political significance. Then he planned to continue connecting the nations' capitals by flying on south to Guatemala, British Honduras (Belize), Honduras, Nicaragua, Costa Rica, Panama and the Canal Zone, Columbia, Venezuela, the U.S. Virgin Islands, Puerto Rico, the Dominican Republic, Haiti and Cuba, before returning to the United States.

Date	Time Hrs. Min	Pass.	Pass.	Total Flights	Total Passengers	Total Time Hrs. Min	Types				Chute Drops Total
"13	27:15	1	0	7429	6108	2229:30	NYP BOLLING TO MEXICO CITY				
"14											
"16	1:35	6	5	7435	6113	2231:05	Morane Monoplane (Gnome eng.)				
"20	2:15	8	27	7443	6140	2233:20	Fairchild F.C.2.				
"21	:45	3	2	7446	6142	2235:05	NYP - Mexican biplane (B.M.W. 160 H.P. eng.) LOCAL				
"22	1:15	4	0	7450	6142	2235:20	NYP LOCAL				
"26	1:00	4	9	7454	6151	2236:20	Ford Tri-Motor (J.S.C.?)				

1927 Date	Time Hrs. Min	Pass.	Pass.	Total Flights	Total Pass-engers	Total Time Hrs. Min	Types				Chute Drops Total
Dec. 28	7:05	1	0	7455	6151	2243:25	N.Y.P. MEXICO CITY - GUATAMALA CITY				17
"30	3:20	1	0	7456	6151	2246:45	N.Y.P. GUATAMALA CITY - BELIZE				

////////// 1928 //////////

Jan.1	2:50	1	0	7457	6151	2249:35	NYP BELIZE TO SAN SALVADOR				
"3	2:05	1	0	7458	6151	2251:40	NYP SAN SALVADOR - HONDURAS				
"5	2:35	1	0	7459	6151	2254:15	NYP HONDURAS - NICARAGUA				
"7	3:25	1	0	7460	6151	2257:40	NYP NICARAGUA - COSTA RICA				
"9	4:05	1	0	7461	6151	2261:45	NYP COSTA RICA - PANAMA CITY				
"10	1:05	4	3	7465	6154	2262:50	P.W.9., - T.M.0-6				
"12	:45	1	0	7466	6154	2263:35	NYP PANAMA CITY - FRANCE FLD. COLON, C.Z.				
"13	2:30	3	0	7469	6154	2266:05	P.W.9.C.				
"14	2:00	1	0	7470	6154	2268:05	P.W.9.C.				
"20	3:10	3	0	7473	6154	2271:15	P.W.9.C.				
"22	1:15	1	0	7474	6154	2272:30	NYP TEST LOCAL 1:15				
"24	1:00	1	1	7475	6154	2273:30	Loening Amphibian				
"25	1:20	1	1	7476	6155	2274:50	Loening Amphibian				
"26	4:55	4	9	7480	6164	2279:45	T.M.0.6 - Douglass Transport - NYP C.Z. TO CARTAGENA, COLUMBIA				

1928 Date	Time Hrs. Min	Pass.	Pass.	Total Flights	Total Passengers	Total Time Hrs. Min	Types	CARTAGENA TO BOGOTA			Chute Drops Total
Jan 27	6:15	2	0	7482	6164	2286:00	Sikorsky Amphibian (2-25 eng's) - NYP				1
"28	:20	2	2	7484	6166	2286:20	Swiss training plane 150 Hisso eng.				
"29	10:50	1	0	7485	6166	2297:10	NYP.				
"31	10:15	1	0	7486	6166	2307:25	NYP CARACAS TO ST. THOMAS, V.I.				
Feb.2	2:10	1	0	7487	6166	2309:35	NYP ST. THOMAS TO PORTO RICO				
"4	3:50	1	0	7488	6166	2313:25	NYP PORTO RICO -				
"6	3:30	1	0	7489	6166	2316:35	NYP SANTO DOMINGO - HAITI				
"8	9:20	1	0	7490	6166	2326:15	NYP HAITI - HAVANA, CUBA				
"10	:20	1	4	7491	6170	2326:35	Fairchild F.C.2.				
"11	:50	3	33	7494	6203	2327:25	Ford Tri-motor.				
"12	2:00	9	81	7503	6284	2329:25	Fokker Tri-motor.				
"13	15:35	1	0	7504	6284	2345:00	N.Y.P. HAVANA, CUBA - ST. LOUIS, MO.				
"14	3:00	1	0	7505	6284	2348:00	NYP ST. LOUIS - LOCAL				

Original pilot's log of the South American leg of the tour.

Instead of planning his flights in ideal weather conditions, as he had done for the Paris flight, he chose to attempt to fly, at the beginning of the trip, through a long December night on the Washington to Mexico City leg. He would schedule his ETAs in advance (usually 2 p.m.), and attempt to hold to that schedule regardless of severe weather as though he were once again on a routine mail flight between St. Louis and Chicago.

No wonder the audiences he spoke to, through translators, were fascinated by his prophesies about the future of air travel.

It was during this visit to Mexico's capital that he met Anne Morrow, daughter of the Ambassador, whom he eventually married.

Some older readers will remember his piloting those Pan American Airways Sikorsky S-38 flying boats developing new air routes in that part of the world not long after this south of the border goodwill tour.

INSURANCE

It appears that on this flight he was covered for fire, property damage and liability. It was underwritten by The Independence Companies, Philadelphia, Pennsylvania.[1]

NAVIGATION LIGHTS

The NYP still did not have proper navigation lights during the south of the border flights.

COURSE PLOTTED BY THE AUTHOR

When working out the plotting of Lindbergh's south of the border goodwill tour, the latest Aeronautical Charts (1999–2000) were used. (See also endnotes.)

As a guide, Lindbergh's flight log, as printed in the book *The Spirit of St. Louis* by Charles A. Lindbergh (pp. 512–13), was used.

To calculate flight distance, with a red pencil I drew a straight line from one point of reference (city, town, geographical location, etc.) to the next point of reference. A measurement in statute miles was recorded. If Lindbergh flew from one city/town in a straight line to the next city/town, I took the measurement; for instance, from the center of the city/town in each case.

All of the straight-line course distances were added up to a total of approximately 9,490 statute miles. To come up with a total actual distance, which would include his circling both cities/towns, airports or other sites, I found it would be difficult if not impossible to measure on any kind of chart. Therefore I averaged such circles as being at a minimum of five miles for one circle, to perhaps ten miles or more for two or more circles.

Lindbergh used only his watch, plus the panel-mounted Waltham 8-day clock (model XA-15J) in the NYP to determine his flight time. But it is not known if he timed his actual flight time from engine start up to engine shut down, or from take-off to landing touchdown time. He did not have a Hobbs Meter or Recording Tachometer, such as is used in modern day aircraft to record flight time.

FLAGS STORY

During this goodwill tour, miniature flags of each country visited were painted on the lower half left and right side nose cowling. There are nineteen flags in all and four logos/emblems of American military groups. Each flag was hand painted in color. Canada is the only country not represented by a flag. The reason is not known.

Countries represented, reading from left to right, top to bottom (three rows) are United States, Mexico, Guatemala, British Honduras (Belize), El Salvador, Honduras, Nicaragua, Costa Rica, Panama, Columbia, Venezuela, Virgin Islands, Puerto Rico, Dominican Republic, Republic of Haiti, and Cuba.

The four emblems represent the United States Marine Corp; 110th Observation Squadron of the Missouri National Guard; 6th Composite Group of France Field in the Canal Zone; and Bolling Field in Washington, D.C.

It appears the first flag painted was for Mexico, possibly on December 14th or later. Somewhere between Mexico City and Guatemala, the American, French, Belgian and British flags were painted on. At Belize a photo was taken showing the Belize flag already painted on the cowling. Thereafter, each flag was added as Lindbergh completed each stop.

It also appears that local artists or sign painters did the hand painting. However, one photo exists showing a man in a suit and dress hat painting on the flag of Costa Rica. Could it be

Lindbergh himself? In another photograph, a military person in white uniform is shown, with a small brush in hand, just after painting on the flag of the Dominican Republic.

CONCLUSION

As the years since have shown, the south of the border goodwill tour message came through, and was successful just as the United States goodwill tour was.

There was a major boom in air travel throughout the Latin American countries, and further development of aviation and aeronautical technology. Further advancement in research, engineering and freight, air mail and passenger volume, and the number of new airports and air routes were documented in the years 1928 and on.

Charles A. Lindbergh was referred to as Carlos Augusto Lindbergh throughout the Latin American countries. They named streets, avenues, boulevards, buildings and other places after the flyer. His name is still remembered and respected there today.

AUTHOR'S COMMENTS

This writer would like to point out some of the difficulties of doing this chapter, so that the reader will understand why certain historical details and facts may not be shown in the manuscript.

After so many years, much information, in addition to photographs, has never been discovered, even after exhaustive and intense research. Often it was only by chance that certain information was found and translated by someone. Certain photographs were also found, but due to a limited budget, such photographs were unattainable. For the same reason, travel to those south of the border countries was not possible.

In addition, not knowing the language made any communication extremely difficult, if not impossible.

Therefore, this chapter will not be in as much detail as was done on the United States goodwill tour. Perhaps in future years a Spanish-speaking scholar will pick up where I left off, and complete the story.

The help I did receive from various sources, without a doubt, is most appreciated, without which this work could not have been written in its present form.

Footnotes

1. Independence Companies, Combination Aviation Policies, No. AC 1107, copy of which is in the author's collection. It covered from May 4, 1927 to May 4, 1928. Premium was $720.

BOLLING FIELD, WASHINGTON, D.C. TO MEXICO CITY

DECEMBER 13–14, 1927
(TUESDAY AND WEDNESDAY)

As he had done for the New York to Paris flight, Lindbergh planned to fly in "not-best-of-weather" conditions. On this trip he would fly through a long December night, schedule his ETA at Mexico City in advance, and attempt to hold to schedule regardless of the weather conditions. This would be similar to the way he flew as an air mail pilot between St. Louis and Chicago, and later on his goodwill tour of the United States.

A nonstop flight from Washington to Mexico City would cover a bit over 2,100 statute miles. The flight was plotted by this author and turned out to be 2,218 statute miles.

He had a Kollsman supersensitive altimeter installed on the instrument panel in the NYP. This may have been done at Teterboro, New Jersey, between October 25 and December 6, 1927 (see also chapter 3). This could also be the same one supposedly installed at San Francisco. No documentation has surfaced to confirm this.

Lindbergh mentioned in his *Autobiography of Values*[1] that Ambassador Morrow was disturbed when he learned of his plans to fly nonstop through the night to Mexico City. Morrow did not want Lindbergh to fly a hazardous trip and felt Lindbergh should do the flight in easy stages. Charles told the Ambassador to leave the flying to him, that it would be all right and not to worry. And he did.

They set the ETA at Mexico City for 2:00 p.m. on December 14, 1927, just as he had done on the U.S. Tour. Permission was granted by the United States Army for Lindbergh to take off from Bolling Field. The airplane had arrived at Bolling and spent six days in one of the Army hangars there, following its servicing at Teterboro.

At about 8 o'clock in the morning Lindbergh met in the home of Major Harvey S. Burwell, commander of Bolling Field. At this meeting was Lindbergh's cousin Captain Emory S. Land, Major Burwell, Captain Ira Eaker and Grover Loening. They took care of miscellaneous chores to help Lindbergh with his special flight.

That morning Lindbergh went to the post exchange to purchase some sandwiches before taking off. He was in a very calm and relaxed mood as he prepared for another long flight. He spent time going over all of his maps, checking every detail of his navigation plan as well as his equipment.

Bolling was a sod field covering an area of 5,000 feet at a field elevation of 10 feet MSL.[2] It was soaked with water after a storm had dropped torrents of rain just hours before his scheduled departure on Tuesday, December 13th. There were pools of water all over the field, mud and other soft spots the flyer had to contend with. Some of this water was hidden by or in the grass.

The flyer was quite concerned about this condition and spent considerable time walking the full length on the morning of his proposed departure to find the most suitable, firm surface on the airfield. When he was satisfied, he had the NYP rolled out of the hangar and prepared for take-off. The airplane had already been fueled with 368 gallons of fuel. He used white flags to mark the soft spots so that he could steer the airplane appropriately over more firm ground as he did the take-off roll.

In a letter to the author, Paul E. Garber, remembered: "I was at the field then and remember how carefully he walked over the field noting details useful during take-off. I recall also that he was annoyed when someone told him his mother was on the phone. He was not annoyed at her, but at being held up in his planning. He had asked specifically that he be undisturbed."[3]

Weather was forecast as wet and hazy, which was to be expected all along his route. It represented average winter conditions of the time.

On this flight he would wear the same gray suit which he had worn in the House when he was awarded the Congressional Medal of Honor.

Bidding him farewell were Major Burwell, Commandant of Bolling Field; Lt. Comdr. H. C. Wick, Lt. Comdr. D. C. Watson, USN Commander of the Anacostia Naval Air Station nearby; and Maj. Clarence M. Young and William MacCracken, both from the Commerce Department Air Section. Others there to see him off were F. Trubee Davison, Assistant Secretary of War for Aviation, and Capt. Emory Scott Land (his cousin), with whom he had spent the previous night and who drove him to the field that morning.

The NYP was made ready for the flight by Staff Sgt. Roy Hooe of the 65th Aero Squadron of the Army Air Corps.

On his take-off run, water from the tires splashed up from the wheels, spraying mud all over the airplane, but mostly to the undersides of the wings and the tail surfaces.

He took off at 12:25 p.m. Eastern Standard Time, taking up a southwest heading into an overcast and out over Virginia. He was reported over Lynchburg, Virginia, at 2:15 p.m., then Waynesville, North Carolina, at 3:30 p.m. He

Bolling Field, Washington, D.C., December 13, 1927, ready to leave for Mexico City. Notice larger wheels and flares on belly of fuselage. JOHN UNDERWOOD

flew by instruments from somewhere over North Carolina starting at about 6:00 p.m., nightfall in the mountains. From that time until the moon would rise five hours later he would be on the gauges.

On his initial heading he paralleled the Blue Ridge Mountains and Shenandoah National Park to his west. He passed north of Charlottesville, Virginia, and as he came toward the Appalachian Mountains he passed north of Roanoke, Virginia. By this time he was flying in an overcast sky condition with heavy rain squalls.

As daylight gave way to evening darkness, he passed in the vicinity of Chattanooga, Tennessee, where he was reported to be over Signal Mountain at 7:15 p.m., crossing into the state of

Georgia. He was further reported over Baldwyn (Prentice County), Mississippi, at 10:00 p.m., then Tallulah, Louisiana, at 12:30 a.m.

Due to the darkness and scattered rain squalls, he did some scud running, flying around the squalls, but still trying to hold his southwestern heading.

During the night he passed over Jackson, Mississippi, and then crossed the Mississippi River near Natchez and into the state of Louisiana.

More than likely he passed several miles north of Lake Charles and then over the Sabine River into Texas at Port Arthur, a few miles south of Beaumont, Texas. He was reported over Port Aransas at 5:00 a.m.

It is not certain at what point he hit the surf of the Gulf of Mexico, but it could possibly have been at Galveston, Texas or some area southwest of there along the shoreline. He did turn a bit westward to put the surf, which he could see in the night, under his left wing. This helped him not only with perspective but orientation. As the overcast became lower he was forced to descend to about two hundred feet above the shoreline. He continued through the night, sometimes climbing, hoping for clear air above the mist and overcast, and sometimes dropping again to follow the coastline. He found the outside conditions to be hot and humid, but somewhat comfortable in his cozy cockpit.

As daybreak was just on the eastern horizon, he passed south of Corpus Christi, Texas, continuing to follow the coastline as it curved southward to the tip of Texas at the Rio Grande. By this routing he

Start of the take-off roll in the soft surface on his way to Mexico City with the help of military men pushing on the struts. LEO B. KIMBALL COLLECTION

would have covered about 1,402 miles from Bolling to Corpus Christi.

Lindbergh continued along Padre Island, several miles east of Brownsville. As daybreak opened into beautiful, clear weather, he crossed the border (the Rio Grande) into Mexico.

Now in a VFR condition he could hold his southward course along the Gulf coast, following the Laguna Madre inland waterway. Finally he passed over the Mexican town of Tampico.

At this point he had just crossed the Tropic of Cancer. It was about here that he again encountered low clouds, and had to climb. For some reason he turned westward. He was apparently attempting to take up a heading to fly direct to Mexico City.

After passing Tampico he was reported over Tantoyuca, in the state of Vera Cruz, at 10:18 a.m. by a Western Union Telegraph Company in San Antonio, Texas.

From this point it appears that he dropped lower to follow the Panuco River, climbing up to about 1,000 feet to get on top of the clouds. From here he set the wrong compass course and must have headed west. Eventually he flew toward the Sierra Madre Oriental Mountains to the west and ended up over the Valley of Mexico on the west side of the mountains. It is possible that he flew over the states of San Luis Potosi, Guanajuato and Michoacan, but this is not confirmed.

While he was lost over Mexico, Lindbergh thought he had made an error to cause this. It is possible that magnetic variation, which on today's charts is 8 degrees E, was the problem. An 8-degree change in heading or compass course can cause an airplane to be off the intended course if the destination is a considerable distance away.

During this time and at 11:20 a.m., he was reported over Huasca, about 60 km from Mexico City. Part of this flight time he was at an altitude of 12,000 feet and over hostile countryside. He probably flew near the town of Queretaro, then south to near the town of Morelis, and then made a wide circle to the left to head east. It was in this area that he spotted Mount Toluca at 15,650 feet MSL. He headed east toward the mountain, flying around the north side, and soon spotted the town of Toluca. In a few minutes he could clearly see Mexico City, and flew directly toward that large national capital. In a few minutes Valbuena Airport came into view. It was located on the bed of an old lake and was flat and long.

Mexico City is located in a bowl-shaped depression in the mountains at 8,000 feet MSL.

Footnotes

1. *Autobiography of Values*, Charles A. Lindbergh, Harcourt Brace Jovanovich, New York and London, 1976. pg. 84.
2. *American Aircraft Directory*, Aviation Publishing Company, 1927, New York, NY, First Edition.
3. Letter to the author dated February 5, 1979 from Paul E. Garber, Historian Emeritus, Smithsonian Institute's National Air and Space Museum.

STOP #1
MEXICO CITY, MEXICO

CAPSULE HISTORY OF CITY

The capital and largest city in Mexico, Mexico City is located in the south-central part of the country and is one of the highest elevation cities in North America.

At one time the Aztec Indians controlled a mighty empire from Tenochtitlan, which they built about 1325 on the site of Mexico City. People have lived in this area for thousands of years.

The Spaniards built the city on the ruins of Tenochtitlan and made it their colonial capital. Spanish invaders came there in 1519 and destroyed the city almost completely in 1521. Their leader, Hernando Cortes, rebuilt the city on these ruins and took over the rest of the Aztec empire for Spain.

The city remained under Spanish control and rule for 300 years. In 1821 Mexico became independent after an Army led by Gen. Agustin de Iturbide took over Mexico City. There were

other wars until 1876 when Gen. Porfirio Diaz led a revolt and seized power. A Mexican Revolution began in 1910, and Diaz resigned the next year. Mexico City has stayed the capital of the country ever since.

8,000 feet MSL.

December 14–28, 1927
(Wednesday through Wednesday, two weeks)

While Lindbergh was flying south and getting lost, one can imagine what was going on at Valbuena Airport with the reception committee, namely the president of the country and the American ambassador.

Lindbergh was 1:40 overdue. He was expected there by 2:00 p.m., and Mexicans by the thousands were already on the field. They came from far and wide by truck, horse, mule, bicycle and foot, jamming roads for miles around.

Lindbergh himself was quite disappointed and realized his tardiness did not demonstrate aviation's reliability. He had been lost in broad daylight with unlimited visibility and a clear sky. He had never been in such a situation before.

It was Wednesday, December 14th, as he came into view from the west, circled the city and the airport, and came in to land at 3:40 p.m., Eastern Standard Time, after a flight of 27 hours and 15 minutes. Valbuena is two and a half miles from the city.

After landing he was greeted by President Plutarco Elias Calles and other officers of the Federation, and Ambassador Dwight E. Morrow. The President said, "con todo carino" (with great affection).

The perimeter of the airport was patrolled by Mexican soldiers with fixed bayonets to control the crowd of over 25,000 excited people awaiting Lindbergh's arrival.

Special telephones were installed to place the flying field in direct communication with the world.

Shortly after he landed, the NYP was pushed into a large hangar, where it would be kept under constant guard until it was time for him to leave on the next leg of the tour.

After confirming the security of the NYP, Lindbergh, the "Americano," was escorted to a platform as a band played the United States National Anthem and then the Mexican National Anthem.

NYP in the hangar at Valbuena Field, "topping off" the oil tank with Mobiloil "B" extra heavy oil, shortly after the flight from Bolling Field. Filling the tank is Vacuum Oil Company sales manager Felix Duran de Huerta. VACUUM OIL COMPANY OF MEXICO, S.A.

The Municipal President, Mr. De Saracho, gave Lindbergh the symbolic key of the town saying, "I place in your hands the keys of the city. You can do anything that you like with them." Lindbergh held the keys for a moment, thanked him, and returned the keys.

Then the Mexican President was introduced. He said,

"It is not only of technological interest and a heroic deed of aviation, but a valuable Embassy of Good Will that the North American people send us. I'm sure that the purpose of sending us its highest representative of youth, faith, and heroism of the United States, was to bring both countries spiritually and materially closer. If I had to guess the purpose of the flight correctly, I can assure you that the results have been positive and immediate.

"I wish to express my most sincere and enthusiastic admiration for a marvelous kind of modern hero; my thanks to him for having accepted my invitation to come to Mexico and become our guest of honor, and

NYP in the hangar at Mexico City. Men in the photo are unknown. SAN DIEGO AEROSPACE MUSEUM

last but not least, my most cordial congratulations to Lindbergh and to the North American country that has the right to feel proud of having created a man like him."

Lindbergh was then introduced, and with his usual simplicity, said,

"I can say that this flight I just completed has been, due to determined circumstances, the most interesting that I've ever carried out. I sincerely mean it. In this case, I had to make use of the navigation instrument (EIC?) more frequently than when I flew to Paris over the Atlantic.

"When I got to Mexico I got lost in the thick fog I found over the region of Tampico. I found great difficulties in orientation due to the imperfection of the maps I brought with me.

"I have to add, because I consider this detail very interesting, that my flight at night developed without any setbacks, in spite of complete darkness. That was not the case during the day, when I deviated from my route going my way from Tampico to the City of Mexico. The mistake that took me away from the route was only mine.

"During the two hours that I covered enormous areas of your land I didn't find an inch of propitious land for an emergency landing and this, of course, was not a comforting feeling. Fields more or less usable are scarce, and I also found that train stations are not, in many cases, indi-

cated as I would have liked it to make my orientation easier, and not always did the names agree with the maps I used for the trip.

"Most of the flight I had to overcome great difficulties that prove the need for intense and special training for flights in unknown regions.

"The fog covered a considerable area. The flight took place in these conditions until entering North Carolina at five-forty in the evening. It was completely dark. I found myself over a mountainous region. It was getting darker by seconds and midnight arrived without moonlight. The sky looked threatening, and it was drizzling until about 10:00 p.m., and I flew through some areas of strong showers.

"For a considerable lapse of time it was

A Mexican mechanic checking over the airplane after Lindbergh's flight from Bolling Field. HARTFORD TIMES

impossible to glimpse anything. Only once in a while a light would shine below.

"On this occasion, I had to fly almost three hours, completely lost, guiding myself only by instinct. During my night flight I had to use the instruments no less than five hours, trying not to deviate from course. Once over Mexican territory I could not trace any route, and the situation started to look serious because the maps of Mexico I had bought in Washington were not detailed.

"When I arrived at the coast of the Gulf of Mexico, I had fog for two or three hours, and there were no points of reference until I had flown a considerable portion of the Mexican coast (literal). In some areas the fog was so dense that I had to fly at low altitude, two or three hundred feet above the beach. There were moments when I could not even see the coast. The conditions were not satisfactory.

"During the flight to Paris I only had a little bit of darkness. This time there were thirteen and a half hours of foggy conditions, flying more by instinct than by reference points. Despite the thick fog, I recognized the city of Tampico by the large number of petroleum tanks. I got to fly at an altitude of fifty feet above the Panuco River, but realizing the fog was really low, I decided to climb again, using my sixth sense to guide me towards Mexico City.

"About the welcome, I only have to say that it was spontaneous, sincere, and emotional, like the ones the people gave in France, England, and the United States at my return from Europe.

"The friendship that exists between aviators from all over the world is a powerful binding force that unifies everybody who is dedicated to fly. There is always something different in each one of these welcomes. The Mexican welcome has been unique, unforgettable, and one that I will always remember."

For over an hour Lindbergh was driven in a parade from the airport, through the throngs of people in the streets of the great city, to Niza, where Lindbergh was lodged at the American Embassy.

Lindbergh was seated in the first car with Mr. Morrow in the rear seat with his wife. In the front seat was Chief of Staff, Gen. Jose Alvarez.

Will Rogers, American humorist, who had made a trip through northern Mexico with the President and Ambassador Morrow, was among the people who greeted the flyer. Lindbergh had the same room at the embassy that was used by Rogers, who moved out on Monday night.

Lindbergh spent part of that first day in the city. He visited the Secretary of Foreign Relations, where he was welcomed by the personnel that were crowding the hallways. He was taken to the great salon of the Chancellery, where he was again welcomed and where Don Genaro Estrada, Assistant Secretary in charge of the office, offered him a glass of champagne.

At 11 o'clock on the 15th he was taken to the office of the President of the Republic in the National Palace (nacional palacio). From there he was escorted to the Benito Juarez Scholar Center, where the inauguration ceremony of the library took place. The library was named after President Lincoln and was a gift from a group of American Friends of Mexico. He was accompanied by Ambassador Morrow and the Secretary of Public Education, Dr. J. M. Puig Casauranc.

In the evening Lindbergh attended a black tie dinner in his honor put on by the House of

Lindbergh is shown in the center flanked on his right by Genaro Estrada and on his left by Dwight Morrow. LEO B. KIMBALL COLLECTION

Representatives. He was asked to say a few words, which he did, saying,

"I did not know this city was so beautiful and its climate so delightful. It seems to be sketched by an artist.

"If everybody in my country had the chance to experience the cordiality of Mexicans towards Americans, I believe they would feel a great friendship towards Mexico. I haven't heard but friendly words for the United States.

"If my flight contributes to improve the relationship between the United States and Mexico, this will make me the happiest man."

Referring to aviation he observed,

"There is a great need for scheduled air services. The terrain is so rough and the mountains make the trip by road or by train so difficult and long that the air routes will have to bring the United States closer to Mexico and to the rest of Central America. Mexico needs a lot from aviation and has the ideal conditions for its development.

"The airport of this city is one of the best I know. Today I learned that the aerodrome is the base of an old lake. It is a good field, firm, with plenty of space to take off in any direction, and as flat as anybody could wish. I wish it could be possible to find a similar aerodrome in New York."

While in Mexico City Lindbergh had the opportunity to visit with Emilio Carranza, whom he had first met at El Paso during the goodwill tour of the United States. Carranza had felt that because Lindbergh had flown down to Mexico as a goodwill gesture, he should reciprocate and fly from his country to the United States as a gesture of goodwill and friendship.

Because of the poor economy of that country, raising money to finance such a venture was very difficult. By working hard he was able to solve that problem. An airplane was ordered to make the flight: a Ryan B-1 Brougham,

outfitted with extra fuel tanks and powered with the trusty Wright J-5 "Whirlwind" engine. It was affectionately named the "Mexico-Excelsior" and registered M-SCOM. Lindbergh donated $2,500 out of his own pocket toward expenses for his friend Carranza.

Unfortunately Carranza lost his life during that trip as he was flying back from New York to Mexico City. He went down in New Jersey, and the Ryan was destroyed.

Carranza's Ryan B-1 Brougham, the *Excelsior*, with Mexican registration M-SCOM. RYAN AERONAUTICAL COMPANY

Capt. Emilio Carranza with Lindbergh taken in the U.S. sometime in July 1928. LEO B. KIMBALL COLLECTION

Lindbergh shown again with Capt. Emilio Carranza by a Ryan B-1 Brougham.
COURT COMMERCIAL PHOTO

FRIDAY, DECEMBER 16TH

On this day Lindbergh was given a chance to fly a Morane-Saulnier 31-A powered by a Gnome engine. He was checked out by Agustin Castrejon from the Mexican Department of Aeronautics. According to Lindbergh's flight log, he flew the airplane for one hour and thirty-five minutes.

On the 18th the flyer was given many gifts including a beautiful matador's cape given by one of the famous matadors (Jose Ortiz) at a bull fight.

He was taken to the floating gardens in Xochimilco and an exhibition of roping and riding at the famous Rancho de Charros on December 19th.

TUESDAY, DECEMBER 20TH

On this day a Cia. Mexicana de Aviacion's Fairchild FC-2 was put at the flyer's disposal by George Rihl, president of that company. It was a small airline flying a route between Mexico City and Tampico. He put on two hours and fifteen minutes.

On one flight in the Fairchild he carried President Calles and Gen. Jose Alvarez, taking them over the beautiful Valley of Mexico. It was the President's first airplane ride.

He also flew Ambassador Morrow; Gen. Alvaro Obregon; Obregon's son Humberto; Pedro C. Caloca; Colonel McNabb, attaché of the American Embassy; Capt. Jose Yanez of the National Air Force; Russel Owen, journalist for the *New York Times* in Mexico; and other high-ranking Mexican officials.

After his flight President Calles said, "Everything was beautiful. During the ten minutes that I flew, I did not feel even a minor discomfort or the slightest upset. I felt so comfortable aboard the airplane that I almost forgot I was in the air. The splendid panorama of the Valley of Mexico seen from above gave the exact notion of the truth. But who does not feel safe flying with Colonel Lindbergh?"

WEDNESDAY, DECEMBER 21ST

On this day while staying at the Embassy, Lindbergh went into the office of Alan Winslow, First Secretary of the American Embassy and himself a distinguished World War I aviator, and said, "Busy? I'd like to go fly." "Sure," agreed Winslow, and the two drove out to Valbuena airport. To avoid the press they did not inform anyone.

Lindbergh first flew several Mexican Army airplanes and then took the NYP over the area for twenty-five minutes. He also flew a Mexican B.M.W. biplane powered with a 160 hp engine. Upon returning he said it was a wonderful day to fly and felt the NYP was in good condition for his next leg to Central America.

Thursday, December 22ND

Word was received that a Ford tri-motor was on its way into Mexico City being flown by prominent Ford Motor Company pilot Harry Brooks, with mechanic Harry Russell. They had as passengers Lindbergh's mother, Evangeline, Will Rogers, Mr. and Mrs. William B. Stout and Mrs. Morrow.

In the early afternoon Lindbergh took off in the NYP to try to find the Ford, which was carrying his mother, and escort the airplane into Valbuena Field. After flying the NYP for one hour, Lindbergh did not find the Ford. He went up again in the NYP on a demonstration flight and flew for fifteen minutes. After two approaches he could not land because of the crowd of people on the field. He flew over to an adjoining field to attract the crowd, then rose again as the first people arrived and made a successful landing. He immediately taxied into the hangar.

At 3:00 p.m. it was reported that the Ford was sighted over Pachuca. It had also deviated off its course over the same area where Lindbergh had navigation problems. Shortly a few Mexican aviators took off and found the Ford and escorted it to a successful landing at Valbuena.

Saturday, December 24TH

Lindbergh spent this day on a mini-vacation, doing some sightseeing and spending some time out at Cuernavaca. He also met unofficially with the local government leaders including the governor of the state of Morelos and others. He requested that he be allowed to return to Mexico City to spend Christmas Day with his mother and the Morrows.

Monday, December 26TH

At 10:20 a.m. that morning Lindbergh flew the Ford tri-motor NC1077 for one hour over the area. He had as his passengers Gen. Joaquim Amara, Secretary of War and Marine, and his wife, Elisa Izaguirre, Mr. and Mrs. William Stout, Will Rogers, and the Morrow family.

Also on this day Lindbergh was given "flight charts" by engineer Juan Guillermo Villasana of the Civil Aviation division of the Department of Communications and Public Works. Lindbergh studied them carefully and marked his route to

Guatemala's capital city.

Part of that day was also spent with the Morrow family, during which time Lindbergh met their daughter, Anne Spencer Morrow, whom he eventually married.

During Lindbergh's stay in Mexico City meeting most of the government officials and business people, he stressed the importance of developing airports and modern aircraft. He gave them ideas and suggestions for developing airline routes in their country as well as to other neighboring countries and to the United States.

At one dinner Gen. Pedro C. Caloca of the Mexican Air Force gave the following toast, in part:

"The Mexican pilots consider you, not as a foreigner, but as a fellow aviator. We are all citizens of this immense country called sky.

"They, better than anyone else, understand the merits of your deed that will be their stimulus and breath in the future.

"By only learning about your visit to our country, we felt an intense emotion in our hearts, and are filled with happiness. And today that we see this magnificent flight accomplished, and we were able to meet the man whose successes have amazed the entire world, our admiration and thanks are overwhelming.

"This country could not have chosen a better Ambassador of peace and of fraternity than you. Our country is a country of tragedies, legends, and that cultivates courage, and makes men that have great heart and character into supermen or heroes.

"Let's hope that your mission of peace and harmony will be welcomed by men of good faith from both sides of the Bravo, and that the route that *The Spirit of St. Louis* has opened will be always crossed by missions like this one; of peace and concord.

"Let's hope that in a near future there will be so many open routes by the pilots of all the countries with missions of love, that the frontiers will disappear and the dream of universal fraternity will be realized."

It was clear that Lindbergh was quite moved by this sincere speech by a fellow flyer and felt extremely comfortable in Mexico, where he was treated so well and accepted as one of them. He

enjoyed himself, played some jokes on some of the Mexican pilots and did not get to bed until after 3 o'clock that night.

During his stay there he was a guest of honor at the athletic festival in the National Stadium. All the schoolchildren of the capital participated in the festival.

Lindbergh's visit to Mexico had a tremendous and lasting effect on the country and its people politically. Mexico had been experiencing a social revolution and needed some change. Indirectly Lindbergh was a key player in that situation. As their guest he was able to convince them of the importance of the development of new and updated air services, the air mail system, and the construction of new airports and improvements to existing flying fields. He also targeted its air navigation system, which was nil at that point, and suggested improvements on other technologies in the industry.

As the result of Lindbergh's goodwill flight, there were signs of better feelings between Mexico and the United States. President Calles took steps to change the oil and land laws of Mexico so that they would be satisfactory to Americans who owned property in that country. The laws had been based on the Mexican Constitution of 1917, which provided that all land belongs to Mexico.

The President also made it known that the United States would permit Mexico to buy airplanes in the United States. Because of the arms embargo maintained by the United States against Mexico, this had not been possible before.

The name "Lindbergh" has had an everlasting effect on Mexico. People still remember his visit, and later generations are continually reminded of what he did.

His name was given to many places such as "Teatro Coronel Lindbergh" (Colonel Lindbergh Theater) in a residential area of Mexico City. There is a bust of the Colonel displayed at Mexico City Airport, along with an impressive mural entitled "Man's Conquest of the Air," by Mexican artist Juan O'Gorman, that honors the flyer. A Mexico City street is named Lindbergh. A tourism school on the same street as the former Embassy and the hotel is also named Lindbergh. In Cuernavaca there is a Dwight Morrow Street and his famous "Casa Manana" is also preserved as a restaurant.

Many of Lindbergh's books and also his wife's books have been translated into Spanish. Lindbergh documentaries are aired on local TV stations, in addition to re-runs of the Jimmy Stewart movie, *Spirit of St. Louis*.

Flight to Guatemala City
Wednesday, December 28th

This was the day Mrs. Lindbergh left to fly back to Detroit in the Ford, along with several other passengers.

At the Embassy Lindbergh was up early and was driven to the airport, arriving there at 5:40 a.m. He spent considerable time preflighting the NYP, which already had 130 gallons of fuel on board.

After saying good-bye to the many people there, including the hundreds of people already on the field to wish him well, he took off at 6:35 a.m. Central Standard Time.

When he left Valbuena he was dressed in a business suit, covered by his usual leather flying coveralls. He had with him some drinking water, a few sandwiches, and a supply of Army emergency rations. He also had a duffle bag stuffed with extra clothes and a leather handbag with toilet articles, shirts, and underwear.

Here and there could be heard, "Adios, Hermanito" (good-bye, little brother).

Climbing slowly due to the fuel load and the high field elevation, he circled over the field and then the city several times and took up a southeast heading in the clear and cool morning air. This would be a straight shot to Guatemala City with no detours. He would be flying over some rough country with little habitation.

At the beginning of this flight he passed by Popocatepetl, Mexico's great volcano. He flew strictly by compass, depending almost entirely on the Earth Inductor Compass. He flew as high as between 7,000 and 12,000 feet, which put him close to the ground in the higher elevations of Mexico and Guatemala.

He encountered early morning fog over some of the valley areas, some of it for as long as fifty miles. His line of flight took him near Puebla, Mexico, and near Tehuacan. He passed south of Presa Miguel Aleman Lake, passing over some mountains that were as high as 10,000 feet or more.

Lindbergh passed south of Jesus Carranza,

the Isthmus of Tehuantepec, and then south of Cintalapa de Figueroa. He came upon Villa Flores, and then passed south of Presa de la Angostura Lake (Belisario Domiguez), passing over the present town of Jallenango. He continued on a southeasterly heading on the north side of the Sierra de Soconusco mountain range.

During the flight he did not see the Gulf of Mexico, but he did get a glimpse of the Pacific Ocean at one point, about fifty miles off his right wing.

He advanced well into the state of Chiapas, then crossing the Guatemala border, passing along the north side of Guatemala's Sierra Madre mountain range.

After breaking into a clear sky, he came within view of Guatemala City. He had been in the air for 7 hours and 5 minutes for the 655-mile flight.

Today Mexico City has one large airport named Lic Benito Juarez International. It is one of the highest airports in Mexico, at an elevation of 7,341 feet MSL. The field has two parallel runways, one of which is 12,966 feet in length. The airport serves all major Mexican airlines as well as international flights. It is located on the southwestern side of Lago de Texcoco, close to the east side of the city. It is not known if it is in the same location geographically as Valbuena.

There are several other satellite airports, single runway fields, or grass/turf airports around the city.

References

Newspapers
New York Times (Globe Democrat)
Joplin News Herald, Joplin, Missouri, Wednesday, December 28, 1927 (price 3 cents), several pages

Publications
Success of Lindbergh's Good-Will Mission to Mexico, by Charles W. Hackett, Professor of Latin-American History, University of Texas (date of publication unknown).
"Lindbergh's Embassy of Good-Will to Mexico," *The Literary Digest,* New York, December 24, 1927.
Aviation Magazine, December 26, 1927, pp 1514, 1515.
"The Third Flight," by Dr. Wesley Phillips Newton, *American Aviation Historical Society* 20: 2 (summer 1975), p. 94.
Emilio Carranza, by Jose Villeta Gomez (facts of publication?)
Emilio Carranza, a 50 anos de su muerte, 1928–1978: Homenaje Al Aviador," author unknown.

Organizations
Minneapolis Public Library, Minneapolis, Minnesota
United Press International, misc. newspaper cutouts
International Newsreel, photographs

People
Lourdes Ramos	Dr. Eusabio Zambrano
Richard A. Washburn	Adolfo Villasenor M.
Santiago A. Flores Ruiz	Harry C. Goakes
Karen Fishman, University of Maryland	

STOP #2
GUATEMALA CITY, GUATEMALA

CAPSULE HISTORY OF THE CITY

Guatemala City, the capital of Guatemala, was founded in 1776. In the Spanish language, Guatemala City is called Ciudad de Guatemala. It is located on a plateau about 75 miles north of the Pacific Ocean, in the south-central part of the country.

The earliest known society was at Las Charas in the Highlands region of the country and dates from the 1000s B.C. Much of the Maya Indian civilization thrived in this country between A.D. 250 and 900.

On September 15, 1821, Guatemala declared its independence and later became part of the Mexican empire but broke away in 1823 and formed the United Provinces of Central America.

4,850 feet MSL.

DECEMBER 28-30, 1927
(WEDNESDAY THROUGH FRIDAY)

The city at that time had its own airport, known as La Aurora Airport. It was located four miles south of the center of the city, bordered by

Here the NYP can be seen flying over "La Aurora," the airport it landed on at Guatemala City, December 28th. *NATIONAL GEOGRAPHIC*, PHOTO BY JOSE QUEVEDO V

a coffee plantation on the east side and a race-track on the northwest side.

The field was at an elevation of 4,854 feet MSL and was approximately 4,650 feet long. It was a level field of firm sod.

There were several hangars, one large enough with an 18-foot overhead clearance. There was a fence along the western edge. Fuel and oil and some repairs were available.

As Lindbergh came over this beautiful city, the sky was clear with some scattered clouds around the horizon and over some of the volcanoes. He had a smooth flight from Mexico City and looked forward to another city and culture.

He let down over Aurora Flying Field and, as always, did a low pass to check the surface. He had planned to climb around and come in for a landing. However, the thousands of people lining the field broke through the barricades as he circled around, and ran out onto the field. Lindbergh made one more low pass and then came in for the final landing. The people crowded around the airplane immediately, as he taxied up to a hangar on the east side. He had just set a record for the first nonstop flight between the two capitals.

The first person to greet Lindbergh was Col. Francisco Amado of the Guatemalan Army, followed by Arthur Geissler, the American Minister, American Embassy Secretary Hawke, and finally Gen. Lazaro Chacon, President of the Republic.

As the NYP was rolled into the hangar, Guatemalan aviators and Army soldiers immediately organized to protect it.

While in this city he was entertained and taken wherever he wished by the officials who were very proud of their city. He was given many ovations, gifts, medals, and honors, including a large banquet on the second evening. Here he was given the opportunity to speak about his first love of aviation, the future of air travel, and the benefits of connecting the Central American countries by air. They loved his talk, cheering and hailing him as their hero and making him an official citizen of their city.

On the morning of Friday, December 30, Lindbergh took off after a preflight at about 6:30 a.m. and circled over the city. Due to poor visibility and fog he could only catch glimpses of the city below through the occasional hole in the clouds.

After leaving Guatemala City he passed just west of the Sierra de Santa Cruz mountains. He set a compass course northeast for a straight flight to Belize. Again he flew over high mountains and passed several miles west of Lago (lake) de Izabal and eventually crossed the border.

He flew east of the Maya Mountains and came to the shores of the Caribbean Sea at about Southern Long Cay, several miles south of Southern Lagoon. He then headed up the coast to Belize City, passing the Northern Lagoon on his left.

As he came upon the coast he had to go to 6,000 feet to clear some fog, even though he tried to go under it and scud run. While on top of the fog bank he had to navigate by compass only. He finally located his position at about 25 miles south of the city along the coast and flew the coast line north. He said that the beach was lined with coconut palms.

Known today as La Aurora International Airport, this field, on the original site, is at an elevation of 4,952 feet MSL and has one single runway of 9,800 feet in length. It serves most domestic and international airlines.

The only other airport close by is a grass field named Tanzania about fifteen miles southeast of the city at an elevation of 3,576 feet MSL.

References

Newspapers
The New York Times–miscellaneous articles
International Newsreel–miscellaneous photographs

Organizations
Karen Fishman libraries of the University of Maryland at College Park

Publications
Joplin News Herald, December 28, 1927, Joplin, Missouri

People
Tony Passannante   Richard A. Washburn
Carlos Rosa Mejia
Alfonso Quinones, Guatemala Embassy, Washington, D.C.

STOP #3
BELIZE CITY, BELIZE

CAPSULE HISTORY OF THE COUNTRY

British Honduras, or Belize, is a very small country on the eastern coast of the Yucatan Peninsula in northeast Central America. Belize is bordered on the east by the Caribbean Sea, at the mouth of a branch of the Belize River. It is bordered on the west by Guatemala and on the northwest by Mexico.

There is little industry because it is covered mostly with swamps and thick forests. The climate is hot and humid. It was Great Britain's only colony in Central America that changed its name when it became independent. It changed to Belize in 1973.

At one time the country was part of the Mayan Empire, which flourished from the A.D. 300s to the 800s. The region was first visited by British log cutters in about 1638. Fort George, built in 1803, is still standing. In 1961 a hurricane destroyed most of Belize City, killing more than 300 people and leaving thousands homeless.

Belize City, the former capital, is the largest city and chief port on the Caribbean Sea. However, Belmopan became the new capital in 1960. Belmopan, located near Belize City, is 15 feet MSL.

DECEMBER 30, 1927 TO JANUARY 1, 1928
(FRIDAY THROUGH SUNDAY)

Belize City did not have an official airport at the time, but on the north side of the city there was a Golf and Polo Club. The site of polo, soccer, and cricket matches, it was commonly known as the Polo Grounds. Lindbergh would be the first person to land his airplane there.

After arriving over the city and circling several times, he came in for a landing at the Polo Grounds, also known as Newtown Barracks. He just missed the telephone wires at the north end of the field, which was only about 1,200 feet long. He had landed at 9:45 a.m. local time (10:45 EST). He was five minutes earlier than his projected ETA of 11:00 a.m. and had been in the air for 3 hours and 20 minutes for the 255-mile flight.

It appeared that the whole population of 113,000 people had come out to greet him, including the governor, Sir John Burdon.

Lindbergh enjoyed the common language of this British country and was impressed with the orderly rows of people along the edge of the field. He did not have to worry about people running out on the field to hamper his approach and rollout after touchdown.

Soon after shutting down Lindbergh was assured the NYP would be heavily guarded by Belize policemen. Lindbergh and the welcoming committee walked the short distance to the veranda of the Golf Club, where the flyer gave a

short talk and was welcomed by the people who witnessed his arrival. Then he was escorted into the governor's waiting automobile for a motorcade into the city and an official reception at the Government House.

The next day he was taken out to St. John's College at Loyola Park by Governor Burdon and also on a launch ride up the Belize River where he visited the Botanical Gardens, no longer in existence today.

Lindbergh is shown checking the engine area and possibly confirming valve clearance after repairing the spring before his departure for the next stop.

While in the city at the airport he discovered a broken valve spring and, because he carried spares, he took care of that himself. He did this in the rolled-up sleeves of his white shirt and while wearing a tie.

The old and rusted broken spring ended up in the collection of fine china of Dr. James Cran. It was almost a sacred relic kept in there dining room's china closet beside their finest china and glassware. Dr. Cran was chairman of the welcoming committee.

An official banquet was given in Lindbergh's honor at the International Hotel, where a band played popular tunes of the time during dinner. The flyer was presented with the flag of the Colony by Lady Sisnett, wife of Chief Justice Sir Herbert Sisnett, in the absence of Lady Burdon, the governor's wife, who was ill.

In his talk Lindbergh recommended the area known as Tillets Pond be developed as an airfield, ten miles from Belize City, which is now the Belize International Airport. He also spoke on the future of air travel, the importance of developing a local airport, and becoming involved with an airline to connect with other Central American countries as well as other continents.

Lindbergh departed for San Salvador, El Salvador, on New Year's Day, Sunday, January 1, 1928. The governor came to the field to see the flyer off on this next leg of his journey. Most of the population was again there to witness the take-off, including a band to provide music for Lindbergh's departure.

A fine example of British discipline, perfect order was maintained again so there was no danger of the NYP's propeller hitting anyone.

Lindbergh landing the NYP during final approach to the Polo field outside of Belize. He is landing into the prevailing wind from the sea.

Lindbergh took off and circled over the field and the city area. He then set his course in rough turbulence south along the coast. The rough air joggled the liquid magnetic compass so he had to rely on the Earth Inductor Compass. The scenery was spectacular with dense green jungle over the lowlands.

As he headed down the coast and over Dangriga, he continued to follow the coastline down past Monkey River Town and Punta Negra. Then he flew over the Gulf de Honduras over tiny keys covered with mangrove and palm trees.

Continuing across the waters of Bahia (Gulf) de Amatique, he again hit the shore of Guatemala between Livingston and Puerto Barrios. He had passed the peninsula of Punta de Manabique off his left wing before landfall.

He crossed some low mountains of the Sierra de Santa Cruz range and over a low valley, and from there the rest of the flight took him over some rough mountain areas, part of the Cordill de Celaque mountains to his left and close to Nueva Ocotepeque, Honduras, near a 9,000-foot mountain peak before crossing the border into El Salvador.

He had difficulty navigating due to a small-scale map.

Belize City has one major airport today Philip S.W. Goldson International Airport, located about seven miles west of the center of the city. It is at an elevation of 15 feet MSL and has a single runway of 7,100 feet. It serves most major domestic and international airlines.

There is also a grass field airport on the north side of the city.

References

Newspapers
Amandala Press

Organizations
Belize Archives Department

Publications
"Lindbergh United the Americas," *The Literary Digest*, 96:3, (New York, January 21, 1928).

People
Neil L. Fraser   Richard A. Washburn
Deanna E. Nisbet   Carlos Rosa Mejia
R.S. Stewart   Anita Lisbey
Charles Gibson   Evan X. Hyde
Emory King   Leopold Balderamos
Janine E. Sylvestre, Embassy of Belize
George Charles Bruno, Embassy of Belize
Raymond H. Barrow, Atty.

STOP #4
SAN SALVADOR, EL SALVADOR

CAPSULE HISTORY OF THE COUNTRY

San Salvador, capital city of El Salvador, is located in the valley of Las Hamacas, in the heart of the earthquake region.

In Spanish El Salvador is called Republica de El Salvador, Republic of El Salvador. The city is located near the west-central portion of the smallest Central American country.

The Pipil tribe was the largest and most advanced of the many Indian tribes that lived in the country before the Spanish conquerors arrived on the scene. They were descendants of the ancient Toltec and Aztec people.

In 1524 a Spanish soldier of Hernando Cortes named Pedro de Alvarado crossed into El Salvador from Guatemala searching for gold and silver. In 1525 Alvarado founded the city of San Salvador de Cuscatlan, now called San Salvador. The whole country was named for Alvarado's final victory over the Indians. For the next three hundred years El Salvador was a Spanish colony.

El Salvador became an independent republic with its own constitution in 1821. From 1913 to 1927 Carlos Melendez and members of his family controlled the presidency.

2,178 feet MSL.

JANUARY 1-3, 1928
(SUNDAY THROUGH TUESDAY)

The local airport of the time was known as Ilopango Airport. It was the airport of entry,

located on the southern side of the railroad, near the western end of Lake Ilopango, about five miles east of the city. The field was at an elevation of 2,178 feet MSL. Its longest runway was 2,900 feet. It was sod, with a slight incline to the west. Fuel, oil and repairs were available on the field.

Lindbergh came into view over this capital city and circled several times. Earlier he had been reported over La Labor at 8:50 a.m. and at 8:53 a.m. over Las Cruces and Metapan. Against Lindbergh's recommendation and wishes, two Salvadorian aviators, Munes and Bondanza, flew out to meet the NYP.

The sky was clear, and there were thousands of people already on Ilopango Field awaiting his arrival. Traffic was heavy but well organized and orderly. They came in autos and carts, by foot, in wagons and on bicycles.

Lindbergh made a low pass over the field to check the surface and came around for his landing at 9:15 a.m. The crowd yelled and waved like no other time in the city's history or to any other foreigner.

After landing and checking the safety of the NYP, he was met by President Señor Romero Bosque, who was waiting to take the flyer to a reception at the presidential mansion.

taken care of.

At a banquet in Lindbergh's honor, the President remarked, "His countrymen will never forget the most glorious of the 'conquistadors' of the air who crossed the blue heavens to be our guest of honor... In the name of my compatriots and my collaborators and on my own behalf we give you a cordial salutation of welcome so that we can pay homage to you and show our admiration and high appreciation."

Lindbergh was taken all over the area, to all the historic sites, and met with many officials and businessmen. He gave his talk, concentrating on the future development of air travel, with emphasis on Central America and establishing airlines down there.

He was given a special visit to the home of Col. Antonio Claramount, Chief of Salvadorian aviation, accompanied by American businessman Samuel Dickson and Col. M.E. Gilmore,

Above: A proud group of military and civilian Salvadorans pose by the NYP during the visit. CASSAGNERES COLLECTION

At left: NYP on Ilopango Field, just after he landed, and was taxiing in. CASSAGNERES COLLECTION

At the reception he was introduced to the Minister of War, Foreign Minister, Undersecretary and military leaders, who all wore very colorful dress uniforms for the occasion. Single and married women were also dressed in their finest attire to welcome the flyer.

During this time Lindbergh expressed his satisfaction at how well his airplane was being

who was the business manager of paving and highways for the city.

At one affair he was given a medal by the President, who said, "We wish to give you this medal in recognition of the progress of aviation you are responsible for. Please accept this medal as a symbol of love that you are leaving here in this land." It was a gold medal with the shield

of El Salvador.

He was quartered in the American Embassy.

Lindbergh was honored with other medals, gifts, and accolades too numerous to mention, and treated as one of their own.

On Tuesday, January 3, Lindbergh was expected to take off between 11 and 12 o'clock from Ilopango Field. It is believed he got into the air about 11:45 a.m.

After departure, Lindbergh slowly climbed to an altitude of 4,000 feet and set a course northeast. He was given a royal send off by a squadron of Salvadorian airplanes as a salute. He was escorted to the border by Salvadoran pilots Munes and Rodriguez, each in his own airplane.

He immediately passed by the north side of Lago Ilopango and then over the town of Cojutepeque and Sensuntepeque, then toward the mountains where the Lempa River forms the boundary between El Salvador and Honduras.

It was on this flight that Lindbergh experienced his roughest and most turbulent ride in the NYP.[1] He just crossed the river when, according to him, "a norther" had caused the strong wind to come over the mountains with thick clouds. For a full 15 minutes he was tossed around more than he had ever experienced before. The NYP was tossed up and down, even on its side, throwing the flyer up against the top of the cabin. He apparently had hung his goggles on the stabilizer control lever, and when he hit the rough air they were thrown up off the lever and finally fell in the back of the fuselage.

Eventually he climbed to 6,000 feet and found much smoother air, just level with some of the clouds. These clouds covered much of the mountains, so he detoured to the south and finally crossed the Goascoran River.[2]

In the cockpit Lindbergh had three maps and so was able to keep track of his position accurately. He had purchased on of the maps in a stationery store, one was from a wall map, and the third was from a page in a magazine. He eventually found two wireless towers and knew he was getting close to Tegucigalpa.

Today the local airport, on the original site, is called Ilopango International Airport, at an elevation of 2,021 feet MSL. It has a single runway 7,347 feet and services all major domestic and international airlines and some commuter and military aircraft.

About twenty miles southeast of the city is El Salvador International Airport, at an elevation of 101 feet MSL with a single 10,500-foot runway. The field serves most major and domestic airlines as well as cargo.

There are several other small grass fields to the south of the city near the coast, and one other about ten miles northwest of the city used for general aviation airplanes.

Footnotes

1. Charles A. Lindbergh, "To Bogota and Back by Air," *National Geographic* 53:5 (May 1928), p. 548.
2. *Ibid*, p. 550.

References

Newspapers
La Prensa, El Salvador

Organizations
   Embassy of El Salvador
   Embassy of the United States of American, El Salvador

People
   Claudia N. de Bartolini
   Col. Baltzar Lopez Hernandez
   Anne W. Patterson   Richard A. Washburn
   Carlos Rosa Mejia   Prof. Gary Kuhn

STOP #5
TEGUCIGALPA, HONDURAS

CAPSULE HISTORY OF COUNTRY

Known for its production of bananas, Honduras is located in the north-central portion of Central America, bordered by the Caribbean Sea on the north, El Salvador on the southwest, Nicaragua on the southeast, and on the northwest by Guatemala.

The Spaniards arrived in the early 1500s, but little is known of its earlier history. The famous Mayan Indian civilization flourished in the region earlier until the 800s. The land was claimed for Spain by Christopher Columbus in 1502. Honduras is a Spanish word meaning "depths" because of the deep waters off the northern coast.

Tegucigalpa, the capital, is located among the central mountains in the south-central part of the country. Its Indian name means "Silver Hill" and it lies on a fertile plain along the banks of the Choluteca River, about 78 miles from the Gulf of Fonseca, an arm of the Pacific Ocean. The city is surrounded by mountains.

Honduras is roughly the geographical center of Central America. Tegucigalpa is one of the few capitals without a railroad.

3,070 feet MSL.

JANUARY 3-5, 1928
(TUESDAY THROUGH THURSDAY)

In 1928 the city had an airport known as Toncontin Field, located on the eastern side of the bend in the highway, in a valley three miles south of the city. The field was grass and clay with a slight slope to the south. Available lengths at the time were 3,260- and 3,610-foot runways. Elevation was about 3,294 feet MSL.

There were two large hangars, each capable of holding several tri-motor airplanes, as well as two smaller hangars on the northeast edge of the field. Fuel and oil were available as well as maintenance of airplanes.

Lindbergh came over the city during a heavy rainstorm and could see from the smoke that several cannons were being fired, although he could not hear the noise. He dropped to a lower altitude and made three passes over the Tegucigalpa Field before touching down.

For the first time in the city's history, all the barbershops and other stores were closed this special day. The local residents were dressed in gala attire and were in a very festive mood.

After landing and being assured of the safety of his airplane, Lindbergh was met by President Dr. Miguel Paz Baraona. He was taken to the Presidential Palace (Casa Presidencial) where he was to be quartered for the night.

The parade was a gala event with many decorations along the streets and on the houses, with "Viva Lindbergh" signs posted everywhere.

While in Honduras he was shown not only the city's historic sites, but also the surrounding area, and entertained by many officials and business people. He was asked to give a talk in which he again stressed the importance of developing aviation, airports and airlines for future air travel.

On Wednesday the 4th at 9:00 a.m., he was given a reception at the Presidential Palace, where the President decorated the flyer. Other officials gave him further honors.

In the afternoon he attended a special session of the Congress, where General Carias, President of the House, addressed Lindbergh: "Colonel Lindbergh, it affords me great pleasure to welcome you. Your visit to our country strengthens the bonds of friendship existing between the great North American nation and the sister republic. The National Congress of Honduras joins with the Honduran people in their manifestations of extreme joy and enthusiasm, deeming it a great honor to pay you sincere homage."

Lindbergh was also honored by the American Minister Summerlin. He was a guest at the Union Club, where they held a dinner and dance.

When Lindbergh planned to depart on Thursday, January 5, weather conditions were perfect with a clear sky and good visibility. He took off from Tegucigalpa at 11:25 a.m. after a thorough preflight and expressing his gratitude

The NYP on the field at Toncontin Field. The man with the glasses may be Vincente Mejia Colindres, President of Honduras. CARLOS ROSA MEJIA AND NORMAN FAIRBANKS

NYP in front of the hangar at Toncontin Field in Tegucigalpa. CARLOS ROSA MEJIA AND NORMAN FAIRBANKS

Lindbergh, in the light hat, in front of the Congress building in Tegucigalpa with government officials and some of the local citizens. CARLOS ROSA MEJIA AND NORMAN FAIRBANKS

NYP warming up for departure from Toncontin Field to fly to the next stop. CARLOS ROSA MEJIA AND NORMAN FAIRBANKS

NYP taking off from Toncontin Field headed for the next stop – Nicaragua. CARLOS ROSA MEJIA AND NORMAN FAIRBANKS

to everyone there.

Prominent aviator of the United Fruit Company, Sumner B. "Sunny" Morgan escorted Lindbergh part of the way to his next stop. Morgan flew the company Fokker Universal "Tela." It was named after the Tela Railroad Company that maintained the flying fields used by that particular airplane at Tela and Tegucigalpa as well as other places.

Lindbergh has carefully planned his route to avoid the conflict between the American Marines and Nicaraguan rebels. He had been warned to fly at high altitudes out of rifle range when over territory where the forces of Augusto Sandino–a pioneer guerrilla tactician of the twentieth century–operated. The U.S. Marines were engaged in crushing a revolt by Sandino's bandits against the regime of Nicaraguan President Dias, the same Dias who, on January 6, would decorate Lindbergh with a gold Medal of Merit and Valor.

Because of the abundance of volcanoes along the route, Lindbergh also planned to do some sight-seeing on this flight. He had seen volca-

The NYP on the right and a Fokker "Universal" on the left at Toncontin Field.
Pilot of the Fokker was Sunny Morgan. CARLOS ROSA MEJIA AND NORMAN FAIRBANKS

noes before but never had the chance to see one from above. He deliberately planned to fly over them.

Because Tegucigalpa was at 3,000 feet MSL, he climbed to 8,000 feet to safely clear the higher mountains and set a course for León near the Pacific Coast. He did encounter a stiff headwind resulting in a slow ground speed.

He flew south, eventually passing near the town of Choluteca after crossing the mountains. He crossed the Honduras-Nicaragua border near the River Negro, which runs into the Gulf of Fonseca to the west. After this he could also see the Pacific coast to the southwest of his route. Coming over León he dropped down in altitude, circling the city several times. He could see people running around to see his airplane as it went over.

His course was well marked by railroad tracks and a line of volcanoes before reaching Managua. The first volcano consisted of three concentric craters within one large one. This was El Viejo at an elevation of 5,800 feet MSL. The second volcano was about 2,000 feet lower and had a large crater, half a mile in diameter, and was fairly level at the bottom. The third volcano was fifteen miles farther on, and he found it to be active, smoking heavily. It was burning on one side, which was very yellow, possibly from

sulfur, and throwing off dense fumes. He wanted to fly down into it but did not have the time, according to one article he wrote (source unknown). The last volcano, also smoking, was Momotombo, close to Managua.

As he passed these behemoths his route took him south of Lago de Managua. Soon he came upon Managua and could see the field quite well. It was large and well marked with many American Marine airplanes lined up along the north side.

Today, on the very same site as the original field, is Toncontin International Airport. It now has a single runway of 3,294 feet in length. It serves most major domestic and international airlines and military operations.

There are several satellite grass airstrips in the outlying areas of the city.

References

Organizations
Embassy of Honduras, Washington, D.C.

People
Salvador E. Rodezno-Fuentes
William T. Pryce   Wendy Griffin
Paul W. Looney   Carlos Rosa Mejia
Richard A. Washburn

STOP #6
MANAGUA, NICARAGUA

CAPSULE HISTORY OF COUNTRY

Nicaragua, the largest country in Central America, is located in the southern part of the continent. It borders on the Caribbean Sea to the east and the Pacific Ocean to the southwest.

The Spaniards arrived in the early 1500s and named the land for an Indian chief and his tribe–both called Nicarao–who lived there. This country was also claimed for Spain by Christopher Columbus in 1502. On September 15, 1821, Nicaragua declared its independence.

Managua, the capital, is located in the southwestern portion on the south shore of Lake Managua (Lago de Managua), twenty-five miles east of the Pacific. It became the capital of Nicaragua in 1855.

195 feet MSL.

JANUARY 5-7, 1928
(THURSDAY THROUGH SATURDAY)

The Managua airport at that time was known as Managua National Airport. It was a military base located on the south side of Lake Managua, about two miles east-southeast of the city near the railroad tracks. This sod field had an elevation of 150 feet MSL. The runway, 2,300 feet in length, ran basically east-west and was nearly level but sloped down near the west end.

Mechanics supplied fuel and oil and did minor repairs.

After circling the city and making several low passes over the landing field, Lindbergh came in for a landing at 2:25 p.m. He did not know there was a twenty minute difference between Honduras and Nicaragua, so ended up behind

schedule when he landed at Managua.

Thirty thousand people were at the field waiting for him. The airfield was lavishly decorated with flowers and bunting, with a huge sign in white block letters that clearly spelled out, "Republica de Nicaragua Bienvenidos," Nicaragua's welcome.

After the NYP came to a stop the Nicaraguan band played the "Star Spangled Banner" in his honor. Thunderous cheers of "Viva los Estados Unidos" followed. He was greeted by the American Charge d'Affairs, Dr. Dana G. Munro. Also there to greet the flyer were President Adolfo Diaz and the American Minister Eberhardt, in addition to many other officials and military personnel. He was hailed by the newspaper, *La Noticia*, as "The Eagle without claws or talons."

According to one report, the people of the area adjacent to Managua, whatever their political affiliations, declared a truce for the day and joined in welcoming the flyer.

Soon Lindbergh was taken to El Tazate, the coffee plantation of a prominent citizen of Nicaragua, who was a graduate of Cornell University in the United States.

Later that afternoon the municipal government gave Lindbergh a reception. Mayor Jose Maria Zelaya presented him with a scroll describing him as the guest of the city and also a commemorative metal. The reception was at the International Club, which was decorated profusely with Nicaraguan and American flags and flowers.

The day was established as an official holiday by General Estrada.

In Lindbergh's usual presentation he said, "I want to thank you for myself and for my country for the honor which you have bestowed upon me here today. I cannot express to you how deeply I appreciate this honor, and I must say that my visit here is one of the most pleasant which I have experienced and will never be forgotten. I want to thank you for the honors you have given me, and I hope in the near future there will be many more flights between the United States and Central America."

Lindbergh took off from Managua at about 11:03 a.m. on Saturday the 7th, and circled the city several times before taking up a heading southeast part Nindiri and Masaya and out over Lago de Apoyo.

Soon he passed just southwest of Isla Zapatera and along the shore of the large Lago de Nicaragua, passing the Isla de Ometepe with its two volcanoes, Concepción and Madera, off his left wing.

Near the little coastal town of Cardenas it is assumed he changed direction slightly to cross the border into Costa Rica close to the town of Colón. He continued on the north side of the Cordillera de Guanacaste mountain range.

He was flying at about 4,500 feet MSL, but at one point over the lake he dropped down to 1,000 feet to fly under some clouds. Due to low visibility and rain clouds at the southern end of the lake, he dropped to 50 to 200 feet above the lake, continuing on at that altitude over a thick swamp area. The rain clouds were so low he had to fly just above the treetops. He knew that he could fly up through the clouds to clear conditions and possibly turn back or hold an instrument course until reaching the mountains, where it might be clearer. He enjoyed flying that low and seeing in the jungle palmetto, mango, and many other types of tropical growth. Lindbergh saw scores of colorful birds in the trees, many in brilliant red, yellow and blue colors. He never saw any people along this rough territory.

After passing a second river he altered his course to the south, through several mountain peaks, one of which was Volcan Barba on his left. Then he passed over the town of Poas.

After another fifteen miles he could clearly see San José. Soon he was circling over the city and then flew out to the airfield. He was a half-hour early for his planned landing at San Jose, so he circled the city a number of times.

When he finally came over the field he noticed long lines of soldiers that were stationed at ten-foot intervals in front of an apparently orderly crowd of several thousand. He figured he could land and taxi up to a pre-assigned position without the danger of hitting anyone. He also noticed that the soldiers had bayoneted rifles to "present arms" which gave him a security that all would be well. (Data on his reception and celebration has not been found by this author.)

The present-day airport for Managua is known as the Augusto Cesar Sandino Airport. It is located about four miles east of the city near the south shore of Lago de Managua, east of the

January 7, 1928, just before leaving for Costa Rica. A Fokker tri-motor can be seen in the background. LT. COL. RUDY SCHWANDA USMC RET. VIA CHARLIE ROMINE

original airport site. The airport is at an elevation of 194 feet MSL and has a single runway of 8,012 feet. It serves some domestic and international airlines, as well as military, general aviation, and helicopters.

Los Brasíles Airport is about three miles northwest of the city, with a single hard-surface runway that runs east-west.

Additional small grass airstrips dot the area to the southeast of the city and elsewhere.

References

Organizations
Embassy of Nicaragua

People
Cesar A. Zamora   Richard A. Washburn
Carlos Rosa Mejia

STOP #7
SAN JOSÉ, COSTA RICA

CAPITAL HISTORY OF COUNTRY

Costa Rica borders the Caribbean Sea as well as the Pacific Ocean, in the southern portion of Central America. It is bordered on the north by Nicaragua and the southeast by Panama.

It received its name from early Spanish adventurers who came in search of gold. Christopher Columbus discovered Costa Rica in 1502. His brother, Bartholomeo, led a group of Spaniards on the coast to establish the first white colony near the present-day Limón. Early Indian tribes were the Boruca and Chorotega. It has often been called a "Banana Republic."

The name means "rich coast" in Spanish. The name of the country in Spanish, the official language, is Republica de Costa Rica, or Republic of Costa Rica. It has very high mountains, high plateaus, and hot coastal plains.

Capital and largest city in the country is San Jose, located in a valley near the center of the country on a plateau at 3,868 feet MSL. It is one of the most attractive of the Central American cities. Due to the high altitude there is a pleasant year-round climate. Coffee growing has been their chief industry.

3,021 feet MSL (average altitude for the country).

JANUARY 7-9, 1928
(SATURDAY THROUGH MONDAY)

The only airport at that time was called Sabana Airport. The field was located a mile and a half northwest of La Sabana, at 2,780 feet MSL,

and was basically sod. The runway was oriented northeast-southwest, and was 2,860 feet long.

They had fuel and oil, no hangar, but did do minor repairs.

Costa Rica has always been a progressive republic with an advanced education system, resulting in a good standard of living. There had been a long period of peace, with able rulers, honest courts, sound land titles, and a well-run public utilities system.

When word was received that Lindbergh was coming, a committee was formed to organize a reception and to control the crowds of people so all could thoroughly enjoy his visit. Special trains were run, free to anyone, and paid for by the government. Thousands of citizens of this prosperous country came from outlying areas to see the aviator. The airport was mobbed with humanity.

Lindbergh came over the area, circled the city, then the flying field, and dropped a note on the landing area, written on a chart, asking that the spectators be moved farther back. Earlier he had sent a note suggesting adequate arrangements must be made to keep the field clear to protect the NYP. Otherwise he would only circle overhead and then continue on to one of the U.S. Army airports in the Panama Canal Zone.

There were an estimated 30,000 people there as he finally came in for a landing at either 2:11 p.m. or 2:18 p.m. The field was mostly a pasture and golf course that had been smoothed and leveled.

As the NYP came to a stop, sweating men and boys surged around the airplane and crammed closer, too close for comfort. Lindbergh was afraid that damage would be done to the fabric and structure. Lindbergh himself was physically lifted high onto the shoulders of the people, and he was half-sitting and half-lying, between bayonets that stuck up like huge needles. Years later Lindbergh said that the hazards of weather, snipers' bullets, and inadequate flying fields had been a minor

problem by comparison.

After the airplane was secured, he was met by President Jimenez and the American Minister, Mr. Davis, and escorted to a waiting car to be driven in a parade through the streets of San Jose to the American Legation (embassy). They passed by welcome signs and buildings decorated in buntings through a shower of confetti and spirals of roses and other flowers thrown from the rooftops of buildings.

While in Costa Rica he was entertained at a bull fight, for which the bull's horns were blunted and the toreadors were weaponless, much to the delight of Lindbergh who, since his youth on the farm in Minnesota, had a special love for all animals.

The famous flyer was entertained, honored and feted in this country and also given an historic tour. At one of the functions the President said, "Costa Rica is your home."

Lindbergh was up early on Monday, January 9 and, after a hearty breakfast and a good night's sleep, was at the airport for his preflight. He finally took off at 8:45 a.m. He circled the field and city several times, then came back over the flying field at about 1,500 feet, over the city again and then headed southeast.

Soon he passed over Cartago, then followed the Reventazon River valley, flying over Turrialba.

There were clouds along the Atlantic coast, so he continued over lower ground, crossing the

The NYP in flight over the Panamanian jungles enroute to Colombia. U.S. AIR FORCE PHOTO

border between Costa Rica and Panama about Bribri. From there he flew on to Almirante and Almirante Bay and over Isle Cristobal, as his course took him over the northern part of Laguna de Chiriqui, the Peninsula Valiente, and the Gulf de Los Mosquitos. He then followed the coastline to about Veraqua and flew a straight easterly course toward the Cordillera Central mountain range.

Lindbergh crossed the northern part of the mountain range, flying between Gatun Lake and Chorrera (the town of La Correra) and from there directly to Campo de Lindbergh at Panama City. He had been in the air for 4:05 minutes.

Today there are two international airports in San Jose, both of which are located only a few miles northwest of the city.

One is Juan Santamaria International, close to Alajuela, at an elevation of 3,021 feet MSL. It has one runway of 9,882 feet and serves most major domestic and international airlines.

The other, Tobias Bolanos International Airport, is closer to San Jose. It is at an elevation of 3,260 feet MSL. No other information was available at this writing.

Just twelve miles southeast of the city is a grass airstrip known as Agua Caliente on the south side of Cartago at an elevation of 4,658 feet MSL.

References

Newspapers
Miscellaneous newspaper articles

Organizations
Departmento Conservacion y restauracion Division de Microfilms

People
Johannes G. Nikkels   Walter Mora Calva
Douglas M. Bielanski   Carlos Rosa Mejia
Richard A. Washburn   Paul W. Looney
Sonia Picado, Ambassador, Washington, D.C.
Martha Virginia de Perea, Embassy, Washington, D.C.

Stop #8
Panama City, Panama

Capsule History of City and Country

Founded in 1903, Panama is the youngest republic in the Western Hemisphere and is the southernmost Central American country. It has low mountain ranges, thick jungles, and fertile green valleys and plains. The name of the country in Spanish, the official language, is Republica de Panama, meaning Republic of Panama. The local people call it the "Crossroads of the World" because it lies on a trade route between North and South America and on the route between the Atlantic Ocean and Pacific Ocean. It is famous for its Panama Canal, which runs through the Canal Zone. The country has a hot climate.

Little is known about the early Indians that lived in the area before the arrival of Europeans. In 1501 a Spanish explorer, Rodrigo de Bastidas, became the first white man to visit the area. The name Panama comes from an Indian word meaning "fishermen" or "plent of fish." Panama gained its independence on November 3, 1903.

As one of man's greatest engineering achievements, the famous Panama Canal crosses Central America to connect the Atlantic Ocean with the Pacific Ocean. The canal runs north-northwest and south-southeast. The United States built the canal, 50.72 statute miles long, during the early 1900s.

Panama City is the capital of the Republic of Panama and is the largest city. It is located at the Pacific end of the canal, on the Bahia de Panama. It was founded in 1519 by Spaniard Pedro Arias de Avila.

40 feet MSL.

January 9-12, 1928
(Monday through Thursday)

It was a clear, dry season in this part of the world, as preparations for Lindbergh's arrival were in full force. They cleared a dirt strip about 1,800 feet long by 600 feet wide, at a site seven miles out of town known as Pina Pina, in the vicinity of Juan Diaz. They named it Campo de Lindbergh. Today the Remon Race Track is lo-

cated there. The field was ready by January 4. U.S. Army Corps aircraft did landing tests with large planes to prove the field's worth.

It was hoped that the visit of Lindbergh to this area would demonstrate aviation's commercial advantages and give evidence of the airplane's new respectability, safety, and potential. The advantages to be gained through rapid air connections to the United States were obvious. Panama would eventually have commercial air communication with their neighbors and the United States and then would come the prospect of the Isthmus becoming a crossroads for ships of the air as it was already for ships of the sea.

Everyone became excited as news of Lindbergh's travels through Central America came over the wires and the date of his arrival approached. This visit was so important that Panama issued a special commemorative postage stamp. The sale would begin on the day of his arrival. They were of 2-cent and 3-cent value

depicting the NYP. It was also announced that a two-day National Holiday would be in effect while Lindbergh was there.

Lindbergh arrived over Balboa, across the Canal to the southwest, and was escorted by Army pursuit airplanes at 1:40 p.m. He circled the terminal city and proceeded to Campo de Lindbergh, flew slowly over the field, did a low pass, and came in for a landing at 1:50 p.m.

The crowds of people along the edge of the field, most of whom had stayed in place, now broke through the police lines, to head out onto the field toward the landing NYP. However, Lindbergh did manage to taxi quickly into a special fenced area, where he came to a stop and shut down the engine. He was greeted by Col. Arango, his Panama Aide de Camp. Arango soon escorted the flyer to a hastily erected presidential stand and introduced him to the Foreign Minister, Dr. Alfaro, who in turn presented him to President Don Rodolfo Chiari. He met there for a short time with the press and then entered the President's car to be driven in a parade through the city streets to City Hall. On the way they passed the Panama Railroad Station, where schoolchildren sang the "Lindbergh March," which was quite emotional. At City Hall on Cathedral Plaza he received the Gold Key of the City of Panama.

Meanwhlie the NYP was under constant guard by both the Panamanian National Police and Panamanian Bomberos (firemen) in that specially made enclosure.

In the evening of the first day

Lindbergh in the NYP on January 9th had just landed and was taxiing in. UNIVERSITY OF MARYLAND

Taxiing in at Campo Lindbergh. Notice Panama firemen in dark shirts, white trousers, and the white line along the ground to guide the pilot in. The crowd is following the Panamanian National Police on horseback. U.S. military in foreground only. CLARE H. COMINS VIA GEORGES G. BOUCHE

A good close-up of the nose of the NYP showing the flags painted on up to this stop. MARK WYNNEMER

The NYP at its final resting place with a man (not CAL) checking the engine and a makeshift ladder for fueling. GEORGE B. ARMSTEAD JR.

Lindbergh was served a light supper at the American Legation, hosted by the U.S. Charge d'Affairs Martin. He also had an audience with the President.

At 11:00 p.m. he was escorted to the Union Club, then went to the Las Bobedas Plaza Reancia for a special performance by Panamanian folk dancers and musicians. Finally he returned to the American Legation for a much needed rest.

The next day Lindbergh was given a sightseeing trip around the area. Also on this day he took President Chiari up for his first airplane ride. After the flight, the President was so impressed he said, "For a man to realize how really insignificant he is in the universal order of things, he must fly." The type of airplane is not known but appears to have been a TMO-6. He flew several other dignitaries as well and flew a PW-9 airplane that day.

Wednesday, the 11th, was Canal Zone Day, and he was asked to call upon Acting Governor Burgess and then did more sightseeing. It was a packed day of meeting people, watching all kinds of demonstrations, and attending luncheons. There was a public reception below the Administration Building attended by over 3,000 people. Lindbergh spoke for a few minutes on the glowing future of aviation on the Isthmus.

Lindbergh was also taken over to Balboa, where he gave a talk on the future of air travel and aviation in general. Also on this day Lindbergh was honored by two thousand school-children at a swimming pool in the city.

There is a report that the President's grand-

Early morning showing a Boy Scout rolling up his bedroll after a night of guarding the airplane. Notice man painting the Panama flag on the nose cowl. PHOTOGRAPHER GOMEZ MIRALLES, VIA THE HERBERT HOOVER PRESIDENTIAL LIBRARY-MUSEUM

Herb Halliday just outside the fence. COL. RET. HERBERT E. HALLIDAY

son, possibly just born, was named after the flyer–Lindy Carlos Parades.

In the evening Lindbergh enjoyed a dinner at Quarry Heights with Panama Division Commander Graves, at his residence.

On Thursday, January 12, after a rousing farewell, Lindbergh took off at 9:45 a.m. from Campo de Lindbergh field and circled over the area several times before heading northeast.

On this short hop he headed up the canal, across Gatun Lake, then changed course and flew directly to Colón, where he circled several times before planning his landing there.

There are six airports in and around the general Panama Canal area. That includes two turf/grass airstrips for general aviation.

The main airport is Tocumen International, at an elevation of 135 feet MSL. It has two parallel (more or less) runways, the longer of which is 10,006 feet. The field is located ten miles northeast of the city and serves most all domestic and international airlines and some general aviation and military aircraft.

General Omar Torrijos Herrera International Airport is just another ten miles in the same direction and is at an elevation of 135 feet MSL. It has a single northwest-southeast paved runway.

Across the canal and southwest of the city is an Air Force base with two parrallel runways. Directly north about ten miles from the city is Calzada Larga Airport at an elevation of 394 feet MSL with one single north-south runway.

A good aerial view of the *Spirit of St. Louis* in its resting place, the many automobiles, people and the reception enclosure to the upper right. CASSAGNERES COLLECTION

Close-up of Lindbergh in the cockpit of the NYP. Notice the large Kollsman "Super Sensitive Altimeter" mounted on the instrument panel just in front of the flyer. MARK WYNNEMER

Aerial view showing the NYP flying over part of the Panama Canal. CASSAGNERES COLLECTION

Can you see the NYP as it flies over part of Gatun Lake in the Canal Zone? CASSAGNERES COLLECTION

STOP #9
COLÓN, CANAL ZONE

Second largest city in Panama, Colón is located on Manzanillo Island, a peninsula overlooking Limon Bay at the Atlantic end of the Panama Canal. It was founded in 1852 by Americans who built the Panama Railroad and named it Aspinwall, after William H. Aspinwall, a promoter of the railroad. In 1890 the Panamanians changed the name to Colón, in honor of Christopher Columbus. Colón in Spanish means Columbus.

Referred to as the Canal Zone, a part of the country of Panama, the "Zone" is a strip of land that lies along or across the country of Panama. The Canal runs through the center of the zone. The United States and Panama signed a treaty in 1903 to establish the Canal Zone. This pact gave the United States the right to build and operate the Panama Canal and to govern the zone. It is interesting to note that the United States never had control over Panama City and Colón, although the cities lie at the ends of the canal. The negotiations to return the Canal to Panamanian control took place in the 1970s and the Panamanians took over in 2000.

25 feet MSL.

JANUARY 12-26, 1928
(TWO WEEKS, THURSDAY THROUGH THURSDAY)

After a forty-five-minute flight from Panama City along the Canal in perfect weather with warm sun and little wind, Lindbergh came over Colón, where he circled several times and made what was described as a perfect three-point landing at 10:30 a.m. He was escorted by several military airplanes of the U.S. Army Air Corps, some of which had the press as their passengers.

He landed on France Field, a modern military airport, operated by the American military. It had newly painted hangars and housed many fighters and bombers for the defense of the canal.

After climbing out of the cockpit, Lindbergh

was greeted by Governor J.D. Arosemena, Inocencio Galindo Jr., who was chairman of the reception committee, and Lt. Col. Arthur G. Fisher. Fisher was an ex-cavalryman who commanded France Field, and was also a rated airship pilot.

The NYP was immediately put into one of the largest hangars to be thoroughly checked over by military aircraft mechanics. One photograph exists in the author's collection, showing it in the hangar, with the full cowling removed, the propeller and spinner assembly and magnetos removed as well. They more than likely did an oil change, checked the spark plugs, mag timing and a general "annual" type inspection for the whole airframe during those sixteen days before he left for the next leg of his tour.

Soon after landing and meeting everyone, Lindbergh was escorted to a waiting car for the parade into town. In the car with him were the Governor and Lt. Robert W. Douglas Jr. of the 24th Pursuit Squadron.

During those days in Panama, Lindbergh was wined, dined, entertained and taken to all the interesting sites.

On Friday, the 13th, he flew a Curtiss PW-9C, accompanied by two other Army airplanes, to Panama City to visit with the famous French flyers, Dieudonne Costes and Joseph Marie Le Brix. They had just flown down from Paris via Africa and across the South Atlantic to Guayaquil, Equador, with several stops along the way for fuel and rest, finally landing at Panama City. They were flying in a French Brequet XIX (19), 600-hp, two-place, open-cockpit biplane.

On the 14th, in a Curtiss PW-9C with Lt. Robert Douglas Jr. and Capt. Arthur Simonin in the same type airplanes, Lindbergh flew west-southwest to the picturesque village of Bouquete, in the state of Chiriqui, for a vacation as a guest of the Army. It was a 200-mile flight. The village was within sight of Baru volcano, shown on today's charts as Volcan de Chiriqui, at a height of 11,396 feet MSL. Lindbergh's disappearance caused surprise throughout the world, as he enjoyed himself away from civilization.

Lindbergh in the NYP being escorted by Army fliers over Gatun Lake on his way to France Field, CZ. U.S. AIR FORCE MUSEUM

France Field, showing Lindbergh in the NYP just after landing. U.S. AIR FORCE MUSEUM

The NYP on the "roll-out" after landing. Notice the windsock in upper middle on top of hangar. U.S. ARMY AIR CORPS

Local men and military people lending a helping hand to guide the flyer in. MARK WYNNEMER

Running up the NYP engine near the large hangars on France Field. CRADLE OF AVIATION MUSEUM

Lindbergh (in dark suit) standing with, from left: Lt. Col. Arthur Fisher, Lt. Dieudoune Costes, Lt. Joseph Marie Le Brix, Capt. Simonin and Lt. Douglass. U.S. AIR FORCE MUSEUM

A wonderful close-up of Lindbergh with his helmet and goggles on. STAM ROBERTSON

The NYP outside one of the large hangars. Notice the patches on the fuselage near the cockpit. MARION J. KIMBRELL

Good photo of the French aviators, Costes and Le Brix, in the cockpit of their Breguet 19. STAM ROBERTSON

The NYP during maintenance in one of the large hangars. The airplane was thoroughly checked over, to get it ready for the next leg of Lindbergh's journey. CLARE H. COMINS VIA GEORGES G. BOUCHE

The NYP next to a Panther Cub, at the time presumed to be the smallest airplane in the world. MUSEUM OF FLIGHT, SEATTLE, WA

Here Lindbergh is shown during the parade through the area. MUSEUM OF FLIGHT, SEATTLE WA

The little group stayed at Wright's Hotel, owned and operated by Mr. and Mrs. "Pop" Wright. While there he and his friends hunted, hiked, fished, rode horseback, played cards and generally relaxed.

On Monday, the 16th, Lt. Col. Fisher flew out to Bouquete to spend several days with the three flyers before they all returned. On Friday, the 20th, they all flew back to France Field, and Lindbergh spent that evening at the home of the Fishers. The next day he was given a tour of Fort San Lorenzo and its ruins, located west of Colón

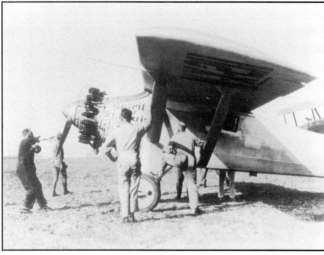

Army mechanics getting ready to check out the engine after and annual-type maintenance was completed.
MUSEUM OF FLIGHT, SEATTLE WA

A wonderful photo of a child by the name of Margaret "Peggy" Hyland, then living in Panama while her father was stationed there, as Chief Mechanic with the U.S. Army Air Corps. She is now Mrs. John Ayala and lives in California. MRS. HELEN H. ZELINSKY

on the coast of the Caribbean.

On the 22nd (Sunday) Lindbergh flew the NYP on a test flight over the area for one hour and fifteen minutes to check it over after its recent maintenance by the Army. On the 23rd he spent the day touring the Gatun Locks and other areas of the canal system, and was shown how it all operated.

On Tuesday, the 24th, in the morning Lindbergh was invited to indulge in that once common Isthmian sport of alligator hunting along the old French Canal with Lt. Douglas. In the afternoon they flew out to the Perlas Islands in a borrowed Navy Loening OA-1A amphibian for an overnight fishing trip. Part of the venture was spent aboard the Canal Zone tug *S.S. Favorite.* They returned the next day to France Field, and it is assumed that Lindbergh spent the remainder of the day resting and planning for his next flight, to Cartagena, Colombia.

Lindbergh left a legacy, serving as the catalyst who popularized commercial air travel, both in the United States as well as, and more specifically, on the Isthmus. Within a few years of his initial flight to Panama, there were 12-hour connections to the United States, and the crossroads of the world's shipping was on its way to becoming one of the aviation centers in that part of the world.

Lindbergh returned in Sikorsky flying boats and pioneered air travel and the air mail services to Latin America. He always drew crowds of admirers, but never again was the thrill the same. His imprint on the Isthmus is indelible.

In the early morning of Thursday, January 26, he took time (according to his log) to fly a Thomas-Morse 0-6 and a Douglas C-1 transport. He then took off in the NYP at 9:26 a.m. for the flight to the old colonial fortress city of Cartagena, Colombia.

After circling over the area a number of times, he headed southeast and south of a large lake and over thick jungle. He passed just a few miles north of Panama City before hitting the Bay of Panama of the Golfo de Panama (Pacific Ocean). He flew along the coast to the east and then southeast to a point south of the Serrania de Canazas mountain range on his left.

Eventually he left the coast and headed east-

southeast and over the Istmo Del Darien valley, over the Serrania del Darien mountain range, and crossed the border into Colombia, striking the Caribbean Sea (Mar Caribe) at about Sapzurro. He then crossed the thirty miles of salt water of the Golfo de Uraba to Pta. Caribana, while cruising along at 1,800 feet MSL. Fighting a headwind, he made a ground speed of about 95 mph, but continued on a northeast heading, passing Golfo de Morrosquillo to the far shore, then north to Cartagena after crossing the Bahia de Barbacoas. He came over the city at 1:45 p.m.

Today there are only two nearby airports in the Colón area. The main one if Enrique Adolfo Jimenez Airport. It is located right outside of the city at an elevation of 25 feet MSL. It has a single north-south paved runway of 6,001 feet. The airport is located on the same site where France Field was.

Across the bay to the west is a general aviation grass/turf airstrip named Sherman Airport. It is at an elevation of 10 feet MSL.

References

Newspapers
Panama American, January 10, 1928
Canal Record

Organizations
The Panama Canal Society of Florida, Inc.
The libraries of the University of Maryland
at College Park

People

Paul W. Looney	George G. Bouche
Merl C. Olmsted	Richard W. "Pat" Beall
Julius Grigore Jr.	George M. Chevalier
R.D. Meyers	Karen Fishman
Carlos Rosa Mejia	Richard A. Washburn
Jodi McKee	Dan Hagedorn

STOP #10
CARTAGENA, COLUMBIA

CAPSULE HISTORY OF CITY AND COUNTRY

Cartagena is the chief seaport on the northwestern coast of Colombia, just below Barranquilla, on the Caribbean Sea. The city was founded in 1533. Cartagena was also known as the old colonial fortress city. The city was named after Cartagena, Spain, the name of which originated from the Carthaginians, who founded the Spanish city in about 225 B.C.

Colombia lies in the northwest portion of the continent of South America. The first people in the area were the Chibeha Indians, who farmed and made pottery. A Spanish explorer, Alonso de Ojeda, discovered Colombia in 1499. The Spaniards named it New Granada, after the home province of Gonzalo Jimenez de Quesada, a Spanish lawyer. The country was claimed by Spain in 1536. It was named for Christopher Columbus, and the name in Spanish is Republica de Colombia or Republic of Colombia. Because of the extreme altitude differences from sea level to its highest peak at 18,947 feet, the climate varies from extreme tropical heat to damp, biting cold.

5 feet MSL.

JANUARY 26-27, 1928
(THURSDAY AND FRIDAY)

At the time of Lindbergh's visit, the only flying field was known as the Boca Grande Field, a military camp. It was an improvised strip in what today is the Avenida San Martin, now the Centro Commercial Bocagrande.

Lindbergh first appeared over the city at 1:40 p.m. and after a low pass across the field, he came around for a nice landing shortly before 2:00 p.m., his planned ETA.

He was met by many of the country and city officials and military personnel. When Lindbergh was assured of the security of the NYP, he was escorted to a waiting automobile to be driven in a parade into the suburb of Isla de Manga, where he was the guest of H.O. Ware, an American businessman. Most likely he was quartered there.

The municipal council of Cartagena declared him the guest of honor of the city. Accompanied by officials of the welcoming committee, he was taken to the Club Cartagena for a reception. At 7:30 p.m. Lindbergh was a guest at a gala dinner. He gave his usual promotional talk

Lindbergh, just after he arrived in Cartagena on Boca Grande military field, and being greeted by the reception people. FUNDACION FOTOTECA HISTORICA DE CARTAGENA DE INDIAS

The NYP is swamped by the multitudes of people in Cartagena. FUNDACION FOTOTECA HISTORICA DE CARTAGENA DE INDIAS

to further the development of aviation and air travel in the area. At the banquet Miss Olga Noguera Davila, Queen of the Students, placed a kiss on Lindbergh, and he turned red and blushed with embarrassment.

The American minister held a reception at the Embassy that evening at 9:00 p.m.

On Friday morning, it appears, Lindbergh flew a Wright J-5 (2) powered Sikorsky S-36 amphibian over the area.

Then after a thorough preflight of the NYP, Lindbergh took off from Cartagena at about 8:00 a.m. He circled over the field and the city, then took up a south-southeast heading. The route took him mostly over lowland at first, before crossing a small mountain range near El Carmen and then passing to the east of Sincelejo, again over more lowland areas.

Telegraph operators in towns that he flew over informed that newspaper of the time. For instance, he was reported over Sincelejo at 10:20 a.m. and 30 minutes later over Caimito, at 1:25 p.m. he was over Puerto Berrio, and at 2:10 p.m. over Yacopi.

For a while he paralleled the Rio San Jorge, near the towns of San Benito Abad and San Marcos, and then Ayapel. Soon the countryside became very rugged with dense jungle.

He located himself at the forks of the Nechi and Cauca rivers, flying parallel with the Rio Nechi for a while, then left the river at about El Bagre, and passed just to the west side of a 2,920-foot mountain peak on his left side. A second peak at the same elevation was at the village of Los Chorros.

Lindbergh with Colombian military and civilian officials, next to the NYP. FUNDACION FOTOTECA HISTORICA DE CARTAGENA DE INDIAS

Continuing over more high terrain he came upon the Magdalena River at about Puerto Berrio. From there he changed to a southerly course, at 2,000 feet, and flew over some more high mountain country, paralleling to the east the Magdalene River and then part of the Negro River, passing to the east side of an 8,800-foot mountain.

He was at 8,000 feet at this point and had found clouds covering the mountains on his left side. He detoured from a direct line to Bogotá to the west to go around the mountains and at 9,800 feet found a clear path that appears to have been just to the west of Alban and Facatativa, until southwest of Facatativa, where he turned directly east toward Bogotá.

He arrived over Madrid Field at 2:00 p.m. and went directly to the city, circling several times and flying back to Madrid, where he landed at three o'clock.

The main airport for Cartagena is Rafael Nunez, located on a peninsula on the north side of the city. It is at an elevation of 5 feet MSL and has a single north-south runway of 8,530 feet. It serves most domestic and international airlines, as well as general aviation, helicopters and some military aircraft.

One grass/turf airstrip by the name of Hormigas is located about five miles northeast of the city.

In case of very poor weather, the alternate airport is Ernesto Cortissoz at Barranquilla, about sixty air miles to the northeast.

A good view of the NYP on the Boca Grande field, again showing the fabric patches near the cockpit.
FUNDACION FOTOTECA HISTORICA DE CARTAGENA DE INDIAS

STOP #11

SANTA FE DE BOGOTÁ, COLOMBIA

CAPSULE HISTORY OF CITY

Bogotá, Colombia, capital of the country, is located more or less in the central western portion, high in the Andes Mountains. Because of its high elevation, the climate is cool and fresh.

The city was founded in 1538 by Gonzalo Jimenez de Quesada, conqueror of the Chibeha Indians. Originally it was known as Santa Fe de Bogotá, a name derived from the Chibeha

Chief Bacata. It became the capital in 1819.

The city is often called the "Athens of America" because of its center of art and learning.

8,659 feet MSL.

JANUARY 27-29, 1928
FRIDAY THROUGH SUNDAY

There was a clear blue sky as Lindbergh came into view over the capital city. He realized

-313-

that he was one hour early and ahead of his schedule. His ETA was three o'clock in the afternoon. So he flew over the area, and the people went wild when they realized who it was and waved enthusiastically at him with white handkerchiefs.

Because he initially came over at a high altitude, part of the time was spent in a spiral, descending lower and lower, until just before 3:00 p.m. he came over Madrid Field. It was like flying into a large basin, as the city is surrounded by mountains.

He landed at exactly 3:00 p.m. Madrid Field is part of the military school and was fairly well-equipped for security requirements and the safety of the NYP, including some hangars. Madrid at that time was known as Aerodromo de Techo (Techo airfield), which was located until 1957 approximately five miles southwest of the modern El Dorado airport.

There were about 15,000 people there to greet the flyer, including government officials, members of the diplomatic corps and military personnel. Madrid Field is at an elevation of nearly 9,000 feet, and was the highest elevation for the NYP to take off and land on during its flying life.

The man in charge of security of the NYP was Lieutenant Gutierrez of the Colombian Army. The Lieutenant had the troops surround the airplane for protection as soon as the engine stopped.

When Lindbergh climbed out of the cockpit, he was hoisted onto the shoulders of some young people, who marcked with him toward the hangars. It was extremely hot that day.

The usual parade left the field and proceeded into town to the Presidential Palace (Carrera Palace) where he was received by the President and other officials. At the palace President Miguel Abadia Mendez presented Lindbergh with the Emblem of the Cross of Boyaca of the First Order. Lindbergh was the first American to gain this recognition from the government. Only ten foreigners have ever received the Cross. The Cross was pinned on Lindbergh's lapel by the President, who said, "We give you this in wishing the American people prosperity and tranquility."

From there Lindbergh was taken to the Ministry of Foreign Affairs, where he was received by Dr. Don Carlos Uribe, the Minister, and from there to the War Office, where he was greeted by General Santander, Chief of Staff. At the War Office he received a gold plaque as a gift from the Colombian Army.

That evening there was a banquet in his honor and a special dance at the Jockey Club. After introductions, he gave a speech stressing the importance of developing air travel and airports in Colombia and creating airlines to connect with the rest of the world.

Most of the next day was spent as a guest of the country. They showed him the historic sites and other special places in and around Bogotá. Also on this day he flew over the area for twenty minutes with Abraham Llevano in a Swiss training airplane powered with a Hispano-Suiza 150-hp engine.

Lindbergh was hosted at a luncheon by Samual H. Piles, the American Minister, that included another guest, Dr. Pidrahita, Mayor of Bogotá.

On Sunday, January 29, the sky was clear, as he prepared to depart from Madrid Field. After a preflight and expressing his appreciation for the country's hospitality, Lindbergh took off at 6:48 a.m. and immediately circled over the field as well as the city of Bogotá, climbing up to gain altitude over the mountains. Heading northeast up the valley toward Cajica and Choconta, he ran into very cloudy conditions. He then continued to Tunja and northwest of Sogamoso where he flew on the other side of a 10,500-foot mountain. He continued up the valley past Curital and was unable to get over the mountains, so he made a 180-degree turn. He spiraled for a while and finally found an open area over the mountains, where he crossed over a ridge between the clouds at 12,000 feet. He came into a clear and flat area. Then he changed his course to fly northeast up the valley and shortly crossed the Rio Casanare. Eventualy he came upon the border of Venezuela at the Arauca River, just southeast of Guasdualito, and followed the Rio Apure to where it meets the Rio Suripa.

There were times when he would drop down to only fifty feet above the ground in the plains area to view the scenery and details of the land. For 400 miles, while flying over this flat plain area, he found few landmarks to check his position. Shortly the Cordillera of Merida mountains appeared on the horizon to his left.

At this point Lindbergh did not know that a

severe storm covered Venezuela's coastal mountains, which would force him to detour. Straight ahead he noticed that clouds covered the lower mountains around Caracas. He held his heading to about San Juan de los Morros and changed his course easterly to fly around the south side of the range. His new route took him just north of Embalse de Camatagua Lake directly to Clarines. Flying for two hours he hunted out an opening to get to the sea.

Just south of Puerto Piritu and about 140 miles east of Caracas, he made another 180-degree turn (west of Barcelona) to fly out over the sea and headed west along the coastline. It was about 4:00 p.m. and the sun was due to set at 6:00 p.m.

Lindbergh was racing time and went full throttle to arrive before dark. He followed the coast along the northern side of the Cordillera de la Costa mountain range, off the coast of Maiquetia, north of Caracas. The air grew rough and the sand beach disappeared. He continued to fly to Puerto Cruz, where he turned and headed inland directly to Maracay, located on the northeast shore of Lago de Valencia.

He landed on Maracay Field a few minuted before sunset.

Madrid Airbase is located on the same site as it was in 1927 and is 8,355 feet MSL in elevation. It has a single northeast-southwest paved runway. The field is still located about fifteen miles northwest of the city.

On the northwest edge of the city near Fontibon is the large Eldorado International Airport, at an elevation of 8,361 feet MSL. It has two parallel runways, both of which are 12,467 feet long. It serves most major international airlines as well as domestic, commuter, and cargo.

Directly north about ten miles is Guaymaral Airport at an elevation of 8,478 feet MSL. It has a single paved runway that runs basically east-west. There are no other airports near Bogotá.

References

Newspapers
  Bogota, Republica de Colombia, Sabado, January 28, 1928
  ABC Propietario; Rennaldo Valencia, Quibdo, January 26, 1928
  El Tiempo, Edicion de Doce Paginas, Bogotá
  El Grafico
  El Espectador

Organizations
  Columbia Embassy, Washington, D.C.
  Fototeca Historica de Cartagena: Fund
  Museo Romantico, Barranquilla, Col.
  Centro de Recursos Informativos, Embassy, USA

People
  Fidel Cano, Press Secretary, Embassy, Wash. D.C.
  Maj. Gen. Hector Hernando Gil Nieto, Bogotá, Col.
  Cecilia Grandos, Directora, Embassy, Bogotá, Col.
  Carlos Rangel, Bogotá, Col.
  M. Longas Tonylow, Medellin, Col.
  Blanca de Vassallo, Barranquille, Col.
  Juan C. Betancur, Pereira, Col.
  Manfred Oeding, Barranquilla, Col.
  Dorothy J. de Espinosa, Cartagena, Col.
  Paul W. Looney   Capt. Tony Vallillo
  Richard A. Washburn   Juan C. Beyancur

(No photos have ever been found for the Bogotá leg of the tour.)

Stop #12
Caracas, Venezuela

Capsule History of City and Country

Caracas, the nation's capital, is located in the north-central part of the country, six miles inland from the port of LaGuaira, on the Caribbean Sea. A Spaniard, Diego de Losado, founded this large city in 1567.

Venezuela is a republic located on the northern coast of South America on the Caribbean Sea. The name is Spanish for "little Venice." Spanish explorers found an Indian village built on wooden poles above the shallow waters of Lake Maracaibo, and the village reminded them of Venice, Italy. The official name of the coun-

try is Republica de Venezuela (Republic of Venezuela). Today it is one of the most modern countries in Latin America.

The Carib Indians were the first people in the area. The country was discovered by Christopher Columbus in 1498, and the next year the Spanish explorer Alonso de Ojeda led an expedition to the area. The Teques indians also inhabited the area. The country received its independence on July 5, 1811.

3,164 feet MSL.

Here is seen the NYP in a hangar on the military field at Maracay, Venezuela. The country's flag has just been painted on the cowling. DICK SHERMAN

JANUARY 29-31, 1928
(SUNDAY THROUGH TUESDAY)

Caracas did not have an airfield at the time–at least there is no mention of one in any reference material found by the author. However, Maracay, located at the northeast corner of Lago de Valencia, did have a military flying field with a hangar. By road Caracas was about fifty miles east, near the south side of the Cordillera de la Costa mountains.

Lindbergh came in low over the field, then came around and landed at 6:10 p.m. after his ten-hour-and-fifty-minute flight from Bogotá. It was the first flight over that route made by any airplane.

The NYP was quickly placed in the military hangar, where Lindbergh spent considerable time discussing its security with the proper authorities.

Meanwhile the Venezuelan dictator, Juan Vincente Gomez, and his friends were waiting nearby for some time, all sitting comfortably under a canopy. Many people there were upset at Lindbergh's concern for his airplane rather than greeting Gomez first.

However, Gomez was not woried and said, "Uh-huh. That's the kind of man I like. He looks after his beast first. He is a cavalier of the skies. He examines his plane as a horseman examines his mount before riding."

Lindbergh did apologize to Gomez for having kept him waiting for a long time. Gomez immediately decorated Lindbergh with the Order of the Liberator, one of the highest honors from that country. It was also referred to as the Order of Liberty, or Order of the Commander.

Shortly Lindbergh was escorted to a waiting car and was driven from Maracay to Caracas. He rode with Gomez and his aides over

a road strewn with roses by the admiring Venezuelans. The flyer spent the night at the United States Legation.

The next day the city gave him a tumultuous welcome with everyone shouting "Viva" until they were hoarse. Beautiful young ladies, teir arms filled with flowers, waved and shouted from many balconies of buildings along the parade route.

Lindbergh received a warm welcome from the people of the capital city of Caracas. He found the crowds much more disciplined than at many of the other places he visited.

While there Lindbergh placed a wreath on the tomb of the great liberator, Simón Bolívar, in the National Pantheon. The inscription read, "From Colonel Charles Lindbergh to the Memory of General Simón Bolívar." Bolívar was considered the George Washington of South America.

Gomez was an interesting fellow who had fathered ninety-seven children. Several of the dictator's children, neatly attired, presented Lindbergh with bunches of flowers. The smiling Lindbergh, obviously pleased while accepting them, said, "Are they natural?" And Gomez replied, thinking Lindbergh referred to the children, said, "Yes, natural, but recognized." (To explain the above, one needs to know that in Venezuela at that time illegitimate children were called "natural" children. They became legitimate when they were legally "recognized.")

Lindbergh was driven to Maracay early in the morning of the 31st, a Tuesday. The NYP's fuel tanks had been filled for the over one-thousand-mile flight to St. Thomas. After a thorough preflight he took off at 6:00 a.m.

He circled the city several times and then took up an easterly heading. He climbed up and over La Victoria and flew directly to the coastline, somewhere near Areanas or Puerto Piritu. He passed just south of Puerto La Cruz and up over some high terrain over Cumanacoa and reached the west shore of the Gulf of Paria, south of Yaguaraparo and Irapa and headed toward the tip of the Peninsula de Paria neaer Puerto de Hierra and its eastern tip.

From this point he changed to a more northerly direction (north-northeast) toward Granada Island of the Grenadine Islands. It was about a hundred-mile overwater flight.

He flew over the island and from there passed to the west of Carriacau and Union Island, continued on the same course, and passed along the west coast of Saint Vincent, a northern unit of the British Windward Islands.

The next island was Saint Lucia, where he went along the west shoreline past Castries, and took a north-northwest heading toward the west side of Martinique. He passed by the city of Fort-De-France, and continued toward Dominica and its west shore. He then flew over Roseau and Portsmouth on Dominica, continuing toward Guadeloupe.

He approached the southern tip of Guadeloupe at about Basse-Terre and La Pointe-Noire. Then he took up a heading more to the northwest, passing just west of Newcastle on the island of Nevis and Basse-Terre on the island of St. Kitts (Saint Christopher). He then passed Saint Eustatius Island toward Saba Island and from there took a direct heading of over 120 miles over water to St. Thomas in 10 hours and 45 minutes, encountering some head winds and some rain. He kept his cruising speed higher than normal due to the head winds because, as usual, he had plenty of fuel capacity.

There are three main airports for the city of Caracas today. The main one is Simon Bolivar International, which is located near the coast of the Caribbean Sea, about four miles north of the city. It is at an elevation of 235 feet MSL and it has two main runways, the longer of which is 11,483 feet. The field is actually located in Maiquetia. It serves most domestic and international airlines as well as commuters, general aviation, and military aircraft.

Within the city limits there is a single paved runway at the General Francisco de Miranda Air Base, owned and operated by the Venezuelan Air Force. It is at an elevation of 2,739 feet MSL.

Fifteen miles south of the city is Caracas International del Centro, at an elevation of 2,145 feet MSL. It is a single east-west paved runway.

At Maracay there are three airports: Mariscal Sucre, El Libertador, and a small grass/turf strip (at Cagua). Mariscal Sucre is at an elevation of 1,338 feet MSL. El Libertador is at an elevation of 1,450 feet MSL, and the grass field is at 1,555 feet MSL.

References

Newspapers
   Miscellaneous newspapers, *Associated Press* and *International Newsreel*

People
   Richard Sanders Allen
   Paul W. Looney
   Richard A. Washburn

STOP #13
ST. THOMAS, VIRGIN ISLANDS

CAPSULE HISTORY OF CITY AND ISLANDS

The beautiful Virgin Islands are located just forty miles east of Puerto Rico, between the Caribbean Sea and the Atlantic Ocean. There are two groups of small islands: the American group consists of St. Croix, St. John, and St. Thomas islands. They are the easternmost pos-sessions of the United States.

Christopher Columbus discovered the islands on his second voyage to the Americas in 1493. He named the group the Virgin Islands in memory of St. Ursula and her 11,000 maidens. He claimed these islands for Spain.

Warlike Carib Indians lived on the island first. A British group of settlers were the first

whites to settle there in 1607. Later several of the islands were transferred to American possession.

Charlotte Amalie is the capital city of St. Thomas, located in the south-central part of the island on the Caribbean Sea. It is the largest city on the island and is the capital of the American Virgin Islands, a harbor city on the Caribbean. It was named for the princess consort of King Christian V of Denmark.

Charlotte Amalie is 40 feet MSL.

Crown Mountain is 1,556 feet MSL.

JANUARY 31-FEBRUARY 2, 1928
(TUESDAY THROUGH THURSDAY)

On January 6, 1928, Governor Waldo Evans had sent a radiogram through the Commandant of the 15th Naval District, Balboa, Canal Zone; "To Col. Lindbergh–The governor and people of the Virgin Islands extend to you a cordial invitation to visit St. Thomas on your way north. We would be honored to have you as our guest."

On January 9, Lindbergh replied, "I accept with pleasure your kind invitation to visit the Virgin Islands. Because my time is so limited, I will be able to remain in St. Thomas two days only, the day of my arrival and the next day. Will inform you of my date of arrival more accurately later."

The governor gathered a group of local officials, citizens, and business people to discuss the upcoming visit, and how they should prepare for the event. The most important factor was to select a suitable and safe field for his landing. They did not have an airport at the time.

The governor asked his engineers to check out sites, and they suggested two possibilities. One was a closely cropped pasture between the Sugar Estate Road on the north and Long Bay Road on the south. This land was made available through the courtesy of Mr. A.H. Lockhart. Already work had begun to smooth out the surface. The other suggestion was the local golf course. It was a small uphill field with mountains at the end. The governor accepted a recommendation from a local pilot that they use the golf course. The golf course was also known as "strip No. 2." Strip No. 1 was the "Sugar Estate."

The first airplane to land on the island was some sort of tri-motor biplane, flown by W.S. Wade, carrying four passengers. It landed on the golf course, flying in from San Juan, Puerto Rico, on January 22.

In preparation for Lindbergh's visit, all of the public places were decorated with plants and flowers. Painters were putting finishing touches on store fronts, and streets were spotlessly cleaned. Flags and bunting were seen everywhere.

The Governor declared February 1 as an official island holiday, and a holiday spirit prevailed.

The roads leading to the golf course were crowded with autos, carriages, bicycles and other transport conveyances as well as people on foot.

It had been raining on and off, but just before Lindbergh was due to arrive the sun broke through and it became sunny and pleasant.

At about 4:20 p.m. signal guns gave a 21-gun salute from the town battery, and the sound of steam whistles from ships in the harbor brought cheers from the waiting throngs of people.

Lindbergh approached from the southeast, a bit low as he approached the island. He found the field and made a low pass to inspect the surface of the short landing area. Then he flew seaward and southward, turned, and came in for the short landing. Guards had difficulty controlling the crowds as they ran out on the field.

He landed at 4:50 p.m., 60th meridian time,

The NYP shown on "strip No. 2," the local golf course with a tarp over the engine to keep it dry from the rain. Notice the fabric patch still there near the cockpit. LEO B. KIMBALL COLLECTION

which is 30 minutes ahead of Maracay time. He made the flight in 10 hours and 15 minutes.

After climbing out of the cockpit he gave instructions for tying down the airplane because there was no hangar. The flyer was escorted to a reception stand decorated with a beautiful wreath of flowers, which was placed around his shoulders by an attractive Miss D. Lamb. He was formally received by the governor and his staff.

In a few minutes Lindbergh and the governor climbed into the latter's official car. The parade of a few autos made its way onto the main street, through the business district of Charlotte Amalie to Government House, where he would be the guest of the island.

There was a press conference there, and one writer was Isidor Paiewonsky, who was nineteen years old at the time. A friend of his, a Navy draftsman/engineer by the name of Schaub, invited him to go to the NYP at the field, where he would paint the Virgin Islands flag on the nose of the airplane.

While on St. Thomas, Lindbergh spent considerable time working on the NYP. In one photograph he can be seen on top of the engine cowling with a screwdriver checking the valves. He noted in pencil on one of his maps (now in the Smithsonian) "greased rockers, installed Uniflow #9 intake valve, greased prop (?), tightened no. 4 intake and exhaust push rod housing. Drained oil. Filled 15 gal. Mobil B oil, fueled 20 gallons in front tank and 30 gallons in rear (main) tank." He was wearing his suit.

It was Thursday, February 2, when Lindbergh preflighted the NYP in the morning to prepare for his flight to Puerto Rico.

He took off from the golf course at 11:45 a.m., circled over the field, then directly over Charlotte Amalie, circling several times.

The governor of the Virgin Islands requested that he fly over St. Croix on his way to Puerto Rico. After leaving St. Thomas he flew over two small islands on a south-southeast heading. The two islands were Turtledove Cay and Saea Island. The flight to St. Croix was 45 statue miles and took only thirty minutes.

He approached St. Croix on its north side, then flew east along the coast to circle over the town of Christiansted and then west to circle over Frederiksted to greet the people of that beautiful island.

Within a few minutes he headed directly northwest to fly the 100 statue miles to San Juan, Puerto Rico.

Lindbergh is shown on top of the airplane as he checked over the engine.

Lindbergh is most likely checking the valve tappets on the Wright J-5 engine before he was to leave for Puerto Rico on February 2.
PHOTO BY R. COLORADO, 1928 VIA MISSOURI HISTORICAL SOCIETY, ST. LOUIS

When he approached the island of Puerto Rico he flew over the smaller Vieques Island (Isle de Vieques) and then over the Pasaje de Vieques (Bay) hitting the shore of Puerto Rico at about Naguabo. Then he flew over 3,524-foot Mount Yungue of the Caribbean National Forest and from there directly to the city of San Juan.

He reached San Juan at 1:55 p.m. (12:55 p.m. Eastern Standard Time "EST") and landed on Escambron Flying Field.

The only airport on St. Thomas today is near Charlotte Amalie. Cyril E. King airport is located at the west central area of the well-known island on the north side of Lindbergh Bay and Brewers Bay. It is at an elevation of 24 feet MSL,

and has a single east-west runway of 7,000 feet. It serves most international airlines as well as commuter, general aviation, helicopters, cargo, and military.

References

Newspapers
   The Daily News, St. Thomas, Virgin Islands
   The St. Croix Avis, Thristians Head, Virgin Islands

People
   Paul W. Looney   Isidor Paiewonsky
   Robert W. Eldred   Richard A. Washburn

STOP # 14
SAN JUAN, PUERTO RICO

CAPSULE HISTORY OF CITY AND COUNTRY

San Juan, capital of the island and the chief seaport, is the largest city on the island. It is located on the northeastern coastline on the Atlantic Ocean. El Morro Castle, begun in 1539 and completed during the late 1700s, lies on a bluff at the entrance to the bay, one of the best harbors in the West Indies. In 1521 followers of Ponce de León founded the city.

About a thousand miles southeast of Florida lies the beautiful island of Puerto Rico, which forms part of the boundary between the Caribbean Sea and the Atlantic Ocean. Puerto Rico is a Spanish name, and in English it means

"Rich Port." In the colonial days it was the name for San Juan, Puerto Rico's capital. The name gradually came to be used for the entire island. It is a popular tourist playground due to its year-round balmy weather. Temperatures range from 73 degrees F. in the winter to 80 degrees F. in the summer.

Christopher Columbus discovered the island in 1493 during his second voyage to the Americas. However, the first settlement was started in 1508 by Ponce de León and fifty of his men at Caparra, across the bay from the present-day San Juan. Columbus named the place San Juan Bautista.

20 feet MSL.

FEBRUARY 2-4, 1928
(THURSDAY THROUGH SATURDAY)

At this time there was a flying field, located along the seacoast, that had what appears to be one wooden hangar. The field, known as the Escambron Flying Field, was at Puerta de Fierra.

As Lindbergh circled over the city and the field, he was given a 21-gun salute, one less than a presidential salute, in addition to sirens and ships' whistles adding to the excitement of the occasion. As he approached the area he was escorted to San Juan by the *Santa Maria*, a West Indian Aerial Express airplane flown by noted pilot Basil Rowe. He landed at 1:55 p.m. (12:55 p.m. EST).

The NYP landing at Escambron Flying Field. MISSOURI HISTORICAL SOCIETY, ST. LOUIS

After securing the NYP in the hangar, he was taken through San Juan's flag-draped streets to a special stand erected in front of the Government House. Here he reviewed a grand parade with marching bands and military units.

During the parade two thousand schoolchildren in mass drills passed by the reviewing stand as a tribute. As they passed they all came to attention and saluted.

He was welcomed by a crowd of 100,000 people, and Mayor R.H. Todd, Chief Justice Emilio Del Toro, Governor Horace Mann Towner, and Col. George H. Estes.

When Governor Towner stepped up to the platform, he said, "Among those honored for great accomplishments and noble virtues, your name will ever be enrolled. Your success has not been won by bloodshed, or by making wars, but in every test of valor and daring your accomplishments are at least equal to any of either fabled or historic hero. You have not caused a single heartbreak or a moment's suffering to others by your rise to fame."

Lindbergh was then escorted to the federal building and the Puerto Rican legislature, where he was proclaimed the honored guest of the city by Mayor Todd. He was given the Medal of Honor.

Puerto Rico was in the process of attempting to obtain independence from the United States. Lindbergh was shown the petition, which he did not comment on. He was not interested in politics unless it had to do with the further development of air travel.

Lindbergh was asked to speak about where he centered only on commercial aviation and its future. He said, "It would be easy to link the island of Puerto Rico with the United States by air and such a service could be started soon. The object of my trip through the West Indies is to investigate conditions with the idea of promoting aviation. Transportation which now requires days and nights will soon be possible in a matter of hours.... I hope this island will devote attention to aviation and co-operate for the betterment of the West Indies."

After the reception Lindbergh retired to the 400-year-old La Fortaleza, which was once the palace of the Spanish Captains General but pres-

Lindbergh is shown with Governor Horace Mann Towner on his left and apparentlly the Governor's wife on his right. The others are Mayor R.H. Todd (center) and Col. George H. Estes with Justice Emilio del Toro. HAROLD J. LIDDIN VIA PAUL LOONEY

into the cockpit, fired up the engine, and took off at 10:57 a.m. (9:57 a.m. EST).

On this flight he was entrusted with a message from the people of Puerto Rico to the people of the United States, making a plea for freedom. No report of his actually doing that has surfaced.

After climbing into a bright sun and circling over San Juan several times, he headed directly west. Flying low along the northern Puerto Rican coast, he spotted a school of sharks and one large sea turtle. Continuing along the coast he left the island at about Aguadilla and then flew across the Mona Passage. He hit the shore of the Cominican Republic at about El Cabo. He was fortunate to have a nice tailwind, causing him to be bit ahead of schedule.

During this flight he found time to write newspaper dispatches and other notes on the back of a hydrographic chart while passing over the east end of Haiti at about 1,600 feet. This is some of what he wrote:

On his birthday, Lindbergh is seen here as he pulls the prop through on the NYP. PHOTO BY HARWOOD HULL VIA MISSOURI HISTORICAL SOCIETY, ST. LOUIS

ently was the executive mansion. He slept late the next morning.

On Friday, the 3rd, he was given a motor touring trip to Fort San Cristobal, the new capital building, the School of Tropical Medicine, and the high school and local university.

Puerto Rican schoolchildren greeted the pilot at Campo del Morro, near the historic stone fort that guarded the entrance to San Juan harbor in Spanish colonial times.

He was a guest at another reception at the Governor's palace, then visited the Rotary Club and the Chamber of Commerce and attended the Puerto Rican carnival, where he was introduced to Edna Coll, queen of the carnival. The queen was dressed in the garb of an aviatrix as a special tribute to the flyer.

On Saturday, the 4th, his 26th birthday, he tinkered with the NYP in the hangar for half an hour before rolling it out to get started for his next stop.

After saying goodbye to everyone, he climbed

I am now at an altitude of 1,400 feet, cruising at 75 mhp at an engine speed of 1,300 rpm.

Oil pressure is 52 pounds (psi), Oil temp 50 degrees Centigrade, angle of attack 2 degrees, compass heading 270 magnetic, 1:20 p.m.

I am increasing the engine rpm to 1,650 and the angle of wings is 8 degrees, air speed 75 mph. Times 1:31 p.m.

At 1:35 p.m. I am at 4,200 feet.

In 14 minutes, I have changed from the warm air close to the ground to a quite cold climate nearly 8,000 feet above where it is necessary to turnon the intake heater (carburetor) to keep up the engine temperature.

Because he was ahead of schedule, he continued past La Romana and along the southern coast of Hispaniola and Santo Domingo and Cristobal, continuing westward. Eventually he crossed Behia (Bay) de Ocoa just south of Azua near Neiva, and across the southern part of Lago Enriquillo to Jimani, making a right turn over Etang Saumatre Lake in Haiti, reversing his course back eastward.

There were countless cumulus clouds in the area along his route, so at this point he elected to climb up to 7,200 feet, occasionally flying through a cloud full of moisture. Water streamed off the NYPs wings and struts. Above all this the sky was quite clear. He finally went up to 8,000 feet to clear the clouds and used his carburetor heater for a while. He climbed again, up to 9,700 feet, where it must have been a bit on the cold side.

A short time later he had descended to a much lower altitude and came over the mountains near San Cristobal, descending farther to the field at Santo Domingo.

San Juan today has two airports. One is the Luis Munoz Marin International, located just outside the city to the northeast. The field is located between the Moscoso Bridge over San Juan Bay and San Jose Lagoon. It is at an elevation of 10 feet MSL. It has two main runways, the longer of which is 10,002 feet. It serves most major international airlines, as well as commuter-type aircraft, general aviation, helicopters and some military and cargo.

The other field is Fernando Luis Ribas Dominicci, located on the north side of the city. It is at an elevation of 10 feet MSL and has a single east-west runway of 4,800 feet. It serves mainly general aviation.

References

Newspapers
The Kansas City Star, Friday, February 3, 1928
El Mundo
San Juan Star

Organizations
Office of the Governor, San Juan, Puerto Rico

People
Paul W. Looney   Harold J. Lidin
Bernardo Vazques   George McDougall
Richard A. Washburn

STOP #15
SANTO DOMINGO, DOMINICAN REPUBLIC

CAPSULE HISTORY OF CITY AND COUNTRY

The city of Santo Domingo is the capital and largest city in the Dominican Republic. The oldest European-founded city in the Western Hemisphere, it is located by the mouth of the Ozoma River on the southern coast of the country. It was founded by Christopher Columbus' brother, Bartholomew Columbus, in 1496 as "Nueva Isabela." From 1936 to 1961 under the dicta-tor Rafael Trujillo, the city was called Ciudad Trujillo.

The Dominican Republic makes up the eastern two-thirds of the island of Hispaniola, while Haiti covers the western end. The Dominican Republic is in the West Indies island group, about 575 miles southeast of Miami, Florida. It is known in the Spanish language as Republica Dominicana.

Christopher Columbus discovered the island

in 1492 on his first voyage to the New World. It is speculated that Columbus is buried on the island at or in the Cathedral of Santo Domingo.

The oldest university in the Western Hemisphere is the University of Santo Domingo, located in that city. It was established by Pope Paul III in 1538 as the University of Saint Thomas Aquinas.

85 feet MSL.

FEBRUARY 4-6, 1928
(SATURDAY THROUGH MONDAY)

Lindbergh circled the city several times, flew on out to the flying field, and made a low pass to check the surface, landing at 2:25 p.m.

There were hundreds of automobiles and thousands of spectators on the field when Lindbergh arrived. They gave him a tremendous ovation. He was met by President Horacio Vazquez and United States Minister Evan E. Young, as well as various other diplomats, consuls, and military figures.

During the welcoming fiesta, young women aboard a float in the parade wore "airplane hats" and "Lindy" neckties whle waving to the flyer as he passed by. There were even small-scale models of the Eiffel Tower and the Goddess of Liberty set up along the parade route into the city.

While in the city Lindbergh attended many official functions, one of which was a call on Archbishop Nouel at the Santo Domingo Cathedral, where he laid a wreath on the Columbus tomb. He was told that it is the oldest in the hemisphere, construction of which began in 1514 and was completed in 1540.

Lindbergh was taken to the castle built in 1510 of Diego Columbus, youngest brother of Christopher, and the castle of San Jeronimo and the Church of St. Nicholas, built in 1503.

At 7:30 in the evening Lindbergh attended a banquet by the municipality of Santo Domingo, later attending a grand ball at the national palace as the guest of President Vazquez.

In the meantime, the NYP was housed overnight in an open air type of hangar without doors, windows or walls, but with a substantial roof overhead to protect it from the elements.

The NYP nose cowling having the Dominican Republic flag painted on. MISSOURI HISTORICAL SOCIETY, ST. LOUIS

The NYP just outside the open air-type hangar with a mechanic pulling down on the propeller as the tail is lifted to move the airplane out of the hangar. MISSOURI HISTORICAL SOCIETY, ST. LOUIS

The NYP in the open air-type hangar at Santo Domingo. MISSOURI HISTORICAL SOCIETY, ST. LOUIS

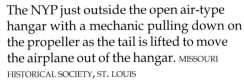

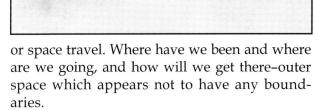

Local mechanics and military personnel moving the NYP out of the hangar before Lindbergh flew to Haiti. MISSOURI HISTORICAL SOCIETY, ST. LOUIS

Lindbergh in the cockpit with his left hand on the magneto switch before departing for Haiti. Note: Kollsman Super Sensitive Altimeter on the instrument panel. MISSOURI HISTORICAL SOCIETY, ST. LOUIS

One photo exists that shows a close-up of the nose area of the NYP in the hangar with the lower cowl removed. Possibly they did an oil change at this time.

It was the famous Caribbean flyer Basil L. Rowe who came up with the idea of having Lindbergh fly the regular WIAE (West Indian Aerial Express) mail from Santo Domingo westward over the route to Port-au-Prince and on to Havana in the NYP. Lindbergh agreed to do this, which makes it the first and only time that mail was officially carried aboard the NYP.

On the 6th Lindbergh took off at 10:50 a.m. local time and circled up over the city before taking a northwest heading. On board were 1,607 pieces of mail for Port-au-Prince and 1,570 pices for Havana, Cuba.

His thoughts drifted to Christopher Columbus and how the times had changed since the sea captain had discovered the land to the west of Europe. He compared the modern airplane with the *Pinta*, the *Nina*, and the *Santa Maria*, two contrasting means of transport. We might do the very same today, comparing the early airplanes with the Super Sonic Transport (SST) or space travel. Where have we been and where are we going, and how will we get there–outer space which appears not to have any boundaries.

On his northwest heading he flew over the extensive tropical plains with the 5,000-9,000-foot-high Cordillera Central Mountains to his left, over Basima and La Vega, eventualy circling over the city of Santiago several times. (Santiago was known then as Santiago de los Caballeros, and was the largest city in the interior of the Dominican Republic.) When over the city he found the airfield and flew low over it

The NYP just before departure for Haiti on February 6th. MISSOURI HISTORICAL SOCIETY, ST. LOUIS

The NYP leaving for Haiti on February 6th. MISSOURI HISTORICAL SOCIETY, ST. LOUIS

and the crowd gathered on its aviation field.

He then took up a heading of west-north-west, toward Cape Haitien, passing on the way the famous Citadel of Christophe. He crossed over the border into Haiti at about Pepillo Salcedo at the northern coastline, and then along the coral reefs to Cape Haitien. He circled low over this early capital of Haiti and from there headed southwest over the citadel of La Ferriere, built more than 100 years ago by the Haitian King Henry Christophe. The fortress is enormous and situated on the peak of a mountain 3,000 feet above the sea.

He came to the Golfe de la Gonave at about Saint Marc and then turned left to head southeast along the coast of the Canal de Saint Marc, passing Arcahale directly toward Port-au-Prince.

There are three major airports in the Santo Domingo city area today. The main one is De Las Americas International, located about fifteen miles to the east. It is at an elevation of 59 feet MSL and has a single runway of 11,002 feet. It serves most major international airlines, some commuters, general aviation and helicopters.

Another field is Herrera International located on the western edge of the city. It is at an eleva-tion of 190 feet MSL and has a single north-south runway of 4,052 feet. It serves mainly general aviation and helicopters.

About ten miles to the east is San Isidro Air Base at an elevation of 111 feet MSL, with a single runway of 7,000 feet. It is strictly for mili-tary operations.

References

Newspapers
Listin Diario
Ultima Hora

Organizations
American Aviation Historical Society Journal, 26:3 (Fall 1981), page 239.
Musuem of the Dominican Man, Santo Domingo
Archivo General de la Nacion "Ano Del Nino"
Embassy, Dominican Republic, Washington, D.C.

People
Jose Chez Checo   Paul W. Looney
Richard Marracino   Holley Mack Bell
Dr. Julio Jaime Julia   Ronald R. Sager
Richard A. Washburn

STOP #16
PORT-AU-PRINCE, HAITI

CAPSULE HISTORY OF THE CITY AND COUNTRY

Port-au-Prince is the capital and largest city in Haiti and is the chief port of the country. Two peninsulas which project westward from the ctiy protect its harbor. It is the center of Haitian life.

Haiti covers the west third of the island of Hispaniola, which lies between Cuba and Puerto Rico in the Caribbean Sea. Much of the country is covered by rugged mountains. The name Haiti comes from an Indian word mean-ing "High Ground." The highest point is Pic la Selle at 8,783 feet MSL. The official language is French.

The country is the oldes black republic in the word and the second oldest free nation in the Western Hemisphere. It has been indepen-dent since 1804. The official names, in French, is Republique d'Haiti (Republic of Haiti).

Christopher Columbus arrived at Hispaniola in 1492. One of his ships, the Santa Maria, ran aground on reefs near the present day city of Cape Haitien. The Arawak Indians occupied the land before the white men arrived. On January 1, 1804, Gen. Jean Jacques Dessalines, the leader, proclaimed the colony an independent country named Haiti.

25 feet MSL.

FEBRUARY 6-8, 1928
(MONDAY THROUGH WEDNESDAY)

Lindbergh had been ahead of schedule and spent extra time circling over the area before coming in over the city. He had first approached

An aerial view of the hangars on Bowen Field. CLINT P. HOUSEL

Here is the *Spirit of St. Louis* upon arrival at Bowen Field at Port-au-Prince. MISSOURI HISTORICAL SOCIETY, ST. LOUIS

Mechanics probably lubricating the axles and bearings and, at right, checking the left wheel more closely. BOB ROCHETTE

from the south.

There was a crowd of 6,000 spectators, all in a holiday mood and dressed accordingly, ...had been waiting anxiously for some time.

Lindbergh finally landed on Bowen Field at Port-au-Prince at 2:00 p.m. American Marine guards and Haitian Gendarmes were there to protect the NYP from the crowds already on the field.

After he had stopped the engine, and before climbing out of the cockpit, he reached back inside and pulled out the mail bag from Santo Domingo to give to the proper authorities.

He was officially met by President Louis Borno of the Republic of Haiti. Shortly after, the President pinned the Haitian Order of Merit on Lindbergh's suit lapel.

Soon the NYP was wheeled into a wooden hangar nearby and guarded. "WE" had been painted high up on the front edifice on the hangar. There were other hangars on both sides of this one that appear to have been of military design and construction.

In several photographs it appears that a problem may have developed with the left wheel. Several mechanics were working in that area with a jack and possibly a grease gun. Perhaps they were just lubricating the wheel bearings and adjusting them as well.

Lindbergh was taken to the national palace, an architecturally pleasing building, set in a park around which the chief public buildings of Port-au-Prince are erected.

No other information has been found describing the details of Lindbergh's stay in Haiti or functions he may have attended.

Lindbergh took off from Bowen Field at 6:35 a.m. on February 8. He had on board three sacks of mail. One bag was from Santo Domingo to Havana, Cuba, and two from Port-au-Prince.

After take-off he circled over the airfield and then over the city of Port-au-Prince several times. He took up a heading to the northwest in the direction of the southeast tip of Ile de la Gonave and over the Baie de Port-au-Prince. He flew along the south shore of the island and changed course slightly to the north, flying directly over the Windward Passage of the Golfe de la Gonave toward Cuba.

He hit the island in the area of Guantanamo Bay, near the United States Naval Base that was established there in 1903, under a lease/treaty agreement between the two countries.

It was about 9:20 a.m. as he flew over this area and into the Guantanamo Valley, covered with fields of sugar cane.

From there he took a more westerly heading, flying over Dos Cominos, just north of Palma Soreano Lake to Cauto. Then he headed northwesterly, flying toward the town of Camaguey. The next leg took Lindbergh over Sancti Spiritus and then just north of the Loma San Juan Mountains (with a peak of 3,773 feet MSL) and over Cienfuegos.

He was seen over Havana (Habana) at 3:40 p.m.

This was his second longest flight since leaving Mexico City, about 728 statute miles.

Today there are two airports for the city of Port-au-Prince. The main one is Port-au-Prince International, located just outside the city limits to the north. It is at an elevation of 121 feet MSL and has a single east-west runway of 9,974 feet. It serves most domestic and international airlines, as well as some general aviation, cargo and helicopter aircraft.

On the very north edge of the city is Bowen Military Airfield at an elevation of 108 feet MSL, with a single east-west runway of 5,100 feet.

References

Newspapers
  Miscellaneous newspaper articles, cut-outs

People
  Paul W. Looney   Clinton P. Housel
  Bob Rochette   Richard A. Washburn
  James E. Ferguson Jr.

Here the NYP is shown in front of the local hangar with "WE" painted on the upper portion. CLINT P. HOUSEL

STOP #17
HAVANA, CUBA
(INCLUDES FLIGHT TO ST. LOUIS)

CAPSULE HISTORY OF CITY AND COUNTRY

Capital and chief port of Cuba, Havana (La Habana in Spanish) is the largest city there. It is located on the northwest coast, about one hundred miles south of Key West, Florida. Spanish colonists built the city in 1519, next to a large harbor. The city was founded by Diego Velasquez in 1515. It became the capital of Cuba in 1552.

Cuba is an island country in the West Indies about ninety miles south of Florida. It consists of one large island and more than 1,600 smaller ones. It is one of the most beautiful islands in the Antilles, which is another name for the West Indies. The people of Cuba call it the "Pearl of the Antilles." High mountains and rolling hills cover about a fourth of the island. The highest point is Pico Turquino at 6,542 feet MSL. At one time is was one of the world's most luxurious and popular tourist centers. But when Fidel Castro came into power in 1959, the economy declined and many of its people have fled the country. Christopher Columbus landed on this island in 1492 and claimed it for Spain. Spaniards began to settle there in 1511.

100 feet MSL.

FEBRUARY 8-13, 1928
(WEDNESDAY THROUGH MONDAY)

Lindbergh landed the NYP on Columbia Field (Camp Columbia) about eight miles from Havana at 4:00 p.m. He taxied over the field to the front of the stand reserved for the reception committee. The crowds were enormous, and the cavalry with drawn sabers, attempted to keep them back, with much difficulty until the NYP could be rolled into a nearby hangar. Infantrymen with fixed bayonets were also needed to keep some semblance of control.

He was greeted by American Ambassador Noble Brandon Judah, Charles Evans Hughes, who was head of the United States delegation to the Pan-American conference then being held in this city, and Ambassador Orestes Ferrara Marino, Secretary of War Ituraldi and General Herrara. Ameri-

The NYP over Columbia Field as Lindbergh checked over the landing site before setting down. UNIVERSITY OF MARYLAND

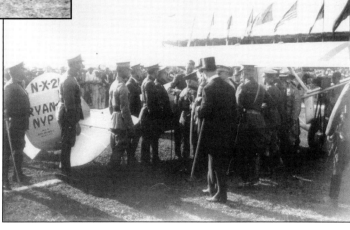

Shortly after Lindbergh landed at Havana being greeted by high officials of the country. UNIVERSITY OF MARYLAND.

Lindbergh is seen here with American Ambassador Noble Brandon Judah; Cuban Ambassador Orestes Ferra Marino and other personalities shortly after landing on February 8. *BOHEMIA MAGAZINE,* HAVANA, CUBA

can Col. Henry Breckenridge, who had been Lindbergh's legal advisor, was also there.

Lindbergh was then escorted to a waiting automobile to be driven to the Presidential Palace, where he was greeted warly with a hardy handshake by President Gerardo Machado. After ceremonies there, he was taken to the United States Embassy by Ambassador Judah, where Lindbergh was given his quarters. There was a reception at the embassy, attended by many Americans who at that time were living in Havana, in addition to some Cuban citizens of note. There were over 2,500 people in attendance.

On the morning of February 9, Lindberth had the NYP thoroughly inspected under the supervision of U.S. Army officers, who happened to be there to inspect the new Cuban flying unit. There was also a technical representative there from the Wright Aeronautical Company for the same reason. He inspected Lindbergh's J-5 Whirlwind engine. Lindbergh cautioned the mechanics to be careful of the hand-painted flags on the nose cowls.

Later that day he attended a luncheon given by Army officers at Camp Columbia, historically famous as the billet of many American soldiers during the Spanish-American War.

On Friday, the 10th, Lindbergh received a medal from the Cuban Secretary of State. At a noon reception at the Central Park he was given the keys to the city from Mayor Gomez. The park was a mass of humanity.

At 1:30 p.m. he was a guest at a luncheon given by the Cuban Aero Club. He flew a Fairchild FC-2 that afternoon. At 4:00 p.m. he attended a reception of the Veterans of the Spanish-American War at the Embassy. At 8:30 p.m. he attended a meeting of the Cuban Geographic Society and at 9:00 that night he attended a state dinner given by the President at the National Theater. Lindbergh's talk at the dinner was the longest one given by him on his entire Latin-American tour.

On the morning of February 11, Lindbergh flew a Ford tri-motor, taking up many local passengers. It is not known what the serial and registration number was, but it appears to have been 4-AT-11, NC1780.

Shown here is the procession of automobiles leaving the field for the palace of President Machado after Lindbergh had landed.
UNIVERSITY OF MARYLAND

He made three flights and carried such notables at Mrs. Charles Evans Hughes, Mrs. Henry P. Fletcher, Mrs. Harold Williamson, Mrs. Joseph Hanna, and Mrs. Cord Meyer. Also carried were Mayor of Havana Miguel Mariano Gomez, Secretary of War Ituralde, Vice-President LaRosa, Dr. Jesus Salazar, head of the Peruvian delegation to the Pan-American Conference, Miss Ituralde and the Misses LaRosa.

About 8:30 a.m. on the morning of the 12th, Lindbergh made another flight in a Fokker trimotor. He had as his passengers President Machado, Mr. Hughes, and several others. It was President Machado's first airplane ride.

The rest of the day was a day off for the flyer, with no more official social commitments. He was taken around Havana and the surrounding area on a tour of historic and other sites.

Sometime after midnight on Monday the 13th, the NYP was rolled out of the hangar, while the Cuban band played a lively march. Lindbergh's luggage and a few sandwiches had already been placed inside the cockpit.

Just after midnight as Lindbergh started the engine before his departure for St. Louis on February 13th.
BOHEMIA MAGAZINE, HAVANA, CUBA

After a thorough preflight, he started the engine, waved goodbye to everyone, and taxied to the far end of the field. After a long run he passed right over the hangar. He circled around the area for about ten or fifteen minutes, and then took up a northerly heading, over the open sea of the Straits of Florida. He had lifted off a 1:35 a.m. (2:35 EST).

The following description of the flight to St. Louis, as plotted, is only approximate, based on information from Lindbergh's writings and miscellaneous other accounts of the flight.

As far as Lindbergh was concerned, this would be a routine flight. His plan was to leave Havana and fly directly to Key West, Florida, up the Gulf of Mexico along the west coast of Florida and then directly to St. Louis. Here is the story, as it was far from routine.

He climbed to 4,000 feet, relaxed in the comfort of his cozy cockpit, and set up an appropriate north-northeast heading. All was well up to a point about halfway across the Straits of Florida. Then the liquid magnetic compass began to rotate, and at the same time the earth-inductor compass needle began jumping back and forth erratically. And what had been a clear night became hazy, with no visible horizon. He was flying strictly on instruments. He checked the turn indicator needle, which was holding in its centered position. Pushing on the rudder pedals showed that the gyroscope was working. This kind of situation of both compasses malfunctioning had only happened one other time. That was during the New York to Paris flight, passing over a storm over the Atlantic Ocean. At that time the liquid magnetic compass only oscillated through an arc of close to 180 degrees. In that situation he got an approximate idea of direction by taking the midpoint of the compass card's swing, and held that heading by the stars above.

In this case however, the liquid magnetic compass rotated without stopping. He considered the earth-inductor compass absolutely useless. He had no idea what his direction of flight was in relation to a compass heading.

As he looked up at the stars, which were only dimly visible in the haze, he could not recognize any constellation. He began to climb from 4,000 feet to a higher altitude, in hopes of finding it much clearer so he could navigate by the stars. he felt that if he could see Polaris, he could navigate with some accuracy. However, the haze got worse as he climbed, and he figured there must be a storm not far beyond, perhaps over the mainland of the United States.

He continued to speculate about what plan he could use to continue navigating toward St. Louis. He finally descended to 1,000 feet, and even then it was difficult to find a horizon, as the sea and the haze blended. On top of all this, the air became rather turbulent, making it that much more difficult to hold any kind of heading.

He still had trouble due to the continued ro-

tation of the compass card. As dawn slowly appeared he noticed a small land mass, which he thought was the Florida Keys, and assumed he had been on course all along, in spite of the compass difficulties. As he followed the shoreline of this land, he could not match it up on his map with anything near Florida, and then wondered if he might have ended up back over Cuba. As he scanned his map further he realized that he must have been over some islands of the Bahamas, about 300 miles off his original course.

As daylight increased, he noticed that what he saw below agreed with his chart of the Bahama islands. He must have been near the Berry Islands, and had crossed over the northern tip of Andros Island.

Somewhere near the northern tip of the Berry Islands he took up, as best he could, a direct heading for St. Louis to the northwest. It appears that with this new heading he may have hit the Florida coast between Daytona Beach and Jacksonville. This course would have taken him over Grand Bahama Island.

Passing over Jacksonville, or possibly slightly west of that city, he would eventually fly a few miles west of Atlanta, Georgia, then northeast of Huntsville, in the northeast corner of Alabama, continuing on west of Nashville, Tennessee, and over Paducah, Kentucky.

Since hitting the Florida coast, he flew into a large storm area and was on instruments most of the time. He would be low, just above the treetops, in and out of the fog, and then he would have climbed up to 7,000 feet to attempt to get into clearer weather.

As he flew over Tennessee and Kentucky, the weather improved, but as he got closer to St. Louis it deteriorated again. He found St. Louis and flew quite low up the Mississippi River along the city's waterfront. In and out of clouds, he finally flew up to the Missouri River to the north of the city and followed it to St. Charles. At this point he picked up a paved road familiar to him and followed it to Lambert Field.

He landed at 5:10 p.m. Central Time, after a flight of fifteen hours and thirty-five minutes.

This was the first nonstop flight between Havana and St. Louis, Missouri.

He dragged the rain-soaked surface of Lambert Field twice, and then finally landed on the firmest part of the field he could find.

Havana today has several airports around the city. The main one is Jose Marti International, a single strip located south of the city at an elevation of 210 feet MSL and a runway length of 13,123 feet. It serves some international airlines, and possibly commuter and general aviation aircraft, helicopters and cargo.

Another field is Playa Baracoa, located to the south at an elevation of 102 feet MSL. It has a dingle runway of 7,546 feet. It serves some airlines and general aviation.

On the western edge of the city is Cuidad Libertad Municipal Airport, at an elevation of 98 feet MSL and a single runway of 6,800 feet. It is a military airport.

Farther west is Santa Fe airport at an elevation of 18 feet MSL with a single runway of 3,000 feet. It serves general aviation.

Farther to the southwest is San Antonio de Los Banos, another military field, at an elevation of 106 feet MSL and a single runway of 11,800 feet.

Another military field is San Pedro, southwest of the city, at an elevation of 262 feet MSL and a single runway of 10,600 feet.

References

Newspapers
The Hartford Daily Times

Organizations
Libraries of the University of Maryland at College Park

Publications
Bohemia Magazine, Havana, Cuba

People
Paul W. Looney   Richard A. Washburn
Angel Guerra Cabrera, editor of *Bohemia*
Karen Fishman, University of Maryland

St. Louis, Missouri

FEBRUARY 13-APRIL 30, 1928

About 700 people were on Lambert Field to greet Lindbergh when he landed at 5:01 p.m. First in line to welcome him back was Harold Bixby of the Chamber of Commerce, in addition to acting Mayor Walter Neun.

Lindbergh was taken in charge by Harry Hall

A well-known photo, produced often, of Lindbergh and the NYP just after his return from Cuba on February 13. CASSAGNERES COLLECTION

Knight and spent the night at Harry French Knight's home (Harry Hall's father).

The next day, Tuesday, February 14, the NYP was flown, according to Lindbergh's flight log, a total of three hours. He flew it over and around the St. Louis area on a demonstration flight for schoolchildren, many of whom were gathered along the Mississippi River. It was reported there were 60,000 children there, and each one was carrying an American flag in order to wave to their hero.

Lindbergh felt that his goodwill tour south of the border demonstrated that airplanes could be used longer and could stand more wear and tear than had been generally believed. He was convinced that airlines could be established between the United States and Central and South America and could be practical and would be established.

The NYP was stored in either a National Guard hangar or one of the Robertson's han-

gars on Lambert Field from February 13 to April 30. The airplane spent a total of forty-six days there, but not much is known about how it was taken care of during that time. More than likely it was serviced and inspected and checked over thoroughly and kept closely guarded.

In the meantime Lindbergh spent his time getting airlines started, flying many different types of airplanes and working as a consultant in the aviation community.

During that time he flew a total of nineteen different airplanes. In his log one can find such names as Ryan B-2, DH-4, Douglas Mail, Travelaire, P.1, Fokker tri-motor, Ford tri-motor, Douglas transport, Fokker Super Universal, Vought Corsair, Fairchild FC-2, Buhl Sesqui Wing, Lockheed, Eaglerock, Swallow, Curtiss Hawk, Curtiss Falcon (one of his favorites), and a Curtiss Robin.

He flew all over the country as PIC in the Ryan B-1X, NX4215, s/n 69, which was built in February 1928 in San Diego.

On Saturday, February 18, he left Lambert Field in a Douglas mail plane at 6:40 p.m. to fly to Springfield, Illinois. With three air mail pilots as passengers, they all planned to attend a dinner there.

A rare photograph, only one ever found, taken during the NYP's extended stay in St. Louis before being flown to Washington, D.C. Left to right are: Sgt. Ralph Meyer; Sgt. George Vonland and Sgt. William Hayward Morton. PHOTOGRAPHER FROM THE 35TH DIVISION OF THE 110TH OBSERVATION SQUADRON OF MISSOURI NATIONAL GUARD, VIA MALCOLM MORTON

This photo was taken at Lambert Field, just before he left for Washington, D.C., on his last flight in NYP. THE WESTERN RESERVE HISTORICAL SOCIETY, CLEVELAND, OHIO

On Monday, April 30, 1928, Lindbergh took off in the NYP from Lambert Field at 9:00 a.m. Soon after take-off he circled the city several times, then took up an easterly heading across the Mississippi River, crossing the northern tip of Carlyle Lake in Illinois.

He crossed the Wabash River and later the Ohio River just southwest of Cincinnati, Ohio.

April 30, 1928, Lindbergh taxiing in at Bolling Field, Washington, D.C. WIDE WORLD PHOTOS VIA LEO B. KIMBALL COLLECTION

After crossing the state of Ohio he came into West Virginia and, nearing the eastern border with Virginia, flew over the Allegheny Mountains, near Front Royal, and began his let down to Washington, D.C.'s Bolling Field.

He landed on Bolling Field after a flight of four hours and fifty-eight minutes.

This last flight was one year and two days after the very first (test) flight off of Dutch Flats in San Diego on April 30, 1927.

One of the last photographs taken of Lindbergh with the *Spirit of St. Louis* shortly after landing at Bolling Field. P.&A. PHOTO

Lindbergh standing with a Bolling Field mechanic, shortly after landing on April 30. WIDE WORLD PHOTOS VIA LEO B. KIMBALL COLLECTION

Aeronautical Charts

Sectional Aeronatical Charts, including appropriate Class B, C, & D Airspace Charts–complete coverage of the United States, published by U.S. Department of Commerce, National Oceanic and Atmospheric Administration, National Ocean Service, Washington, D.C. 1999-2000 issues. Scale 1:500,000 (1" = 8 statute miles).

World Aeronautical Charts, CG-21, CG-20, CH-23, CH-24, CH-25, CJ-26, CJ-27, CF-19, published by U.S. Department of Commerce, National Oceanic and Atmospheric Administration, National Ocean Service, Washington, D.C. 1999-2000 issues. Scale 1:1,000,000.

Operational Navigation Charts, J-24, J-25, K-25, K-26, K-27, L-25, L-26, L-27, L-28, M-24, M-25, M-26, M-27, M-28, N-25, N-26. Published by the Defense Mapping Agency Aerospace Center, St. Louis Air Force Station, Missouri, Revised 1980. Scale 1:1,000,000.

USAF (United States Air Force) Jet Navigation Chart, published by the Aeronautical Chart and Information Center, United States Air Force, St. Louis, Missouri–JN45, JN46, JN47N, JN61N, JN62. Scale 1:2,000,000.

Hydrographic Office Publication No. 195, "Naval Air Pilot of Central America," United States Government Printing Office, Washington, D.C., Notice to Aviators, No. 13, 1937, corrected to July 1, 1937 (via Carlos Rosa Mejia, Miami, Florida).

Approach Plates by Jeppesen for appropriate airports at cities where Lindbergh landed. Used for general references.

Road Maps

The Caribbean, Central America & South America, American Automobile Association, Heathrow, Florida, 1999-2000 edition.

Puerto Rico road map Map Easy, Inc., Wainscott, N.Y.

Mexico, Nelles Maps, Nelles Verlag Gmbh, Munchen, Federal Republic of Germany, Scale 1:2,500,000.

Kuba (Cuba), Freytag & Berndt, Artaria, 1071 Wien, Germany, Scale 1:1,250,000.

Travelers Map of Mexico, National Geographic Society, September 1994, Washington, D.C. Scale 1:4,358,000 or 1 inch = 69 miles.

South America, National Geographic Society, Washington, D.C., October 1972. Scale 1:10,700,000 or 1 inch =169 miles.

Emergency Equipment Aboard NYP

Pliers	First Aid Kit
Screw driver	Tropical medicines
Wrench	Seven cans of rations
Knife	Aluminum pot
Machete	Bullion cubes
Gloves	Canteen
Rifle	Fifty rounds of ammunition
Pack straps	Leather flying suit
Poncho	Walking boots
Tarpaulin	Flying boots
Two flashlights	Helmet & goggles
Match case	Sewing kit

Emergency equipment was wrapped in the tarpaulin and stored in the fuselage behind the cockpit.

People

Paul W. Looney	David C. Weiss
Richard A. Washburn	Jodi McKee
Carlos Rosa Mejia	Dennis G. Holt

Lindbergh's Last Airplane Flight

In my previous book, *The Untold Story of,* The Spirit of St. Louis, I covered what the last airplane was that Lindbergh flew as PIC (Pilot in command) and what little information I had at the time regarding his last flight after he had become terminally ill.

Since that time I have uncovered further information. Here are the details.

He had flown on United Airlines flight #897 from New York via Chicago to Honolulu International Airport (HNL), arriving on August 18, 1974. From Honolulu he was flown to Hana, Maui, Hawaii, by Valley Isle Aviation, an air charter company based on Maui, at the request of Sam Pryor. Pryor was a close friend of the Lindberghs and dealt with Valley Isle frequently.

They were to meet the United Airlines DC-8 and make the transfer on the ramp. Valley Isle pilot Wray Fleming flew a Beechcraft 55 Baron, N1022V, to pick up Lindbergh, his wife, Anne and their son, Land. The Baron, the early model 55, had a large baggage door on the left and by folding down the left rear seat, Lindbergh's stretcher was able to be loaded in that way. Mrs. Lindbergh sat next to Fleming in the co-pilot seat and Land rode in the right rear seat.

A few days later Fleming picked up son John and flew him to Maui to be at his father's bedside.

CHARLES A. LINDBERGH
37 Broadway
New York City

May 31, 1933

Dear Dr. Abbot:

I have expressed twenty-two (22) additional maps which were used on the Caribbean Flight of the Spirit of St. Louis. The flight started at Washington, D.C. and ended at St. Louis, Missouri. When you receive these, the institution will have a total of thirty-six (36) maps used on this flight.

I am enclosing with this letter the peep sight which belongs on the rifle you received several weeks ago. Also the match box, which to the best of my knowledge, was the one carfied on the Caribbean Flight. As I stated in one of my letters, the match box I sent was a duplicate. I would appreciate having this box substituted and the other returned to me.

You now have practically the complete equipment of the Spirit of St. Louis, as it ended the last flight before being placed in the Smithsonian. I flew it from St. Louis directly to Bolling Field, where it was disassembled and taken to the Institution. I am sending this equipment to the Smithsonian Institution with the understanding that it will be accepted and cared for under the same agreement as that covering the Spirit of St. Louis.

It is my request and understanding that neither the Spirit of St. Louis, nor any part of its equipment, will ever be removed from the Museum for temporary exhibition elsewhere.

Sincerely yours,

/s/ Charles A. Lindbergh

Dr. C.G. Abbot
Smithsonian Institution
Washington, D.C.

Encs.

(This letter was retyped here for readability but is an exact replica. Any errors are from the original.)

CORREO AEREO ESPECIAL POR
LINDBERGH
EL ESPIRITU DE SAN LUIS

PRIMER CORREO AEREO
SANTO DOMINGO - HAVANA
Vuelo especial "LINDBERGH" con el
"Spirit of St. Louis"

B. L. ROWE

c/o LAWRENCE A COLMAN
MANZANA DE GOMEZ 343
HAVANA, CUBA.

In February, 1928, while surveying the "Lindbergh Circle" in the West Indies for PAA with the Spirit of St.Louis, Lindbergh flew three bags of mail for Basil Rowe, who was piloting an accompanying plane. These were: Santo Domingo to Port au Prince, Santo Domingo to Havana, and Port au Prince to Havana, all addressed to Rowe.

POSTE ARERIEN SPECIAL POUR
LINDBERGH
"ESPRIT DE St. LOUIS"

B. L. ROWE

c/o LAWRENCE A COLMAN
MANZANA DE GOMEZ 343
HAVANA, CUBA.

These three types were the only official airmail ever flown on the Spirit of St.Louis. Much of it was water-damaged and lost in a hurricane shortly thereafter,

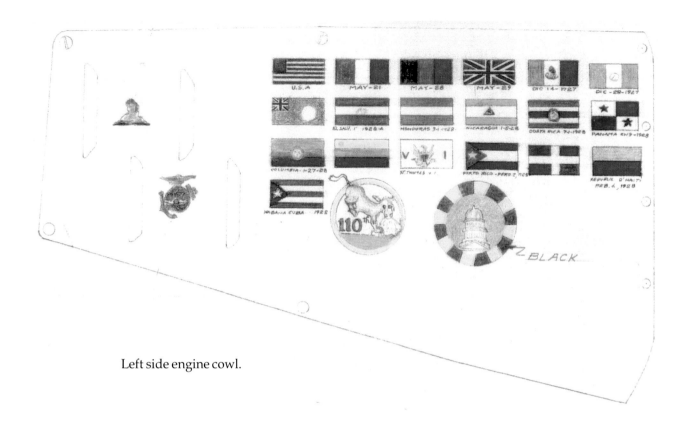

Left side engine cowl.

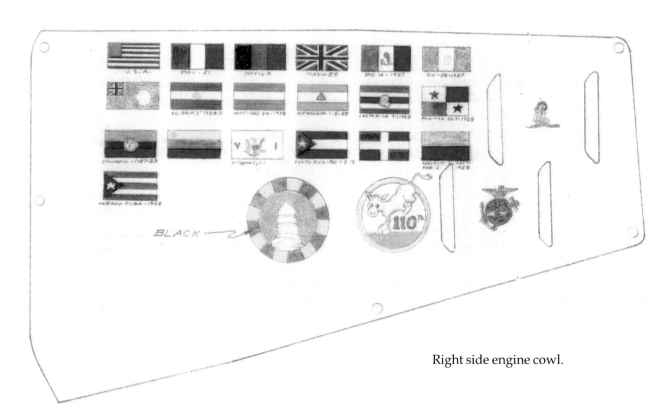

Right side engine cowl.

DATA FOR MARKINGS, COLOR AND INSIGNIA - RYAN *SPIRIT OF ST. LOUIS*

All surfaces are silver aluminum color.
All lettering is black.

Engine cowling insignia:
The following flags of countries which the *Spirit of St. Louis* visited are shown on both the right and left cowl in their appropriate colors. Left to right, top to bottom, as follows:

U.S.A. – France – Belgium – England – Mexico – Guatemala – British Honduras – El Salvador – Honduras – Nicaragua – Costa Rica – Panama – Columbia – Venezuela – Virgin Islands – Puerto Rico – Dominican Republic – Haiti – Cuba

The unit insignia on the cowl are colored as follows:

   1. Bolling Field, Washington, D.C.
      White Capitol done against background enclosed in a circle with alternating segments of yellow and black.
   2. Missouri National Guard, 110th Observation Squadron.
      Gray mule on white background with green grass, enclosed in yellow circular border.
   3. Marine Corps Insignia – Haiti unit.
      Red western hemisphere globe with gold wings and anchor.
   4. Sixth Composite Group, France Field, Canal Zone.
      Head and shoulders figure of swarthy, black-haired pirate with white shirt over brown propeller.
All cowl insignia was painted on the *Spirit of St. Louis* during flights made after the transatlantic flight.

Left side engine cowl.

Renderings of the lettering on the NYP engine cowl as it actually appears on the left and right. Notice the subtle differences in some of the letters ie. the "S" and "R" in Spirit. HAND-DRAWN BY AUTHOR

Right side engine cowl.

NATIONAL AIR AND SPACE MUSEUM SMITHSONIAN INSTITUTION

WASHINGTON, D. C. 20560

June 6, 1977

MEMORANDUM FOR: Messrs. Collins, Zisfein, Whitelaw, Durant, Chamberlain, Miss Scott

SUBJECT: Inscriptions on "Spirit of St. Louis" cowling

We have had several inquiries lately on exactly what inscriptions are inside the cowling of the "Spirit of St. Louis." Attached are sheets which repeat the scratched-in inscriptions, complete with misspellings, strange dates, and so on.

We are making arrangements through Bill Good to have these inscriptions photographed; some special techniques will no doubt be required.

Walt

Walter J. Boyne

Attachments

cc: Mr. Lopez

On engine cowling around cylinders:

P. R.	L. B.
L M	J. B Bobin
A. H. L	P C. Nations
W. D	Haiti
W. B. 28	Sgt. Psierra
	Feb. 11, 1928

On prop spinner:

Prest Rose
1946
May.28

West Indies
Express

John Daley
    Frank E. Field
        Canal Zone, Jan 19
                1928

Lela Williams
    St. Louis, Mo.

Miss
    F. Rohr
        3722 Art Zona
        San Diego, Cal.

F. C. Mitchell
4453 – 39th St.
San Diego, Cal.

Pop Daly – Canal
Zone

Right hand side cowl

W. G. E.
W. G. Edwards Portland

JNO R. Lester
    San Diego

Fred Maguda

Fred Rohr
    San Diego, Calif.

Original builders of this cowling.

Top Cowling

December 13, 1927

To: C. A. Lindbergh

    With sincerest hopes
that you may be
successeul (sic) we thank
you for en-
trusting us with the
work of preparing your
plane for the flight.
        Very truly yours,
            R. H. Hooe
            S. Borecki
            U. E. McQuade
            C. L. Rockenbaugh
            I. L. Kallmyer

D. H. Stewart
written across above

Bibliography

Aero Digest Magazine, March 1928, "Lindbergh Ends Latin-American Tour."

Aircraft Owners and Pilots Association, Frederick, Maryland.

Aircraft Year Book, 1927-1928, Aeronautical Chamber of Commerce of America, Inc., New York City.

Aviation, December 26, 1927, "Lindbergh Flies from Washington to Mexico City."

Aviation Publication Service, Del Mar, California.

Davis, Kenneth S., *The Hero: Charles A. Lindbergh and the American Dream*, Doubleday & Company, Inc. New York, 1959.

Flight Guide, by Airguide Publications, Inc., Long Beach, California, Volumes I, II, III, 1999-2000.

The Flying Magazine, November and December 1927, printed in Mexico and written in Spanish, translated to author by Lourdes Ramos.

Hagedorn, Dan, *Alae Supra Canalem, Wings Over the Canal*, Turner Publishing Company, Paducah, Kentucky, 1995.

Hart, Arthur A., *Wings Over Idaho*, Historic Boise, Inc., Boise, Idaho, 1991.

Jeppesen Sanderson, Inc., Englewood, Colorado.

Keyhoe, Donald E., *Flying with Lindbergh*, Grosset & Dunlap, New York, 1928. Published by arrangement with G. P. Putnam's Sons.

Komons, Nick A., *Bonfires to Beacons*, Smithsonian Institution Press, Washington, D.C. & London, 1989.

Lindbergh, Charles A., *Autobiography of Values*, Harcourt Brace Jovanovich, editor William Jovanovich, coeditor Judith A. Schiff, 1976, 1977, 1978.

_____, *Spirit of St. Louis*, Charles Scribner's Sons, New York, 1952.

The Literary Digest, January 21, 1928, "Lindbergh United the Americas," New York.

Miller, Francis Trevelyan, *Lindbergh, His Story in Pictures*, Anniversary Edition, G.P. Putnam's Sons, New York–London, 1929.

National Geographic Magazine, Washington, D.C., Volume LIII, Number One, January 1928, authored by Lt. Donald E. Keyhoe, U.S.M.C. (retired).

_____, Volume LIII, Number Five, May 1928, "From Bogota and Back by Air," by Col. Charles A. Lindbergh.

Navy Air Pilot: Central America, corrected to July 1, 1937, Hydrographic Office under the Authority of the Secretary of the Navy, United States Government Printing Office, Washington, D.C., 1937. Publication No. 195.

Reinhold, Ruth M., *Sky Pioneering, Arizona in Aviation History*, The University of Arizona Press, Tucson, Arizona, 1982.

Road Atlas, American Automobile Association, Heathrow, Florida, 1999-2000.

Sectional Aeronautical Charts, including appropriate Class B, C, & D Airspace Charts. Complete coverage of the United States (37 copies), published by U.S. Department of Commerce, National Oceanic and Atmospheric Administration, National Ocean Service, Washington, D.C., 1999-2000 issues. Scale 1:500,000 (1 inch = 8 statute miles).

Sikorsky, Igor I., *The Story of the Winged – S*, an autobiography, Dodd, Mead & Company, New

York, 1944.

Tourbook, American Automobile Association, AAA Publishing, Heathrow, Florida, 1999-2000 issues covering all of the United States, used in preparing the history of each city or town that Lindbergh visited.

VFR Navigation Chart–Calgary, Canada. Scale 1:500,000, February 2000, Published by Geomatics Canada Department of Natural Resources

Western Flying, January 1928, "The Colonel Repeats" by Richard J. Probert.

_____, February 1928, "The Colonel Abroad" by T.E. Stimson.

_____, March 1928, "Odysseys of the Air" by Richard J. Probert.

Wiley, Frank W., *Montana and the Sky*, Montana Aeronautics Commission, 1966.

World Book Encyclopedia, Field Enterprises Educational Corporation, Chicago, London, Paris, Rome, Stuttgart, Sydney, Tokyo, Toronto, 1974. All volumes covering the history of each individual city or town that Lindbergh visited.

Yale University, Manuscripts and Archives, Sterling Memorial Library, New Haven, Connecticut.

About the Author

Ev Cassagneres is the internationally recognized historian of Ryan aircraft, and preeminent specialist on the *Spirit of St. Louis*. He has devoted over 45 years to the study of both.

He has authored countless magazine articles on Ryan airplanes. He has authored five books: *The Spirit of Ryan*, a detailed history of the Ryan Aeronautical Company; *The New Ryan*, a company history having to do with the Ryan ST and SC respectively; *Supplement A*, the individual histories of all Ryan ST series airplanes; *The Untold Story of the Spirit of St. Louis*, a detailed history of that famous airplane. That book is Part I with this book being Part II.

A highlight of his writing career has been meetings with Charles A. and Anne Morrow Lindbergh, both of whom showed much interest in Ev's aviation history research work.

Cassagneres is a licensed professional pilot with single, and multi-engine land, sea and instrument ratings. He has been flying for over 60 years in more than 50 antique classic as well as modern single and multi-engine types of airplanes, with a total flying time of over 6,000 hours. He presently owns and flies a 1953 classic Cessna 170B.

Part of his flying career was during the early days of the Old Rhinebeck Aerodrome in New York, as "Solo" the flying clown, doing aerial antics in Cole Palen's 1936 Aeronca C-3. Later he flew air shows in a standard Piper J-3-C65 "Cub."

He served in the U.S. Army (1st Cavalry Division) on the front lines of Korea, where he was awarded two Purple Hearts while under fire. Ev was also a bicycle racer and seven-time Connecticut Senior Champion, having retired undefeated. His records include an unbroken 200-mile national endurance/speed record.

The author leads an active life as a swimmer, hiker, cross-country skier and snowshoer, camper, photographer, ethnic and classical music lover (he plays a Celtic Bodhran drum), and model airplane and ship builder. He actively does traditional English, Scandinavian and Contra dancing. In his 1945 Old Town HW wood and canvas canoe Ev can be found on local lakes and rivers. He is president of his own firm, Aero-Draft, and Bluebird Aerial Photography Division of Aero-Draft, and does consulting work for Yale University.

Cassagneres currently lives in Connecticut.

Index

319
USS Memphis–223